Persuasion
Reception and Responsibility

THIRTEENTH EDITION

CHARLES U. LARSON
Northern Illinois University, Emeritus

WADSWORTH
CENGAGE Learning·

Australia • Brazil • Japan • Korea • Mexico • Singapore • Spain • United Kingdom • United States

WADSWORTH
CENGAGE Learning·

**Persuasion: Reception and Responsibility,
Thirteenth Edition, International Edition**
Charles U. Larson

Senior Publisher: Lyn Uhl

Publisher: Monica Eckman

Development Editor: Larry Goldberg

Assistant Editor: Rebekah Matthews

Editorial Assistant: Colin Solan

Media Editor: Jessica Badiner

Marketing Program Manager: Gurpreet Saran

Manufacturing Manager: Marcia Locke

Manufacturing Planner: Doug Bertke

Rights Acquisition Specialist: Mandy Groszko

Internal Designer, Production Management, and
Composition: PreMediaGlobal

Interior Image: shutterstock 69545452
© Fazakas Mihaly

Cover Image: © shutterstock

International Edition:

ISBN-13: 978-1-133-49053-1

ISBN-10: 1-133-49053-0

Cengage Learning International Offices

Asia
www.cengageasia.com
tel: (65) 6410 1200

Australia/New Zealand
www.cengage.com.au
tel: (61) 3 9685 4111

Brazil
www.cengage.com.br
tel: (55) 11 3665 9900

India
www.cengage.co.in
tel: (91) 11 4364 1111

Latin America
www.cengage.com.mx
tel: (52) 55 1500 6000

UK/Europe/Middle East/Africa
www.cengage.co.uk
tel: (44) 0 1264 332 424

Represented in Canada by Nelson Education, Ltd.
www.nelson.com
tel: (416) 752 9100/(800) 668 0671

Cengage Learning is a leading provider of customized learning
solutions with office locations around the globe, including Singapore,
the United Kingdom, Australia, Mexico, Brazil, and Japan. Locate your
local office at: **www.cengage.com/global**

For product information and free companion resources:
www.cengage.com/international
Visit your local office: **www.cengage.com/global**

Printed in the United States of America
1 2 3 4 5 6 7 16 15 14 13 12

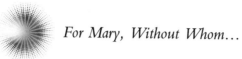 *For Mary, Without Whom...*

Brief Contents

PART III   Applications of Persuasive Premises   307

Contents

PART III Applications of Persuasive Premises   307

11 The Persuasive Campaign or Movement   308

Preface

I'm not sure many students (if any) really read the prefaces of their textbooks, and I have my doubts about how many instructors actually consult the preface as they consider the various options to adopt for their classes. The preface is supposed to tell the reader why the book was written, to whom it is aimed, the things that should be learned, what is new to this edition, and to give thanks to those who helped during the writing and review process.

I recall writing the preface to the first edition of this book almost 40 years ago in the 1960s. That was a decade during which cultural critics felt the country was on the edge of a nervous breakdown. There were three major assassinations of political and social leaders—President Kennedy, his brother Robert, and Rev. Martin Luther King, Jr. There had been race riots and demonstrations to end segregation, other political and social assassinations, and then there was the ongoing war in Vietnam and ever growing worldwide opposition to it and to our government. There was the drug culture, hippies, free love, home-grown militias, and the women's liberation movement with its strikes, demonstrations, and bra burnings. They were truly scary times. The persuasion texts on the market focused on how to prepare and present a persuasive speech and related the various theories to that task. But research in receiving told us that people spent almost twice as much time listening to persuasion as they did presenting it. As a result, I set out to prepare the receiver for various kinds of persuasion—advertisements, political speeches and demonstrations, mass movements, mass media, and governmental propaganda (at that time mainly devoted to the war and race relations). Remember at that time there were only three national television channels, radio, newspapers, magazines, billboards, brochures (or "broadsides"), and leaflets distributed in various ways. So we needed (and still need) training for the deluge of persuasion coming at us from every direction.

Since that first edition, however, and especially since the most recent edition, the changes have been breathtaking for both receivers and senders or sources.

Think about some of them for a minute: the personal computer; the multiplication of media, such as the number of channels on almost any topic on TV; the many personal communication devices that vie for our attention like cell phones, texting devices, tablets, the Kindle and it imitators, iPods, Wi-Fi, Skyping, and who knows what comes tomorrow?

As a result, this edition adds a secondary and new focus that incorporates many of these communication technologies. We do this by emphasizing the degree to which persuasion is shaped and carried by social networking media (SNM) or "one to several" media that can spread persuasion by "word of mouths," which can then spread to many in a viral process that allows audience comment, input, and feedback. This is quite different than the traditional "one to many" media like TV or newspapers that do not offer much chance for audience feedback (except for the rare letter to the editor or purchase behavior). So the receiver can now become the source in this new focus of the thirteenth edition. Another emphasis which runs through this edition is upon the elaboration like-lihood model (ELM), which describes how receivers process the persuasive messages coming from them via traditional media and SNM. Aside from that rather monumental change, the organization of the book is pretty much as it has always been but with many new examples and visuals demonstrating the points being made and theories being discussed. Let's look at that organization briefly.

Part I consists of six chapters.

Chapter 1: "Persuasion in Today's Changing World." The first chapter defines how we shall use the word "persuasion" after looking at various definitions other theorists have used. In addition, it gives you a brief model with which to analyze most of the persuasion coming at you. It originated with communication scholar Hugh Rank and is a handy model that quickly and easily applied to a variety of communication contexts—advertising, politics, interpersonal persuasion, and so on.

Chapter 2: "Perspectives on Ethics in Persuasion." Chapter 2 focuses on one of the most important and essential topics for both persuaders and receivers: ethics. Dr. Richard Johannesen is a nationally recognized expert in the question of what is ethical for persuaders to do and not do and how receivers can react. He discusses a variety of ethical systems and/or theories and how they can be applied in many different contexts, ranging from propaganda and advertising to feminism and sexist language to cyberspace and your personal character. Remember, SNM have only been around for a short while, and unethical uses of them have already caused swindles of several kinds (such as identity theft), suicides (caused by impersonating an important someone like a lover or a parent), and have even been used in organizing revolutions in the Middle East and elsewhere.

Chapter 3: "Traditional, Artistic, and Humanistic Approaches to Persuasion." Dr. Joseph Scudder, another nationally known expert in both traditional and social science theories of persuasion, begins his chapter with the theories of Aristotle (whom we consider the father of the field of rhetoric) and covers theorists from him up to modern rhetorical theorists. He also covers applications of rhetoric/persuasion to such issues as the women's movement, the environmental movement, global warming, and other past and current social theories and movements.

Chapter 4: "Social Scientific Approaches to Persuasion." Chapter 4, also by Dr. Scudder, covers theories and research done from the social scientific viewpoint including the ELM (one of the central themes running through this book) by Petty and Cacciopo and other dual process theories. Scudder also covers variable analytic and compliance gaining theories and gives the reader alternatives to dual process models throughout the chapter.

Chapter 5: "The Making, Use, and Misuse of Symbols." Chapter 5, like the rest of the book, is by your major author where I explore the power of the English language and how it relates to other persuasive symbols as our most commonly used symbolic device. I also consider how it relates to symbolic action as opposed to actual action, and look at a variety of language theories including those of Suzanne K. Langer, Kenneth Burke, and general semantics and semiotics as ways to analyze and create persuasive messages. Finally, I explain the power of metaphor in persuasion and give a model for analyzing and creating metaphors in traditional media as well as SNM.

Chapter 6: "Tools for Analyzing Language and Other Persuasive Symbols." Chapter 6 discusses and gives tools for analyzing and creating the functional, semantic, and thematic dimensions of persuasion. It also elaborates further on analyzing persuasion via semiotics, metaphors, and deconstruction. Included in this chapter are many examples of persuasion and the ELM, and the uses of SNM.

Part II consists of four chapters that discuss the various kinds of appeals that can be made in persuasive messages and how to find and analyze them. These appeals are:

1. Process premises or psychological appeals to the emotions.
2. Logical or content premises which appeal to one's logical or rational self.
3. Culturally ingrained cultural premises.
4. Nonverbal premises or messages in persuasion.

Chapter 7: "Psychological or Process Premises: The Tools of Motivation and Emotion." The first of these premises are appeals to one's physical and emotional needs and covers theories by Packard, Maslow, and others, and points out how these premises are processed in the ELM and how they are often used in messages communicated via SNM. The second process premise includes appeals to one's emotions and covers the emotions of fear, guilt, anger, pride, happiness, and joy. The third process premise is the kinds of appeals that are made to one's attitudes and covers the functions of attitudes, the differences between attitudes and behavioral intentions, and the differences between attitudes and opinions, as well as the differences between attitude formation and information processing, and how attitudes operate in interpersonal communication, especially via SNM and the ELM. The fourth process premise relates to how we seek to maintain consistency among and between our attitudes and focuses on the process of dissonance and dissonance reduction, as well as consonance, consonance maintenance, and enhancement.

Chapter 8: "Content or Logical Premises in Persuasion." Chapter 8 focuses on the issues of evidence and reasoning, the bases of our government and laws. Beginning with a discussion of what constitutes proof, it goes on to look at three types of evidence: direct experience, vicarious experience, and rationally processed evidence. We then look at seven types of reasoning or proof, moving from evidence to proof or conviction. Following a brief discussion of how statistics and testimony can be misused, we explore some of the most commonly encountered fallacies and logical syllogisms. The chapter concludes with an analysis and demonstration of Toulmin's format for logical or content premises.

Chapter 9: "Cultural Premises in Persuasion." As its title implies, Chapter 9 examines the cultural premises in persuasion. These premises are ones that our culture ingrains in us from a very young age and reinforces in us throughout our lives. These cultural premises are seen in the cultural images and myths that are acted out in various scenarios or myths that act as parables that become persuasive to our audiences. They can also be seen in how we judge a person's character or image and in the cultural values we hold and believe in over long periods of time.

Chapter 10: "Nonverbal Messages in Persuasion." Chapter 10 gives students of persuasion a number of deeply ingrained patterns of behavior which almost have become logical premises for most persuaders. Discussion of these messages includes a consideration of such things as facial expression, bodily communication, physical appearance, artifacts, vocal features, touch, and the use of chronemics or time. All of these are probably processed in the peripheral channel of the ELM but are nonetheless logical to us, as in "You can't trust someone who can't look you in the eyes." And nonverbal messages, as we shall see, can even be expressed in the wording of messages sent via SNM.

Part III consists of four different applications or contexts in which we must deal with modern persuasion via the ELM and the other models we have considered as well as via the media for social networking.

Chapter 11: "The Persuasive Campaign or Movement." Chapter 11 begins with an examination of the persuasive campaign as opposed to single-shot persuasive messages. Campaigns go through phases or stages that stretch across time with a beginning, middle, and an end—especially political campaigns. But even longer lasting campaigns, such as those on behalf of products, good causes, or ideologies, go through these stages. They all involve an overall goal that is accomplished by devising strategies that can be put into action using certain tactics. For example, Claussen's brined (as opposed to cooked) pickles had a goal to gain sales. Its strategy was to use TV for the first time ever. Its major tactic was to demonstrate its crispness compared to its most popular competitor by demonstrating the limpness of the competitor versus its own crispness by trying to bend both brands in half in the TV spot. The chapter also looks in depth at the five stages in a model developed at Yale—identification, legitimacy, participation, penetration, and distribution. This Yale model is then applied to political, product, ideological, and idea campaigns from the past and we discuss how they involve the ELM. The chapter then speculates how SNM can be used in campaigns of the three types and gives recent examples. Finally we consider another model for campaigns called symbolic convergence theory.

Chapter 12: "Becoming a Persuader." Chapter 12 has probably had the most significant change since the massive popularity of SNM. It really has given advice on how to make a formal public persuasive presentation in the past (which most of us rarely must do). In previous editions, we also briefly touched on using persuasion in interpersonal communication (something which we frequently do). However, with the advent and enormous spread of SNM and their powerful and even global impact, the idea of becoming a persuader has prompted extending the concept and advice to that medium. So not only does the chapter give you guidance for preparing and delivering both a formal persuasive "one-to-several" presentation and an informal "one-to-one" persuasive interpersonal message, the chapter now gives you some guidance in doing both when you are using SNM to deliver a persuasive message in a "one-to-a-spreading" private, but potentially public audience. This is an unfamiliar type of persuasion for most of us until recently, but it certainly has changed the communication landscape. As a result, this chapter is probably the most changed and the most focused on SNM. Many of the concepts or steps used in the public "one-to-many" approach parallel the persuasive SNM messages and these similarities are emphasized, as is the act of processing the information by both one receiver and by many. The informal "rules" of both often are identical and the channels of the ELM used to process the information in these persuasive messages are frequently similar too.

Chapter 13: "Modern Media in Persuasion." Chapter 13 deals with modern media in persuasion and traces human behavior and changes brought on with the innovations in media of human communication. This began with the spoken word, and moved on through the written and printed words, the electronic word, and on up to our present-day interactive word as shown especially in SNM. The chapter reviews and explains the work of two giants of twentieth century media theory—Marshall McLuhan and Tony Schwartz—as well as explains several other more modern media theories. It then considers several aspects of how the Internet has changed persuasion theory and practice in recent times. This chapter also has been markedly changed by the spread of SNM. They are presently perhaps the most interactive of media in an already interactive culture. The way these media messages are processed—in the central versus the peripheral channels of the ELM—is also considered.

Chapter 14: "The Uses of Persuasive Premises in Advertising." Chapter 14 begins with examples of the varied tasks advertising can perform in addition to "building the brand," like identifying qualified leads, creating traffic, promoting features and benefits, and inducing trial of the brand. The chapter goes on to differentiate and demonstrate the differences between advertising, sales promotion, packaging, and positioning, and relating all of them to the process of achieving TOMA, or "Top of Mind Awareness," which is the key to final sales of the brand. After considering some of the problems of an over-communicated society, the chapter discusses the need for several kinds of research including demographics, sociographics, psychographics, ethnographics, and others. The chapter then investigates the various kinds of "weasel words" and misleading and deceptive claims used in advertising, as well as the implication for future advertising the receivers will face. In closing we consider the use of sexual and subliminal advertising techniques and speculate how SNM will make us the most advertised society in history.

INSTRUCTIONAL AIDS IN THIS EDITION

In addition to the features already mentioned, each chapter has a number of useful aids to student learning, including an initial listing of "Learning Goals" to prepare the student for what will be included in each chapter and what they should expect to know when they have finished it. The chapters each end with a listing of "Key Terms" which they should be familiar with and able to explain and exemplify. To further reinforce our emphasis on persuasive ethics, each chapter has an "Application of Ethics" that relates that chapter title or topic to some ethical issue or concern. And finally, each chapter ends with a series of "Questions for Further Thought" intended to induce class discussion and consideration on the topic.

To help the student identify key concepts throughout the non-text parts of the book (e.g., boxes and visual figures), we have included eight icons throughout the text. These are placed with appropriate boxes and figures to indicate places for the reader to pause and reflect on applications of the material to the contemporary world. These icons represent different ways to examine persuasion. Sometimes more than one icon appears indicating the content may be considered through multiple lenses.

1. Interactive icons represent the fundamental understanding of persuasion as co-creation between the maker of a message and its receiver. The persuasive message is not static. We need to understand changes as information is exchanged. Increasingly, the interaction may go beyond communication of two people face-to-face in real time. It is common for consumers to now communicate their needs such as putting a newspaper on vacation hold by interacting with a program on a computer system. (This icon is also used whenever a Web search is encouraged.)

2. The receiver icon indicates a persuasive situation where subtle connections are suggested by the message creator, but those constructions may rely more on affective or emotional bases in the receiver's mind rather than logical premises. This icon often flags situations where persuasive messages work in the background of a person's mind rather than in explicit arguments and are probably processed in the peripheral channel of the ELM.

3. Critical thinking icons ask readers to render judgments of persuasive situations using a specific persuasive concept. Many of these questions may not have a clearly right or wrong answer. Although many of us may see the situation as having a right answer from our perspectives, others may see it differently. Critical thinking probably occurs in the central path of the ELM.

4. Global icons indicate situations where the persuasive principle under discussion has implications across national boundaries. Some persuasive practices are not universal. Various countries may have different preferences in customs, tastes, and societal assumptions. For example, norms vary greatly about assumptions regarding time and how quickly a decision may come in response to a persuasive message.

5. A multicultural icon indicates that differing views of a particular form of persuasion may exist for persons from different cultures. Multicultural differences may exist within the same country or across national boundaries.

6. Social network media icons designate persuasive situations particularly suited to the use of communication media involving social interactions that usually go beyond the simple dyad. Persuasive communities are emerging not only on Facebook, but through user-generated recommendation sites like Amazon or TripAdvisor.

7. Ethics icons involve moral value judgments about the desirability of persuasive behaviors. An important skill to develop is learning to approach persuasion from the ethical perspective of others who differ from our own moral assumptions. Such perspective-taking is important to developing respect for others.

8. Propaganda icons represent biased influence efforts that make no attempt to negotiate meaning. They are not interactive and do not involve the co-creation process. They make little or no effort to present a balanced argument. Such influence attempts are often ideological or political in nature and represent the imposition of ideas rather than a true persuasive process.

As mentioned earlier, many examples, boxes, and visual figures have been changed and brought up to date or are entirely new to this edition. This is in partial response to requests for more coverage of visual persuasion and to make the text more interesting and applicable to contemporary persuasion. Naturally we have also reported on new developments in the various subfields of the communication discipline and have particularly on some that we feel will influence our world most in the coming years. They include:

1. Increasing cultural diversity. While some politicians and religious leaders complain of the opening of the doors of sexual preference, race, religion, and gender, we believe that this trend will continue for the foreseeable future. It will also continue to breed controversy and problems that can best be solved by ethical and wise persuasion on the parts of all sides.

2. New technologies, especially communication technologies, will be blasting past us and calling all to try to keep up with these sometimes breathtaking innovations (e.g., micro-miniature drone aircraft the size of a dragonfly that recharges its batteries by landing on electric wires and delivers bacteriological techniques such as Israel's new Mosquito and Mosquito 1.6; B.B.C., One Minute News, 3/26/2004).

3. There will be more and more interactive social media networks and both receivers and persuaders will have to be careful what weapons of persuasion they choose to decide to use on these powerful messengers.

Those were scary days in the late 1960s and early 1970s, and people were wondering if the country was having a nervous breakdown. That's when the first edition of this book was published, filling a massive vacuum in the teaching of persuasion and thus shooting it to record sales levels. Those days haven't gone away. They've just morphed into more frightening, potentially dangerous, and possibly enormously helpful times in which ethical and responsible receivers and senders will be needed. It is our hope that those senders and receivers will be you.

SUPPLEMENTS

Instructor's Resource Manual: This guide is designed for beginning as well as seasoned instructors. It includes additional suggested classroom exercises and test questions for each chapter.

PowerLecture for *Persuasion: Reception and Responsibility*: This dynamic presentation tool offers the perfect software to help you present outstanding lectures. It includes book-specific Microsoft PowerPoint slides, which feature text and art, plus the ability to import information from previously created lectures. Additionally, an electronic copy of the Instructor's Resource Manual and ExamView Computerized and Online Testing are available with PowerLecture. Create, deliver, and customize tests and study guides (both in print and online) in minutes with this easy-to-use assessment and tutorial system. ExamView offers both a "Quick Test Wizard" and an "Online Test Wizard" that guide you step by step through the process of creating tests—you can even see the test you are creating on the screen exactly as it will print or display online.

ACKNOWLEDGMENTS

Anytime someone revises a long-selling textbook the final product is due to the wisdom, words, and efforts of many persons. Let me acknowledge several of those persons here. Becky Hayden was the initial editor of *Persuasion: Reception and Responsibility* and deserves special note for recognizing that there might be a market for a receiver-oriented book. That prediction has proven true in edition after edition. This edition and earlier versions could not have happened without the help and input of my two co-authors and colleagues, Richard L. Johannesen, who revised Chapter 2, including explanation and advice, especially regarding SNM. Joe Scudder revised Chapters 3 and 4, including the most current updates and especially those regarding SNM and ELM. Thanks to both Joe and Richard. Thanks also to Cengage Learning and especially Monica Eckman, publisher,

Larry Goldberg, development editor, and to Ashley McDonald, copyeditor for PreMediaGlobal.

And of course many thanks to the many folks in production, permissions, design, and marketing at Cengage. And thanks to the several colleagues from other universities and colleges who reviewed and offered many wonderful and helpful suggestions. They are Michael Arrington, University of Kentucky; Barbara Breaden, Lane Community College; John Giertz, Bakersfield College; Susan Gilpin, Marshall University; Kathy Magrino, Rider University; Karin Sergel, Kutztown University; and Clay Warren, The George Washington University.

Finally, I offer special thanks to the students and teachers who will hopefully profit from adopting, reading, and discussing the thirteenth edition of *Persuasion: Reception and Responsibility*.

Charles U. Larson

Theoretical Premises

1

Persuasion in Today's Changing World

LEARNING GOALS

After reading this chapter, you should be able to:

1. Identify and explain the importance of social network media (SNM) and give examples.

2. Identify several definitions of persuasion (including the one used here) that have emerged across time and briefly explain the theoretical implications of each.

3. Identify, explain, and use the Internet and several interactive media other than SNM, such as video games.

4. Identify and explain instances of doublespeak, deception, and scamming in contemporary mass and interactive persuasion including SNM.

5. Recognize our increasing cultural diversity and make attempts to interact with persons who are culturally different from you.

6. Define advocacy and propaganda and give current examples used in current events and issues.

7. Explain common ground and how it operates in interpersonal, public, mediated, and interactive media, and understand how you use them in your varied persuasive encounters with others.

8. Explain the SMCR (source-message-channel-receiver) and ELM (elaboration likelihood model) styles/models of communication and their dynamics, and why each is relevant in the current day.

9. Identify persuasive messages that are primarily processed in the central and peripheral information-processing channels and how many subconscious or nearly subconscious messages are processed via the peripheral channel. This is important to note because both types continue to affect us long after our first exposure; one such example is the Nike logo.

10. Identify instances of Rank's intensifying and downplaying strategies in persuasion targeted at you today—on television, online, and in SNM.

11. Develop your abilities to engage in self-protection using the Rank model.

12. Become a regular follower of your personal, local and the global effects of SNM.

OUR CHANGING PERSUASIVE WORLD

We are engulfed in a sea of information, and most of us are trying to make persuasion ROCK, but there is much more information out there, especially in cyberspace, than we can ever hope to process. And most of us are exposed to a series of messages on a given topic, brand, or cause—not just a single shot. As a result, the overall message of the persuasive campaign comes to us in bits that are jumbled so we, as receivers, have to assemble or co-create the persuasion. Even more difficult is to evaluate our options and make choices, while putting to use tools of analysis in being persuaded or in persuading others. Of course much of the information flooding us is useless, and we can safely ignore most of it. For example, we need to know about emerging energy sources in order to estimate global warming, the remaining supplies of other existing fuels, and our position as a nation in the world, among other issues. This information helps us make rational choices—some easy and some difficult—such as the new ways our government is dealing with countries such as India and China that are emerging from second- or third-world status. In this text, our focus is on how the central form of influence in our lives—persuasion—is used to prompt our votes, purchases, donations, and other actions like recycling, installing solar panels, or adopting a new technologies. So now more than ever we need to engage in what might be called "defensive listening," a term we shall return to in future chapters. It promotes what is called "critical thinking," which is a characteristic highly prized by employers and others.

We also live in a new age of electronic, digital, and interactive media, such as the recent rise in social networking sites—Facebook, MySpace, Twitter, and others. Mass media have long been with us—at least since the printing press—but in today's highly media-rich and technological culture, persuasion gains new power. Through the tremendous growth of electronic communication and social networks, these forms of media have made it easier for us as individuals to influence others by voicing our opinions about any topics or potential choices. We are becoming sources of persuasive messages much earlier than ever—even in fairly recent times.

Furthermore, we are able to spread our messages far wider than ever before. Go to a socially networked media if you already belong to something like Facebook (or join one if you are not), and you will begin to realize how wide the scope is of such a medium, and how important you are as both a sender and a receiver of persuasive communication. For example, a soldier fighting a war in a foreign land e-mails his family and friends recounting for them what things are *really* like on the scene, and they can respond to information that the mainstream media don't report. That same soldier can also blog about their war experiences and what is happening on the battle ground, reaching a mass audience that far extends beyond his or her immediate friends and family. His or her reality can be spread by friends, friends of those friends, and so on, becoming what experts call "viral persuasion." These messages can easily spawn a mass movement to end the war. This type of response actually happened in France in 2010 when its government tried to increase the retirement age from 60 to 62 years of age. There were huge demonstrations and national slowdowns of the transportation of goods and people. There was massive and global press coverage and even violence against property—all related to

these viral and personal messages from individuals delivered via some kind of **social network media (SNM)** or the Internet—one was viewed over 1 billion times (see Weblink 1.1). (You can access this and all of the other chapter 1 weblinks through your companion website for *Persuasion*, chapter 1 resources.)

Meanwhile, we receivers are faced with ethical decisions about how to behave in similar situations, or what to believe and pass on, and how to determine how reliable a person may be as an eyewitness. We might pass this information on in a blog or an SNM and wonder whether our biases should enter into our evaluation of the issues of war, citizen casualties, life and death, and similar serious issues. Evaluating the individual, as both persuader and "persuadee" (the receiver), is one major theme of this book. Another theme we'll also pursue is the degree to which **interactive media** (see Figure 1.1) plays a role, and what happens when the receiver is able to actively participate, influence others, and is moved to action. We have always had some of these interactive media (for example, letters to the editor or public forums, media "talk shows," and others), all of which can persuade. But recently, interactivity in media has ballooned and multiplied. You can now use the Internet to voice your opinion to thousands, give suggestions for the solutions of problems, or ask questions of actors in a television series about their characters, the ongoing plot, or discuss your own hunches about the show. You can also use interactive media to get professional and amateur counseling on personal problems ranging from where to get your car repaired to what to do in case you have had your identity stolen, or on how to manufacture bombs or amphetamines. In short, there are countless interactive relationships in which any individual can participate. While these media offer us the opportunity to participate in important decision-making processes like purchasing, voting, joining, supporting, or donating, thus "democratizing" society, they also can "dehumanize" us, because these media are programmed to track individual actions and results as never before.

FIGURE 1.1   The number of SNM available staggers the mind.

SOURCE: iStockphoto.com.

Let us consider a rather recent and surprising example of how real these media can be in creating a "virtual world" in which many moral, ethical, and even legal issues can arise from one of these interactive (though not socially networked in this case) media (see Box 1.1).

BOX 1.1   Interactive Hunting

Liveshot.com, a website no longer active, was used as an interactive hunt for big game—wild boar, antelope, deer, bear, and other species. (For similar content, go to Weblink 1.2.) It allowed persons from remote locations to interact with a robotic telescope and rifle to locate and then target game by using a mouse that allows the "hunter" to manipulate a real rifle located in Texas where the "hunt" takes place. The hunter visually looks for targets using a webcam. When one is found, the user manipulates (that is, aims) the robotic rifle and squeezes its trigger. One of Liveshot's earliest users was a quadriplegic man who hadn't hunted in 17 years, and who did the aiming and shooting via a computer mouse operated by puffs of air he blew into a tube. By the way, he wore camouflage. ("All Things Considered," NPR, 2005.)

The example described in Box 1.1 raises troubling ethical questions. Should the virtual hunter have had a hunting license? How could one tell if he was poaching or not? What other uses of this kind of interactivity can you imagine? It's not really social networking, is it? Interestingly enough, in late 2010, MySpace announced that it was no longer a social networking site but an "entertainment destination." Taken together with the questions—ethical and others—brought up by the "Liveshot" website, we have to seriously consider the uses to which SNM are being put. Do they constitute a possible threat to various individuals? Are they truly credible? How fast and widely do they spread? How do they psychologically affect their users?

Another powerful theme in our study of a persuasion world is the degree to which our culture reflects increasing cultural diversity. **Cultural diversity** (that is, the increasing numbers of persons from other cultural backgrounds, races, ethnicities, sexual preferences, educational levels, political and religious beliefs, and so on) calls for us to make adjustments in all forms of communication, but especially in persuasion. Many times the communication results of cultural diversity are very positive. For example, in Gillette, Wyoming, the Prairie Winds organization regularly hosts a cultural festival with ethnic food, dancing, music, art and craft demonstrations, and hundreds of attendees can participate in any of them (*News Record*, 2005). Unfortunately, sometimes the results of miscommunication across diverse cultures are tragic. For example, in 2004, a Hmong deer hunter in Wisconsin murdered five people because he misunderstood a persuasive attempt to convince him that the deer stand he was using belonged to someone else. He was found guilty of killing them and is now serving a life sentence without chance of parole.

Today, new immigrants to the United States face various appeals from their own culturally diverse backgrounds, and undoubtedly they will join, vote, believe in, and donate as do their countrymen. We are especially aware of differences emerging from cultures that embrace the Muslim religion, such as the role and dress of women, particularly Muslim women. Challenging these cultural differences can lead to disruption and further division; for example, some types of the clothing worn by Muslim women—the burka—were totally banned in France, thus sparking sometimes violent demonstrations. Another way to respond to cultural differences is to persuade via compromise or by offering something new. In 2007, swimsuit manufacturers tuned in to reach a new Muslim market segment by offering a model called a "Burkini." Such cultural differences can apply to existing subcultures as well. For example, Latinos respond to persuasive appeals of their reference groups, and the same applies to African Americans, Asians, and Pacific Islanders, among others. Consider a few of the many decisions you make while pursuing your degree that may involve cultural diversity: to enlist in ROTC, to move out and rent your own place, how to choose your major, what committees or clubs you will join, whether to wear the school colors, to join the Young Democrats or Young Republicans, to vote, or to join a cause. We all bring our own cultural and psychological values and needs to these decisions, and thus our choices will inevitably be culturally diverse.

A fourth overall theme to be pursued in this book is the increasing presence of various kinds of **propaganda** or **advocacy** in recent times. **Propaganda** is a word that we hear quite often. *Webster's Collegiate Dictionary* defines propaganda as "… ideas, facts or allegations spread deliberately to further one's cause or to damage an opposing cause." The three key words here are "spread," "deliberately," and "cause." Wikipedia defines it as a set of messages designed to influence large numbers and warns that it is selective and that it "… presents facts selectively in order to … produce an emotional rather than a rational response to the information provided." The key words here are "selectively" and "emotional." As you can see, the word "propaganda" carries a lot of negative baggage and seems to bring up images of a heavy-handed ministry of propaganda forcing ideas and beliefs down the throats of its citizenry (see Figure 1.2). In today's world, however, most propagandists say they are using **advocacy** or are persuading for or against a certain "cause." This distinction makes it seem less heavy-handed; but it is

FIGURE 1.2

Although this propaganda dates to WWII, it exemplifies the one-sidedness and heavy-handed approach to propaganda.

SOURCES: Galerie Bilderwelt/Getty Images; Keystone/Getty Images; INTERFOTO/Alamy; Bettmann/CORBIS.

not always easy to establish what is propaganda and what isn't. In fact, some would even claim that advertising or branding is propaganda because it promotes the free market system. Its originators are probably really promoting a brand, not a dogma or a political belief set (except during political campaigns). For our purposes, we will consider things like the fairly objective documentary film by former Vice President Al Gore about global warming, *An Inconvenient Truth*, and the responses of its critics, as a kind of mid-level propaganda. This classification is apparent when compared to the more heavy-handed *Sicko* and *Capitalism: A Love Story*, by Michael Moore, which focus on the weaknesses in the American healthcare and economic systems. And at the most heavy-handed end of the scale might be the video and audio messages of Osama Bin Laden to his followers and the public, or the claims of the essentially power-less Iranian President Mahoud Ahmadinejad. He claims that the Holocaust never happened and links that to his rejection of to Israel's "right to exist" (Klein, 2007).

In addition to a global world that is facing a crisis of ethics, and is engulfed by new media, we are also in an age of increasing advocacy and propaganda. Everywhere someone is advocating their personal agenda or that of a group—global warming, war on Iran, increasing the capital gains tax, feeding the poor, taxing the rich, the Tea Party, hydrogen energy, or prevention of cruelty to plants by some gardeners are only a few of the many issues that people are fighting for every day.

As noted earlier, the word "propaganda" carries loads of negative baggage. There are five key characteristics of propaganda—things which set it off from other kinds of persuasion. It exhibits all of the following, which again you will see in other places than this initial introduction:

1. It is ideological or it carries and promotes a belief or system of attitudes that is dogmatic. That system is the one and only way to believe—no other system is acceptable.

2. It uses the mass media to deliberately spread its belief system in order to convince and recruit ever larger and larger groups of "true 'Tea Party' believers." They are frequently fanatical about the belief in the existing system. In this way it becomes a mass movement.

3. It conceals one or more of the following:
   a. the source of the message (e.g., a political party, a religion, an economic system, etc.)
   b. the true goal of this source (e.g., attainment of power, discrimination against a minority, violence against a group or belief set, etc.)
   c. the other side of the issue or other perspectives from which to view the issue
   d. the techniques being used to promote the message (e.g., subliminal cues, music, uniforms, or so-called "impromptu" marches or meetings)
   e. the result if the source reaches its goal (e.g., tyranny, secret surveillance of the citizenry, the abolishment of personal rights like privacy, habeas corpus, or even national sovereignty)

4. It aims at uniformity of belief and behavior. In this way it is like mob psychology.

5. It usually circumvents the reasoning process and substitutes emotional argument and the hatred of stereotypes for totally illogical reasoning (e.g., Jews for the Nazis, Jihadists in contemporary times).

So one can advocate one side of an issue and still not do any (or only one or two) of these things, which characterize propaganda, and still be just "advocating." True propaganda is *unethical advocacy on behalf of an ideology using largely emotional argument that conceals in order to assemble a mass movement on behalf of or against that ideology.* And we are seeing increasing amounts of it in recent times, and are likely to see more in the future, perhaps because of our increasing cultural diversity.

The key for the critical persuadee or audience is to receive both honest advocacy and unethical propaganda and be able to distinguish between them. That will help us all to make better and wiser decisions when faced with important issues that will affect more than just us as individuals. And a few minutes of examining blogs or radio and television political talk shows will demonstrate propaganda at work in today's world on all of these levels. In the following chapters, you will find current examples and tools that are helpful in locating and analyzing it. You will also find interactive examples of propaganda and various "propaganda boxes" that we include (for instance, Weblink 1.3), where you will find a lengthy multimedia piece of propaganda concerning the building of a mosque at "Ground Zero" in New York. Notice the one-sidedness and heavy-handedness of the both the videos and posters there (especially the anti-Nazi cut from Charlie Chaplin's first talkie, *The Great Dictator*).

Persuasion and Its Ethical Challenges Today

At the same time that we face an anytime-anywhere world of advocacy, propaganda, and persuasion, we are also experiencing a crisis in personal and public ethics. In fact, two authors call us a

"Pinocchio Nation" (Donaldson & Wamberg, 2001). The topic of ethics will be dealt with in depth by Dr. Johannesen in chapter 2, but for now let's just consider how this crisis has developed to its present-day dimensions. We have recently faced almost unprecedented lying and unethical decision making by our government and elected officials, our corporations, our religious institutions and leaders, and by other individuals in our everyday lives. There have always been duplicitous and deceitful advocates and propagandists in all of these institutions, but since the turn of the new millennium and its technological innovations like SNM, the dimensions of these problems mushroomed, as seen in the book entitled *The Post-Truth Era* (Keyes, 2004). Just a few recent examples demonstrate this point:

1. World-class corporations, accounting firms, and business leaders lied and cheated to help bilk thousands of law-abiding and trusting citizens—employees, retirees, and investors—of not only their money but of their faith in the future and of business in general (examples include Enron and Arthur Anderson, LLP, among others).

2. World-renowned religious spokespersons, television evangelists, everyday clergy, lawyers, counselors, and school teachers were unmasked as child molesters, unfaithful spouses, or as financially greedy to the extreme throughout the past decade, and continuing on into the next in all likelihood.

3. Our governments have clearly and repeatedly lied to us about the wars in Iraq and Afghanistan, the resulting use of governmentally approved forms of torture (thus thumbing the country's nose at the global community), and illegal invasions of our privacy. We have also

seen numerous unethical, if not illegal, means of gaining and maintaining the highest political office locally, and the use of these positions by such officials to line their own pockets as well as those of their friends at local, state, national, and global levels.

4. A number of studies show that individual honesty has deteriorated in recent times. Individuals in general seem to have much lower standards of honesty and ethical behavior, whether in the honest filing of income taxes, academic honesty, plagiarism, marital fidelity, business dealings, marketplace transactions, and in many cases of personal relationships (Cook, 1996, Callahan, 2004, Keyes, 2004, and Ekman, 1999).

So, based on the examples above, and for many reasons in general, we need to train ourselves as critical receivers, if for no other reason than to deal with the "post-truth," globally unethical environment that we face on a daily basis (see Box 1.2).

For example the viral technique persuades on at least two levels: purchase of the product and forwarding the "fun" interactive site. Can you think of other persuasion where this viral approach might be exploited? What about political campaigns? Barack Obama's 2008 presidential campaign used Facebook and MySpace to raise over $31 million, with 80 percent of it in gifts under $100 (Tumulty, 2007), suggesting contributions were largely from individual middle class voters and not corporations, unions, or other PACs. Other politicians are following Obama's lead. What about religious appeals? Worthy causes? What are the ethical implications of using "fun" media to hook consumers or urging them to spread the message? Is it "propaganda" in your mind? (See Box 1.3.)

BOX 1.2 **What Is Propaganda?**

You have read two dictionary definitions of propaganda. Now view a video that explains propaganda giving several devices that are frequently used in propaganda. You will find out why some could argue that even sober driving is dangerous. Refer to Weblink 1.4.

BOX 1.3   **Becoming an Advertising Medium—Ethical or Unethical?**

"Viral marketing" is a new form of interactive persuasion. It turns the audience into an advertising channel as each receiver spreads the message online like a (benign) virus resulting in an "epidemic" of interactive persuasion. The technique resembles a chain letter. First the advertiser places an entertaining and interactive message (such as a game) on the web and directs consumers to visit the site, which also contains links from which to choose. One of these is "send this site to a friend." The consumer frequently does just that because it is fun and easy to share things like games. One such site is sponsored by Burger King (see Weblink 1.5), which promotes their chicken products as opposed to the Whopper. The site has someone dressed in a chicken suit, and viewers can command the chicken to run, fly, hop, and skip, and other simple movements. If asked to perform a distasteful or obscene act, the "chicken" confronts the screen and shakes its finger at the "naughty" user. Try it; it's fun. Then send it to a friend – see, there I just sent you a viral message!

New media—especially the Internet and digital formats—have resulted in a whole new game of social "Monopoly." Nowadays, the most desirable piece of Monopoly property—equivalent to the "Boardwalk"—is the Internet, taking advantage of websites, blogging, hogging, and new media devices, procedures, and related confounding changes that easily baffle us. The focus of the popular TV series "Boardwalk Empire" was on Atlantic City's Mafia-run boardwalk during Prohibition are again familiar. But that's where the action and where the money is. Cellular phones that can photograph, videotape, text, and interact with instantaneous speed are surely more breathtaking than Monopoly's B. & O. Railroad. They are in a way more frightening than the sci-fi novel *Brave New World*, whose author, Aldous Huxley, was mainlining LSD on his deathbed ("Hippie," The History Channel, 10/23/07). He predicted the new filmic technique he called "the feelies" wherein one could be electronically made to feel the physical hurts and pleasures of the characters in today's movies. (Huxley, 1932). Where previously the convenience of having a mobile phone just to make calls anywhere, anytime was an amazing development, now we're accustomed to cellular phones that can photograph, videotape, text, access the web, and provide any kind of information instantaneously. And as soon as one technology is introduced, improvements and further developments are already being explored. These possibilities are exciting, and people gravitate toward the use of such media and technology. Princeton professor, Dr. Ed Felton predicts that within ten years "… we'll see a $100 device that fits in your pocket and holds all the music ever recorded," (Levy, 2007). He also observes that the digital book has already become a reality. Amazon first released its version with the "Kindle"; it is only 3 years old and already has been duplicated by other companies. It's about the size of a paperback and adjusts font size for the reader while holding several hundred books at a time. It also tracks your reading habits—time of day, time spent on a page, type of material read, and other variables ("All Things Considered" 12/15/10, NPR). Even with this fairly new technology, it's constantly being improved with new features added with each new version.

Another theme covered is the degree to which we humans process these massive chunks of information we constantly receive. Do we process them emotionally or logically? The question of how we process emotion goes back a long way, as we shall see. Aristotle talked of the different ways of processing and producing information. He used the term *pathos* to refer to the emotional side of persuasion and the word *logos* to refer to the logical side. By pathos (and to some degree *ethos* as well), he meant those arguments that appealed to the "emotions, the passions, or the will," while logos appealed to the intellect or rational parts of our minds. A more recent explanation of this phenomenon is called the elaboration likelihood model of persuasion (Petty and Cacciopo, 1986), which we and most other sources refer to as the ELM. The model deals with information processing and argues that we use one of two "channels" or routes to process information. One is called the "central processing route" and resembles Aristotle's logos in that it is used for extended, complex, and important pieces of information like the news item, the financial information on one's home mortgage, tuition rates, and other information that needs to be studied and researched consciously. The "peripheral processing route" is used for processing (perhaps evaluating), and for storing less important information, like the 15-second television spot ad or various logos like the Nike "swoosh" and jingles that pepper our eyes and ears each day. As we study persuasion in all of our chapters, the ELM will apply to the information we use in our everyday and our specialized lives, whether it be in ethics, language use, arguments, media, or advertising— to name a few—and when we develop our own persuasion to deliver to others, whether it be in a public speech, a comment on a Facebook wall, a tweet, or a text or voicemail message. Some messages will be important—even essential for us as receivers and for the receivers we intend to

persuade—and other information will be almost trivial; but over time, this information will affect our purchasing, voting, joining, and donating decisions. When we make such decisions we do so using information processed in one channel or the other or in some cases from both. For example, you all know which charitable organization stands on street corners at holiday time with red kettles and ringing bells, just like you all know that the generic name for facial tissue is "Kleenex" and for photocopying is "Xerox," because that "peripheral" information has been processed by you so many times that it has become generic for the type of product or cause involved. You don't stop and ask yourself: "What does the Salvation Army really do with this money?" Therefore, it's important to examine the degree to which we mentally elaborate on and store both the important information that we process, and that which almost passes unnoticed but affects us nonetheless. We will discuss such examination as one of the themes of this book. For example, which channel do you think will be used to process the new images of diseased patients, tissue, or the DNA of cancer patients depicted on cigarette packaging? Where do you think the earlier warnings on cigarette packages were processed? (See Box 1.4.)

BOX 1.4   ## Interact with Propaganda

Log on to the Internet and enter the word "Propaganda" into a search engine. Go to the "Propaganda - Source Watch" option and explore some of the more contemporary uses of propaganda techniques, like the U.S. government's publication of comic books targeted at the conflicts in the Middle East. What do you think of the "green washing" technique, in which environmental issues are appropriated by corporate polluters for image building? This is done with the use of words we unconsciously process, like "Our shipping containers are made of 100 percent recycled materials." Browse through a variety of key words and techniques links to learn more about the enormous number of new propaganda techniques that are now being used (for example, buzz words, "Astroturf blogging" or the

creation of false blogs to make messages appear as if they came from grass roots organizations). Other examples include the "echo chamber," in which bogus or conscripted news sources are paid or rewarded in some other way to present seemingly unbiased issues that actually mirror the positions of the politician, advocate, propagandist, or corporation; or the use of stealth-marketing, in which low-budget campaigns are waged to promote candidates and brands. What about photographic manipulation (where photo ops are created or existing photos are altered to make propagandistic points) and others? You will be amazed at the burgeoning propaganda that is just now coming to the attention of scholars and the public in general.

> ## BOX 1.5   Multicultural = There Are Many Others
>
> Get a slight feel for our multicultural world, how we have become a global community, and the related issues that have developed as a result by looking at Germany—a country that should still be feeling guilt from its participation in the Holocaust. It recently claimed it had too many "outsiders" and "foreigners" living in their country. All
>
> Things Considered, NPR, October 24, 2010). You might try to explore the topic by entering the words "Germany," "racism," and "foreigners" in the search engine and looking at a few of the resulting websites. There you will encounter and view the many unpleasant facets of our multicultural "family."

Persuasion in a Multicultural World

As can be seen in the crisis over immigration reform and various discriminatory actions against certain minorities, not only in our country but elsewhere, we live in a world that is composed of many cultures, be they racial, religious, related to gender or sexual preference, nationality, or even modes of dress or grooming. Each of these cultures and subcultures has its own set of values and beliefs; and at the same time each shares some of the same things with the new culture as a whole. We need to take into account not only those values that we share with others but also where we differ, if we are to avoid tragedies (like the example previously noted about the Hmong hunter in Wisconsin). This awareness is especially vital when we persuade or evaluate persuasion via SNM, where personal and public agendas are being debated. When that is the case, both persuading others and being persuaded by them becomes doubly complex. We may say to ourselves (and perhaps unwittingly to others) that someone is late because he or she is operating on the accepted values of their own subculture (at one time this was called CPT or "colored people's time), and that this is a valid excuse. But we need to remember that not everyone thinks this is okay; bosses, drill instructors, judges, bankers, and many others would not accept such an explanation. Although such explanations may not always be excusable, at the same time, we need to make sure that the action we suggest in our persuasion takes into account that some cultures place a much higher value on some characteristics, circumstances, or morals, than do others. For example,

different cultures have differing opinions on males versus females when making business decisions, making major purchases, and even voting decisions; or for some it might be vital that a proposed solution to problems had better contain an "escape hatch" so that those from another culture can engage in "face-saving" options, because that is important in that culture (see Box 1.5). In other words, within the process of persuasion, it is essential to keep a balance of what is important to you, and what is valued by those with whom you are engaging. Such differences in values can often constitute the circumstances that can lead to misunderstandings and failure, or if handled well, success.

Persuasion as Protection in a Deceptive, Doublespeak, and Dangerous World

We have had to live in a deceptive and dangerous world ever since Adam and Eve tried to lie about eating the forbidden fruit—I wonder if it was rhubarb. Ever since then, however, we have become increasingly more skillful and sophisticated in deceiving others in order to succeed in duping them. (Dr. Johannesen will discuss lying and deception and their ethical dimensions in depth in chapter 2.) However, in all likelihood, we have not become increasingly sophisticated in spotting and saying "No, thanks—maybe another time" to the scam, the swindle, the political deception, the cheat, or the hoodwink. Just the other day, I learned via email that I was the winner of a lottery I hadn't even entered, and I won it twice in the same day, and all I had to do was send a cashier's check to cover the transfer of funds. How can someone believe that they have won a lottery that they haven't even entered? (See Figure 1.3.) And how can they be foolish enough to send thousands of dollars into an unknown address? Yet, we read time after time that people who appear to be bright and educated are snookered by this relatively new scam. All of these cases and many others bear

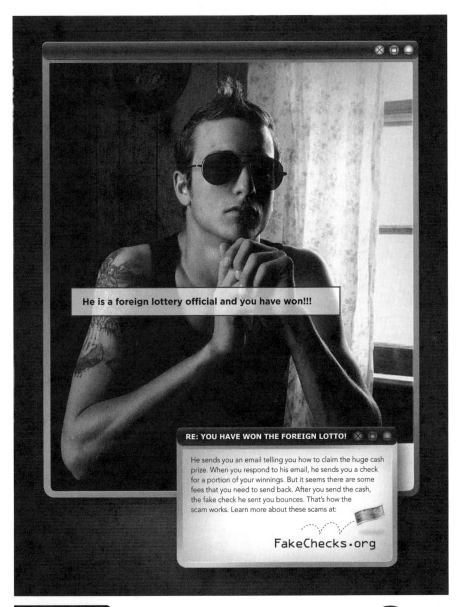

FIGURE 1.3 "He Is a Foreign Lottery Official and You Have Won!!!" What techniques of persuasion were used or ignored in this ad warning others of a scam that often succeeds?

SOURCE: National Consumers League, Inc.

witness to the need to become critical and skeptical persuadees or receivers in the deceptive and dangerous world we face—especially since the introduction of interactive media and SNM. We face several kinds of deceit. A new one to me was a telephone call supposedly from a collection agency. They said that I had been turned over to collection by my cell phone provider. Supposedly I was overdue by only $110. I asked them to resend the bill, but they asked if I wouldn't rather settle this over the phone by credit card? Luckily I had left my wallet several rooms away and asked the caller to hold while I went to get my credit card. By the time I returned, the so called "collection agency" had hung up. What was the scam? They wanted my credit card number. I checked with the cell phone provider, and found that I was up to date on my bill.

Doublespeak.   This book advises that your job as a receiver and as a sender is to engage in **"response-ability,"** or your ability to wisely and critically respond to the persuasion you encounter and to make wise choices and ethical decisions when you both process and craft persuasion. It would have been good in past times for persuaders and audiences to have response-ability. If they had, many tyrants might not have risen to power, and wars might have been avoided. The National Council of Teachers of English (NCTE) recognized this need for people to engage their response-ability when it instituted its regular conferences on **doublespeak**, which it defined as deliberate miscommunication and which the *American Heritage Dictionary* defines as "evasive, ambiguous, high-flown language designed to deceive." NCTE conferences point out kinds of doublespeak that might be used by sources and interpreted by receivers, and also granted awards for the year's most outrageous examples. *Euphemism* is an example. It means "words to distort or soften reality." In 2007, a U.S. Senator was accused of "cruising" for a homosexual encounter (a case of euphemism already) by reaching under the toilet stall in a public restroom at the Minneapolis airport and tapping his feet in order to establish contact with another potentially gay person. He denied doing this, saying that he merely reached under to retrieve a piece of dropped toilet paper and that he did his "business" from a "wide stance," meaning that he had made the initial signal of putting his foot into the territory of the next stall and tapping it. Chicken purveyors use euphemism when they claim that their frozen product is "deep-chilled, not frozen." In politics and business, "user fees" replaces "tax increases" or "price hikes," which are also examples of euphemism. Law enforcement officials refer to "a person of interest" when they really mean a suspect, and school officials talk of a "reduction in force" or RIF when they mean they are laying off teachers (see Weblink 1.6). Maybe we are being faced with a new kind of "euphemasia" in the early twenty-first century—so how can we as sources and receivers deal with this ubiquitous perversion of language? We shall see.

In a persuasion-riddled world such as ours, you would not need defensive training if all persuaders were open, ethical, and honest. Too many, however, try to persuade by using doublespeak, which comes in many guises. One way to protect ourselves is to become aware of these guises as they occur in propaganda, advertising, political discourse, and elsewhere. You need to learn what the "half truth" technique of doublespeak is and how it works. As its name implies, it only tells half the story (and so resembles propaganda). An example might be our military telling the public that the United States is "making progress" in Iraq or Afghanistan. What does that mean? Well, if we look at what has been brought out in Congressional inquiries, it means that "in some places and at some times, certain indices of progress have appeared to have happened." But it didn't mean progress as a whole was made or that the war was nearly over. Though several years later President Obama did remove 50,000 "combat forces" from Iraq in 2010 (which wasn't exactly clear as a sign of progress either, because the term "combat forces" was potentially misleading). And in some critical Afghanistan provinces, as much as 90 percent of citizens were unaware of the events of September 11, 2001 (see Weblink 1.7).

The use of *jargon* is yet another kind of double-speak. Because it is highly technical or specialized language, it confuses the receiver and as such is frequently seen in advertising, political rhetoric, and economic propaganda. Consider the definition of political jargon given by this online dictionary (see Weblink 1.8). Many politicians like to use other phrases to categorize themselves and others. For example, a "birther" is someone who doubts the ability for President Obama to be in office because his birth certificate could potentially not be valid. Another phrase of political jargon, "undocumented workers," usually refers to illegal immigrants. Most of these phrases become terms used in popular culture as well, as political issues spill over into more personal issues in the everyday lives of people.

The list of political jargon terms continues infinitely: new ones are being coined by political figures every day. The way to tell if something is a part of political jargon is to question whether the phrase or term really means what it sounds like. Instead, ask if there is an added connotation that comes as a subtext for the word (see Weblink 1.9).

Consider the term "ethnic cleansing," which actually referred to mass murder but used words that sounded almost antiseptic. What can the average receiver do about doublespeak? I recommend (along with many others) asking the following questions about any persuasion being received or planned:

1. Who is speaking to whom?
2. Under what conditions?
3. Under what circumstances?
4. With what intent?
5. With what results?

If you cannot answer *all* these questions with ease, or if you feel uncomfortable with the answers, or if you cannot determine any answer to them, you are probably dealing with doublespeak. You had better be prepared to delve deeper, or if you are sending a message and can't answer these questions, you'd better think about cleaning it up a bit.

Of course, doublespeak isn't confined to the world of politics. CEOs at Enron, AIG, WorldCom, and others were experts at using doublespeak to confuse and bilk investors, employees, governmental officials, and the public by convincing them that "liabilities" were "assets," that "spending" meant "earning," and many more examples. As a result, many employees and investors lost hundreds of thousands of dollars including all that they had saved for retirement. Although the CEOs went to jail, the risks are still out there. You will find doublespeak elsewhere—in sales pitches, in your interpersonal persuasion with friends and relatives, in the classroom, at church, in politics, and economics—no area of interest is immune, so be on guard for what the words *really* mean—especially on SNM, since we are not exactly certain of how this new type of media really can work for good results or for those that are not so good.

Scams. Another kind of deception in our dangerous world of persuasion is the **scam**, which again has been with us for ages—since Cain successfully cheated Abel out of his birthright for something mundane like a bowl of porridge. The typical scam relies heavily on persuasion, first in convincing the person to be scammed that the persuader or scammer is credible and believable (as noted in Figure 1.3), and then in the steps taken to complete the scam. We will discuss credibility at length in several places later but sincerity, trustworthiness, and believability are good synonyms for now, and it is important to remember that many elements of credibility or ethos are probably processed in the peripheral channel of the ELM, passing our conscious notice almost imperceptibly. In the next step, the scammer persuades the target that the scheme is likely to succeed and yield plentiful rewards by playing on the human motive of greed. This is frequently done by using statistics or testimonials, both of which we also discuss later. Then the scammer must persuade the person to make some kind of commitment—usually financial (see Figure 1.3 once again). Other kinds of scams involve persuading a person to donate or pledge to a good cause such as a "walk" for the poor or some disease like HIV. This type of scam usually also persuades the audience of the credibility or the reasonableness of the plan, and of course the generous rewards. Then comes the key commitment step. Sometimes it is minimal—like signing one's name to an online petition. Other times it involves only a minimal financial donation, but this usually leads to larger and larger ones. Interestingly, having a list of donors in advance and amounts given or pledged really helps get the bucks. Identity theft is another type of scam as noted in the example of the so-called "collection agency." It is sometimes accomplished by "phishing" in order to gain sensitive information that can be used to masquerade as someone else. Frequent aliases are PayPal, eBay, or online banking fronts, and more recently SNM have been used for identity theft (see Weblink 1.10). Identity theft usually involves persuading the target to give up key identity information because the fake bank says it needs the password or account number to verify its records. Again, credibility is critical, and once key info is known, the pieces in the scam fall into place.

Finally, another and far more dangerous kind of scam is the corporate or governmental scam or swindle. A few of these scams come to mind in both the corporate and the government arenas. They are Enron, the world's largest energy broker; WorldCom, the second largest long-distance company; Adelphia, a major cable provider; Arthur Andersen, one of the five top accounting firms in the United States; and the entire mortgage banking system, which triggered the housing bubble and the "Great Recession" of 2007—?

Self-Protection.   Both business and governmental scams have been with us for a long time, going back to the founding fathers and moving on to the swindling of the Native Americans, Credit Mobilier, Teapot Dome, the Great Depression, recent timber and oil swindles, and the list goes on. Step one is to establish the credibility of the source. After all, who wouldn't trust our government or most major corporations—look at all the regulations and oversight! The key persuasive step is similar to that in the individual scam, which is to convince the public—voters, investors, vendors, or employees—that everything is being conducted honestly. That's

the purpose of having oversight committees or regulators like the SEC. The commitment step is almost irrelevant in corporate or government scams because the public has already committed to the company, office holder, or corporation.

The critical thing to keep in mind regarding any of these deceptions, ranging from doublespeak to outright scams and swindles, is that **self-protection** is the only weapon the average person has with which to defend themselves. Again, that's the magic bullet for combating these stings—to train you to be skeptical and responsible persuadees or audience members. Shortly we will investigate a handy model and tool that you can use to begin to become such an audience member, but first let's set the historical context for the study of persuasion and examine some of the theoretical foundations for its examination. We shall begin by looking at how persuasion has been defined from the time of the ancients until the present.

DEFINING PERSUASION: FROM ARISTOTLE TO ELABORATION LIKELIHOOD

Definitions of Persuasion

The ancient Greeks were among the first democracies to systematize the use of persuasion, calling it "**rhetoric**." They studied it in their schools, applied it in their legal proceedings, used it in their Senate, and employed it to build the citizen-based self government in their city-states. Aristotle was the primary information broker and persuasion theorist of those times, authoring more than 1,000 books and categorizing all of the types of knowledge in the known world including persuasion. He was basically the "Secretary of Education" for his childhood friend, Alexander the Great. Among the areas of knowledge he studied and defined was rhetoric, which he defined as "the faculty of observing in any given case, the available means of persuasion." And, according to Aristotle, persuasion consists of artistic and inartistic proofs. The persuader controls **artistic proof**, such as the choice of evidence, the organization of the persuasion, style of delivery, and language choices. **Inartistic proof** includes things not controlled by the speaker, such as the occasion, the time allotted to the speaker, or things that bound persons to certain action, such as undeniable facts or statistics. Also important to note are tactics of getting compliance by questionable means like torture, tricky or binding contracts that are not always ethical, and sworn oaths; but all of these methods actually coerce the receiver into compliance to one degree or another instead of actually persuading them. We know today that coercion or torture results in low commitment, which results not only in the lessening of desired action, but a reduction in the likelihood of attitude change.

According to Aristotle, persuasion succeeds or fails based on three basic types of artistic proof, as noted earlier. First, persuasion depended on a source's credibility, or **ethos**, which is why the testimonial is such an effective persuasive tactic in much advertising. Second was the use of emotional appeals, or **pathos**, usually found in the kinds of colorful language and imagery used by the persuader, or in the emotional level of evidence cited in speeches, ads, documentaries, and so on. Again we find this to be true in modern times; witness the language used in many contemporary political speeches as well as in most advertisements—print and electronic—for the brands we are urged to buy, the candidates for whom to vote, or the causes that we are urged to support with donations, pledges, or action. Finally, the idea of using logical or rational appeals, or **logos** in Aristotle's words, was a persuasive tactic that employed the arguments or reasons for actions that the populace deemed most logical. Examples today are the use of statistics on behalf or against a given policy of government or a brand or other issue. The use of historical precedent or analogies to promote a given policy, and the opinions and advice of well-known experts on a given topic or issue, are also examples of appeals to logos. Of course, most persuaders use a combination of all three of these tactics (Roberts, 1924),

and we see all of them being used in both ethical and unethical persuasion in our contemporary world. Even though Aristotle never dreamed of such a thing as an SNM, we find these proofs being used there as well. Aristotle also thought that persuasion is most effective when based on the **common ground**, or the shared beliefs, values, experiences, and interests existing between persuaders and persuadees that could be established by any or all of the above tactics. This shared territory or common ground permits persuaders to make certain assumptions about the audience and its beliefs, such as assuming that using certain patterns or types of language, emotions, and logic will be most effective. This concept is still true when working within social networking. When you send a message to a "friend" urging them to take a certain action, you assume they share well-accepted patterns of logic, language, and emotions.

Assuming these beliefs, Aristotle advised persuaders to use **enthymemes**, defined as "a form of argument in which the first or major premise in the proof remains unstated by the persuader and, instead, is supplied by the audience" (Larson, 2010). This form of proof is also a powerful claim for believing the socially networked messages that we receive. Many of the chapters to follow explain broad examples of such commonly-held major premises. A familiar example is "All men are mortal; Socrates is a man; therefore Socrates is mortal." Today's persuaders need to identify common ground between themselves and their audience using such patterns, or locating those major premises probably held by most audiences and that can be used in effective enthymemes (see Figure 1.4).

Roman students of persuasion added specific advice on what persuasive speaking ought to include. Cicero identified five elements involved in the preparation and presentation of persuasive messages (public speeches for him). They were: (1) inventing or discovering evidence and arguments, (2) organizing them, (3) styling them artistically, (4) memorizing them, and (5) delivering them skillfully. Both Aristotle's and Cicero's definitions focus on the sources of messages and on the persuader's skill and art in building a speech. Little

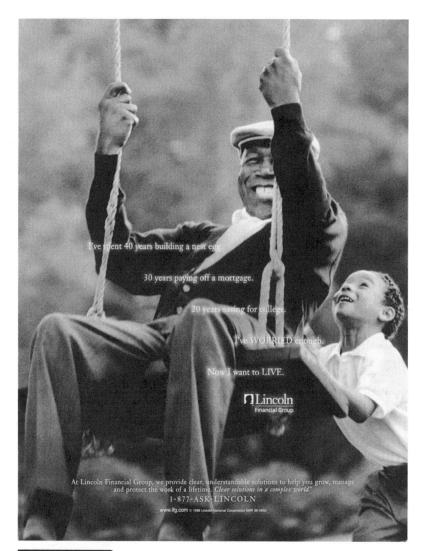

I've spent 40 years building a nest egg.

30 years paying off a mortgage.

20 years saving for college.

I've WORRIED enough.

Now I want to LIVE.

∩Lincoln
Financial Group

At Lincoln Financial Group, we provide clear, understandable solutions to help you grow, manage
and protect the work of a lifetime. *Clear solutions in a complex world.*
1-877-ASK-LINCOLN
www.lfg.com © 1998 Lincoln National Corporation SMR 96-9962

FIGURE 1.4   The Lincoln Financial Group establishes common ground in
this advertisement between the company and any person of any race or ethnicity
who is approaching retirement. Note the satisfied and happy looks on both of the
faces and the healthy appearance of both persons (a non-verbal emotional appeal).
This resonates with the desire to have a happy, healthy retirement and helps build
the common ground. Note also the examples referred to in the ad copy: "40 years
building," "30 years paying off," and "20 years saving," each of which would probably
resonate with any potential retiree, and the idea that "Now I want to LIVE," (clearly
both a logical and emotional appeal—they can occur at the same time). These
words continue building common ground between the company and the
potential customer.

SOURCE: Used by permission of the Lincoln Financial Group.

© Cengage Learning 2013

attention is paid to discovering details about the audience in ways similar to modern demographics, sociographics, or psychographics. In the communication discipline, we consider these stages in speech preparation "rhetorical" approaches to the study of persuasion because they grew out of the rhetorical traditions of the Greeks and Romans.

Later students of persuasion reflected the changes that accompanied the emergence of print and electronic media like the newspaper, magazines, radio, film, and television, and the emerging social sciences that followed World War II. These new media resulted in the emergence of powerful leaders—even some dictators—in many places around the globe including the United States, Germany, Italy, Spain, Japan, Russia, and elsewhere, as well as the re-emergence of heavy doses of powerful propaganda, as noted in the propaganda boxes throughout this book.

Over 50 years ago, communication scholars Winston Brembeck and William Howell (1952) broke new theoretical ground after WWII when they described persuasion as "the conscious attempt to modify thought and action by manipulating the motives of men toward predetermined ends." Prior to that time, persuasion was often thought to consist mainly of logical arguments; but that was not the case with what happened to cause WWII, which consisted of demagogic persuasion communicated via new media unfamiliar to the audience (radio and film) and from powerful communicators (Hitler, Roosevelt, many radio and film personalities, and others), and it persuaded the defenseless audience. The audience had become more important than it ever was to the ancients.

In Brembeck and Howell's definition, we see a notable shift from impersonal logic in persuasion toward a focus on the more personal and "emotional" means of persuasion—those that stimulate the internal motives of the audience. Twenty years later they re-defined persuasion as "communication intended to influence choice" (1975), reflecting the interest on the idea of *influence* in the social sciences.

Literary critic and language theorist Kenneth Burke (1970) also defined persuasion in an intriguing way. His definition was an imaginative one. He said that persuasion was really the artful use of the "resources of ambiguity" usually revealed in an artistic—and frequently emotional and dramatic—format. Burke believed that if receivers feel they are being spoken to in their "own language" and hear references to their own beliefs and values, they tend to develop a sense of **identification** with the persuader, and believe that the persuader is like them—a concept close to Aristotle's "common ground." In Burke's theory, when persuaders try to act, believe, and talk like the audience, they create a bond with listeners, who will identify with them and will follow their advice on issues. He also noted that such identification occurs most readily when wrapped in a drama, a story, or other kind of narration that humans naturally find interesting and engaging (Burke, *A Grammar of Motives*, 1970 and *A Rhetoric of Motives*, 1970). We see this format in many, if not most, advertisements and in much political, religious, economic, and other advocacy and propaganda, ethical and unethical. It has led to a set of communication and persuasive theories called "narrative" ones (see Fisher, 1987; Campbell, 1972, 1991).

Taking our cues from Aristotle, Burke, and others, persuasion is defined for our purposes here as *the process of dramatic co-creation by sources and receivers of a state of identification through the use of verbal and/or visual symbols.* This definition implies that persuasion requires intellectual and emotional participation between both persuader and the audience that leads to shared meaning and co-created identification, usually via a dramatic form. Communication professor and researcher Herbert Simons and his colleagues (2010) agree and call this result "co-active persuasion." Notice that, like our definition, co-active persuasion is receiver or audience oriented and situational, relying on similarities between persuaders and persuadees. It appeals to things acceptable to the persuadee, thus inducing action. Because of the process of co-creation, all persuasion thus consists of **self-persuasion** to some degree. We rarely act in accordance with isolated elements of persuasion unless we participate or interact in the process logically, emotionally, and perhaps dramatically. The words "process," "co-created," and "identification" are central in this definition and draw on both Aristotle and Burke.

Take for example an instance that took place on the N.I.U. campus. A female art major was reported missing after friends noticed that she hadn't returned from a visit to a local forest preserve/park where she had told them she was going to gather material for an art project. Two days later, police reported that they had found some cremated "human remains" in the park and some of the girl's possessions nearby (a camera and art portfolio case). What sort of drama is the average receiver going to co-create using such "facts"? You are probably co-creating a story about them right now. Let us now examine a few of the well-known theories in persuasion that relate in one way or another to our dramatic-oriented definition, and the mystery of the missing art student.

The **elaboration likelihood model** (ELM), which we noted earlier, is a theory that serves as an organizational model of persuasion and has resulted in many significant changes in the way theorists view persuasion. It serves as a central model throughout this book. Social psychologists Richard Petty and John Cacioppo (1986) suggested the ELM as a cognitive model in which persuasion takes one of two routes. In the **central information processing route** the receiver consciously and directly focuses on the persuasive communication while mentally elaborating on the issues and actively seeking more information and facts. In the case of the missing art student, the part of the drama processed in the central route would include seeking information on how old the remains were, the DNA of the remains, the DNA of known samples of tissue from the victim, and other factual bits of data. This requires significant effort on the part of the receiver. The audience of the persuasive message searches out the issues, supporting evidence, alternatives, respective costs and benefits, and other potential outcomes. In this case, the additional information sought might involve the friends of the missing art student. Who were they? What were their reputations? If their reputations were poor, maybe they're good suspects.

At other times, persuasion requires only a momentary period of concentration on an issue—a good price on a brand of detergent, whether to engage a lawn service, choosing the color of a sweater, what channel to tune, or was the missing student attractive? According to the ELM, this persuasion occurs in the **peripheral information processing route**. There, information may be processed almost instantly or just by the senses, without direct focus or research of the logic of the decision. It is usually prompted by minor and seemingly unimportant cues—a phrase of music that accompanies a television spot, a single word or metaphor in a news report (for example, the word "remains" in the art student incident), or the color and shape of a package on the store shelf. We decide to buy Cracker Jacks at the ball park to get the "free" prize (though we know there has never been a good one in over 120 years) and because they are mentioned in the song "Take Me Out to the Ball Game" that is traditionally sung at the middle of the seventh inning at most games. Few people are "dying" to get their hands on Cracker Jacks prizes—it requires no skill and they are usually worthless. We really don't think about these cues thoroughly in any logical way—if we did we'd probably just settle for singing the song. At any given moment, there are millions of pieces of such trivial or peripheral information available to us, but we consciously attend to only a few of them and only process the rest in a kind of subconscious way where they lie dormant until a decision must be made on Cracker Jacks or whatever the item or issue (the "remains" in the art major's case were later reported to have been parts of a leg bone, a few teeth, and bits of ashes from a cremation of a human body). The peripheral route resembles a sponge. We soak up persuasive information and may act on it, but more likely, we remain unaware, unconscious, and unfocused on it in any direct or effortful way until we need it to decide something, and then the sponge is squeezed (in our example, when the university reported that the case was a suspected homicide, that the perpetrator might still be in the area, and advised students to therefore follow certain security precautions, the drama developed rapidly). The peripheral route usually contains shortcuts for decision-making and mostly includes emotional rather than logical appeals; for example, jumping to the conclusion that the student was raped and murdered. Instead of focusing on different variables or facts in persuasion, the peripheral processing in the ELM focuses on the processes that go on during the overall act of persuasion. As noted above, it fits with one of the central ideas of this book: We are bombarded by more information than we can possibly process in any given situation and hence must learn to focus on, study, and elaborate on critical pieces of information, and leave the others to less intensive study or unconscious

"shortcuts"—what Cialdini (2008) calls the "Click, Whirr" response.

The authors of the ELM believe that because we focus or elaborate on some issues more than others, those we choose are far more likely to affect our attitudes, more than the peripherally processed messages that we unconsciously bypass or only consider briefly if at all. Therefore, more "powerful" persuasion occurs with more complete elaboration.

However, we maintain that even slightly elaborated- upon issues still make impressions on us, and because they are more emotional (and perhaps narrative), more unconscious and "subliminal," they can also affect our attitudes toward making final decisions or forming opinions. These changes will not be as consciously or as powerfully believed as those considered in the central processing route, where the attitudes that are formed will last longer, predict behavior better, and combine to form attitude networks. At the same time, and as noted earlier, attitudes formed in the peripheral routes are more likely to be prompted out of us by small, seemingly insignificant cues, such as those found in television advertisements (e.g., jingles). We really don't think about thirty-second television spots, but they probably affect our purchasing or voting behavior. And in both routes a number of factors can affect our elaboration and the resulting attitudes. For example, if we ourselves have a certain health problem—say diabetes—we are far more likely to pay attention to the television ads and to read the magazine articles about the problem that would usually be considered peripheral information to others. That is why most major pharmaceutical companies have recently begun using heavy doses of television and print advertisements. The television advertisements are told like stories, building the drama, leading to the presentation of the drug that will solve whatever ailment they have depicted. Their traditional marketing strategy had been to load doctors with a ton of "free samples" to give to patients, who usually adopted them and became regular users. This idea worked to some degree, but not nearly as well as the ads that told the story or drama of users of the drug and urged the consumer to ask their doctor for the free sample, thus co-creating the message of the drug's positive effects with the pharmaceutical company and the doctor. Doctors can testify that these ads do work. The consumers/patients would have been unaware of those names previously without the ads. Would the industry have continued spending millions of media dollars on such ads if they didn't work? But are the ads ethical? These are the kinds of questions critical receivers need to ask.

What are the methods receivers might employ to protect themselves in this confusing world of elaborated-upon central and peripherally processed information and persuasion? Let's try a method for doing this by asking ourselves what criteria are needed for responsible persuasion to occur.

CRITERIA FOR RESPONSIBLE PERSUASION

How does cooperative and co-creative persuasion happen? These are two things that we need in being responsible persuadees. We should try to assure that they have the best chance of occurring. Three conditions seem to increase the chances that responsible receivers make wise and knowledgeable decisions. First, responsible persuasion is most likely to occur if both parties have an equal opportunity to persuade and approximately equal access to the media. That is why SNM have changed the world so much. Most of us have access to them. However, if one side imposes a gag rule on the proponents of the other side (as is the case in many international economic, military, and ideological conflicts we experience today, such as in Iran and China), the balance of access is affected. The advocates of one side have unlimited access to those media, and as a result, the receivers get an unbalanced view of the issues. Unfortunately, this happens all too often in our global world. Second, it would be much simpler if persuadees would reveal their agendas in advance to the audience. Again, this does not happen often in our global world. Iran doesn't reveal why they want nuclear weapons. To bomb Israel?

To bully some other Arab states in the Middle East (recent Wiki leaks suggest this)? Or to retaliate against the United States? Their agenda is unclear; thus persuasion is impossible.

In an ideal world, persuaders would also warn their audiences of any possible negative side effects of their advocated policies. It would be similar to what drug companies are forced to do. For example, we should have been warned that invading Iran (the persuader's advice) could result in a loss of world prestige, higher gas prices, highly motivated terrorists, and easy recruitment for al-Qaeda. This is precisely what happened in the case of Iraq. Unfortunately, such warnings are not typically given, which is why the third and final criteria is important. This essential element is for critical receivers to test the assertions made by the persuaders, test their evidence against alternate sources, and withhold judgment until all of the facts are in. And even if the first two criteria—equal advocates with equal access to the media and revelation of agendas—are not operating fully, critical receivers can make the difference.

In every upcoming election, we are all likely to see negative ads and false assertions being made by many candidates. We need to question them! As Kathleen Hall Jamieson (1992) observed over two decades ago: "All forms of campaign discourse were becoming alike ... assertion was substituted for argument and attack for engagement" (p. 212). Today, she probably thinks things have become worse. There is more assertion versus argument, and more personal attack versus true issue engagement. It is the job of the critical receivers—you and I—to insist on and carefully examine accurate sources, arguments, and a clash of ideas, instead of charges and countercharges. So let's keep that in mind as we examine how persuasion differs from other forms of influence.

THE SMCR MODEL OF PERSUASION

The simplest model of communication, and one of the oldest and most widely referenced, is Shannon and Weaver's (1949) **SMCR model** (see Figure 1.5). The model began with the early study of

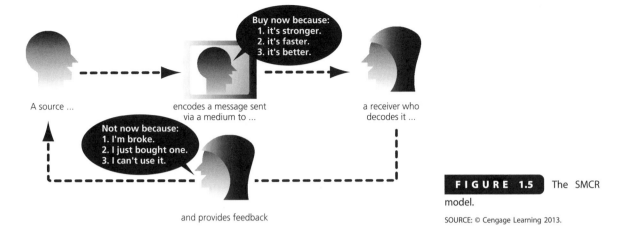

A source ...

encodes a message sent via a medium to ...

a receiver who decodes it ...

and provides feedback

FIGURE 1.5 The SMCR model.

SOURCE: © Cengage Learning 2013.

cybernetics and how information processing technology works; it contains these essential elements:

- A source (S) (or persuader), who or which is the encoder of the message. The code can be verbal, visual (or both), musical, and it might also be encrypted and secret.

- A message (M), which is meant to convey the source's meaning through any of the codes.

- A channel (C), which carries the message. It might be print or electronic and might have a distracting noise which makes deciding more difficult.

- A receiver (R) (or persuadee), who or which decodes the message, trying to sift out channel noise, and adding his or her (or its) own interpretation all the elements that add up to communication.

Let's apply the model to a television ad for a new brand of automobile. Suppose you tell a friend that the words used in a TV ad for the new Chevy Volt (a totally electronic vehicle) emphasize how huge the car seems when it really isn't all that spacious. In this case, you help your friend to form an opinion by explaining a source-related aspect of persuasion—in this case word choice: "Volt—Big Enough to Be a Virtual Party Car!" Then you alert your friend to the doublespeak or "code" in the ad. It is the claim that Volt is "A Virtual Party Car!" You ask what the words "Virtual" and "Party Car" *really* mean, and thus you focus your friend's attention on the message itself. You also point out that skillful video editing and the use of special effects to enhance the meaning of the message, and that using *Mardi Gras* as a background is intended to make it seem huge and fun. Here, you focus on the persuasive impact of the channel that conveys the persuasive information. Finally, you might ask your friend why he or she thinks the Volt will automatically result in fun times, a party atmosphere, and accompanying personal popularity. With this final question you focus your friend's attention on the receiver element of the model and what he or she (or you) bring to decoding the communication. Because persuasion is a process, being a critical receiver means being prepared for all four elements: the motives of the source (obvious or disguised), message elements (verbal and visual symbolic meanings or codes), the channel or medium effects that are used to send the message (electronic, print, or interactive/interpersonal) and finally the interpretations the receiver brings to the source's argument(s).

Try using several of these tools to determine a source's motives. For example, language choice often tips us off to the source's intent. The ideas that the source thinks are persuasive to the audience almost always appear expressed in the words, metaphors, and visuals used. Are they questions or exclamations? Are they short, punchy, and attention getting? Or are they long and soothing? For instance, Schick introduced a "cosmetic" razor called the "Personal Touch." It is clear to whom the product was targeted, and the language used in ads was a tip-off. What do the words "cosmetic," "personal," and "touch" tell you about Schick's view of its potential customer pool? Was it aiming at a "macho" man or at feminine women? Do the words suggest that Schick is giving them the special attention they've always deserved? They tell us that the brand is targeted to females, and the motive is to make them feel special when considering buying a razor. Analyzing the source's message provides the receiver with two benefits. First, it alerts us to the persuasion being aimed at us. Second, it reveals things to us about the source that can help us when that source becomes the target of our own persuasion—for example, when we may want to persuade a feminine audience. Other tools to help us analyze the intent of the message include the source's beliefs about receivers' needs and emotions, the evidence contained in persuasive messages, and considering how that evidence relates to the persuasive goal. Later, we will also consider the layout, graphics, and wording of ads. For example, consider an ad placed across the country by the International Fund for Animal Welfare (IFAW) in Figure 1.6.

Do you really know what can go into a simple fish sandwich?

Fish caught by Canadian Fishermen who also kill the baby seals. Your purchase of a McDonald's or Burger King Fish Sandwich could help buy the boats, hard wooden clubs, and guns used by the seal hunters as they turn from fishing to the cruelty of killing adult and baby seals.

If you made a pledge today not to buy fish sandwiches from McDonald's or Burger King unless you were assured by the companies listed below that no Canadian fish was used . . . your decision would save the seals. Canadian fishermen would have to stop sealing since they are totally dependent on their fish sales, with seal hunting a tiny sideline in comparison.

Canadian Globe and Mail of 13 March 1984, had this to say of IFAW's call for a worldwide boycott of Canadian fish: ". . . But what really has the officials spooked is the U.S. market. (There) The International Fund for

Animal Welfare (IFAW), which spearheads the anti-sealing protest worldwide, has started pressing U.S. purchasers not to take Canadian fish. The U.S. market is worth $1-billion a year to Canadian fishermen and the fast-food business in the United States is about a fifth of that market. Canada fears that, if one U.S. fast-food chain caves in to the protestors, all will surrender."

Over 15,000 seals, mostly babies just 2-4 weeks old, have been clubbed or shot over the last 28 days . . . and yet the Canadian Minister of Fisheries says there is no baby seal hunt.

You have it in your hands to save the baby seals today.

Please write or telephone one or both of the companies listed below and seek an assurance that they will not purchase Canadian fish until the Canadian Government passes a law banning the seal hunt forever.

Mr Fred L Turner,
Chairman of the Board,
McDonald's Corporation,
McDonald's Plaza, Oak Brook, Illinois,
IL 60521
Tel. 312/887-3200

Mr J Jeffrey Campbell, Chairman,
Burger King Corporation,
7360 North Kendall Drive,
Miami,
Florida FL 33156
Tel. 305/596-7277

SAVE THE SEALS
NO TO CANADIAN FISH

To the International Fund for Animal Welfare
I'll put animals first . . . I'll do my part to help you fight the baby seal hunters.
Enclosed is my tax-exempt contribution to IFAW in the amount of:
☐ $10 ☐ $15 ☐ $25 ☐ $35 ☐ $50 ☐ $100 ☐ $500 Other $ _____
We need hundreds of gifts this size to save the baby seals forever.
Name _____
(please print)
Address _____
_____
Zip Code _____

International Fund for Animal Welfare
169 Main Street, Yarmouth Port,
Massachusetts 02675 U.S.A.
Our financial statement is available to contributors
IFAW

Our boycott campaign needs your support. We cannot succeed without your funds, to carry our boycott to every community in America.
A copy of the last financial report filed with the Department of State may be obtained by writing to: N.Y. State Department of State, Office of Charities Registration, Albany, N.Y. 12231 or IFAW.

FIGURE 1.6   Ad encouraging people to boycott fish sandwiches to stop the killing of harp seals.

SOURCE: 1984 Historical IFAW Advertisement courtesy of the International Fund for Animal Welfare.

The IFAW opposes the harvest of baby seals in Canada. This is a highly emotional issue since the young seals are clubbed to death when they climb up on the ice floe to be initially nursed. After they are on the ice and helpless, they are "harvested" to be used in fur garments.

Consider the copy in the ad. "Do you really know what can go into a simple fish sandwich? … Fish caught by Canadian Fishermen who also kill the baby seals. Your purchase of a McDonald's or Burger King Fish Sandwich could help buy the boats, hard wooden clubs, and guns used by the seal hunters as they turn from fishing to the cruelty of killing adult and baby seals." The words such as "hard wooden clubs" and the visual of the men battering the cute baby seal alert you to the underlying emotional persuasion being used. This should prompt one to investigate the facts more fully, because emotional appeals are more likely to be biased, incomplete, propagandistic, or unethical. Even more importantly, they are processed in the peripheral channel of the ELM where they are not analyzed in any detail, and become embedded in the subconscious. Research reveals that actually very few Canadian fishermen are also baby seal hunters; and clubbing the seals is actually the least painful means of the "harvesting" of them. Furthermore, the ad doesn't mention the furs of the seals are the object of the hunt, not their flesh, which is not used in the fish sandwich as the words and visuals suggest. Furthermore, they are mammals, not fish and therefore wouldn't go into a fish sandwich anyway. The connections are weak at best; notice the underlined weasel words—*some* Canadian fishermen also hunt seals and so *some* of the fish (not seals) they catch *could be* in a fish sandwich. It's a real stretch. Looking carefully at the message should prompt you, as a critical persuadee, to get the other side of the story. It also alerts you to the kinds of effects that the print channel has on persuasion. A similar appeal using radio would probably fail, because radio lacks the visual imagery needed (the fish sandwich, the baby seal, and the brutal clubbing). Imagine a TV ad documenting the harp seal slaughter. Would this make the message more or less effective? I believe it would have been

terrifically persuasive. The dramatic nature of TV makes us more vulnerable to certain types of messages, such as humorous ones, demonstrations, exaggerations, comparisons, and before and after appeals. Video and audio footage of the clubbing of the seals would certainly raise audience emotions.

Finally, the SMCR model suggests we need to look at ourselves to determine what kinds of motives, biases, and perspectives we bring to the persuasion. What fascinations, needs, and desires do we add in the process of co-creation? How do we interact with the message and the medium used? Does our cultural heritage shade the meaning of the message? Do we inherently oppose the killing of innocent, harmless, helpless animals? Are we grossed out about eating them by mistake? Remember that *communication tactics* flow from *communication strategies*, which in turn flow from overall *communication goals*—there is a three-part process going on: goal setting, strategy planning, and the final tactical design.

PERSUASION AND OTHER THEORIES OF INFLUENCE

Of course, persuasion is not the only form of influencing others. Aristotle differentiated between artistic and non-artistic means of getting others to follow our advice—there were coercive means like torture, legal means like contracts, and promissory means like oaths, to name a few.

The Theory of Reasoned Action

Another theory of persuasion is primarily based on the central processing channel of the ELM. Communication researchers Fishbein and Azjen (1980) were dissatisfied with the inability of shifts in attitude to predict subsequent shifts in conscious and desired changes in behavior. Habitual, mindless, or scripted behavior is ruled out of this theory. It focuses on volitional behavior—those actions that you and I choose to enact or reject. A key concept in the theory is the *behavioral intention*, which is the result of individual influences such as our feelings, attitudes or predispositions, and our cultural norms. Cultural diversities may also affect behaviors. Take, for instance, my or your actions in regards to practicing safe sex.

Individually, we may think it is a good practice for health reasons, to avoid unwanted pregnancy, and to prevent the spread of disease. We have been advised to do so by trusted sources like our physician. However, once we get to college we learn that practicing safe sex is not that cool or fun, and it is not the norm for our fellow classmates and friends. Now what do we do? Do we listen to the health warnings or do we follow the crowd? The theory predicts that our actions will flow from what we planned or intended to do beforehand. These *behavioral intentions* rest upon the strength of our beliefs about health risks involved and our evaluations of those beliefs. The other half of the behavioral intention rests upon cultural norms or patterns. If the persons in our fraternity think safe sex is laughable, that may change our initial intention to even carry condoms. The cultural norm also interacts with our motivation to comply. Would I rather feel secure against infection or pregnancy, or do I want to feel accepted as part of the group? These factors then lead to a pre-behavior intention. I say that it can't hurt to be prepared—after all that's the Boy Scout motto—so I might as well carry condoms. In this case the personal rather than the cultural factors play the major role, and my ultimate action or behavior will probably be to carry condoms. But what if I'm a dedicated Catholic? Then cultural diversity enters in and that may change my behavior. The theory has been particularly predictive in issues involving health and safety (wearing seat belts, breast self-examinations, etc.) (Fishbein & Ajzen, 1991). The theory basically says that I use my reasoning abilities to balance my individual beliefs and values with those of my surrounding culture when taking voluntary action in response to a persuasive request.

Narrative Theories

A final set of theories briefly examined here and elaborated on in later chapters are called *narrative theories*. Their basic premise is simple, and most would agree with it—human beings are instinctually storytellers. They are like the Ancient Mariner who stops the traveler to insist that he listen to the old man's tale of the curse of the albatross he killed while at sea. We human beings, as sources of persuasion, are impelled to convince others of the rightness of our position(s) by recreating the story of how we came to believe as we do: "Let me tell you how …" As receivers, we are also more affected by, likely to remember longer, and are probably more likely to take action on persuasion if it is packaged in a story format. That is the basic premise for 95 percent of all television spot advertisements and probably a high percentage of most other persuasion we face on a daily basis. They tell us the tragic or comic story of the person whose company didn't have health insurance and who, as a result, lost everything. It is also frequently the story behind most political candidacies. Obama Barack began his political race for the presidency in 2007, but preceded it with two books entitled *Dreams from My Father* and *The Audacity of Hope* (2006), in which he traced his roots and told how they led him to a political life and a belief that he could do something about today's political and public woes. Public opinion at the time widely supported the invasion of Iraq in 2003. This belief was based largely on the "story" of a tyrant who repeatedly flaunted the United Nations and world opinion, used poison gas on his countrymen, committed other acts of genocide, and was developing nuclear weapons. The narrative played well for a time though it was finally recognized mainly as a constructed hoax. In another example, many persons were convinced or persuaded to donate money to assist the victims of Hurricane Katrina and especially the citizens of New Orleans based on the story of how they had been displaced from their homes. This rise in donations resulted when it was revealed that the tragedy could be traced to faulty plans by the Army Corps of Engineers, and the federal government, FEMA, and even the president seemed to forget about the disaster. And of course it also dovetailed with the past experiences of citizens who have been discriminated against because of their race—prime territory for co-creation. Thousands of more recent narratives about people losing jobs and not finding another are told every day. We could continue with hundreds of other examples where the power of the story worked both for persuaders and on persuadees.

The point of these theories is not to advise the use of the narrative, the dramatic, and the personal story in trying to persuade others (though that would be good advice). Instead, it is to caution receivers against being too willing to accept such persuasion simply because it is packaged in an attractive narrative. As noted earlier, we will encounter these theories in more depth as we move along. Now let us try to differentiate persuasion from other forms of influence. In the final analysis, we want to learn about what gets us to do the things we do, and believe the things we believe. Most communication scholars agree that persuasion usually relies on communication that attempts to change another person in some way. Some suggest that the attempt must succeed to be considered persuasion, others disagree. Most agree that persuasion requires participation by a sender and a receiver. Persuasion usually succeeds when it adapts to the receiver's world—the situation, the context, the culture and its norms, and the receivers' emotions and motivations. Figure 1.7 illustrates the relationships among various forms of influence that often confuse the new student of persuasion. The importance of each type of influence probably varies substantially from person to person and according to the context. The central point of this diagram is that many forces (including persuasion) bring change to our lives.

Those who study persuasion don't always distinguish among these forms of influence. In many discussions, "influence" and "persuasion" are used interchangeably. We need to distinguish among several terms related to persuasion, including: influence, coercion, compliance-gaining, acquiescence, behavioral modeling, and information integration.

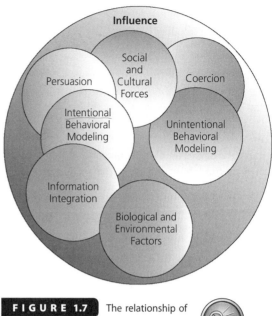

FIGURE 1.7 The relationship of persuasion to other forms of influence.

SOURCE: © Cengage Learning 2013.

Influence refers to the ways in which certain things alter a person's attitude or behaviors. There are several ways that attitudes or behaviors may change. (See the best-selling *Influence: Science and Practice* by Robert B. Cialdini, 2008.) For example, many fans adopt the styles or behaviors of their pop idols. This represents influence through behavior modeling. Similarly, many adults are embarrassed when their young child uses profanity in public—profanity that was overheard at home. This is also an outcome of behavioral modeling, though probably an unintended one. In contrast, most parents consciously try to model more positive behaviors for their children, hoping to "persuade" them to emulate those behaviors. Persuasion always entails some degree of choice. In contrast, coercion, another form of influence, always uses some level of force—physical or psychological—to gain compliance. A usually benign form is when peer pressure forces an individual to change attitudes or behaviors. But it can also be dangerous, when peers persuade us to do something illegal or unethical. **Coercion** also has levels. At one extreme, it is being held at gunpoint, facing the threat of terrorism, or even being exposed to torture. A slightly less direct use of force might be blackmail, threatening to harm another's reputation by revealing secret information, or to intimidate someone in other ways like cyber bullying. Propaganda is also another form of influence—usually psychological versus logical—and, as we have already seen and shall continue to see throughout this book, it is frequently extremely effective. Propaganda can often change entire cultures as it did in Hitler's Germany or as in some Islamic sects. It doesn't usually use direct or physical influence, but instead uses some level of psychological reward (such as promising heavenly bliss for martyrdom). Or it may predict dire consequences. People weren't physically forced to oppose Al Qaeda, but after 9/11 and other terrorist acts, they felt compelled to label and oppose the enemy, resulting in much generalized anti-Islamic prejudice. Propaganda usually does that; it convinces us to label others as undesirable or hated, and then to scapegoat them. It then urges taking actions against them—imprisonment, death, discrimination, and so on. As noted above, *Webster's Collegiate Dictionary* defines propaganda as "ideas, facts, or allegations spread deliberately to further or to damage an opposing cause." Notice the use of the key words "deliberate," "spread," and "cause." The propagandist acts deliberately, not by chance, and tries to extend his or her message as widely as possible—usually using some mass media. This probably will include more recent forms of media such as SNM. The propaganda message promotes or opposes some ideology. Most advertising, while deliberate, doesn't promote or oppose a cause but uses facts, ideas, or allegations to promote a *brand* or to oppose a competing brand. However, in some cases advertising is quite propagandistic, as in political ads.

Persuasion and coercion represent two ends of a continuum ranging from free choice to forced choice. Although terrorism uses coercion, the co-creation of states of identification between source and receiver doesn't often result. Persuasion of a different sort can occur as an unexpected result; for example, acceptance of cultural diversity suffered after terrorist attacks around the globe. Many people feared air travel—especially if other passengers appeared to be of Middle Eastern extraction; this was demonstrated even as recently as 2010, when a minority NPR celebrity was fired because he admitted he felt uneasy on airplanes if other passengers were dressed in Islamic fashion.

In other words, events can be a form of influence, though not always in the hoped-for direction. Influence can also occur when a person chooses a certain action in return for some future concession, known as political favor swapping: "You scratch my back and I'll scratch yours." In such a case, persuasion occurs in making a political deal because some common ground was reached; but few of the involved *really* changed their minds. Information integration and analysis is yet another route to influence that doesn't involve real persuasion. For example, a retail manager may change his or her inventory management behavior after learning that quarterly sales in certain product categories (e.g., seasonal items) were up or down in the past quarter or last year in the holiday season. Again, persuasion is not really involved, since neither co-creation, common ground, nor interactive communication occurred. And something overheard in a conversation, read in the newspaper, seen on TV, or via a SNM may lead to changes in behavior; but this is not persuasion for the same reasons.

Co-creation is central to our definition of persuasion. Persuasive contexts extend beyond public-speaking situations, but all involve some kind of co-creation. For instance, most advocacy and related propaganda, protest marches, decision-making get-togethers, staff meetings, sales presentations, and mass media events all involve some level of co-creation. With all of these kinds of influence (including persuasion), some of it is going to be unfair, untrustworthy, and even unethical. How can responsible influence occur in today's confusing world? Let's examine an easy-to-use model that will help us, as receivers, to ensure that such persuasion—whether by mass or social media—can occur so that we can spot its opposite—irresponsible or unethical persuasion—when it occurs.

RANK'S MODEL OF PERSUASION: A FIRST MEANS OF SELF-PROTECTION

As noted in our discussion of doublespeak, the National Council of Teachers of English (NCTE) seeks ways to teach students to identify doublespeak and to become critical receivers of it and other kinds of persuasion. Researcher Hugh Rank (1976) long ago offered a useful model for doing just that. He noted even back then that: "These kids are growing up in a propaganda blitz unparalleled in human history… Schools should shift their emphasis in order to train the larger segment of our population in a new kind of literacy so that more citizens can recognize the more sophisticated techniques and patterns of persuasion" (p. 5). Rank's easy-to-use, analytical tool is called the **intensify/downplay model**, and its goal is to help you to become more critical and analytical receivers. It defines and gives examples of four often-used major persuasive strategies and six associated tactics frequently used by persuaders, which critical receivers can identify. Remember that a persuader's **goals** are implemented in the **strategies** he or she chooses, and these strategies are put in place using certain **tactics**. It is similar to the layers of an onion with goals on the outside, strategies in the middle, and tactics at the center.

Rank maintains that persuaders employ these major strategies to achieve their goals. One of Rank's major strategies is for persuaders to **intensify** certain positive aspects of their product, cause, or candidate, or some negative aspect of the competition. Another of his strategies is for persuaders to **downplay** certain negative aspects of their brand, cause, or candidate, or the positive aspects of the competing brands, causes, ideologies, or candidates. Often, they do both. Figure 1.8 illustrates this model. Persuaders choose from four strategies of action.

Notice that many of these tactics are probably processed via the peripheral route of the ELM; for example, this can happen whenever persuadees or receivers give evidence or reasoning little thought or serious consideration. Nonetheless, the misleading evidence or reasoning is making what the pros

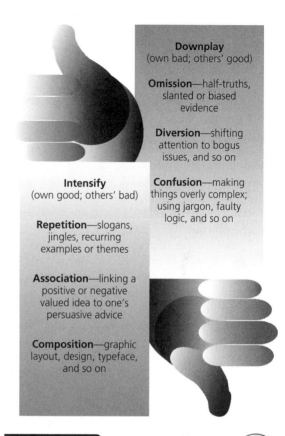

Downplay
(own bad; others' good)

Omission—half-truths, slanted or biased evidence

Diversion—shifting attention to bogus issues, and so on

Confusion—making things overly complex; using jargon, faulty logic, and so on

Intensify
(own good; others' bad)

Repetition—slogans, jingles, recurring examples or themes

Association—linking a positive or negative valued idea to one's persuasive advice

Composition—graphic layout, design, typeface, and so on

FIGURE 1.8 Rank's intensify/downplay schema.

SOURCE: © Cengage Learning 2013.

call "impressions" or "brand contacts." And these remain imbedded in your unconscious or subconscious minds until the moment you decide to purchase, vote, donate, or join. We will discuss this further when we address subliminal persuasion and/or neuromarketing.

Basically, persuaders use tactics such as **repetition**, **association**, and **composition** to intensify their own good points or the bad points of the opposition. They use the tactics of **omission**, **diversion**, and **confusion** to downplay their own bad points or the good points of the opposing brands, candidates, causes, or ideologies. Any one of these tactics can be used logically or emotionally, and can employ interactive or more traditional media to accomplish the persuader's intentions. Again, many are processed in the peripheral channel of information processing and remain hidden and unconscious until decision time. We have seen these tactics in the powerful propaganda of the Nazis, and continue to see them in the propaganda surrounding the war on terrorism, the immigration issue, the wars in Iraq and Afghanistan, and other policy issues that continue to emerge, as well as in more harmless persuasive attempts like advertisements on behalf of certain brands, letters to the editor, and so forth.

Persuasive strategy, then, is an overall step-by-step program for reaching some persuasive goal. Strategy also dictates tactics or the specific kinds of arguments, evidence, or points the persuader makes. For example, politicians want to persuade voters to support their candidacy (the goal), so they try to make the audience feel good about particular platform plans (the strategy), and the candidate's own character and past record (the tactics). For years, Claussen's dill pickles used the tactics of print advertising to sell the crunchiness of the pickle (an uncooked but heavily brined pickle) compared to the competition (cooked or canned pickles that had little "crunch"). Crispiness was hard to demonstrate in print so they turned to a TV advertising tactic—the demonstration. There they showed the saggy competition being bent in half without breaking and compared its sagginess and sogginess with the Claussen's pickle's snap (sound "sweetened" by experts). Sales improved almost immediately.

Intensification

Persuaders either want to look good in the eyes of the audience—the voters, joiners, donors, or potential customers—or they want their opponents to look bad in the same person's eyes. Some tactics intensify the persuader's own good points ("He's always been on the right side of environmental and immigration issues"). Others intensify the bad points of the other guy, thus making the persuader look good by comparison ("He didn't tell us the truth on the tax increases or the mega-dump in our town, so don't trust his opinions on global warming").

Repetition. One way to intensify good or bad points about a product, person, or candidate is to repeat them over and over again. That's why slogans, jingles, and logotypes work. For example, Energizer batteries "keep going and going" in TV spots, magazine ads, and even on their packages, and have done so for decades; this advertising campaign probably will continue to "keep working and working." We repeatedly are warned against transfats in our diets; and we know that Lexus is "in the pursuit of perfection" by heart. All of these are examples of the power of repetition in persuading people—either intensifying one's own good or intensifying the opposition's bad points—again mainly in the peripheral route of information processing.

Association. Another tactic for intensification is association, which operates in three steps. It (1) links a cause, brand, or candidate (2) to something already liked or disliked (3) by the audience. Thus, the cause, brand, or candidate becomes identified with the thing liked or disliked and the favor or disfavor "rubs off." As a result, it is likewise liked or disliked. Or consider that politicians know that we have fears about privacy, so they refer to secrecy and warrant less surveillance by our government. Here association works the other way; something not liked (invasion of privacy) is associated with the politician or party to be defeated. In commerce, advertisers associate a certain athletic shoe with a well-known professional athlete, everyday people who exercise, or with a person in a wheelchair as Nike did in one of their ads. NFL athletes regularly testify during game breaks as to the good aspects of the United Way. These associations intensify the good aspects of the shoe or the United Way and show that one needn't be an athlete to benefit from the shoe or to promote the good causes to which the NFL is committed, also reinforcing—what a bunch of good guys—the character of the organization. Visual cues can also create association. That's why candidates are pictured in front of the Lincoln

Memorial or the Capitol. Video footage can intensify the good aspects of the United Way or other good causes (for example, showing a star quarterback playing with kids), and the bad aspects of world problems by showing videos of starving children.

Composition.   The third and final tactic of intensification uses physical composition of the message to emphasize one's own good points or the other guy's bad points. This usually involves the use of nonverbal or visual means that are processed via the peripheral channel of the ELM and takes several forms. Altering the makeup of the printed word (as in changing "U.S.A." to "U.$.A.") sends the message that the nation is only interested in money. Altering the composition of a candidate's publicity photo often manipulates meaning. A low camera angle makes the candidate look larger than life and tells us to look up to him or her. Altering the layout of an advertisement intensifies persuasive outcomes. For example, the upper-right and lower-left corners of a magazine page or a poster or video screen are considered "fallow" (or less productive), and thus not likely to get full reader attention. The eye only glances at them momentarily, so guess where the tobacco industry usually puts the required health warning? In those fallow corners. A good example of composition being used is seen in Figure 1.9.

These cases also exemplify the use of the peripheral route of the ELM in persuasive appeals, and as a result we don't put much time, effort, or research into processing them. Furthermore, they also demonstrate the age of advocacy in which we live when a health clinic feels it must advertise that it is a "good citizen" in the community. Other principles we have discussed are also reflected here. What are they? What common ground has been co-created? To give you an idea of how persuaders also use composition to compare and contrast, consider the following hypothetical TV spot against a candidate:

> To intensify the politician's bad points, an ad superimposes his or her image on a picture of a polluted river or a filthy harbor

in the home district. To emphasize the negative identification and to encourage further emotional interaction with the spot, a muted off-key version of "America the Beautiful" might accompany a voice-over talking about the incumbent's lack of social responsibility. The polluted river or harbor, the background, the music, and the voice-over combine to "compose" the ad's co-created meaning.

Another example of intensification is seen in most "before and after" ads for consumer products dealing with appearance; they use composition to show us the good points about the brand that inevitably changes things for the better (for example, whiter teeth, thinner bodies, and happier babies). You can use Rank's intensification as a starting place in becoming a critical receiver by identifying the strategies and tactics used by persuaders in achieving their strategy of intensification. So the tactics of repetition, association, and composition are all effective in implementing the communication strategy of intensification of one's own good or the other's bad points.

Downplaying

Sometimes persuaders want to avoid intensifying or calling attention to something because it undermines their persuasive goal. The government doesn't tell us over and over about the billions of dollars being overpaid by the Department of Defense (for example, $171 for a hammer or $600 for a toilet seat), and it opposes other persuaders who repeat those figures. And car advertisers avoid promoting the good mileage results of the competing brand. This strategy carries over to other kinds of persuasion as well. No brand advertises its high trans-fat composition or its detrimental dyes; instead they advertise its meaty appearance that will thrill, not kill, your pet or you. Downplaying can soften the persuader's own weak points while downplaying a competitor's strong points. The car manufacturer advertises its good styling, built-in GPS, and audio-direction to destination advice, but avoids telling us about the competition's

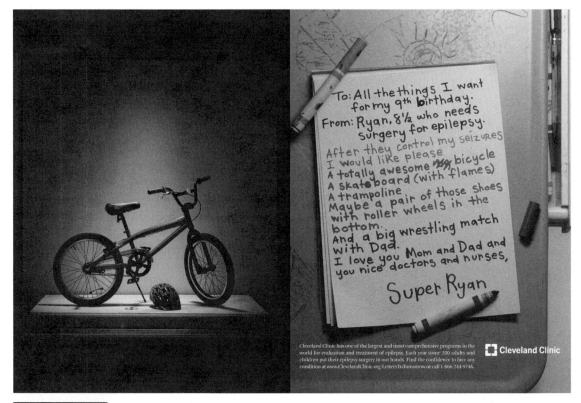

FIGURE 1.9   This ad for Cleveland Clinic is another example of how composition persuades. Note Ryan's confident handwritten message—"After they control my seizures...."—the tear in the page and his scribbled-over mistake the act of a young boy, thus making his determination to recover from epilepsy all the more moving. Now compare those elements of the ad with his wishes for a "totally awesome bicycle, a skateboard (with flames), a trampoline, and a big wrestling match with Dad," all of which will be fulfilled because of the quality care he will receive at Cleveland Clinic. Cleveland Clinic is world famous in its treatment of epilepsy and many other serious health problems of children and adults.

SOURCE: Courtesy of Cleveland Clinic.

superior safety features. The politician, who knows he or she made a bad decision on a certain vote, tries to avoid mentioning it. Let's look at some tactics used in the strategy of downplaying: **omission, diversion**, and **confusion**.

Omission.   Some persuaders simply leave out critical information to avoid highlighting their own shortcomings or the competitor's strengths. Not telling the whole truth about an issue is one

way to use omission. For example, the government didn't reveal the questionable quality of their "intelligence" on Weapons of Mass Destruction (WMD) in Iraq. That qualifies it as propaganda in that it conceals its source and thus results in invalid beliefs. As a result, we went to war for at least a decade—longer than any other previous war fought by the United States. Who knows how many lives, how much oil, metals, dollars, and other valuables it cost and

BOX 1.7 **Cultural Diversity and Persuasion**

To become familiar with the many issues that are intertwined with our increasing diversity as a country, go to Weblink 1.12 and explore the content and authors of various diversity-related documentary videos. Visit the video by Jean Kilbourne entitled "Killing Us Softly," which addresses the many ways in which advertising forces women to value attractiveness, sexuality, and gender stereotypes, thus making women and children vulnerable to violent abuse. Kilbourne claims that advertisers are the real pornographers of our times. Other interesting options include "The

Politics of Love in Black and White," which explores the problems of interracial couples; and "Colorism," which investigates the caste system that operates in Black communities based on features, hair, and lightness of skin shade. Take a look at "Tough Guise," which focuses on the relationship between gender and violence. Other titles will interest and sensitize you to persuasion and diversity as well as to what is being left out (omission) or given as a misleading issue (diversion), and so on, using the Rank model.

still does cost? Omission also occurs in many advertisements—for instance, in those for foods. Live photographs of some kinds of food are frequently unappetizing—lettuce wilts, ice melts, red meat color fades to gray, and so on. As a result, there is an occupation known as "food cosmetics" in which the expert uses a variety of techniques to make the food look better (for example, photographs of salads look crisper if coated with hair spray, and photographs of floor tile adhesive look more appetizing than actual chocolate pudding). The officials of a charitable organization omit telling potential donors that the administrative costs for dispersing the charitable donations exceed 90 percent of the actual donations themselves. Our propaganda-filled world has many examples of omitting the crucial information for getting audiences to make apparently logical or reasoned decisions, such as the one noted above. For instance, in the case of a horse slaughtering business in Dekalb, Illinois, advocates for its closure omitted telling the readers that since the closure of two similar plants in Texas, the number of horses found tied up in forest preserves or state and national forests to starve and painfully die had sky-rocketed. In the same debate, opponents mentioned that with the closing of U.S. slaughterhouses, thousands of the animals were sent to Mexican facilities. There the animals are not disposed of in a humane way but instead are stabbed in the spinal cord and must wait in pain for final slaughter. This kept

them paralyzed, easy to control and resulted in "fresher" meat for the consumer.

Omission also means avoiding mention of the opponent's strengths. It is hard to imagine a toy manufacturer mentioning that kids love the competitor's doll or train set more than their own brand. Likewise, it is rare that a politician would emphasize the opponent's honesty, hard work, and sincerity. And it would be foolish for a bank to note that other banks or credit cards offer better interest rates. So the tactic of omission is a critical way to downplay either one's own flaws or the opposition's strengths. Can you identify examples of omission from today's news reports?

Diversion. Diversion consists of shifting attention away from an opponent's strengths or one's own shortcomings this time not through omission, but by using substitute issues to divert the receiver's scrutiny. Persuaders frequently use humor to shift attention. Making a joke of the competitor's image ("He's the Charlie Chaplin of Community Leaders") diverts attention from the issues to the person (an example of what is called an *ad hominem* as we shall see later). In another advertising example, "Headon," over-the-counter headache "medicine" diverts attention from its bad points (time to take effect, messiness, etc.) by diverting our attention to its ease of application. Toyota doesn't mention that it is a foreign brand, or had to do hundreds of thousands of recalls in 2010 due to faulty accelerator problems that caused stuck accelerators and led to many fatal accidents. Instead Toyota focuses its ads on the U.S. factories that assemble the foreign-made parts instead of shipping the work offshore. The polluting power company diverts attention from its use of high sulfur coal to its support of "Save the Species" programs. And the clever politician avoids mentioning his or her early support for the now unpopular wars in the Mid-East to their longtime support and promotion of saving the environment. Diversion can also redirect audience attention from the major issues of a debate to inconsequential ones, and thus siphons valuable time away from discussion and interaction between the persuader and persuadee. This happened in the longtime debate over immigration. Some politicians focused the debate on the impossibility of transferring ten million illegal aliens back to their home countries. Other office holders focused the debate on the effectiveness or ineffectiveness of putting some sort of a fence or wall along the Canadian and Mexican borders. This option diverted attention and downplayed the major difficulty in solving the complex issues of dealing with the large numbers of persons involved. I crossed the Canadian border on a daily basis while canoeing and fishing in the Boundary Waters Canoe Wilderness Area (BWCWA) and in fact literally "exploited" Canadian natural resources by using deadfall wood from the Canadian side of the lake for my campfire held in the United States. That example could short circuit the "Border Fence" diversion pretty quickly and serve as a diversion as well.

Confusion.   Another downplaying tactic is to create confusion in the audience's mind. Using technical jargon that the receiver doesn't understand creates such confusion. For example, the Department of Defense has a jargonized term called BRAC. That's an acronym for "Base Realignment and Closure," a term sure to confuse. It actually means closing a base in one state and moving it to another, which naturally has good and bad results for both places; but the term confuses and camouflages the resulting effect the action will have on jobs, traffic, behavior problems, and other issues.

Another way to create confusion is by weaving an intricate and rambling argument that evades the real issues results in audience confusion. Yet another device for confusing persuadees is the use of faulty logic. Consider the logic used in the following claim: "Mr. Taco has delicious food—look at how clean its kitchen is!" The weak connection is apparent, but it will probably confuse some potential customers. It is what is called a "red herring" because it simply doesn't follow or isn't part of the school of thought of regular "herrings." Does cleanliness equal delicious food? It may be that clean kitchens don't ever produce good-tasting food.

A governmental example occurred when the White House declared in 2005 that it had adopted 37 of the 39 reforms recommended by the 9/11 commission. Sounds like a very logical outcome, doesn't it? However, one of the rejected recommendations was that the United States should comply with the internationally recognized Geneva Convention's standards on humane treatment of prisoners. These outlaw torture as a means of extracting information from captured terrorists. The United States was engaging in torture widely and sometimes secretly "subcontracting" its torture to other countries. As a result, many foreign governments now refuse to cooperate with the United States' "War on Terrorism," fearing that they will be labeled as also violating the international agreement. And there are other ways to confuse the persuadee, as we shall see. Taken together with the other tactics of downplaying as well as those of intensification, we see that clever persuaders have many options beyond the use of confusion when considering how to persuade gullible and uncritical audiences. So it is incumbent on us to train ourselves to be critical receivers as we encounter contemporary persuasion in our interactive and socially networked world.

A METHOD OF SELF-PROTECTION

In his discussion of doublespeak, Rank (1976) offered some advice about how to detect the

Intensify own good	Intensify others' bad
1. ____	1. ____
2. ____	2. ____

Downplay own bad	Downplay others' good
1. ____	1. ____
2. ____	2. ____
3. ____	3. ____

FIGURE 1.10   Intensify/downplay scorecard.

SOURCE: © Cengage Learning 2013.

flaws of persuaders who use various tactics to intensify or downplay: "When they intensify, you downplay. When they downplay, you intensify." A way to follow Rank's advice systematically is to divide a sheet of paper into quarters, as shown in Figure 1.10, and then enter the kinds of downplaying and intensifying going on in the message(s). Simply seeing these items makes you more alert to the kind of manipulation going on. It becomes a kind of "scorecard" for immunizing oneself to deceptive minds of doublespeak. Try using the self-protection method on an advertisement or a current political speech. When the ad or speech downplays something, you intensify its shortcomings. And when it intensifies something, you downplay the intensification. We will discuss a number of other tools of analysis as we proceed, but Rank's intensify/downplay tool seems a useful general tool of analysis to employ when first faced with a persuasive blitz.

REVIEW AND CONCLUSION

If you now feel more alert to the possible ways persuaders manipulate you, congratulations! You're already on your way to becoming a more critical, doubting, and skeptical receiver. You now need to arm yourself with some tools of analysis that make for wise consumers of persuasion. Rank's model is a good beginning, but there are more ways to tune our critical abilities, and there is a bonus for learning them. Seeing what works in what circumstances, and with what kinds of people—yourself and others—helps you prepare to persuade others when encountering similar circumstances. Skillful consumers of messages learn to be more effective producers of messages. As we move ahead, apply the tools of persuasive analysis on your own and in the study questions at the end of each chapter. Use the diversity, propaganda, SNM, ELM, and interactive media boxes as well as the learning

goals, key terms, and applications of ethics. Also, explore the Internet and research issues via a search engine. Examine the ways in which persuasion operates on the interpersonal level. Every day you make decisions in non-public settings. Your parents may try to persuade you to avoid certain occupational fields, to seek a summer job, or to put off a purchase. You need to decide to heed or reject your parents' choice of your career/major in college on the basis of your interpersonal communication with them. Rank's model helps here too. Identify what your parents intensify and downplay. Do the same thing with other interpersonal relationships—roommates, friends, colleagues, the government, your boss, advertisers, your "friends" on Facebook, MySpace, and other SNM. Then try to spot the kinds of symbols that lead to or discourage identification. Critical analysis of interpersonal persuasion helps you to make informed decisions. People are persuaded daily in the public arena through advertisements, speeches, radio and TV programs, newspaper and magazine articles, and the Internet. But we also need to remember that, in addition to the world of the marketplace and political and ideological realms, persuasion also takes place in our personal lives and we need to become critical receivers in those venues as well.

KEY TERMS

After reading this chapter, you should be able to identify, explain, and give an example of the following key terms or concepts:

social network media (SNM)	artistic proof	central information processing route	downplay
interactive media	inartistic proof	peripheral information processing route	repetition
cultural diversity	ethos	SMCR model	association
propaganda	pathos	influence	composition
advocacy	logos	coercion	omission
"response-ability,"	common ground	goals	diversion
doublespeak	enthymemes	strategies	confusion
scam	identification	tactics	
self-protection	self-persuasion	intensify	
rhetoric	elaboration likelihood model		

APPLICATION OF ETHICS

The Ethics of Omission. A homeowner needs to sell his home but is hesitant to inform realtors or prospective buyers that there has been a mold problem in the basement in the past and that it could become a toxic variety. Presently it only smells in damp weather and is soon removed by spraying bleach and washing down the basement. What should the homeowner do? (1) Spray the basement, list the house for sale, and not mention the mold problem. (2) Spray the basement and mention the problem and the present solution to both buyers and realtors. (3) Hire a toxic mold expert to find out if the mold really is likely to become toxic and discover what can be done about it if it is indeed toxic. (4) Don't spray the basement since the weather is now dry and simply list the house as "For Sale by Owner." What are the ethical problems in this case? How would you characterize each of the homeowner's options in terms of what has been discussed in this chapter?

QUESTIONS FOR FURTHER THOUGHT

1. If you or someone you know recently made a major purchase (for example, an automobile, an MP3 player, iPhone, or a digital camera), identify the context in which persuasion occurred. Where did the persuasion take place? In the showroom? Through a television ad? Interpersonally, such as in discussing the purchase with a friend or on an SNM? What kinds of appeals were made? What characteristics were intensified? Downplayed? Was the persuasion emotional or logical, or both? Was it processed in the central or the peripheral channel of information processing? What did you learn from the careful examination?

2. Much persuasion occurs in interpersonal contexts. Examine one of your interpersonal relationships, such as that between you and your parents, your roommate, a teammate, a "friend" from an SNM or a fellow member of an organization or church. Describe how, when, and where persuasion operated in the relationship. What characteristics about yourself have you intensified? Downplayed? What about the other person's intensification? Downplaying? Which tactics worked best? Repetition? Association? Omission? Where in the ELM did the processing occur?

3. Beginning with the definition of persuasion offered in this chapter, create your own model of persuasion that reflects all the important elements of the definition given here.

4. Identify three types of persuasion you recently processed, and analyze each according to the definition offered in this chapter and the ELM (such as an advertisement, a television talk show, a sermon, or an interpersonal relationship). What verbal or visual symbols were used? Did you interact with the message? What did

the persuader intend? Which information processing route (peripheral or central) operated for you? What created identification or common ground for you? What was intensified? Downplayed? Using which tactics? Repetition? Association? Composition? Omission? Confusion? Diversion?

5. Describe the tactics of intensification, and explain how they work. Give examples of their use on television, in print, on radio, by politicians, and by advertisers.

6. Enter the word "propaganda" in a search engine and look at some historical and contemporary examples. How do they differ? What did the audience of the times (such as WWI or WWII) identify with? How did the propaganda create common ground with the families of soldiers in each of the World Wars? How was it accomplished in the contemporary examples (such as the wars in Iraq or Afghanistan). Now do the same thing with the term "advocacy." Do they both get processed in the same channel of the ELM?

7. Describe the tactics of downplaying and explain how they work. Give examples of their use on television, in print, on radio, by politicians, and by advertisers.

8. Identify a current "propaganda blitz" (for example, the war on terrorism, the emigration issue, the real estate bubble bursting, unemployment, or budget deficits) going on in the media coverage of an event or issue. Which route in the ELM was employed? Which (if any) of the five characteristics of propaganda (such as concealing source or results) is operating? Describe current examples of the strategies of intensification and downplaying that seem central in the "war on terrorism"

propaganda. What tactics of intensification or downplaying are used regarding environmental issues? Are they ethical or unethical? Are any issues involving cultural diversity involved? Are SNM being used?

9. List some of the interactive media or SNM you use. How many of them came about in recent times—say since 2000? How many of them preceded the Internet? Have they reduced or eliminated other means of communication that you have used in the past?

10. Have you noticed the ways in which we are becoming a more diverse culture? How does that affect the persuasive process?

 You can access your online resources at the companion website for *Persuasion.* Log in at **http://www.cengagebrain.com**.

2

Perspectives on Ethics in Persuasion

RICHARD L. JOHANNESEN

Northern Illinois University

LEARNING GOALS

After reading this chapter, you should be able to:

1. Discuss the importance of ethical issues and standards in the persuasion process.

2. Recognize the complexity of making ethical judgments about persuasion.

3. Apply five ethical perspectives for judging persuasion.

4. Apply specific ethical criteria for assessing political communication and commercial advertising.

5. Recognize how moral exclusion functions in unethical persuasion to harm people of diverse

nations, cultures, religions, genders, and sexual orientations.

6. Recognize how interactive and social network media pose significant ethical issues for persuasion.

7. Understand the distinction between lying and deception.

8. Start developing your own workable and justifiable ethical framework or code of ethics for evaluating your persuasive choices of means and ends and those of other persuaders.

Students enrolled in persuasion courses frequently are preparing for careers in advertising, sales, law, journalism, business, or politics. But students interested in such careers may be surprised by the extremely negative perceptions people have of the ethics and honesty of persons in such professions. The November 2010 Gallup Poll of perceived honesty and ethics of 22 professions ranks the following 11, in descending order, as lowest in perceived ethicality: bankers, TV reporters, newspaper reporters, local officeholders, lawyers, business executives, state officeholders, advertising practitioners, members of Congress, and finally, tied at the bottom, lobbyists and car salespeople (see Weblink 2.1). (You can access this and all of the other chapter 2 weblinks through your companion website for *Persuasion*, chapter 2 resources.)

Evidence abounds that supports public concern over the decline of ethical behavior. A May 2010 Gallup Poll of citizen perceptions of moral values in the United States found that 83 percent of respondents rated the current state of moral values as only fair/poor and 76 percent thought the level of moral values was declining (see Weblink 2.2). The Josephson Institute of Ethics conducted a 2009 survey of almost 7,000 persons ranging in age from teenage to over fifty. A significant conclusion was that the "vast majority of respondents of all ages believe that young people lie, cheat, and steal more than previous generations but teens and young adults are considerably more likely to believe this than older adults" (see Weblink 2.3).

The 2010 Report Card on the Ethics of American Youth by the Josephson Institute was a survey of over 40,000 high school students. The results show a puzzling contradiction. On the one hand over 92 percent of those surveyed said that it is "important for me to be a person of good character," that "trust and honesty" are important in personal relationships and in the workplace, and that they are satisfied with their own "ethics and character." On the other hand, in stark contrast, 80 percent admitted that they had lied to a parent (54 percent two or more times) and 61 percent lied to a teacher (34 percent two or more times) about something significant in the past year. Eighty percent admitted (60 percent two or more times) that they had copied another's homework. And 10 percent admitted they lied on three to ten questions in the survey (see again Weblink 2.3). In his book, *The Cheating Culture,* David Callahan (2004) documents a "pattern of widespread cheating throughout U.S. society," observes that people "not only are cheating in more areas but also are feeling less guilty about it," and concludes that most of the cheating "is by people who, on the whole, view themselves as upstanding members of society" (pp. 12–14).

CASE STUDY

Imagine that you are an audience member listening to a speaker—call him Mr. Bronson. His aim is to persuade you to contribute money to the cancer research program of a major medical research center. Suppose that, with one exception, all the evidence, reasoning, and motivational appeals he employs are valid and above suspicion on any ethical grounds. However, at one point in his speech, Bronson knowingly uses a set of false statistics to scare you into believing that, during your lifetime, there is a much greater probability of you getting some form of cancer than is actually the case.

To help our analysis of the ethics of this hypothetical persuasive situation, consider these issues. If you, or society at large, view Bronson's persuasive goal as worthwhile, does the worth of that goal justify his use of false statistics as one means to achieve his end? Would Bronson's use of a fear appeal (emotional scare tactic) be ethical if the statistics were true rather than false? Does the fact that he consciously chose to use false statistics make a difference in your evaluation? If he used the false statistics out of ignorance or a failure to check his sources, how might your ethical judgment be altered, if at all? Should Bronson be condemned as an unethical person or an unethical speaker, or, in this instance, just for use of a specific unethical technique?

Carefully consider the standards you would employ to make your ethical judgment of Bronson. Are your standards purely pragmatic? (In other words,

should Bronson avoid false statistics because he might get caught?) Are they societal in origin? (If he gets caught, his credibility as a representative would be weakened with this and future audiences, or his getting caught might weaken the credibility of other cancer society representatives.) Should he be criticized for violating an implied ethical agreement between you and him? (You might not expect a representative of a famous research institute to use questionable techniques, and so you would be especially vulnerable.) Finally, should his conscious use of false statistics be considered unethical because you are denied the accurate, relevant information you need to make an intelligent decision on an important public issue?

In what ways does Bronson's intentional use of false statistics as a scare tactic appeal to *both* information processing routes of the ELM model of persuasion? In what ways might Rank's model of persuasive strategies and tactics be helpful in judging the ethics of Bronson's false appeal?

IMPORTANCE OF ETHICS

As receivers and senders of persuasion, we have the responsibility to uphold appropriate ethical standards for persuasion, to encourage freedom of inquiry and expression, and to promote public debate as crucial to democratic decision making. To achieve these goals, we must understand their complexity and recognize the difficulty of achieving them. One purpose of this chapter is to stimulate you to make reasoned choices among ethical options in developing your own positions or judgments.

Ethical issues focus on value judgments concerning degrees of right and wrong, virtue and vice, and ethical obligations in human conduct. Persuasion, as one type of human behavior, always contains potential ethical issues, for several reasons:

- In persuasion, one person, or a group of people, attempts to influence other people by altering their beliefs, attitudes, values, and actions.

- Persuasion requires us to make conscious choices among ends sought and rhetorical means used to achieve the ends.

FIGURE 2.1   This Coca Cola ad for its *BURN* high energy drink was used in Italy.
If this ad were used in the United States, would it be considered as unethical,
just in poor taste, or just humorous? Why?

SOURCE: Courtesy of Advertising Archives.

- Persuasion necessarily involves a potential judge—any or all of the receivers, the persuader, or an independent observer.

As a receiver and sender of persuasion, you will evaluate the ethics of a persuasive instance based on the ethical standards you are using. You may even choose to ignore ethical judgment entirely. People often cite several justifications to avoid direct analysis and resolution of ethical issues in persuasion:

- Everyone knows the appeal or tactic is unethical, so there is nothing to talk about.

- Only success matters, so ethics are irrelevant to persuasion.

- Ethical judgments are matters of individual personal opinion, so there are no final answers.

However, potential ethical questions exist regardless of how they are answered. Whether you wish it or not, consumers of persuasion generally will judge your effort, formally or informally, in part by their own relevant ethical criteria. If for no other reason than the pragmatic motivation of enhancing your chance of success, you would do well to consider the ethical standards held by your audience. This chapter should increase your understanding of how ethics relates to our networked, interactive, media-saturated world, our multicultural global world, and a world of doublespeak and propaganda (see Figure 2.1).

Now we turn to the concept of ethical responsibility. What is it and what are some of its components?

ETHICAL RESPONSIBILITIES
OF PERSUADERS

Persuaders' ethical responsibilities can stem from statuses or positions they have earned or have been granted, from commitments (promises, pledges, agreements) they have made, or from the consequences (effects) of their communication for others. **Responsibility** includes the elements of fulfilling duties and obligations, of being accountable to other individuals and groups, of adhering to agreed-upon standards, and of being accountable to one's own conscience. But an essential element of responsible communication, for both sender and receiver, is the exercise of thoughtful and deliberate judgment. That is, the responsible communicator carefully analyzes claims, soundly assesses probable consequences, and conscientiously weighs relevant values. In a sense, a responsible communicator is "response-able." She or he exercises the ability to respond (is responsive) to the needs and communications of others in sensitive, thoughtful, fitting ways (Freund, 1960; Niebuhr, 1963; Pennock, 1960; Pincoffs, 1975).

Whether persuaders seem intentionally and knowingly to use particular content or techniques is a factor that most of us consider in judging communication ethicality. If a dubious communication behavior seems to stem more from an accident, a slip of the tongue, or even ignorance, we may be less harsh in our ethical assessment. For most of us, it is the *intentional* use of ethically questionable tactics that merits the harshest condemnation.

On the other hand, we might contend that, in argumentative and persuasive situations, communicators have an ethical obligation to double-check the soundness of their evidence and reasoning before they present it to others; sloppy preparation is no excuse for ethical lapses. A similar view might be advanced concerning elected or appointed government officials. If they use obscure or jargon-laden language that clouds the accurate and clear representation of ideas, even if it is not intended to deceive or hide, they are ethically irresponsible. Such officials, according to this view, should be obligated to communicate clearly and accurately with citizens in fulfillment of their governmental duties. As a related question, we can ask whether sincerity of intent releases persuaders from their ethical responsibility to use fair means and effects. Could we say that if Adolf Hitler's fellow Germans had judged him to be sincere, they need not have assessed the ethics of his persuasion? In such cases, evaluations are probably best carried out by appraising sincerity and ethicality separately. For example, a persuader sincere in intent might use an unethical strategy.

American culture emphasizes dual concerns for maximizing the latitude of freedom of communication and for promoting responsible exercise of that freedom. In the United States we have a long history of First Amendment and Supreme Court protection of freedom of speech and press. At the same time, citizens generally expect that freedom to be used in ethically responsible ways. Often we may observe or experience a tension between communication freedom and responsibility, and we have to decide which one should take precedence in a particular situation.

The **freedom versus responsibility tension** might occur when we, as individuals, carry to an extreme the now traditional view that the best test of the soundness of our ideas is their ability to survive in the free and open public "marketplace" of ideas. We might take the mistaken view that, as individuals, we have no responsibility to test the ethicality of our persuasive techniques and goals before we present them. We incorrectly assume that the logical and ethical soundness of our ideas need only to be evaluated through their ability to survive in the marketplace in competition with other ideas and differing viewpoints. Such a view could lead each of us to ignore our ethical responsibilities as persuaders because, supposedly, the marketplace ultimately will render the necessary judgments. However, we must remember that while we do have First Amendment protection of our persuasion, each of us also has the responsibility to exercise that freedom in an ethical manner (adapted from Meiklejohn, 1948, pp. 73–74).

Questions about how far persuaders should go in adapting their message to particular audiences focus on a special type of ethical responsibility. We now examine this issue.

Adaptation to the Audience

What are the ethics of adapting to the audience? Most persuaders seek to secure some kind of response from receivers. To what degree is it ethical for them to alter their ideas and proposals to adapt to the needs, capacities, values, and expectations of their audience? To secure acceptance, some persuaders adapt to an audience to the extent of so changing their own ideas that the ideas are no longer really theirs. These persuaders merely say what the audience wants to hear, regardless of their own convictions. During the 2007–2008 Republican presidential primary campaign, for example, candidate Mitt Romney was criticized by opponents and the media for changing his views on significant issues depending on the audience he attempted to persuade. One political cartoonist (Horsey, 2007) satirically depicted Romney as saying: "And on torture, immigration, and taxes, I'll adopt any viewpoint that'll get me elected. So you don't need to worry about my beliefs. I don't have any." In contrast, some persuaders go to the opposite extreme of making little or no adaptation to their audience. They do not take serious account of the nature of their audience, no matter whether that audience is much like them or whether it reflects cultural or religious diversity. To the audience, the speaker, writer, or advertisement seems unconnected to them or unconcerned about them.

Some degree of adaptation for specific audiences in language choice, evidence, value appeals, organization, and communication medium is a crucial part of successful and ethical persuasion. No absolute rule can be set down here. Persuaders must decide the ethical intermediate point between their own idea in its pure form and that idea modified to achieve maximum impact with the audience. The search is for an appropriate point between two undesirable extremes—the extreme of saying only what the audience desires and will approve, and the extreme of complete lack of concern for and understanding of the audience. Both extremes are ethically irresponsible (Booth, 2004, pp. 50–54). In this era of heightened awareness of ethnic, racial, and religious diversity, persuaders face significant practical and ethical choices concerning the appropriate degree of audience adaptation. And just because we may use informal SNM to influence others does not lessen our ethical responsibilities in adapting to our audience of one or many.

A frequent ethical question facing persuaders is: Does the end justify the means? How should we answer that question? What are some guidelines for answering it?

The Ethics of Ends and Means

In assessing the ethics of persuasion, does the end justify the means? Does the necessity of achieving a goal widely acknowledged as worthwhile justify the use of ethically questionable techniques? We must be aware that the persuasive means employed can have cumulative effects on receivers' thoughts and decision-making habits, apart from and in addition to the specific end that the communicator seeks. No matter what purpose they serve, the arguments, appeals, structure, and language we choose do shape the audience's values, thinking habits, language patterns, and level of trust.

To say that the ends do not *always* justify the means is different from saying that the ends never justify means. The persuader's goal probably is best considered as one of a number of potentially relevant ethical criteria from which we select the most appropriate standards. Under some circumstances, such as threats to physical survival, the goal of personal or national security may *temporarily* take precedence over other criteria. In general, however, we can best make mature ethical assessments by evaluating the ethics of persuasive techniques apart from the worth and morality of the persuader's specific goal. We can strive to judge the ethics of means and ends *separately*. In some cases, we may find ethical persuasive tactics employed to achieve an unethical goal; in other cases, unethical techniques are used in the service of an entirely ethical goal.

Consider this report in the *Chicago Tribune* (April 12, 2000, sec. 1, p. 3):

> More than one-third of doctors surveyed nationwide admit deceiving insurance companies to help patients get the care they need. Their tactics include exaggerating the severity of an illness to help patients avoid being sent home early from

FIGURE 2.2 How might Bovee's questions apply for evaluating the justifications here?

the hospital, listing an inaccurate diagnosis on bills and reporting non-existent symptoms to secure insurance coverage. More than one-quarter, 28.5 percent, said it is necessary to "game" the system to provide high-quality care.

Does the end of securing high-quality care for patients justify use of such deceptive communication tactics? Why or why not?

Although discussed in the context of journalistic ethics, the six questions suggested by Warren Bovee (1991) can serve as useful probes to determine the degree of ethicality of almost any means-ends relationship in persuasion (see Figure 2.2).

Here are the questions in paraphrased form:

1. Are the means truly unethical/morally evil or merely distasteful, unpopular, unwise, or ineffective?

2. Is the end truly good, or does it simply appear good to us because we desire it?

3. Is it probable that the ethically bad or suspect means actually will achieve the good end?

4. Is the same good achievable using other more ethical means if we are willing to be creative, patient, determined, and skillful?

5. Is the good end clearly and overwhelmingly better than the probable bad effects of the

means used to attain it? Bad means require justification whereas good means do not.

6. Will the use of unethical means to achieve a good end withstand public scrutiny? Could the use of unethical means be justified to those most affected by them or to those most capable of impartially judging them?

Perhaps now we can better answer the question: In persuasion, does the end justify the means? Certainly we see more clearly some of the issues and options involved.

The ethics of persuasion are important both for persuaders and for receivers of persuasion. We turn now to special ethical responsibilities for audiences.

ETHICAL RESPONSIBILITIES OF RECEIVERS

What are your ethical responsibilities as a receiver of or respondent to persuasion? An answer to this question stems in part from the image we hold of the persuasion process. Receivers bear little responsibility if the persuader views them as passive and defenseless receptacles, as mindless blotters uncritically accepting ideas and arguments. If audience members actually behave as viewed by the persuader, then they have little or no responsibility to understand accurately and evaluate critically. In this view, they have minimal power of choice and almost automatically must agree with the persuader's arguments. In contrast, we can see persuasion as a transaction or co-creation in which both persuaders and persuadees bear mutual responsibility to participate actively in the process. This image of persuadees as active participants suggests several responsibilities, perhaps best captured by two phrases: (1) reasoned skepticism and (2) appropriate feedback.

Reasoned skepticism includes a number of elements. It represents a balanced position between the undesirable extremes of being too open-minded or gullible, on the one hand, and being too closed-minded or dogmatic, on the other. You are not simply an unthinking blotter "soaking up" ideas

and arguments. Rather, you exercise your critical thinking capacities actively to search for meaning, to analyze and synthesize, and to judge soundness and worth. You do something to and with the information you receive: You process, interpret, and evaluate it. Also, you inform yourself about issues being discussed, and you tolerate, even seek out, divergent and controversial viewpoints, the better to assess what is being presented.

As a receiver of persuasion, you must realize that your accurate interpretation of a persuader's message may be hindered by attempts to impose your own ethical standards or cultural values on the persuader. Your immediate, gut-level ethical judgments may cause you to distort the intended meaning. Only after reaching an understanding of the persuader's ideas can you reasonably evaluate the ethics of his or her persuasive strategies or purposes.

In this era of distrust of the truthfulness of public communication, reasoned skepticism also requires that you combat the automatic assumption that most public communication is untrustworthy. Just because a communication is of a certain type or comes from a certain source (e.g., a government official, political candidate, news media figure, controversial blog, or advertiser), it must not automatically, without evaluation, be rejected as tainted or untruthful. Clearly, you must always exercise caution in acceptance and care in evaluation, as emphasized throughout this book. Using the best evidence available, you arrive at your best judgment. However, to condemn a message as untruthful or unethical solely because it stems from a suspect source is a type of judgment that threatens the soundness of our decisions. If we reject a message, it must be after, not before, we evaluate it. Like a defendant in a courtroom, public communication must be presumed to be ethically innocent until it has been proved "guilty." However, when techniques of persuasion do weaken or undermine the confidence and trust necessary for intelligent, public decision making, we can condemn them as unethical.

As an active participant in the persuasion process, you need to provide appropriate feedback to persuaders. Otherwise, persuaders are denied the relevant and accurate information they need to make decisions. Your response, in most situations, should be an honest and accurate reflection of your true comprehension, beliefs, feelings, or judgment. It might be verbal or nonverbal, oral or written, immediate or delayed. A response of understanding, puzzlement, agreement, or disagreement could be reflected through your facial expressions, gestures, posture, inquiries, and statements during question-and-answer periods and through letters or e-mails to editors or advertisers. In some cases, because of your expertise on a subject, you may even have an obligation to respond and provide feedback while other receivers remain silent. You need to decide whether the degree and type of your feedback are appropriate for the subject, audience, and occasion of the persuasion. For instance, to interrupt with questions, or even to heckle, might be appropriate in a few situations but irresponsible in most others.

SOME ETHICAL PERSPECTIVES

We will briefly explain five major ethical perspectives as potential viewpoints for analyzing ethical issues in persuasion. As categories, these perspectives are not exhaustive, mutually exclusive, or given in any order of precedence. For a more extensive discussion, see Johannesen, Valde, and Whedbee (2008).

As a receiver of persuasion, you can use one or a combination of such perspectives to evaluate the ethicality of a persuader's use of language (such as metaphors and ambiguity) or of evidence and reasoning. You can also use them to assess the ethics of psychological techniques (such as appeals to needs and values) or the appeal to widely held cultural images and myths. The persuasive tactics of campaigns and social movements can also—indeed must—be subjected to ethical scrutiny.

Human Nature Perspectives

Human nature perspectives probe the essence of human nature by asking what makes us fundamentally human. They identify unique characteristics of human nature that distinguish us from so-called lower forms of life, characteristics that we can then use as standards for judging the ethics of persuasion. Among them are the capacity to reason, to create and use symbols, to achieve mutual appreciative understanding, and to make value judgments. The underlying assumption is that we should protect and nurture such uniquely human characteristics so that persons better can achieve their individual potential. We can assess the degree to which a persuader's appeals and techniques either foster or undermine the development of a fundamental human characteristic. Whatever the political, religious, or cultural context, a person would be assumed to possess certain uniquely human attributes worthy of promotion through communication. A technique that dehumanizes, that makes a person less than human, would be unethical.

In 1990 in Florida, a U.S. district court judge declared obscene the album *As Nasty As They Wanna Be* by the rap group 2 Live Crew. But in a local trial in Florida that same year, three members of the group were acquitted of obscenity charges for performing the songs. These incidents are part of a larger controversy concerning lyrics that explicitly refer to the sexual and physical abuse and debasement of women and that attack ethnic groups. For example, lyrics on the *Nasty* album vividly describe the bursting of vaginal walls, the forcing of women to have anal or oral sex or to lick feces, and such acts as urination, incest, and group sex. Similarly sexually violent lyrics can be found in songs by such individuals and groups as Judas Priest, Great White, Ice-T, and Guns n' Roses. And bigotry against immigrants, homosexuals, and African Americans surfaces in the Guns n' Roses song, "One in a Million." Can you think of lyrics to current songs or rap that are similar to those just discussed?

Regardless of whether such lyrics are judged obscene or whether they are protected by the freedom-of-speech clause of the First Amendment, many would say that they should be condemned as unethical (Johannesen, 1997). Such lyrics treat women not as persons but as objects or body parts to be manipulated for the selfish satisfaction of males. Thus, they dehumanize, depersonalize, and trivialize women, they celebrate violence against them, and they reinforce inaccurate and unfair stereotypes of women, homosexuals, and ethnic groups. How do you believe a human nature perspective on communication ethics might be used to assess such lyrics?

Political Perspectives

The implicit or explicit values and procedures accepted as crucial to the health and growth of a particular political system are the focus of **political perspectives**. Once we have identified these essential values for a political system, we can use them to evaluate the ethics of persuasive means and ends within that system. The assumption is that public communication should foster achievement of these basic political values; persuasive techniques that retard, subvert, or circumvent the values should be condemned as unethical. Different political systems usually embody differing values leading to differing ethical judgments. Within the context of U.S. representative democracy, for example, various analysts pinpoint values and procedures they deem fundamental to the healthy functioning of our political system and, thus, values that can guide ethical scrutiny of persuasion therein. Such values and procedures include enhancement of citizens' capacity to reach rational decisions, access to channels of public communication and to relevant and accurate information about public issues, maximization of freedom of choice, tolerance of diversity and dissent, honesty in presenting motivations and consequences, and thoroughness and accuracy in presenting evidence and alternatives.

Hate speech is a broad label that includes communications that degrade, belittle, humiliate, or disrespect individuals and groups based on their race, ethnicity, nationality, religion, sex, or sexual orientation. Hate speech truly warrants our concern as an issue central to respect for diversity in our nation. In the late 1980s and early 1990s, the issue of hate speech on college and university campuses illustrated the tension between the right of freedom of speech and the ethically responsible exercise of that right.

On one campus, eight Asian-American students were harassed for almost an hour by a group of football players, who called them "Oriental faggots." On another campus, white fraternity members harassed a black student by chanting, "coon," "nigger," and "porch monkey." On yet another campus, a white male freshman was charged under the school's speech code with racial harassment for calling five black female students "water buffaloes."

In response to hate speech incidents, many colleges and universities instituted speech codes to punish hateful and offensive public messages. Among the forms of expression punishable at various schools are these:

- the use of derogatory names, inappropriately directed laughter, inconsiderate jokes, and conspicuous exclusion of another person from conversation

- language that stigmatizes or victimizes individuals or that creates an intimidating or offensive environment

- face-to-face use of epithets, obscenities, and other forms of expression that by accepted community standards degrade, victimize, stigmatize, or pejoratively depict persons based on their personal, intellectual, or cultural diversity

- extreme or outrageous acts or communications intended to harass, intimidate, or humiliate others on the basis of sex, sexual orientation, race, color, or national origin, thus causing them severe emotional distress.

We call your attention to two websites that provide reliable information about hate groups that promote hate speech. Check the Hate Groups Map on the Southern Poverty Law Center website and surf its various links to see the nature and extent of such groups (see Weblink 2.4). On the Anti-Defamation League website (see Weblink 2.5) type in the search window: poisoning the web. Then click on "Table of Contents" to surf the various listings.

Whether hate speech is protected by the First Amendment and whether campus speech codes are constitutional, we should evaluate specific instances of hate speech for their degree of ethicality (Johannesen, 1997). We can use various ethical perspectives (such as human nature), but how might we use the values and procedures central to a U.S. democratic political perspective to judge hate speech?

Situational Perspectives

To make ethical judgments from a **situational perspective**, it is necessary to focus *regularly and primarily* on the elements of the specific persuasive situation at hand. Virtually all perspectives (those mentioned here and others) make some allowances, on occasion, for the modified application of ethical criteria in special circumstances. However, an extreme situational perspective routinely makes judgments only in light of *each different context*. This perspective minimizes criteria from broad political, human nature, religious, or other perspectives, and avoids absolute and universal standards (see Figure 2.3). Among the concrete contextual factors relevant to making a purely situational ethical evaluation are these:

- the role or function of the persuader for receivers

- expectations held by receivers concerning such matters as appropriateness and reasonableness

- the degree of receivers' awareness of the persuader's techniques

- goals and values held by receivers

- the degree of urgency for implementing the persuader's proposal

- ethical standards for communication held by receivers.

From an extreme situational perspective, for instance, we might argue that an acknowledged leader in a time of clear crisis has a responsibility to rally support and thus could employ so-called emotional appeals that circumvent human processes of rational, reflective decision making. Or a persuader might ethically use techniques such as innuendo, guilt by association, and unfounded name-calling as long as the receivers both recognize and approve of those methods.

Berry's World

"It's exciting to be part of a firm that's on the cutting edge of 'MORAL FLEXIBILITY.'"

FIGURE 2.3

How might situational ethics apply here?

SOURCE: Berry's World: © by NEA, Inc.

Legal Perspectives

From a **legal perspective**, illegal communication behavior also is unethical, but that which is not specifically illegal is ethical. In other words, legality and ethicality are considered synonymous. This approach certainly has the advantage of making ethical decisions simple: We need only measure communication techniques against current laws and regulations to determine whether a technique is ethical. We might, for example, turn for ethical guidance to the regulations governing advertising set forth by the Federal Trade Commission (FTC) or the Federal Communications Commission (FCC). Or we might use Supreme

Court or state legislative criteria defining obscenity, pornography, libel, or slander to judge whether a particular message is unethical on those grounds.

However, many people are uneasy with this legalistic approach to communication ethics. They contend that obviously there are some things that are legal but ethically dubious. And some social protesters for civil rights and against the Vietnam War during the 1960s and 1970s admitted that their actions were illegal but contended that they were justifiable on ethical and moral grounds. Persons holding such views reject the idea that ethicality and legality are synonymous, view ethicality as much broader than legality, and argue that not everything that is unethical should be made illegal.

To what degree, then, can or should we enforce ethical standards for communication through laws or regulations? What degrees of soundness might there be in two old but seemingly contrary sayings: "You can't legislate morality" and "There ought to be a law"? In the United States today, very few ethical standards for communication are codified in laws or regulations. As we have indicated, FCC or FTC regulations on the content of advertising represent the governmental approach. But such examples are rare compared with the large number of laws and court decisions specifying the boundaries of freedom of speech and press in our society. Rather, our society applies ethical standards for communication through the indirect avenues of group consensus, social pressure, persuasion, and formal-but-voluntary codes of ethics.

Controversies surrounding computer communication on the Internet illustrate not only the tension between freedom and responsibility but also the pressures to apply legalistic approaches to ethics and to create formal codes of ethics. Should you be free to say or depict anything you want, without restriction, on the Internet, in e-mail, in blogs, or in SNM? What is your view on how ethical responsibility for computer communication on the Internet should be promoted? Through laws? Through institutional and professional codes of ethics (Box 2.1)?

Dialogical Perspectives

Dialogical perspectives emerge from current scholarship on the nature of communication as dialogue rather than as monologue. From such perspectives, the attitudes participants in a communication situation have toward each other are an index of the ethical level of that communication. Some attitudes are held to be more fully human, humane, and facilitative of personal self-fulfillment than others (see Johannesen, 1971; Johannesen, Valde, & Whedbee, 2008; Stewart & Zediker, 2000).

Communication as dialogue is characterized by such attitudes as honesty, concern for the welfare and improvement of others, trust, genuineness, open-mindedness, equality, mutual respect, empathy, humility, directness, lack of pretense, nonmanipulative intent, sincerity, encouragement of free expression, and acceptance of others as individuals with intrinsic worth regardless of differences of belief or behavior.

Communication as monologue, in contrast, is marked by such qualities as deception, superiority, exploitation, dogmatism, domination, insincerity, pretense, personal self-display, self-aggrandizement, judgmentalism that stifles free expression, coercion, possessiveness, condescension, self-defensiveness, and

---

BOX 2.1   A Legalistic Perspective?

University officials, perhaps on your campus, have debated whether to apply to the Internet and e-mail activities of students existing campus speech codes that prohibit hate speech and harassment, or whether to formulate special codes of computer communication ethics to guide student use. On your campus, what official policies (set how and by whom?) govern ethically responsible communication on the Internet? How adequately and appropriately do these policies speak to specific issues of communication ethics? Do these policies actually seem to address matters of legality more than of ethicality?

the view of others as objects to be manipulated. In the case of persuasion, then, we examine the persuader's techniques and presentation to determine the degree to which they reveal an ethical dialogical attitude or an unethical monological attitude toward receivers.

How might a dialogical ethical perspective apply to intimate interpersonal communication situations such as between friends, family members, lovers, and spouses? Or consider some of the popular interactive media such as e-mail, chat rooms, blogs, cell phone text messaging, and Microsoft Xbox. For example, blogs (short for weblogs) facilitate extensive participation between blogger and users. One 2005 estimate indicated that 8 million American adults have created their own blogs, almost 32 million indicate they read blogs, and over 14 million say they have responded to a blog. Blog activity has been compared to a conversation or a seminar (Primer, 2005, pp. 15–16). How might we apply ethical standards rooted in a dialogical perspective to evaluate communication via blogs or social network media such as Facebook, Twitter, or Formspring (Box 2.2)?

With knowledge of the preceding ethical perspectives (human nature, political, situational, legal, dialogical), we can confront a variety of difficult issues relevant to ethical problems in persuasion. As receivers constantly bombarded with verbal and nonverbal persuasive messages, we continually face resolution of one or another of these fundamental issues. To further help us grapple with such issues, we next consider some traditional advice on ethics which most of us have heard at one time or another—The Golden Rule.

THE GOLDEN RULE AND THE PLATINUM RULE

"Do unto others as you would have them do unto you." Most of us probably are familiar with this statement, which we have come to know as **The Golden Rule**. Persons familiar with the Christian religious tradition may think the Golden Rule is unique to that religion. In the New Testament we find: "And as ye would that men should do to you, do ye also to them likewise" (Luke 6:31; also see Matthew 7:12). However, some version of the Golden Rule is found in the sacred literature of the major world religions, including Hinduism, Confucianism, Taoism, Zoroastrianism, and Jainism. For example, in Judaism: "What is hateful to you, do not to your fellow men." In Islam: "No one of you is a believer until he desires for his brother that which he desires for himself." In Buddhism: "Hurt not others in ways that you yourself would find hurtful" (Kane, 1994, p. 34; Samovar, Porter, & Stefani, 1998, p. 269).

One interpretation of the Golden Rule is that we should only do *specific actions* to others if we would allow them to do the same specific actions to us. Another interpretation would not require mutually specific actions but would require that the *ethical principles and standards* that we follow in relating to others are the same ethical principles we would expect others to follow in relating to us (Singer, 1963). Versions of the Golden Rule have been advocated not only by the major world religions but also by non-religious philosophers.

BOX 2.2 **Dialogue and Social Network Media**

The question-and-answer format of Formspring, they say, builds on our "curiosity about one another" to facilitate "engaging, authentic conversations between our community members." Go to the Formspring website (see Weblink 2.6) and click first on "Community Rules" and then click on "Safety Tips." Read both of these sections carefully. In what ways might the rules and advice in them work over time to build a kind of dialogic communication between users? Now consider the fact that both posers of questions and responders to questions can choose to remain anonymous. How might that fact help or hinder dialogic communication?

Thus a contemporary philosopher, Marcus Singer (1967), concludes: "The nearly universal acceptance of the Golden Rule and its promulgation by persons of considerable intelligence, though otherwise divergent outlooks, would therefore seem to provide some evidence for the claim that it is a fundamental ethical truth."

However, in the context of ethnic and religious diversity and of intercultural and multicultural communication, Milton Bennett argues that the Golden Rule best applies *within* a culture or group that has wide agreement on fundamental values, goals, institutions, and customs. In other words, the Golden Rule assumes that other people want to be treated in the same way we do. But this assumption is not automatically applicable in diverse intercultural and multicultural communication. Too often in such situations we may focus primarily or solely on our own values or preferences to the exclusion or minimization of values and preferences of others that differ from ours. As an alternative (or perhaps supplement) to the Golden Rule, Bennett (1979) offers **The Platinum Rule**: "Do unto others as they themselves would have done unto them."

Certainly the Platinum Rule forces us to take into serious account the values and preferences of others, especially others unlike us, perhaps through empathy for or imagining of their experiences and worldviews. But we need to be careful that we do not interpret the Platinum Rule as requiring us automatically and unquestioningly to do what others want us to do. In making our final decision about what and how to persuade, even on social network media, we should carefully weigh the ethical guidance embodied in both the Golden Rule and the Platinum Rule. Then we should decide which takes precedence in our particular situation.

LYING AND DECEPTION

Is it ever ethical to **lie** or be **deceptive**? To this question some people would respond with a resounding no, never! Others would respond with less certainty and recognize the possible complexity of the question.

Some would say it depends on the *definition* of lie or deception. Are lying and deception synonymous or is deception a broader concept than lying? Some would say it depends on the *intention or motive* of the liar. Is the motive self-serving for the liar or is the liar's intent to serve a more noble goal or acknowledged good? Some would say it depends on the *circumstances or context* of the lie. Does a unique situation justify a lie that usually would be condemned as unethical? And some would say that the degree of good or bad *consequences* of the lie should justify or condemn the lie. The short-term and long-term consequences should be judged not primarily by the liar but by those lied to and/or impartial observers. For example, if we are telling a "little white lie" to spare the feelings of a friend who is emotionally unstable, that lie might not be defined as a "real lie" or might be viewed as justified by intent and circumstances.

Bear in mind that lies and deception may occur in a wide variety of persuasive types, techniques, and formats such as oral or written statements, images, gesture and facial expression, omission of information, silence, and implication and suggestion. Note also that perceptions of lying and deception often are culture-bound and punishments for them may vary between cultures and between co-cultures within a larger culture. A statement or image that one culture views as a lie or deception may not be defined the same way in another culture. Also of importance is the difference between intent/motivation and a lie being *intentional* rather than accidental or out of ignorance or incompetence. Often a lie or deception that is not presented knowingly or consciously may be viewed as less blameworthy than one presented intentionally.

A helpful source on some of the issues discussed above is *Lying and Deception in Human Interaction* by communication scholar Mark Knapp (2008, pp. 3–18, 41–46). Knapp offers pragmatic advice for anyone contemplating presenting a lie. Assume your lie will be discovered sooner or later. The potential liar should consider the following questions: "What is the worst thing that is likely to happen if your lie is discovered—to you and to others? Are you willing to live with the consequences? Will you admit and be accountable for your lie? How will you defend it?" (p. 58).

BOX 2.3 **Casino Deception?**

In gambling casinos you will find row after row of five or seven slot machines in separate clusters, each designated as penny, two-cent, nickel, dime, quarter, fifty-cent, or one-dollar machines. On occasion there will be a row of five machines with the two on each end being one-cent machines and the middle one being a one-dollar machine. This arrangement occurs at several places in the casino.

There is no lying here since each machine accurately states its monetary designation. But what about nonverbal deception? Who ordered the placement of these five slots in this particular order? What is the intent of this placement? What are several arguments you could use to conclude that intentional deception is involved and that this particular type of placement is unethical?

For our purposes in this chapter we describe **lying** as the intentional presentation in verbal and/or nonverbal form of a claim as true that we know to be false. **Deception** is broader and includes any intentional behavior that misleads, misinforms, or misdirects. Deception is the broader category that includes lying. All lies are deceptive but not all deception is through lies (Box 2.3).

Some of the views of philosopher Sissla Bok (1979) provide insights concerning the nature, functions, and evaluation of lies. She does see deception as a broader category that includes lies. In her book, *Lying: Moral Choice in Public and Private Life*, she evaluates lying in varied contexts: white lies; lies in a crisis for the public good; lying to liars and enemies; lying to protect confidentiality; lying for the welfare of others; lies in social science research on humans; and lying to the sick and dying. Among the excuses people use to justify a lie or deception are: avoiding harm to ourselves or others; producing benefits for others; promoting fairness and justice; and protecting the truth by counteracting another lie, by furthering a more important truth, or by preserving the confidence of others in our truthfulness (pp. 78–94). Often people attempt to justify their lies and deceptions by saying they promote some higher good. The acknowledged good end served, they contend, justifies use of ethically questionable means.

Bok focuses on the importance of telling the truth (as we know it) and avoiding lies whenever possible. Her basic assumption is that trust in some degree of truthfulness is a "*foundation* of relations among human beings; when that trust shatters or wears away, institutions collapse…. *Whatever* matters to human beings, trust is the atmosphere in which it thrives." Bok also assumes that there always is a **negative presumption against lying**. She argues that lying always carries an "initial negative weight," that "truthful statements are preferable to lies in the absence of special considerations," and that "lying requires explanation, whereas truth ordinarily does not" (pp. 32–33).

Lies, says Bok, increase the power of the liar and weaken the power of persons deceived by altering those persons' choices in significant ways. First, the lie may obscure or hide some goal the deceived persons sought. Second, the lie may obscure or eliminate relevant alternatives that should be considered. Third, the lie may misinform concerning benefits and costs of probable consequences. And fourth, lies may falsify the level of confidence or certainty that deceived persons should have about the choice.

There also are potential negative consequences for the liar, whether, for example, the liar be an individual, a commercial ad agency team, or political communication advisor to a candidate. First, resorting to lies may weaken the liar's sense of self as an ethical person. Second, additional lies or deceptions may be needed to preserve the initial lie. Third, lying may increase the temptation to use lies or deception on other topics in the future (p. 55). Fourth and finally, we can add, if caught the lie or deception may damage the reputation or credibility of the liar whether the liar is an individual, group, or institution.

Deception and lies often are associated with common perceptions of propaganda and a demagogue. We turn now to a more detailed examination of ethical issues in propaganda and demagoguery.

ETHICS, PROPAGANDA, AND THE DEMAGOGUE

Is **propaganda** unethical? The answer depends upon how we define propaganda. A simplistic answer, sometimes resorted to in the heat of clash of opposing viewpoints, is to claim that my communication is persuasion but my opponent's/enemy's is propaganda.

Recall the definition (key characteristics) described in chapter 1. (1) Propaganda is ideological—it promotes one and only one way to believe. (2) It employs various mass media to spread its belief system to ever larger masses of fanatical "true believers." (3) It conceals one or more of the message source, the true goal of the source, the other sides of the issue, the persuasive techniques being used, and the actual consequences of putting the belief system in action. (4) It aims at mass uniformity of belief and behavior. (5) It usually circumvents the reasoning process and relies heavily on irrelevant emotional appeals and hatred of stereotyped opponents. Thus the definition used in this book views propaganda as an unethical persuasion process (also see Black, 2009, pp. 143–144).

In his book, *The Idea of Propaganda*, scholar of philosophy and communication Stanley Cunningham (2002, pp. 176–178) argues that propaganda is "an inherently unethical social phenomenon" because it undermines the significant values of truth and truthfulness, reasoning, and knowledge; because it sidesteps voluntary choice and human agency; and because it "exploits and reinforces society's moral weakness." Because propaganda violates the normal communication expectations

(implied ethical contracts) of trust, truthfulness, and understanding, it is best characterized as "counterfeit or pseudocommunication." He also describes the various "deep-structured constituents and enabling conditions" that mark propaganda.

Propaganda, contends Cunningham, is constituted by a "complex array" of deficiencies or shortcomings that undermine justified knowledge. We paraphrase and summarize those characteristics here. Propaganda plays on complexity and stimulates confusion; exploits expectations; poses as valid information and accepted knowledge; constructs belief systems of tenacious convictions that defy questioning; offers false or artificial assurances and certainties; distorts perceptions; disregards truth and truthfulness as values necessary for accurate knowledge and understanding; subverts "rationality, reasoning, and a healthy respect for rigor, evidence, and procedural safeguards"; promotes ignorance and passive acceptance of unexamined beliefs; and uses truths and information as mere instruments rather than as ethical ideals in themselves.

Today the label **demagogue** typically is used to render a negative ethical judgment of a persuader. Too often, however, the label remains only vaguely defined; the criteria being used to evaluate a person as a demagogue are unspecified (Box 2.4).

You now are invited to consider the following five characteristics (taken together) as possible appropriate guides to determining to what degree a persuader warrants the label demagogue (Johannesen, Valde, & Whedbee, 2008, pp. 114–115).

1. A demagogue wields popular or mass leadership over an extensive number of people.

BOX 2.4   Who Is a Demagogue?

Consider the following hypothetical description of a politician: He is the perfect example of a demagogue, combining true-believer certainty, raw pursuit of power, blue-collar populism, chameleon-like adaptability, and blunt, sometimes crude, persuasive appeals (adapted from

Lesher, 1972). Are each of the characteristics listed truly appropriate criteria for judging a demagogue? Why or why not? Are there any appropriate criteria omitted? Given the criteria listed, would you label this politician as a demagogue?

2. A demagogue exerts primary influence through the medium of the spoken word—whether through direct public speaking to an audience or through speaking via radio, television, or on the Internet.

3. A demagogue relies heavily on propaganda defined in the negative sense of intentional use of suggestion, scapegoating, irrelevant emotional appeals, and pseudo-proof in order to bypass human rational decision-making processes.

4. A demagogue capitalizes on the availability of a major current social cause or problem.

5. A demagogue is hypocritical. The social cause serves as a mask or persuasive leverage point while the actual primary motive is selfish interest and personal gain.

Several cautions are in order when applying these guidelines. A persuader may reflect each of these characteristics to a greater or lesser degree and only in certain circumstances. A key determination would be whether the alleged demagogue shows a high degree of all the characteristics most of the time. A persuader might fulfill only several of these criteria (such as items 1, 2, and 4) and yet not be called a demagogue. Characteristics 3 and 5 seem to be central to a conception of a demagogue. How easily and accurately can we determine a persuader's actual motives? Should we limit the label "demagogue" solely to the political arena, or could it apply to religious figures, radio/TV talk show hosts such as Rush Limbaugh and Glenn Beck, or Internet bloggers such as Ariana Huffington? Go online and Google these persons' names to see if you can locate sources that discuss them as demagogues.

ETHICAL STANDARDS
FOR POLITICAL PERSUASION

Directly and indirectly, we are daily exposed to political persuasion in varied forms. For example, the president appeals on national television for public support of a military campaign. A senator argues in Congress against ratification of a treaty. A government bureaucrat announces a new regulation and presents reasons to justify it. A federal official contends that information requested by a citizen action group cannot be revealed for national security reasons. A national, state, or local politician campaigns for election. A citizen protests a proposed property tax rate increase at a city council meeting. What ethical criteria should we apply to judge the many kinds of political persuasion?

During the latter half of the twentieth century, traditional American textbook discussions of the ethics of persuasion, rhetoric, and argument often included lists of standards for evaluating the ethicality of an instance of persuasion. Such criteria often are rooted, implicitly if not explicitly, in what we previously described as a political perspective for judging the ethics of persuasion. The criteria usually stem from a commitment to values and procedures deemed essential to the health and growth of our system of representative democracy.

Of all the ethical criteria for varied types and contexts of persuasion described in this chapter, the following 11 are the most generally applicable for you to use as a persuader and persuadee. Do not look on these standards as limited only to political persuasion. They can apply to a wide variety of persuasive efforts in which you engage or to which you are exposed such as Internet blogs and SNM. Consider adopting (and modifying) these standards as your own *starting point commitment* to ethical persuasion (also see Sellers, 2004; Baker & Martinson, 2001).

What follows is my synthesis and adaptation of a number of traditional lists of ethical criteria for persuasion (Johannesen, Valde, & Whedbee, 2008, pp. 28–29). Within the context of our own society, the following criteria are not necessarily the only or best ones possible; they are suggested as general guidelines rather than inflexible rules, and they may stimulate discussion on the complexity of judging the ethics of persuasion. Consider, for example, under what circumstances there might be justifiable exceptions to some of these criteria. Also bear in mind that one difficulty in applying

BOX 2.5   Checking the Facts

On the FactCheck.org website go to the article "Toss-Up: Missouri Mudslinging" (see Weblink 2.7). This 2010 Missouri U.S. Senate race focused on claims by both candidates that their opponent had engaged in unethical behavior. FactCheck concluded that both candidates distorted facts in their TV ads. Read the complete analysis by FactCheck. How adequate are distinctions made between clear-cut lies versus other types of deception? Which of the 11 ethical criteria for political persuasion suggested in this chapter might apply to particular ads?

these criteria in concrete situations stems from differing standards and meanings people may have for such terms as *distort, falsify, rational, reasonable, conceal, misrepresent, irrelevant,* and *deceive.*

1. Do not use false, fabricated, misrepresented, distorted, or irrelevant evidence to support arguments or claims.

2. Do not intentionally use specious, unsupported, or illogical reasoning.

3. Do not represent yourself as informed or as an "expert" on a subject when you are not.

4. Do not use irrelevant appeals to divert attention or scrutiny from the issue at hand. Among the appeals that commonly serve such a purpose are smear attacks on an opponent's character, appeals to hatred and bigotry, innuendo, and emotionally loaded terms that cause intense but unreflective positive or negative reactions.

5. Do not ask your audience to link your idea or proposal to emotion-laden values, motives, or goals to which it actually is not related.

6. Do not deceive your audience by concealing your real purpose or self-interest, the group you represent, or your position as an advocate of a viewpoint.

7. Do not distort, hide, or misrepresent the number, scope, intensity, or undesirable features of consequences or effects.

8. Do not use emotional appeals that lack a supporting basis of evidence or reasoning or that would not be accepted if the audience had time

and opportunity to examine the subject themselves.

9. Do not oversimplify complex situations into simplistic two-valued, either/or, polar views, or choices.

10. Do not pretend certainty where tentativeness and degrees of probability would be more accurate.

11. Do not advocate something in which you do not believe yourself.

FactCheck.org is a non-partisan project of the Annenberg Public Policy Center of the University of Pennsylvania. It evaluates the factual accuracy of public statements by political candidates, public officials, and news reports. In evaluating the advertisements of various state and national 2010 political campaigns, they found numerous "twisted claims and distortions of reality" and some "pure fabrication" (Box 2.5).

ETHICAL STANDARDS FOR COMMERCIAL ADVERTISING

Consumers, academics, and advertisers themselves clearly do not agree on any one set of ethical standards as appropriate for assessing commercial advertising. Here we will simply survey some of the widely varied criteria that have been suggested. Among them you may find guidelines that will aid your own assessments.

Sometimes advertisers adopt what we previously called legal perspectives, in which ethicality is equated with legality. However, advertising executive Harold Williams (1974) observed:

> What is legal and what is ethical are not synonymous, and neither are what is legal and what is honest. We tend to resort to legality often as our guideline. This is in effect what happens often when we turn to the lawyers for confirmation that a course of action is an appropriate one.
>
> We must recognize that we are getting a legal opinion, but not necessarily an ethical or moral one. The public, the public advocates, and many of the legislative and administrative authorities recognize it even if we do not (pp. 285–288).

Typically, commercial advertising has been viewed as persuasion that argues a case or demonstrates a claim concerning the actual nature or merits of a product. This view is reflected in the formal codes of ethics of professional advertising associations, such as the American Advertising Federation. Many of the traditional ethical standards for truthfulness and rationality are applicable to such attempts at arguing the quality of a product. For instance, are the evidence and the reasoning supporting the claim clear, accurate, relevant, and sufficient in quantity? Are the emotional and motivational appeals directly relevant to the product (Box 2.6)?

The American Association of Advertising Agencies' code of ethics was revised in 1990. As you read the following standards, consider their level of adequacy, the degree to which they are relevant and appropriate today, the extent to which they are being followed by advertisers, and how they reflect truthfulness and rationality criteria. Association members agree to avoid intentionally producing advertising that contains the following:

- false or misleading statements or exaggerations, visual or verbal

- testimonials that do not reflect the real choices of the individuals involved

- price claims that are misleading

- claims that are insufficiently supported or that distort the true meaning or practicable application of statements made by professional or scientific authority

- statements, suggestions, or pictures offensive to public decency or to minority segments of the population.

What if ethical standards of truthfulness and rationality are irrelevant to most commercial advertising? What if the primary purpose of most ads is not to prove a claim? Then the ethical standards we apply may stem from whatever alternative view of the nature and purpose of advertising we do hold. Some advertisements function primarily to capture and sustain consumer attention, to announce a product, or to create consumer awareness of the name of a product. Many advertisements aim primarily at stimulating in consumers a positive or feel-good attitude about the product through use of metaphor, humor, fantasy, and fiction (Spence & Van Heekeren, 2005, pp. 41–53). What ethical criteria are most appropriate for such attention-getting or feel-good ads?

What ethical evaluation of effects and consequences would you make of an advertisement for

---

BOX 2.6   The Story of Stuff Project

The mission of *The Story of Stuff Project* is to build a social movement to transform current wasteful and polluting systems of production and consumption into ones that foster "ecological sustainability and social wellbeing." Go to *The Story of Stuff* website and view the eight minute video titled "The Story of Bottled Water" (see Weblink 2.8). This video is an argument against unethical ads and practices of the bottled water industry. Why, or why not, were you persuaded about the industry? What industry ads were ethically questionable and why? Also explain whether the project itself used claims or techniques that were ethically questionable.

Fetish perfume in *Seventeen*, a magazine whose readers include several million young teenage girls? The ad shows an attractive female teenager looking seductively at the readers. The written portion of the ad says, "Apply generously to your neck so he can smell the scent as you shake your head 'no.'" Consider that this ad exists in a larger cultural context in which acquaintance rape is a societal problem, women and girls are clearly urged to say "No!" to unwanted sexual advances, and men and boys too often still believe that "no" really means "yes."

What harmful individual and societal consequences may stem from ads that negatively stereotype persons or groups on the basis of age (old and confused), sex (women as sex objects), or culture (backward)? Our frequent exposure to such ads may indeed influence the way we perceive and treat such stereotyped persons and the way the stereotyped persons view themselves and their own abilities (Spence & Van Heekeren, 2005, pp. 54–69). "Therefore, insofar as stereotyping in advertising degrades people as persons and harms their personal dignity by degrading the societal group to which they belong, stereotyping violates people's rights to freedom and well-being and hence is unethical" (p. 68).

Commercial advertisements sometimes can be criticized for containing ambiguous or vague elements. But concern about vagueness and ambiguity in persuasion is not limited to commercial advertising. Now we examine the more general ethical implications of ambiguity and vagueness.

THE ETHICS OF INTENTIONAL AMBIGUITY AND VAGUENESS

"Language that is of doubtful or uncertain meaning" might be a typical definition of ambiguous language. **Ambiguous** language is open to two or more legitimate interpretations. **Vague** language lacks definiteness, explicitness, or preciseness of meaning. Clear communication of intended meaning usually is one major aim of the ethical communicator, whether that person seeks to enhance receivers' understanding or to influence beliefs, attitudes, or actions. Textbooks on oral and written communication typically warn against ambiguity and vagueness; often, they take the position that intentional ambiguity is an unethical communication tactic. For example, later in this book, ambiguity is discussed as a functional device of style, as a stylistic technique that is often successful while ethically questionable.

Most people agree that intentional ambiguity is unethical in situations in which accurate instruction or transmission of precise information is the acknowledged purpose. Even in most so-called persuasive communication situations, intentional ambiguity is ethically suspect. However, in some situations, communicators may believe that the intentional creation of ambiguity or vagueness is necessary, accepted, expected as normal, and even ethically justified. Such might be the case, for example, in religious discourse, in some advertising, in labor-management bargaining, in political campaigning, or in international diplomatic negotiations.

We can itemize a number of specific purposes for which communicators might believe that intentional ambiguity is ethically justified: (1) to heighten receiver attention through puzzlement, (2) to allow flexibility in interpretation of legal concepts, (3) to allow for precise understanding and agreement on the primary issue by using ambiguity on secondary issues, (4) to promote maximum receiver psychological participation in the communication transaction by letting receivers create their own relevant meanings, and (5) to promote maximum latitude for revision of a position in later dealings with opponents or with constituents by avoiding being locked into a single absolute stance.

In political communication, whether from campaigners or government officials, several circumstances might justify intentional ambiguity. First, a president or presidential candidate often communicates to multiple audiences through a single message via a mass medium such as television or radio. Different parts of the message may appeal to specific audiences, and intentional ambiguity in

| BOX 2.7 | **Ambiguity and Confusion** | |

Recall from chapter 1 Rank's intensify/downplay model for critically analyzing persuasion. In general he does not attach ethical judgments to the tactics of repetition, association, composition, omission, diversion, and confusion. We could infer that in a specific situation concrete examples of each tactic might be ethical, ethically questionable, or obviously unethical. But think more deeply about the tactic of confusion. Might it be the case that intentional promotion of confusion *always* is ethically questionable or obviously unethical? What are some examples of persuaders promoting confusion in the minds of receivers that you would judge to be unethical? What is your justification? Try to identify some examples of intentional promotion of confusion that you would consider to be *wholly ethical*. Finally, what is the relationship between promotion of confusion and promotion of ambiguity/vagueness as discussed in this section?

some message elements avoids offending any of the audiences. Second, as political scientist Lewis Froman (1966) observed, a candidate "cannot take stands on specific issues because he doesn't know what the specific choices will be until he is faced with the necessity for concrete decision. Also, specific commitments would be too binding in a political process that depends upon negotiation and compromise" (p. 9). Third, groups of voters increasingly make decisions about whether to support or oppose a candidate on the basis of that candidate's stand on a single issue of paramount importance to those groups. The candidate's position on a variety of other public issues is often ignored or dismissed. "Single-issue politics" is the phrase frequently used to characterize this trend. A candidate may be intentionally ambiguous on one emotion-packed issue in order to get a fair hearing for his or her stands on many other issues (Box 2.7).

During the 2004 presidential campaign, George W. Bush frequently charged his opponent, John Kerry, with "flip-flopping" on significant issues. That is, Bush claimed that Kerry often changed his position on issues and thus was inconsistent or ambiguous. Is it automatically unethical for a politician to change her or his position on an issue? Why or why not?

In some advertising, intentional ambiguity seems to be understood as such by consumers and even accepted by them. In your opinion, what might be some ethical issues in the TV ad for a popular beer, in which Sergio Garcia, a famous professional golfer, acts as a kind of secret agent?

He sneaks into a plush party to meet a sultry, sexy-looking date.

> SHE: "What took you so long?"
>
> HE: "Tough drive."
>
> HE: "How's your game?"
>
> SHE (IN A SEXY VOICE): "Oh, there's nothing like a good up and down."

THE ETHICS OF MORAL EXCLUSION

Moral exclusion, according to Susan Opotow (1990), "occurs when individuals or groups are perceived as outside the boundary in which moral values, rules, and considerations of fairness apply. Those who are morally excluded are perceived as nonentities, expendable, or undeserving; consequently, harming them appears acceptable, appropriate, or just." Persons morally excluded are denied their rights, dignity, and autonomy. Opotow isolates for analysis and discussion over two dozen symptoms or manifestations of moral exclusion. For our purposes, a noteworthy fact is that many of them directly involve communication. Although all the symptoms she presents are significant for a full understanding of the mind-set of individuals engaged in moral exclusion, the following clearly involve persuasion:

- showing the superiority of oneself or one's group by making unflattering comparisons to other individuals or groups

- denigrating and disparaging others by characterizing them as lower life forms (vermin) or as inferior beings (barbarians, aliens)

- denying that others possess humanity, dignity, or sensitivity, or have a right to compassion

- redefining as an increasingly larger category that of "legitimate" victims

- placing the blame for any harm on the victim

- justifying harmful acts by claiming that the morally condemnable acts committed by "the enemy" are significantly worse

- misrepresenting cruelty and harm by masking, sanitizing, and conferring respectability on them through the use of neutral, positive, technical, or euphemistic terms to describe them

- justifying harmful behavior by claiming that it is widely accepted (everyone is doing it) or that it was isolated and uncharacteristic (it happened just this once)

An example may clarify how language choices function to achieve moral exclusion. The category of "vermin" includes parasitic insects such as fleas, lice, mosquitoes, bedbugs, and ticks that can infest human bodies. In Nazi Germany, Adolf Hitler's speeches and writings often referred to Jews as a type of parasite infesting the pure Aryan race (non-Jewish Caucasians or people of Nordic heritage) or as a type of disease attacking the German national body. The depiction of Jews as parasites or a disease served to place them outside the moral boundary where ethical standards apply to human treatment of other humans. Jews were classified or categorized as nonhumans. As parasites, they had to be exterminated; as a cancerous disease, they had to be cut out of the national body.

Another example of moral exclusion is the genocide (attempted extermination of an entire ethnic group) that occurred in the African nation of Rwanda in 1994. In about 100 days, some 800,000 people were slaughtered, most by being hacked to death with machetes. The ethnic Hutus in power organized soldiers and ordinary citizens to murder ethnic Tutsis (men, women, and children), many of whom had been friends and neighbors. While there are multiple causes or influences that led to the massacre, clearly the language of moral exclusion was a contributing factor. A lengthy government propaganda campaign using radio programs fostered in the minds of the Hutus a view of Tutsis as less than human, as prey "for hunting expeditions," and as "cockroaches" to be squashed. For horrifying yet routine examples of this process, we urge you to read Jean Hatzfeld, *Machete Season: The Killers in Rwanda Speak* (2005). To experience the hate-filled atmosphere at that time, view the fact-based films *Hotel Rwanda* (2004) and *Beyond the Gates* (2005).

Michael Ramirez is a conservative political cartoonist. He has received two Pulitzer Prizes (1994 and 2008) for his editorial cartoons. On June 25, 2007 he published an editorial cartoon in the *Investor's Business Daily* that prompts further discussion of the moral exclusion process (Figure 2.4).

Note that while the word *Iran* is very clear on the sewer cover the word *extremism* is much less clear. Also note that there are masses of cockroaches streaming out of the sewer to infest other mid-east countries such as Iraq, Afghanistan, Pakistan, Syria, Lebanon, and Israel. How easy would it be for a viewer of this image to conclude that *all* Iranians (not just extremists) are cockroaches (less than human vermin)? What might be the normal solution for the problem of cockroaches spewing from their breeding ground in Iran? Drop a bug-bomb down the sewer? Or, by implication, drop a nuclear bomb on Iran? In judging the ethics of this cartoon, how much does it matter whether Ramirez *intended* the above interpretation? A collection of a large body of his editorial cartoons, including this one and those that won him the Pulitzer Prizes, is Michael Ramirez, *Everyone Has The **Right** To My Opinion* (2008). For a wide-ranging analysis of examples of moral exclusion see Erin Steuter and Deborah Wills, *At War With Metaphor* (2008).

Even headlines we encounter daily in newspapers or magazines may reflect (perhaps unconsciously) the process of moral exclusion. Carefully consider the headline discussed in Box 2.8.

FIGURE 2.4   Ramirez editorial cartoon and moral exclusion.

SOURCE: By permission of Michael Ramirez and Creators Syndicate, Inc.

BOX 2.8   **Moral Exclusion in a Headline**

The headline "An Eskimo Encounters Civilization—and Mankind" appeared in the Tempo section of the *Chicago Tribune* (May 29, 2000). Can you identify two ways in which the words in the headline reflect a process of moral exclusion? How do these words place people outside the categories where human ethics normally apply? Hate speech, as discussed earlier in this chapter, and racist/sexist language, examined in the next section, also illustrate the process of moral exclusion. In what ways does hate speech embody the moral exclusion process?

The Ethics of Racist/Sexist Language

In *The Language of Oppression*, communication scholar Haig Bosmajian (1983) demonstrated how names, labels, definitions, and stereotypes traditionally have been used to degrade, dehumanize, and suppress Jews, Blacks, Native Americans, and women. Bosmajian's goal was to expose the "decadence in our language, the inhumane uses of language" that have been used "to justify the unjustifiable, to make palatable the unpalatable, to make reasonable the unreasonable, to make decent the indecent." Bosmajian reminded us: "Our identities, who and what we are, how others see us, are greatly affected by the names we are called and the words with which we are labeled. The names, labels, and phrases employed to 'identify' a people may in the end determine their survival" (pp. 5, 9).

"Every language reflects the prejudices of the society in which it evolved. Since English, through most of its history, evolved in a white, Anglo-Saxon, patriarchal society, no one should be surprised that its vocabulary and grammar frequently reflect attitudes that exclude or demean minorities and women" (Miller & Swift, 1981, pp. 2–3). Such is the fundamental position of Casey Miller and Kate Swift, authors of *The Handbook of Nonsexist Writing*. Conventional English usage, they argued, "often obscures the actions, the contributions, and sometimes the very presence of women" (p. 8). Because such language usage is misleading and inaccurate, it has ethical implications. "In this respect, continuing to use English in ways that have become misleading is no different from misusing data, whether the misuse is inadvertent or planned" (p. 8).

To what degree is the use of **racist/sexist language** unethical, and by what standards? At the least, racist/sexist terms place people in artificial and irrelevant categories. At worst, such terms intentionally demean and put down other people by embodying unfair negative value judgments of their traits, capacities, and accomplishments. What are the ethical implications, for instance, of calling a Jewish person a "kike," a Black person a "nigger" or "boy," an Italian person a "wop," an Asian person a "gook" or "slant-eye," or a thirty-year-old woman a "girl" or "chick"? Here is one possible answer:

> In the war in Southeast Asia, our military fostered a linguistic environment in which the Vietnamese people were called such names as slope, dink, slant, gook, and zip; those names made it much easier to despise, to fear, to kill them. When we call women in our own society by the names of gash, slut, dyke, bitch, or girl, we—men and women alike—have put ourselves in a position to demean and abuse them (Bailey, 1984, pp. 42–43).

From a political perspective, we might value access to the relevant and accurate information needed to make reasonable decisions on public issues. Racist/sexist language, however, by reinforcing stereotypes, conveys inaccurate depictions of people, fails to take serious account of them, or even makes them invisible for purposes of such decisions. Such language denies us access to

necessary accurate information and thus is ethically suspect. From a human nature perspective, it is also ethically suspect because it dehumanizes individuals and groups by undermining and circumventing their uniquely human capacity for rational thought or for using symbols. From a dialogical perspective, racist/sexist language is ethically suspect because it reflects a superior, exploitative, inhumane attitude toward others, thus denying equal opportunity for self-fulfillment for some people.

A Feminist View on Persuasion

Feminism is not a concept with a single, universally accepted definition. For our purposes, elements of definitions provided by Barbara Bate (1992) and Julia Wood (1994) are helpful. **Feminism** holds that both women and men are complete and important human beings and that societal barriers (typically constructed through language processes) have prevented women from being perceived and treated as of equal worth to men. Feminism implies a commitment to equality and respect for life. It rejects oppression and domination as undesirable values and accepts that difference need not be equated with inferiority or undesirability.

Sonja Foss and Cindy Griffin (1995) develop an "invitational rhetoric" rooted in the feminist assumptions that (1) relationships of equality are usually more desirable than ones of domination and elitism, (2) every human being has value because she or he is unique and is an integral part of the pattern of the universe, and (3) individuals have a right to self-determination concerning the conditions of their lives (they are expert about their lives).

Invitational rhetoric, say Foss and Griffin, invites "the audience to enter the rhetor's world and to see it as the rhetor does." The invitational rhetor "does not judge or denigrate others' perspectives but is open to and tries to appreciate and validate those perspectives, even if they differ dramatically from the rhetor's own." The goal is to establish a "nonhierarchical, nonjudgmental, non-adversarial framework" for the interaction and to develop a "relationship of equality, respect, and appreciation" with the audience. Invitational rhetors make no assumption that their "experiences or perspectives are superior to those of audience members and refuse to impose their perspectives on them." Although change is not the intent of invitational rhetoric, it might be a result. Change can occur in the "audience or rhetor or both as a result of new understandings and insights gained in the exchange of ideas."

In the process of invitational rhetoric, Foss and Griffin contend, the rhetor offers perspectives without advocating their support or seeking their acceptance. These individual perspectives are expressed "as carefully, completely, and passionately as possible" to invite their full consideration. In offering perspectives, "rhetors tell what they currently know or understand; they present their vision of the world and how it works for them." They also "communicate a willingness to call into question the beliefs they consider most inviolate and to relax a grip on these beliefs." Further, they strive to create the conditions of safety, value, and freedom in interactions with audience members. Safety implies "the creation of a feeling of security and freedom from danger for the audience," so that participants do not "fear rebuttal of or retribution for their most fundamental beliefs." Value involves acknowledging the intrinsic worth of audience members as human beings. In interaction, attitudes that are "distancing, depersonalizing, or paternalistic" are avoided, and "listeners do not interrupt, confront, or insert anything of their own as others tell of their experiences." Freedom includes the power to choose or decide, with no restrictions placed on the interaction. Thus, participants may introduce for consideration any and all matters; "no subject matter is off limits, and all presuppositions can be challenged." Finally, in invitational rhetoric, the "rhetor's ideas are not privileged over those of the audience." (Also see Gorsevski, 2004, pp. 75, 164.)

In concluding their explication of an invitational rhetoric, Foss and Griffin suggest that this rhetoric requires "a new scheme of ethics to fit interactional goals other than inducement of others to adherence to the rhetor's own beliefs." What might be some appropriate ethical guidelines for an invitational rhetoric? What ethical standards seem already to be implied by the dimensions or constituents of such a rhetoric? For example, invitational rhetoric respects the value and freedom of the others to whom the persuasion is addressed and in doing so avoids moral exclusion. Also such rhetoric reflects a type of dialogic communication as discussed earlier in this chapter.

A few scholars with a feminist viewpoint explore ethical issues concerning the Internet and cyberspace (e.g., Adam, 2005). Our next topic examines general issues of Internet ethics from several ethical viewpoints.

ETHICAL ISSUES IN CYBERSPACE

What ethical standards should apply to communication in cyberspace—in the realm of the Internet, e-mail, blogs, chat rooms and social network media (Box 2.9)? We can get guidance and suggestions from several sources (e.g., Berkman & Shumway, 2003; Cavalier, 2005; Hamelink, 2000; Johnson, 2001; Wolf, 2003). Some of the "Ten Commandments of Computer Ethics" formulated by the Computer Ethics Institute are particularly relevant. For example, "thou shalt not: use a computer to harm other people; interfere with other people's computer work; snoop around in other people's computer files; use a computer to steal; use a computer to bear false witness against others; [or] plagiarize another person's intellectual output" (reprinted in Ermann, Williams, and Shauf, 1997, pp. 313–314).

In *The Weblog Handbook*, Rebecca Blood (2002, pp. 85–87, 114–121, 135–137) contends that "the weblog's greatest strength—its uncensored, unmediated, uncontrolled voice—is also its greatest weakness." Also she laments that there "has been almost no talk about ethics in the weblog universe." Blood thus is aware of the tension between freedom and responsibility in this form of Internet communication. At several points in her book, she suggests principles to highlight ethical responsibilities both for creators of and participants in the various types of blogs: (1) "Publish as fact only that which you believe to be true. If your

BOX 2.9 **False Photo on Facebook**

Imagine that you and your close friend both have home pages on Facebook. Without your knowledge your friend uses a photograph of you instead of your friend's own photo on her/his home page. After finding out, how would you feel about your friend's action? Because of this action, have you lost trust in your friend? Why? Is your friend's action unethical? Why? Does the use of your photo constitute lying to persons who have access to your friend's home page? Why? In what ways might issues of motive, context, consequences, and intentionality apply to this example?

statement is speculation, say so." (2) "If material exists online, link to it when you reference it. Online readers deserve, as much as possible, access to all of the facts." (3) "Publicly correct any misinformation." If you discover that one of your links was inaccurate or one of your statements was untrue, say so and correct it. (4) "Write each entry as if it could not be changed; add to, but do not rewrite or delete any entry.... Changing or deleting destroys the integrity of the network." (5) Disclose any possible or actual conflict of interest so that audience trust is not undermined. (6) Clearly label biased or questionable sources, otherwise readers will lack necessary information to assess the merits of the source. (7) Respect other people's privacy. It is ethically questionable to repeat without permission someone's instant message, chat-room or real-life conversation, or e-mail. (8) Question someone's facts or arguments but don't personalize your attack by denouncing her or his stupidity or other personal characteristics. (9) Consider carefully the arguments and evidence presented by others and try to represent their positions fairly and accurately.

Advertising and marketing specialists increasingly capitalize on the interactive capacities of the Internet and of interactive television to create a two-way "conversation" between product and consumer. On the Internet, Java and Shockwave technologies facilitate interactive ads. Video on demand and personal video recorders (such as TiVo) afford opportunities for interactive television ads. But much of the contact, such as banner ads and pop-ups on the Internet, is not truly a conversation (Spence & Van Heekeren, 2005, pp. 96–107). "One-way unsolicited communications from advertisers to consumers, especially when they

are conducted without the consumers' consent, are not 'interactive' and not 'conversations' even if the advertisers mislabel them as such. And insofar as they invade the consumers' privacy they are ethically unjustified" (p. 104).

Let's consider the ethical implications of several terms often used in the context of the Internet. *Cookies* are used by various types of websites to collect information about the browsing behavior of visitors to that site but to track that information without the visitor's knowledge or approval. How we conceptualize such processes influences whether they may have ethical dimensions. Are cookies like a clerk asking for our zip code so a store can do more efficient market analysis or are they an intrusive "stealth" surveillance technique? Are they like cameras in a store to help catch shoplifters or like a camera in our home watching what we do in private? (Adapted from Johnson, 2001, pp. 9–10). *Spam* is a type of promotional e-mail sent to large numbers of users all at the same time but it has not been requested by those e-mail users. On what grounds, and why, might it be considered unethical? Or is spam simply irritating "junk mail" but not considered unethical?

Going viral describes rumors, controversial statements, and provocative photos or videos that are quickly picked up, rapidly spread, and widely diffused through blogs, e-mail, and social network media such as YouTube and Twitter. This rapid virus-like spread often occurs without any consideration of factual accuracy or personal/media ethical responsibility. In analyzing the "Whoppers of Campaign 2010," FactCheck.org notes that the claims they were most frequently asked to verify "don't always come from the mouths of politicians, or even their TV ads.... The falsehoods circulate widely by e-mail, forwarded by people who don't know or don't care that they are spreading misinformation the way a virus spreads disease" (see Weblink 2.9).

As social network media, Facebook, YouTube, Formspring, and Twitter are not simply neutral conduits of messages. They facilitate intentional efforts to influence or persuade others, not just allow for self-expression. Of course ethical issues arise concerning these vehicles of persuasion. In his book, *Watching You-Tube*, media critic Michael Strangelove (2010) observes: "Videos within YouTube are littered with racist, sexist, misogynist, homophobic, anti-Semitic, and obscene hate speech" (pp. 119, 107). And the process of moral exclusion often functions in additional ways. "Comparisons between a politician and Hitler or the devil are common within YouTube" (p. 147).

It could be argued that Twitter, by its very structure, encourages deception and lying in political persuasion. Consider the reasoning of FactCheck.org. "For providing false and misleading information, the 30-second TV spot crafted by a seasoned media consultant is still king. But there's another medium this campaign year that makes the content of a TV ad seem like the Lincoln-Douglas debates. We're talking about Twitter.... It provides its users with 140 characters to make a point—enabling them to oversimplify and exaggerate. In politics this is considered an asset, and both parties have taken to the social networking site" by using "designated party twitterers" to reinforce misperceptions about opponents or make clear-cut lies (see Weblink 2.10). The structure of Formspring allows both posers of questions and responders to questions to choose to be anonymous. This feature may encourage such unethical communication as hate speech and bullying. Two frequent postings on Formspring are "you should kill yourself" and the claim or rumor that one person has hooked up with another person (Eldeib, 2010).

Standards, criteria, and guidelines are central to much of the earlier discussion in this chapter, and shortly we will present a framework of questions that can improve your ethical judgment. But now we discuss the often-neglected role of your own formed ethical character in creating and evaluating persuasion.

ETHICS AND PERSONAL CHARACTER

Ethical persuasion is not simply a series of careful and reflective decisions, instance by instance, to persuade in ethically responsible ways. Deliberate application of ethical rules is sometimes impossible. Pressure for a decision can be so great or a deadline so near that there is insufficient time for careful deliberation. We might be unsure what ethical criteria are relevant or how they apply. The situation might seem so unusual that applicable criteria do not readily come to mind. In such times of crisis or uncertainty, our decisions concerning ethical persuasion stem less from deliberation than from our formed "character." Further, our ethical character influences what terms we use to describe a situation and whether we believe the situation contains ethical implications (Hauerwas, 1977; Johannesen, 1991; Klaidman & Beauchamp, 1987; Lebacqz, 1985).

Consider the nature of **moral character** as described by ethicists Richard DeGeorge and Karen Lebacqz. As human beings develop, according to DeGeorge (1999), they adopt patterns of actions and dispositions to act in certain ways.

> These dispositions, when viewed collectively, are sometimes called *character*. The character of a person is the sum of his or her virtues and vices. A person who habitually tends to act as he morally should has a good character. If he resists strong temptation, he has a strong character. If he habitually acts immorally, he has a morally bad character. If despite good intentions he frequently succumbs to temptation, he has a weak character. Because character is formed by conscious actions, in general people are morally responsible for their characters as well as for their individual actions (p. 123).

Lebacqz (1985) observes:

> ... when we act, we not only do something, we also shape our own character. Our choices about what to do are also choices about whom to be. A single lie does not necessarily make us a liar; but a

series of lies may. And so each choice about what to do is also a choice about whom to be—or, more accurately, whom to become (p. 83).

In Judeo-Christian or Western cultures, good moral character is usually associated with habitual embodiment of such virtues as courage, temperance, wisdom, justice, fairness, generosity, gentleness, patience, truthfulness, and trustworthiness. Other cultures may praise additional or different virtues that they believe constitute good ethical character. Instilled in us as habitual dispositions to act, these virtues guide the ethics of our communication behavior when careful or clear deliberation is not possible.

The Josephson Institute of Ethics conducted a 2009 survey of almost 7,000 persons ranging in age from teenage to over fifty. This ethical integrity report examined the degree to which attitudes and habits of young people carried over into their adult behavior. Here are some typical findings. Respondents who believed that lying and cheating are a necessary part of success, when compared with those who did not believe this, were: two and one-half times more likely to have deceived their boss on a significant matter during the past year, more than three times as likely to have misrepresented themselves on a resume in the past five years, three times as likely to have misrepresented or omitted important facts during a job interview, and twice as likely to lie in significant personal relationships. Respondents who cheated on high school exams two or more times (compared to those who did not cheat) were: twice as likely to have deceived their boss, more than twice as likely to have lied or mislead on a resume, three times more likely to have misrepresented relevant facts on a job interview, and three times more likely to have filed a false insurance claim. Respondents who believed that lying and cheating were a necessary part of success and respondents who cheated on exams in high school (both compared to those who did not) were much more likely to have made an unauthorized copy of music or video in the past year. Michael Josephson, the founder of the institute, believes the survey demonstrates that "character counts now and in the future

and that values and habits formed in school persist" (see Weblink 2.11).

When we evaluate a person's ethical character in light of a specific action or persuasive technique, there are five issues or dimensions that may aid us in reaching a judgment. These issues may apply in varying degrees to a wide variety of persons, such as family, friends, coworkers, business leaders, leaders of volunteer or social organizations, or elected or appointed government officials. That is, these issues apply to anyone in whom we place our trust and whom we assume to have certain responsibilities in their roles. The dimensions aid our critical thinking about character.

First, we consider the *citizen-politician issue.* Should the ethical standards we expect of politicians be the same or higher than those for the average citizen? Why? Second, the *private-public dimension* warrants consideration. Is the behavior that is ethically at issue relevant to the duties or responsibilities the person has in the public realm? Or is the behavior purely a personal and private matter and not appropriate for public examination? Third for consideration is the *past-present dimension.* Should we be most concerned about recent behavior? Or should unethical behavior in the past also be of concern? How far past is past? Should we overlook a "youthful indiscretion" but worry more about unethical behavior of the mature person? Fourth, we must consider the *once-pattern issue.* Should we overlook a one-time unethical behavior ("we all make mistakes") while taking very seriously evidence of a pattern or habit of unethical behavior? What if the one-time mistake was intentional rather than unintentional? Is evidence of a pattern of unethical behavior a sign of a serious character flaw, such as poor judgment or hypocrisy? Fifth, the *dimension of trivial-serious* must be evaluated. Is the unethical behavior trivial and minor or is it serious and significant? Should we make allowances for minor ethical mistakes but not make allowances for major, serious, clearly harmful ethical errors? A careful consideration of these five issues/dimensions may help us reach clearer and more precise judgments about a person's ethical character (even our own) when that character is in question because of unethical persuasion.

Members of organizations frequently pattern their own communication behavior and ethical standards after those persons in leadership roles for the organization. The ethical or unethical behavior of leaders significantly influences the organization's ethical climate. A reasonable expectation by members would be that leaders should embody the standards presented in the organization's code of ethics. A leader with weak ethical character, however, may not embody those standards.

Consider the Enron Corporation scandal and collapse in the first years of this century. In July 2000, Kenneth Lay, the founder, chairman, CEO of Enron, sent all employees a 65-page code of ethics. Honesty, candor, and fairness were to mark the company's relations with its various stakeholders. Respect and integrity were basic values. Thus, "ruthlessness, callousness, and arrogance" were condemned, and open, honest, and sincere relationships were stressed. Kenneth Lay's signed introduction to the code emphasized that business must be conducted in a "moral and honest manner." He concluded by noting "Enron's reputation finally depends upon its people, you and me." How ironic, then, that in May 2006 Kenneth Lay was convicted in federal court of various charges that involved lying and deception about Enron's profits and debts (for a copy of the code of ethics, see Weblink 2.12).

IMPROVING ETHICAL JUDGMENT

One purpose of this book is to make you a more discerning receiver and consumer of communication by encouraging ethical judgments of communication that are specifically focused and carefully considered. In making judgments about the ethics of your own communication and the communication to which you are exposed, you should make specific rather than vague assessments, and thoughtful rather than reflexive, "gut-level" reactions.

The following framework of questions is offered as a means of making more systematic and firmly grounded judgments of communication ethics. Bear in mind philosopher Stephen Toulmin's (1950) observation that "moral reasoning is so complex, and has to cover such a variety of types of situations, that no one logical test ... can be expected to meet every case" (p. 148). In underscoring the complexity of making ethical judgments, in *The Virtuous Journalist*, Klaidman and Beauchamp (1987) reject the "false premise that the world is a tidy place of truth and falsity, right and wrong, without the ragged edges of uncertainty and risk." Rather, they argue: "Making moral judgments and handling moral dilemmas require the balancing of often ill-defined competing claims, usually in untidy circumstances" (p. 20).

1. Can I specify exactly what ethical criteria, standards, or perspectives are being applied by me or by others? What is the concrete grounding of the ethical judgment?

2. Can I justify the reasonableness and relevancy of these standards for this particular case? Why are these the most appropriate ethical criteria among the potential ones? Why do these take priority (at least temporarily) over other relevant ones?

3. Can I indicate clearly in what respects the communication being evaluated succeeds or fails in measuring up to the standards? What judgment is justified in this case about the degree of ethicality? Is the most appropriate judgment a specifically targeted and narrowly focused one rather than a broad, generalized, and encompassing one?

4. In this case, to whom is ethical responsibility owed—to which individuals, groups, organizations, or professions? In what ways and to what extent? Which responsibilities take precedence over others? What is the communicator's responsibility to self and to society at large?

5. How do I feel about myself after this ethical choice? Can I continue to "live with myself" in good conscience? Would I want my parents or mate or best friend to know of this choice?

6. Can the ethicality of this communication be justified as a coherent reflection of the

communicator's personal character? To what degree is the choice ethically "out of character"?

7. If called upon in public to justify the ethics of my communication, how adequately could I do so? What generally accepted reasons or rationale could I appropriately offer?

8. Are there precedents or similar previous cases to which I can turn for ethical guidance? Are there significant aspects of this instance that set it apart from all others?

9. How thoroughly have alternatives been explored before settling on this particular choice? Might this choice be less ethical than some of the workable but hastily rejected or ignored alternatives?

Remember that this framework for ethical judgment is not a set of inflexible and universal rules. You must adapt the questions to varied persuasive situations to determine which questions are most applicable. Also, this list may stimulate additional questions. The framework is a starting point, not the final word.

REVIEW AND CONCLUSION

The process of persuasion demands that you make choices about the methods and content you will use in influencing receivers to accept the alternative you advocate. These choices involve issues of desirability and of personal and societal good. What ethical standards will you use in making or judging these choices among techniques, contents, and purposes? What should be the ethical responsibility of a persuader in contemporary society? Obviously, answers to these questions have not been clearly or universally established. However, we must face the questions squarely.

In this chapter, we explored some perspectives, issues, and examples useful in evaluating the ethics of persuasion. Our interest in the nature and effectiveness of persuasive techniques must not overshadow our concern for the ethical use of such techniques. We must examine not only how to but also whether to use persuasive techniques. The issue of "whether to" is both one of audience adaptation and one of ethics. We need to formulate meaningful ethical guidelines, not inflexible rules, for our own persuasive behavior and for use in evaluating the persuasion to which we are exposed.

KEY TERMS

After reading this chapter, you should be able to identify, explain, and give an example of the following key terms or concepts:

ethical issues	situational perspective	negative presumption against lying	racist/sexist language
responsibility	legal perspective		feminism
freedom versus responsibility tension	dialogical perspective	propaganda	invitational rhetoric
	The Golden Rule	demagogue	going viral
human nature perspectives	The Platinum Rule	ambiguous	moral character
	lying and deception	vague	
political perspectives		moral exclusion	
hate speech			

APPLICATION OF ETHICS

Assume that you are employed in the public relations department of a large corporation. Your supervisor assigns you to present a series of speeches to community groups in a city where your company has just built a new production facility. In the speech prepared by your supervisor, you will describe the services and advantages of the plant that will benefit the community. But during a visit to the plant to familiarize yourself with its operation, you discover that the plant cannot actually deliver most of the services and advantages promised in the speech. Should you go ahead and present the speech as your supervisor prepared it? Should you refuse to give it at all? What changes might you in good conscience make in the speech? Should you make any changes with or without your supervisor's approval? What ethical standards might you use in making your decisions? Why? What additional ethical issues might confront you in this situation? (Adapted from McCammond, 2004.)

QUESTIONS FOR FURTHER THOUGHT

1. What ethical standards should be used to evaluate commercial advertising? Describe a current ad or ad campaign that you believe is unethical and justify your judgment.

2. The website of the Center for Media and Democracy presents evaluations of the public relations "spin" of both political and corporate communications (see Weblink 2.13). Search the site for cases under such topic headings as ethics, rhetoric, or propaganda. What is your judgment of the ethics of a public relations example you select from this site?

3. How might a particular actual or hypothetical argument that a worthwhile goal (end) justifies use of unethical persuasive techniques (means) be viewed as an example of the Situational Perspective?

4. What current prominent person might warrant the label of demagogue? What is your justification?

5. What current example of public persuasion might illustrate the tension between freedom of communication and ethical responsibility? How?

6. How might cell phone text-messaging be used by a student (or by students) in unethical ways during an in-class written exam? Why do you consider these uses to be unethical?

7. What ethical standards do you personally believe should guide communication on the Internet?

8. How does hate speech illustrate the process of moral exclusion?

9. Sometimes the necessity to lie in order to be successful in business is justified by the saying "business is business." What does that saying imply to you? Would you accept that saying as a general justification for lying in the workplace? Why or why not?

10. Recall the discussion in chapter 1 of the elaboration likelihood model (ELM) of persuasion. In the central information processing route, the receiver of persuasion consciously and directly focuses on relevant issues, supporting evidence, alternatives, and probable consequences. Give some examples of concrete appeals in the central information processing route that you would consider to be *unethical*. Why? In the peripheral information processing route, the receiver reacts

to emotional appeals, short-cut cues as reminders of something, unconscious yet influential triggers of values, and seemingly insignificant bits of information on the fringes of our awareness. Give some examples of concrete appeals in the peripheral information processing route that you would consider to be *unethical*. Why?

11. Go to Weblink 2.14 and read this analysis of the evidence and argument on both sides of the debate on global warming/climate change. What are some issues of communication ethics discussed? What standards could you use to judge these instances as unethical? Or, as an alternative, Google the topic "climategate" and select to read an article that seems to be evaluating facts and claims on one side or the other. What types of unethical communication/persuasion can you identify and on what grounds do you judge them as unethical?

 You can access your online resources at the companion website for *Persuasion*. Log in at **http://www.cengagebrain.com.**

3

Traditional, Artistic, and Humanistic Approaches to Persuasion

JOSEPH N. SCUDDER
Northern Illinois University

LEARNING GOALS

After reading this chapter, you should be able to:

1. Discuss the foundations in Aristotle's *Rhetoric* that guide contemporary persuasion and marketing.

2. Assess what Plato's dialogic approach adds to the practice of persuasion today.

3. Evaluate the merits of Quintilian's argument of the necessity of the good character of the persuader.

4. Explain Robert Scott's epistemic approach in relationship to Aristotle's and Plato's approaches.

5. Articulate how Burke's dramatistic approach differs from early approaches to persuasion.

6. Describe Fisher's reasons for developing his narrative approach and apply Fisher's criteria of coherence and fidelity to recent persuasive narratives.

7. Identify the objections to Fisher's narrative approach.

8. Discuss whether visual rhetoric exists and how a critic can view it.

9. Contrast the differences between traditional rhetorical scholars' approach to social movements and those taking a more contemporary approach.

10. Distinguish social movements that use persuasive tactics and nonviolent methods in contrast with those using violent means.

Nostalgia still exists among many college students. In fact, it is difficult to persuade many in the job market to think about jobs in locations with more opportunities that would take them far from their families and friends. Yet, contemporary persuasion reveals biases toward people who are attractive, activities that are popular, material goods with bling, and things that are new. Older apartment complexes, antiques, mechanically sound cars with an outdated style, mature politicians, and vacations to historical sites are more difficult to sell to those in a younger demographic group. As a result, Chapter 3 has less natural appeal to most college students than many of the other chapters that clearly have relevance to their future. This is unfortunate because the foundations established by the people in this chapter are critical tools for how those in the Western world think, process information, form values, and see the world. Persuasion still addresses many of the same basic human motivations they addressed: the promise of a better life, the security of our country and homes, the joy of children, the love of family and friends, the desire for justice, and the respect of others.

Blind spots, however, do exist in these early classics. They did not deal adequately with confronting powerful others—especially those in leadership positions involved in oppression. Nor did they address the multicultural face of persuasion. The absence of women as persuaders is evident. Of course, persuasion was limited predominately to face-to-face and written communication; it is hard to imagine a world without electronic media. Thus, this chapter considers a wide range of persuasive approaches from the early traditional ones to more recent humanistic approaches exposing the exploitation of persons pushed to the margins of society.

ARISTOTLE FRAMED PERSUASION
AND OUR WAY OF THINKING

Aristotle (384 BC–322 BC) was a remarkable person. He receives my vote as the person who has most influenced the way we think in the Western world.

Alexander the Great put Aristotle in charge of the educational system of Greece. He established an ambitious program cataloguing everything known about the world at that time. Even more impressive is the continuing impact Aristotle continues to have on our way of thinking. Much of what we now consider to be the way a rational person operates has its foundation in Aristotle. He clearly established deductive and inductive patterns of reasoning that continue as essential parts across all parts of modern universities from the sciences to the humanities. Although we now consider these patterns of reasoning to be common sense, there are cultures in many parts of our world who still do not organize their worlds in a linear pattern of thinking that we now label as Aristotelian. One must read several of his books to get a good understanding of his importance to our current day. Yet, those studying communication will find a good introduction to his linear pattern of organizing in his *Rhetoric*, which is considered by many to be the single most important work ever written on the study of persuasion.

As a point of clarification, rhetoric as found in Aristotle's work (called *Ars Rhetorica* in Greek) is loosely considered to be a synonym of our term "persuasion," but rhetoric also has other meanings for scholars in English and literature departments. It is widely believed that the materials in this book were lectures or materials for his students rather than a book as we know it.

The formal study of persuasion has its early roots in ancient Greece where city-states valued the right of their citizens to speak on issues of the day. That is not to say that free speech was widely encouraged across all social classes and all persons, but it was the place where freedom of speech became a well-established principle. Aristotle did not invent rhetoric or persuasion, but he described effective persuasive practices as he saw them. Whatever its original intent, the content of what Aristotle provided on the subject of persuasion has relevance today when his principles are adapted to fit contemporary society. The next section summarizes key features from the *Rhetoric* that remain central to the practice of persuasion today.

Adaptation to Context and Purpose

Aristotle recognized that one approach to persuasion did not fit all situations. He proposed that a persuasive speaker must adapt to the context. In today's advertising and media markets, we talk about market segments and target audiences in a 24/7 media-saturated environment. Although mass media were not yet invented, Aristotle recognized **segmented audiences** long ago when he saw that it is important to customize the message strategies to the specific target. Three contexts dominated his thinking: (1) **forensic discourse** considered allegations of past wrongdoing in the legal arena; (2) **epideictic discourse** treated present situations that were often ceremonial focusing on praise or blame; and (3) **deliberative discourse** dealt with future policy, with special attention to the legislative and political realms. Adaptation was not just to the place or setting but also to the purpose of the activity that would happen there. Each of these contexts imposes certain constraints or expectations about appropriate procedures and behavior. Legal procedures in U.S. courts are carefully prescribed. The legislatures at national and state levels not only have procedures that need to be followed for the conduct of business, but also have standards of behavior expected of its members. Ceremonies like weddings and funerals also have expectations that differ across cultures and contexts, but these expectations are very important to many communities of those involved. Funeral ceremonies

---

BOX 3.1   **Westboro Baptist Members' Use of Inappropriate Persuasive Attempts at Funerals Draws Fire**

Fred Phelps and members of his congregation at West-boro Baptist Church provide evidence of the outrage that can occur when a group uses tactics inappropriate to the ceremonial context of the funeral. One of the more publicized controversial events happened when members of the Westboro Baptist church protested at the funeral of Gerorge Tiller, MD in 2008. He was targeted because he was a doctor who sometimes performed late-term abortions. This act was even more shocking because Doctor Tiller was shot while attending church. What is your personal reaction to the messages on the signs of the protestors found in the picture in Figure 3.1? Explain why this event was very hard to reconcile for most persons holding pro-life beliefs.

---

do not typically get much attention unless high profile individuals are the focus. Recently, however, funerals have become a frequent site for protests (see Box 3.1 and Figure 3.1). Rights of free speech come into conflict with a family's need to mourn in a dignified ceremony. A key factor in judging the success of persuasion in an epideictic context is whether the message is appropriate for the occasion. Most people do not think protests at funerals are appropriate.

The group has protested nationwide at over 30,000 funerals, including those of American soldiers killed in the line of duty in Iraq. The group claims these deaths are the result of God's punishment for our nation's tolerance of homosexuality.

Churches and other religious organizations clearly have First Amendment rights to address societal issues—they were important voices in struggles for civil rights in the 1960s—but these protests test the limits of the First Amendment right of free speech. Such protests would likely not exist without the presence of mass media. These uses of persuasion clearly involve the ethical issue of hate speech previously described in Chapter 2. Here we see a case of propaganda that is manufactured through the complicity of the media. An emerging strategy is to block the visual presence of such protestors by having volunteers hold tall placards in front of the protestors while encouraging media outlets to ignore the protests that have nothing to do with the event. These incidents do raise ethical issues of media coverage of hate speech where the coverage furthers the goals of hate groups.

Aristotle's three types of discourse remain relevant today, though we pursue many other contexts and market segments with our persuasion. Entertainment and media play dominant roles in our society that had limited impact in Aristotle's world, and persuaders today are challenged to understand the similarities and differences between each new generation and its predecessors. For example, advertisers have paid premiums in the past to reach the coveted segment of 18- to 39-year-olds, but persuasive strategies are changing now to follow the next age cohort of 40–59, because those in the Baby Boom represent a large and lucrative market. The important point is that Aristotle recognized that successful persuaders match appropriate persuasive tactics to the context.

Audience Adaptation and a Common Universe of Ideas

Keep in mind that the world in Aristotle's time did not have the luxury of facts, statistics, research studies, and government reports that we have today. Speakers in that time had to create much of their proof from the world that existed around their audiences. Aristotle assumed that listeners would hold ideas in common. That is, certain types of stock appeals could be used to gain the attention of audience members. In Book I, Chapter 5, of the *Rhetoric* (pp. 37–38), Aristotle makes one of the earliest statements about the approach-avoidance tendencies of individuals. He proposed that speakers should promote things that bring happiness and speak against those that destroy or hamper happiness. Aristotle's popular appeals included having one's independence; achieving prosperity; enjoying maximum pleasure; securing one's property; maintaining good friendships; producing many children; enhancing one's beauty; attending to one's health; fostering one's athletic nature; and promoting one's fame, honor, and virtue. With some updating for our current world situation, most of these appeals remain effective today. Aristotle recognized that

many of the things in this list are external and others are internal. Tapping into common cultural values such as patriotism is commonly used, but many tire of draping every issue in the national flag. See Box 3.2 for an international example of using common cultural themes as persuasive devices.

In later parts of the *Rhetoric,* Aristotle provides examples of persuasive devices, such as maxims or sayings, with broad appeal to audiences. In Book II, Chapter 21, for instance, he introduces a maxim that is much like a saying that Tony Soprano might use today: "Fool, who slayeth the father and leaveth his sons to avenge him" (p. 138). In advocating the use of maxims for listeners who love to hear universal truths in which they believe, Aristotle is advising the persuader to reinforce what the audience already knows. He

BOX 3.2   Pura Vida in Costa Rica: Drawing on Cultural Values and Dangers of Exploiting Them

Observant visitors to Costa Rica begin to see the phrase *pura vida* immediately upon arrival. The phrase is loosely translated as "pure life." The phrase appears extensively at bus stops and elsewhere in an ad campaign for Imperial beer. The tourist industry promotes Costa Rica using the phrase in its promotional materials as well as on most tours that visitors take. There is an element of propaganda here. Costa Rica benefits from visitors who go home thinking of the country as *pura vida*. The phrase, however, is deeply embedded in the culture—it is not a creation of the advertising industry. Costa Ricans use it as a common greeting or farewell.

Costa Ricans using this phrase are not saying everything is actually good in Costa Rica. They often use it as their way to create more pleasant thoughts in a less than optimum situation. Some backlash, however, is happening in the country because of the commercialization of the phrase. Many people do not want to see it in commercial advertising or on the shirts of tourists. This is a key point for those using campaigns with some element of propaganda. Many younger adults in San Jose embrace the term, while many of their older counterparts are less sanguine about its use except with those persons they know well. So persuaders need to be sensitive to overusing common cultural understandings because negative sentiment toward the message may develop, and the message may be counterproductive. Tour organizers in Costa Rica can be heard using this phrase with a bus of anxious tourists when the tour has to alter its planned itinerary after the tour is in progress. Such a strategy does little good when a major feature of an expensive excursion cannot be visited or a volcano cannot be seen because of fog or the clouds.

says, "The orator has therefore to guess the subjects on which his hearers really hold views already, and what those views are, and then must express, as general truths, these same views on these same subjects" (p. 139). The point today is not that we need to learn the use of maxims, but that we must learn to adapt our messages to the world of our listeners.

Today's advertisers still use themes that resonate with the lives of consumers. For example, milk is one of the most common items in a refrigerator in the United States. The California Milk Processor Board (2011a) originated the *Got Milk?* campaign in 1993 that has been one of the most recognized advertising campaigns in the past two decades. In 2008, they revamped their campaign with a new look on the Internet, such as in the new *Get the glass campaign* (see Weblink 3.1). (You can access this and all of the other Chapter 3 weblinks through your companion website for *Persuasion,* Chapter 3 resources.)

Adapting to the audience's views raises ethical issues. Crass commercialization of major holidays in the United States sometimes dilutes the impact persuaders make with their messages, because many people believe the true sentiments of these holidays are lost in the overabundant advertising that pervades these occasions. Speakers, however, are sometimes put into a double-bind when making a public address on a memorable day. To not acknowledge a memorable day may seem insensitive to some groups, while acknowledging it may be viewed as not feeling the events or persons memorialized were not important. Advertisers often attempt to appeal to a cultural theme they think will resonate with consumers such as patriotism. Perhaps the use of the U.S. flag in political and commercial advertising has been overdone. The *Pura Vida* campaign in Costa Rica shows the use of cultural themes is not always welcomed (see again Box 3.2).

Types of Proof

In the *Rhetoric,* Aristotle focused on what he called the artistic proofs or appeals that the persuader could create or manipulate. For example, persuaders create emotional moods by their choice of words and images, and heighten the mood by varying their vocal tone, rate, and volume. Aristotle identified three major types of artistic proof—ethos, pathos, and logos—which remain remarkably current in today's world. It should be noted that many scholars see all three of these types of proof as rational or cognitive appeals rather than three distinct ways to persuade an audience. Remember that there were fewer inartistic proofs, such as statistics and scientific evidence, in those times. It is useful to explore the types of proof more closely.

Ethos.   Before the speaker actually makes a persuasive presentation, the audience holds an image of the persuader. Even if the persuader is totally unknown to the audience, members will draw certain conclusions based on what they see—body type, height, complexion, movements, clothing, grooming, and so on. If the audience already knows the speaker, he or she may have a reputation for being honest, experienced, and funny. Aristotle called this image or reputation of the speaker **ethos**. A contemporary example of the use of ethos appears on eBay, one of the most profitable electronic commerce sites on the Internet. One-line reports from individuals involved in past transactions form the basis of buyers' and sellers' reputations. Users of the site earn such reputations without even seeing others or having verbal interaction. The speaker in a television program might deliberately make eye contact with various audience members and with the television cameras because eye contact can be an important element in a person's believability. Trust and credibility are salient issues today in the wake of prominent scandals from Wall Street to the White House.

What establishes a person's reputation, however, often varies from person to person. Many people may feel goodwill toward Bill Gates, cofounder of Microsoft, and his wife when they learn that the Gates have donated over $20 million to a charitable foundation that is one of the leaders in combating AIDS and other diseases in Africa. On the other hand, many computer professionals loathe Microsoft's business practices. Ethos involves many complex elements that are not always predictable. For example, former Speaker of the House Newt Gingrich was unfaithful to his wife even as he was criticizing President Clinton for being immoral. Gingrich was unable to sustain his political career after publication of the damaging information, but President Clinton survived impeachment. When a person's ethos is in question, it rarely happens without also creating an emotional reaction. This leads us to the next type of artistic proof.

Pathos.   We typically consider Aristotle's use of the Greek word **pathos** to describe what we now call emotions. He recognized that emotions come into play as appeals are made to the things people hold dear.

Aristotle recognized that carefully chosen language is part of a successful persuasive strategy. He promoted the use of emotional expression because it makes the audience share feelings with the speaker (Book III, Chapter 7). Moreover, Aristotle understood that when the audience shares similar feelings about the topic, the speaker can use more emotionally charged language. He emphasized the importance of **metaphor** in conveying new ideas and facts through images of the familiar: "It is from the metaphor that we can best get hold of something fresh" (p. 186). However, not just any metaphor would do for Aristotle; rather, the metaphor needed to be so lively or active that it made those hearing it actually see things. Of course, metaphors can be overdone. Like any other form of language, the metaphor must be appropriate. Modern political discourse uses lots of metaphors. Rank's system discussed in Chapter 1 is a very good way to think about metaphors in political contests. Some metaphors are used to intensify a candidate's good characteristics and other metaphors are used to intensify the opponent's weaknesses. Metaphors may downplay a candidate's weaknesses or an opponent's strengths.

Although Aristotle addresses the use of pathos in persuasion, he was wary of it. His writing about the use of emotion has a bit of an antiseptic quality about it. Even today it is difficult for professors teaching persuasion and argumentation to capture the dynamic role of emotion in persuasive discourse. Rational discussion about the emotional component of persuasion can never fully capture it. Fortunately, the pathos of many important persuasive events over the past 70 years has been preserved, in part, by film, recordings, and video. Even then, the real-life experience of a persuasive event can never be fully re-produced, just as the claustrophobic feeling of being trapped in a mass audience during a popular music event cannot be re-produced. One has to be there to fully experience the pulsing sensations of gigantic speaker towers penetrating your body and the mass of bodies pressing on yours.

Despite the limitations of Aristole's cerebral approach to pathos in persuasion, later scholars have undertaken more detailed considerations of the emotional nature of the audience. Now we recognize that it is not only the pathos evident in the delivery of the message but also the emotional energy brought by an audience in its context. High levels of emotion have been common in the persuasive messages of prominent religious leaders of the past and present, such as Jonathon Edwards, Billy Graham, Martin Luther King, Jr., and Minister Louis Farrakhan, but part of the definition of persuasion in Chapter 1 as co-creation involves a jointly created emotional environment. Yet the danger exists that listeners will perceive the prominent use of emotion as excessive. Howard Dean's bid to become the Democratic candidate for the presidential race in 2004 was severely hindered by his very emotional speech, deemed by some to be "over the top," given after his loss in the Iowa primary.

Pathos may involve the content of the appeal itself to the presence of injustice and suffering. Justice was one of the widely held virtues noted by Aristotle that often gives rise to emotions when it is violated. In a contemporary example, much animosity remains among average middle-class investors who saw large portions of their savings evaporate after the collapse of large Wall Street investment companies in 2008. A strong sense of injustice still appears in editorials, blogs, and letters to editors from hard-working people who have had to delay their retirements.

Emotionally-laden, persuasive appeals are also evident in recent protests of immigrants in the United States as well as Europe, but counter-protests are often as emotionally laden where legal residents express their frustration of bearing the costs of local schools and hospitals for illegal immigrants. It is clear that the consideration of pathos continues as an important consideration to how persuasive appeals are delivered. Failure to do so may mean the failure of the content of the message that Aristotle addressed in the last of his three types of proof.

Logos.   Appeals to the intellect, or to the rational side of humans, are represented by the Greek word **logos**. Logos relies on the audience's ability to process evidence in systematic ways and to arrive at valid conclusions. The persuader must predict how the audience will do this and thus must assess their information-processing and conclusion-drawing patterns.

Although Aristotle was very involved in starting rigorous scientific investigations of the natural world, he and others in his time did not have the body of scientific evidence that we have today to serve as the foundation for well-reasoned arguments. They had to rely more on artistic proofs they constructed from reasoning, rather than inartistic proofs that were evident from observations of scientists and researchers. They frequently used a form of reasoning called an **enthymeme**. Aristotle describes it as following the form of what the study of logic today would call a **syllogism**, which we will study more in a later chapter. Syllogisms begin with a major premise such as:

> Advertising is unethical if the audience does not have the capacity to evaluate the claims being made.

This major premise is then associated with a minor premise:

> Young children have not developed the ability to evaluate the merits of commercial messages on television.

This, in turn, leads to the conclusion:

> Television advertising is unethical when targeting as consumers young children who cannot evaluate the claims being made.

In Book II, Chapter 22, Aristotle also recommends that the persuader be an expert on the facts in order to use such reasoning effectively:

> The first thing we have to remember is this. Whether our argument concerns public affairs or some other subject, we must know some, if not all, of the facts about the subject on which we are to speak and argue. Otherwise, we can have no materials out of which to construct arguments (p. 140).

Clearly, substance was important for Aristotle. Persuasion was not just a bag of tricks for pulling the wool over people's eyes. You can find logical appeals operating in your daily life. Politicians use events and examples to persuade you to believe a certain view or to vote in a certain way. Financial advisers use graphs and tables to persuade you that their investment options are superior to others. Often, college recruiters provide potential students and their parents with examples of jobs filled by recent graduates and their starting salaries, and information regarding the reasonable costs of their institutions, as well as potential sources of financial aid. In each case, the persuader is betting that you will process the information logically and predictably.

Yet the form of the argument may not appear to you to be exactly like the one in the example. Consider a syllogism that Aristotle quotes: "Thou hast pity for thy sire, who has lost his sons: Hast none for Oeneus, whose brave son is dead?" (p. 145). Sometimes the language does not follow the format exactly. Let's consider this example again in contemporary language:

> You have pity for a father whose sons have died (major premise).
> The brave son of Oeneus is dead (minor premise).
> You should have pity for Oeneus (conclusion).

So enthymemes or syllogisms may leave out one of the premises or have parts in slightly different order. Nevertheless, the pattern of reasoning is there.

Places of Argument. Contemporary market research attempts to identify consumers' major premises. With these in mind, marketers design products, packaging, and advertising that effectively develop *common ground* and hence the co-creation of persuasive meaning. Aristotle used the term **topoi** to refer to places or topics of argument that are a good way to establish common ground. Persuaders identify these "places" and try to determine whether they will work for a particular audience. Consider a few of these topics and identify where contemporary persuasion uses them.

- *Arguments as to degree, or "more or less":* Will candidate A be more or less trustworthy than candidate B? Are less costly Lee jeans more or less durable than Levis?

- *Past fact:* Has an event really occurred? Did a person commit the alleged crime? This tactic is very important in the courts, where a prosecutor must prove that a crime occurred and that the accused committed that crime.

- *Future likelihood:* Is something likely to occur in the future? This argument focuses on probabilities. For example, colleges attempt to recruit students by arguing that the earnings of those with a college degree are substantially higher than the earnings of those without a college degree.

Yet Aristotle recognized that it was not simply the structure of the syllogism, but the language used within it, that was persuasive. His focus on language merits attention.

Despite many possible contemporary applications Aristotle's *Rhetoric* provides for our practice of persuasion, there are some frequently noted limitations. A danger exists of making Aristotle's *Rhetoric* a cookie cutter. If Aristotle were alive, he would probably say that it is a starting point for instruction. Many modern scholars such as Kenneth Burke have taken Aristotle very seriously as long as his principles are adapted to current situations and contexts.

Simply considering it a formulaic approach much like a cookbook clearly ignores much of what is happening in the persuasive situation. Simply thinking of evidence in terms of logos, pathos, and ethos is very simplistic. Things about some persuasive events that truly compel us by their passion, sincerity, and conviction become rather lifeless when dissected in terms of breaking them into logos, pathos, and ethos because the whole is greater than the sum of its parts. There are aspects of delivery and performance in some masterful persuasive messages, such as the *I Have a Dream* speech, delivered by Dr. Martin Luther King, Jr., that have to be experienced. Such persuasive attempts are simply difficult to understand without hearing and seeing the message as it was delivered. So we have to consider persuasion as a living event, but for instructional purposes we need to examine the component parts that fall short of comprising the overall experience.

In sum, Aristotle's principles of persuasion are remarkably contemporary and provide the foundation for modern persuasion research. Granted, there are portions that have little relevance today and that reflect values our society does not embrace. Yet his principle of adapting the message to the context recognizes that changes in persuasive messages should occur as the context changes. Now we turn to alternative points of view.

PLATO'S DIALOGIC APPROACH

The contemporary practice of persuasion owes a large debt to Aristotle. It was presented first in this chapter because it continues to dominate the design of persuasive messages and campaigns. Aristotle's linear approach to persuasion continues to work well when dealing with the physical, observable world where facts or clearly advocated values are apparent. There are, however, debates over many contemporary issues that have core ideas and assumptions that are contested. That means there are issues or assumptions that have good arguments on more than one side of the issue. There may or may not be a correct answer that can be established as truth.

The current health care debate in the United States is an example. Some politicians firmly believe that universal health care should be a fundamental right for citizens of the United States. Recent legislation is moving in that direction. Others who disagree sometimes apply the pejorative label *Obamacare* to this legislation and they have vowed to reverse it. They often advance several major arguments against the recently passed health care legislation. They see this new entitlement as too expensive and further deepening our national debt. It is viewed as a major threat to the survival of small businesses who cannot afford it. Universal health care is also argued to be a threat to the present quality of health care. Aristotle's approach to persuasion does not adequately address these contested situations. There are very good arguments on many sides of the health-care issue that are not right or wrong.

Plato's dialogic approach is a process that is better suited than Aristotle's for exploring contested values and deeper assumptions about the meaning of life. Plato believed that as humans we do not see absolute truth directly, but only glean indirect images, glimpses, or shadows of the truth. Plato used dialogue, or the **dialectic method**, to pursue these truths. Dialogue is a form of discussion where the parties ask and respond to questions from the other parties involved. Plato frequently used dialogues in his writing that began with a question that defined the terms. The answers to the questions introduce the issues followed by a cross-examination from another party. In the end, some resolution results in changes, with each side of the issue demonstrating increased understanding of each position. Beyond an elitism that favored philosophers and excluded women, Plato's dialectic method promoted discovery and open public discourse.

Plato devoted a lot of attention to the concept of truth. In the *Gorgias,* he expressed little respect for rhetoric as it was commonly practiced because he viewed it as a skill used more to flatter, appease, disguise, or deceive than to discover truth and identify the important things in life. Plato presented the ideal speaker, in Socrates' dialogues with Phaedrus, as one who seeks the best interests of the listeners rather than advancing self-interests.

Plato clearly articulated that the facts of the situation do make a difference. Consider one dialogue between Socrates and Phaedrus. Socrates pointed out that merely calling a donkey a horse does not make it a horse (Plato, 1937, p. 263). So Plato did not believe that truth was relative. There were material facts that one simply could not ignore. Beyond the factuality of these mundane details, Plato's writings present a view of Truth that we sometimes call *big T truth,* in which absolute and certain truths exist, but are obscured from our direct view.

SCOTT'S EPISTEMIC APPROACH

Plato's perspectives remain very important to communication ethics and dialog as presented in Chapter 2. Rhetorician Robert L. Scott (1993) bemoans the dominance of the Aristotelian tradition: "In general what may be called 'Aristotelian instrumentalism' has dominated thinking about rhetoric and the teaching of it ... I am suggesting that the dominant attitude ... should be drastically altered" (p. 121). Scott objects to truth being presented as an objective package, as if it were a possession or commodity. He suggests that **truth** is never certain, whether in the realm of science or public affairs, but he differs from Plato here in that he advocates

truth with a small t. For Scott, rhetoric is a process of constant discovery in which truth is seen as moments in "human, creative processes" (p. 133). This perspective is known as **epistemic** or as a way of coming to know about things.

Although truth can be stable at times, according to Scott it cannot be static in an ever-changing, 24/7, multicultural world. Many discoveries come during our rhetorical encounters with others. Scott's perspective has many similarities to that of existential thinkers, who argue that truth is experienced in the lived moment and cannot be possessed forever. In an email exchange with him, he said he was not uncomfortable being described in these terms. For Robert Scott, knowing is more than possessing facts; the experiences we have while communicating with others are very important.

Seeing persuasion as a process of constant discovery is a key principle for students of persuasion to learn. Many persuasive situations are interactive with an exchange of many questions, offers, and counter-offers. One quickly learns when purchasing a car that the true price is not what is first quoted. The true price emerges in the bargaining process. The price the next customer is charged may be higher or lower than you pay. Robert Scott's perspective clearly shows us why simply learning a set of tactics of persuasion is not enough. It seems as if this more personal approach to persuasion should have prevailed as the preferred method. Why, then, has Aristotle's influence on persuasion been greater?

Although that question cannot be answered with certainty, interactive, personal approaches are not suited to many mass communication media such as television, radio, newspapers, and direct mail. Aristotle's methods can be adapted more readily to marketing and advertising, which are more efficient methods for reaching unseen consumers. Beyond the efficiency issue is the issue of certainty. It is much harder to explain or sell an approach that cannot speak with certainty. That is why sound bites are so important for the presentation of political candidates in the media. This does not mean, however, that we should ignore the lessons from Plato and Scott. Truth and trust are clearly in vogue in the aftermath of some of the biggest ethics scandals ever seen in corporate life. Sound bites will not be sufficient means to promote trust. Yet flaws in the moral integrity of those in the public are not new. We look at Quintilian's focus on character next.

QUINTILIAN'S FOCUS ON CHARACTER

Quintilian established a public school of rhetoric in Rome in the first century AD. Although there are many useful things for persuaders in his 12-volume work, *Institutio Oratoria,* he probably remains most noted for his focus on the character of the speaker.

Many parallels exist between the credibility of public figures in the first century and today. Corruption and illegal activity was a problem then as it is now. For persuaders, a central problem was believing what those in the public eye had to say. A crisis of trust existed then about believing anything said by public figures, just as it does today.

Quintilian was unusual in that he began his *Institutio Oratoria* by focusing on the character of the person rather than establishing the truth of the content. He opens the book with the following statement:

> Let the orator whom I propose to form, then, be such a one as is characterized by the definition of Marcus Cato, a good man skilled in speaking. But the requisite which Cato has placed first in this definition—that an orator should be a good man—is naturally of more estimation and importance than the other. It is important that an orator should be good because, should the power of speaking be a support to evil, nothing would be more pernicious than eloquence alike to public concerns and private.

Although the logic of Quintilian's argument for the importance of character probably suffers because of all the exceptions he covers such as a lawyer providing a defense for a guilty individual, it is important from the standpoint that he acknowledged the character problem was present for believing persuaders in that early period. Just as in the days of the Roman Empire, establishing believability is a critical burden of the persuader today. Professional sports seem to be particularly plagued with credibility crises (see Box 3.3).

| BOX 3.3 | **Believability in the Sports Steroid and Doping Controversies** | |

The persuasive face of an effects-oriented, bottom-line world is clearly seen in the substance-abuse scandals of the sports world. The steroid crisis in professional baseball came to a critical point with the release of the Mitchell report in December 2007. Although home-run leader Barry Bonds had received the most scrutiny of any major league baseball player in recent months regarding steroid use because of his breaking of Hank Aaron's home-run mark, pitcher Roger Clemens became the focus after being named in the Mitchell Report as one of the professional players that an informant implicated in the scandal. Clemens admits that he was injected with B12 shots, but denies he intentionally used steroids. He appeared on *60 Minutes* to defend his reputation.

The stripping of the Tour de France title from Floyd Landis and the conviction of Olympic standout Marion Jones for perjury regarding the use of illegal substances are other examples of high profile sporting figures accused of using performance-enhancing substances. Lance Armstrong remains under a cloud of suspicion for the use of performance-enhancing techniques, even though drug tests never provided credible evidence of illegal behavior. A recent *Time* magazine cover story has resurrected these charges. Several questions are prominent for persuaders regarding players named in reports without legal bearing such as the Mitchell Report. First, what are legitimate sources of evidence appropriate for such documents? Second, what persuasive tactics could be used to protect one's reputation for a person accused unjustly? Is it impossible for an unjustly accused player to prove the negative that he or she is really innocent?

See the Mitchell Report at Weblink 3.2.

BURKE'S DRAMATISTIC APPROACH

Kenneth Burke, whom we noted earlier in Chapter 1 and will revisit later, is considered to be the most influential rhetorical scholar of the modern era. He continues to wield major impact upon communication scholarship even though he was a literary scholar and critic. Burke's perspective on persuasion has probably influenced the perspective of this book more than any other, outside of Aristotle. His approach was important to the definition of persuasion in Chapter 1 and will be referenced in future chapters as well. Most of this section considers his book, *The Rhetoric of Motives*.

A prolific writer with extraordinary breadth, his **dramatistic** approach cannot be neatly captured in a short statement. His perspective clearly emphasizes the performance aspect of persuasion as opposed to the scientific orientation presented in the next chapter. In other words, the art of persuasion is at its best in his writings. In one of the better articles regarding Burke's work, Marie Hochmuth Nichols maintains that Burke draws upon his study of motivation by using key terms from drama. Perhaps the most prominent of these terms are labeled the **pentad**. The pentad includes: the **act** or the description of what takes place; the **scene** providing the background or context of the act; the **agent** or the person who performs the act, the agency, or the means or instruments of accomplishing the act; and the **purpose**. Burke proposed that combinations of the elements of the pentad commonly occur with one being a primary and the other being a secondary motivation.

One should guard against only considering Burke's pentad as a tool to break a situation into its component parts. A key factor for Burke is the dynamic of the interaction of the parts. Significantly influenced by the alienation and destruction of World War II, Burke focuses on healing the divisions among people. The term **identification** that was a focus of the definition of persuasion presented in Chapter 1 of this text clearly focuses on establishing those things that are common among us. Beyond the immediate task of persuasion in his discussion of identification and the **autonomous**, Burke took care to place a persuasive act in its larger context and its impact on the community. In this discussion, it is very clear that Burke just does not see persuasion as a set of tools to accomplish an end. That is, the component parts clearly do not comprise the whole.

Interestingly, Burke draws much from Aristotle, but indicates those principles need a makeover to be more relevant to current cultural contexts. Burke suggests that readers often fail to see that Aristotle was often highly dramatistic in his context. A key element, often lost in the consideration of other persuasive approaches, is that persuasion is a performance. Persuasion cannot be separated from actually doing it. There is a clear experiential element in his approach. Like a theatrical play, the play can be performed many times, but a shift in situation and attitudes of the audience changes the effectiveness of the play.

His emphasis on identification makes the dramatistic approach not just experiential, but also relational. His dramatistic approach suggests to those who study persuasion that much of what is important in persuasion is found in relationships among the actors and the actual enactment or use of persuasion. These are intangible elements that are often missed in the analysis of persuasive events. Consider what dramatic elements that appear in the story of Professor Randy Pausch in Box 3.4 might be missed when using an Aristotelian approach to analyze it. The next perspective approaches the narrative with some similarities to Burke, but is cast in terms quite different.

FISHER'S NARRATIVE APPROACH

Communication theorist Walter Fisher (1978) shook up the dominant assumptions in the communication discipline by suggesting that humans are "as much valuing as they are reasoning animals" (p. 376). Fisher (1984, 1987) challenged the dominance of the **rational world paradigm**, which assumes people are essentially rational

BOX 3.4   Randy Pausch's Last Lecture: Really Achieving Your Childhood Dreams

One of the most moving contemporary examples of a persuasive narrative to inspire people to action was given by Professor Randy Pausch at Carnegie Mellon University on September 18, 2007. To view this lecture, go to Weblink 3.3. If the link does not work, search on Google for Randy Pausch.

Professor Pausch was diagnosed with pancreatic cancer in September 2006 and given only a short time to live. Although he claims that his first objective was to record these comments for his children, the lecture clearly attempts to inspire others to a different way of thinking about life. Consider whether this video is better analyzed as a dramatistic

event as Burke would suggest or with Fisher's narrative approach. The fidelity of Fisher's narrative approach clearly comes through in this lecture where Randy Pausch talks about his experience of achieving his childhood dreams through the many relationships he has had. The combination of humor, passion, irreverence, emotion, and real-life tragedy make it a real-life tragedy for this gifted man and his family. It is nearly impossible to watch this event without being affected personally by it. Consider whether you can truly ever say again that it was merely rhetoric after watching this lecture. Professor Pausch died on July 24, 2008.

individuals basing their decisions on the quality of arguments and evidence. In his narrative theory, Fisher (1978, 1984, 1987) proposed instead that we can better understand behavior using the story, drama, or narrative as an analytical device, and then casting the persuasive event in narrative terms. At the core of this perspective is the belief that the drama or story is the most powerful and pervasive metaphor that humans can use to persuade and explain events. Fisher (1984) described the **narrative paradigm** as a synthesis of argumentative and aesthetic themes, challenging the notion that rhetorical (persuasive) human communication must be argumentative in form and evaluated by standards of formal logic; thus, the narrative paradigm subsumes rather than denies the rational world paradigm.

So what was it that bothered Fisher so much that he decided to take on many in the established tradition? Part of Fisher's mission appeared to be to change the trend in scholarship that was increasingly focusing on the elite rather than the common. Fisher was frustrated with the way attention had shifted to technical argument that excluded most people; in his view, it was elitist. In this respect, Fisher differs from Plato. Fisher wanted to return to the rationality of everyday argument where consideration is given to the narratives of all members of the community—not just to the specialized few. Those skilled in technical aspects of argument often use such skills to

reveal the deceptive side of persuasion. Lawyers may use technical arguments from legal statutes to prevent clients from being convicted, but such technicalities do not persuade many familiar with the situation that the accused is actually innocent. Fisher's narrative approach gets more to the core of what constitutes believability.

A second motivation was his desire for a more vital communication field that returned to the roots of human experience—a very existential idea. The story became such a recognized focus of Fisher's argument that those new to the study of his narrative paradigm often overlook his focus on the human experience as the generative force behind the narratives. It bothered Fisher that traditional approaches to communication often lost the soul and conviction of the human experience by dissecting the text with systems of formal logic and argument. The difference is like that between studying the human body in anatomy class by dissecting cadavers and studying it by examining living people—both approaches have value, but one misses the lived experience.

Fisher proposed that narratives succeed or fail depending on whether they have coherence and fidelity. **Coherence** refers to the way the story hangs together and thus has meaning or impact. **Fidelity** relates to whether it rings true with the hearer's experience. With a coherent story, almost everyone understands its premises or the points it tries to make. The story is told artistically, and it is believable.

Coherence relies on the degree to which the story is consistent. Consistency means that the story is logically organized or told. In other words, we generally don't know the outcome of the story or the fate of the characters until the story is complete (i.e., it has a beginning, middle, and end in the most traditional cases). In consistent narratives, the characters have good reasons for doing what they do, and the impact of the situation or setting of the story also makes sense.

Fidelity in a narrative is similar to coherence but focuses more on whether the story seems realistic and is the kind of thing that really happens. It presents a rationale or **logic of good reasons** (Fisher, 1978) for the setting, plot, characters, and outcome of the narrative. Fisher presented several benchmarks of narratives demonstrating good fidelity. First, they deal with human values that seem appropriate for the point or moral of the story and for the actions taken by the characters. Next, the values seem to lead to positive outcomes for the characters and are in synch with our own experiences. Finally, the values form a vision for our future. Persuasive narratives cut across a broad expanse of human behavior. They appeal to our native imagination and feelings. Consider how fidelity is conveyed in Randy Pausch's last lecture (see again Box 3.4).

Narratives can also form communities of identification that together lead to a common worldview. Because of this, they have been a central part of most if not all ideological movements throughout history. For example, America's founding fathers promoted a narrative of freedom and an inherent set of human rights that continues to be important for our expected conduct today.

Although many welcomed the discussion opened by the narrative paradigm, Fisher met resistance from those who had built careers on the rational world paradigm. For example, Barbara Warnick (1987) challenged Fisher's criteria as being so context-dependent that listeners would need extensive knowledge of the situation before attempting to understand a narrative. In her opinion, Fisher's

standards allow so much room for interpretation that they leave the theory open to the inconsistencies of personal judgment. Others such as Rowland (1989) were not convinced that narrative encompasses as much of the communication domain as Fisher maintained.

Much territory in the narrative paradigm remains unexplored regarding bridges across differing cultures, but negotiating our different cultural narratives seems to be a good starting place to understand our differences. Whether or not the narrative paradigm is the single dominant organizing paradigm in the way communication operates is questionable, but Fisher did articulate a descriptive approach to persuasion that better captures the human experience of the average person than the more technical approach that appears to have become elitist in its assumptions. Despite the imperfections of the narrative paradigm, narratives are one of the most powerful persuasive tactics available. At times, good stories counter many facts. Fisher's narrative theory helps us understand this. The key point here is that you should never underestimate the value of a good story that resonates with its hearers.

VISUAL RHETORIC

Visual rhetoric continues to be a contested issue among rhetorical scholars. Given that no propositional arguments exist, many rhetoricians do not think visual rhetoric exists independently from verbal or textual arguments. Nevertheless, a few rhetorical scholars advocate for the necessity of considering the visual elements of rhetoric. Blair (2004) articulates arguments against the consideration of visual rhetoric as a distinct area, but provides his own arguments for its pursuit. He suggests that images are often used to make impact beyond that which is spoken or written. More specificity is, however, found in the work of Sonja Foss (1994).

Professor Sonja Foss (1994) was one of the first rhetorical scholars to create a concrete schema to evaluate visual imagery. She immediately attacks the need to establish intention in its historical sense, "a work, once done, stands independent of its production, and the intentions of artists or creators are irrelevant to critics' responses…. (p. 215)." She suggests that the first step in the schema is for the critic to assign a function to the visual item by interpreting the physical data that are evident. This is followed by an assessment of how well that function is executed. Finally, reflection is made on its legitimacy, soundness, and the resulting consequences.

First, consider the following image (see Figure 3.2) taken by Associated Press photographer Eddie Adams on January 31, 1968 for which he won a Pulitzer Prize. Foss's first principle is complex when applied to this photo. In the historical context it was a news photo. Traditional rhetorical scholars would carefully document the historical situation involved in the photograph. Foss's approach focuses more on the here and now. The photo still has impact that is important in Foss's view. If this is the first time you have seen this picture, it probably evokes an emotional reaction from you that words

could not do very easily. It may convey an impression about the Vietnam War that you have not experienced. What about things in this photo seem to make you react emotionally? For many it involves the close distance of the shooting. The cold expression of the person pulling the trigger and the facial expression of the person shot probably establish a slightly different mood for each observer, but most people probably feel somewhat somber after viewing it. In a larger image, it is possible to see the bullet exiting the head of the person who was shot. Depending on what you perceive to be the function of this photograph from an analysis of the internal characteristics, you would make a judgment about how well those functions were implemented. In her third step, there are several questions to be answered. Is it legitimate that this photo was ever published? Several issues continue to be debated about war photographs and whether they should be published (see Decker, 2007). From the standpoint of consequences of this photograph, it continued to have consequences for the shooter,

FIGURE 3.2   Adams' Pulizer prize winning photograph of Nguyễn Ngọc Loan executing Nguyễn Văn Lém published on February 1, 1968 (Associated Press).

SOURCE: Eddie Adams/AP Photo.

General Loan, for the rest of his life and for the photographer.

More traditional communication scholars would likely investigate the intent of the photographer and the historical context. The photographer's reaction a few years later reflects on the consequences of taking this picture. Adams said,

> I won a Pulitzer Prize in 1969 for a photograph of one man shooting another ... The general killed the Viet Cong; I killed the general with my camera. Still photographs are the most powerful weapon in the world. People believe them, but photographs do lie, even without manipulation. They are only half-truths. (Picture Power, 2005)

Adams followed General Loan as part of his assignment after this incident. The photographer regretted the personal impact it had on General Loan, who pulled the trigger. He concluded that General Loan should be considered a hero—not a murderer. General Loan came to the United States and established a restaurant that he later closed after his past was revealed. Thus, the consequences of publishing this photo have been well articulated.

Yet it is important to note Foss's point about the intent of the photographer and the Associated Press who distributed it. The average viewer had little information about the central people pictured. The stories of those in the photograph were not well known immediately; so the newsworthy elements of the photo were not well understood at the time. Viewers were left to form their own impressions without the information needed to interpret the picture. It is very hard to assess the impact that this picture had at the time, but many claim that the picture was a turning point in perceptions about U.S. involvement in the war (see Story behind a picture, 2011). The U.S. military were not directly involved in this incident, so the impact that viewers took away from this picture at that time was often not rooted in the facts or motives of the situation. The lasting impressions you take away from this picture will probably be more grounded in the picture itself than the historic background information given. Perhaps the history will shape the impression you take away from this potent image. I find that

both Foss's approach and the more traditional approach bring out different experiences for me. Both are valuable.

Visual communication from a persuader's perspective involves many perceptual tools that visual artists use daily. A comprehensive treatment of these tools is not possible here, but many are covered in Paul Martin Lester's (1995) volume *Visual Communication: Images with Messages*. Lester describes how light, color, and the typefaces used communicate differently. Ethical issues are involved when creative techniques are used to alter images that may have appeared quite differently in the original photograph. In one of the most famous image manipulation controversies, the June 27, 1994 *Time* cover used digital manipulation to picture O.J. Simpson as much darker in his police photo than did the *Newsweek* cover using the same image. Many thought *Time*'s manipulation made him look more sinister or evil. Since that time, it is usually considered to be unethical to alter an image when one is representing it as factual, such as before and after pictures used to demonstrate the effectiveness of a product. Some skirt the edges of ethical standards by using a real, but unflattering picture for the before picture while showing a picture where a person may be more stylishly dressed and more nicely groomed after using a product.

POWER-ORIENTED PERSPECTIVES

Themes challenging the authority and power of the dominant culture run through the final group of perspectives covered in this chapter. These approaches allow us to look at a persuasive situation from the position of groups that are not in power. Such approaches address voices of the oppressed and those advocating for causes that do not have their own voice.

Social Movements

The recent toppling of governments in Tunisia and Egypt through the influence of masses of youthful protestors has brought again to the forefront the study of social movements. A common approach of rhetorical scholars in the Vietnam era (see Andrews, 1980; Bowers & Ochs, 1971), social movements can be seen as influence attempts with the power of the people behind them. This label, however, does not apply to a single rhetorical method or approach. When social movements have involved violence, such as our own American Revolution, such movements have gone beyond persuasion to coercion. The non-violent civil rights marches in the 1960s led by Dr. Martin Luther King, Jr. used powerful rhetoric backed by the power of those supporting him; but there were other radical elements in the same time period advocating the violent overthrow of an unjust government, some of which involved using violence to make points that went beyond persuasion. Thus the term "social movement" is typically a label to designate a critical mass of people coming together to address problematic actions. Various disciplines, such as sociology and political science, take very different approaches from those taken in communication to the study of social movements, but they all typically address abuses of power. These perspectives also offer reasons why some persuasive campaigns have failed with groups that are not in the majority. Current protests for immigration reform in the United States have yet to gain the kind of traction that happened in response to the civil rights protests of the 1960s.

Current scholars of social movements are divided—often breaking down by the age of those doing the research. A substantial group of scholars still falls into those following traditional approaches. The classic work of Bowers and Ochs (1971) has been updated recently (see Bowers, Ochs, Jensen, and Schulz, 2010). Their current approach still suggests that social movements go through progressive phases of petition, promulgation, solidification, polarization, nonviolent resistance, and escalation/confrontation, but not necessarily going through each one or in the same order. The authors suggest the pattern of the activists depends upon the means of resistance used by the other side. The interactive nature of activists and those who resist them is described aptly in the case of the Democratic National Convention in Chicago in 1968. An important change since the original

edition is their argument that we have entered a new era in social movements. They suggest the new era was seen in the 1999 protest in Seattle against the World Trade Organization (WTO). The use of the Internet and more sophisticated patterns of organization are noted as big differences at these protests.

Bowers and associates are very open about questions that still linger about rhetoric and social movements. An unresolved issue is whether there was one movement or several separate movements for the protests at the Democratic National Convention in 1968. It is unclear whether it matters that there were at least three major groups of protestors in Chicago— some clearly committed to nonviolence and some not. Even though the groups had not coordinated their activities, the cumulative impact that was mediated by media may have been more important. The WTO protests are even more difficult to assess because some of the diverse organizations began to cooperate well in advance of the WTO meetings in Seattle. The question of how to identify a social movement continues for the new generation of rhetoricians studying those events.

A different approach has been emerging among a new generation of communication researchers studying social movements. Although some attention is still given to the great speakers and speeches of the day, the current generation of communication researchers is more likely to examine current societal problems and how discourse contributes to them or ignores them entirely. One of the new generations of scholars is Karen Lee Ashcraft (2005), who considered the discourse of commercial airline pilots as revealing their occupational identities setting them apart as the elite members of the organization. Dana L. Cloud (2001) argues that a new capitalism requires scholars to examine a new era of social movements. That is, the United States is no longer characterized by manufacturing in the traditional industrial sense where there was a tall hierarchy of management and clashes between unions and owners. Instead we manufacture in other countries who supply our material needs in a digital world.

Environmental communication is one focus of this new generation of scholars. Phaedra Pezzullo

(2007) builds on Robert Cox's (2010) extensive treatment of environmental communication with her book, *Toxic Tourism*, where she describes tours given of toxic sites around the United States. She particularly focuses on the rhetoric of the leaders of these tours. Economic issues are revealed, with many of these toxic sites existing in lower income regions.

It will be interesting to see how this new generation of communication scholars will study the discourse of the many sites of political unrest around the world. In the case of recent regime changes in Tunisia and Egypt, broadcast media have televised many personal accounts of the economic despair of this younger generation. These young citizens clearly played a large part in the civil unrest that led to the overthrow of their governments. This leads to a discussion of the Marxist critique.

Critical Theory

Many of this new generation of rhetorical scholars focusing on the inequities and injustices in the United States and around the world consider themselves critical theorists. Critical theory focuses on inequitable situations and injustices. These approaches typically have some roots in the work of Karl Marx. Marxist theorists address the issue of economic power as it exists in capitalistic countries such as the United States, Japan, and Germany. They believe that those who control the means of production (the bourgeoisie, or power elite) also control and determine the nature of society.

Such elite circles were as prominent in Plato and Aristotle's time as they are in developed nations today. Even though most scholars recognize that Marxism has failed as an economic system, this new generation of communication scholars recognizes that power imbalances exist in most countries where a large percentage of the resources are controlled by the top one percent of the people. In essence, they believe that capitalism has failed much of society as well. They attack what they call they belief in *neoliberalism* rooted in the work of Adam Smith where global free trade trickles

down for the benefit of all. The bottom line is the elite profit by exploiting workers and dominating them in a variety of ways. This is where the old saying *the rich get richer and the poor get poorer* comes into play.

How does this all relate to our study of persuasion? Much of persuasion discussed in this book has ties to capitalism in terms of buying and selling. Some see persuasive tactics as naturally biased toward maintaining the economic well being of the elite. For example, workers are enticed to produce so they can earn wages, which then permits them to purchase the essentials and become part of the American dream. This produce-earn-purchase cycle creates a never-ending and ever-increasing necessity to work in order to produce and, in turn, earn wages in order to buy products. So, in the eyes of some, the materialism of the American dream actually enslaves us. People sometimes miss really crucial things in life, like the importance of family and friends, while pursuing material wealth. Even though the authors of this book are not critical theorists, we do see societal problems resulting from a very materialistic world. Perhaps 20 percent among us are struggling financially. Most of us living in the United States are part of the consumer culture where we use a disproportionate share of the world's resources.

Other connections should also be fairly obvious. Because political power is needed to maintain economic power, the power elite must find members willing to run for political office and support their campaigns with money, volunteers, and other things necessary for political persuasion. Politicians elected in free elections still must maintain the support of average voters, and thus must remain in touch with their needs. Workers and citizens sometimes can exercise their own persuasive power about their working conditions through nonviolent protest marches (see Figure 3.3). These are turbulent times. The words of Bob Dylan's third album, *The Times They Are a-Changin'* are still as true today as they were then.

Sometimes even the use of excellent persuasive tactics will not be able to reverse the desire for change in a poor economy. The recent events in

Egypt reveal the flaws in an economic system that cannot maintain high levels of employment even for the population as a whole. The situation is even worse when college graduates, who have pursued a path that was supposed to be the route to a better life, cannot find good jobs. This situation is present in many countries around the world. As this

text is being written, young adults with college degrees in many parts of Europe face unemployment rates of 25 percent or more. A poor economy had much to with the large political swing seen in the national political elections in 2010 in the United States. Prospects are not as dire for new college graduates in the United States, and opportunities do exist, but finding a good job remains difficult even as economic recovery is expanding.

Radical Movements

Here we should ask a key question: Is moving from verbal to physical confrontation ever justifiable? Physical confrontation means crossing the line from persuasion to coercion. Currently, the debate continues over the ethics of physical confrontation. It is difficult to bring about change in large corporations when lax government regulations support many environmentally unsound practices. Violence and protests are two of the few avenues of influence available to groups with few economic resources and little political clout to bring about change in problematic actions of large organizations. So groups of radical environmentalists such as Earth First! drive spikes into trees, knowing that loggers may be seriously injured when their chainsaws hit the spikes. Cut brake lines appeared on corporate vehicles of a seafood company that was not conforming to environmentally sound policies. Radicals set fire to the Two Elks Lodge in Vail to protest the actions of a company they believed to be environmentally unsound. Most environmentalists reject such tactics, but the radical fringe does not think change will come in time to save our planet without the use of extreme measures.

The question of whether intimidation, harassment, force, and violence are justifiable has no easy answer. Keep in mind that the American Revolution involved the use of armed revolt. The difficulty of addressing the use of force is reflected in the different philosophies embodied by Dr. Martin Luther King, Jr., and Malcolm X. Dr. King promoted nonviolence as the means for change, but even nonviolent protests were a means of coercion. Cities and businesses were closed for a period of time when protests and boycotts were used. Malcolm X went further. He advocated armed self-defense and revenge against the Klan and other white terrorists. It is easy to understand Malcolm X's point about not taking abuse from white people anymore when we consider that over four thousand black people were lynched in the South in the decades following Reconstruction (see Burns, 1990).

These violent tactics draw attention to serious issues. Although they are forms of influence, they are not persuasion.

REVIEW AND CONCLUSION

Aristotle's *Rhetoric* created the dominant pattern of persuasion that held for centuries, but alternative models in the tradition of Plato view persuasion in a different way. Traditional forms of persuasion have many limitations, including the impression that those using them often do so in manipulative ways. Quintilian introduced a corrective element by insisting that personal character is the center of socially redeeming discourse. Credibility crises in professional sports illustrate the importance of character as an issue in the media. Alternatives to the traditional approaches include processes of discovery in which the best interests of all parties are identified. Burke, who introduced the dramatistic approach, sees persuasion in a larger performance context. Narratives represent an alternative way of seeing the world—the persuasive nature of a good story and true personal experience, such as the last lecture of Randy Pausch, should not be underestimated. Increasing attention to visual rhetoric demonstrates that persuasion is not only through verbal and written means. Power also plays an important role in persuasion. For example, in social movements, persuasion is used by those who have less power in society to address those who have more power. Critical theory represents another way of thinking about the abuse of power in society. Whether or not one agrees with all this perspective advocates, there are things we should all consider in its approach as we live in a very politically unstable world. The message of these latter perspectives is that greater attention must be paid to situations in persuasion studies in which the interests of some groups are ignored by more powerful others. Also, sometimes even those students without many financial resources can do something about creating a better environment. Bob Dylan's lyrics from 1964 summarize our turbulent times, *the times they are a-changin'*.

KEY TERMS

After reading this chapter, you should be able to identify, explain, and give an example of the following key terms or concepts:

segmented audiences	logos	dramatistic	autonomous
forensic discourse	enthymeme	pentad	rational world paradigm
epideictic discourse	syllogism	act	
deliberative discourse	*topoi*	scene	narrative paradigm
ethos	dialectic method	agent	coherence
pathos	truth	purpose	fidelity
metaphor	epistemic	identification	logic of good reasons

APPLICATION OF ETHICS

Assume a major tobacco company is recruiting you to work in its advertising unit. Realizing that public perception of its products is becoming more hostile, the company wants you to create an advertising campaign that you believe violates no ethical boundaries, effectively promotes tobacco products, but improves relations with the public at the same time. Discuss which perspectives in this chapter you could use to create an ethical campaign that meets these criteria. Is such a campaign possible?

QUESTIONS FOR FURTHER THOUGHT

1. What would your reaction be to the Westboro Baptist Church if they were protesting at a funeral of one of your friends?

2. For today's generation in college, which of the three dimensions of credibility makes the most difference to you for evaluating someone as a parent? A professor? A boss?

3. How would you define the character of a good person if you think Quintilian has a point about the character of the speaker?

4. What examples of hate speech as described in Chapter 2 are found in the violations of sanctity of the funerals by members of the Westboro Baptist Church?

5. What are Walter Fisher's big issues with communication approaches in the Aristotelian tradition? How does his approach solve or fail to solve these issues?

6. Is there more to analyzing a narrative than assessing coherence and fidelity in Randy Pausch's last lecture? Might not this lecture be better analyzed by Burke's dramatistic approach than by Fisher's?

7. When examining visual rhetoric such as photographs from various events whether happy or tragic, what do you think about Professor Sonja Foss's schema to analyze visual artifacts? Do you think the creator's intent is important?

8. How have new media such as Facebook and Twitter changed social movements such as those toppling governments in Egypt and Tunisia?

9. Was the burning of Two Elks Lodge at Vail by radical environmentalists justified as a means to convince others of the environmental tragedies that are created by ski resorts? When is violence justified in a protest? Why?

 You can access your online resources at the companion website for *Persuasion*. Log in at **http://www.cengagebrain.com**.

4

Social Scientific Approaches to Persuasion

JOSEPH N. SCUDDER
Northern Illinois University

LEARNING GOALS

After reading this chapter, you should be able to:

1. Describe the major theories and approaches used by social scientists to study contemporary persuasion.

2. Compare and contrast the dominant dual-process models: the elaboration likelihood model and the heuristic-systematic model.

3. Show what the expectancy-value theories, the theory of reasoned action, and the theory of planned behavior do that the dual-process theories do not accomplish.

4. Evaluate whether Zajonc's mere exposure principle poses a fundamental problem to the major cognitive approaches.

5. Explain the connection of the memory and the activation of attitudes to persuasion.

6. Indicate why efficacy may be more important than the actual fear generated through fear-inducing tactics.

7. Illustrate how the use of anchors through tactics such as decoy effects may make political candidates appear more or less favorable.

Social scientific approaches to persuasion emerged only recently compared to the foundations of persuasion discussed in Chapter 3. They study persuasion using modern empirical methods. The term **empirical** refers to the practice of validating knowledge by experience or observation. Most empirical studies of persuasion use statistical methods to analyze experimental results, surveys of persuasive behaviors, or actual behaviors. Changing attitudes and behaviors are typically the focus of empirical studies of persuasion.

This chapter is not intended to be a complete history of empirical studies of persuasion. Rather, the intent is to show how past and recent empirical approaches by persuasion researchers lead us to our current knowledge of how persuasion operates in our contemporary world. First, we turn to models of persuasion that are frequently used in research from a social science perspective today.

MODELS OF CONTEMPORARY PERSUASION

Persuasive models propose how variables and processes are connected. Some models are overarching frameworks that are more explanatory. That is, they are intended to explain how persuasion works in the big scheme of things. They are validated in different ways than more specific perspectives that are tested for their ability to predict specific outcomes.

DUAL-PROCESS MODELS

According to social psychologists Shelley Chaiken and Yaacov Trope (1999), **dual-process models** propose two qualitatively different modes of information processing that operate in making judgments and decisions. The first is a "fast, associative, information processing mode based on low-effort heuristics," and the second is a "slow, rule-based information processing mode based on high-effort systematic reasoning" (p. ix). The second route is similar to traditional understandings of persuasion we considered in Chapter 3. Dual-process models, however, challenge the dominant rational world paradigm we met in Chapter 3, which assumed that people primarily reasoned their way to persuasion through careful consideration of arguments and evidence. A big reason for moving to dual-process models is that we have known for some time that humans are limited information processors. That means people can only handle so much information at one time (see March & Simon, 1958). Moreover, dual-process models moved persuasion to a more dynamic process orientation. We consider the two dual-process models that command the most attention: (1) the elaboration likelihood model and (2) the heuristic-systematic model.

The Elaboration Likelihood Model (ELM)

We saw in Chapter 1 that social psychologists Richard Petty and John Cacioppo (1986) articulated a dual-process theory they called the **elaboration likelihood model (ELM)**. The ELM revitalized researchers' interest in persuasion. Elaboration in the ELM refers to the conscious scrutiny we use in making an evaluative judgment and requires both the motivation and the ability to process information. They place elaboration on a continuum whose ends are two different routes of information processing. The **central route** forms the high end of the continuum. It is information processing that occurs "as a result of a person's careful and thoughtful considerations of the true merits of the information present" (p. 3). It is a slower, deliberative, high-effort mode of information processing that uses systematic reasoning. When persons use the central route, it is clear that they are consciously engaged in thinking. Petty and Wegener (1999) maintain not only that the greater amount of thinking is done at the high end, but also that elaboration at the high end uses a kind of thinking that adds something beyond the original information. People

are making the best-reasoned judgments they can make based on their scrutiny of the information available.

Even though you possess exceptional ability to process information, that ability goes to waste if you are not motivated to process the information. This motivation may, however, happen in different ways for different people. Demonstrating relevance and importance are two key factors of motivation to centrally process a persuasive message. In other words, a persuader must be able to answer the question, *why should my target audience pay attention to this message?* Beyond importance and relevance, Petty and Cacioppo proposed that another component of cognitive motivation to process information is a general trait that some persons enjoy thinking and others do not. They called this trait the **need for cognition (NFC)**. It ranges from one extreme where persons enjoy thinking to the other where others wish to avoid cognitive effort. So some people naturally like to think and analyze across situations, whereas others prefer not to expend any more energy thinking than is necessary. NFC often is tested as an independent variable that predicts other persuasive outcome variables that are often called dependent variables.

At the low end of the elaboration continuum, people use the **peripheral route** of information processing, requiring much less cognitive effort and sometimes surveying less information than in the central route. The peripheral route may also rely on simple classical conditioning, or the use of mental shortcuts or rules of thumb. It often occurs as the result of some simple cue in the persuasion context, such as an attractive or handsome source like Angelina Jolie or Brad Pitt promoting their movie.

Persuasive messages bombard us constantly through the peripheral route, such as the brand names displayed on shoes or clothing, or the sponsorship acknowledgments at events we attend. The constant reinforcement of these brands often happens without our conscious awareness; we take the information in like a sponge soaking up water. For example, find the repeated cue in the picture I took of a street café in Buenos Aires (see Figure 4.1).

Such cues are typically processed by the peripheral route, except in situations like in this book where your attention is directed to them. I call this the "sneaky route" to persuasion because brands and other messages often are stored in our memory outside our conscious awareness. In a persuasion class a few years ago I asked if anyone had seen the first political commercial for an election more than two years away. One student said she had seen it, but had not paid attention to it. I asked her what she remembered. She recalled every important aspect of the commercial's message—even though she had not been carefully thinking about it. It is often harder to actively resist this type of persuasion because the tactics are not always obvious—especially to children.

So peripheral cues that promote brand preferences and our habits often lead us to process information peripherally. For instance, when asked at a fast-food restaurant what you want to drink, you may respond automatically, "Diet Coke." Most consumers do not evaluate all the choices carefully or even ask what they are. Strong brand preferences reduce the central processing necessary.

The ELM, however, does not provide much help in determining which people will rely heavily on brands and which make purchase decisions based on price (see Box 4.1). A sale price of $3.99 for a case of Diet Pepsi may lead a person with a preference for Diet Coke to change brands that week. Others may select generic diet colas because they use a different decision rule like "get the most volume for the least money." Sometimes other factors such as a strict budget, organizational regulations, or our insurance plans may influence the brands we buy.

Peripheral processing covers a large range of behaviors. For example, the speech rate of individuals influences the way we perceive them, with some evidence suggesting that we prefer rates as fast as or faster than our own. The use of physically and socially attractive persons in advertising also reflects an appeal to peripheral processes. Sometimes, appeals to peripheral processes are more useful in drawing our attention to the message than in altering our perception of its content.

Petty and Cacioppo's ELM rests on the assumption that people are motivated to process information because they want to hold correct attitudes, or at least those perceived as being correct in light of social comparisons and norms. Petty and Cacioppo also believe that various factors can affect the direction and number of individuals' attitudes

BOX 4.1   **Brand Influences**

What influences your choice of brands or labels? Think about purchases you made or influenced in the past month. Did you choose brand names or generic products? Do you have a brand preference for any of the following items: toothpaste, shampoo, pizza, car, gas, computer, soda, athletic shoes, clothing shops, hamburger, French fries, or ketchup? If you do have preferences, where did they originate for you?

and enhance or reduce argument strength. For instance, if an attractive or highly credible source opposes flag burning, that factor could increase or decrease the weight you might give to the Supreme Court's decision that flag burning is legal. The ELM also suggests that as people increase scrutiny through the central processing route, peripheral cues have less impact, and vice versa. This controversial proposition represents a marked difference from our other dual-process model, the heuristic-systematic model.

The Heuristic-Systematic Model (HSM)

Similarities are apparent between the ELM and the **heuristic–systematic model,** or **HSM** (Chaiken, Giner-Sorolla, & Chen, 1996). The HSM proposes a **systematic processing route** that represents a comprehensive treatment of judgment-related information. It is a slow, high-effort reasoning process bearing strong resemblance to the central processing route in the ELM. The other route, the **heuristic processing route**, is a fast, low-effort process that relies on the activation of judgmental rules or heuristics. Heuristics are mental rules of thumb that are not the most accurate procedure, but often very useful to deal with common situations; they are adaptive strategies that help us reduce the time it takes to make decisions. For example, to calculate the distance around a circle we often multiply the diameter of the circle by 3 to get a rough estimate instead of a more precise value for π of 3.14159. The HSM proposes the sufficiency principle whereby people attempt to strike a balance between minimizing cognitive effort and satisfying their goals.

Sometimes heuristics are used because we have too many options or too much information is presented to us. As previously mentioned, humans are limited information processors and can only handle so much information in their memory at one time. Psychologist George Miller (1956) first proposed that a person could only hold from five to nine chunks of information in his or her memory at one time depending on the person and the type of task. Memory limits are probably much lower for many types of persuasion. It is important for persuaders to keep this in mind when designing their messages. Persuaders have sometimes intentionally presented massive amounts of information to make it almost impossible for consumers to process all of that information systematically, thus forcing them to resort to heuristics. Ethical questions exist when consumers are presented with large quantities of information.

We do, however, use heuristics daily. Instead of trying to remember the exact rules of right-of-way when two people come to a stop sign at the same time, many people simply wave the other person through the stop sign to avoid having to think too much. Some heuristics can be very misleading, like the saying that moss only grows on the north side of a tree—this simply is not true. A much better heuristic if you are lost in a forest is the fact that the sun rises in the east and sets in the west, but even this is not much help when you are lost and it is cloudy or dark.

In the HSM, systematic processing and heuristic processing operate independently and may occur simultaneously. This is probably the largest difference between the ELM and the HSM. In the ELM, there is an inverse relationship between the use of the central and the peripheral routes—as one rises, the other falls. In the HSM, we assume that people could make systematic use of some evidence at the same time they are using heuristics for other information. For example, you could make the judgment using systematic processes that a member of your work group made a good argument for doing a project a certain way, while at the same time you were making a judgment using heuristic processes about the attractiveness of that group member.

Choosing whether the ELM or HSM is a better model to explain the persuasion process can be difficult and probably varies with the situation.

Whichever dual-process model one might prefer, the decision process can become so complex that identifying when each process is in operation can be difficult. In complex decisions a person might use central decision processes for some components such a price comparison, peripheral processes for how the item looks and feels, and heuristic processes for asking others about their preferences. Examine Box 4.2—what parts of this process are better handled by the ELM, and which parts are more closely related to elements of the HSM?

The impact of receiving too much persuasive information has not received much empirical study. It is clear, however, that people respond differently to large amounts of information. Some prefer a restaurant menu with only three choices to one that has ten pages of options. According to the ELM, the motivation of an individual to process the information is a key factor. Overloading central or systematic information processes should result in a shift to peripheral or heuristic processing. Traditional advice for creating persuasive presentations recommends the use of supporting visuals to assist understanding. After all, isn't redundancy better? We simply cannot make the blanket assertion that the use of visual aids with persuasive messages is always a recommended practice. Images in multimedia presentations may require so much attention to process that they detract from the message content rather than enhance it (see Box 4.3). That is, graphics may interfere with the interaction between the person speaking and the person listening. Some backlash is occurring against the use of PowerPoint© because viewers may pay so much attention to writing and recording the information

---

BOX 4.2   Complexity of Buying a New Cell Phone

Choosing a new cell phone is a complex set of persuasive processes for some buyers, but a very quick process for others. Some buyers begin by reading recommendations on the Internet to gather information. Many start by visiting stores where one is typically given a brochure and a pitch by a salesperson; and, for some, they buy with about an hour of considering the options. Others start by asking friends how they made the decision to buy their phone.

For those making a very careful decision evaluating all the evidence, a person must not only consider features that are necessary on the phone, but the quality of service available through the cell phone service as well as the prices for various features like texting, local minutes, long-distance minutes, a data plan, and roaming charges. One also has to consider length of plan commitment and whether buying insurance on the phone makes sense. This is even more complex when buying a plan for a large family where monthly cell phone bills for the new smart phones may run over $300 per month. An optimal thinking process will

include considering how the cell phone will be used, scrutiny of the options, price comparisons, and an evaluation of the service provided to customers of each plan. Some of this information will be centrally processed, but the way the phone looks, feels, and sounds often makes impressions beyond central or systematic processing.

Many people, however, simply do not have the ability or the motivation to evaluate all of these factors. Some decisions might not be considered important enough to carefully process all of the information available or the issue might be the limited time available. Under such conditions, consumers may take the recommendation of *Consumer Reports* or that of a friend or relative who uses one of these products or services. Relying on the recommendation of others we trust or an expert requires only a small amount of central or systematic processing. Moreover, the actual experience of others we trust may be a better guide than representatives of the company as to whether reception and coverage work well in the location where they will be used.

| BOX 4.3 | **Graphics May Detract from the Message** |

Conventional wisdom suggests that a picture is worth a thousand words, but psychologists Kurt Frey and Alice Eagly (1993) provide evidence that even vivid elements in the persuasive messages may reduce the message's effectiveness when they result in low scrutiny of the message. We know from other research on split attention effects that misplaced graphics may direct attention away from the main point of the message. In your experience, when do graphics aid understanding and when do they distract audiences from the point of the message? Are there times you don't know what the speaker is saying because you are looking at the graphic?

on the slides that they do not, or cannot, process what the information means at the same time. Again, humans are limited information processors and can only handle so much at one time. The attention given to PowerPoint© may prevent many listeners from hearing all that a persuader is saying. It may be that information overload is the reason behind the tendency some researchers have found for visual cues to override what is said. Clearly, more research is needed regarding the processing of visual forms of persuasive messages and whether they enhance or detract from the oral or written persuasion that accompanies them. Simpler may be better.

THE UNIMODEL

Not all persuasion researchers have been fans of dual-process models. Kruglanski and Thompson (1999) argue that two routes are not necessary. They suggest in their unimodel of persuasion that the two routes are just two different ends of a continuum, running from more complex evidence requiring more elaboration to very simple evidence requiring little thought to process it. Although critics (see Lavine 1999; Manstead, A.S.R., and van der Pligt, 1999) do find some merits to the issues raised in the arguments for a unimodel, it is not as radically different from the dual-process models as it first appears. Petty, as one of the originators of the ELM, agrees with many of the points raised by Kruglanski, but does not think those issues lead to requiring a single dimension (see Petty,

Wheeler, and Bizer, 1999). Whether or not one believes there is a better case for a dual-process model or for the unimodel, they agree that different types of processing are happening for persuasion involving complex information versus simple cues. Most of these researchers agree that complex information requires greater thinking than simple cues.

THE AUTOMATIC ACTIVATION OF ATTITUDES AND IMPLICIT MEMORY

Others take a radically different approach to attitude formation and change in the persuasive process. For the purposes of this chapter, attitudes are the positive, neutral, or negative evaluations a person holds of objects, activities, people, or institutions. Attitude change is one of the simplest types of persuasion. Shifting an attitude from neutral to positive or negative may not lead to immediate behavioral change, but it may begin a broader change in the network of information stored in one's brain.

Most models of persuasion do not attempt to integrate prior memory into the persuasive process. Although pre-tests are often given in experiments to control for past perceptions stored in the brain, most models of persuasion such as dual-process models do not attempt to connect the present to the past. Psychologist Russell Fazio (1989) is different. He believes attitudes can be triggered automatically, without deliberation. This perspective has important applications in persuasive messages intended to overcome resistance to change. For example, it allows us to understand why it is difficult to change our attitudes about our addictions, health practices, and use of stereotypes.

The automatic activation perspective treats the mind as a place where a massive amount of information is stored. As in a library, some of this information is easy to access. Most pieces are connected by pathways to other pieces of information, and accessing one piece may activate others connected to it. Connections vary in strength, and those we make regularly will typically be more accessible in our memories than those we access rarely, just as places we travel frequently become easier to find. Fazio and an associate (see Roskos-Ewoldsen & Fazio, 1992) found that highly accessible items in memory were more likely to be recognized in a visual display and sometimes interfered with a visual search for other items.

All memory, however, is not accessible. Fazio (see Olson & Fazio, 2001) and his colleagues have investigated implicit attitude formation where some individuals have learned rules or associations during another task, but they are unable to verbally express conscious knowledge of it. Implicit memories are those that affect people's behaviors without deliberate intentions to behave in that way. Although measuring implicit attitudes has sometimes been problematic (see Capner, Scarcia, and Graham, 2007), it continues to be one of the more investigated areas in attitude change and behavior. Thomson, Milliken, and Smilek (2010) have recently confirmed the impact of implicit memory with an actual behavior measure. Students were involved in a task involving the generation of the names of states. Students were more likely to generate the names of little-known states that were presented in a class 8–10 weeks prior than those in classes where the names of those states were not mentioned.

So why should persuaders be so concerned about implicit memory? First, it has big implications for public health programs attempting to change problematic behaviors creating large public health problems like smoking and obesity. Changing eating and smoking habits likely requires changing many connections in our implicit memories and in our associated memory networks that lie outside conscious awareness. Establishing new behaviors means creating new pathways in our minds for accessing positive attitudes and behaviors that we learn to prefer to the old ones. This does not happen overnight. Understanding this process is very important in resisting persuasive attempts that automatically trigger certain processes for us. Think about the checkout aisles of supermarkets and the items placed there. Many of us have chosen items in the store while waiting in checkout aisles. Although candy and drinks trigger appetites across most age groups, many children know parents are particularly vulnerable to a request for a candy treat that is stimulated by an item in the checkout area. Fortunately, some markets have established candy-free checkout lanes so parents can avoid them.

A new reason to be concerned about associated memory networks and implicit memory is the increasing amount of time spent on the Internet searching with Google, visiting social media like Facebook, or watching new media sites like YouTube. Little empirical research has investigated the impact of new media on our associated memory networks or our implicit memory. Prominent product placements in movies and television programs have implanted several products and brands in our memories (see Box 4.4). Similarly, we should expect that new media are likely to be infiltrating our conscious and unconscious memories with many brands—particularly at sites like YouTube. Groupon.com or your local web coupon site is probably in your conscious awareness already despite its recent entry to the advertising world.

MERE EXPOSURE

Robert Zajonc's (1968) **mere exposure** research is so simple that we might debate whether it is a model, just as the debate continues whether Pluto should be reinstated as a planet. The principle behind it is a straightforward idea: Repeated exposure to a stimulus results in more favorable evaluation of that stimulus. In other words, the more we

BOX 4.4   Product Placements Skirt New Technology

Much pressure was placed on the consumer electronics industry to not introduce in the United States the technology to record programming on television while eliminating commercials—even though it was available elsewhere. Consumers can now avoid most of the commercials on television by recording the programs and watching them later. This commercial-zapping feature reduces the persuasive impact of commercials on television. The impact of commercials had already been reduced by the remote control that allowed viewers to flip channels during commercial breaks.

Product placement in televised programming and in movies cannot be removed by technology; thus, product placement is increasingly attractive to advertisers. Apple computers appeared in 30 percent of the top-grossing movies of 2010 and Glock handguns continued their long-running tradition of being the weapon of choice in movies and on television (see Sauer, 2011). Within Fazio's system, more frequent appearances of such product placements should keep those products activated in the associated memory network.

are exposed to something, the more we are likely to be favorable toward it. In a classic study, Zajonc asked participants to pronounce a series of Turkish nonsense words. In varying the frequency of times of pronouncing each word, he found that more frequently pronounced words received more favorable evaluation. He reported the same pattern for different photographs of men and for Chinese-like characters. Favorability increased substantially up to about ten exposures and continued to increase at slower rates until reaching 25 repetitions. Other studies of mere exposure suggest a point of diminishing returns whereby more repetitions yield no benefit and sometimes become counterproductive, with people getting bored with overexposure.

Robert Bornstein's (1989) meta-analysis of over 200 studies indicated that the mere exposure phenomenon appeared reliably across many different types of stimuli and objects. Moreover, Bornstein found that the mere exposure effect tended to be larger when stimuli occurred in a subliminal manner—too quickly to be consciously recognized. The very interesting finding in this analysis is that rapid exposure below the level of consciousness had greater impact than some stimuli that were consciously recognized. Given that there is much skepticism over subliminal advertising and its effectiveness, this line of research demonstrates that at least subliminal effects can be effective. Recent studies of priming behavior confirm that attitudes change in response to visual materials presented below the level of conscious awareness.

There is little doubt that mere exposure makes information very accessible simply through repetition, but there is much disagreement as to *why* it occurs. Certainly there are similarities to the implicit attitude change research that we previously discussed. Zajonc frequently used the mere exposure findings to argue against the primacy of cognition; that is, to argue against the idea that everything—especially emotion—has to begin with explicit cognitive thought processes. He instead argued that affect needed no prior cognitive preferences for activation. Although Zajonc's contentions about the primacy of affect were not widely embraced when cognitive psychology was dominant, perspectives are emerging that incorporate arguments from both sides. Psychologist Icek Ajzen (2001) suggests that a multicomponent view of attitudes is becoming more popular among attitude researchers; that is, more researchers see the importance of considering the roles both affect and cognitions play in changing attitudes. Affect may be a more important influence on the development of some attitudes, and cognition in the formation of others. Some evidence suggests that we rely more on our feelings when our feelings and our beliefs do not agree (see Lavine et al., 1998). The evidence clearly supports the mere exposure principle, but there are obvious exceptions where repeated exposure may have the opposite effect, such as at my home, where the same satellite company keeps calling even though we are on the national "do not call" registry.

BOX 4.5   Glock Handgun Promotions on YouTube.com

You may be aware that YouTube.com has become a place where many products are featured in detail. Few are more detailed than Glock handguns. Over 10,000 videos of Glock handguns are posted on YouTube. One video called *2x Full Auto Glocks* has been view almost 11 million times over the past three years. This video probably appeals to those who are excited by the rapid fire of guns rather than those concerned about a weapon for home defense. Another very emotional presentation can be found on YouTube at *"Ted Nugent—Kiss My Glock"* where rock star Teg Nugent bashes "anti-gun liberals." *Glock Top Models* is a more objective presentation about the best choice of the many variations of models, but it has only been viewed about 300,000 times in the past year since it was posted. This video is long at 41 minutes, but very informative if one is in the market for a handgun.

Interestingly, YouTube posts advertisements at the bottom of the videos that sometimes are links to other advertisers or those opposing such messages. As this is being written, an advertisement appears on *Glock Top Models* called the *9mm Will Not Save You*. Other balanced or counter discussions may also be found on YouTube as well, but the pro-Glock videos will be the overwhelming exposure one receives when typing "Glock" into the YouTube.com search box.

Today's mass media regularly use mere exposure. Its application to politics is especially worth noting. Psychologists Joseph Grush, Kevin McKeough, and Robert Ahlenng (1978) examined political campaigns for political newcomers and low-visibility offices. They found a significant connection between increasing the exposure of unfamiliar candidates through greater campaign spending, and winning the election. Although it is frustrating to those who want voters to base their decisions on the issues, the use of short commercials with sound bites makes sense for candidates unfamiliar to the masses.

Before beginning the next section, no author of this text is advocating the possession of handguns or the banning of their possession. Possession of handguns is a complex issue even when the weapons are possessed legally. The point of this section is to demonstrate that exposure to products may come from sources beyond advertisers. These sources may aid in the persuasion of consumers to purchase or not purchase various products.

Mentions of products in news media provide exposure that may drive sales. For example, Glock handguns, referred to in Box 4.4 as product placements, have been mentioned frequently in the news media as the weapon of criminals or as the weapon used by law enforcement. In the case of the shooting of Congresswoman Gabrielle Giffords in 2011, the sales of Glock handguns "skyrocketed" as they did after the shootings at Virginia Tech (Hartenstein, 2011). Congresswoman Giffords acknowledged on the campaign trail that she owns a Glock and is a rather good shot.

Exposure is extensive on other non-advertiser sites on blogs and websites, but one of the most frequented sites is YouTube.com (see Box 4.5). From a mere exposure standpoint, it is unclear how length of a video enters into the change of attitudes. Some YouTube videos are one or two minutes while others are 30 minutes or longer. Some are outrageous and others are predominately informative. The mere exposure perspective does not give much guidance about the ways that length and quality of arguments are important to this approach.

EXPECTANCY-VALUES MODELS

Theory of Reasoned Action (TRA)

Martin Fishbein died in 2009. It was a great loss for persuasion research. He had been a professor of psychology and communication as well as working previously at the Centers for Disease Control. The legacy of his work on persuasion continues to have impact worldwide. His work has impacted public health practices around the world—perhaps more than any other persuasion researcher. It is hard to measure his impact on public health initiatives—especially the impact on the reduction of HIV transmission. The many tributes to his impact give some measure of the man (see Yzer, 2010).

Fishbein (see Fishbein & Ajzen, 1975, 2010) along with his former student Icek Ajzen developed the theory of reasoned action (TRA) to solve the especially difficult problem of finding significant **attitude-behavior relationships**. That is, researchers have frequently found low or no relationship between attitudes and behavioral change resulting from persuasive messages. For example, many smokers report that smoking is bad for their health and that it may eventually kill them, but if you ask them whether they intend to stop, they may say no or maybe in the future. So our attitudes may be negative toward the dangers that behaviors pose, but our attitudes toward the solutions to avert the dangers are negative, neutral, or so weakly positive that we do not start a program to change our behavior. Martin Fishbein and Icek Ajzen (1981) suggest that attitudes have been defined so generally that it is no surprise there are mixed results for finding the attitude-behavior relationship. Instead, they propose that our **behavioral intentions** toward *changing* our behavior are the most important predictor of actually changing behavior, not our attitudes toward the behavior itself (see Figure 4.2).

They criticize past attitude research for not measuring specifically enough and for measuring the wrong predictors. Behavioral intentions are clearly the central feature that distinguishes this approach from all other attitude research. Many other parts of the TRA appear also in other perspectives.

As the model in Figure 4.2 indicates, the behavioral intention is a product of two assessments: (1) a person's attitude toward a behavior and its importance to him or her; and (2) the normative influence on an individual and its importance to the individual. First, we consider the individual's attitude toward the behavior. Notice that the top line of the model in Figure 4.2 deals with the individual's processing of the issue. The attitude is the judgment of whether an individual considers the behavior to be positive or negative—what researchers call valence. The valence is multiplied by the probability of success of the advocated action and also by the importance of the behavior.

The expectancy component of the model arises from the individual's assessment that engaging in the advocated behavior will be effective or successful. There are many reasons why something might be judged as having a low likelihood of success. One may be that the statistical odds are against success. For instance, most individuals with a job would not consider a persuasive message from an

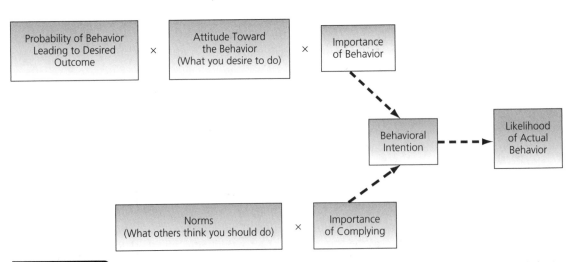

FIGURE 4.2   The Fishbein and Ajzen theory of reasoned action (TRA) for the prediction of intentions and behavior.

email advocating buying lottery tickets as part of their retirement plan because there is not a high likelihood that playing the lottery will result is a profit rather than a loss. Another reason some persuasive messages may be rejected is the poor track record of product claims in that category such as health supplements. For example, claims that the goji berry will produce the promised health benefit are rejected by many because claims for many health-related products have not been substantiated. Yet another reason that individuals will reject a solution is because they do not believe they are capable of following the plan or the regimen. Various aspects of efficacy will be discussed later.

The value aspect of the expectancy-value label comes, in part, from the importance of the advocated behavior or outcome to the individual. Typically, the principle applies that behaviors that are more important will lead to higher behavioral intentions and actual behavior, but this is not always the case. Buying bananas today will often precede a more important, but expensive purchase like a new car. Herein lies a limitation of the model, it does not work for prioritizing which valued behaviors should take place first. It is, however, useful for addressing everyday decisions as they happen.

Moving to the bottom line of the model in Figure 4.2, **normative influence** is a person's belief that important individuals or groups think it is advisable to perform or not perform certain behaviors. This type of influence comes from important persons in one's life. It may be one's family, significant other, friends, co-workers, bosses, employees, or peers. It is whoever's opinion is important to you. Normative pressure may simply be the desire to please one individual. For instance, a person in my family started flossing her teeth regularly because she did not want her dental hygienist again to tell her she was not doing a good job of flossing. Weight Watchers also uses normative pressures in its weight loss programs. Participants do not want the scale to go up instead of down at their weekly weigh-in.

The other component on the bottom line of the model is the importance of complying with the norms or the wishes of others. People vary greatly in the degree to which they consider the opinions of others. Some care whether others will think an item of clothing will look good to others while others only care whether they like it. When it comes to choosing a marriage partner, some would choose not to marry a person of another religious faith because it would upset the family, but others view it as the sole decision of the two persons joining together. If two people do join together with the blessings of their families, struggles of still remain when the desired format of the wedding for the persons being married differs from the expectations of the families of those being married.

In many cases, some combination of influences from the top and bottom lines in Figure 4.2 makes the difference. Compromises over wedding plans do happen. In other contexts such as in health care issues, many people are motivated to stop smoking or to lose weight for their own health, but also because they want to live long enough to to support their children and to see their grandchildren. The model reminds us that persuasive decisions often are embedded in a social network.

The big point to remember is that behavioral intent is the best predictor of actual behavior. There are big implications for this feature of the model. For those doing opinion research with intent to predict outcomes, it is imperative that a researcher asks what behavior a person intends to do such as for which candidate the persons intends to vote rather than how one would rate the candidate on a 7-point scale ranging from negative to positive.

Although TRA has had tremendous impact, limitations of the model have become evident when trying to apply it to some context. As a result, Icek Ajzen introduced a variation on the model.

Theory of Planned Behavior (TPB)

Ajzen proposed modifications to TRA in his **theory of planned behavior (TPB)** (see Ajzen, 1991, 2001). Ajzen (2010) maintains that theory of reasoned action is one type of TPB. In TPB, he added a third factor, **perceived behavioral control**. The original TRA worked well in conditions where individuals perceived a strong personal sense of control over their behaviors, but it became apparent after several studies that in many situations people felt little control. This addition of perceived control better articulated whether people really expected that a particular outcome would happen if they tried. So you may resist your doctor's recommendation to lose weight if you have tried many diets, but never have been able to control your love of regular soda, your tendency toward binge eating, your nervous eating when you are not hungry, and your disdain for vegetables. TPB has proven to be superior to TRA in situations where athletes are provided a new training regimen. Ailsa Anderson and David Lavallee (2008) found that perception of behavioral control significantly improved the prediction of adherence to a new physical conditioning program; and thus, TPB was superior to TRA in predicting the degree to which athletes would adhere to the new conditioning program.

Overall, TRA and TRB have been strong predictors of changes in behavior (see Armitage & Christian, 2003; Ajzen, 2001). They have had broad application in health care and have had good success in predicting condom use, safe-sex behaviors, use of illegal substances, adherence to taking prescribed medications, the wearing of safety helmets, use of dental floss, and physical activity. No other theoretical perspective on persuasion and attitude change compares to the successful predictions of behavior of these two expectancy-value approaches. However, it has been difficult to predict when TPB actually was an improvement over TRA. Psychologist Alicia Munoz-Silva and associates (2007) present very complex findings in a comparison of TRA and TPB in predicting condom use among students from Portugal and Spain. TPB was superior to TRA in the prediction of behavioral intent to use condoms, but not their use. Moreover, the attitudes toward condoms were more predictive of women's intent to use condoms, but normative influence and perceived behavioral control were more predictive to use condoms for men.

Of all the persuasive approaches to behavioral change, the TRA and TPB appear to have the clear edge in predicting behavior, but they are far from perfect. Some of the components of the models may not be truly independent. For example, a person may devalue the importance of an activity because it is perceived a high level of performance is never personally attainable. Some of us may have been very good at playing a sport or a musical instrument in high school, but we did not continue in college because we did not believe we had the ability to compete at the higher level. Measurement challenges remain for these models. Better procedures are needed for incorporating relevant personal beliefs and measuring relevant normative influences.

NORMS-BASED MODELS

Norms-based approaches to behavioral change have similarities to the expectancy-values models, but they only focus on the normative force in the persuasive argument. Past research results have been mixed in regard to the success of norms-based campaigns (see Greene, Campo, and Banerjee, 2010). Many persuasive campaigns use norms to demonstrate that individuals selecting the recommended behavior are in the majority. One such campaign to fight alcohol abuse is used at our university to show that the majority of students do not participate in binge drinking. Another normative approach being used at our university shows that females do succeed at calculus and actually receive higher grades than their male peers. Measuring the success or failures of these approaches is very difficult because other interventions were happening at the same time. When we cannot rule out that the other factors may have influenced the outcomes, researchers say the results are confounded. That it, we cannot disentangle the true impact of a persuasive intervention.

Questions arise about the success of norms-based programs because their impact is often modest at best. As is often the case when the effectiveness of persuasive campaigns is assessed, success is in the eye of the beholder. Programs such as DARE and abstinence-based campaigns to reduce early sexual activity have advocates who look at the results and see success while critics look at the same numbers and see program failures. Some critics suggest that sensation-seeking individuals may find attempts to create fear or negative stereotypes about performing a problematic behavior to be motivation to try it (for a review see Kang, Cappella, and Fishbein, 2009).

SINGLE VARIABLE APPROACHES TO PERSUASION

Now that we have explored some of the prominent models in contemporary persuasion research involving multiple variables, we turn to single variables of interest to many researchers. Although some of them have been discussed in the prior models, these variables merit additional attention.

Many of these variables first gained attention in the early years of empirical persuasion research. Carl Hovland established a program of research investigating the relationship of communication to attitudes now known as the Yale Communication and Attitude Change Program.

The Yale group assumed that people would change their attitudes if provided with sufficient reinforcement in support of the change. In other words, people need motivation to process information that will change their existing attitudes and the actions that flow from them.

Source Effects

The Yale studies particularly focused on the source's credibility or believability and the source's attractiveness to the receiver. In terms of today's dual-processing framework, source credibility usually influences attitude change through the peripheral or heuristic route, but central processing of a person's credibility could occur when a controversy erupts. For example, many people have centrally processed the credibility of controversial professor Ward Churchill (see Box 4.6).

Research in the 1960s proposed several dimensions of credibility, but expertise, trustworthiness, and attractiveness continue to be the most widely investigated. The Yale researchers conducted credibility studies in which the same message was attributed to persuaders having various kinds of reputations. A message about smoking and lung cancer, for example, was attributed either to a college sophomore or to a doctor from the surgeon general's office. Not surprisingly, greater attitude change occurred when the audience believed the message was coming from the doctor as opposed to the student. A critical point found in these studies is that the effect of speaker credibility may decline over time if the content of the message becomes separated from the source in the hearers' memory. This is a particular problem with messages we hear only once.

Hovland and his colleagues called the decaying link between message and speaker's credibility the **sleeper effect**. It can work to a speaker's disadvantage

---

BOX 4.6   **Credibility May Be Centrally Processed: The Case of Ward Churchill**

Ward Churchill's remarks about the United States deserving the 9/11 attacks generated a lot of controversy. Many called for his firing from the University of Colorado. Is the fact that Professor Churchill is a Cherokee and was chairman of the department of ethnic studies at University of Colorado more likely to be a central or peripheral processing issue? His ethnic heritage as a member of one of the most abused Native American peoples certainly provides a different perspective that draws attention as does his position at a prestigious university. This is certainly a case where credibility of the speaker is not simply a peripheral cue for those who read his entire remarks. A search of the web will reveal many materials for and against the decision of the university to not fire him.

when his or her credibility is initially high, because it means that high credibility can be lost over time. However, the sleeper effect may work to the speaker's advantage when initial credibility is medium or low but very strong arguments are offered, because people may remember the strong arguments and forget about the credibility factor. Although subsequent research on the sleeper effect has yielded mixed outcomes at times, it generally provides support for the idea. The meta-analysis of the sleeper effect by Kumkale and Albarracin (2004) found that persuasion did increase over time for persons initially exposed to a less-credible source when the quality of the message arguments were initially judged as strong. Thus, years of research tend to support the original formulation of the sleeper effect by the Yale researchers (see also Allen & Stiff, 1998). Consistent with the more contemporary ELM, persuasion was stronger when recipients of the persuasive messages had the ability and motivation to scrutinize the message. This issue of the motivation of the listeners is one of many places where the ELM refines our understanding of past research without questioning the foundations of the original concept. Many questions remain about how it works. For instance, research is not conclusive as to whether information is even stored in memory when the credibility of the speaker is very low or the relevance of the information is low.

A review of five decades of credibility research (see Pornpitakpan, 2004) supports the conclusion from the Yale studies that high-credibility sources are generally more persuasive than low-credibility sources. High-credibility sources often enhance the impact of high-quality evidence. Yet, the review notes a reduction or reversal of the impact of high-credibility in

some conditions. For example, high-credibility sources appear to be less effective where motivation to process the message carefully is low. Notice that the motivation of the receiver again becomes a qualifying factor of the general finding. Another consideration is the position currently held by the target audience. High-credibility sources may be more important to use in situations where the message is advocating substantial changes from positions currently held than when attempting to get only minor changes from current positions. High-credibility sources have also been found to be more persuasive when using threats or presenting negative opinions.

A trustworthy source for one group may not carry the same weight with another group. In some contexts expertise is a better route to establish credibility, but it must appear certain and have little ambiguity. One of my family members who was experiencing back pain received conflicting recommendations from two surgeons with extensive expertise in back surgery. In this case, there was great ambiguity, it was not clear which expert had the best recommendation, and the advice from both surgeons was discounted. The two conflicting experts negated the influence of each other. The person turned to people she trusted for advice.

Another important factor in determining the credibility of a source is the degree to which the source is similar to us. Using similarity in persuasive appeals is usually attempting to appeal to peripheral processes rather than making it an explicit focus. Many organizations use visual appeals to provide evidence that other people like them are part of their organization (see Box 4.7).

BOX 4.7 **Nonproportional Representation of Ethnicity in University Publicity**

Universities are engaging in fierce competition for the best high school students. One of the ethical questions arising in these recruiting efforts is the representation of students of various ethnicities on brochures and websites, in proportions that differ from the actual proportion of students on campus. Universities know that students are more likely to feel more at home when there is a critical mass of others with similar backgrounds. So, is it ethical for a university comprised of 90 percent Caucasians to display pictures in their recruitment brochures and on the web where a spectrum of persons from other ethnicities are represented at much higher rates than they would be represented in the actual student body?

Yet building unwarranted trust is a common, but unethical appeal to similarity that operates through peripheral rather than central processing. Frauds often occur when persons pose as group members or enlist the help of actual group members. Such tactics are called **affinity scams** because they exploit the trust and friendship existing in groups whose members have much in common. In a Ponzi (pyramid) scheme new investor money is used to pay off earlier investors, who may make a very good return on their money and so unwittingly convince other potential investors that it is a good deal. One scam bilked $2.5 million from a group of 100 Texas senior citizens who were asked to switch safe retirement savings to securities promising a higher investment return. Consumers from close-knit groups or communities must be especially wary of deals proposed just because several of their trusted associates participate. Offers that look too good to be true deserve more examination in the central route of processing.

The Yale studies also considered whether the height of a source leads to more or less attitude change, how the rate of delivery affects persuasion, and when eye contact produces desired effects. Taller persuaders were rated more believable and more trustworthy than shorter ones. Standards of attraction clearly vary by culture, gender, and sometimes by generation. The general assumption is that attraction is routinely processed in the peripheral or heuristic routes, but it may be centrally processed when explicit focus is placed on it (see Box 4.7).

Attractiveness goes beyond physical characteristics. Have you ever heard someone remark that a person is "beautiful, but too high-maintenance for my tastes"? For many, attractiveness includes prestige, social standing, and influence. What are some other attractiveness factors? Persuaders delivering their messages in halting or introverted ways tend to exert less effect on attitudes than those who deliver their speech in smooth and extroverted ways. Gender influences acceptance as well. Although results are mixed, attractive same-sex persuaders are often rated as less credible than attractive persuaders of the opposite sex.

Message Effects

The Yale studies considered the impacts of several message effects on persuasion, not all of which were new to researchers.

Primacy-Recency Effects. One of the oldest findings of persuasion research, presented by psychologist F. H. Lund in 1925, claimed that the most important piece of evidence should come first. We call this the **primacy effect**. The **recency effect**, that is, information most recently presented, also has been found to have significant impact. Whether the primacy or the recency effect is more effective has received substantial attention. Hovland (1957) reported that the primacy-recency issue is not so straightforward. They found the first speaker did not necessarily have an advantage over the second speaker. However, the primacy of negative information has an important role in impression formation—it is particularly difficult to overcome negative information presented first.

The time frame is important in predicting whether primacy or recency effects prevail. It appears that recency effects often decay over the longer term but may be relevant in short-term situations. Research within the ELM framework suggests that listener motivation plays a large role in the processing of information and in determining the impact of primacy-recency effects. The order of the content appears to make little difference to those with high motivation to process who carefully scrutinize messages, but recency effects appear to play a greater role than primacy effects for persons less motivated (see Petty, Wegener, and Fabrigar, 1997). Again, notice that listener motivation is an important factor in the primacy-recency debate.

Message Bias and Two-Sided Arguments. Sometimes persuaders must address people who hold views that are neutral or may be contrary to their own. Should the persuader present one side or two sides of an issue? We call this aspect of persuasion, where only one side or all sides of an issue are considered, **message-sidedness**. Hovland (1957) suggested that it may be wise to first introduce the negative arguments people are already considering. Such tactics launch a preemptive strike against unfavorable information that persuaders expect the hearers may already possess. In the dual-processing framework, using two-sided arguments encourages listeners to centrally process information. Consider United Airline's ad campaign strategy dealing with its filing for bankruptcy. The campaign attempted to establish that travelers need not fear flying with United and it promoted the company's new beginning. The ad engages readers to process this information centrally rather than peripherally. It gets the lingering issue of the airline's bankruptcy out in the open.

Allen's (1998) meta-analysis of message-sidedness considered 70 studies involving over 10,000 people. It indicated that two-sided messages are more effective than one-sided messages when they refute the opposition's arguments. Even those holding similar values are likely to benefit from two-sided messages. Such messages inoculate those whose belief systems are not yet mature by forewarning them of the dangers out there. They may also generate more support against the opposition, much like a pep rally. However, it is not enough merely to mention the positions of the other side; the persuader must refute those positions. Biased information processing suggests that the need to use two-sided messages depends largely on the goals and motivation of the persuader.

Biased information processing occurs when decision-makers favor a certain position and interpret the world in light of that position. They are not giving objective or fair consideration to all possibilities. For example, an employee who has worked for Ford Motor Company for 25 years may be so loyal to Ford that she or he would never think of buying a vehicle from a competitor. Other people come from families who have been Democrats or Republicans for generations and will tend to evaluate persuasive political messages from the biases of those long-standing traditions. Some biased processing occurs because people have a lot more facts and information stored in their memories for activation of one side of an issue than others (see Petty and Wegener, 1999). If you prefer an Apple computer and have used one for years, you probably have a lot more knowledge of Apple computers than of its competitors. You can

probably articulate far more features of the Apple system and why you would be most comfortable buying another Apple computer. The same would be true if you have been a loyal user of Microsoft Windows. So, long-standing ties with products, services, and institutions often lead us to have substantially more information about them. When the quality of information accessible in our memories is very lopsided, objective processing is less likely unless we recognize and correct this deficiency.

According to psychologist Shelley Chaiken and her associates (1996), objective and biased processing originate from different motives. The HSM distinguishes among accuracy, defense, and impression motives. Two-sided messages are appropriate when the goal is to present an accurate assessment such as when making a hiring recommendation from a pool of several qualified candidates. One-sided messages, however, are perfectly fine in persuasive situations where a person is defending a position or trying to maintain an image with important others. For instance, one-sided messages are fine at a political rally that people have paid $1000 per plate to attend—those are not people who have to be convinced to support the candidate. Similarly, Petty and Cacioppo (1979) propose that biased processing is likely when the issue at hand is relevant to the target of the message and that person holds a vested interest; but objective processing is more likely when relevance is high, but the person has no vested interest in the outcome or little knowledge about the topic. Consequently, persons with large investments in a company are more likely to favor that company's products. They often do not try to do a fair comparison with the products of the competition. This biased-processing tendency is a critical problem with many boards of directors at large corporations. Biased processing appears to be more common when persuasive messages contain ambiguous information or arguments of mixed quality rather than clearly strong or weak arguments (see Petty and Wegener, 1999).

Inoculation.   Inoculation is probably the foremost strategy for helping others resist persuasion. In the persuasive context, **inoculation** is the practice of warning people of potentially damaging information or persuasive attempts that will probably happen in the future. This is typically done by giving them a weakened version of the threats and dangers in arguments, practices, or behaviors they will encounter in the future. Michael Pfau (see Pfau et al., 2001) highlights the robust nature of inoculation and demonstrates the multiple and surprising ways of accomplishing it across contexts. Increasingly, political campaigns use it to warn their supporters that attempts will be coming from opponents to turn them to "the dark side." Inoculation provides a heuristic strategy to get people to ignore persuasive attempts from the opposition without careful processing of those messages, rather like throwing away junk mail unread.

The Influence of Mood and Affect on Biased Processing.   It is fairly common for persons taking their first persuasion class during the holiday season to ask whether holiday music and holiday decorations that attempt to put people in a happy mood are an effective strategy for store sales. Although such holiday features appear to bring more shoppers to major urban centers known for such displays, such as New York City and Chicago, the exact impact of mood on specific purchases is less clear. A review of several studies of mood and its impact on the processing of information by psychologists Herbert Bless and Norbert Schwarz (1999) indicates wide agreement for the proposition that people will pay more direct attention to specific information when they are in a neutral mood or are sad. Generally, anger does not encourage objective processing. In contrast, positive moods or happy moods appear to encourage less careful analysis and greater reliance on heuristic processes or stereotypes. Thus, positive or happy moods increase the likelihood of biased rather than objective processing of information. Bless and Schwarz argue that these differences in processing may be due to the increased motivation to process information in negative situations where systematic processes are required to handle problematic situations. They suggest that persons in good moods have little motivation to expend the energy to systematically process information unless other goals require it. Moreover, they suggest that the less-

efficient processing we may do when in a positive mood results from using past experiences and ways of coping with the world. Others, such as psychologists Mackie and Worth (1989), however, maintain that being in a good mood limits information processing capacity because it activates a large amount of positive material in our limited processing capacity; and thus, it is an information capacity issue. The general conclusion is that we make greater use of heuristics and stereotyping in positive moods and do more scrutiny of specific information under neutral or sad moods. Yet several exceptions to these general conclusions have emerged (see DeSteno et al., 2004; Nabi, 2002; Mitchell et al., 2001; Petty & Wegener, 1999; Pfau et al., 2001; Wegener, Petty, & Smith, 1995).

Fear and Drive Reduction

Inducing **fear** continues to be one of the most studied tactics in persuasion research. Hovland, Jams, and Kelley laid the foundation in 1953 by proposing that the use of fear would increase the likelihood of persuasion, because compliance reduces emotional tension. The drive-reduction model is a more specialized version of the **pleasure-pain principle**—that is, people are attracted to rewarding situations and seek to eliminate uncomfortable conditions. Janis (1967) summarized the use of fear appeals and the drive-reduction model:

> Whenever fear or any other unpleasant emotion is strongly aroused, whether by verbal warning or by a direct encounter with signs of danger, the person becomes motivated to ward off the painful emotional state and his efforts in this direction will persist until the distressing cues are avoided in one way or another. Thus, if the distressing threat cues do not rapidly disappear as a result of environmental changes, the emotionally aroused person is expected to try to escape from them, either physically or psychologically (pp. 169–170).

Hovland and his associates (1953) suggested that the fear appeal is effective only if it is sufficiently intense to create a drive state that recipients believe can be effectively countered by the recommended action. This perception that the threat can be handled is now called **efficacy**. If the negative outcome seems insubstantial to the receiver, then its effectiveness is likely to be negligible. Likewise, if the credibility of the person issuing the threat or warning is low, less compliance occurs.

Controversy remains over whether using more fear is better. In the most famous fear appeal study of all time, Janis and Feshbach (1953) studied fear appeals in a dental hygiene context. They found that too much fear arousal can be less effective than more moderate fear arousal. Janis (1967) attributed these effects to an inverted U-shaped curve measuring reaction to fear appeals. That is, high levels of fear (the top of the inverted U-curve) lead to defensive avoidance, but low levels of fear are not enough to induce attitude change. Thus, Janis maintained that using moderate levels of fear produces optimal results. This U-shaped reaction is sometimes called the **boomerang effect**. This effect only occurs when it can be established that persons have changed their minds as a result of a persuasive intervention. The term is often used loosely and inappropriately. It should not be used to refer to messages to which people tune out or turn off. Research regarding fear appeals often has suffered from having no pre-test measures to validate whether participants have actually reversed their prior attitudes. So it is difficult in many cases to interpret unexpected results of fear-inducing studies when no pre-test is conducted. Note this very important point, the inability to establish a boomerang effect, does not mean that negative effects do not arise from messages attempting to produce fear or anxiety.

The superiority of moderate fear appeals has not received support from two meta-analyses by communication researchers. Paul Mongeau (1998) reviewed 28 fear appeal studies involving over 15,000 individuals. He found significant and consistent links between the use of fear appeals and attitude change; that is, more fear is more effective than less fear. Kim Witte and Mike Allen (2000) qualified Mongeau's conclusions, proposing that strong fear appeals coupled with high-efficacy messages produce the greatest behavioral change. Perhaps even more important is their conclusion that strong fear appeals with low-efficacy messages lead to **defensive avoidance** where people try to avoid, ignore, or minimize the issue if they cannot do anything about it. In other words, they tune out the message. These results suggest that efficacy and perception of substantial fear are central to whether fear appeals succeed or fail; strong fear messages alone are not enough. Witte (1992) provides a clear articulation of these processes in the extended parallel process model (EPPM) of fear appeals.

Witte's (1992) EPPM builds on the findings and limitations of Leventhal's (1970) parallel response model and Rogers' (1975) protection motivation theory. Witte's EPPM proposes that fear appeals invoke two processes: threat appraisal and perceived coping appraisal. The first process assesses the danger presented by the threat and how urgent it is to attend to it. So, if a park ranger sees a rattlesnake ahead on the path while conducting a nature walk, she might choose to take another path or go ahead of the group and encourage the snake to go elsewhere with her walking stick. The ranger's action removes the actual danger. The second process of fear control happens when the threat is judged to be real, but it is perceived that the remedies will not be totally effective. For example, it can be a terrifying experience to be caught out on a large body of water in a sailboat during a thunderstorm producing lots of lightning. The tall mast on the boat makes it an attractive target. After you do all you can do to secure the boat and take as much cover as possible, coping with the fear is all you can do. Ineffective fear control in a serious situation leads to the production of anxiety and stress. Recently, communication researcher Ruan Goei (2010) and associates report the value of the EPPM model in promoting asthma interventions with school children in Michigan.

Research by psychologist David Roskos-Ewoldsen and his research team (2004), however, failed to support the EPPM and the conclusions of Witte and Allen (2000). They studied fear appeals in an attitude accessibility framework (see the earlier discussion of Fazio, 1989) that examines how easy it is to access information stored in our brains that fear appeals generated. They studied fear-inducing messages regarding breast cancer and messages advocating the efficacy of self-breast exams. Their results indicate that high-efficacy messages ("you can do something about the problem") produced greater accessibility to attitudes stored in the brains about the adaptive behavior (doing the exam), but high fear-inducing messages appeared to decrease the accessibility of attitudes toward the threat itself. In other words, you could make the information regarding the effectiveness of doing breast cancer self-exams more prominent and focused without creating greater perceptions of the high danger of breast cancer itself. This finding revives the debate about whether producing more fear is better to change attitudes. More research is necessary to determine whether these results are limited to certain contexts or more generally challenge the conclusions of Witte's EPPM.

Why so much attention to fear appeals? Fear appeals are one of the most common persuasive devices encountered by consumers today. In a class lecture at our university, a product manager at a telecommunications giant acknowledged that one of the firm's most common sales techniques is to use fear, uncertainty, and doubt—also known as **FUD** (see FUD-counter, 2001). The origin of the term is attributed to Gene Amdahl, who claimed that salespeople at IBM tried to instill fear, uncertainty, and doubt in the minds of potential customers

who were considering Amdahl computer products. Using FUD tactics also may be a component of propaganda campaigns where appeals are made to people to support various causes such as saying no to drugs or smoking (see Box 4.8). Such causes have good intentions, but some programs appear more like indoctrination rather than discussion of the issues behind these problematic behaviors. Clearly, FUD tactics will not disappear any time soon, but the ethics of using them, especially in messages directed to senior citizens, need more debate.

Shock tactics are often considered a form of fear tactic because they do have similar anxiety producing effects. Although they are not usually intended to be persuasive, horror movies may use tactics intended to shock, disgust, and induce fear. Several advertising campaigns have intended to shock to promote their products, but only limited empirical evidence of its impact exists. Dahl, Frankenberger, and Manchanda (2003) note the widespread use of shock appeals in public health campaigns promoting awareness of breast cancer, AIDS, domestic violence, seat belt safety, and alcohol abuse. They studied the effectiveness of shock advertising for HIV/Aids prevention. Their study suggests that offending the audience often means breaching "norms for decency, good taste, aesthetic propriety, and/or personal moral standards" (p. 269). Their results confirmed that norm violations "heightened awareness of shocking advertising content" (p. 275). Their results also indicated that the shock condition produced greater recall than the information and fear conditions. So, the violation of norms that we hold can

| BOX 4.8 | **Mixed Perceptions of Propaganda Using Scare Tactics** | |

Think about campaigns using fear to reduce the use of illegal drugs, deaths from drunk driving, and infections from HIV/AIDS. Some schools show videos of the tragic consequences of mixing alcohol with driving. Others show the consequences of unwanted teen pregnancy resulting from unprotected sex. Abstinence programs such as DARE attempt to gain commitments of students to not use drugs. The goals of many of these programs are motivated by good intentions,

but there is no room for discussion or true two-way dialogue about the issues with many proponents of these approaches. Thus, many of these well intentioned programs are propaganda. This does not mean that such propaganda is all bad, but advocates of such approaches usually are not open to changing their minds. Mixed opinions exist of the effectiveness of using scare tactics. Has persuasion using fear appeals led to change in your behavior or of anyone you know?

produce dissonance that draws attention to activities violating norms.

It appears that shock appeals actually attract younger audiences because they violate traditional norms and establish individualism. Although the reasons vary, using shock-oriented, dissonance-producing may help gain attention for a persuasive message as well as encourage cognitive processes such as message elaboration and message retention, but many ethical issues remain to be resolved. On the other hand, many of us avoid those using graphic images to dislodge people from their comfortable positions on important issues by changing the channel or turning the page.

Anchor Effects

The book *Social Judgment* (Sherif & Hovland, 1961), the final volume of the Yale Studies in Attitude and Communication, marked the end of an era, along with Hovland's death that year. **Social judgment theory** focuses on how we form reference points, or what Sherif and Hovland called "anchors." The **anchor** is an internal reference point with which we compare other persons, issues, products, and so on that we encounter. Every issue has an anchor at any given time. Research compares the consumer's original anchor to an anchor established later by a persuasive communication.

Perhaps the most important contribution of social judgment theory is the idea that the anchor really represents a range of positions rather than one single point. Thus, "the individual's stand on a social issue is conceived as a range or a **latitude of acceptance**" (pp. 128–129). The anchor is a range of positions acceptable to persuadees, including the most acceptable one. Yet it also includes the **latitude of rejection**, which is the range of positions that persuadees find objectionable, including the most objectionable one. Moreover, research indicates that highly ego-involved individuals have very narrow latitudes of acceptance and very broad latitudes of rejection, so that the likelihood of changing the minds of highly ego-involved people is very small. The best chance of persuasion is a message advocating a position within the hearer's

latitude of acceptance and only a small distance away from the position he or she holds. One of persuaders' more important tasks is determining whether various groups of people have firmly set anchors on positions that relate to the issue at hand.

An important question is how these anchors are established. Although anchors come into our lives in many ways, the people around us in our early childhood experiences provide some of the early anchors in our lives through patterns of behavior labeled *norms*. It is common for younger siblings to desire what their older siblings have at the family table. Most of us still find special foods from our childhood comforting in times of distress, like macaroni and cheese or ice cream. Perhaps these foods remind of secure and safe times with our family. As we mature, it is natural to want things our peers have or to do things our peers do to fit into the culture.

Anchors, however, may be manufactured by persuaders. A common anchor is the **manufacturer's suggested retail price (MSRP)** which is also known as the full retail price. Most customers rarely pay full retail price for many items. The MSRP is usually the upper anchor or limit a customer should pay, but in many cases it is an artificially high number to make the actual price being charged appear more reasonable. Many manufacturers create a line of very high-end products that are very expensive, a range of mid-level products of very good quality, and a low-end line of products that provide significantly less benefits or are inferior to the mid-range products. The central intent of many manufacturers is to sell a high volume of the mid-level products with a few upper-level customers being a welcome bonus. Auto manufacturers often limit sales of their base models to less than two percent of total sales and customers may have long waiting times for a base model to become available. Even though it is difficult in many cases to actually see a base model on the lot of an automobile dealer, the base model does serve as a point of comparison for additional features a customer gets in a mid-range or high-end model. General Motors (GM) perfected this anchoring strategy by creating divisions catering to differing price-points of customers with Chevrolet division being the anchor for its basic customer and the Cadillac division serving as its upper-end anchor as its definition of luxury. The company's goal was to elevate customers to higher quality lines as their ability to spend more on a vehicle became a possibility. All strategic development of anchors, however, has not been in the retail or corporate environment. Many have suggested that some political candidates for major offices serve an anchor function labeled the **decoy effect** that makes certain major candidates look better (see Box 4.9). It remains unclear the degree to which candidates with little chance of winning are encouraged to enter political races to make other candidates look better, but the social comparison process happens whether the process has been intentionally manipulated or not.

Self-Efficacy and Efficacy

Although **self-efficacy** has been discussed in the TPB, it warrants further attention because it is one of the most researched elements of persuasion over the past decade. Self-efficacy is being used an important component in programs to improve student math proficiency, smoking cessation programs, weight-loss programs, and drug rehabilitation programs. Psychologist Albert Bandura has been credited with being the originator of the concept (see Bandura, 1977). He frames self-efficacy as an individual believing she or he is capable of a successful performance. That is, a person believes she or he

can perform sufficiently to attain certain goals. Bandura (1993) articulates four major processes through which self-efficacy operates: cognitive, motivational, affective, and selection processes. Cognitive processes are the primary thought processes dealing with self-confidence. The motivational component also is presented as a cognitive process where humans set goals and plan. The affective processes are described in terms of managing the stress and anxiety that happens in pursuit of our goals. Finally, the selection processes involve making choices that maximize the other three processes.

These four processes are not, however, four disconnected, independent functions. His framework is very complex and uses many other theories to support them including expectancy-value approaches, social learning, and attribution theory. All of these processes taken together result in the degree to which a person believes she or he can accomplish the established goals.

Sometimes the term self-efficacy is used interchangeably with **efficacy**. These terms have different meanings for many persuasion researchers with efficacy being the wider term including all reasons that a person uses to determine whether an action will likely be effective. Efficacy has previously been discussed as a component in persuasion attempting to induce fear. So, self-efficacy is a sub-class of the more general category of efficacy.

Both efficacy and self-efficacy are important terms in many types of persuasion. First, you have to believe a solution will work to meet your goal. One of the most problematic categories of consumer

BOX 4.9 **Ethics of Decoy Effects in Politics**

An interview with *Washington Post* columnist Shankar Vedantam on National Public Radio examining the decoy effect in political races discussed how a third-place candidate may impact the choice of the number one candidate. He suggests perceptions of characteristics of Democratic candidate John Edwards in the race had an impact on perceptions of candidates Clinton and Obama. He maintains that characteristics of a third option can either improve the image of certain front-

running candidates or detract from them. In essence, the third candidate provides an anchor against which to judge the number one and two candidates. In some races a third party candidate enters the race with financing that appears to have ties to another party. The third party candidate might pull more votes from one candidate than the other. Is it ethical for a political party to encourage other candidates to enter the race who they believe may pull votes from a front runner?

electronics is the point-and-shoot digital camera. It is a product category expected to be take better pictures than the camera in a cell-phone, but more convenient than the more expensive DSLR cameras. Problems with picture quality of the pocket digital cameras often center around poor inside pictures, where people are often blurry because of motion in low-light situations and the camera shutter not taking the picture quickly. The inability of the camera to take quality pictures in low-light situations is an issue of efficacy. Most small digital cameras do not perform well in low-light situations even in the hands of a professional photographer. When a product cannot do reliably what a consumer needs to do, this is a problem with efficacy.

The situation is different when a person moves to a digital SLR camera and appropriate external flash attachment in the $750 price range. Other than a defective camera, there is no reason why a new Canon Rebel camera with the appropriate flash matched to the camera will not take excellent pictures inside one's home, except operator error. Many consumers stay away from the better cameras

because they have a lot of settings that they do not believe they can master. This is an issue of self-efficacy. There is nothing wrong with the camera—it is the limitation of the user. As a response, Kodak has developed a line of Easyshare cameras that have few controls on the cameras and are connected easily to a computer to share the pictures with others.

Problems with complicated products do not stop with consumer electronics. The health care industry has many products that must be used correctly to be effective. Most forms of contraception are highly effective in laboratory tests when used according to instructions; however, the effectiveness when used by actual consumers is much lower. For example, many people don't know or forget that antibiotics can interfere with the effectiveness of birth control pills. They also can make people more sensitive to the sun and more susceptible to sunburn. Others stop taking their antibiotics as soon as they start feeling better. Both efficacy and self-efficacy play roles in making effective health care decisions.

REVIEW AND CONCLUSION

There is little question that the ELM has been a catalyst in the last three decades of persuasion research. Still, no single theory addresses every persuasive situation. Some, such as the ELM and HSM, address larger (macro) issues regarding overall approaches to persuasion while others address very specific (micro) persuasive situations at the tactical level, such as approaches intended to arouse fear or shock. Often we need multiple perspectives to explain different parts of a persuasive situation. One of the objectives of this chapter was to emphasize that the most appropriate persuasive tactics for a given situation depend heavily upon the motivation of the audience to listen and analyze carefully. The use of more statistics and evidence is unlikely to be effective when the audience is not listening. Thus, attempting to beat people into submission until they start listening is probably not the best first

line of action. Another objective was to make it clear that much attitude change and persuasion takes place through peripheral or heuristic processes so that as consumers of persuasion you will become more aware of what is happening below your conscious awareness. The mere exposure research should cause us to examine what kinds of persuasive effects are happening from just seeing brands and icons frequently. Moreover, we need to consider what impact new social media such as YouTube.com and Facebook may be having on our attitudes.

Despite the many persuasive trends found over a number of years, it is also important to recognize that such findings are fallible. Although research findings typically represent a greater likelihood that specific persuasive strategies or tactics will produce predictable reactions, there are often important factors like the motivation of the audience to listen and daily events that create some unpredictability in every persuasive situation.

Although others may disagree, I award the title of the most effective predictor of behavioral change to the expectancy-values approaches by Martin Fishbein and Icek Ajzen. No other approaches have been as widely adopted in persuasive

campaigns—particularly those that are health related. The importance of affect in the persuasive situation is gaining more respect from researchers but still needs better integration in the mainstream approaches. These theories in this chapter are representative, but not a complete consideration of the persuasion literature. We will revisit many of these perspectives throughout the remainder of the book.

KEY TERMS

After reading this chapter, you should be able to identify, explain, and give an example of the following key terms or concepts:

empirical

dual-process models

elaboration likelihood model (ELM)

central route

need for cognition (NFC)

peripheral route

heuristic-systematic model, or HSM

systematic processing route

heuristic processing route

mere exposure

attitude-behavior relationships

behavioral intentions

normative influence

theory of planned behavior (TPB)

perceived behavioral control

norms-based approaches

sleeper effect

affinity scams

primacy effect

recency effect

message-sidedness

biased information processing

inoculation

fear

pleasure-pain principle

efficacy

boomerang effect

defensive avoidance

FUD

social judgment theory

anchor

latitude of acceptance

latitude of rejection

manufacturer's suggested retail price (MSRP)

decoy effect

self-efficacy

efficacy

APPLICATION OF ETHICS

We frequently encounter the manufacturer's suggested retail price (MSRP) on price tags in retail stores, on products in show rooms, and in advertisements. Except in situations where the final selling prices are carefully controlled by the manufacturer, most consumers do not pay the full MSRP. When sales promotions and members' discounts are applied, consumers often pay half the MSRP and sometimes as little as a

fourth of this amount. The large discrepancy between the MSRP and what consumers actually pay can be viewed as a form of consumer fraud. Most astute consumers understand that the MSRP provides psychological support to justify purchases and it aids in combating buyer's remorse. If consumers knowingly participate in such deception, is the use of the exaggerated MSRP an ethical persuasive practice?

QUESTIONS FOR FURTHER THOUGHT

1. An ethical issue raised by the ELM is determining when children develop the ability to centrally process persuasion at a level that allows them to make informed choices. In what situations should parents allow their children to make their own choices about purchases like cereal, toys, and clothing?

2. Given that attractiveness has proven to be a valuable factor in persuasion, what can people do in persuasive situations to make up for the fact that they are not among the beautiful people in this world?

3. Put yourself into the role of the parent of a teenager who has just obtained his or her license. What inoculation strategy might you use to try to persuade your teenager not to drink and drive?

4. Do you believe norms-based approaches can work to combat undesirable behaviors in young people? Why or why not?

5. Many universities provide a large booklet of information regarding parking policies on campus that many students, staff, and faculty never read. How might such documents be redesigned to be more effective at persuading students, staff, and faculty to comply with the regulations?

6. If you are not sensitive to handgun issues, search for the sites mentioned in Box 4.5 regarding the Glock handgun. What is the impact of the Ted Nugent site on you versus the more objective presentation?

7. Why are there so many more videos on You-Tube against gun control than for limitations on gun ownership?

You can access your online resources at the companion website for *Persuasion*. Log in at **http://www.cengagebrain.com**.

5

The Making, Use, and Misuse of Symbols

LEARNING GOALS

After reading this chapter, you should be able to:

1. Identify significant human developments that were made possible via language.

2. Identify several unique facts about the English language.

3. Explain and give examples of eloquence.

4. Explain why language is symbolic action.

5. Give examples of the use and misuse of linguistic symbols.

6. Discuss Langer's theory about language use.

7. Discuss the general semanticists and their theories and goals.

8. Demonstrate how an emotion-laden sentence can be defused using the extensional devices suggested by the semanticists.

9. Discuss Burke's notions of identification, substances, and the role of language as a cause of guilt.

10. Explain semiotics and its use of terms such as text, code, signifiers, and signifieds.

11. Identify cases where your language in using SNM affected the overall meaning that your audience perceived.

12. Navigate your way from one page on Facebook to another and learn about friends of your friends, especially as to how they use language.

A uthor, language columnist, and critic Richard Lederer (1991) observes:

> "The boundary between human and animal—between the most primitive savage and the highest ape—is the language line. The birth of language is the dawn of humanity; in our beginning was the word. We have always been endowed with language because before we had words, we were not human beings. [Words] tell us that we must never take for granted the miracle of language" (p. 3).

Throughout history, the uniquely human ability to create **symbols** made possible most if not all of our major cultural advances, and this is more true than ever in the current age of social networking. Words begin in infancy (see Figures 5.1 and 5.2) and continue being central to everyday life as we mature, and we as persuaders need to recognize these word/symbols (as well as visual or other kinds of symbols) for what they are and what they do to us in order to accomplish persuasive results.

Symbols can be many things, not just words; pictures, art works, music, advertising logos, and team emblems are a few examples. The dictionary definition of a symbol reads: "Something that represents something else by association, resemblance, or convention" (*American Heritage Dictionary,* 2005). However, the most widely used type of symbol is probably language or words. I like to use the term word/symbols to remind me that language is usually symbolic.

And we all use words on a regular basis, yet we aren't all artists, musical composers, or advertising and PR designers. As a result, we tend to overlook the importance and the tremendous power of symbols like words and language choice in persuasion and elsewhere. Since words stand for or represent things, ideas, and feelings, we also tend to react to words as if they actually are the things they only represent. For example, Kenneth Burke, a noted language theorist, called the use of language "symbolic action," by which he meant when you say it, you have done it symbolically (at least). Take name-calling, for example; if someone calls me a dumb Swede, I am likely to get angry and perhaps

FIGURE 5.1 The alphabet was a major technology for communication—even for children.

SOURCE: © Shelley Dennis/iStockphoto.com.

at least examine some of my less than intelligent decisions and actions. In its most malignant uses, such name-calling can prove fatal. Witness the Missouri teenager who committed suicide in 2007 because of names she was called online on her MySpace account. The name-caller was not a person she knew—but the parent(s) of a former friend. Symbols and language are powerful stuff as history has repeatedly demonstrated. Patrick Henry's words before the Virginia House of Burgesses ring poetic and persuasive: "I know not what course others may take sir, but as for me give me liberty or give me death!" (To hear the entire prelude to Henry's peroration read by a professional, go to Weblink 5.1.) (You can access this and all of the other Chapter 5 weblinks through your companion website for *Persuasion,* Chapter 5 resources.) You'll note

Henry is poetic and persuasive even before the most often quoted "Give me liberty or give me death" section (2:35 minutes).

With the ability to use word/symbols for communication, humans were enabled to live very differently. With this ability they could form tribes, enact rituals, trade with one another, and persuade. Through language humans could create culture, and with the use of visual and verbal symbols, communicate. Communication facilitated the specialization of labor and the recording of oral history. Language not only allowed humans to create culture, but with the use of visual and verbal symbols, they could communicate. Language also allowed humans to engage in less-constructive behaviors such as lying, teasing, breaking promises, scolding, demeaning, propagandizing, and cyberbullying (such as in the suicide case noted above), to name a few. And with the development of writing and print, people found that promises, treaties, and legal contracts could be both made and broken, and laws could be used for evil as well as good. The title of the book, *Deeds Done in Words* (Campbell & Jamieson, 1990), indicates that language serves as a frequent surrogate for action. Researcher and professor Neil Postman (1992) maintains that language is an "invisible technology" or a kind of machine that can "give direction to our thoughts, generate new ideas, venerate old ones, expose facts or hide them" (p. 127). And this universal technology is closely linked to language theorist Kenneth Burke's words (1966) when he said that humans are "symbol making, symbol using, and symbol misusing" creatures. This ability to use symbols—whether words, pictures, music, or art—lies at the heart of persuasion. As a result, receivers must carefully analyze the verbal, auditory, and visual symbols being used or misused by the many persuaders around us, including those using SNM to reach us. As noted in Chapter 1, we must engage in "defensive listening" if we are to avoid swindles, scams, and political and personal errors. We need to ask whether the word/symbols and the accompanying visuals, sound effects, and so on prompt logical or emotional meanings, and if they are centrally or peripherally processed in the elaboration likelihood model (ELM) also mentioned in several places earlier. For instance, imagine a TV advertisement for a brand of beer. It probably uses verbal, visual, and musical or lyrical (auditory) symbols. Visually, the screen displays a group of youthful males and females drinking bottles of the powerful malt liquor plus energy drink, Four Loco, and having fun while watching a football game and maybe hoping to meet an important someone. Musically, we hear the Four Loco jingle. Verbally, the voiceover tells us what we should treasure and seek out: "Love Those Hot Moments—So Just Go Loco!!!" The word in the jingle almost guarantees fun and certainly a high energy, potentially sexual relationship. Together, these various kinds of symbols show that people who drink Four Loco enjoy a certain life-style, are happy-go-lucky, sexually motivated, hot, and models to be emulated.

In addition to words alone, persuaders frequently use artistic metaphors (which are a kind of symbol, such as the "Nike swoosh") to emphasize their points in dramatic ways. These can either intensify or downplay the points being made. For example, two books on the issue of the right to privacy use metaphors in their titles: *No Place to Hide* by Robert O'Harrow (2005), and Daniel Solove's *The Digital Person* (2005). Both titles imply in their metaphors that we face two dangers—a loss of privacy and that we are becoming mere ciphers or digits. We discussed both topics briefly in relation to the use of SNM, ethics, propaganda, and the ELM. They also relate to the humanistic as well as the social science theories related to the process of persuasion (see Chapters 2–4). Recent research on persuasive metaphors shows that their use increases persuader credibility, and that they operate best when their theme is reiterated throughout the persuasive message, especially if used initially and in the conclusion (Sopory and Dillard, 2002). This is especially so if the metaphors are universal or archetypal; in other words, ones that can be understood over time and across cultures, such as the light and dark family. In these cases, light is generally associated with positive pleasures, good, knowledge, and uplifting emotions or ideas; dark is generally associated with mysterious, unknown, potentially dangerous, potentially exciting, and maybe potentially evil actions or events. By examining various metaphors and other symbols used in persuasion, we accomplish several things:

1. We discover the persuader's pattern of use or misuse of symbols.

2. We discover the persuader's stylistic preferences, what they reveal about his or her motives, and how they can intensify or downplay.

3. Knowing these things, we can anticipate the kinds of messages likely to come from this persuader in the future and be prepared for them.

One reason we can infer a great deal from how a person uses word/symbols to persuade is because the making of symbols is so highly ego-involving. In other words, because it is a creative act, it is our opportunity to be "artists" of sorts. When we make a symbol, we own it—it belongs to us, has our stamp of ownership on it, and it reveals a good deal about us. It tells others how we think and respond to events and issues. And our metaphors also tend to reveal our motives. The same thing happens when others try to persuade us. They create symbols (usually language) and metaphors, and as a result they "own" their creations. Through their choice of symbols, they reveal things about themselves. For example, what could we infer about a persuader—say an editorial cartoonist—who continually used dark metaphors, referred to conspiracies working against us, and chose visual symbols that involved predatory creatures like sharks or wolves? We might well conclude that the cartoonist was paranoid, felt him- or herself to be in the minority on public opinion, and was distrustful of others. So you see, critical receivers need to know something about symbols, particularly word/symbols, and how to read them for clues regarding the persuader's motives.

What sorts of metaphors are being used in the messages you receive on SNM that you use? Where are they processed in the ELM? I recently displayed on my Facebook page a picture of the corpse of a creature I found necessary to shoot. It was repeatedly bothering my dog and sending him into crazy fits of barking and snarling at various bushes on our property. The critter was at least four feet in total length. I asked receivers to name it and gave them a hint or two: it was a marsupial; its feet had no claws; it had a long, rat-like tail; and its teeth looked ferocious. I got a quick and rather clever response—"Awesome Pawssum!" What do you think of the respondee's relationship with me? What was artistic about his metaphor? You see word/symbols reveal things about us...and others.

Let's look a little deeper into the enormous power that lies in the English language in particular, and how it rules the global, multicultural, interactive, 24/7 networked world in which we live; a world that is saturated with advocacy, propaganda, constantly changing media, increasing ethical challenges, and doublespeak. And in regard to the ELM, we know from history that language cues, metaphors, and what we call "eloquence" have often acted as the powerful emotional cues that are processed in the peripheral channel. These emotional and peripheral cues prompt our action in significant, if unconscious, ways similar to the ways in which the words of Patrick Henry brought on a response to the British tyranny (see Weblink 5.2 for his entire text). We will examine several examples of these powerful central and peripheral cues in the following discussion, but first let's look at the English language itself. After all, it is the dominant linguistic force in the world today, accounting for overwhelming percentages of language used in scientific knowledge, research journals, diplomacy, international trade, and travel, and in the vast majority of existing and likely to be produced computer files. If a person can't speak or read English today, flipping burgers is likely to be their future occupation.

THE POWER OF THE ENGLISH LANGUAGE

In his book *The Miracle of Language,* Lederer (1991) offers many observations about the power of the English language (the common denominator for most persuasion that we process and much that is sent around the world today). His observations warn us not to take language or word/symbols for granted. His advice is more poignant than ever given the burgeoning presence of persuasion in contemporary culture, and also given the many changes we have seen in communication technologies since he first noted his observations over 20 years ago. Consider just a few of them:

1. Of almost 3,000 languages in existence today, only 10 are the native language of more than 100 million people, and English ranks second in the list only behind Chinese. It is the first language of 45 countries, and its second-language users outnumber its native users, making it a truly global tongue (pp. 19–20). As such, it is a powerful tool without which one is extraordinarily disabled.

2. English is the language of most of the world's books, newspapers, magazines; in two-thirds of all scientific publications; and in 80 percent of all stored computer texts (p. 20).

3. English has one of the richest vocabularies—there are over 615,000 words in the *Oxford English Dictionary*—not including newly invented slang such as the word "skank" which has metastasized into hundreds of other words like "skankbutter," "skanksta," or "skankin!!" (see Weblink 5.3 for a sample). Or consider the many new technical terms that come into play on almost a daily basis—the iPhone, blogs, mouse, or tweets. Compare that with the mere 100,000 words in the equivalent French dictionary, the 130,000 in Russian, or the 185,000 in German. It is also an economical language requiring far fewer words to translate Mark's gospel in *The New Testament* than any other language. The same goes for the rest of *The Bible* as well as many other important documents. And translators prefer using English above any other language when doing their work.

4. English is now the international language of science, business, politics, diplomacy, literature, tourism, pop culture, and air travel. Iranian pilots flying Iranian airliners over Iranian air space who communicate with Iranian flight controllers must use English, not their native language. And the same is true of the airspace over every other country in the world (p. 30).

5. Non-native speakers report that English is the easiest second language to learn (p. 28). Lederer also demonstrates the power of a permanent aspect of the English language and its syntax. He asks random students to arrange five words—***Lithuanian, five, scholars, Shakespearean***, and ***old*** in proper order to make syntactical sense—try it yourself. Everyone comes up with the same order: "five old Lithuanian Shakespearean scholars." The adjective string begins with the most specific and runs to the least—a syntactical rule we each learn early in life. There are Shakespearean scholars in countries other than Lithuania just as there other kinds of scholars, and not all of them are old.

Or consider the variances in meaning when one uses spoken as opposed to written English. In spoken English, try to determine the difference between "no notion" and "known ocean," or between "buys ink," "buys zinc," and "buys sink" or between "meteorologist" and "meaty urologist." What are the differences between "cat's skills," "cats' kills," and "Catskills," or between "tax" and "tacks"? Figure 5.5 demonstrates these differences in a humorous way. This last example resulted in a humorous blooper in a term paper. The student wrote, "The American Revolution came about because the British put tacks in the tea." So, as persuadees, we must consider whether the persuasion is coming to us in written or spoken language or via visual symbols. In other words, the channel plays an important part in our development of meaning and deciding how to react to it, as seen in Figures 5.5 and 5.7. Another example comes from a relatively recent form of communication in which you all probably engage—texting—a cumbersome means used to communicate and one which has a much higher likelihood for being misunderstood than speaking does. (See for example

BOX 5.1   **Interactive English**

Go to Weblink 5.4 and explore the many interesting and fun ways interactive media can help you improve your use of the English language. One of the many activities at the site is the daily display of a new idiom. If you don't know what an idiom is, consider this one: "As different as chalk from cheese." What do you suppose it means? At the site there is a daily famous quote and a chat group where you can leave or receive a message about the use of English. You can trade English language lessons with students from other countries.

For example, Oman will trade lessons in Arabic with you. You can leave your term papers or other texts there for free critiques. Try to solve the word puzzles and learn new slang words. The site also lists good English schools in eight countries and offers students budget travel hints. And there is even an online wizard who can read your mind. You will learn much about the English language there. You may want to invent your own words as Shakespeare did (see Figure 5.3).

Weblink 5.5.) As a result we need to pay much more careful attention to the word/symbols we use when writing and sending a message than we do when sending it in the spoken channel.

LANGUAGE, ELOQUENCE, AND SYMBOLIC ACTION

Eloquent persuasion always seems unique, fresh, exciting, and somehow emotional. It strikes us as capturing the moment, and it may even prophesy the future. As seen from Figure 5.3, the talented wordsmith can invent such eloquence, or he or she might borrow it. Take the speech made by Martin Luther King, Jr., on the night before he was assassinated where he said that God had allowed him "to go up to the mountain top," and that he had "seen the Promised Land," but that he doubted that he would get there with his followers (see Figure 5.4). His words have an obvious Biblical reference to Moses leading the children of Israel out of bondage but not being allowed to pass into the Promised Land. He concluded, "But, I am happy tonight! I'm not fearing any man! Mine eyes have seen the glory of the coming of the Lord!" Although the words were not wholly original (they were drawn from the *Old Testament* and Julia Ward Howe's "Battle Hymn of the Republic"), his use of them was prophetic, emotional, effective, and probably processed in the peripheral channel of the ELM.

FIGURE 5.3   Other words coined by Shakespeare include *amazement, bump, clangor, dwindle, fitful, majestic, obscene, pious, road, flibbertygibbet, slugabeat,* and *useless.* Can you invent some words of your own?

SOURCE: Word for Word by Michael Atchinson. Reprinted with Permission.

As you can see, King was a charismatic and impressive speaker. To hear the speech he gave the night before he was assassinated, go to Weblink 5.6.

SOURCE: Time & Life Pictures/Getty Images.

Today we find many groups using and misusing linguistic symbols in dramatic ways on buttons, badges, or bumper stickers. Many of them are emotion laden and hence peripherally processed. Consider a few: "Think Globally; Act Locally," "Guns Don't Kill; People Do," or "Da Bears." Others use license plates as a medium to make symbolic declarations about themselves and the times: IM N RN, REV BOB, BMW BFD, 3MTA3 (hint—use a mirror), I M SX C, MR X TC, 3NON (read upside down), XME OUT, TACKY, GWS WAR, IMVAIN2, DON HI, DZ BLND, IH8 MYX, 400 GPA, and CRE 8TV.

In each of these messages, its inventor is symbolically making a revealing statement about themselves. Researchers note that persons displaying bumper stickers or wearing T-shirts with product, cause, or candidate labels imprinted on them will buy the products, donate, or vote for the candidate, cause, or brand they are promoting far more often than those who don't display the words. Making the symbolic statement equates with action in their minds, and their words become deeds or substitutes for action. As Burke (1966) observed, "Language is symbolic action," and we often act out what we speak.

Language can also be misused, as in euphemisms like the deaths of Afghani and Iraqi civilians that were labeled "collateral damage," in operations "Rolling Thunder" and "Enduring Freedom" (both names are also examples of euphemisms in doublespeak), and in the words "surgical air strikes," which made the enormous damage sound neat and clean. Market researchers decided to use the words "recipe for success," for example, to assure working women who use Crisco that they are indeed "cooks" and not merely "microwavers." They just thaw and reheat meals. A great pair of words, "budget gourmet," describes an inexpensive, okay, prepackaged meal.

The use of a message's particular verbal and visual symbols is another reason language requires careful analysis. Consider the demeaning and dehumanizing language used by anti-Semitic persuaders in past (and perhaps in present) examples of propaganda in referring to Jews and other minorities. Words such as "vermin," "sludge," "garbage," "lice," "sewage," "insects," "scum," "slime," and "bloodsuckers" were frequently used by the Nazis and others. What do we do with such creatures? We **EXTERMINATE** them—as in the extermination of over six million in the Holocaust. The recent influx of

FIGURE 5.5

As this cartoon demonstrates, language used in its spoken form can be quite different from its use in its written form.

SOURCE: Reprinted by permission of Aaron Johnson.

immigrants from the Middle East has spawned similar linguistic venom: "camel jockey," "dot head," "pak head," or "Q-tip," all of which demean and dehumanize others. We need to remember that "ethnic cleansing" still occurs, and that language serves as the major weapon for dehumanizing others before killing or torturing them and worse. In less dramatic settings, word/symbols like "spic," "greaser," "beaner," and "spans" create emotional responses and also devalue persons of Hispanic heritage.

What do the word/symbols "lady doctor" imply? That the doctor is not as good as a male physician? That the doctor is in the business only for the fun or sport of it? Why does "lady" convey so much meaning and evoke emotional responses? Perhaps the speaker means a gynecologist.

Communication scholar Dan Hahn (1998) points out how language depicts males as sexual aggressors and females as stalked prey or passive entities. Consider a few examples in which the language of seduction becomes the language of stalking: the male is described as "a real animal" or unable to "keep his paws off her," while the female is "a real dish" or "a real piece of meat" to be "turned on" or a "gash" to be "cranked."

Recently we have become sensitized to the use (and misuse) of Native American references in athletics—the Braves, the Redskins, the Chiefs, the Fighting Illini, and the Seminoles—all of which were perfectly acceptable until persuadees were sensitized to their use. And as Figure 5.5 demonstrates, confusion can frequently arise from similarities and differences between the spoken word as it sounds and as it might be interpreted in its written form.

The world of marketing provides many examples of the persuasive power in language choice. Brand names often reveal manufacturers' attitudes toward customers. For instance, Oster Corporation markets a "food crafter" instead of a "food chopper," which tells us that Oster takes a gourmet approach. (Chopping sounds like work. Crafting? Now, that's art.) One can easily sense the emotional flavor of these words and why they are processed almost unconsciously via the peripheral channel of the ELM. They certainly reflect doublespeak. Smoking certain brands of cigarettes can also make a gender statement—Eves and Virginia Slims are for her, not for him; he's better off with Marlboro or Camels. (See Box 5.2.)

BOX 5.2 **Interact with Vanity Plates**

Go to Weblink 5.7 and read about the series of 154 actually issued California license plates that tell the entire story of Oedipus Rex. Report back to class. While you're at the site, explore some of the very funny vanity plates imagined or real—enjoy.

LANGER'S APPROACH
TO LANGUAGE USE

To become truly responsible receivers of persuasion, we need to identify the uses and misuses of symbols, especially in the language used by politicians, advertisers, employers, and other persuaders. A useful approach to the study of language is based on the work of philosopher and language pioneer Suzanne K. Langer (1957). She recognized the power of word/symbols, and like Lederer and others, she believed that the ability to create and use language distinguishes humans from nonhumans. Language lets us talk and think about feelings, events, and objects even when the actual feelings, events, or objects are not physically present. Langer associates two concepts with this capacity—signs and symbols. Signs indicate the presence of an event, feeling, or object. For instance, thunder signals lightning and usually rain. My dog goes into a panic at the sound of thunder—lightning struck close to her as a pup, so she tries to hide from it. If she could process symbols, I might talk to her about thunder and explain the futility of trying to hide from it. Only the comforting tone of my voice (another sign) seems to calm her down. We know that the red traffic light at an intersection signals potentially dangerous cross traffic. Though color blind, "guide" or "leader" dogs recognize the red light by its location on the top of the traffic signal

and even learn to stop the person they are leading, but you cannot teach them to recognize the symbolic link between the red light and the words "cross traffic"—a much more complex connection. As Langer (1957) put it, "Symbols are not proxy of their objects, but are vehicles for the conception of objects" (p. 60). Because of our ability to use symbols, you and I understand the presence of danger by such things as the color red, the word "danger," or the skull and crossbones on a bottle. Using symbols seems to be a basic human need. Even persons unable to write, hear, or speak make symbols using visual signs, hand motions, and other symbolic means, as Helen Keller demonstrated though both blind and deaf.

Some symbols have a common meaning upon which most people agree. Langer called such symbols **concepts**, in contrast to **conceptions**, which she used to refer to any particular individual's unique meanings for the concept. All human communication and hence all persuasion relies on concepts and conceptions. So, naturally, the possibility of misunderstanding always presents itself. How might the activities in Box 5.3 reflect map and territory differences?

Langer also introduced three terms to be used when discussing meaning: "signification," "denotation," and "connotation." **Signification** means a sign that accompanies the thing being considered. So the skull and crossbones symbol on a bottle signifies "Danger—Poison!" **Denotation** refers to the

---

BOX 5.3   Brand Names: Discursive or Presentational?

Developing brand names entails more effort than you would think. It is no accident that Snuggle—a fabric softener—has a teddy bear as its logo. When you see Snuggle on the shelf, you probably do not think of actually "snuggling" up with a good book and a cup of coffee, but you might put a package of it in your shopping cart and feel good about having done so. Cues or information processed in the peripheral channel of the ELM has probably been at play in your purchase. There is no string of words to be followed when you look at the brand, its logo, or its packaging, but many times there is a story there. The brand's

name is a presentational symbol. Observe the brand on your next shopping trip. Now consider this metaphoric brand name—Thera-Flu—a cold medicine meant to be taken as a hot drink before you go to bed. There is no evidence (other than 24/7 media-saturated examples) that the brand works any better than any other nighttime cold medicine having similar ingredients. However, the brand is threatening sales of Nyquil, the first over-the-counter nighttime cold medicine on the market. Why? Perhaps there is a presentational (or metaphorical) media explanation (Feig, 1997).

FIGURE 5.6 What is the denotation of this visual symbol? What is its connotation?

SOURCE: www.shutterstock.com.

common and shared meaning we all have for any concept (see Figure 5.6); we all have similar meanings for the concept of "profit" versus loss, unless some scoundrel CEO redefines his or her definitions of the terms and calls profit "risk" or "investment in the future" and then chooses to use it to build mansions for personal use or simply embezzles it—this happened to me in an ad agency in which I was a partner in the recent past. **Connotation** refers to a private, metaphorical, emotional (and perhaps propagandistic) meaning for any concept such as "profit," which for me means revenue that exceeds overall costs, but which for the crooked CEO may mean "...the amount of money he or she can skim from overall revenue without it showing up on a financial statement." The denotation of the word would be the dictionary definition of the word "profit" as "the amount of return on an investment after all expenses have been deducted" (*American Heritage Dictionary*, 1985). Recent history has shown us just how cleverly words like "profit" can be used to scam others. I already reported my recent experience with the words "collection agency" and the telemarketing scam I almost fell for. In that case the connotation of the words "collection agency" almost scared me out of my socks. Why? What things are associated with those word/symbols? Why would they scare me?

The connotation of the word is our personal and individual conception of danger. For example, because of my Minnesota background, I find

blizzards to be dangerous; but someone from Florida might not, and the obverse would be true for my connotation for the word "hurricane." And of course, we are increasingly facing culturally diverse connotations for words and concepts. For example, China thinks of itself as extraordinarily egalitarian. However, professor and marketing consultant Barry Feig (1997) reports that a flourishing trade exists there for counterfeit labels for high-priced and high-status brands of bicycles. Chinese workers remove their low-end labels and substitute the high-status ones. Few persons in China own autos, but most have bicycles, and most of them are quite ordinary—almost generic. The fake labels are symbols that communicate status (connotation) in a society where status differences supposedly don't exist (denotation). Langer also maintained that meaning is either "discursive" or "presentational." **Discursive symbols** are usually made up of sequential, smaller bits of meaning that unfold across time to yield ultimate meaning. They are like advocacy or propaganda that occurs step by step. Musically, this would be equivalent to movements in a symphony. In a drama it would be the unfolding of a plot. For our purposes, discursive symbols usually occur in the form of language and the development of meaning in a sentence, paragraph, chapter, and so on. **Presentational meaning**, on the other hand, occurs all at once and the message is experienced in its entirety at one time, such as when one looks at a painting, architecture, or a statue; or when one experiences a ritual or an emotional gasp of approval to eloquent language use. In this way it resembles a metaphor that is recognized all at once and is best fit for a media-saturated dramatic world. Thus, some of the "meaning" in any advertisement is discursive (the slogans, jingles, plot, and ad copy), while some is presentational (the graphic layout, logos, fonts, and photos or pictures). Similarly, some of the meaning in a political campaign occurs discursively (the speeches, press releases, and interviews), while some is presentational (the way the candidate looks, his or her image, the candidate's artful use of language, or the pictorials and music in spot ads). That's why politicians employ the services of speech writers and image consultants to get you processing their advocacy/propaganda in both the peripheral and the central information processing channels of the ELM and repeatedly in a 24/7 networked world. Box 5.3 illustrates the differences.

GENERAL SEMANTICS AND LANGUAGE USE

Beginning with the landmark work *Science and Sanity* by Count Alfred Korzypski (1947), language scholars known as general **semanticists** began a careful and systematic study of the use of language and meaning. Korzypski had been an intelligence interrogator questioning prisoners for intelligence about the enemy. He specialized in de-briefing spies and double or even triple spies, so it is not surprising that he became fascinated with language use and its true meanings. Apparently with the de-briefing of Al Qaeda suspects, the difficulties with determining true meaning from tricky language choices is still with us. Even with the use of water-boarding and other forms of torture, which most experts agree is ineffective at getting to the "truth" of a situation, deciphering the truth is difficult. Korzypski and his colleagues intended to devise tools for improving the understanding of human communication and to encourage careful and precise uses of language and when they were occurring. Most of these scholars were from academic departments of English or psychology. Their theory grew out of the difficulty in determining what double spies really meant when they communicated something. The semanticists wanted to train people to be very specific in sending and receiving words, to avoid the communication pitfalls such as stereotyping, over-generalization, euphemism, and others. Such word/symbols had led to the rise of demagogues like Hitler and Stalin in many countries prior to WWII. For instance, the general semanticists believed people needed to learn to be aware that the word/symbol appeals made by most advocates and propagandists were only **maps** or inner perceptions of places, persons, or things and not true **territories** or realities. A map is what exists in our heads, but a territory is what physically exists in the real world, as we shall see later in an extended metaphorical example and in future chapters. You might have an image of a certain place, experience, or event. That image is only a map, which probably flows from our media-saturated world of advocacy and propaganda. That place, experience, or event may not really or even closely resemble your map of it at all. In fact, if you were to visit the place or experience the event, you might not even recognize it. With the advent of such interactive media as virtual reality, Internet gaming and dating, the home shopping network, and telemarketing, receivers face an increased blurring of map and territory. This of course can lead to Internet deception like "phishing," which is the gathering of personal (financial) information or other scams and swindles. As a result, we need to heed the advice of the semanticists more than ever because much of the interactive world is virtual. Remember, interactive messages are only maps, not territories, even though we confront them daily. Considering them otherwise is bound to lead to misunderstandings and worse.

Take the case of stereotyping. Stereotypes are supposedly unreliable. No member of a class or group is exactly like any other member. To counter the miscommunication that can result from stereotyping all Muslims in the same way, for instance, we need to heed Korzypski's reminder that "the map is not the territory." In other words, our internal conceptions of other persons, ethnic groups, and ideas will differ widely from the actual persons, groups, things, and ideas. Korzypski and his colleagues recognized the difference between an event, object, or experience and any individual's conception of it. In their scheme, the word "map" equates to Langer's "conception," and the word "territory" equates to "objective reality" or close to Langer's "concept." Our faulty maps get expressed through the language we create to convey them, and they usually miscommunicate in some way. For the general semanticists, the real problems occur when people act as if their maps accurately describe the territory, thus turning the map into the territory. Following the bombing of the World Trade Center, many persons refused to fly on airplanes if persons of Middle Eastern abstraction or appearance were on board. In a way these stereotypes serve as maps or metaphors for certain special classes of people.

Korzybski believed that we all carry thousands of such maps or connotative metaphors around in our heads that represent nonexistent, incorrect, or false territories. We probably refer to them via the peripheral channel and react emotionally, not logically, to such persons or events. To demonstrate this concept for yourself, write down the name of a food you have never eaten, a place you have never been, and an experience you have never had. These words serve as maps for unknown territories. You probably think that fried brains would feel slimy and gooshy in your mouth. In reality, they have the texture of well-scrambled eggs and are frequently scrambled together with eggs. From that reality, we have invented the concept of having "fried" one's brains on drugs. What about your map for skydiving or for being a rock star? What about your maps for various ethnic groups? What about your map for places that you have only visited via the Internet? What about some occupation you are considering for your major?

In most cases, your maps will be very different from the territories as they really exist. Our mental, visual, and word maps present a real problem in communication, and especially in persuasion. Just as persuaders must discover our common ground of ideas so they can persuade us, they also must identify the maps we carry around in our heads. Then they must either play on those maps (using our misperceptions to their advantage) or try to get us to correct our faulty maps as Figure 5.7 illustrates. Only then can they persuade us to buy, vote, join, or change our behavior. Our faulty maps are frequently expressed through language and often by using metaphors. We create and use words to communicate and to build our maps, and then we often behave in accordance with what might be very faulty perceptions. We react to these words as if they are true representations of the territories we imagine. The semanticists called this a **signal response**, which is equivalent to my dog trying to hide from lightning whenever she experiences the sign or signal of thunder. Signal responses are emotionally triggered reactions to symbolic acts (including language use), and these responses play out usually in the peripheral channel of the ELM as if the act were actually being committed. Some time ago an example of the signal response occurred when an official in the Washington, DC city council and aide to the then African-American mayor was removed from the council

WAY UP NORTH, WHERE THE HUSKIES GO BY AL O

HEY EVANS, DID YOU EVER GET A RESPONSE FROM THE NORTHERN STAR ABOUT THE ARTICLE YOU SUBMITTED?

YEA, GRANT, I JUST GOT AN EMAIL FROM ONE OF THE EDITORS, "DEAR BOO"...

MY NAME AIN'T BOB...

HA HA HA! WHAT AN IDIOT, LOOK, HE SPELLED "BOB" WITH TWO "O"s

FIGURE 5.7 It is clear that Bob doesn't understand the map/territory distinction.

SOURCE: Used with permission of Al Ochsner.

because he used the word "niggardly." Now, the dictionary definition of the word is "unwilling to give, spend, or share … stingy, scanty, or meager" (*American Heritage Dictionary,* 1985). But because the word sounds similar to a racial epithet—the "**N**" word—it prompted a signal response among members of the council, even after a definition of the word was given. The semanticists were accurate about the power of the signal response (National Public Radio, 1999). Signal responses are also a prime objective of the propagandist.

The semanticists also wanted to train senders and receivers to be continually alert to the difference between signals and symbols so that they would not be misunderstood by receivers. In other words, they wanted to train not only responsible and ethical receivers but such senders as well. Semanticists also try to isolate and specify meaning in concrete terms. Let's examine a fairly inflammatory sentence that might be used by either an insensitive sender or an anti-student propagandist. Then we will try to defensively defuse it using the techniques of the semanticists and those of responsible receivers. Suppose the sender tells you, "College students are addicted to technology—especially texting—which some persons think is irresponsible to others, and as a result they judge you as antisocial, self-centered, and selfish." Your response will probably be negative, because of the connotations of some of the words used; "selfish," "anti-social," and "addicted," for sure, and maybe "irresponsible" as well. Semanticists would advise us to use what they call **extensional devices**, or techniques for neutralizing or defusing the emotional connotations that often accompany words by adding information that makes my meaning clear to you and others. One extensional device in my word/symbol use would be to identify the specific college students I have in mind. Semanticists call this **indexing**. In this case, the statement would change to something like, "College students, who have everything paid for by their parents, are addicted to technology—especially texting—which some persons think is irresponsible to others, and as a result, they judge you as anti-social, self-centered and selfish." That would calm some of you because it means that

you aren't irresponsible to everyone, but to certain special others, and that you aren't irresponsible in all ways. You probably know fellow students who have everything paid for, including lots of "extras" that you don't get while you work summers and part-time during the year to help defray costs. But the sender still would not be as clear as possible, according to the semanticists. They would further urge him or her to use an extensional device called **dating**, or letting you know the time frame of my judgment about college students. Using dating, they might say something like, "College students who have everything paid for by their parents and who were in college when texting and Facebook were introduced are addicted to technology—especially texting—which some persons think is irresponsible to others, and as a result, they judge you as anti-social, self-centered, and selfish." That might cool you down a little more because now there is only that special set of college students enrolled from 2000 to 2009, and that's not you; but there might still be some dissatisfaction with the statement.

Here is where the extensional device semanticists call **etc**. comes into play. This device is meant to indicate that we can never tell the whole story about any person, event, place, or thing. Using this device, senders might say, "College students who have everything paid for by their parents, and who were in college when texting and Facebook were introduced, are addicted to technology—especially texting—which some persons think is irresponsible to others, and as a result, they judge you as anti-social self-centered, and selfish, among other things." Of course, it's getting to be a long sentence and could be divided, but the important thing is that being anti-social, self-centered, and selfish aren't their only attributes. For example, they also might be "societally concerned about environmental issues," "worried about honesty," or any of a number of other positive attributes. This brings us to the final extensional device—**the use of quotation marks.**

The semanticists would advise using an extensional device called **quotation marks** whenever using word/symbols in a special way. They indicate

© Cengage Learning 2013

© Cengage Learning 2013

| BOX 5.4 | **Is the United States Too Pro-Israel—Our Propaganda?** | |

Enter the words "Israeli Propaganda" in any search engine and and peruse several of the items listed there. You will soon learn about how our country discriminates against citizens of Arab countries and propagandizes about Arab actions against

Israel are neglected in the world press. And the testimony comes from various experts including a U.S. congressman, *Newsweek,* and *Time* journalists, former *ambassadors* to these countries, former government officials, and others.

that the sender is using those flag words in their own way, which isn't necessarily your own way. For example, their use of the word "selfish" might relate to the students' unwillingness to help other students succeed in class. Or it could relate to their unwillingness to volunteer in the community or to do any of a number of other things that wouldn't necessarily match your meaning for the word "selfish." The sender's sentence might now read, "College students who have everything paid for by their parents, and who were in college when texting and Facebook were introduced, are addicted to technology—especially texting— which some persons think is irresponsible to others, and as a result, they judge you as 'anti-social,' 'self-centered,' and 'selfish,' among other things." Now you would probably probe for my meanings for the emotional words, or you might even agree with the sentence. Does Box 5.4 help you understand the extensional devices and the ideas of the semanticists? Why or why not?

Using extensional devices in decoding persuasion helps us make sure the maps in our heads more closely resemble the territory to which we refer. Persuaders need to design specific, concrete extensional messages, especially when using emotionally charged or abstract words for which there can be many meanings. More important, even if they don't, defensive persuadees need to consider whether they are being appealed to via the map or the territory. Abstract words such as "power," "democracy," "freedom," "morals," and "truth" are particularly vulnerable to misunderstanding and are probably best communicated using a familiar metaphor. Unethical persuaders and propagandists often intentionally use abstract or emotionally

charged language to achieve their purposes. It is our task to remember the map/territory distinction and to use extensional devices as we attend to symbols. We must remember that receivers also have "response-ability" or the ability to respond, as noted earlier in Chapter 2 and elsewhere. That might mean asking probing questions of the persuader or of oneself when exact meaning is unclear.

BURKE'S APPROACH
TO LANGUAGE USE

Perhaps no language theorist or critic wrote as many treatises in as wide a variety of fields or with as broad a knowledge of human symbolic behavior as Kenneth Burke. Recall that we first met him in Chapter 1, and that he is associated with many narrative theories, which we have now encountered several times. He focused on language or word/symbols as they are used to persuade people to action. He defined persuasion as "the use of language as a symbolic means of inducing cooperation in beings that by nature respond to symbols," (Burke, 1970, p. 43). This active cooperation is induced by what he termed **identification**, a concept similar to Aristotle's "common ground" and our use of "co-creation," as noted in Chapter 1. According to Burke, identification develops through the linguistic sharing of what he called **sub-stances**.

He divided that word/symbol into its prefix *sub,* meaning "beneath," and *stances,* which refers to one's physical, emotional, experiential, and philosophical "grounding" or "places" on which to stand or to take a stand. In other words, identification rests on the beliefs, values, experiences, and views of the self that we share with others, or with our groundings or our basic and first principles. Burke noted that these sub-stances or "places" emerge in the word/symbols we use to define things, persons, and issues. Critical receivers of persuasion need to pay particular attention to the words, images, and metaphors that persuaders use to create (or undermine) identification. Our self-concepts are made up of various kinds of symbolic and real possessions, including physical things (clothing, cars, and books), experiential things (work, activities, and recreations), emotions, and philosophical possessions (beliefs, attitudes, values), which we need to examine and defend. Identification with others develops to the degree that we symbolically share these possessions. In other words, we identify with persons who articulate a similar view of life; who enjoy the same kinds of activities; who have similar physical possessions, lifestyles, beliefs, attitudes; and who have similar emotional responses to events. For example, gun owners are generally staunch supporters of the Second Amendment and probably belong to the NRA. If we identify with persuaders, we naturally tend to believe what they say and probably follow their advice. Thus, the job of persuaders is to call attention to those sub-stances or basic beliefs and

experiences that they share with receivers. As a result, conservative politicians will try to remind us that they are like us ("of the people") and own guns too, advertisers will depict brand users as like us—the target market. The receivers' job, in turn, is to critically and defensively examine these sub-stances to see whether they truly are shared values and beliefs or whether the persuader merely makes them appear to be shared. We probably will need to think about these things in the central path of the ELM examining their logic, and the evidence used to support them. Defensive persuadees need to decode persuaders' messages for their authenticity, and determine whether the messages reflect or resonate with persuaders' real beliefs and values or are merely convenient metaphorical concoctions. Frequently, these artistic creations rely on the persuader's skill with language. Let's explore the concept of sub-stance further (see Box 5.5).

To Burke, most persuasive attempts to describe our "essential parts," are always revealing. All words have emotional shadings and reveal the various degrees of our feelings, attitudes, values, and judgments. For example, take the word "manipulate." It carries a lot of potentially negative meanings, although its denotation is quite benign. Wikipedia defines it as social influence involved with changing people's minds—not too terrible? But then Wikipedia is not always a good source, is it? Yet some of its links for the words include "abuse, puppeteer,

---

BOX 5.5   Language and Cultural Diversity

Did you know that only four countries in all of Latin America have populations greater than the Latino population of the United States, which is now about 22.5 million? Or did you know that there are more Asians in the United States than there are in Cambodia, Laos, Hong Kong, and Singapore combined? Or did you know that at some point in this century, Latinos will outnumber non-Latinos? These are just a few of the many facts mentioned by Nido R. Qubein. He is an internationally known consultant, award-winning speaker, president of High Point University, and he sits on the boards of several Fortune 500 companies. He is chairman of a

national public relations firm, Business Life Inc., and CEO of the Great Harvest Bread Company. He came to the United States as a teenager, with no contacts, no English language skills, and less than $50 to his name. He travels the globe and urges his audiences to remember that "people from different backgrounds send and receive messages through cultural filters," and that the same words, facial expressions, and gestures have different meanings depending on one's cultural heritage. You may want to access his home page at Weblink 5.8. There you can listen to him speak, get samples of his video and audio tapes, and get free articles written by him.

BOX 5.6 **Is Persuasion Bad: Changing People with Word/Symbols**

"If you give people a gun, they will kill someone." What's wrong with this conditional premise? (Hint: See Chapter 8 on logical premises.) Is it true about teaching people to persuade with clever language? Explore the Internet and learn more about this quandary.

propaganda, mind control, fraud, and brainwashing" which seem to capture the word's meaning pretty well. Not too harmless, eh? Check out the words "emotional manipulation" in any search engine and you will discover how terribly harmful manipulation can be. Check out the word symbols in a "real" dictionary like the *American Heritage College Dictionary*. Examining persuasive language not only can tell us about ourselves but it can also tell us such things as which sources to believe and which to check and many things about the persuaders who solicit our interest, support, and commitment (see Box 5.6).

Burke further suggested that symbolic activities like the use of word/symbols inevitably cause people to have feelings of guilt. From the beginning, language automatically led to rule making and moralizing—in fact from infancy on we learned the meaning of "No!" Because we all break the rules or don't measure up to moral standards at some time, we experience some degree of guilt. Burke argued that all human cultures exhibit patterns that help explain guilt, and the development of language in each of us is foremost. For example, the word "puppy" is clearly not an actual puppy, so word/symbols that name what something is, inherently lead to the idea of what something is not—**the negative**. The negative then leads to sets of "thou shall nots," whether supernatural, parental, spousal, or societal. Inevitably, we fail to obey some of these negatives and again experience shame and guilt. "No" is one of the first things we learn as children, and we realize that it means we just displeased someone. We hear "No, no, no," over and over, and then we begin to use it ourselves. It gives us power, and we go about

testing the extent of that power during the "terrible twos" especially. So some language can induce feelings of guilt in the audience, which becomes a powerful motivator. For example, persons who have been abused frequently feel guilt or shame for such things as being raped or beaten. Why? Probably because the word "SHAME" or some variant (e.g., ashamed, mortified, humiliated, sorry, disgraced, embarrassed, etc.) is being used to describe them/us or their/our behavior. Most likely, we first hear of shame from our parents, who tell us that we should feel it when we do something that displeases them. This powerful word/symbol—shame!—can then be tied to other issues like the feelings we might have at being tricked or fooled by terrorists, politicians, or a friend/lover. Whenever we hear persuasion that uses some variation of "shame," we need to listen carefully because someone is probably laying blame on us, and it is probably unjustified; further, it probably describes what the persuader feels in regard to the issue. This isn't to say we never truly do wrong—just that we all have blame laid on us, and it is a great motivator, hence a powerful persuader.

The second behavioral pattern that contributes to guilt relies on the principle of hierarchy, or "pecking order." It happens in all societies and groups, and it leads to either jealousy of others or to competition with them. We rarely (perhaps never) reach the top of the pecking order and we feel guilty about that as well. A third source of guilt is our innate need to achieve perfection. Unfortunately, we all fall short of our own goals and then feel inadequate and ashamed for not doing our best. This shame makes us feel guilty about not living up to our own or others' expectations. The persuader tells us that we could have done better if only we had really tried instead of only giving a half-hearted effort, or if we used the brand or voted for the right candidate. How do we rid ourselves of this shame and resulting guilt? In most religions, guilt is purged symbolically—we offer up a sacrifice or engage in self-inflicted suffering, confession, penance, or by trying to "make up for it." In everyday life we may offer up a scapegoat, laying the blame on him/her or it/them. But the handiest and most flexible, creative, artistic, and universal means to whip guilt is through language. We usually try to get rid of guilt by talking about it—in prayer, or to a priest, to ourselves, to a counselor or authority figure, or to someone with whom we identify. Consider how frequently persuaders offer us symbolic ways to alleviate our guilt. The parents who feel guilty about being absentee after school is out can take their family on a week's vacation to Disney World. The imperfect child tries to do better at school by using the Internet and spending more time studying and doing extra credit assignments, or by watching less TV or playing fewer video games. The weak-willed nation can purge the national guilt by following the new "tough and demanding" leader as Germans did with Hitler and which Americans have done repeatedly in this century.

In summary, persuasion via identification works because we all share sub-stances and because we all experience guilt. In processing persuasion, try to recognize that persuaders create identification by referring to shared sub-stances—preferred beliefs, lifestyles, and values. They motivate us by appealing to our internal and inevitable feelings of inadequacy, shame, or guilt. Process the substance of and evidence for their arguments, especially when you receive one of those blame-laying word/symbols via an SNM, which is likely to feel more personal than any mass media can make you feel. Examine the word/symbols and images in advertisements, sermons, political appeals, and other messages, reminding yourself of the strategies being used to create identification and also feelings of imperfection, shame, and guilt.

THE SEMIOTIC APPROACH TO LANGUAGE USE

Semiotics is another field concerned with the generation and conveyance of meaning (see Figure 5.8). A number of scholars are associated with this "science" of meaning. These semiologists

FIGURE 5.8 Bob doesn't get the meaning of the word "euphemize."

SOURCE: Used with permission of Al Ochsner.

apply the tools of linguistics to a wide variety of texts—verbal and nonverbal. Linguists usually study meaning as it occurs in word/symbols but they also see meaning in art, architecture, civil and private events, and so on. Almost anything can be a "text" that has one or more meanings; semioticians talk about the "meaning" of a doctor's office, a meal, a TV program, a circus, or any other verbal or nonverbal symbolic event. They also try to describe the underlying meaning in any of these, which they call the "subtext" of any symbolic act. For example, what is the subtext for "America's Next Top Model"? Some things are obvious. The importance of being slim and beautiful is clear, but what about the probable ethnicity of the next top model? It used to be nearly always Caucasian, but what is the expected body type? It seems to me that they all need to visit an all-you-can-eat buffet for their morning, noon, and evening meals and to load their plates. What are their family values? Their political leanings? Who knows (because they don't follow politics)? These and other "subtexts" may be there in the program, but probably are not so clearly.

According to semiotic theory, all texts convey meaning through **signs** or **signifiers**. A signifier in a restaurant could be the presence or absence of a hostess. It signifies that either we are to wait to be shown to our table or that we can select our own in the case of the absent hostess. **Signifieds** are the things (events, rules, etc.) to which the signifiers refer. These signifiers interact with one another in meaningful and sophisticated, but not obvious, relationships, or sign systems, which make up the "language," or "code," of the text. What are the signifiers in "America's Next Top Model"? Probably the styles of clothing, the body shapes of the contestants, the sponsors of the program, and the fact that there is racial diversity amongst the "winners" in the show. Certainly there will be no obese contestants (see Figure 5.9). Will there be any with disabilities? Will they be college educated?

These codes (and others like them from any text—celebrity behavior, sports, films, political events) can be inferred from the text's signs, codes, and signifiers. For example, consider your classroom as a text having its own signifiers and signifieds—some linguistic and some visual, some logical and some emotional. The room usually has an institutional "meaning" signified by the type of walls, lighting, boards, and the cork and metal strip above the black, green, and white boards. Blackboards and plaster walls usually signify that the building is an old one. Green or white boards and cinder block walls signify a newer building. The kinds of student desks (with or without arms), whether they are made of wood or artificial material, the arrangement of the room (e.g., desks in rows vs. groups), and the physical objects in the room (an overhead vs. a video projector) are all signifiers that tell us about what to expect when entering this "text." There may be a clock on the wall, signifying that time is important here, and it may be in view of the students or only to someone facing the back of the room (usually the teacher). Consider several of the codes embedded in various texts. For example, a simple code is the use of black and white hats in old cowboy movies to indicate the good guys and the bad guys. Pages being blown off a calendar in a movie signify the passage of time, and there are other examples. In a way these codes are quite similar to metaphors for purposes of communicating meaning.

In a semiotic approach to the study of meaning, we try to read each message from several perspectives: (1) the word/symbols that are or are not spoken, (2) the context in or from which they are spoken, (3) the actions that are or are not taken, are or are not approved of, and (4) the other signifiers in the message—visuals, colors, costumes, tone of voice, music, background settings, furnishings, and many other "layers" upon layers of meaning that might be there. Examples include facial expressions, models, their body posture, and many others. Enter the words "semiotic analysis" into a search engine and you will find many varied and fascinating examples of the analysis of meaning there as well as links that will provide material for an interesting term paper on the peripheral path, subliminal, and/or semiotic cues in persuasion.

FIGURE 5.9 America's Next Top Model cast members. In all likelihood, the signs in the program flow from our 24/7, media-saturated, advocacy- or propaganda-filled world, and also reflect a multicultural world and value system.

SOURCE: AP Photo/Jennifer Graylock

More and more marketing and advertising research is being conducted from a semiological approach, according to Curt Suplee (1987) of the *Washington Post,* who notes: "When advertising is great advertising, it fastens on the myths, signs, and symbols of our common experience and becomes, quite literally, a benefit of the product… As a result of great advertising, food tastes better, clothes feel snugger, cars ride smoother. The stuff of semiotics becomes the magic of advertising." For many other examples see Weblink 5.9. Semiotics also can help us understand where a persuader is coming from and what his or her agenda might be. What is the semiotic meaning of the following letter sent to the chair of my department?

Dear Professor Jones,

I am interested in directives as to how one may proficiency out of the speech requirement. Having been advised to seek counsel from you *specifically*—I sincerely hope you will not be displeased with my enthusiasm by asking this indulgence. There is a basis for my pursuing this inquisition as I am an adept speaker with substantiating merits. I will be overburdened with more difficult courses this fall—at least they will be concomitant with my educational objectives in the fields of Fine Arts and Languages. It would be a ludicrous exercise in futility to be mired in an unfecund speech course when I have already distinguished myself in that arena. I maintained an "*A*" average in an elite *advanced* speech course in High School. I am quite noted for my bursts of oratory and my verbal dexterity in the public "reality"—quite a different platform than the pseudo realism of the college environs. There is a small matter of

BOX 5.7   **An Interactive Short Course on Semiotics**

Go to Weblink 5.10, if you want to get an "A" on an extra credit paper in this course and enjoy an interestingly illustrated short course on the terms and methods of semiotics that show us a lot about advertising. Use the lessons and terms you learn there to create a well-written semiological analysis of some type of advertising such as fashion, beer, sports, home furnishings, or cosmetics. Be sure to follow the entire short course through all of the "continue" links.

age—I shall be twenty-two this fall. I am four years older than the average college freshman. I am afraid that I would dissipate with boredom, if confined with a bunch of teenagers. Surely you can advise something that would be a more palatable alternative?

Yours sincerely,

P.S. Please do not misconstrue this *inquiry* as the enterprise of an arrogant student, but one who will be so immersed in serious intellectual pursuits that the *speech* requirement will be too nonsensical and burdensome.

If ever a student needed to learn about communication, it was this individual. But what does the language usage here tell you about the writer of the letter? Semiotic analysis tells us much. She (yes, it's a female author) uses 64-dollar words—perhaps a code for insecurity—but she seems unsure about her choice of words, as shown by using italics for certain high falutin' words, which indicates that she has her own special meaning for them. She also misuses some words. For example, she says that she is pursuing an *inquisition* when she means an *inquiry*. An inquisition is a tribunal for suppressing religious heresy. She says she has *substantiating merits* when she probably means that she has *substantial reasons* for being excused from the course. She seems uncertain about what she means as she italicizes, capitalizes

and puts words in quotes as if they have a special meaning for her. These and other signifiers add up to the semiotic meaning of the letter, which is that the author is insecure and hopes to impress the recipient of the letter.

So the study of semiotics and its tools, terms, and methods is another tool of language that can help alert us as receivers to the persuasion that is targeted at us (see Box 5.7). Like the earlier theories discussed above, it can also be used to craft the language we use in trying to persuade others. Let us now take a brief look at one of the most powerful and artful of all language devices used in persuasion—the metaphor.

LANGUAGE, METAPHORS, AND MEANING

Most language theorists agree that of all the figures of speech, the **metaphor** is the most powerful, most persuasive, most memorable, and most likely to require truly artistic language creativity. The Merriam-Webster online dictionary defines metaphor as "... a word or phrase literally denoting one kind of object or idea is used in place of another to suggest a likeness... (as in drowning in money)."

Literary critic I.A. Richards long ago distinguished between two key parts of any metaphor—the **tenor** or subject of the metaphor (peace-loving) and the **vehicle** (doves carrying olive branches) or the means of embodiment or transmission of meaning (from the Latin "vehere" meaning "to carry"). Since then, many other language theorists and critics have used his system. For example, take the experience of drowning in money in the metaphor cited above by the online dictionary. Drowning serves as the vehicle for the tenor or subject/idea of having an overwhelming abundance of money. Another way to put it is that the tenor is equal to the vehicle. In the words of the semanticist, they are map and territory. In a way, a metaphor is a small sentence. In the example "drowning in money," the metaphor states that "an overabundance of money is as fearsome as drowning—it makes on feel trapped and useless." The metaphor creates a new image or concept by tying the familiar or the subject (tenor) to a less familiar image (vehicle) and herein lies its creativity, its persuasiveness, and in semiotic terms, its code(s) or subtext(s).

A good and persuasive metaphor is one in which the vehicle can be readily and repeatedly "mapped" or traced back to the tenor, and preferably on several dimensions. In the example above, the vehicle (drowning) maps back to the tenor (an overabundance of money) in several ways. First, the sensation of drowning is related to being surrounded by the threat of water. Another dimension of drowning is a feeling of helplessness and an inability to escape the threat. Third, drowning is probably a lonely experience where one feels that only he or she can remedy the situation. Finally, experiencing drowning or near drowning probably feels like one is pursued by the water. Now, can we determine if any or all of these dimensions "maps" back to the tenor (an overabundance of money)? If we are to believe the stories of persons who say they are cursed by too much money, (these dimensions of feeling surrounded by the overabundance; feeling helpless to divest oneself from it; cursed or pursued by it; and reliant only on the self to escape the curse), then indeed the vehicle "maps" back to the tenor quite well and there

are several such maps. (See Weblink 5.11 and explore the "metaphor" link for further illumination.) Clearly most of us haven't experienced near drowning, so while the repeated mapping is good, a broad familiarity with the vehicle doesn't exist. That's why the most effective and persuasive metaphors are broadly familiar to the audience as well as being repeatedly "mapped" to the tenor on several dimensions. In this way metaphors are related to the semiotic terms "signified" and "signifier," or the terms "concept" and "conception" discussed earlier.

In their broadest level of familiarity, metaphors can be what are called "archetypal," which means they have universal and cross-cultural themes. Many persons, at different times in history and faced with differing circumstances, can relate to and are familiar with these themes. Some examples are the dark/light, hot/cold, quest/journey, sailing/navigating, water/fertility, seedtime/harvest, and the life/death families, to mention only a few. You can see that these experiences are shared by large numbers of persons from diverse backgrounds and cultures. In other words, they have broad familiarity or applicability. As a result, they provide ideal places in which to design or create persuasive metaphors and an important place to see how they might be effective in persuading you and others. (See Weblink 5.12 for further explanation and definitions of a number of other speech terms related to eloquence and persuasiveness.) Let's identify one of many archetypal families that could be put to use in persuasion. Remember that the key to determining the persuasiveness of metaphors is to identify and isolate the tenor(s) and vehicle(s), then to see how broadly familiar they are to the audience(s), and finally to see how many ways the vehicle(s) can be "mapped" back to the tenor(s). For example, take the seedtime/harvest family and its relation to our election cycles wherein the spring primary season leads to the autumnal general election. Spring is a time of testing candidates so they can be "winnowed" or thinned out to the two (or more if there are independents) "best" presidential and vice presidential candidates for the general election in November. A primary candidate might use this invented metaphor.

It is now spring and we are testing the seeds of our platform so that we will reap a full harvest and the best fruits of our labors. Some seeds will fall by the wayside to be consumed by the birds of the air and the beasts of the field. Others fall on parched land and will wither and die. Some fall among brambles and will be choked with cares and pleasures. Happily, some will fall on good ground and take root and will yield the accomplishments of this administration and the first fruits of the "New Democracy," which will be the theme of the Larson administration—let us plant now so that we can bring the harvest in!

The applicability of this metaphor (that the election process is both seedtime and harvest) is clearly broad and understood by persons of many backgrounds, cultures, and times. And to an American audience also familiar with biblical references, it rings of the parable of the sower and his seed from the *New Testament*. Does the vehicle (planting and harvest) connect in people's minds with the tenor (the election process)? Anyone who has planted a garden (and many who have only experienced that act vicariously) will map back to the reference to spring as planting time and will also map to the fact that not all sowed seeds (or tested ideas or proposals as in "seeds of thought") will develop to be fully productive and ultimately harvested. So here are at least three "map/territory" connections. Another "map" from the vehicle (planting/harvest) to the tenor (elections) is the seed that is either eaten (or stolen by the other candidates) or disregarded (ignored by the electorate). Yet another "map" flowing from the vehicle is the seed that is overshadowed by other problems (cares and pleasures of the day). And finally the seed that takes root on good ground (ideas that are favored by the electorate and the press) maps back to tenor to become the best (or the first fruits) potential

accomplishments leading to a "New Democracy" or the campaign theme followed by the action metaphor of bringing in the autumnal harvest. In other words, this should be a highly effective and widely accepted metaphor for the election campaign—clearly understood and widely resonated with by the voter.

And metaphors can be visual as well as verbal. For example, during the 1936 Olympic Games in Berlin, Germany, Hitler wished to dramatically and metaphorically express the vision/version of his administration and country. He tried to combine two powerful nonverbal metaphors to express the overall metaphors of "Germany is a peaceful nation" and "German is a powerful nation." He used the release of 20,000 doves in the opening ceremonies for the peaceful metaphor, and at the same time he had cannons fired to express the "powerful" metaphor. Unfortunately the "vehicles" of each visual/auditory metaphor conflicted. The result was that the doves became nervous and frightened by the "power" metaphor of cannons being fired and "crapped" on the athletes and audience—an unfortunate visual, "sensual," and auditory metaphor for Mr. Hitler's propaganda—probably processed in both channels of the ELM. (Hildebrand, 2010, p. 32).

Literary critic I.A. Richards, as noted above, long ago distinguished between two key parts of any metaphor—the tenor (or subject of the metaphor—peace-loving and powerful Germany) and the vehicle (doves and cannons) or the means of embodiment or transmission of meaning (see Figure 5.10). However, in this case the metaphor "backfired" (excuse the pun). This is a danger with all metaphors—they can be used against you. So Hitler's visual and auditory metaphor—"Germany is peace seeking and yet powerful"—due to the doves becoming nervous. It might now be stated that "Germany is nervous, and you can scare the crap out of it with a show of power." This would have been a good lesson for many of the world diplomats of the next four

Tenor	Vehicle	Dimensions
Love	Island	Separated, idyllic
Time	Money	Trade, interchange
House	Home	Safety, familiarity
To persuade	To plant	To put in, to nuture
Opportunity	A thing	Can be examined, grasped
Anger	Storm	Energy, danger
New	Raw	Unchanged, original
Superiority	Above	Position of power

FIGURE 5.10　This chart shows how the vehicle creates new meaning when paired with the tenor. Here you can see a few ways that the tenor and vehicle in a metaphor create a new meaning composed of both elements. Can the new meanings be "mapped" back to the tenor?

SOURCE: www.changingminds.org/techniques/language.

years. They repeatedly appeased Hitler's demands instead of demonstrating a show of power.

What are some of the other archetypal metaphors that we might encounter as responsible receivers, and how can we analyze them as well as the other uses of language discussed above?

Try to create a few metaphors that might help explain some current event or issue. The chart in Figure 5.10 will give you a few ideas to start (see Weblink 5.13). The above-noted website also categorizes some interesting varieties of metaphors that may give you more ways to understand and create metaphors of your own. For example, take the physical senses, as in "the meeting ended on a sour note," which uses the senses of taste and hearing (as in music), or the sense of smell as in "he reeks of an ashtray." Or take the sense of touch as in "hold onto that thought," "let's put on the squeeze," or "he's a pain in the neck." Recently, the idea of building a huge fence along both the Mexican and Canadian borders was proposed as a means of controlling the huge influx of illegal aliens. While fishing in the Boundary Waters, my grandson wanted to know if we were illegal aliens when we crossed the international boundary running down the middle of the lake. We were in our canoe. A metaphor to debunk the fence proposal might be something like, "Canoes jump the Canadian border daily—a few strokes and you're over the 'fence.'" And there are other analytical tools to get at the meaning of some metaphors or to create some when you are the persuader, and other uses and techniques of using word/symbols.

In Chapter 6 we will explore some of them and devise specific tools of analysis that have been developed from the theories and concepts discussed here.

REVIEW AND CONCLUSION

By now, you probably have deeper appreciation for human symbol making, use, and misuse, and for the power of language as a tool of persuasion—especially the English language. You might realize how much meaning you can uncover when you critically analyze the symbols used in persuasion. It takes time and effort to decode discursive and presentational persuasion, to locate the meanings being used to create a state of identification, to determine the difference between the map and the territory, and to learn the many semantic and semiotic codes operating in various kinds of texts as well as the powerful effects of metaphors. To become a responsible persuadee, you need tools to assist you in analyzing the many persuasive messages and language techniques targeted at you. Knowledge of these variables will help you when trying to persuade others as well. Chapter 6 focuses on some tools for doing this.

KEY TERMS

After reading this chapter, you should be able to identify, explain, and give an example of the following key terms or concepts:

symbols	presentational meaning	dating	signs
concepts	semanticists	etc.	signifiers
conceptions	maps	quotation marks	signifieds
signification	territories	identification	metaphor
denotation	signal response	sub-stances	tenor
connotation	extensional devices	the negative	vehicle
discursive symbols	indexing	semiotics	

APPLICATION OF ETHICS

Here is the situation: An interpreter arrives a few minutes before a court of law is called to order. He wants to speak to the defendant, who is a non-English speaker, to determine if using Spanish instead of English will be acceptable. The defendant lets the interpreter know that Spanish is a second language for him (his first language is an indigenous dialect), but that he understands the interpreter and proceeding in Spanish is acceptable. The interpreter has three options: (1) tell the judge of the situation and that Spanish interpretation is acceptable to the defendant; (2) say nothing and proceed with the interpretation in Spanish since the defendant has said it is okay with him; or (3) inform the defendant's attorney and let him decide how to proceed. Which option seems most ethical to you? Does the interpreter have any ethical obligation to inform the judge? Is he ethically obliged to say anything?

QUESTIONS FOR FURTHER THOUGHT

1. Why is symbol making such a powerful human activity? Give several examples of how symbols create high involvement in people. Are symbols logical or emotional? Are they processed centrally or peripherally?

2. What is meant by Burke's phrase "symbol misusing"? Give some examples of the misuse of symbols. Is propaganda a misuse?

3. Why is the English language so powerful?

4. Why is a red stoplight a sign to a leader dog, and how is that "meaning" different from the words "red stoplight" or "dangerous cross-traffic"?

5. What did Suzanne Langer mean when she said that symbols are the "vehicles for the conception of objects"?

6. What is the difference between signification, denotation, and connotation?

7. What is the difference between a presentational and a discursive symbol?

8. What is the difference between a map and a territory, according to the general semanticists? Give an example of one of your food maps. One of your geographic maps? One of your experience maps?

9. When then-President Bill Clinton said that he had never had "sexual relations" with "that woman" (he'd had fellatio with intern Monica Lewinsky, it was later learned), was this an ethical use of language? Why or why not?

10. What is a signal response? Give several examples.

11. What are the extensional devices recommended by general semanticists? What purpose do these devices serve? Give examples.

12. What did Kenneth Burke mean by "identification"? By "sub-stance"? By the "need for hierarchy"? By "guilt"? How do these concepts explain why language is so important in persuasion and in living life?

13. What is the difference between a signifier and a signified? What is a code? Give examples of simple codes from the worlds of sports, politics, and/or advertising.

14. What is a metaphor and why is it likely to be persuasive? What are its parts?

15. What is the tenor in a metaphor? What is the vehicle? What is "mapping" back?

16. Is it ethical for advertisers to use guilt to get us to buy? Why or why not? Give some examples.

6

Tools for Analyzing Language and Other Persuasive Symbols

LEARNING GOALS

After reading this chapter, you should be able to:

1. Identify the three dimensions of language focused on in this chapter and give examples of each that you have found or invented.

2. Discuss the powers of symbolic expression in persuasion.

3. Give examples of tools of analysis for each of the dimensions of language.

4. Explain the pentad and give examples of each term in contemporary persuasion.

5. Explain and give examples of god, devil, and charismatic terms in contemporary persuasion.

6. Explain and give examples of archetypal metaphors being used in contemporary persuasion.

7. Explain the difference between the pragmatic and unifying styles and give examples of each from contemporary persuasion.

8. Explain and identify metaphors, archetypal metaphors, the tenor and vehicle, and "mapping" of the various vehicles back to their tenors.

9. Explain semiotics and discuss how texts and codes work. Explain an "open" text and how it relates to the process of co-creation as key to the definition of persuasion given in Chapter 1.

Now that you have some perspective on the making, use, and misuse of symbols, and an appreciation for the power of **language** (and the English language in particular), let's consider several ways to analyze both verbal and nonverbal persuasive symbols. Such analysis helps us to reject misguided, fallacious, and deceptive messages. We mentioned several recent examples, such as the nonexistent "WMD" in Iraq, the lies of CEOs and the corrupt practices of their corporations who bankrupted their companies while getting rich in the process, and the official rejection of global warming by the highest officials in the land until it was almost too late. All of these used persuasive language, and we'll face many more examples in the future, so receivers need to learn about language use and to use tools of language analysis that can uncover deceptive persuasion. In more modern terms, receivers need to acquire the tools of deconstruction in order to uncover potentially misleading and harmful persuasion.

The cube in Figure 6.1 represents three of the many dimensions of language. They are (1) the **semantic dimension** (the meanings for a word), (2) the **functional dimension** (the jobs that words can do, such as naming), and (3) the **thematic dimension** (the feel and texture of words like "swoosh" or metaphors like "the whole nine yards" that are probably processed in the peripheral channel of the ELM). Following our consideration of these dimensions, you will find a discussion of several tools useful in analyzing each dimension and several examples of such analysis. Notice that the cube consists of many smaller cubes, each representing a word or set of words having its own unique semantic, functional, and thematic dimensions. Now consider this line of ad copy: "Sudden Tan from Coppertone Tans on Touch for a Tan That Lasts for Days." On the functional dimension, the words "Sudden Tan" name a product. Semantically, much more is suggested. The word "sudden" describes an almost instantaneous tan, and, indeed, the product dyes skin "tan" on contact. The ad's headline—"Got a Minute? Get a Tan"—is superimposed over before-and-after photos of an attractive blonde who has presumably been dyed tan. On a thematic level, the words do even more. The word "sudden" sounds and feels like the word "sun," so the brand name sounds like the word "suntan" and notice the repetition of the consonant sounds of "s" and "t" that are central to the word "suntan," which is the benefit promised by the brand.

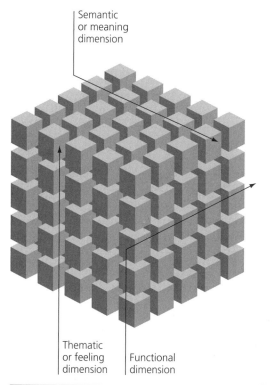

Semantic or meaning dimension

Thematic or feeling dimension

Functional dimension

FIGURE 6.1   This figure shows three of the many dimensions of language that are at work when persuadees decode or deconstruct the many persuasive messages of our 24/7 and media-saturated world.

SOURCE: © Cengage Learning 2013.

Consider these examples of thematic language use.

- The "Kero-Sun" heater burns kerosene and warms your house like the sun.

- Have a "Soup-erb Supper" with a package of Hamburger Helper's beef-vegetable soup.

- Try "My Mom's Meatloaf Mix—Meat Loaf that Tastes Like Home."

- Presto named its popcorn popper "The Big Poppa," which sounds like popcorn being popped.

- Satin Cigarettes are so Smooth and Silky.

Each example demonstrates one or more of the three dimensions of language depicted in the cube

above—the functional dimension, the semantic dimension, and the thematic dimension. Let us explore these dimensions more fully.

THE FUNCTIONAL DIMENSION: WHAT DO THE WORDS DO?

Words can do many things. They can motivate action, identify causes and effects, and lay or deflect blame. During a trial in which an abortionist and the woman who had the abortion faced charges of manslaughter, language functioned in several ways. The defense referred to attempts to abort the fetus early in the pregnancy (months before the trial), by saying, "After two unsuccessful attempts...." The prosecutor used active verbs and pronouns, saying, "They tried twice...they were unsuccessful." This language helped to lay blame on the woman and the doctor. In one case, the function of the words blunted the accusation because the unsuccessful attempts weren't anyone's fault. In the other, it focused blame on both the woman and the doctor, which was the prosecution's aim.

The functional dimension also has powerful potential to simply shift our focus (Andrews, 1984). Take, for example, the function of defining, which can "frame" or set the perspective for the persuasive appeal. As communication scholar Dan Hahn (1998) observes, "Definitions are like blinders on a horse: They focus attention on some aspects while blinding us to others" (p. 53). For example, consider the quarantining of trade to a country to stop shipping into and out of its ports, such as we did in the past and probably will do in the future. You could call such an action a "blockade," which (in the eyes of the world) is considered an act of war. Now, call the actions "sanctions." That's what the United States did when it outlawed trade by American companies with Iran, Iraq, and North Korea, portraying these nations as part of an "axis of evil" that had sinister worldwide motives. These word choices (i.e., "sanctions" and "axis of evil") served at least three functions. First, they signaled to the three nations, and others that objected to the sanctions, that the United States wasn't necessarily interested in all-out war (though we ultimately did invade Iraq with unsuccessful and even damaging results). Second, they gave a justification for the resulting hardships being endured by the populace of the three countries. Finally, they vilified the three nations as "outlaws" in the world community. So the words served several functions—reassuring world fears, placing and deflecting blame, and the building of a negative image for the three nations. In another example, Hahn points out the meanings associated with the label "middle class." For some, the term means those earning between $20,000 and $70,000 per year (pp. 61–62). In reality, 40 percent of persons making less than $20,000 per year call themselves middle class and one third of those making $150,000 in a year also call themselves middle class. (See Weblink 6.1.) (You can access this and all of the other Chapter 6 weblinks through your companion website for *Persuasion,* Chapter 6 resources.) To others "middle class" means a lifestyle that includes a house, two late model cars, dinner prepared at home, and membership in the local YMCA. But for others it would include new luxury sedan, membership in a golf club, a summer cottage, a speed boat, frequent restaurant meals, and a winter cruise. So an important dimension of persuasive language is the functions, tasks, or jobs that the words perform, and the reality of the issues or facts remains fluid.

Communication researcher Robert Cialdini (2008) observes that some language functions to compensate for our personal feelings of insecurity or low self-worth. He notes that "the persistent name dropper" is a classic example (p. 173); name droppers bolster their own self-esteem by knowing important personalities. So bolstering is another function of words. Sometimes, words create fear that can be very persuasive. Consider how the United States responded to the fear appeals associated with terrorism—it formed an entirely new cabinet-level agency for "Homeland Security" to fight terror, implement cooperation between formerly independent intelligence agencies, and allocate funds to very small towns where terrorism is not likely. For example, there are several Homeland Security checkpoints along lakes along the wilderness Gunflint Trail in Northern Minnesota, where there are no clear demarcation lines of the Canada border between United States and Canada, as such lines frequently lie in the middle of huge lakes. There is only one road out of the wilderness reserve. No one who lives in the area has ever seen a Homeland Security agent at any of the checkpoints. So while the name of the agency makes us feel secure, it does nothing to step illegal aliens or terrorists from entering the United States; in fact, someone who was planning terrorist bombings in California entered the United States illegally across the Canadian/U.S. border (See Weblink 6.2). In another successful example, a "Got Milk?" ad claimed: "One in five osteoporosis victims is male. Luckily, fat free milk has the calcium bones need to beat it." The words create fear in the male reader who uses this new knowledge to change his behavior. So naming potential problems interacts with the reader and prompts fear and a motivation to take action—drink more milk. Figure 6.2 is an example of a nuclear propaganda poster that uses fear appeals.

Cialdini (2008) identifies several other functions that language can perform. These include the function of creating deference or blind obedience to authority. Cialdini says that the use of titles can also function to convey authority. Today, we hire an "administrative assistant" not a "secretary," and the new name functions to build the employee's self-worth. Another function Cialdini identifies is the power of language to create "the scarcity effect." Consider the phrases "Price Good Only While Supplies Last!" or "Act Now! Only a Few Left." These phrases function to convince the persuadee that the product is in short supply. This creates a sense of urgency and prompts the prospect to take action. So language has a functional dimension that refers to the number of the jobs or functions language can perform while persuasion is going on, and it has a second dimension dealing the meaning (s) of words. Consider a less benign example, the shooting of Democratic Congresswoman Gabrielle Giffords and 18 others, and of whom five were killed, including a nine-year-old girl. Former

FIGURE 6.2

Why should this be more fearful after the Japanese nuclear disaster?

SOURCE: © K.J. Historical/CORBIS.

governor of Alaska and vice presidential candidate, Sarah Palin, had a map posted on her website which "targeted" the Congresswoman's district in the "crosshairs" of a sniper rifle and used the words "bull's eye" and "reloading" for the 2012 elections. Many media sources criticized her for use of such examples and tied the language to the shooting. (See Weblink 6.3.) The argument here is that one of the functions that language can prompt is the use of violence.

THE SEMANTIC DIMENSION: WHAT DO THE WORDS MEAN?

The semantic dimension explains the various shades of meaning given to language. For example, in the abortion case discussed earlier, the defense won a ruling that censored the use of the terms "baby boy" and "human being" and allowed only the word "fetus" to be used by the prosecution. What a difference. We react very differently to the word "fetus" than we do to "baby boy." Or take the example of a person saying, "I'm really anxious to visit you again." What they really mean is that they are "eager" to see you and are unlikely to experience any bit of anxiety over the visit. Clearly, choosing words with the proper semantic meanings can be critical to the interactive co-creation of persuasive meaning in a multicultural world, especially where misunderstandings are all too frequent. The right choice can also make all the difference when communicating via an SNM, and semantic distinctions are probably processed in the peripheral channel, thus making their impact almost subconscious.

Word choice also provides clues about the source's underlying intentions (see Figure 6.3). It is not surprising that words like "questionable business practices" would raise suspicions in the audience even though they do not function to lay blame. And recall my knee jerk response to the words "collection agency." If a persuader says, "I'm responsible" versus "I'm culpable" versus "I'm guilty," receivers are going to have very different levels of response. Some experts like Lucille Magdalena advise that it's easier to apologize than to ask permission when making management decisions in organizations. But you do have to be careful about your choice of words for the apology—especially on SNM where the receiver doesn't usually get a lot of nonverbal cues like facial expression, body tension, posture, and so on (see Weblink 6.4).

So the words a persuader chooses can make a huge difference. Word choice also provides clues about the source's underlying intentions. It is not surprising that words like "questionable business practices" and "insider trading" convey different meanings than the words used by industry critics, which include terms like "looting" the company's pension fund, "destroying employee security," "auditing flimflams," "black market bribery," "cyber-fraud," "influence peddling," and "corporate sharks drawn in a feeding frenzy by the smell of blood."

When we talk about the meanings words have we need to remember Humpty Dumpty from *Alice in Wonderland*. Like many persuaders, he held that "When I use a word, it means just what I choose it to mean—neither more nor less." So when persuaders choose to use certain words in our 24/7 doublespeak world, receivers need to examine them carefully, not only for what they do (their functional dimension) but for their various shades of meaning (their semantic dimension), because to the persuaders they mean just what they choose them to mean—"neither more nor less." As a result they reveal much about the persuader and his or her beliefs and intentions. We will look at several tools to get at both the functional and semantic dimensions of the language used in persuasion a bit later, but for now, let us turn to the thematic

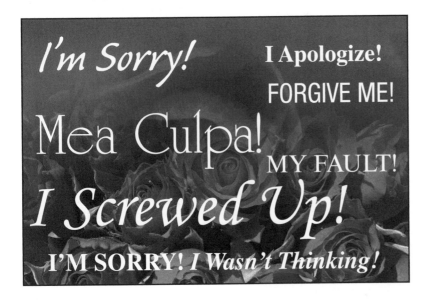

FIGURE 6.3
Here are just a few of the ways to apologize. Which wordings would work best when you have insulted someone via an SNM like Facebook where the insulting message on the recipient's wall can be read by anyone on the network?

dimension of language to discover how words can convey not only meanings but feelings and sensations, sometimes via one of the five senses.

THE THEMATIC DIMENSION:
HOW DO THE WORDS FEEL?

In addition to having functional and semantic meanings, some words also have a feeling, a texture, or a theme to them. You almost physically sense them. Onomatopoeic words sound like their meaning. For example, listen to the feel of "shush," "whir," "rustle," "buzz," "hum," "ding," "bang," "bark," or "boom." You'll find some enjoyment and possible grist for a term paper on onomatopoeic words at Weblink 6.5.

Somewhat less obvious thematic examples rely on **assonance**, or the repetition of vowels or vowel sounds—for example, "the low moans of our own soldiers rolled across the battlefield like the groans of the doomed." Or a Hoover vacuum: "It beats; it sweeps; it cleans." **Alliteration** is similar except that it relies on the repetition of consonants, as in the familiar motto of the recycling movement "Reuse, reduce, recycle"; or brand names like Banana Boat or Calvin Klein; or ad slogans like "Renting is Better than Buying at Blockbuster." Both alliteration and assonance are favorite tools of advertising. They're fun to hear and repeat. This phrase uses both: "Flash with a rash, gimme my cash, flickin my ash …" (See Weblink 6.6.)

By carefully considering the functional, semantic, and thematic dimensions of any persuasive message, we exercise our response-ability as receivers. Even if our interpretation of a message doesn't match the persuader's, the analytic process we apply to persuasive messages helps ensure the responsible reception of persuasion.

METAPHORS, ARCHETYPES,
AND THEIR MEANINGS

We briefly introduced the persuasive power of metaphors back in Chapter 5, but to review briefly:

1. They are memorable and the more times repeated, the more so.

2. They have two parts: the tenor, which is the "topic" (e.g., the "passing of time"), and the vehicle, which gives a meaning or image of the topic (e.g., "time flies").

3. They can be used to persuade, especially in advertising and political persuasion (e.g., "We have a puppet government").

4. Metaphors can be "indirect claims" and might be visually conveyed. (For example "Metropolitan Life protects you like an umbrella" in a bad storm shown by, Snoopy holding up a Met Life umbrella. Who needs more protection than poor naive Snoopy? (See Figure 6.4 for another example.)

5. Receivers need to analyze metaphors to discover the persuader's meaning and intentions. Sometimes, metaphors and other figures of speech can also produce a texture or theme at the same time as they perform a function and carry a meaning. The use of powerful metaphors creates thematic meaning or texture.

According to communication researcher Michael Osborn (1967), wartime British Prime Minister Winston Churchill repeatedly used what Osborn termed archetypal (universal) metaphors of "light" to characterize the British military and citizenry and "dark" ones for the enemy. In a speech during WWII, he said,

> If we stand up to him [Hitler], all Europe may be free and the life of the world may move forward into broad, sunlit uplands. But if we fail, then the whole world, including the United States, including all that we have known and cared for, will sink into the abyss of a new Dark Age made more sinister, and perhaps protracted, by the lights of perverted science.… Good night then: sleep to gather strength for the morning. For the morning will come. Brightly will it shine on the brave and the true, kindly upon all who suffer for the cause, glorious upon the tombs of heroes. Thus will shine the dawn (pp. 115–126).

WHY DO YOU THINK
EVERY PACKET CARRIES A GOVERNMENT HEALTH WARNING?

Issued by the Scottish Health Education Unit

FIGURE 6.4

This visual metaphor conveys the tenor or topic (smoking = death) using the vehicle (a cardboard coffin with a cigarette warning printed on it).

SOURCE: Image Courtesy of The Advertising Archives.

Archetypal metaphors usually refer to common substances or events like light and dark, birth and death, and rite of passage, and frequently are associated with the sacred or profane. Some familiar ones include references to fire, water, and blood. President George W. Bush repeatedly used the fire metaphor to characterize the hoped- for rise of democracy in the Middle East and elsewhere in the world where freedom's "flames need to be fanned." Opponents of the invasion into Iraq declared that it would take a long time to "wash the blood" from America's hands. Metaphoric language can carry a lot of persuasive cargo (see Figure 6.5).

As we noted in Chapter 5, the study of metaphor is extensive and revealing. Recall that every metaphor has at least two parts—the tenor or subject/idea of the metaphor and the vehicle or the means of transmitting or expressing the new concept or meaning of the tenor/idea. In that way the metaphor is like a sentence that basically says, "Idea/Tenor X is similar to Image/Vehicle Y in several ways." In the Bush example above the sentence "explaining" the metaphor would read something like: "Fledgling democracies

Metaphor

Being very busy at work is like being **covered with things** or **surrounded by** something such as water or the ground, so that you cannot move easily.

They keep **piling** *more work* **on me.** ♦ *I'm* **up to** *my* **eyes/ears/ eyeballs/neck** *in work.* ♦ *I'm* **drowning** *in paperwork.* ♦ *I have got a lot of work to* **wade through.** ♦ *I'm* **snowed under** *with work.* ♦ *I don't have time to* **turn around.** ♦ *We're absolutely* **swamped** *at the moment.* ♦ *We've been* **inundated** *with phone calls.* ♦ *They* **buried/immersed** *themselves in their work.*

FIGURE 6.5   Enough said!

SOURCE: Extract from www.macmillanenglish.com © Macmillan Publishers Limited 2011. Used by Permission.

are like a spark that needs to be carefully urged along in order to develop into a full fire that is self sufficient." Recall also that metaphors are artful and hence persuasive to the degree that their vehicle "maps" back to the tenor in ways to which the audience can relate and respond. In other words, the truly persuasive metaphor seems just right for the occasion—it couldn't be said any better. So persuadees need to pay attention to the metaphorical strategies being used by persuaders as well as the functional, semantic, and thematic ones.

THE POWER OF SYMBOLIC EXPRESSION

Symbolic expression affects emotions and/or the intellect, but it sometimes has actual physical effects. For example, the kinds of linguistic symbols people use and respond to can affect their health. People who use expressions such as "I can't stomach it," "I'm fed up," or "It's been eating away at me now for a year" are more likely to have stomach ulcers than others (*Chicago Daily News,* 1972). Symbolic days like birthdays have dramatic effects. In nursing homes, more persons die during the two months after birthdays than during the two months before (Lewis & Lewis, 1972). Thomas Jefferson and John Adams both died on the Fourth of July, a date of tremendous significance for both of them (Koenig, 1972). Some people die soon after the death of a loved one—and sometimes from the same disease. Symbolic sympathy pains can become real (Koenig,

1972; see also Weblink 6.7). According to Seigel, the words we say to ourselves can also cure disease and even stop hemorrhaging (1989).

Burke (1960) makes an argument that language is symbolic action, and that may be an explanation of why words have almost magical possibilities. We know that words are central to most religious beliefs (for example, see John 1:1, and Genesis where God speaks with each act of creation) and words are usually spoken at and central to sacramental enactments (i.e., marriage or the burial of the dead) in most if not all religions. Words are also important in law (the defendant must plead and speak the words "guilty" or "not guilty" unless handicapped, and the verdict and sentence must also be spoken). Not only do symbols deeply affect individuals, but they also serve as a kind of psychological cement for holding a society or culture together. Traditionally, a sacred hoop representing the four seasons of the earth and the four directions from which weather might come served as the central life metaphor for the Lakota Indians. The hoop's crossed thongs symbolized the sacred tree of life and the crossroads of life. A Lakota holy man named Black Elk (1971) explained the symbolic power of the circle for his people:

> You have noticed that everything an Indian does is in a circle, and that is because the Power of the World always works in circles, and everything tries to be round. In the old days when we were a strong and happy people, all our power came to us from the sacred hoop of the nation and so long as the hoop was unbroken the people flourished.... Everything the Power of the World does is done in a circle.... Even the seasons form a great circle in their changing and always come back again to where they were. The life of a man is a circle from childhood to childhood and so it is in everything where power moves. Our tipis were round like the nests of birds and these were always set in a circle, the nation's hoop, a nest of many nests where the Great Spirit meant for us to hatch our children (p. 134).

Black Elk believed that his tribe had lost all its power or "medicine" when forced out of traditional round tepees and into square reservation houses.

What symbols serve as the cultural cement for our way of life: the flag, the Constitution, the home, competition, and sports? What are the symbols that unite our diverse cultural segments? What might someone of Chinese heritage use for cultural cement? References to wisdom and age occur frequently in Chinese literature from the past to the present. What about persons of Indian extraction? Moslems? Hindus? Buddhists? Eastern Europeans?

A good place to find the central symbols of our culture is in the language used in advertisements, if the particular culture uses advertising. In marketing advertisement services, particularly to new emigrants from other cultures, I have found that in some cases, they have no concept of what an advertisement is or why a business should use one. That makes sense at least in countries of the former Soviet Union. When all goods are in short supply, there is no need for a merchant to advertise that his business has something in supply. I recall seeing a huge truckload of bananas drive up to a street market in Leipzig, East Germany and watching it sell out its entire inventory in less than five minutes. The string shopping bag that people used to take the fruit away was called a "perhaps," to be used just in case something was available. It didn't matter what was for sale. If something became available, buy it whether you needed it or not. When the inventory ran out, the dealer posted a sign saying "Pause."

This is obviously very different from the case in American culture. Here, goods are in strong supply, so we must advertise other reasons (other than "availability") to prompt consumers to buy. In fact when many persons from the former Soviet Union are taken to an everyday supermarket on a visit to the United States, they are surprised by the supply of product. No market in Russia has so many oranges, so much bread and pastry, never so much meat. But this is normal for us in the United States. As a result, most ads must promise a benefit to the consumer beyond mere availability. Ads must elaborate on the benefit, provide proof, and give a call to action—usually to purchase. Benefits must

reflect our wants and not just our daily needs. Elaboration and proof for taking action, such as purchasing, probably reflect our need for knowledge. And we are an action-based society, as we shall see when we discuss cultural premises. To be short and concise, the ads and slogans "distill" or simplify complex ideas. This "boiling down" of meaning is a figure of speech called **synecdoche**, and politicians frequently use it. They know that concise words and phrases often become part of the evening news, thus acting as unpaid advertisements. The words also suggest a common denominator between persuader and persuadee. Shakespeare used the device in his play *The Tragedy of Julius Caesar* when Mark Antony addresses the Roman Senate with these words: "Friends, Romans, Countrymen, lend me your ears." Of course he is not really talking to all his friends, all Romans, or all Countrymen—he is using his words to indicate all of them in a synecdoche, and the result is he addresses them in a special way. In an ad in *Newsweek,* the AARP used the slogan "Let's Not Stick Our Kids with the Bill!" referring to its opposition to proposed changes to the Social Security system. The phrase unified members and nonmembers of the organization to object to the proposed changes. It did not refer to all kids individually but to the whole population of "kids" who might have to pay the bill someday in the future.

Political rhetoric also reflects our cultural values. Two important words used by politicians are "freedom" and "equality." As columnist David Broder (1984) noted, "Words are important symbols, and … 'freedom' and 'equality' have defined the twin guideposts of American Democracy" (p. 41). The words have the thematic qualities to stir patriotic emotions. However, they are not rated the same by all persons. As Broder notes, "Socialists rank both words high, while persons with fascist tendencies rank both low; communists rank 'equality' high but 'freedom' low, and conservatives rate 'freedom' high but 'equality' low" (p. 41). Considerable power in linguistic symbols resides in their functional, semantic, and thematic dimensions. Not only do words reveal motives, but they also affect our self-image and express cultural ideals. Let's examine tools for analyzing these dimensions of language in persuasion.

TOOLS FOR ANALYZING PERSUASIVE SYMBOLS

Becoming aware of the three dimensions of language, metaphors and other figures of speech, as well as non-verbal symbols, helps us to become responsible receivers of persuasion. We also need to become increasingly aware of the interactive world of film, architecture, and other persuasive forms, as explored in Box 6.1. We can use various tools for the analysis of persuasion to focus our critical eyes and ears on more specific aspects of language symbols. Let us now explore some of the tools of analysis for these three major dimensions of language in persuasion.

Tools for the Functional Dimension

Two tools for analyzing the functional dimension of language symbols in persuasion are language critic Richard Weaver's grammatical categories (especially regarding sentence and word types) and the effects of word order or syntax in sentences.

Weaver's Grammatical Categories. Language theorist and pioneer Richard Weaver (1953) suggested that the type of sentence preferred by an individual offers clues as to that person's worldview (the way the person uses information and comes to conclusions). Weaver discussed some persuaders' preference for simple sentences, compound sentences, or complex sentences.

Simple sentences express a single complete thought or point and must contain one subject or noun and one action word or verb and an object: "He hit the ball." Persuaders who prefer simple sentences don't see the world as a very complex place. Such a person "sees the world as a conglomerate of things… [and] seeks to present certain things as eminent against a background of matter uniform or flat" (p. 120). The simple sentence sets the subject off from the verb and object. There is a clear foreground and background in simple sentences, and they highlight cause and effect or the familiar advertising appeal "Before…. After." (see Box 6.2).

Compound sentences consist of two or more simple sentences joined by a conjunction such as "and" or "but." Weaver observed that the compound sentence sets things either in balance ("He ran, and he ran fast") or in opposition ("He ran, but she walked"). The compound sentence expresses

---

BOX 6.1   Meet Mediamatic.Net

Go to Weblink 6.8 and find numerous examples of how our new digital world is changing not only the persuasive symbols in language but in other forms of symbol making such as interactive film, virtual reality, diagramming a speech in space, mob-tagging discourse, architecture as a

criminal act, and video letters, and many other fascinating items on language and other symbols. Be sure to visit the Mediamatic Supermarket while you're there, play some of the video games available for free, and learn how to get a Mediamatic t-shirt.

BOX 6.2   Interactive Cause and Effect Games

Go to Weblink 6.9 and play with the sample sentences using cause and effect reasoning. You will also enjoy the Rube Goldberg cartoon at Weblink 6.10. Can you identify cause

and effect there? And you will get some good advice for writing a cause and effect or before and after term paper or essay.

either resolved or unresolved tension. According to Weaver, it "conveys that completeness and symmetry which the world ought to have" (p. 127). Persuaders using compound sentences see the world in terms of opposites or similarities. When you encounter compound sentences, try to identify the tension and the symmetry (or lack of it) in them.

Complex sentences also contain two or more distinct components, but not all the components can stand alone as complete simple or compound sentences. Some of the elements in the sentences rely on another element in the sentence to be fully understood. Once, in speaking about word choice, Mark Twain used a complex sentence: "Whenever we come upon one of these intensely right words in a book or a newspaper, the resulting effect is physical as well as spiritual and electrically prompt" (Lederer, 1991, p. 128). The first portion of Twain's sentence ("Whenever... newspaper")

could not stand alone; it is dependent on the last half of the sentence ("the resulting...prompt"), which could stand alone. The complex sentence features an intricate world with multiple causes and effects at the same time—dependency and independency or completeness and incompleteness. Weaver (1953) said it "is the utterance of a reflective mind" that tries "to express some sort of hierarchy" (p. 121). Persuaders who use complex sentences often express basic principles and relationships, with the independent clauses more important than dependent ones, as in these examples:

> If the temperature stays at about freezing, then we can join the polar bear club for a dip in the lake.
>
> I told him that his new print on the wall looked like an interesting prehistoric drawing of a fish....

"The Power and Mystery of Naming Things" by EVE ENSLER

an essay from

THIS I BELIEVE

EDITED BY JAY ALLISON AND DAN GEDIMAN IN ASSOCIATION WITH n p r

FIGURE 6.6

What would you name your first-born male? Your new puppy? Your used car? Why?

SOURCE: Macmillan Audio.

(For a fun time go to Weblink 6.11 and learn some lessons in grammar in this hilarious take-off on the recent film *Inglourious Basterds*).

Weaver (1953) also had some observations about types of words. For example, people react to **nouns** (which are defined as the name of a person, place, or thing) as if they were the things they name. Nouns "express things whose being is completed, not…in process, or whose being depends upon some other being" (p. 128) (see Figure 6.6).

A persuader's noun use can reveal clues to his or her perceptions of things. When persuaders reduce persons to the level of things or objects by name calling, they do so for a reason—to deal with the people as objects, not as subjects or human beings.

According to Weaver, **adjectives** function to add to the noun, to make it special. The dictionary defines adjectives as "words that modify nouns…by limiting, qualifying or specifying" (*American Heritage Dictionary*, 1985). For example, "the little blue Ford hybrid with the Alabama plates" limits, qualifies, and specifies which vehicle we mean. For Weaver, adjectives were "question begging," and showed uncertainty. If you must modify a noun, you're uncertain about it in the first place. To Weaver the only certain adjectives are dialectical (good and bad, hot and cold, light and dark). Examining a persuader's adjective use can reveal his or her uncertainty and what they see in opposition to what. **Adverbs**, to Weaver, are words of judgment. The dictionary defines adverbs as "words that modify verbs, adjectives, or other adverbs" (*American Heritage Dictionary*, 1985). Adverbs represent a community judgment that helps us to agree with what the persuader thinks we believe and often in "ly." For example, adverbs such as "surely," "certainly," and "probably" suggest agreement. When persuaders say, "Surely we all know that thus-and-such is so," they imply that the audience agrees with them. Such adverbs encourage interactive co-creation.

Syntax or Word Order. In addition to using word or sentence types to analyze persuaders' messages, we can look at the syntax used. **Syntax** is defined as "the pattern or structure of the word order in sentences or phrases." How can that have a persuasive effect? Word order can either alert or divert the reader/listener. Consider the difference between these two sentences:

> "Before bombing the terrorist headquarters, we made sure the target was the right one."

> "We were sure the target was the right one before bombing the terrorist headquarters."

In the first sentence, the dependent element occurs at the beginning of the sentence ("Before…") and alerts the reader/listener to the conditions needed before taking action. The independent element expresses the main point of the sentence. In the second sentence, the action comes first, and the dependent element comes second and focuses the attention of the listener/reader on the justification for the action.

Some persuaders place emotional or surprising words at the beginning of a sentence to reduce the impact of what follows. The audience focuses on the evidence because of the emotionality of the claim. For example, the speaker might say, "There is no greater hypocrite than the animal rights advocate who opposes the use of animals in research labs during the day and then goes home and has beef, pork, or chicken for dinner!" The readers/listeners know beforehand that the claim is about hypocrisy, and they focus on the reasons for the claim. The sentence is dramatic and creates a puzzle—"There is no greater hypocrite than whom?" we ask ourselves. We wait for the answer.

The other side of the coin is the speaker who diverts attention from the evidence by hiding the claim at the end of the sentence. This makes the audience wonder where all this evidence is leading. The speaker says, "The animal rights advocate who opposes the use of rats in the research lab and then goes home to eat beef, pork, or chicken is the kind of hypocrite we don't need in this country!" The drama of the sentence is shriveled, and the power of the evidence is diminished because the audience wonders about the speaker's destination—what is their point?

Communication scholar L.H. Hosman (2002) notes that language variations affect one of three elements of the persuasion process: "judgment of speaker, message comprehension and recall, or attitude toward the message" (p. 372), and that these effects are crucial in information processing. This, of course, brings us back to the elaboration likelihood model (ELM), and the old debate over the comparative effectiveness of emotional appeals (peripheral processing) and logical ones (central processing). Hosman also reports that active sentence structure influences perceived believability, clarity, appeal, and attractiveness in print advertisements in different ways than does passive sentence structure: "The nature of a sentence's grammatical construction or of a narrative's construction has important persuasive consequences" (p. 374). Sentence structure and word choice can reveal the persuader's motives and indicate information-processing channels being used in the ELM.

Tools for the Semantic Dimension

While the functional dimension carries important verbal and nonverbal meanings, the semantic dimension of co-created interactive meaning carries the bulk of persuasion in most messages.

Strategic Uses of Ambiguity.   Some think it unethical for persuaders to communicate in intentionally ambiguous ways, but they quite often do just that. They try to be unclear, vague, and general to allow for the broadest possible degree of common ground, identification, and co-creation of meaning. During the 2008 campaign for the presidential nomination, almost every candidate's slogan on both the GOP and the Democratic sides involved the word "change" (examples include, "Change We've Been Waiting For," "Our Time For Change," "Change That We're Ready For," and "Change We Can Believe In"). Obviously, they all didn't mean the same thing by that word. They used this exciting but ambiguous word because they wanted each receiver to fill in his or her own private meanings or connotations for the word, thus "owning" the concept of change. This strategy results in the maximum number of interpretations and thus creates the largest potential audience for the persuader's brands, candidates, or causes. It also pleases as many and offends as few persons as possible. Receivers need to identify intentional ambiguity

being used in persuasive messages, and then they need to analyze the persuader's reason(s) for using the ambiguous term(s).

Persuaders use several methods other than using ambiguous words to create strategic ambiguity. One is to choose words that can be interpreted in many (often contradictory) ways. A politician may support "responsibility in taxation and the cost of educating our youngsters." Those who think teachers are underpaid might hear this as a call for increasing funding for education. Those who hold the opposite view could as easily interpret the statement as meaning that education spending needs to be cut. The key word that increases ambiguity is "responsibility." The speaker or writer does not say what cause he or she favors. Another ambiguous word is "astronomical," as in: "The budgetary implications of the war in Iraq are astronomical." Does this mean millions or billions or hundreds of billions of dollars? Depending on one's position, each meaning might result.

Another way to create strategic ambiguity is to use phrases like "noted authorities on the subject seem to concur that…," which appear to lend support and credibility to the persuader's point. Another way is to refer to several topics at once and imply that they are parallel or equivalent. "Truth" and "justice" are examples. The persuader might say that his program will "provide justice for all because it is based on truth," when, in fact, injustice can flow from truth as well as false thinking.

Of course the most fertile field for the use of persuasive ambiguity is advertising. Most ads include both words and pictures and can thus imply multiple meanings through each or both of these media. The simplest use of ad ambiguity is the testimonial. We see a picture of a celebrity—say a professional athlete wearing a certain brand of athletic shoe, and we are supposed to conclude that the shoe caused the athlete's success. Why aren't there any ads showing the celebrity and other kinds of sports equipment— shoulder pads, hockey stick, athletic supporter? Obviously, there is a much smaller general audience for shoulder pads than for athletic shoes, and there are fewer obvious differences between brands. Communication scholar E.M. Eisenberg (1984) held that strategic uses of ambiguity can also help get agreement on things like mission statements and at the same time allow individuals to interpret the statements as the persuader hopes.

In some cultures, ambiguity is considered offensive. There, listeners want to "cut to the chase" and stop wasting time. Persuadees in other cultures (such as Japan) value talking around the point and establishing a relationship before talking business. Still others want to mull things over and look at the issue from several perspectives.

Persuaders also create ambiguity when they juxtapose or combine words, phrases, and or visuals in startling ways that present issues in a new light. For example, the term "born again" is persuasive to many people. It suggests that the person's earlier religious beliefs were weak, and that their conversion caused the person to be spiritually re-created. Some "born again" politicians and journalists labeled themselves the "Moral Majority," thus creating persuasive intentional ambiguity. The term was ambiguous because the group wasn't a majority but a minority, yet it had great persuasive appeal. Another highly ambiguous term is "moral decay." It reminds us of "tooth decay," which nobody likes. In the area of advertising, visual and verbal juxtapositions can create ambiguous meanings that permit receivers to co-create and achieve persuader goals in efficacious and efficient ways, thus demonstrating another face of our 24/7, media-saturated world.

How can we defend ourselves against ambiguous persuasion, both visual and verbal? Paul Messaris (1997), communication researcher, scholar, and director of the Visual Communication Laboratory at the Annenberg School of Communication at the University of Pennsylvania has some advice. First, he advises recognizing that the visual image is meant to be a print for a previously real physical image and that there are connections between the two—real and co-created. In a magazine ad for the Paris Casino, the original was the presence of two face cards—the queen of diamonds and the jack of spades. Prior to the image we see in the magazine, they were real, separate, and without character— simple face cards in a simple deck on the playing table. But the new image transforms them as Messaris says will happen. The new image gives them life that excites the viewer. They become man and

woman, seducer and seduced, lovers-to-be sometime in the future—in a new image we cannot see. The transformation happens in one place only—the Paris Casino in Las Vegas where similar transformations await us all. That's the visual persuasion that we experience as we turn the page. In the twinkling of an eye, sex rules the day there. "Most people do not actively seek out exposure to advertising" (Messaris, p. 5), so unless something is done, we quickly slip past ads like Paris and the queen and jack liaison. As a result, advertisers must continually find new ways to attract and hold, however briefly, our attention, and that is what the Paris ad does. Messaris points out that "… one of the surest ways of attracting the viewer's attention is to violate reality" (p. 5), which is precisely what the Paris ad does with the addition of the seduction theme.

We could devote an entire chapter to visual persuasion and indeed many of the examples and discussions throughout this book call your attention to the impact of visual images, but suffice it to say that truly critical receivers don't just "flip the page" when encountering persuasion of any kind. Instead, they remember that we live in an advocacy/propaganda-riddled world that is filled with persuasive deceptions that are results oriented, ethics be damned. They are ubiquitous, and always present. Instead of being oblivious to this kind of persuasion we need to take that second look and try to mind-read the persuader's purposes and tactics. They are trying to guide us into a world of strategic ambiguity as Burke calls it. Recall that the semanticists advise using increasing specificity about and concrete elaborations on any ambiguous terms. They advise using extensional devices to clarify meaning. Semioticians go further and advise us to seek meanings in persuasive "texts" by digging into various verbal and nonverbal "codes" and signifiers in the text. Doing so helps determine the real thing being "signified," not the reality being violated. Keep in mind that it is your response-ability that will protect you from the unethical persuader.

Make no mistake about it, advertisers will use semiotics, reality violation, semantic trickery, and any other strategy to devise global marketing and

BOX 6.3   Semantics, Propaganda, and Diversity

Go to Weblink 6.12. There you will find a detailed discussion loaded with examples and explanations of how language is used as a tactic for producing three kinds of propaganda: hypnotic propaganda, semantic propaganda, and cognitive propaganda. Hypnotic propaganda attempts to mesmerize the audience by avoiding any highly emotional terms or words so that the reader or listener must add his/her own interpretation—an interpretation that has been carefully pre-programmed by their culture. Semantic propaganda relies on deletions, generalizations and distortions in order to make the audience believe the map is the territory. Cognitive propaganda relies on language that leads to highly emotional reactions such as fear, hate, anger, and so on, some of which appeal in far different ways to diverse cultures. Additionally, the article discusses propagandistic language strategies for each type. If you are required to write a paper in this class, here is an excellent place to start including excellent examples, clear organization, and common-sense discussion of the propaganda topic as well as related references.

advertising strategies (Domzal & Kernan, 1993), and we need to discover and then continually apply tools of analysis. For example, examining the denotations and connotations of persuasive symbols also helps us study the semantic dimension of language. Other tools address the semantic dimension of language. Among the more useful tools addressing the semantic dimension of language is the dramatistic approach suggested by Kenneth Burke, which we will now explore. Note how it helps reveal things about propaganda, as shown in Box 6.3.

Burke's Dramatism.   In addition to his ideas on language discussed in Chapters 1 and 5, Burke offered students of persuasion a theory and a tool for analyzing the semantic dimension of language. He called his theory **dramatism**, and his tool of analysis the **pentad**. Dramatism maintains that the basic metaphor used by humans to explain various situations is the narrative story or drama. Burke (1960) thought of the drama as "a philosophy of language" capable of describing and analyzing a wide variety of human symbolic acts such as language use. He focused on the differences between action (which is motivated) and motion (which is not motivated). Basic bodily functions, such as sweating or digestion, are unmotivated non-symbolic acts. Action requires motivation, and the ability to use language symbolically is surely such a motivated act. We bring the action into being, and language is the tool we use, thus a kind of symbolic action—it is motivated. Burke

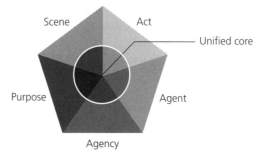

FIGURE 6.7   The five elements of dramatism ultimately affect one another, and each emerges from a common unified core—the drama itself. Notice that one can move from one term to another in 10 ways by returning to the central core—the ratios—and that all five terms terminate in the center of the diagram where the entire meaning of the drama is revealed.

believed that we choose words because of their dramatic potential and that different individuals find certain elements in the drama more potent than others do, though all terms begin and terminate from the same source as seen in Figure 6.6. Those who favor epic dramas differ from those who favor psychological ones. Burke's model, the dramatistic pentad, as its name implies, has five central elements that one might favor and that work together in balance or imbalance to give life to the drama: scene, act, agent, agency, and purpose (see Figure 6.7).

Scene includes physical location, the situation, time in history or time in life, social place, occasion, and other elements. The scene could be something like "Campaign 2012," "the Oval Office," a website, New York City on the day 3,000 people were killed by a terrorist attack, or *The Oprah Winfrey Show*. Any of them can be ripe scenes for a drama. Scenically oriented persons feel the scene should be a "fit container" for the action, or that heroic actions occur in heroic settings and vice versa. That's why foul deeds in film are usually conducted in dark and sinister settings with proper music accompaniment. Scenic persons also believe that changes in the scene will cause other changes—if the scene for assassination of a powerful Muslim political leader is a holy mosque, the meaning of the act will be far different than if it were done on a military base or in an open-air market. Time, as an element in the scene, would also be important—if it were time for the twice daily prayers to Mecca, for example, versus a state banquet or a wedding. If the scene was "family" they would be unlikely to approve of nonfamily characters in that scene. For example, take into account the reactions to Brittany Spears arriving late and perhaps intoxicated or under the influence of drugs when the scene was a hearing about getting custody of her children. Her action caused the presiding judge to rule against her and to recommend rehabilitation. The Clinton-Lewinsky sex scandal was distasteful less because it happened and more because the Oval Office of the White House was the container for the action. If their liaison had occurred at a motel or a private residence, there would not have been such a great hue and cry for impeachment. Clinton had besmirched sacred ground. That's where Ms. Lewinsky and the then president performed oral sex—certainly not a fitting scene for sexual dalliance. The Lincoln Memorial was a "fit" scene for Martin Luther King's historic, "I Have a Dream" speech. The setting helped make the speech memorable. And the scene of Barack Obama's unexpected win in the Iowa caucuses (a rural, Midwestern, almost 100 percent white, farm state) made the victory of an urban, black, Chicago lawmaker all the more dramatic and exciting for his supporters and surprising for the rest of the audience.

Act refers to any motivated or purposeful action that occurs within the scene. In persuasive messages, the verb is the best indicator of the act. After all, verbs are defined as words that describe acts or actions; thus, looking at the verb is the best place to start applying the term "act" to your analysis. The words and actions taken by a person, and their appropriateness for the scene, ultimately affect outcomes. This kind of balance/imbalance between act and scene happens in all kinds of persuasive contexts—advertisements, films, speeches or sermons, public documents, news stories, and so on—and again they affect our interpretation of the actions. Why, for instance, did the 9/11 terrorists pick the twin towers in New York and the Pentagon in Washington, D.C. to use as targets for their acts? Why use passenger airplanes? What if they had picked the Sears Tower in Chicago and the Denver Mint? What if they had used tourist buses as the vehicles to carry the bombs? How would the "persuasion" of their action have been different? The act must "fit" the scene, and if it doesn't, the meaning of the act shifts.

Agent is Burke's term for the person or group of persons who take action in the scene, and again the balance or imbalance between them and the acts they perform and the scenes in which they perform them affects their persuasive meanings. If the assassination at the mosque is done by a street beggar, its meaning is far different than if the assassin is a rival member of the leader's own party. What if the NBA official who was caught gambling on games at which he officiated had been black instead of white? What if he had a family with mob connections? How would the meaning of his action have changed? Agents are the actors or characters who make things happen (the police officer, the corrupt politician, the terrorist, a particular celebrity figure, and so on), and they too must "fit" or be in balance with the action and the setting for a certain persuasive message to result. If not, a very different interpretation will emerge, and the results will be altered dramatically.

Such balanced or unbalanced matches of agents with acts and scenes occur frequently in advertisements as well. For example, examine Figure 6.8.

FIGURE 6.8 This ad for Calvin Klein's Secret Obsession clearly focuses on the **agent** and her obsession with the brand or the agency in getting others to notice her via the peripheral sense of smell.

SOURCE: Image Courtesy of The Advertising Archives.

You will see that there is a clear focus on the agent and nearly every other element in the pentad is missing. But why include the bottle of Secret Obsession? It is clearly the agency through which she can express herself to others using at least the sense of smell that will be processed by others in their peripheral channel and thus passed by almost unconsciously, but with enhanced effect of her attractiveness. In this sense (using Burke's terms), it is a balanced agent–agency ratio. And remember that all sorts of factors such as hatred, instinct, greed, or jealousy sometimes motivate agents, and these too can alter meanings. Countries and organizations (e.g., UN peacekeeping forces, the NRA, al-Qaeda, or pro-choice groups) can also act as agents and can

alter meaning. If the 9/11 attacks had been perpetrated by militia organizations within the United States, there would not be a war on terror but one on militarist groups. After all, that's what occurred following the attack on the Murrah Federal Building in Oklahoma City a few years prior to the 9/11 tragedies—it killed almost a thousand innocent persons and the deed was done with a bomb (though it should be noted that officials began looking for persons of Middle Eastern abstraction immediately following that attack—why?). Agent-oriented persuaders believe that strong, honest, committed, and well-intended individuals determine the outcome of important events and even of history, as was the case of the fourth hijacked airliner on 9/11/01. It was taken over by the passengers and crew. What would have been the interpretation if they had failed and the hijackers had hit the White House or the Capitol? On the other hand, agent-oriented persons believe that unthinking, deceitful, or dishonest agents cause bad outcomes. Was NFL star quarterback Michael Vick simply no good, and that's why he loved dog fighting and gambling? And was that sufficient to imprison him and dismiss him from play, thus postponing his star-potential career that was worth millions to him each year? If he hadn't been a celebrity, would he have received the same punishment? How different were his acts from the several CEOs who lied and cheated regarding the financial health of their companies in order to line their own pockets? After all, their actions bankrupted their companies, their companies' retirement plans, and the retirement future of thousands of employees. Again, the elements of the pentad must fit or the meaning is altered.

Agency is the tool, method, or means used by persuaders to accomplish their ends. Some auto companies now focus on development of the fuel cell and hydrogen energy or the hybrid gas/electric models as agencies to solve our dependence on fossil fuels. In Shakespeare's *Hamlet,* the prince uses the play within a play as the agency to establish his uncle's guilt. Calvin Klein uses nudity and prepubescent females as agencies to draw attention to Obsession "Night for Men" cologne. Wheaties uses pictures of famous athletes on its packages to promote the brand as the "Breakfast of Champions." Communication strategies can also act as agencies (such as intensifying one's own good points or others' bad ones or a politician focusing on his or her humble beginnings). Certain diplomatic agencies like boycotts, street protests, general strikes, walking out of a conference, or sanctioning a country can act as agencies, and can also result in historical outcomes such as war. There is some reason to believe that the sanctioning of Japan prior to WWII was one cause of the attack on Pearl Harbor, for example. Recently some groups have proposed boycotting gasoline from companies that import oil from countries that gouge the United States (e.g., Shell, Exxon, Amoco) or that oppose us, such as certain countries in the Middle East. They advise consumers to favor companies that purchase their oil from South American countries (e.g., Marathon, Conoco, Sinclair). The boycott was proposed using an e-mail chain letter format to spread the word. The chain letter and the boycott were both agencies used to promote the supposed purpose of the action, which was to reduce prices (see Weblink 6.13).

Purpose is the reason an agent acts in a given scene using a particular agency. The persuader's true purpose can be more or less apparent in the persuasion. The U.S. Army's old, very persuasive, and highly successful recruiting slogan, "Be All That You Can Be" suggested that the purpose for enlisting was improving your skills to maximize your potential, a likely reason for volunteering in the post-draft era. Its later slogan, "Join the Army of One," suggests a different purpose for enlisting—to make an individual difference and develop your skills. More recently it advertises "Army. Army strong," which seems to involve the agent-purpose pairing of terms of the pentad wherein the agent joins to become strong as the purpose. In another example, the amount of aid sent by the Bush administration to victims of a disastrous Indonesian tsunami was low compared to that sent by much smaller countries. Critics in this country and abroad interpreted the action as meaning that the administration was less interested in helping others than in saving money. The administration was embarrassed by the criticism and later upped its donation—the purpose of the criticism. What is the purpose in promoting the use of Botox and Lasik eye surgery? What was the purpose in 2008 of centering the themes of almost every candidate for nomination on the key term "change," regardless of which party they were in? What is your purpose in choosing Facebook over MySpace? Why engage in blogging? Why purchase an SUV? All of these decisions involve the agent-purpose pair of terms from the pentad.

These five elements can also help develop a persuasive strategy in various interpersonal relationships. For example, suppose you are trying to get a friend to accompany you and others on a wilderness canoe trip. Your friend is a total amateur at canoeing and so is understandably somewhat reluctant about going, especially so far from civilization. You might emphasize the scenes that your friend will experience—the undisturbed nature and its environment, the vastness of the uninhabited wilderness lakes and streams, the thrills of going through rapids, or the quietness of the trip across satin smooth lakes at sunrise (see Figure 6.9).

An alternative strategy would be to focus on the act, describing the kinds of terrain you will be crossing on portages, the interactions between other

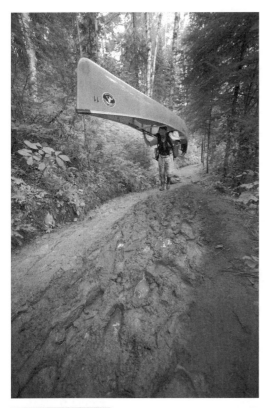

canoeists around the campfire in the evening, or the fun of stripping for an afternoon swim and diving off huge rock outcrops or boulders into crystal clear waters (see Figure 6.10).

You might choose to focus on the agents who will accompany you on the trip—describing the musicians with their harmonicas and guitars singing an endless repertoire of hilarious songs and telling uproarious jokes and stories (see Figure 6.11).

If you chose to feature agency, you might mention the new ultra-light Kevlar canoes that slide through the waters like a smooth sleek creature, that can be portaged with minimal effort, and that afford you the chance to cast lures into previously un-fished ideal spots for huge walleyes (see Figure 6.12).

Finally, you could feature purpose by telling your friend how in 10 short days they will develop marvelous new skills, muscles, and stamina. Or you might focus on the memories and stories of the trip that will remain in your friend's mind—the meals more delicious in the wild than they could ever be back home, the immensity of the nighttime sky and its stars and borealis, the thrills of near accidents, the big fish that got away, and the multitude of wildlife that visited your campsites and beachfronts (see Figure 6.13).

FIGURE 6.10   The act of portaging may be the motivational catalyst to join the trip.

SOURCE: Layne Kennedy/Corbis.

FIGURE 6.11
Maybe the agents you go with will be the motivator.

SOURCE: Vladimir Piskunov/iStockphoto.com.

FIGURE 6.12

Equipment is one agency for the trip.

SOURCE: Norbert Eisele-Hein/ PhotoLibrary.

Burke compared the five terms in pairs, or "ratios," to identify a persuader's "key" term. For example, the scene can be compared with each of the other terms one at a time, and we can determine which term seems most important or favored by the persuader through a process of elimination. For instance, if scene supersedes act, agent, and agency, but not purpose, we can then infer that purpose is a good candidate for the persuader's probable key or ultimate term. But then purpose must be compared to act, agent, and agency to see if it supersedes those terms of the pentad. The end result of this process of residues will most likely focus in on the persuader's key/ultimate term and will help to predict future persuasion coming from that person, thus preparing you as a receiver to critically receive their messages.

There are 10 possible such ratios or pairs of terms. In *Hamlet,* for example, the dramatic tension created in the scene–act ratio comes from the fact

FIGURE 6.13 The ultimate purpose of the trip!

SOURCE: David Ryznar/Shutterstock.com.

that Hamlet's mother has married his uncle (the act) during the period of mourning (part of the scene) for Hamlet's father, the king, who has died mysteriously. His uncle inherits the throne and marries Hamlet's mother less than one month after the funeral (also part of the scene). Clearly the scene has been tainted by the act. In fact, to the young prince it might seem as if were almost orchestrated by his mother and uncle/stepfather. Disturbed by this imbalance, Hamlet curses his mother, and says to his friend Horatio, "She married. O, most wicked speed, to post with such dexterity to incestuous sheets!" He seems to consider her act as being motivated by an illicit purpose—to commit adultery with her brother-in-law. Later, Hamlet asks Horatio whether he came to court for the funeral or the wedding, and expresses his anger and perhaps his suspicions in these bitter words: "Thrift, thrift, Horatio! The funeral baked meats did coldly furnish the marriage tables." So the scene–act ratio is flint and steel ready to strike a tragic spark, as it does when the play ends with Hamlet's mother, his uncle and now king, Hamlet's lover, her brother and father, and Hamlet himself all dead on the palace floor; all of this must occur in order to undo the dramatic tension caused throughout the play by the scene-act imbalance introduced in the opening scene when the ghost reveals his murder to Hamlet. To begin to imagine the applicability of the pentad in the development of electronic media that came or will come after TV, consider how it might work in "virtual reality" (Larson, 2010).

We also frequently see the persuasive power of the scene-act ratio in advertisements. For example, in a Super Bowl Pepsi ad in 2010, an eager, nerdy tailgater is kidded by a guest bully who asks for a can of Pepsi. However, the nerdy tailgater has a weapon of his own—a Pepsi cooler that fires a perfect spiral can of Pepsi into the bully's crotch and another into his face. The scene should be a good natured one, but the bullying and the retaliation clash.

Scene can also interact with the other elements of the pentad. In the scene-agent ratio, balance or imbalance again can indicate potent persuasion or high drama—comedy, tragedy, or melodrama. In Hitchcock's classic film, *Psycho,* viewers see a

scene-agent and perhaps an agent-purpose imbalance. Norman Bates (Anthony Perkins), innkeeper at the Bates Motel where Marion Crane (Janet Leigh) has decided to stop, acts strangely when Marion starts to register. (She has just stolen $50,000 from her employer and is thus understandably nervous.) Norman tells Marion that he has "stuffed" all the animal specimens in the motel office. He also says that he likes "stuffing" things. Then we see him spy on her through a secret peephole in the eye of one of the specimens. This is not the behavior of a normal motel owner. It makes the audience uneasy. What is the agent-purpose ratio telling the viewer? Does this happen every time someone registers at the motel? This uneasiness implies the strong possibility of danger. Maybe she should continue on to the next motel, even though she is tired and the weather is bad. The tension caused by the scene-agent imbalance is increased when we hear Norman and his "mother"/"mummy" (whom he has also "stuffed") arguing at the Victorian house near the motel (see Figure 6.14). We want to warn Marion to at least to lock the bathroom door. Hitchcock uses scene-agent tension throughout the rest of the film to keeps the audience on the edge of their seats. It usually arises because we, the audience, infer the imbalance between the scene (a run-down motel) and the act that is going to happen—murder by a "mummy" mother.

Any of the other ten possible pairs of elements of the pentad (act-purpose, act-agency, scene-purpose, scene-agency, and so forth) might be

FIGURE   6.14   The imbalance in the scene–act ratio in Hitchcock's film classic, *Psycho,* heightens dramatic tension.

SOURCE: Used with permission of Doug Walker.

examined to discover a persuader's key term or element. Burke believed that a persuader's key term infuses every aspect of life—home, family, job, political choices, and philosophy of life. Identifying a persuader's key terms or elements alerts us to the motives of and reasons for the persuasion and helps us predict future persuasive appeals. As you encounter persuasion, try to listen for the key term being used.

Tools for the Thematic Dimension

We've seen that the thematic dimension of language is that quality in certain words or sets of words that gives them a texture or "feel." Onomatopoeia is one type of linguistic "feeling" or texture, but there are others. While words do have a variety of semantic meanings and syntactical functions, their most important persuasive aspect is their ability to set a mood, a feeling, or a tone or theme for the persuasion. For example, Abraham Lincoln set the theme for his famous Gettysburg Address with these words: "Four score and seven years ago

our forefathers brought forth on this continent a new nation, conceived in liberty and dedicated to the proposition that all men are created equal." How far less stirring the speech would have been if he had said, "Eighty-seven years ago the signers of the Declaration of Independence started a new country designed to assure us of freedom and equality." The two sentences have equivalent semantic and functional meanings, but the obvious difference between them lies in their texture. We also noted how the repetition of consonants (alliteration) or vowels (assonance) carries thematic meaning. The advertisements for Satin cigarettes, for example, used alliteration to create a thematic meaning for the brand: "Smooth, silky, satin cigarettes." Or consider the slogan for Lexus: "The relentless pursuit of perfection." It sounds unstoppable. Cohen's use of alliteration is also apparent in Figure 6.15; the slogan "12 party pleasers in puff pastry" is almost fun to say.

Thematic meaning also can come from the use of metaphors or onomatopoeia, which we covered earlier in Chapter 5. Let's turn now to several other

FIGURE 6.15

What is the use of alliteration here?

SOURCE: www.cuisineinnovations.com.

tools for discovering the thematic meaning in persuasive messages, including finding metaphorical themes; noting the use of **sensory language**; looking for god, devil, and charismatic terms; identifying the pragmatic and unifying styles; and use of semiotics to determine the thematic meanings of nonverbal symbols or "signifiers."

Metaphorical Style.   Persuaders set the mood for persuadees by repeatedly using certain sounds, figures of speech, and images. Recent research on the effects of metaphors shows that using them increases the credibility of the persuader because they make the persuader seem more dynamic and interesting. This is especially so when the source uses only a single metaphor instead of multiple ones (Sopory & Dillard, 2002). Dan Hahn (1998) applies another archetypal metaphor—that of water as a dangerous image. Notice the positivism and the negativity of the underlined water images:

> Due to *foggy thinking,* the tide has been *running against freedom* and we are *sinking* in a *swampland of collectivism.* Therefore, despite the detractors who say *don't rock the boat,* the campaign we launch here will *set the tide running* again in the cause of freedom. The *past will be submerged, and* we will travel *democracy's ocean highway* where freedom will accompany *the rising tide of prosperity* (p. 115).

Hahn reminds us of other associations we have with the water metaphor. It is life giving and is also the basic element from which life emerged (p. 115). Other archetypal metaphors include references to wind and windstorms, blood and blood bonds, the locomotive as representative of the industrial age and the driving force of the economy, and the boxing ring or the horse race as stand-ins for any of life's contests and struggles. Roads and maps also serve as metaphors for planning (for example, "the roadmap to peace" in the Middle East or the map of Iran being over run by cockroaches used by Johannesen back in Chapter 2). Metaphors also help in **framing** the issue or topic to give the audience a way of seeing things.

For example, imagine a persuader trying to inform the audience about the AIDS crisis in Africa, where grandparents are now raising most children due to the premature deaths of the parents. A good metaphor might be warfare, with the persuader saying, "We're in the early stages of the battle here with the veterans of past battles having to fight to the bitter end. It's not going to end with a single decisive weapon." The audience sees the fight against the disease is likely to be a long one with no real miracle cures. Ray Gozzi says that the medium of television is really a metaphor for "life is a drama" (1999) and quotes media ecologist Neil Postman adding a unique twist to McLuhan's metaphorical claim that "the medium is the message" by transforming this metaphor into "the medium is the metaphor." We will look at some tools for the analysis of metaphors a bit further on. Suffice it to say, they can haul a lot of persuasive freight in advertising, politics, interpersonal relations and elsewhere. What metaphor might be created to explain SNM?

Sensory Language.   Courtroom communication expert Stephanie L. Swanson (1981) maintained that most effective lawyers rely on words that relate to one or more of the five senses: sight, sound, touch, smell, and taste. She speculated that jurors respond to the particular sensory information channel they prefer. How could a persuader use these preferences? Suppose an attorney asks three witnesses to describe an automobile accident. The witness preferring the auditory channel might say something like, "I was walking down Oak Street, when I heard the screech of brakes, and then a sickening sound of crashing glass and metal, and someone screamed." The witness who prefers the visual channel might say, "I saw this blue Beamer coming around the corner practically on two wheels. Then he hit the brakes, and it looked like the car slid sideways toward me. Then I saw his front end make a mess of the little Geo." The witness who prefers the kinesthetic channel might say, "I had this feeling that something was about to happen, and when it did I felt frightened and helpless, and I cringed as the cars crumpled up like scrap paper." Swanson advised attorneys to "listen closely to the sensory language used by your clients and … try to respond in kind—matching the sensory language of the other person" (p. 211). She suggested attending to the kinds of words used by individuals during the juror selection process—then "tailor your language to your listeners' primary sensory channel. You can 'paint a picture' for a visual person, 'orchestrate the testimony' for an auditory person, and 'touch the heart' of the kinesthetic individual. Using sensory language lets the jurors feel that your discourse is directed toward them individually" (p. 211). The use of sensory language acts like an interactive medium, and it increases the likelihood for the co-creation of meaning. Thus, in trying to identify a persuader's use of the thematic dimension of language, explore the sensory language used in the persuasion. In another example, author Elie Weisel described the hanging of a young boy as follows:

> To hang a young boy in front of thousands of spectators was no light matter. The head of the camp read the verdict. All eyes were on the child. He was lividly pale, almost calm, biting his lips. The gallows threw its shadow over him…. We looked at the flames in the darkness. There was an abominable odor floating in the air….

That night the soup tasted of corpses. (See Weblink 6.14.)

Go through the quote, and you will find language used that refers to sight, sound, smell, taste, and touch—all used in a few well chosen and used words of sensory language.

God, Devil, and Charismatic Terms. Another thematic or textural element of style in persuasion is the development of families of terms. Persuaders like to divide the world into tidy categories that prompt co-created meanings. Richard Weaver (1953) held that one of these category sets is made up of **god terms** and **devil terms**. These terms can be seen in action in Figure 6.16. Although terms or labels make up only parts of propositions, they often link with other terms or labels to shape a message or a persuasive argument. Weaver defined a god term as an expression "about which all other expressions are ranked as subordinate and serving dominations and powers … its force imparts to the others their lesser degree of force" (p. 211). Persuaders repeatedly refer to such terms and even fashion their **visual persuasion** in accord with the god term. Weaver saw a god term as an unchallenged word (or phrase) demanding sacrifice or obedience. He used three terms as examples of god terms: "progress," "fact," and "science."

aochsner@northernstar.info

FIGURE 6.16 It is clear that giving parking tickets is a god term for the evil queen, but getting a parking ticket from any of her helper dwarfs is a devil term for her.

SOURCE: Used with permission of Al Ochsner.

Progress still persuades, but is hampered by negative associations—pollution, for example. Science lost some of its credibility in recent times also, due to negative associations such as nuclear power or genetic engineering. Change was such a god term in the campaign of 2008 and was usually in the largest font on signs, direct mail appeals, or background materials at televised news conferences, and others.

Devil terms are just the opposite. They are "terms of repulsion" and express negative values. As Weaver put it: "They generate a peculiar force of repudiation" (pp. 210–215). Today's god and devil terms include the *environment, green, the family, security, terrorism, deficit spending, politically correct, technology, change, ditto-heads, surfing the web, budget surplus, budget deficit, consumer debt, foreclosure, diversity,* and many others that emerge almost daily. God and devil terms can vary in a diverse culture. For example, Western culture places considerable value on the term "forgiveness," considering it the correct response when one is wronged. Middle Eastern cultures believe "forgiveness" is a devil term—the sissy's way out. For them, the god term when wronged is "revenge," as their history for thousands of years has shown and will probably continue to show. Such god and devil terms alert you to potential persuasive appeals aimed at you or that you might choose to use in your own persuasion.

As we move further into the new millennium, other god and devil terms are emerging. Some of the more recent god terms include *family/family values, low fat, rule of law, green vehicles, air security, financial security, education, phased retirement, weight loss, nutrition, fuel cell, hybrid car, electric vehicles, bioenergy,* and *debt free.* Try to discover others as you search for the thematic dimensions of words or terms used in advertising or political and ideological statements.

Weaver said that the connotations of certain negative terms can sometimes be reversed, making the terms neutral or even positive. Take, for example, the expression "wasted" or "getting wasted." Its use during the 1970s referred to killing Viet Cong or others perceived to be the enemy. In the recent film, *Rules of Engagement,* the Marine colonel

accused of 83 counts of murder almost convicts himself when he orders his men to "waste the motherfuckers," referring to the hostile crowd using guns to attack the U.S. Embassy in Yemen. Later, "wasted" referred to getting drunk or "stoned." Today, "wasted" has recovered much of its original meaning of "squandered" and refers to such topics as the squandering of corporate trust, thrown away energy, and lost credibility among others; and the term is referred to in reference to current political and economic issues as in: "Bush wasted his 'political capital' after the 2004 election," or "Arthur Anderson wasted its longtime credibility when it verified the corporate book keeping practices of Enron. As a result the firm went bankrupt, or "The war in Iraq has wasted our grandchildren's inheritance."

Weaver described another kind of term that he called the **charismatic term**, defined as "terms of considerable potency whose referents it is virtually impossible to discover. Their meaning seems inexplicable unless we accept the hypothesis that their content proceeds out of a popular will that they shall mean something" (p. 48). His examples are the words "freedom" and "democracy," which have no apparent concrete referent but still seem to have great potency and serve as god terms for U.S. foreign policy. As noted earlier, the god term "change" was powerful in the 2008 election and may well become a charismatic term for facing the future problems of global warming, the credit crisis, depletion of the productivity of our land and seas, the oil crisis, and others.

The terms "budget surplus" and "fanning the flames of freedom" became charismatic recently; and most agreed back in 2000 that a "budget surplus" was great after decades of "budget deficits" (a devil term). Initially, nearly everyone agreed on the wisdom of "saving social security," but later the term lost its power. An older candidate for a charismatic term is "recycling." With the growing awareness of declining natural resources, the concept of recycling applied to a host of things, such as paper, plastic, aluminum, glass. Probably the most famous use of charismatic language emerged during the early years of WWII, and probably the most famous orator of that period was England's prime minister, Winston S. Churchill. Listen to his use of charismatic language in his first speech of his office:

> I have nothing to offer but blood, toil, tears and sweat. We have before us an ordeal of the most grievous kind. We have before us many, many long months of struggle and of suffering. You ask, what is our policy? I can say: It is to wage war, by sea, land and air, with all our might and with all the strength that God can give us; to wage war against a monstrous tyranny, never surpassed in the dark, lamentable catalogue of human crime. That is our policy. You ask, what is our aim? I can answer in one word: It is victory, victory at all costs, victory in spite of all terror, victory, however long and hard the road may be; for without victory, there is no survival.

You can hear why he was able to rally an England suffering from defeatism to one with a new spirit. This is the power of charismatic language and terms.

Pragmatic and Unifying Styles. Persuaders tend to rely on one of two persuasive styles—pragmatic or unifying. Pragmatic persuaders want to convince neutral or opposition listeners. They want to change minds instead of reinforcing existing beliefs. Politicians speaking at a news conference rather than at a rally of their supporters tend to favor the **pragmatic style**. Unifying persuaders use a different style because they want to motivate people who already believe what they're going to say; they just reinforce beliefs to whip up enthusiasm, dedication, or encouragement. Thus, when Rush Limbaugh, Howard Stern, Bill O'Reilly, Chris Matthews, and others speak to their respective television and radio audiences, they use the tactics of the unifying speaker—their audiences already believe them. The problems for pragmatic persuaders are clear—they must change opinion before expecting action. **Unifying style** persuaders can be much more idealistic, emotional, with fewer objective claims and data than the pragmatic persuader.

What stylistic devices typify these extremes? The unifying persuader can focus on the "then-and-there"—on the past or future—when things were ideal or when they might become ideal. Because the audience fills in the blanks, abstract language choice works well for unifying persuaders, and their language frequently is poetic, emotional, and filled with imagery that excites the imagination. Although the unifying persuader is a sounding board for the audience and provides them with the gist of the message but not the details, the audience co-creates with unifying persuaders' messages. Audiences sometimes participate by yelling encouragement or by repeating phrases to underscore their words: "Right on." "Amen, brother." "Tell it like it is." "Hill—oh—ree!" or "Huck—aaah—bee!"

Pragmatic persuaders need to win the audience, and so avoid appealing to abstract ideals or emotions. They use concrete words, and focus on facts instead of undisputed issues. They avoid "then-and-there" terms. Rather, they focus on real aspects of immediate problems of the "here-and-now," orienting their message to the present instead of the future to focus on facts, problems, solutions, and statistics instead of an idealistic future or past. Their messages pass through the central information-processing route of the ELM instead of the peripheral route, as is the case for unifying persuasion. Consider these words of a pragmatic persuader, Barack Obama, describing his feelings about a fairly emotional but realistic topic, "Standing up to Terror," upon receiving the Nobel Peace prize. He said:

> …mindful of what Martin Luther King said in this same ceremony years ago—"Violence never brings permanent peace. It solves no social problem: it merely creates new and more complicated ones." As someone who stands here as a direct consequence of Dr. King's life's work, I am living testimony to the moral force of nonviolence. I know there is nothing weak—nothing passive, nothing naïve—in the creed and lives of Gandhi and King. But as a head of state sworn to

protect and defend my nation, I cannot be guided by their examples alone. I face the world as it is, and cannot stand idle in the face of threats to the American people. For make no mistake: evil does exist in the world. A nonviolent movement could not have halted Hitler's armies. Negotiations cannot convince al Qaeda's leaders to lay down their arms. To say that force is sometimes necessary is not a call to cynicism—it is a recognition of history; the imperfections of man and the limits of reason. (See Weblink 6.15.)

The language is concrete and prosaic, the references are here and now, and the persuader is trying to change the audiences' mind instead of uniting them. The pragmatic and unifying styles depend on the needs of the audience and the demands of the occasion, not on the needs of the speaker.

TOOLS FOR
ANALYZING METAPHORS

We have mentioned the power of the metaphor several times already and have briefly explained how they work in a variety of stages in the persuasive process—attracting attention, providing emotional arguments, retaining messages and prompting action to mention a few. Let us now explore a few ways the average receiver can analyze and process them. Recall that a metaphor is like a sentence in which a familiar thing, emotion, experience, and so on, is made clear by comparing it to a less familiar thing, emotion, experience, and so on. A simple example would be: "OK team, let's give it the whole nine yards this time." So the first thing receivers should do when analyzing the metaphors used in any persuasive message is to identify the tenor and the vehicle, and then ask themselves if they are appropriate—do they work together in any meaningful and persuasive ways? This requires finding out where the metaphor came from. Online research gives a plausible explanation "…the phrase

comes from the length of WWII machine gun belts…." (see Weblink 6.16).

Recall that we also mentioned "mapping" of metaphors back in Chapter 5. The next step in analyzing metaphors in persuasion is to identify as many ways that the vehicle "maps" back to the tenor. It is plausible that the vehicle means "use up all your ammo" on the enemy. However, there are several other explanations or mappings. For example, "the whole nine yards" crops up in many contexts, which isn't surprising, as there are many things that can be measured in linear, square, or cubic yards—and there are also yard-arms, steelyards, etc., to account for (see again Weblink 6.16). Another tool for the analysis of metaphors and their persuasiveness is the metaphor checker (see Weblink 6.17). It posits that you can ask three essential questions of a particular figure of speech thought to be a metaphor and if the three questions can all be answered in the affirmative, then you have a metaphor. Positive answers also give a strong indication of the power of the metaphor. The three questions are:

1. Is the statement figurative instead of literal? For example, the statement, "love is a flower," is clearly figurative since love is not a flower; versus the statement, "love is a feeling," which is literal, so it is not a metaphor.

2. Is it an equation? Are its two parts being made equal? Again take the statements "love is a flower" and "love is a feeling." In this case the answers are yes for both statements, but "love is a feeling" did not get an affirmative for question 1, so it is not a metaphor.

3. Can it be expanded figuratively? In the two statements again, "love is a flower" can be expanded—love is a red, red rose; love is a fragrant bloom; love is a fast fading blossom; and so on. All are figurative expansions of the original. In the case of "love is a feeling," any expansion will be literal, not figurative, such as "love is an emotion" or "love is a physical response."

So what about the "nine yards" metaphor? Is it figurative as used? Yes, as the team is being addressed, and it may need yardage to gain a first down, and the phrase relates to ammunition or weapons. And a team's talents are frequently thought of as its weapons, so the metaphor "maps." Is it an equation? Give the opposition the team should use "all our weapons/ ammunition." The answer again is "yes." Finally can the supposed metaphor be expanded figuratively? Again the answer is "yes" as in, "give them the whole nine yards in one long burst—don't just strafe them."

In addition, metaphors—unlike similes—imply an exact similarity, not an approximate one, and as a result similes always have the words "like" or "as" in them (for example, "My love is like a red, red rose" or "My vacation was as short as a dream," as opposed to "My vacation was a dream"). Finally, metaphors are not idiomatic or untranslatable (for example, "Nuts!" or "Nuts to you!" are untranslatable). In fact, the German Army High Command was baffled by General McAuliffe's response of "Nuts!" and couldn't interpret it as a highly negative response to their demand that he surrender his army during the Battle of the Bulge in WWII. In fact he might have said, "Nuts!! You are going to get our whole nine yards, you dirty krauts!" and they would have been even more baffled.

Metaphors can also be visual (Larson, 1982). In a way, the ad for Paris casino is a powerful metaphor that says, "Paris is seductive." The same is true of many other advertisements, television programs, music, and movies. Identify the tenor and vehicles in them and you're on your way! And metaphors exist for practically any issue or event—in fact enter the word "metaphor" and select "images" for any issue or event into a search engine, and you'll find lots of examples.

We briefly discussed archetypal metaphors in Chapter 5, recognizing that they were cross-cultural, not time bound, easy to relate to, and widely applicable. Our example there was Osborn's discussion of the "light/dark" family of metaphors as they occurred in a speech by Winston Churchill. We also used the planting and harvest archetypal family to craft a pretty effective campaign message. Other archetypal families include the bound/free metaphor, water (as we also in Chapter 5), the spreading, consuming, or epidemic metaphor (e.g., disease or trouble such as cancer metaphors and fire metaphors), and the predator metaphor (e.g., the corporate shark, devouring the marketplace). This is especially true with interactive media as seen in Box 6.4.

SEMIOTICS, SIGNIFIERS, SUBTEXTS, CODES, AND DECONSTRUCTION

We referred to the field of **semiotics** earlier as a way to study meaning. Its most important contemporary theorist and renowned novelist is Umberto Eco. He proposed that the process of "signification" (or the giving of meaning to a "sign") has four elements:

1. The objects or conditions that exist in the world (e.g., a busy intersection).

2. The signs available to represent these objects or conditions (e.g., a traffic light and warning sign stating, "Warning—Busy Traffic Ahead").

BOX 6.4 **Visual Metaphors, Interactive Media, and Vampires**

Vampire power is the energy that electric devices, such as your computer, draw even when not in use. How to warn against this waste was the question, and IGo (a power management system) decided to advertise its services using the visual metaphor of a woman's neck apparently having being sucked of blood by a vampire with three teeth instead of two. The wounds looked very much like a grounded electric outlet. This ad was followed up by an app at its website (found at Weblink 6.18) where an augmented and virtual reality graphic of a grounded electric plug splatters blood on your screen "face" when you hold it up to your webcam.

3. The set of choices among signs, or the repertoire of responses available for use (e.g., one can choose to obey the green and red traffic lights, to disobey them, or to proceed on yellow keeping the warning sign in mind).

4. The set of rules of correspondence that we use to encode and decode the signs we make and interpret when we communicate (e.g., almost every driver—there are some dunderheads—understands warning signs and the meaning of the three colored lights in a traffic light).

This final characteristic most directly relates to the goal of this course, which is the discovery of the various **codes**, **meanings**, or **sets of rules** used by persuaders and understood by persuadees in the process of co-creation. Eco also believed that "open texts" were always open for new or alternate meanings or interpretations and that good literature or good persuasion is always open to the process of co-creation.

To exemplify an easy code that is open to alternate interpretations, we know that when a stage manager lowers the lights and asks us to turn off our cell phones and pagers, and to unwrap our candies, then the event is about to begin; this is an example of a code. But it could also mean "do not disturb your neighbor during the play" or "there are some persons dumb enough to leave their cell phones on during the play so we are forced to make this announcement."

In fact, during my mother's funeral service, a lady in the front row left hers on even after it had disturbed the service with its initial "ringing." She received three more calls that she answered and had conversations on—all during the service. How rude and stupid! I felt like going to her seat, taking the phone and stomping on it. As a persuadee, what meaning could you assign to such actions—hers in not turning off her phone and mine in wanting to stomp on it?

We participate in our own persuasion by "agreeing with" the code(s) the persuaders use. For instance, I agree with the stage manager, so I turn off my phone but don't unwrap my candies—I bring candies that don't require unwrapping (e.g. lemon drops in a packet).

We become critical consumers of persuasion by continually striving to uncover and reveal these codes and then to evaluate them (Eco, 1979). For example, do I need to unwrap opened lemon drops when they are in a metal box in my shirt pocket? Can I just put my cell phone on vibrate so I know when an important call comes in?

We find more subtle examples of codes in some advertisements. For example, consider the ad for Bostonian shoes in Figure 6.17. What codes operate in this ad? Some seem obvious, but others are more subtle. In fact, some codes found in the ad embed themselves within other codes. The most obvious code is that the ad tries to sell the product, although the kind of product is not so clear. But after some consideration, we discover that the product is men's shoes. Another less obvious code is that the product is an upscale one, as indicated by the composition and copy of the ad and the price of the shoes—$105. The ad is understated, with little actual ad copy. Finally, the illustration is distinctively "fine art" in its composition. Within these codes, we find a more subtle code that is only implied and never directly stated. This code signifies the lifestyle that goes with the product. The shoes merely serve as an emblem of that lifestyle. What do we see in this photograph? Clearly, it is the "morning after" a satisfying night of lovemaking—perhaps in a fine hotel (notice the coffee cups and pastries on the bed, the negligee on the well-rumpled bedding, the indentations on both pillows). The lifestyle includes a fine home or hotel room (notice the expensive furniture and the framed photographs on the nightstand in the upper left corner). This lifestyle includes expensive accessories such as the Rolex watch and the Mont Blanc pen on the dresser. The stylish suspenders, the theater ticket stubs slipped into the frame of the mirror, and the picture of a beautiful wife under the tickets signify a lifestyle that values the arts, stylishness, beauty, and physical attractiveness (note the snapshot of the man, bare-chested and muscular). Clearly, this ad carries a lot of meanings, "signified" by the verbal and nonverbal symbols being used (or perhaps misused). Its persuasive message must be decoded and then meaning is

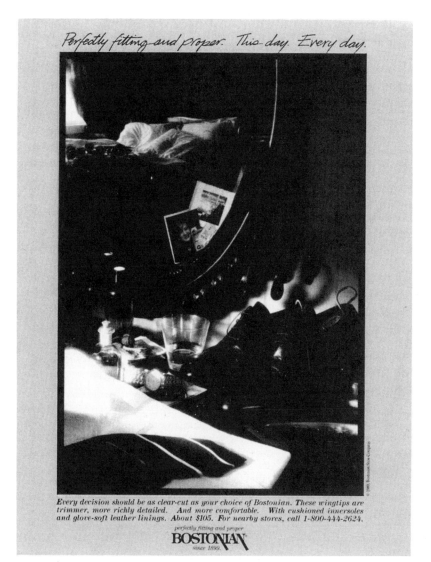

Perfectly fitting and proper. This day. Every day.

Every decision should be as clear-cut as your choice of Bostonian. These wingtips are trimmer, more richly detailed. And more comfortable. With cushioned innersoles and glove-soft leather linings. About $105. For nearby stores, call 1-800-444-2624.

perfectly fitting and proper

BOSTONIAN
since 1899

FIGURE 6.17

What messages are implied by the "code" of physical objects in this ad (theater tickets, rumpled bedclothes, articles of clothing that seem to have been hurriedly discarded, an empty cocktail glass, and so on)?

SOURCE: Reprinted by permission of the Bostonian Shoe Company/Copyright Clarks.

co-created based on agreed upon and shared semiotic codes. The signifiers, or collection of objects in the room, probably trigger emotional values that the audience holds dear. It is not propaganda, but borders on advocacy and is surely an example of our 24/7, media-saturated world, and the success depicted indicates that the wearer of Bostonian shoes is a winner in a results-oriented world.

Although analyses like this are fun and intrigue us, they are difficult to carry out without some kind of systematic methodology. The fields of theoretic (e.g., reading Eco or Pierce) and applied semiotics (e.g., advertising and image/political consulting) expanded rapidly in recent times and are used in political campaigns, advertising, public relations, religion, and elsewhere. A method of researching audiences/consumers and at the same time creating messages that are "open" to co-creation is the use of focus groups. Here consumers discuss the brand, the packaging, its name, its appearance, feel, and so on, and their words are used in the persuasive copy for an ad promoting the brand—true co-creation. As receivers we need a simplified way to pin down the uses (or misuses) of symbols, and the following brief discussion of the semiotic approach to language and meaning gives us yet another tool for discovering the important first premises emerging from language preferences and the images molded from them. By the way, most of these meanings are processed in the peripheral channel of the ELM, and we are only dimly aware of them unless we pause and do a deeper analysis. They also can produce alternate meanings, especially in a multicultural world like ours. Consider the detailed meaning described by Buissac concerning a familiar and seeming meaningless act of entertainment—the circus in Box 6.5. From a semiotic point of view, it contains signifiers, codes, and subtexts, and can be deconstructed to arrive at an entirely new meaning other than an act of entertainment for "children of all ages."

TUNING YOUR EARS FOR LANGUAGE CUES

Consumers of persuasion need to become vigilant when processing and responding to persuasive messages in our ethically challenged world of advocacy and propaganda. In the course of this vigilance, one of the most important things persuaders can do is tune their ears to language for various clues to style and motives—to the codes of deceptive, sometimes multicultural, and results-oriented world of persuasion. Using some of the tools described in this chapter helps. Applying the study questions at the end of this and other chapters also helps. There are at least three specific strategies you might use to make yourself more critical of style and to "decode" persuaders:

1. **Role-play the persuader.** Assume that you are the persuader. Or assume that you are a

---

BOX 6.5   **Semiotics and the Culture of Circuses**

Semiotician Paul Buissac (1976) offered some fascinating examples of codes in his semiotic analysis of circus acts, illustrating this idea of an easily discernible code understood by "children of all ages" around the world:

> Wild animal, tightrope, and trapeze acts never occur back-to-back in the circus ... they are always interspersed with clown acts, small animal acts, magic acts, or the like. If a daring act is canceled, the entire order of acts needs to be altered because of audience expectations, tension reduction, and the need to communicate that the world is alternately serious and comedic ... Death-defying acts also have a code—usually a five-step sequence. First, there is the introduction of the act by the ringmaster (a godlike figure able to control not only the dangers but the chaos of the circus). This introduction, with its music, lights, and revelation of dazzling and daring costumes, is followed by the "warm-up," in which minor qualifying tests occur: The animal trainer, dressed as a big-game hunter, gets all the animals to their proper positions; the trapeze artist, with his beautiful assistants, can easily swing out and switch trapeze bars in mid-air; the tightrope walker dances across the rope with ease.

Then come the major tests or tricks: getting the tiger to dance with the lion, double trapeze switches, and walking the wire blindfolded. Having passed these tests, the circus performer then attempts the 'glorifying,' or 'death-defying,' test. It is always accompanied by the ringmaster's request for absolute silence and, ironically, by the band breaking the critical silence with a nerve-tingling drum roll. Then comes the feat itself: The animal tamer puts his head into the lion's mouth; the trapeze artist holds up a pair of beautiful assistants with his teeth, demonstrating his amazing strength; and the blindfolded tightrope walker puts a passenger on his shoulders and rides a bicycle backward across the high wire. Frequently, there is a close call: An unruly tiger tries to interfere with the "head-in-the-mouth" trick, there is a near miss on the trapeze or a stumble on the high wire, and so on. Once the glorifying test is passed, the ringmaster calls for applause as the act exits and then returns for a curtain call. This sequence is a 'code' we all understand" (n.p.)

Suppose the circus tent caught fire. What would be the appropriate code for the ringmaster to use in order to reduce panic?

BOX 6.6 **Diversity and Semiotics**

Semiotics and cultural diversity are a particularly hot topic just now, and many websites will pop up when by you enter the words into any search engine. Sample the links found there and discover how many things apply to semiotics. You might also enter the words "semiotics" and "cultural studies" in any search engine and discover more.

persuader from a different cultural background (see Box 6.6). Now, you shape the persuasion he or she presents in your own personal style. For example, if you are supposed to favor high salaries for professional football players, frame a pragmatic message for half-hearted believers, those who are neutral, or others who are only moderately opposed. Would you mention the shortness of most players' careers? After all, they receive a relatively low overall salary if calculated across a lifetime, especially when compared with team owners or even CEOs of medium-sized corporations. You might compare ball players to professional entertainers, who also make several million dollars per year for relatively little actual work time. Be sure to include job requirements such as training camps, weekly practices, body building, and so on. If your audience were the players' union, you might bypass the numbers and use highly emotional and abstract language to motivate them—create images of club owners as rich bloodsuckers who use up the best years of an athlete's life and then dismiss them to the trash heap of history with inadequate health insurance for the injuries they may have had during their on-the-field careers. You would probably use then-and-there language, and refer to concrete statistics and examples that favor the agent, not the agency, and to the new goals or the purpose of the group. And you might want to use emotional metaphors of broken-down race horses being sold off to secondary careers where they suffer endlessly. Doing this role-playing can alert you to the original persuader's true purposes and to their favored tactics as

well. At the very least, you will be on your way to becoming a highly trained and critical receiver.

2. **Restate a persuasive message in various ways.** Ask yourself, "What other ways could I say this?" Try to determine how these alternatives change the intent and effects of the message. Try using the parts of Burke's pentad. For example, take the following slogan for Grand Marnier Liqueur: "There Are Still Places on Earth Where Grand Marnier Isn't Offered After Dinner." The words appear on a photo of a deserted island. The appeal is scenic. An agent-oriented version of this slogan claims that, "People of Taste Offer Grand Marnier." A purpose-oriented version might read, "Want to Finish the Conference? Offer Grand Marnier." An agency-oriented version might say, "Grand Marnier—From a Triple-Sec Recipe." The act-oriented message emphasizes action by saying, "Make a Move—Offer Grand Marnier." And appropriate settings or visual persuasion would serve as the backdrops for the ads instead of the deserted island.

3. **Attend to language features in discourse.** Don't allow yourself to passively buy into any persuasive advice without a thorough inspection of the tactics being used. Instead, get into the habit of looking at each message's style. Analyze messages on billboards, in TV commercials, the language used by your parents when they try to persuade you, the wording on product packages, or in the phrases used in discussions between you and friends, enemies, or salespersons. Start listening not only to ideas

but to word strategies, pentadic focus, the visual and verbal metaphors, and so on. In other words, examine the packaging of those ideas. Focusing on these features gives you an intriguing pastime, and helps develop an ear for stylistic tip-offs.

Communication scholar Arthur Asa Berger (2005) offers a methodology for doing semiotic analysis, and he provides a fairly simple checklist. First, he advises us to consider the persuasion aimed at us as "texts" to be read, and then to start looking for clues. He has a checklist of questions to ask when trying to read persuasive texts:

1. Isolate and analyze the important signs in the text.
   a. What are the important signifiers?
   b. What do they signify?
   c. Is there a system that unifies them?
   d. What codes can be found (e.g., symbols of status, colors, or music)?
   e. Are ideological or sociological issues being addressed?
   f. How are they conveyed or hinted at?
2. Identify the central structure, theme, or model of the text.
   a. What forces are in opposition?
   b. What forces are teamed with each other?
   c. Do the oppositions or teams have psychological or sociological meanings? What are they?
3. Identify the narrative structure of the text (i.e., if a "story" is being told, what are its elements?).
   a. How does the sequential arrangement of events affect the meaning? What changes in meaning would result if they were altered?
   b. Are there any "formulaic" aspects to the text (e.g., hard work leads to success, justice prevails, or honesty gets its reward)?
4. Determine whether the medium being used affects the text, and how.
   a. How are shots, camera angles, editing, dissolves, and so on used?
   b. How are lighting, color, music, sound, special effects, and so on used?
   c. How do paper quality, typefaces, graphics, colors, and so on contribute?
   d. How do the speaker's words, gestures, and facial expressions affect meaning?
5. Specify how the application of semiotic theory alters the original meaning ascribed to the text.

REVIEW AND CONCLUSION

Responsible receivers of persuasion relate to the language and images persuaders choose. They gain insight by looking at the semantic connotations of the words being used. They look at word order, or syntax, and at the frequency of various parts of speech. The degree of ambiguity used by the persuader is often revealing, as in the dramatistic analysis suggested by Burke. The motifs and verbal and visual metaphors chosen by persuaders often reveal motives. Persuadees also need to look at the god, devil, and charismatic terms used, as well as the choice of pragmatic versus unifying styles. Finally, try to apply the semiotic approach to the interpretation of persuasive messages to uncover their codes and signifiers. (See Figure 6.18.) All these critical devices improve with role-playing, restating, and developing awareness of the words, styles, and ideas used in co-created speech, TV ads, films, political slogans, social movements, package designs, visual print advertisements, public relations appeals, and other acts of persuasion.

FIGURE 6.18   Using the semiotic approach in Berger's checklist, uncover the meaning of this ad. Note that the woman has "lost" items from her pockets—a passport, the keys to an Audi, credit cards, a picture of herself drawn by her child, jewelry, aspirin, a champagne cork, a $100 bill, and other signs. What do they signify? How old is this woman? Is she sentimental? Busy?

SOURCE: Reprinted by permission of *Ms. Magazine*, ©1992.

KEY TERMS

After reading this chapter, you should be able to identify, explain, and give an example of the following key terms or concepts:

semantic dimension	complex sentences	act	visual persuasion
functional dimension	nouns	agent	charismatic term
thematic dimension	adjectives	agency	pragmatic style
assonance	adverbs	purpose	unifying style
alliteration	syntax	sensory language	semiotics
synecdoche	dramatism	framing	
simple sentences	pentad	god terms	
compound sentences	scene	devil terms	

APPLICATION OF ETHICS

Considering Richard L. Johannesen's description of ethical standards in Chapter 2, do you consider the strategic use of ambiguity ethical, unethical, or dependent on the persuader's goal and the ultimate outcome? What if ambiguity convinces you to make an unwise purchase decision? What if government reports are ambiguous about the sources of intelligence used to justify the use of U.S. troops? What if they claim this is to protect their sources or to protect national security? What if optimistic but incomplete research about possible cures for a disease gives the individual sufferer a reason to hope?

What might be some ethical standards for the strategic uses of ambiguity? Support your proposed standards and apply them to sample cases like those in the preceding paragraph to demonstrate how well they might work. What shortcomings, if any, did you discover in your proposal?

QUESTIONS FOR FURTHER THOUGHT

1. Transcribe the lyrics of a popular song. Now analyze them according to the functional tools presented in this chapter. Is there a preference for a certain word type? A certain sentence structure? Is the message ambiguous or concrete? Is it propagandistic? What metaphors are used? Explain.

2. Describe several semantic tools. What do you think is the pentadic perspective of the current president of the United States? Of your instructor?

3. Describe the tools for a thematic or textural analysis of language, and use them to analyze the persuasion occurring in a recent political campaign. What do these analyses tell you about the candidate? Do they fit the definition of "propaganda"? Try the same thing with a recent advertising or P.R. campaign.

4. What god terms work for your parents? What about their devil terms? Where are they processed in the ELM? Shape a request for something from your parents expressed in their god

terms. What god terms motivate the user of the interactive medium being sold on Weblink 6.19 where you can hunt big game via a computer?

5. How do unifying persuaders differ from pragmatic ones? Find examples of each type of persuader in your class, in persuasive attempts of the past, or in defenders and opponents of some issue in your community. What differences exist between these two types? Which style seems more or less likely to carry unethical persuasive appeals? Describe the differences between semantics and semiotics. Which seems more objective? When might it be appropriate to use each approach? Do you use semantics and semiotics to both analyze and create persuasive messages and, if so, how?

6. What is the difference between a text and a symbol? What is the difference between a signifier and the signified? What kinds of things might be considered a text? What could act as a code? Why are some books and films or TV series so predictable? Would you consider them open or closed texts?

7. If language use serves as a medium of communication, describe its interactivity. How is it used when delivered via interactive media? Describe some cultural differences in symbolic language use within subcultures.

8. Are you a user of SNM? If so, why? If not, why not? Do you know any non-users of SNM? Ask them why or why not. Do you think SNM isolate you from others? Or are they just the opposite—putting you into social interaction more than when you didn't use them?

9. Are you becoming more aware of the increasing cultural diversity in our country? Give examples. Do these differences affect the way you live? The values you hold?

Identifying Persuasive First Premises

7

Psychological or Process Premises: The Tools of Motivation and Emotion

LEARNING GOALS

After reading this chapter, you should be able to:

1. Identify, explain, and give examples of Packard's hidden needs. Give current examples as used in everyday communication and SNM.

2. Identify, explain, and give examples of Feig's hot buttons. How do they operate in your everyday life and on SNM?

3. Identify, explain, and give examples of several positive and negative emotions. Which are most powerful for you, especially on SNM?

4. Explain the difference between attitudes, opinions, behavioral intentions, and behavior.

5. Explain and give examples of each of the levels in Maslow's pyramid of needs. Who do you know who seems to be self-actualizing?

6. Explain and give examples of cognitive dissonance. Where is it operating in your everyday life and in SNM and where are they processed in the ELM?

7. Explain and give examples of consonance. Where is it operating in your everyday life and on SNM, and where are they processed in the ELM?

8. Discuss the ethics of appealing to the emotions, needs, and attitudes held by persuadees.

9. Why are SNM more likely to contain appeals to process premises?

This chapter examines what are commonly called appeals to the emotions or the will. We will look at four kinds of emotional appeals:

1. appeals to deeply held needs, physical or psychological

2. appeals to positive and negative emotions

3. appeals to attitudes and opinions

4. appeals to psychological states of balance or consonance and imbalance or dissonance.

Some persuasion theorists distinguish between logical and emotional appeals, arguing that they represent opposite ends of a continuum and that the "better" appeals are the logical ones. This explanation assumes that persuasive appeals are either one thing or another and that the two types of appeals operate separately and independently. It is easy for us to think that both "rational" and "emotional" persuasion occur all at once or as a result of some key phrases, statistics, a sensational speech, the known qualities of the persuader, or other factors. While some persuasion does occur this way, it is rare, and far more often true persuasion occurs over time, step-by-step, and incrementally.

In recent times, we've seen that most persuasion depends in part on self-persuasion, usually occurs incrementally or bit by bit, and often includes many kinds of communication. Few even were aware of global warming a decade ago. Then a few persons began to hear of it, and we began to hear of some of its symptoms: decreased size of polar ice caps, increased water levels in oceans, more volatile weather patterns, threats to some species, and so on. Probably the most effective piece of the picture was Al Gore's film, *An Inconvenient Truth*, for which he won the Oscar and a Nobel Prize. Thereafter, further evidence supporting the existence of global warming; the declaration by the United Nations that global warming did exist; and finally even the recognition of global warming (but not its causes) by former doubters such as President Bush, various political groups, Ann Coulter, and other conservative media personalities made the issue finally real for many doubters via this incremental process. In spite of all this, there are still many—on the political right, especially—who believe global warming is a leftist conspiracy to draw attention from other real problems like Muslim Jihad or Russian influence in the world, a conspiracy by the oil-rich countries of the world and others. One "emotional" appeal might have served to capture receivers' attention. A series of "logical" arguments might then have reinforced the first appeal and led to the final decision, belief, and/or behavior. Such changes are part and parcel of a 24/7, media-saturated world of advocacy and propaganda. In fact, both sides of the issue accuse the other of propagandizing in unethical ways, and so the persuasion process on global warming continues.

The point is that no conclusion has or will be reached in a single moment or as the result of a single persuasive appeal or event (unless it might result from a global catastrophe such as a series of violent changes in weather patterns, flooding of coastal cities, etc.). No, these conclusions are far more likely to be incremental and ongoing and will probably never result in 100 percent agreement on the issue. In all likelihood, they will involve the processing of information in both the central and the peripheral routes of the ELM and will involve heavy usage of SNM.

In a far less dramatic and more "normal" example that demonstrates both points about the ELM is called "Volunteers in America," which asks people to donate their cars to the organization because the money earned from selling the car helps place neglected and abused children in safe and nurturing homes. Is the appeal emotional or logical? Well, it has elements of both. The emotional appeal is about helping kids get better treatment in a good environment. Then too, helping others makes most of us feel good about ourselves. But there are some logical reasons for donating your car. For instance, you can get a tax deduction for the donation and you are not responsible for delivering the car or making sure it is in running order—the organization has free pick-up within 48 hours and they repair it before sale. The real question is not whether this is a logical or emotional appeal, but whether you process the message centrally or peripherally. In this case, the peripheral route

processes (the "feeling good" part) and the central route processes (the tax break, the 48-hour pick-up, and the repair) are the emotional and logical parts of the persuasion respectively. On which will you base your decision to donate or trade in?

In this chapter, we are going to examine several emotional appeals or major premises that tap into the psychological or emotional processes operating in the peripheral route of the ELM for each of us. These appeals rely on (1) human needs, (2) human emotions, (3) attitudes, and (4) the psychic comfort or discomfort that normal people always feel over the decisions they make. We call these appeals **process**, or **emotional premises** or **appeals** because they target psychological and emotional processes that operate in most people. When we call them premises, we are referring to their uses as major premises in enthymemes. When we refer to them as appeals, we are talking about how they operate in the persuasive worlds of politics, advertising, public or interpersonal persuasion, and elsewhere. It is probably okay to think of the words *process, premises,* and *appeals* as nearly synonymous. All are sub-types of persuasion that get at our psychological processes rather than our logical or reasoning abilities. For example, most of us have fear-based emotions that cause psychological tension, and we eagerly take action to relieve this tension. So advertisers work to generate fears about our grooming, potential for success, and acceptance/approval by others, and then they offer us products that supposedly relieve those fears and tensions. For example, consider the mouthwash Listerine. Initially, it was used as a powerful surgical antiseptic, a floor cleaner, and a cure for gonorrhea. It wasn't until the 1920s that it was marketed as a cure for halitosis—an obscure word for bad breath (Levitt & Dubner, 2005). A headline in one of its early ads read, "Got halitosis? Listerine mouthwash makes your breath kissing sweet" (see Figure 7.1).

Psychological appeals or process premises also operate in business, marketing, advertising, sales promotions, politics, interpersonal communication, and ideological persuasion where a variety of fears might be developed—fear of losing one's job, fear of going bankrupt, fear of voting for a candidate

FIGURE 7.1 The invented "disease" of halitosis helped Listerine grow its brand even though it had only been previously used as an antiseptic floor cleaner and a cure for gonorrhea.

SOURCE: John T Takai/Shutterstock.com.

who will mess up and so on. Then the persuader offers us a "cure" for the fear—unemployment insurance, stricter business accounting practices, or the candidate who they are supporting.

Process or emotional premises operate when we buy a product because of brand loyalty, brand name, a memorable slogan, a catchy jingle, or even packaging. Recall the Snuggle fabric softener example from Chapter 5? The brand name was cuddly, as was its logo of a stuffed teddy bear, and these were the elements that appealed to the prospect's emotions and desires to be psychologically and physically comforted. Process premises also operate in more serious situations than the right fabric softener, such as enactment of homeland security laws, appeals from prison reform candidates to reduce subsequent crimes being committed against us, from advocates for a candidate they claim to be reliable, or from advertisers trying to convince us to make major purchase decisions for a new car or home. Emotional premises appear in everyday interpersonal persuasion between neighbors, spouses, parents and children, siblings, lovers, bosses, and employees.

The first such premise we will examine is the appeal to real or imagined needs that we might have as individuals or as groups. In some cases (such as physical needs for the basics of human existence), the needs really do exist and we will die if they are not met. In other cases (such as being considered masculine or feminine or being thought of as competent and ethical), we won't die if the need is not met; but we won't feel content either, so psychological or imagined needs can be motivating and persuasive as well.

NEEDS: THE FIRST PROCESS PREMISE

Each of us has our own set of individual needs. As noted, some of them are critical; we cannot live without things like food, water, clothing, and shelter. Others are not critical; we can get along without approval from others. And not everyone's needs have the same priority. I might need group approval while you might need symbols of success. Diverse cultural roots can also influence the priority of our needs, but most needs resemble those of many other people, so various theories of motivation apply to the general population. Many appeals focus on needs, which when satisfied lead to our overall sense of well-being (for example, success on the job, being liked, or having religious faith). Without the satisfaction of these needs (or some substitute), we feel frustrated, anxious, afraid, or even angry, and tension results. We infer these needs from patterns of behavior that presumably satisfied and happy people exhibit. Because other people seem concerned about being successful, we quickly infer a need for the physical symbols of success like a Jaguar, a summer place, a large home, a happy family, or a feeling of religious salvation. Persuasion in today's changing world usually focuses on promoting or selling symbolic ways to meet people's physiological and emotional needs. Some products, such as self-improvement courses, really can help individuals make a better impression on the boss, but what people buy, vote for, or support doesn't usually have such direct effects. Someone may drive a BMW and enjoy what he or she believes to be the admiring looks they get from other drivers. Our support for a candidate may relate to a need for approval from others or a need for self-esteem—the candidate's supporters are our friends or neighbors, and they appreciate our support. And we feel good about ourselves because our support for the good candidate just might "make a difference." Or we might feel good if we exhibit the traits of good children, parents, or responsible persons of a certain religious faith, or maybe just of being a good citizen.

If the persuader relying on the needs process premise analyzes audience needs or emotions incorrectly, persuasion sometimes boomerangs. For example, an advertiser, assuming that travelers needed and wanted tough luggage, produced an expensive TV spot in which the luggage was handled roughly while being loaded onto an airplane and then accidentally falling out of an open cargo door on the plane in flight, plummeting down 30,000 feet, landing on some rocks, and bouncing into the air. When the luggage was opened, the camera showed the undamaged contents. The ad seemed persuasive. However, sales of the brand plummeted following its initial test airing. Why? Focus group interviews revealed that most, if not all, people have some level of fear that their flight might crash, and they resented the idea that their luggage would survive when they wouldn't. So the emotions of fear and resentment serve as powerful motivators to encourage or deter purchase, as might emotions like anger, jealousy, hatred, joy, or love. Sometimes brand preferences are based on such

illogical factors. I avoided automatic transmissions for years because my father said they weren't as good in snow and ice. Persons of the Jewish faith avoided purchasing any product by the Ford Motor Company because old Henry Ford supported an anti-Semitic organization that claimed there was a worldwide Jewish conspiracy to monopolize the financial industry. My spouse only uses Downy because she thinks its odor pleases me when in fact, I can't smell it and really don't sniff my clean laundry that much.

To discover why consumers respond as they do, advertisers, political candidates, and others use **motivation research** to zero in on our needs. Motivation research, or MR, is based on the social sciences and the study of marketing rather than on our traditional political, ideological, or rhetorical traditions, and it grew rapidly after World War II along with the revolutionary new medium of television. In his best-selling book, *The Hidden Persuaders* (1964), Vance Packard, author and advertising theorist, reported that a majority of the hundred largest ad firms in the country used psychoanalytic motivation research to discover deep-seated psychological needs and responses. Other persuaders, such as public relations executives and fund-raisers, also turned to psychological theories to discover receivers' motives, emotions, or needs, and then they tied products, candidates, and causes to those motives and needs. Packard held that much motivation research "… seeks to learn what motivations or **hidden needs** influence people in making choices. It employs techniques designed to reach the subconscious mind because preferences generally are determined by factors of which the individual is not usually aware. In most buying situations the consumer acts emotionally and compulsively, and unconsciously reacts to images which they subconsciously associate with the product" (p. 5).

One expert and critic said, "The cosmetic manufacturers are not selling lanolin; they are selling hope … we no longer buy oranges, we buy vitality. We do not buy just an auto; we buy prestige" (p. 5). Packard says that motivation researchers assume three things about people: (1) they don't always know what they want when making a purchase; (2) you can't rely on what they say they like or dislike; and (3) they don't usually act logically when they buy, vote, or join.

Motivation research reflects the symbolist tradition in psychology rather than the experimental tradition, the tradition that symbols are just as or more important than real things to most people. Advertising and marketing researchers use focus group interviews, surveys, psychological tests, and so on, to get consumers to describe the fears, pleasures, or fantasies they associate with brands and ads. Other researchers ask people to complete sentences or do word associations about the brand. Though initiated to the marketing industry over 75 years ago, this trend continues in more sophisticated forms using more technologically advanced techniques (e.g., the galvanic skin response, MRIs), and recent research about consumer behavior confirms many of the claims made by Packard so long ago. This kind of motivational research is still with us but now uses sophisticated techniques that take cultural diversity into account and use demographic, socio-graphic, and psychographic techniques, as well as interactive media, to involve the receiver. They know, for example, that the subscribers to MySpace are less educated than users of Facebook; less interested in upscale sports (e.g., golf, squash, or polo), equipment, and fashion than Facebook subscribers, who avoid less sophisticated activities

(e.g., fishing, bowling, or gardening); and if they join the armed forces, MySpace subscribers will be enlisted persons rather than officers. NYU professor Neil Postman (Freedman, 1988) long ago observed that: "Advertisers … desperate to keep you tuned to their pitches, (are) trying some new tricks. Many of these commercials have more impact on the subconscious level" (p. 5).

Ad agencies often enlist psychologists and neurophysiologists to produce the desired effects (Freedman, 1988). For example, Amherst Incorporated developed a research instrument called the Motivation and Attitude Profile (MAP) and used it to market goods, services, and politicians. Amherst's creative director describes the idea behind MAP this way: "People are driven by their emotions—it's not about fact or logic. Increasingly, the only button you press is an emotional one. You find out what their needs are and you discover how to reflect those needs" (Booth, 1999, p. 32). Products as varied as Häagen-Das ice cream, Volkswagen, and life insurance rely on psychographics, which is a research technique that identifies the psychological reasons for purchase behavior. Whether we call it motivational research, lifestyle research, hidden persuaders, or psychographics, using the process amounts to the same basic idea—finding hidden or obvious needs and developing the products and ads to fulfill those needs (see Box 7.1).

B O X 7.1   Consumer Insight—Getting into Your Head

A Chicago-based nationwide marketing company, Claritas, used psychographics and lifestyle data to develop its PRIZM system. PRIZM is a marketing tool that identifies more than 60 market segments across the United States with names that reflect the inner psychological needs of the consumers in each. Take, for example, the segment called "Pickups and Gun Racks." Persons in "Pickups and Gun Racks" tend to live in manufactured housing or mobile homes and are heavy users of generic or house brands of sweetened soda pop. If they purchase lingerie, it tends to be from Frederick's of Hollywood. Their most recent

financial transaction is the purchase of a lottery ticket. They obviously have different needs from those of the people in the segment "Town and Gown," and these needs, in turn, differ from those of the people in the segment "Red, White, and Blue Collar." For persons in "Town and Gown," the most frequent financial transaction is the use of an ATM. If they purchase lingerie, it is frequently at a department store or Victoria's Secret, and most of them live in houses, apartments, dorms, or fraternity and sorority houses. PRIZM is a popular tool among many consumer marketing firms.

Packard's "Compelling Needs"

One approach to the needs premise was Packard's "**compelling needs**," which were based on his observations on the rapidly evolving advertising industry of the motivation research era. He claimed that these needs were so powerful that they *compelled* people to buy, and he identified eight such compelling needs that advertisers used to sell products. We still see them in use today, although with far more sophistication than Packard described—digital images, morphing, special effects, color psychology, and other techniques, all of which allow today's marketers to design ads promising that the product, brand, or service will provide real or symbolic fulfillment of these compelling needs (such as Nutri-System, Air Jordans, the Hummer, and Viagra).

Marketing consultant Barry Feig (1997) discusses such process premises and notes that advertisers are looking for the **hot buttons** that will motivate people and prompt purchase behavior. Feig defined hot buttons as verbal or visual appeals that cause receivers to become emotionally involved with a product or brand rather than responding rationally to product/brand reality. For example, he claims that new car purchases frequently result from the test drive and the new car smell, not from any hard research into performance, which though readily available is often ignored or simply overlooked. The purchaser becomes emotionally involved with the feel, smell, sounds, and styling of the new car and puts aside other factors like mileage, warranty, auto magazine ratings, or *Consumer Reports*. Some clever persuader found a way to package that new car odor in an aerosol spray that can be used to sell used cars more effectively on the same emotional bases. Feig's own work in the 1990s verified nearly all of Packard's hidden needs occurring in today's advertising, and he also found other needs not noted by Packard that still get at our hot buttons via process premises. Let us now examine a few of Packard's emotional needs. He called them "compelling needs," and they are even more effective in today's world.

The Need for Emotional Security. Packard's first compelling need was for **emotional security**, which is defined as feelings of anxiety about the future and feelings of insecurity about our personal welfare and safety in the near future as well in the more distant one, as seen in Figure 7.2. These feelings emerge whenever our world becomes unpredictable, and we then try to dispel the unpredictability in symbolic ways. Today, we are seeing this kind of insecurity in persons who fear the loss of their jobs, foreclosure on their homes, global warming, the Jihadist movement, new emerging and competing economies like China and India, and the skyrocketing costs of energy. Originally, Packard attributed this need for emotional security to the Great Depression, but we can fast-forward to the emotional fears of today's citizenry and can predict their longevity into tomorrow's citizenry. Let's look back a bit and see what it was Packard originally identified as that day's causes for emotional insecurity.

During and following the "Great Recession" beginning in 2008, people desperately wanted to avoid the insecurity of unemployment, the inability to make ends meet, mortgage foreclosure, and other potential calamities to their well-being. Unlike the last decade of the 20th century, when the opposite was the case, people suddenly stopped spending in excess in 2008. Before, people had predictable employment at good wages; they spent regularly for the "extras" like cruises, club memberships, and dining out; and they bought larger and larger houses ("McMansions," some called them). It seemed that everyone went into debt using easy credit while they tried to prepare for retirement homes at the same time. And then, the bubble burst and the mortgage meltdown happened (see Weblink 7.1). (You can access this and all of the other Chapter 7 weblinks through your companion website for *Persuasion,* Chapter 7 resources.)

And many went "upside down" in their home loans. It got so bad that the U.S. government had to loan billions to large banks and mortgage firms to keep them out of bankruptcy. And the phenomenon was global. No wonder people felt emotionally threatened and insecure. The need for emotional security still exists. We are stuck in two seemingly "unwinnable" wars that suck up our treasure, lives, and resources. Terrorism seems unstoppable and is

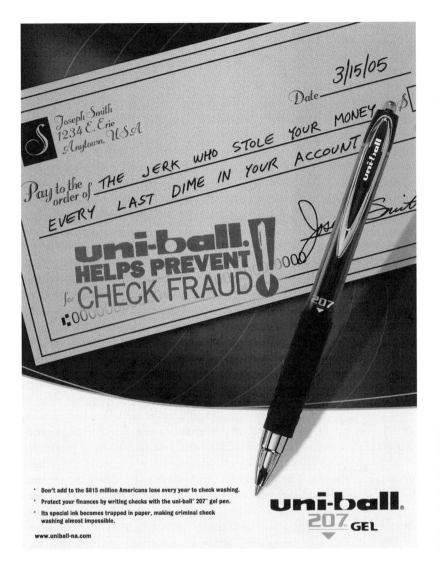

FIGURE 7.2

This ad plays on our inherent feelings of insecurity, especially in an age of identity theft and other means used to defraud people.

SOURCE: Sanford Corp.

certainly unpredictable. Identity theft is mushrooming, making everyone feel insecure. AIDS threatens the economic future of the continent of Africa and elsewhere, and dangerous pollution fouls our environment hourly as it contributes to global warming, which may cause global flooding that will destroy large parts of many countries. Furthermore, the world economy seems precariously balanced. If oil prices continue to escalate, the stock market might crash, resulting in another Great Depression. With mergers, downsizing, and outsourcing, job security

continues to be a worry for many people, and literacy rates have dropped to less than 70 percent from earlier highs over 90 percent, making it hard for many people to get any job other than flipping burgers. And we all feel that somehow we are losing our right to privacy. How do the mass mailers and telemarketers know so much about us? Since 9/11/01, why can the U.S. government wiretap our phones and intercept our mail?

No wonder we search for substitute **symbols** of security. Deodorants promise us secure social

HOMELAND SECURITY TERROR THREAT LEVEL

HYSTERICAL APPROVAL RATING CRITICALLY LOW CREATE IMMEDIATE DISTRACTION	Red
EXAGGERATED AXE ITEMS FROM BILL OF RIGHTS DETAIN TOKEN MUSLIM SUSPECTS	Orange
FABRICATED ANNOUNCE VAGUE BOMB THREAT FROM EVERDAY HOUSEHOLD ITEM	Yellow
SPECIOUS ENTHRALL PUBLIC WITH ZEALOUS RHETORIC ABOUT FREEDOM-HATERS	Blue
UNSUBSTANTIATED MAINTAIN PARANOIA THROUGH PATRIOTIC CALLS FOR VIGILANCE	Green

FIGURE 7.3 The various colors (shown as shades in this book) are merely symbols of security levels.

SOURCE: Chris Pirazzi; www.Lukertech.com.

relationships. Self-improvement courses promise better job security. Retirement planning programs offer financial security for an uncertain future. These and other products and services act as minor premises in the process premise-driven enthymemes mentioned in previous chapters, which have as a major first premise the belief that "security is good." Brand X promises security in some minor way; therefore Brand X represents a sense of security. As a result, we buy it. It is only "symbolic security," but that stands for something (as seen in Figure 7.3).

Even in interpersonal relationships, the need for security causes people to search for commitment. At first, "living together" seemed to be a liberating lifestyle, but this idea is now questioned by some, because there is no security without commitment. Author Stephanie Staal (2001) points out that the divorce rate of those who live together before marriage is 50 percent higher than the rate for those who did not.

We all face unpredictable change, and that makes us vulnerable to persuasion that promises some symbol of security—a good investment program, membership in respected social groups, safety derived from security systems, owning a weapon, or interpersonal confidence stemming from trusting and reliable relationships. Feig (1997) equates this need for security with a universal hot button he calls the "desire for control."

The Need for Reassurance of Worth. We live in a highly competitive and impersonal world in which we often feel like mere cogs or numbers in some database (for example, that's all you are to the university or college you attend). Homemakers, blue-collar workers, salespersons, service workers, managers, and others increasingly need to feel that they are accomplishing something of value and are appreciated by others for the work they do either voluntarily or out of necessity or commitment. (See Figure 7.4.)

Packard called this the need for **reassurance of worth**, which is defined as a feeling that we are valued by others. This need forms the basis of many persuasive appeals, from ads promising to make us better parents, spouses, or friends to appeals for volunteers in good causes. An old but interesting study asked managers and workers to rate 10 factors in job satisfaction. Managers rated wages, fringe benefits, and working conditions at the top, but workers placed them at the bottom. They rated "appreciation for work done" at the top, followed by "my boss listens to me," and "fellow workers." Feig (1997) verified the existence of the reassurance of worth need, saying, "Consumers need to feel good about themselves and fulfill their self-images—it's a basic human need" (p. 14).

Based on hundreds of interviews, sociologist Robert Bellah and colleagues (1985) concluded that most contemporary Americans see themselves in a race for material goods, prestige, power, and influence. They separate themselves from others and find self-worth in material things. Ethics author Kathleen Sibley (1997) noted the feelings of distrust felt by many employees when they learned of a company policy of monitoring employee e-mail. They felt more like objects than like subjects or

FIGURE 7.4 According to Packard's theory on compelling needs, everyone wants to be valued as someone of worth.

SOURCE: StockLite/Shutterstock.com; bikeriderlondon/Shutterstock.com; Tim Graham/Alamy; gerenme/iStockphoto.com; Bart Coenders/iStockphoto.com.

persons. When we feel less and less important as individuals, we become vulnerable targets for persuasion that promises reassurance of worth. Reassurance of worth has its cultural implications also. Schiffman and Kanuk (1997) observed that Asian-Americans are very brand loyal, but especially so when the brand lets it be known that they are welcome and that their patronage is appreciated, shown by offering preferred customer cards, premiums, and so on. Other ethnic subcultures value bargaining, and still others value quality over price.

The Need for Ego Gratification. Packard found that many consumers not only needed to be reassured of their basic worth, but they also needed **ego gratification**, which he defined as feelings of self-

importance and having one's ego stroked. In a widely run ad targeted at the traveling business-woman—showing the woman in a courtyard hotel room by Marriott—the ad focuses on the woman getting all the extras from Marriott, including Internet access, fine furnishings, and even a cup of coffee served in a china cup instead of a Styrofoam one. Marriott also emphasizes that they cater to female business travelers and especially to those from different ethnic groups, thus reinforcing the growing importance of females and ethnic diversity in the workplace. Earlier ads by Marriott usually showed white male executives as customers who get all these extras.

Satisfaction of the need for ego gratification comes from a variety of sources, including friends,

FIGURE 7.5   Satisfaction of any need provides self-gratification.

SOURCE: Juniors Bildarchiv/Alamy.

coworkers, neighbors, parents, groups, institutions, and ourselves (see Figure 7.5).

Feig (1997) called this need the "I'm better than you" hot button, and emphasized that consumers display the possessions that build their egos and meet this need. Persuaders often target groups whose members feel that they have been put down for some time, such as teachers, police officers, firefighters, and postal or social workers. After 9/11, the media brought many of these groups into a well-deserved public spotlight. They got ego gratification from being featured on TV, in newspapers, and on the covers of news weeklies. Such groups can also now get special rates on their mortgages, grants in aid to help them buy homes, and other benefits showing national appreciation for public service.

Persuaders frequently sell products, ideas, and candidates by targeting an out-group's ego needs in personal ways that appeal to self-perception. Take family values, for example. From the late 1960s until the late 1980s, the traditional family was out of style. Communal living was popular, as

was living together. Those who remained committed to the ideal of the traditional family felt like outcasts. From the 1990s to the present, persuasive "pro-family" appeals succeeded in presidential campaigns, religious appeals, public relations, and the marketing of products promising a restoration of family values. Feig (1997) called this need the "family values" hot button, and noted that marketers sell a vision of the family as we all wish it would be. Similarly, politicians know how to stroke the egos of appropriate groups of targeted potential voters. In the 2008 primaries, for instance, Arkansas governor Mike Huckabee repeatedly emphasized his conservative social values and that he rejected the theory of evolution. Not surprising then that he won all of the religious southern states in the "Super-Tuesday" primaries. Mitt Romney emphasized his experience in the business world, and Hillary Clinton emphasized her longtime belief in universal health coverage. All of them were making the "I'm like you" point, as is seen in Figure 7.6 where the milk drinkers' egos are stroked. Earlier, one Republican female candidate for governor used ego gratification with two widely differing audiences, making the same point on similarity with the audience but nonverbally. For a GOP women's luncheon she arrived by limousine, wearing a conservative dress and scarf, and ate chicken salad for lunch. Afterward, she changed her clothes to a black leather jacket, boots, gloves, and pants, and then drove a Harley to the Young Republicans club at a nearby college. She got rave reviews at both events (National Public Radio, 2002).

The Need for Creative Outlets.   In our modern technocracy, few products can be identified with a single artisan. This was not always the case. For example, until the Industrial Revolution, craftsmen such as cabinetmakers created a piece of furniture from beginning to end—it was their unique product. The same applied to blacksmiths, silversmiths, and other craftsmen. They all could point with pride to their product. That is not often the case today, which is why we feel a need for **creative outlets**. Packard saw this need being met by offering substitute creative activities that would replace

Make ours doubles.

My sister and I hate to lose—nutrients, that is.
So we drink milk. It has 9 essential nutrients active bodies need.
You might say it's the only thing we serve.

got milk?

FIGURE 7.6   The Fluid Milk Promotion Board strokes the ego of average citizens by making them feel special, hinting that they are sophisticated, and suggesting that they can avoid health problems by drinking three glasses of milk a day.

SOURCE: Image Courtesy of The Advertising Archives.

the creations previously produced by individuals. They felt less and less creative in many ways, and they needed to find ways to express their own unique creativity. Packard said persuaders targeted this need for creative outlets by promoting products and brands related to hobbies, crafts, and social activities. Today, more than half the population works in the service and information industries, where most important products are intangible and not really very creative. There is no actual creation of anything, and more work is now being accomplished through technologies, such as robots and assembly lines of machinery. Despite this technology, people still need to demonstrate their own

creativity—a need that Feig (1997) identified as the "excitement of discovery" hot button—so they engage in gardening, gourmet cooking, home decorating, art, music, or collecting and restoring antiques. Take a look at the articles included in almost any women's homemaking magazine, and you'll find several ideas for meeting the need for creative outlets.

The Need for Love Objects.   Packard noted that people whose children have grown up often feel a need for **love objects**. These "empty nesters" feel lonely and unneeded when the last kid goes off to college, gets a job, or gets married. Empty nesters fill their love needs in various ways such as doing volunteer work, devoting more time to their jobs or hobbies, or becoming a big brother or sister or a foster grandparent. Persuaders target these empty nesters in a variety of ways. For instance, many older persons get pets to serve as substitute love objects. They coddle them, spoil them, and even dress them up. The pet food industry targets "gourmet" lines to such persons who bring home Premium Cuts, Tender Vittles, Beef 'n Gravy, Tuna Surprise, or Chicken Spectacular. The food sounds and even looks like something a human might consume. Feig (1997) calls this the "revaluing" hot button, and he predicts a major increase in products that attempt to fill this need as the baby boomers approach retirement and an empty nest (see Figure 7.7).

The Need for a Sense of Power or Strength.   More than members of other cultures, most U.S. citizens seek emblems of potency or a **sense of power or strength** in symbolic ways. Packard defined this as the need for a personal extension of one's *perceived* power or strength, rather than true power or strength. For example, the bigger the car or outboard motor, the better; snowmobiles, ATVs, Jet Skis, Hummers, SUVs, and Harley Davidson motorcycles sell because they give the user this sense of power. Whether the brand is a double-triggered chain saw (see Figure 7.8 and note how he holds the chainsaw) or a Hummer, an increased perception of power is the central issue. Stanley Tools sells "heavy duty" tools, not wimpy, "light duty" hammers and

aochsner@northernstar.info

©2005 Al Ochsner/All Rights Reserved

FIGURE 7.7 This cartoon is based on a true incident. A wounded goose was taken in and nursed to health by an assistant to NIU's president, who was single and nearing retirement.

SOURCE: Al Ochsner.

wrenches. Similarly, Americans seem to elect politicians who do macho things. In fact, any major candidate for the presidency must demonstrate physical strength in some way. And as males approach midlife, they often engage in macho activities like bungee jumping or bodybuilding.

The Need for Roots. One of the predominant features of modern society is mobility. Individuals employed by any large firm will probably have to move several times during their careers, and most persons have three or more careers during their lifetime. In the decade following graduation from college, the average graduate moves a dozen times, usually crossing state lines at least once. Few persons remain at "home" for their entire lives. As a result, most persons feel a **need for roots**, symbolic or real. The need for roots is defined as feelings of homesickness and a yearning for family-centered activities. When individuals move away from home, especially if it is some distance, there are some pieces of home that they can take along with them. Brand loyalty, which develops most strongly between the ages of 18 and 24, is a reminder of home; and recent college graduates have one of the highest levels of brand loyalty, which is why my university agreed to give Pepsi exclusive "pouring rights" on campus. Only Pepsi

products (e.g., Mountain Dew, Lipton Tea) can be sold or served on campus. All materials used to serve the brands (cups, straws, napkins, etc.) must have the Pepsi logo imprinted on them. Pepsi gave over $8 million to the scholarship fund for this right, knowing that brand loyalty would develop. I suggested we could charge a couple of million more if we required professors and instructors to wear Pepsi-imprinted gear—after all, it's a game of "brand impressions," isn't it?

The need for roots and the sense of brand loyalty also helps explain **line extensions**, or the development of new products based on old and familiar brands. We feel more at home buying the new Quaker Oats Squares or granola treats than another brand because of the familiar, friendly, and old-fashioned face of the Quaker Man promising "An honest taste from an honest face." (See Figure 7.9.) He serves as an emblem of our tradition, our need for an "old-fashioned" hearty breakfast, and our need for a sense of roots.

The nice thing about brand names is that they are portable—we can take them to a new home anywhere. The Lane Furniture Company appealed to the need for roots and emotional ties to home by offering newlyweds a Lane cedar chest to "take part of home" with them when they married. We've already noted the appeal politicians make to family

Stands Alone!

THE PERFECT CEREAL FOOD FOR ALL SEASONS.

Can't you Eat Breakfast? Try a Dish of Quaker Oats. You'll like That. Cheap, too!
But It couldn't be any better if It Cost a Guinea a Pound.
Appetising and Easily Digested.   Better than Meat.
Goes Further and Costs Less.

Quaker Oats

Sold Everywhere. In 2-lb. Packets Only.

FIGURE 7.9   The old Quaker man
provides reassurance.

SOURCE: The Advertising Archives.

FIGURE 7.8   Powerful motors and
machines often give consumers an
artificial sense of masculinity and power.

SOURCE: Gala_Kan/Shutterstock.com.

values. The trend toward increasingly mobile and fragmented lives is likely to continue. As a result, the need for roots remains an important motivator, and advertisers, politicians, and ideologues continue to use it in their persuasive appeals to us. Feig (1997) equates this need with his "family values" hot button and notes, "Quality time with families is still of utmost importance to Americans." Schiffman and Kanuk observe that in some subcultures (such as Asian–American and Latino) family and roots stretch across several generations. In this regard, The *New York Times* noted the trend of taking generations of family on road trips (Feig, 1997).

The Need for Immortality.   None of us wants to believe in our own mortality. The fear of growing old and dying clearly drives the healthy-living industry, which promotes such things as good nutrition, stress reduction, exercise, and a healthy lifestyle overall. Packard suggested that this need for immortality grew out of the need to maintain influence or control over the lives of family members. The breadwinner is made to feel that by purchasing life insurance, he or she obtains life after death in the form of continuing financial security, which will help the kids go to college even if he or she isn't there (see Figure 7.10). Other products make similar appeals to the fear of death. For instance, Promise margarine will keep you healthy longer because "Promise is at the heart of eating right." And Nivea's Visage face cream will make your skin "firmer, healthier, and younger" for only

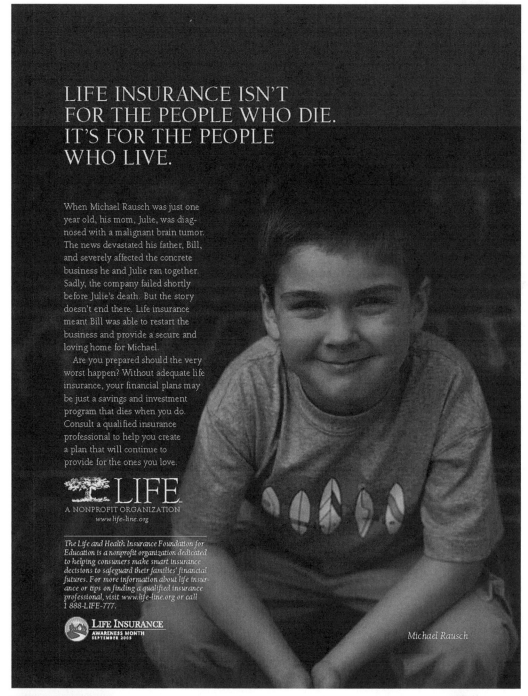

LIFE INSURANCE ISN'T
FOR THE PEOPLE WHO DIE.
IT'S FOR THE PEOPLE
WHO LIVE.

When Michael Rausch was just one
year old, his mom, Julie, was diagnosed with a malignant brain tumor.
The news devastated his father, Bill,
and severely affected the concrete
business he and Julie ran together.
Sadly, the company failed shortly
before Julie's death. But the story
doesn't end there. Life insurance
meant Bill was able to restart the
business and provide a secure and
loving home for Michael.

   Are you prepared should the very
worst happen? Without adequate life
insurance, your financial plans may
be just a savings and investment
program that dies when you do.
Consult a qualified insurance
professional to help you create
a plan that will continue to
provide for the ones you love.

LIFE
A NONPROFIT ORGANIZATION
www.life-line.org

*The Life and Health Insurance Foundation for
Education is a nonprofit organization dedicated
to helping consumers make smart insurance
decisions to safeguard their families' financial
futures. For more information about life insurance or tips on finding a qualified insurance
professional, visit www.life-line.org or call
1 888-LIFE-777.*

LIFE INSURANCE
AWARENESS MONTH
SEPTEMBER 2005

Michael Rausch

FIGURE 7.10   This ad appeals to the need for immortality by assuring readers that even if they are no longer there, they will still be able to influence the lives of their survivors.

SOURCE: LIFE Foundation.

pennies a day. As the ad executive noted in an earlier quote, we aren't buying lanolin, we are buying hope—hope for a little more immortality (see Figure 7.10). This need for immortality seems particularly relevant in our modern technocracy. The much talked-about "midlife crisis" is an example. This occurs when people realize that "time marches on," that they have probably passed the halfway point in their lives, or when they confront some other major life event such as the death of a parent. As a result, many try to start over; they get divorced, quit or lose their jobs, buy sports cars, run off with someone half their age, and speed away in the sports car, determined to make a new life as a ski bum, thus underscoring their indestructible youth. They want to be young again, or at least to enjoy some of the experiences they missed along the way. Frequently, they engage in dangerous activities such as skydiving, whitewater rafting, wilderness thrills, or hot air ballooning.

There are many other persuasive appeals that succeed because they are somehow tied to the desire for immortality (Lafavore, 1995). Feig (1997) calls this the "self-nurturance and the ability to stay ageless and immortal" hot button, and noted that older persons are more willing to spend money on things that make them feel better about themselves, than they are on some of the essentials of life.

We now turn to perhaps one of the most well known models of human needs that was first described more than 50 years ago, and it is still going strong (Rowan, 1998). For a recent update about this relevance, go to Weblink 7.2.

Maslow's Hierarchy of Needs

Abraham Maslow (1954), a well-known psychologist and pioneer in the discipline, long ago offered a simple starting point for examining people's needs. His theories about the power of human needs are judged by many to be as relevant for persuasion today as they were when he first described them. In fact, many have been adapted to management training, humanistic psychology, education, and so forth. Nancy Austin (2002), a California management consultant, maintains that, though the theory

may be over a half-century old, "for modern managers looking to pump up performance, it still has zing." Robert Zemke (1998), the senior editor of the journal *Training,* notes, "It's ironic that this '50s psychologist with no head for business played such a central role in the development of the psychology of management and the thoughts of modern managers." In 1998, Maslow's daughter published a revision of his work, entitled *Maslow on Management,* which was greeted with rave reviews (Rowan, 1998). And Schiffman and Kanuk (1997) say that in spite of its age, "Maslow's hierarchy is a useful tool in understanding consumer motivations and is readily adaptable to marketing strategy" (p. 100). An entirely new field of management psychology called "Eupsychian Management" has grown out of Maslow's original ideas (see Weblink 7.3). Some of Feig's hot buttons equate to Maslow's need levels. Despite its vintage, Maslow's hierarchy still has much to teach us. Maslow theorized that people have various kinds of needs that emerge, subside, and then reemerge. In his hierarchy of needs, the lower levels of the hierarchy represent the strongest needs, and the higher levels the weaker ones (see Figure 7.11). Maslow did not believe that higher needs are superior to lower needs; rather, they are less likely to emerge until the stronger lower needs have been met. The base of the pyramid represents universal needs or beliefs about which there is unanimous agreement. As we move up the pyramid, we find needs or beliefs on which there may not be unanimous agreement and on which individuals place varying degrees of value. As a result, there is an upward dynamic in Maslow's hierarchy, which means that as powerful needs are met, less potent ones emerge. Maslow called this upward dynamic **prepotency.** In other words, weaker needs (such as the need for self-respect) emerge only after stronger needs (like food or shelter) have been filled. Don't try to persuade a dehydrated person to dress up before having a drink of water. The need to slake our thirst is prepotent, and until it is fulfilled, we ignore other needs. As time passes, the earlier needs also reemerge again. For example, the needs for food or water emerge and then recede as we eat or drink, and will reemerge at a later time.

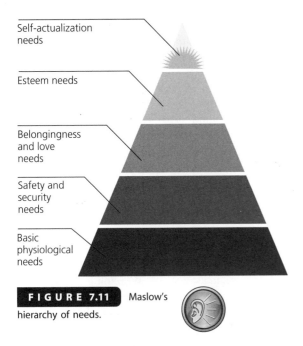

Self-actualization
needs

Esteem needs

Belongingness
and love
needs

Safety and
security
needs

Basic
physiological
needs

FIGURE 7.11   Maslow's
hierarchy of needs.

Basic Needs.   The bottom level of Maslow's pyramid contains the strongest needs we have, our **basic needs**, which he defined as the physiological things required to sustain life: regular access to air, food, water, shelter, sleep, and so on. Until these needs have been met, we don't usually concern ourselves with higher needs. However, basic needs can motivate behavior. For example, the person who is starving can be motivated to do all sorts of unusual things to secure food, ranging from stealing it to eating insects. And we know that the need for air can cause drowning victims to panic and drown not only themselves but also their potential rescuers. Shelter is another basic need and one strong enough to motivate persons to take drastic and apparently illogical action, such as burying themselves in a snow bank in below zero weather, and the need for air was demonstrated by the pyramidal piles of corpses left in the Nazi death camp gas chambers—the gas—Zyklon-B was heavier than air.

Security Needs.   The second level of Maslow's pyramid is the **need for security**, which he defined as the ability to continue to fill the basic needs of life. We can look at these needs in several ways. If we fear losing

our jobs (as is the case for many in recent times), we have a strong need to obtain income security; therefore, we try to find a more secure job, or we save money for hard times. During the recent mortgage meltdown, many feared losing their homes and sold their houses at drastically deflated prices, even when they weren't in real danger of foreclosure. Even if we have job security, we still might feel insecure about maintaining our personal safety because of the rising crime rates in our neighborhood or rental complexes now taking "Section 8" applicants. We might take drastic action to ward off criminals by keeping a gun on the nightstand or perhaps by moving to a gated community. Even when we feel secure in our community, we still might feel insecure because of world politics. We fear that our country is vulnerable to terrorists, who may manage to soon acquire nuclear, biological, or chemical weapons. Or we fear that our leaders are considering unwise military actions against another country. Those not technically trained for the computer age have a realistic fear of being out of date and soon out of a job. Political analysts explained several recent election results as related to fears of economic displacement. In the interpersonal realm, we have a need for "social security," or the continuing acceptance by others. In other words, the need for security emerges and reemerges as various threats to our security become evident (see Figure 7.12).

Today, insecurity, like change, is one of the few predictable things in life. Eight of every ten jobs being filled by tomorrow's college grads don't even exist today. It's almost impossible for someone to prepare for the future because the rate and pace of change is accelerating so quickly. Computer technology now becomes obsolete in less than a year. No one can keep up with all the new (and frequently essential) information about jobs, health, communities, and a host of other personal and social issues. This need is similar to Feig's "desire to control" hot button. Feig says this need explains home-based businesses, because in them you can become your own boss and avoid layoffs.

Belongingness and Affiliation Needs.   Once our security needs have been met, we become aware of needs on the third level of the pyramid—**belongingness or affiliation needs**, which are

BREAST CANCER BEGINS EVEN SMALLER THAN THIS. THAT'S WHY YOU NEED A YEARLY MAMMOGRAM, ESPECIALLY AS YOU GET OLDER. MAMMOGRAMS CAN DETECT LUMPS TOO SMALL FOR YOU TO FEEL AND EARLY DETECTION MAY SAVE YOUR LIFE, SO CALL 1-800-ACS 2345.

GET A MAMMOGRAM.
EARLY DETECTION IS THE BEST PROTECTION.

FIGURE 7.12 The need for security is the appeal used in this ad from the American Cancer Society.

SOURCE: Reprinted by permission of the American Cancer Society.

defined as the need to interact with others and to identify with some group. A number of options are open to us to meet our need for association. Usually, individuals go beyond the family and workplace and become members of groups with which they want to affiliate, such as service groups, places of worship, the PTA, bowling leagues, or golf and health clubs. Generally, we limit the number of groups we join, and we are active members in only a few. Feig (1997) identified the "need for belonging" as another of his hot buttons and noted that "Americans are the 'joiningest' people in the world." He advises doubters to examine the number of membership cards in their wallets if they don't think this is so (p. 29). The flip side of belonging and affiliation needs is the recent trend toward isolation, which has been hastened by the personal computer and the Internet where one can be isolated for hours at a time—even days for true addicts. A number of people and organizations are concerned about the tendency of people to cocoon or isolate themselves. In his article "Bowling Alone" (1995) and his follow-up book, *Bowling Alone: The Collapse and Revival of American Community* (2000), Robert Putnam observed that more and more persons join what he calls checkbook groups such as the Citizen's Utility Board, the Sierra Club, or the American Association of Retired Persons. Belonging only requires that you write a check, because the groups rarely if ever meet. Membership is down in civic and fraternal groups like the Lions, Elks, and Moose Clubs, and fewer people bowl in leagues, preferring to "bowl alone."

Like physiological and security needs, the need to belong often interacts with other needs and continues to reemerge throughout our lives. Also, what fulfills our belonging needs differs at various points in our lives and will probably change across time. It may be important to belong to a fraternity or sorority when we are in college, but after graduation, these affiliations fade and are replaced by job-related associations or other social activities. Later, when we have families, other affiliations tend to be more important to us, and we join community groups, school organizations like the PTA, or a group within our religious organization. In this context, a recent trend is the emergence of "mega-churches" like the Mariners Church of Newport Beach, California. This church offers programming for various market segments—grief therapy, Gen X activities, and seminars on a variety of topics like twelve-step recovery, divorce dynamics, and the parenting of adolescents—all served up with cappuccino and scones. The need to belong will always be with us because humans by nature are social beings.

Love and Esteem Needs.   Once we satisfy our affiliation or belonging needs, we feel the emergence of needs in the fourth level of Maslow's model, which he called **love and esteem needs**, defined as the need to be valued by the members of the groups with which we affiliate—our families, fellow workers, friends, church congregation, and neighbors. Once we are part of a group, we want to feel that the group values us as a member and as an individual. We are happy when our families understand and admire the things we do. In her recent book *My Life So Far,* Jane Fonda quotes Oprah Winfrey as naming this need the "Please Disease" (2005), and describes it as a lifelong and unending desire to do things that will please our parent(s) (even if they are deceased) and bring us a sense of their love or esteem. The esteem need is also a reemerging one. That is, when we find that we are needed, loved, and esteemed by our family, our need for esteem does not fade away—instead, its focus shifts, and we now want to feel needed by our co-workers, our boss, and our friends.

Many product appeals offer a kind of symbolic substitute for esteem. For example, as Figure 7.13

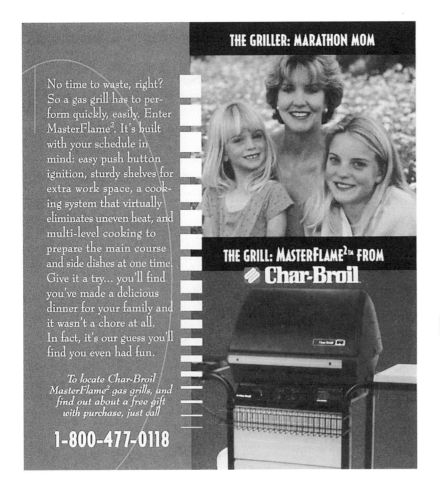

FIGURE 7.13

Esteem needs are the key appeal in this ad claiming a Char-Broil gas grill allows the mother to whip up a great meal for her kids, and she feels good about that.

SOURCE: Char Broil.

shows, the kids will hold Mom in high esteem if she uses a certain brand of gas grill.

At various times, a person's esteem seems rooted in conspicuous consumption for purposes of display. At other times (e.g., wartime), conspicuous consumption borders on being unpatriotic. However, important events and life experiences can change the way people satisfy esteem needs. For instance, recent political, financial, and religious scandals have shaken people's faith in traditional institutions and their leadership's ability to show esteem. What kind of esteem for employees and stockholders does the crooked CEO have? Schiffman and Kanuk (1997) note that the Asian-American subculture is highly motivated by esteem needs and therefore they are strivers, particularly in terms of education. People realize that working in community can help them meet their esteem needs. In fact, "community" has become a kind of god term.

Self-Actualization Needs. Maslow put **self-actualization needs** at the top of his pyramid (thereby implying that they rarely emerge). He defined self-actualization as the achievement of one's full potential or capability. At first, Maslow believed that individuals could live up to their potential only when all four of the lower needs had been met. It is hard for young people on the way up to think about self-actualization, just as it is difficult to meet love or esteem needs if individuals

don't belong to some group that can offer love or esteem. But in reality, self-actualization is an integral part of everyone's life. In fact, later in life Maslow said another need—the need to help others find self-actualization—emerged in some persons. Feig labeled this need "the desire to be the best you can be" hot button, and he identifies several examples, including the pride we all had as children when we brought home our gold-starred papers from school— they were proof of self-actualization. Poor Cardinal Sicola in Figure 7.14 won't get to self-actualize because of his name.

Maslow later came to see self-actualization as occurring through what he called "peak experiences" in life. These events allowed individuals to enjoy and learn about themselves, or experience something they had only dreamed of previously. Thus, the person who ventures into the wilderness and learns to be self-reliant and not to fear isolation enjoys a peak, or self-actualizing, experience. When people take their first job after high school or college and discover that they have abilities that are of value, they probably experience a degree of self-actualization. Cultural trends also affect the ways in which we seek to satisfy our self-actualization needs. Social critic T.J. Jackson Lears (1983) noted that the search for ways of identifying ourselves and our potential came about when the United States shifted from being a culture of production to a culture of consumption; that is, in moving from a

aochsner@northernstar.info

FIGURE 7.14 The humor here is based on Cardinal Sicola's inability to self-actualize.

SOURCE: Al Ochsner.

BOX 7.2   **Interactive Marketing and Human Needs**

Go to Weblink 7.5 and discover how marketing experts are delving into human needs using interactive media. The home page you will discover there will show you how marketers use interactive media to appeal to human needs and emotions. Explore the various options, including how the

Watson Communication Group plans and executes advertising strategies for various clients such as Levi Strauss, Microsoft, cosmetic dentists, skin care specialists, and others. You will see how human needs and emotions are being tapped by persuaders of all sorts.

---

secure farm existence to an unsettling urban isolation, we experienced a loss of traditional values and chaotic changes in our lifestyles. The result, Lears claimed, was the search for a "therapeutic ethos," or an identity that would let us be at ease with ourselves, one that would permit us to self-actualize. To a large extent, this therapeutic ethos offers inner harmony, reduced feelings of emptiness, and hope for self-realization through patterns of consumption. As you are exposed to various persuasive events, whether public or interpersonal, try applying Maslow's model to them, and see whether it sheds light on the needs that people feel and that may motivate their actions and persuade them. You may want to experiment with persuading another person using several levels of Maslow's model. If the person doesn't seem motivated by appeals to security, try appealing to basic or belongingness needs.

Uses of the Needs Process Premise

In our search for the first premises that serve as springboards for persuasion in enthymemes, human needs demonstrate one area of our vulnerability to persuasion. Whether we identify them using Packard's compelling needs, Maslow's hierarchy, Feig's hot buttons, or some other model, we all experience strongly felt needs that require some sort of satisfaction. Satisfaction of some of these needs come to us through various kinds of media—especially SNM. (See Weblink 7.4.) Persuaders frequently tie minor premises to these powerful needs and allow audiences to complete the enthymematic argument by drawing the conclusion. As persuadees, we must consider the persuasive

requests made of us from the perspective of our own needs. And as persuaders, we should examine the current needs of those we wish to influence. If we do that, we are more likely to succeed and to do our audience a service by giving them a way to satisfy their needs.

It is important, however, to be ethical in appealing to audience needs, especially in an ethically challenged world. As persuadees we need to ask, "Is this appeal to my true needs ethical or not?" thus practicing our response-ability, and we need to ask the same questions when we take on the role of persuader. A good way to train yourself to evaluate appeals from this critical perspective—as persuadee or persuader—is to restate persuasive messages, such as TV commercials or political appeals, from the perspective of the Packard, Maslow, Feig, or other need models. As first premises on which persuasion can be built, psychological and physiological needs are powerful motivators, and they are frequently used in our world of advocacy and propaganda. See Box 7.2.

EMOTIONS: THE SECOND PROCESS PREMISE

Another kind of psychological or process premise relates to our emotions (see Box 7.3). Appeals to our emotions are the second of four such process premises including needs. What does it mean when, in the midst of a discussion, someone says, "You're just being too emotional about this"? It may mean that they have noticed a physical change in your behavior. Perhaps your voice changes in timbre or

BOX 7.3 **Disney, Emotions, and Propaganda**

Go to Weblink 7.6 and watch an eight-minute video "Reason and Emotion" on wartime propaganda. Emotion is personalized as a caveman and a naughty and sexy young girl. Why? Reason is personalized as a nerdy fellow with big eyeglasses and as a spinster schoolteacher. Why? If you wish you can also view several WWII animated cartoons (or parts thereof) from Disney. Now enter the words "Institute for Propaganda Analysis" and review the seven techniques of propaganda introduced by the Institute, beginning with the link entitled "Name Calling." Try to determine which of their techniques, as well as the needs and emotions discussed in this chapter, are being played upon in the initial Disney film and the optional clips from the other cartoons.

volume, your face gets red, you begin to show a nervous tic, or your eyes reveal anger.

Or they might be responding to the fact that you have started rattling off statistics and sound like a courtroom attorney. Borchers (2005) refers to these two symptoms of being emotional as demonstrating the physiological and the cognitive dimensions of emotion. In the **physiological dimension**, you feel a change in the way your body is responding to the situation. You feel your voice change in timbre, your face flush, and your facial expression change. (See Figure 7.15.) With the **cognitive dimension** of emotions, the changes in you are not physical responses, they are perceptual changes in the way you think about a person, an issue, or a situation. These cognitive changes are usually expressed verbally. We are probably born with the physiological dimension of emotions hardwired into our brains. However, we must learn the cognitive dimension and how to express what emotions we are feeling. We learn these things from experiences, parents, authority figures, friends, or role models whom we observe in films, on television, or elsewhere. In both the physiological and the cognitive dimension, there are cultural variations (Porter and Samovar, 1998), particularly when our emotions are publicly displayed. We can see this in ethnic stereotypes of the emotional, gesticulating Italian or the authority-driven German. You probably have learned that the British are very polite even when expressing anger, whereas other ethnicities might be outright rude.

In both the physiological and the cognitive dimension, we are dealing with models for understanding and reacting to our feelings and beliefs. Nabi (2002) maintains that emotions have five basic components: (1) cognitive evaluation of a situation, meaning that we are aware and have thought over the situation; (2) physiological arousal, or a change in bodily functions, such as an adrenalin rush; (3) motor expression, or what we physically do about the situation; (4) motivational intentions or readiness, or what we are prepared to do and

FIGURE 7.15 Facial expressions frequently reveal emotional needs.

SOURCE: STUART WALKER/Alamy.

plan to do and why; and (5) a feeling state in the subject, such as when you feel happy or disappointed (p. 290). You have learned to "bite your tongue" or to "count to ten" when feeling the emotion of anger, either from experience or more likely from parents or authority figures. Let's examine a few emotions that most persons feel or respond to in some way and see how persuaders use them to move us to action.

Fear

Fear is one of the most familiar emotions that we experience. Initially, you learned to be afraid when you did something wrong and angered someone else—usually a parent—and were punished for the behavior. As time passed, you learned that other situations and events can also lead to negative outcomes, and you became fearful of a number of things such as disease, injury, loss of property, or personal embarrassment to name a few. Nabi (2002) says that fear includes a threat to our physical or psychological self that is out of our control, and that it has the power change attitudes (pp. 291–292). (See Figure 7.16.)

Sometimes the fear appeal works powerfully, but at other times it boomerangs, especially if it is too strong to stomach, inappropriate for you in your situation, or simply is unbelievable. Politicians have used fear appeals in negative television advertisements in campaign after campaign, and 2012 will probably not be any different. In the 2008 presidential campaign, President Bush implied that a vote for his opponent would lead to a loss of national security. Fear appeals are also common in marketing communication. For example, the insurance industry tells us to be afraid of financial loss. We are told that we need insurance for everything from floods to identity theft, the need for long-term medical care, or national disasters like Hurricane Katrina in 2005, which made New Orleans essentially uninhabitable and resulted in billions of dollars in insurance claims. Personal grooming ads emphasize the possible loss in prestige that comes from teeth that aren't white enough, underarm odor, or poor taste in choice of clothing. And

cause-related persuasion frequently uses fear appeals in campaigns advocating family values, safe sex, and national security. In most uses of fear appeals, the persuader must first convince persuadees of the probability of the threat before offering a means (usually a product or practice) of avoiding it and then demonstrating that the proposed solution will work. As receivers of fear appeals, you need to carefully examine the probability of the threat, the difficulty of taking the proposed actions to dodge the threat, and the evidence that these actions will prevent the problem.

Guilt

As we observed elsewhere, guilt is a powerful motivator in persuading others to vote, purchase, donate, or join. Guilt usually comes from a realization that we have violated some rule or code of conduct but can reduce the guilt by atonement or punishment. Borchers (2005) defines guilt as "a psychological feeling of discomfort that arises when order is violated" (p. 195). Guilt frequently arises out of some kind of interpersonal situation— we have wronged our parents, children, spouse, friends, or the community, and we must set things right. For example, the politician claims that we have underfunded education, and many poor kids are left behind, doomed to failure. We can atone for the mistake by having nationwide competence tests, eliminating tenure for teachers, and getting actively involved in our children's learning. If we missed an appointment, we can send flowers or an "I'm sorry" card. If we have engaged in unsafe sex, thus endangering our partner, we can notify that partner and vow to engage in preventive actions in the future. The best way to prevent drug usage by teens is for parents to ask where the teen is going, who will be there, when they expect to come home, and whether adults will be present. That advice is part of a cause-related campaign sponsored by the Partnership for a Drug-Free America and is about avoiding guilt in the future. Its slogan is: "Parents: The Anti-Drug," and its ads emphasize the guilt a parent can feel if their child becomes a drug user.

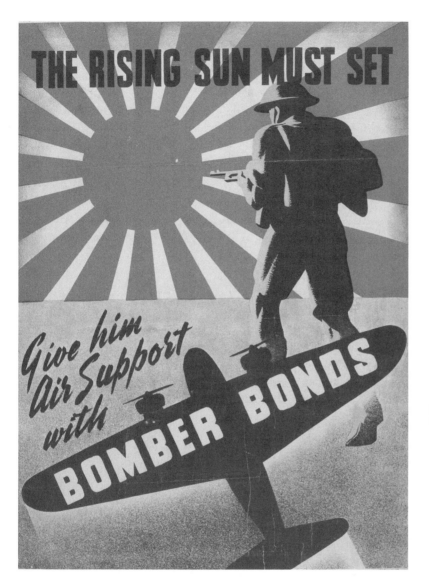

FIGURE 7.16

Appeals to the emotion of fear have been one of the most researched issues in persuasion, but the conclusions of the research are often contradictory.

SOURCE: Gift of Mr C H Andrews, 1967/Museum of New Zealand Te Papa Tongarewa/GH014048.

Nabi (2002) notes that the causes of guilt vary greatly across religions and cultures. In some cultures, "losing face" is about the worst thing a person can do. In others, dishonoring one's elders is the big guilt button. Receivers need to recognize guilt appeals for what they are and then determine what they need to do to reduce their own sense of guilt and try to avoid guilt if possible, as seen in Figure 7.17.

Anger

We usually become angry when things don't go our way. When we face some obstacle that keeps us from reaching our goal or that harms us or loved ones, we become frustrated; and we want to strike out at those who make things difficult for us. Anger is also very powerful. Nabi (2002) noted that anger generates high levels of energy and sometimes leads to constructive problem solving and often prompts

THINK HOW MUCH YOUR KIDS COULD DO IN LIFE. NOW THINK HOW DOING POT COULD STOP THEM.

Reliable evidence shows that marijuana today is more than twice as powerful on average as it was 20 years ago. It contains twice the concentration of THC, the chemical that affects the brain. Pot can turn your hopes and dreams for your kids into a nightmare of lost opportunities.

It can start with messing up in school. Kids who regularly smoke marijuana can develop symptoms of what psychologists call an "amotivational syndrome," which in plain English means:

- *decreased energy and ambition*
- *shortened attention span*
- *lack of judgment*
- *high distractibility*
- *impaired ability to communicate and relate to others*

And pot can cause a whole lot more problems than just doing badly in school. But the good news is that kids whose parents get involved with them are far less likely to do drugs.

So lay down a few laws for your kids. And the sooner the better, because the average age when teens first try marijuana is under 14 years old. To learn more, call 1-800-788-2800 or come to the web site.

PARENTS.
THE ANTI-DRUG.
`theantidrug.com`

OFFICE OF NATIONAL DRUG CONTROL POLICY/PARTNERSHIP FOR A DRUG-FREE AMERICA®

FIGURE 7.17   This ad by the Partnership for a Drug-Free America uses the avoidance of future guilt to persuade.

SOURCE: Reprinted with permission of The Partnership for a Drug-Free America.

careful analysis of messages (p. 293). Take the sentence, "What did he mean by saying that I was naive?" You might get angry over being called naive, but you seek to get down to the actual meaning of the accusation, which is usually a constructive use of your anger.

We see appeals to anger in politics and cause-related persuasion—advocacy or propaganda—and in some types of marketing and advertising. A significant proportion of the population was fearful and angry enough following 9/11 that in 2003 that they supported President Bush's decision to go to war in Iraq. The justification for the action was that Iraq had caused the disaster because it harbored terrorists and had hidden Weapons of Mass Destruction (WMDs), and we wanted to strike

back to remove the problem and punish the country for the tragic attacks. In hindsight, we clearly needed more careful analysis of the situation and the facts by critical receivers. The "striking back" was enormously costly in human and national wealth, plunging us into the longest war in our history and the largest deficits in history in our national budget, not to mention the pain and costs of the deaths and injuries suffered by the troops. Many of these costs will continue to exist for decades, such as the physical or psychological injuries. Furthermore, the invasion didn't result in fewer terrorist attacks, but, in fact, it may have led to an increase in the number of suicide bombers (including women and children) in Iraq and elsewhere, and may have been used to recruit new members of terrorist organizations. Another example occurred in the late 1990s, when employees, stockholders, and retirees became angry with CEOs who looted their company's resources and pension funds. Many Wall Street bankers and CEOs of financial organizations subsequently were awarded obscene annual bonuses that outraged many. Some of them went on a crusade to reform the Securities and Exchange Commission, and they succeeded. They used cause-related persuasion to recruit supporters and donors by appealing to the anger felt by those who were cheated by the crooked CEOs. In Illinois, an organization called the Citizen's Utility Board (CUB) regularly receives donations by appealing to the anger felt by consumers when utility rates are arbitrarily raised. On an intrapersonal level, some people are angry with the way they look, even if it's their own fault. An organization of obese people is now bringing suit against food manufacturers for not disclosing ingredient information that might lead overweight individuals to avoid the products (see Figure 7.18). We have also recently seen persons in middle age go to orthodontists to have braces put on their crooked teeth. Perhaps they were angry with their parents, who didn't take care of the problem earlier in adolescence; but now they are willing to pay for the improvement themselves. So anger frequently serves as a motivator in persuasion. Other negative emotions include envy, hatred, and disgust (Nabi, 2002).

Pride

On a more positive note, persuaders appeal to pride to enact legislation, sell products, and prompt joining an organization or donating to a particular candidate or good cause. A feeling of pride usually includes taking credit for some positive outcome in our lives. As a result, people become expressive about their accomplishments and may make announcements about their good deeds. Sometimes this causes resentment in those who haven't achieved as much, so persuaders need to be careful about using appeals to pride. And cultural differences affect the emotion of pride. Nabi (2002) reports that collectivist cultures (such as China's) "respond more favorably to pride-based appeals" (p. 296) than do cultures that are more individualistically based (such as the United States). We can find pride appeals in many persuasive contexts. Politicians tout the accomplishments of their administrations or programs. Cause-based pride appeals are intended to make the potential donors feel proud about making a donation to the good cause, and frequently use testimonials from persons helped by the good cause. And of course many products promise to make consumers feel proud when they use the brand to improve their appearance. For example, Neutrogena Skin Clearing Tint uses a pride appeal when the ads urge consumers to "Rethink makeup ... now, don't cover up. Clear up." The ads give the brand credibility by using the words "Dermatologist Recommended" together with the pictures of two young females who are presumed to use the product and who appear not to have acne or blemishes.

Happiness and Joy

Happiness and joy are obviously similar. Happiness is associated with a mood, and joy indicates a positive emotional response to such happy events. For our purposes they are synonyms. Happy persons are positive about their future, confident, sharing, and trusting, and they seem to attract other persons (Nabi, 2002). We can all think of persuasive happiness appeals made by advertisers who link use of their brand with happy outcomes and satisfied consumers. Estee Lauder's Pleasures and Pleasures for Men ran a three-page fold-out ad in the May 2005 issue of *Cosmopolitan*. It had no copy aside from the name of the brand. Instead it showed nine pictures, seven of which focused on the members of a young family. The other two pictures were of cherry blossoms and a puppy. The implied conclusion was for consumers to use the brand and be as happy as these folks. Politicians promise better, happier, sharing, and more trusting times if we enact their policies on the economy, health care,

Obesity:

~~"Epidemic"~~

~~"Problem"~~

~~"Threat"~~

~~"Issue"~~

"Hype"

Americans have been force-fed a steady diet of obesity myths by the "food police," trial lawyers, and even our own government.

Learn the truth about obesity at:

ConsumerFreedom.com

The Center for Consumer Freedom is a nonprofit organization dedicated to protecting consumer choices and promoting common sense.

FIGURE 7.18

This ad by the Center for Consumer Freedom builds on the anger that overweight persons have felt throughout their lives.

SOURCE: Used with permission of The Center for Consumer Freedom.

the environment, education, and other issues. Cause-related advertising usually implies that support for a cause such as "Save the Children" or "Gun Ownership Rights" will bring the joiner or donor a sense of well-being, self-respect, and happiness, instead of a sense of guilt for ignoring the issue. Nabi (2002) also says that appeals to happiness frequently use humor in advertising because of its ability to distract audience attention and cause laughter (p. 296). Other positive emotions that persuaders can invoke include relief, hope, compassion, and many others.

ATTITUDES: THE THIRD
PROCESS PREMISE

In Chapter 4 we looked at how researchers use a variety of theories to explain attitudes. One unifying element among these theories is that attitudes can and do serve as the unstated major premises in persuasive enthymemes. We also noted that attitudes act as predispositions to behavior, so holding an attitude or a set of attitudes makes us ready to take action. However, while attitudes are sometimes excellent predictors of behavior, at other times they are not. Psychologists Martin Fishbein and Icek Ajzen (1975) now believe that a better predictor of behavior is what they call the **intention to behave**. When the person tells you how he or she intends to act, the person is prone to act that way. By articulating their intentions, they have already acted symbolically.

The initial series of studies into the effects of attitude were conducted by researcher Carl Hoveland and over 30 of his colleagues at Yale in the 1950s and 60s (Hoveland et al., 1953). They identified a series of stages through which information must pass in order to effect persuasion. Stage 1 was **attention** (for if no one paid attention to the information, it could not persuade). Stage 2 was **comprehension** (for if no one could understand the information, it could not persuade—not necessarily true for information passed through the peripheral channel of the ELM). Stage 3 was **retention** (for if no one remembered the information it could not persuade—again not so in peripherally processed information as in the ELM). The final stage was **action** (for if you did not act on the suggested behavior, persuasion did not occur—again not

true in the peripheral channel and not true in many other circumstances like when the persuasion goal is simply to make people aware). So while quite incomplete, the Yale studies and the Yale stage model did initiate an ongoing series of studies conducted elsewhere and by different researchers that persists up until today, some of which produced significantly predictive results (such as the fear appeal studies), and they led to more and more sophisticated definitions of attitudes. (See Box 7.4.)

For example, psychologists Alice H. Egley and Shelley Chaiken (1993) define an attitude as "a psychological tendency that is expressed by evaluating a particular entity with some degree of favor or disfavor" (p. 1). The important word here is "tendency," by which they mean "an internal state that lasts for at least a short time" (p. 2). Since the attitude is internal (in our heads), we must infer it by using "evaluative responses." Evaluative responses include expressing "approval or disapproval, favor or disfavor, liking or disliking, approach or avoidance, attraction or aversion, or similar reactions" (p. 3). Researchers into consumer behavior identified a social function served by attitudes. For instance, they asked whether family, friends, authority figures, or celebrity figures affect our attitudes toward a brand, candidate, or ideology. They concluded that socially significant persons do influence our attitudes (Schiffman and Kanuk, 1997), and note that mass media exposure correlates highly with the formation of consumer attitudes (pp. 260–262). Advertising researcher Shavitt (1990) maintained that attitudes serve both social and utilitarian functions. In researching audience reactions to advertisements, he found that the social functions of attitudes in the ads tell us what persons

---

BOX 7.4	**The Stage Model and Super Bowl Ads**

Go to any search engine and enter the words "super bowl ads." Select from any of the links there and carefully examine several of these spots from different years. Try to determine

if they get attention, can be remembered, and/or are accepted or acted upon. Does the stage model help you as a receiver in analyzing these multimillion dollar ads?

responding to the ads were like and in all likelihood what sorts of appeals would prompt them to action. For example, the ad might claim that discriminating people prefer high-fiber diets to high-fat, low-carb Atkins diets that only temporarily take off pounds. If we want to be a discriminating and slimmer person, we adopt the eating habits of other discriminating and slim persons.

Utilitarian functions of attitudes stress the features and benefits of the product. An ad might claim that the Honda Prius gets up to 60 miles per gallon, and it is extremely quiet in the electrically powered mode. Two utilitarian elements operate here—mileage and quietness. This also fits with elements of the ELM model. For example, psychologists De Bono and Harnish (1988), Petty and Wegener (1998), and others found that for high self-monitoring individuals (those who were usually very aware of why they were responding to an ad), an attractive source of persuasion usually triggers

elaborate processing of the message. For low self-monitoring individuals (those who were barely aware of even responding to the ad), elaborate processing is more likely to occur only if an expert rather than an attractive source conveys the message. This makes sense. If you are a high self-monitoring person, you do not want to blunder simply because a celebrity recommends the product. That makes you seem impulsive in the eyes of others. So you do serious investigation of the product in the central processing route. Low self-monitoring persons respect expertise more than advice from a celebrity, and they avoid looking foolish by relying on the recommendation of the expert.

We usually find attitude objects in the persuader's requests for action or offers of products, ideas, candidates, beliefs, and so on. (See Figure 7.19.)

For example, recently many Americans started flying the flag and displaying patriotic bumper

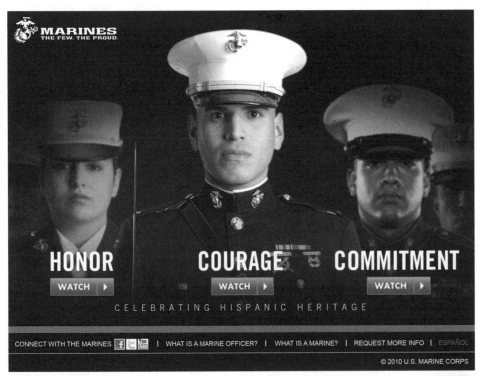

FIGURE 7.19 Ads like the this one use the nature of the three persuaders and Hispanic receivers' attitudes toward them to convince people to be recruited in the Marines.

SOURCE: http://www.hispanicmpr.com/?s=hispanic+heritage+month.

stickers, yard signs, and other emblems with slogans like "United We Stand" or "These Colors Won't Run." These displays are in response to political persuasion emphasizing the value of patriotism. These attitude objects serve a social function because they announce the person's attitudes. This, in turn, causes alignment or identification with others who feel the same way and helps to foster interpersonal relations and influence. The attitude object of the flag, bumper sticker, or sign serves as part of the appeal; and we follow suit if we want to identify with them. The obverse is also true: If we want to distance ourselves from jingoistic patriotism, we won't follow the requested action and may even display a "Get Out of Afghanistan!" sign in our yard. This reduces the possibility of forming interpersonal relationships with superpatriots.

Attitudes have an important social function since they can either foster or discourage social networking. Nelson (2001) notes that the social function of attitudes in organizations (especially businesses) can make or break the organization. And according to Schrader (1999), the social function of interpersonal influence is largely dependent on the goal complexity of appeals. In other words, if the persuader's advice is too complicated, we judge his or her attempts to influence us as unworkable, incompetent, or inappropriate. As a result, the social function of attitudes often affects persuasive outcomes.

Attitudes, Beliefs, and Opinions

As noted in Chapter 4, Rokeach (1968) pointed out that individual beliefs range from primitive and strongly held to those based on authority and not as strongly held. These belief sets cluster and form **attitudes** that fall into two categories: (1) attitudes toward objects or issues and (2) attitudes toward situations. Both predispose us to action, but they also might confuse us when they conflict with one another. For example, when parents protest the presence of a student with AIDS in their children's school, attitudes toward the object (the infected student) and toward the situation

(the possibility of infecting my own children) can either conflict or converge. When the two attitudes conflict, the parents sympathize with the victim; but they don't want their child infected.

Opinions resemble beliefs but are far more fickle; as opinion polls demonstrate, opinions can change overnight. We have opinions about politicians, what they say in campaigns, and their actions taken after assuming office. These opinions change, especially if the politician blunders, loses to Congress on an issue, or supports a corrupt friend. Usually, the politician's errors lead to low voter ratings and sometimes rejection at the polls. But opinions are fickle and unpredictable. For example, during Bill Clinton's impeachment trial, his ratings in the polls actually went to an all-time high in spite of the sordid sex scandal. Why? Rokeach's theory helps explain the riddle. People had a highly negative attitude toward Clinton's sexual dalliance (attitude toward object). But they had highly positive feelings about other issues like the economy, low unemployment, budget surpluses, and a bullish stock market (attitude toward situation). These opinions conflicted with their feelings about the scandal, and the economy won out. More recently President Obama lost public opinion polls when he decided not to lead the campaign for an air free zone over Libya during the attempted revolution there (see Figure 7.20). This action conflicted with his campaign and other public promises to protect citizens of the world from dictatorial action of human brutality against their decisions. He let the French take the lead on this action, then joined in and allowed his military to make naval rocket attacks on the headquarters of Libya's dictator, Moammar Khadafi.

Social psychologist Zimbardo and his colleagues (1976, 1991) note that attitudes are "either mental readiness or implicit predispositions that exert some general and consistent influence on a fairly large class of evaluative responses" (p. 20). A school of advertising research, known by the acronym DAGMAR, suggests that ad agencies ought to **d**efine **a**dvertising **g**oals for **m**easured **a**dvertising **r**esults (Colley, 1961). In other words, establishing positive attitudes toward a brand serves as the goal of advertising, not instant purchase behavior. The idea is that if consumers have an improved image of a product, they will probably buy it sometime in the future. Therefore, if the marketer can change their attitudes, purchase eventually follows. Unfortunately, this attitude-behavior link sometimes flip-flops, perhaps because of intervening variables that also affect purchase behavior such as time of day, attractiveness of the offer, a store display, price, or background music. Even in experiments with these causes filtered out, attitude and behavior do not consistently link.

The Functions of Attitudes

Attitudes can have several functions. For example, they have a cognitive or knowledge function because we aren't born with attitudes but must learn them. Consider our attitudes about being environmentally responsible. How did they come about? Probably we first learned about air and water pollution and the dangers that they bring. Then we learned about recycling and what it can achieve. Then we learned that endangered species may act as early warnings about what might ultimately happen to humans. Only after learning all of these things do we finally form an overall attitude toward environmental responsibility. Likewise, some advertisements also persuade by teaching. A mutual fund company advertises that it is "no load" and goes on to explain what that means— customers don't have to pay commissions when they make investments. Persuadees learn the value of this and form a positive attitude toward that company, and they decide to use the company when they make investments. The same learning operates in political or cause-related campaigns. For example, since the March of Dimes no longer supports polio research (the disease has been nearly eradicated), it must teach potential donors that now it supports research into premature births—the leading cause of infant mortality. The receiver learns about the organization and its purposes and only then forms an attitude toward it and ultimately decides whether or not to send a donation.

Attitudes also function to influence our emotions and feelings, and thus they have what has been termed an **affective function** or an emotional outcome. For instance, our attitudes about the development of hydrogen fuels affect how we feel about this new source of energy. If we equate hydrogen energy with the hydrogen bomb, we experience fear and may actively oppose its production. Some ads target the affective dimension, or emotions. For example, how did *The Sopranos* affect viewers' attitudes and emotions toward mob figures? Chris Seay, a Christian minister, worried about his wife's response when he rushed home from church activities to watch the nudity and profanity-filled fourth season. He ultimately convinced her that the show was about "faith, forgiveness and family values." That nifty bit of persuasion got him out of his affective dilemma (Pinsky, 2002).

Finally, attitudes have a behavioral function in that they prepare us to take certain actions. Because we hold certain attitudes toward air and water pollution, we may choose to recycle, to not buy a gas guzzler, or to use biodegradable detergents. The behavioral function of attitudes affects what we do about these issues. Some ads aim at changing attitudes in order to prompt behavior change. Two goals of advertising are to create traffic in a store and to get consumers to try a brand. The advertiser offers huge discounts or special events, such as the visit of a celebrity, to create traffic. They may send a free sample or offer an attractive rebate with a purchase. Few people reject anything that is free or cheaper, so they give the brand a try. The marketer's hope is that visiting the store will prompt impulse purchases or that satisfaction with the performance of the brand will lead to brand loyalty and future purchases.

Attitudes and Intention

As we noted earlier, the work of Fishbein and Ajzen (1975) added the concept of **behavioral intention** to the research on attitude and behavior change. Here, a fairly consistent set of results emerges. Attitude change usually precedes what people say they intend to do. As noted above, when people articulate what they intend to do, they have already acted symbolically. Nonverbally, when the person clips or saves a coupon, he or she has already "bought" the brand. Likewise, the person who displays a bumper sticker in favor of a certain candidate will show up at the polls to vote for that candidate on election day. Knowing this, politicians urge people to display

bumper stickers, buttons, and yard signs to guarantee their votes rather than trying to persuade others who may be undecided.

Attitudes and Interpersonal Communication/ Persuasion

There are several other dimensions of attitude change and the subsequent behavior puzzle. One of these is the degree to which attitudes function as tools of interpersonal communication or persuasion, or both. In other words, do expressions of attitudes have more to do with fitting ourselves into a comfortable position with others than they do with our ultimate behavior? Eiser (1987), a critic of attitude research, puts it this way: "One of the main shortcomings of many attitude theories is their emphasis on individualistic, intrapsychic factors to the relative neglect of the social and communicative context within which attitudes are acquired and expressed" (p. 2). In other words, we overtly express attitudes in order to get along with and identify with others. (See Figure 7.21.)

Attitudes and Information Processing

The focus on human information processing in the ELM, which serves as a unifying model throughout this book, also relates to behavioral intentions. We

FIGURE 7.21 What sort of relationship is suggested here?

can't look at attitudes and behavior without also looking at how audiences process such persuasive information. One of the first questions to ask is whether the audience even comprehends the message. In the central path, they usually do comprehend the message and may even research it. In the peripheral path, they probably don't. For example, "cents off" coupons as persuasive information fit with several memory networks in our minds, such as whether we already use the brand, how often, and whether the coupons are valuable enough to justify clipping them. Peripheral cues may prompt behavior. For example, people will clip more coupons if there is a dotted line around the coupon and clip even more if there is a little scissors on the dotted line. And there are diversity issues to be concerned with in deciding whether or not to offer coupons. For example, Latinos tend not to clip coupons because they associate them with food stamps, a social stigma in their subculture. So if an advertiser is targeting Latinos, that advertiser should not use coupons but may want to emphasize the warranty or quality instead.

Research into how information is stored in our long-term memory (LTM) is fairly recent, and most researchers agree that information is usually stored in networks and in the form of key words, symbols, and relationships. A good organizing device for LTM is to make one's persuasion episodic in nature, probably due to the power of the narrative or story form. For example, we all have been late for an appointment and find ourselves stuck behind the slowest driver on the road, who also misses all the green stoplights. Imagine a television commercial to promote Compoz, an over-the-counter treatment for settling people's nerves. This episode could act as a script for the commercial. The ad opens with the character realizing that he or she has nearly missed a doctor's appointment. We see them rush out to the car, get in, and speed off, only to get behind the slowpoke. They glance nervously at the clock and begin having a silent "conversation" with the slow driver. They are about to commit road rage, but instead they take a Compoz tablet. The ad closes with the slow driver turning at the next intersection and the product's slogan, "For those nerve-racking occasions, try Compoz." At the behavior stage of the ELM (voting, buying, joining, or donating), the critical episode is retrieved from LTM and provides persuadees with good "reasons" for taking action.

The ELM model has prompted a multitude of research insights into the process of persuasion since its introduction. Researchers S. Booth-Butterfield and J. Welbourne (2002) suggest that the model "has been instrumental in integrating the literature on source, message, receiver, and context effects in persuasion and has also been a springboard for new research in this domain" (p. 155). Although people want to have "correct" attitudes, the degree to which they will elaborate on an issue vanes from individuals and situations; but the following patterns remain clear.

1. A number of variables affect attitude change and can act as persuasive arguments, peripheral cues, or attitudinal positions.

2. When motivation or ability to elaborate decreases, peripheral cues become more important and carry the persuasive load. For example, persons who are uninterested in the implications of diversity will rely on stereotyping.

3. Conversely, as motivation or ability to elaborate on a claim increases, peripheral cues lose impact. For example, if our new boss is ethnically different from us, we devalue stereotypes.

4. The persuader affects consumers' motivation by encouraging or discouraging careful examination of the argument or claim. The persuader says, "April 15 is only a week away, so bone up on the new tax laws," instead of saying, "At your income level, you might as well use the short tax form 1040EZ and file online."

5. Issues and arguments flowing from the central processing path persist, predict actual behavior best, and seem resistant to competing persuasion. Persuasion using process premises is likely to follow the peripheral path, whereas persuasion using reasoned premises is likely to be processed in the central route. Petty and Cacioppo's (1986) chart in Figure 7.22 depicts various options and routes.

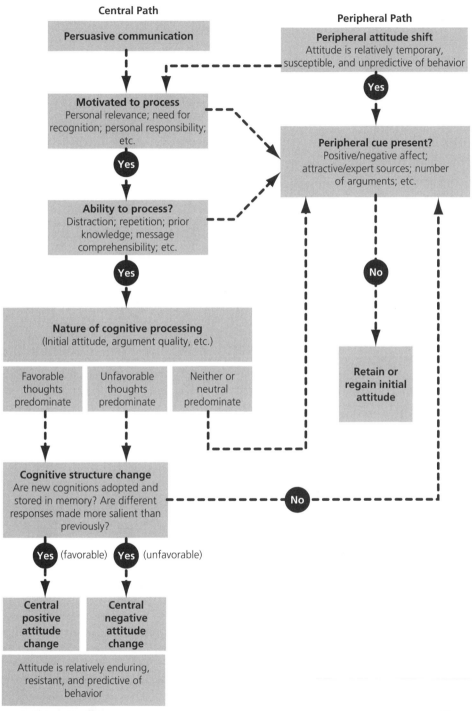

Central Path

Persuasive communication

Peripheral Path

Peripheral attitude shift
Attitude is relatively temporary, susceptible, and unpredictive of behavior

Yes

Motivated to process
Personal relevance; need for recognition; personal responsibility; etc.

Yes

Peripheral cue present?
Positive/negative affect; attractive/expert sources; number of arguments; etc.

Ability to process?
Distraction; repetition; prior knowledge; message comprehensibility; etc.

Yes

No

Nature of cognitive processing
(Initial attitude, argument quality, etc.)

Favorable thoughts predominate

Unfavorable thoughts predominate

Neither or neutral predominate

Retain or regain initial attitude

Cognitive structure change
Are new cognitions adopted and stored in memory? Are different responses made more salient than previously?

No

Yes (favorable)   **Yes** (unfavorable)

Central positive attitude change

Central negative attitude change

Attitude is relatively enduring, resistant, and predictive of behavior

FIGURE 7.22 Decision flow in Petty and Cacioppo's elaboration likelihood model.

| BOX 7.5 | Ten Lenses and the Diversity Channel |

In his book entitled *The Ten Lenses: Your Guide to Living and Working in a Multicultural World* (2001), Mark A. Williams, author and founder of The Diversity Channel (a diversity training company), discusses how human emotions vary in organizations and institutions. He describes and explains 10 "lenses" or perceptual filters through which most of us view our diverse world. There are the **assimilationists**, who believe that all diversities should behave like regular Americans, and then there are the **cultural centrists**, who believe that we must not tamper with the diversity of others. The **meritocrats** believe that if you work hard enough and pull yourself up by your bootstraps, you will achieve your goals regardless of your race, ethnicity, or other aspects of diversity. The **victim/caretakers** believe that bias will forever hold down persons of diverse origins. The **colorblind** believe in ignoring cultural differences and seeking the true value of any individual whose diversity differs from the majority.

The **elitists** believe that it is their destiny and their right to be superior to others of varying diversities. The **integrationists** believe that the best way to break down biases and stereotypes is to merge persons of various diversities in the workplace and elsewhere. The **multiculturalists** want to celebrate our diversity—the more diversity we have, the better things will be for everyone. **Seclusionists** want to distance and protect themselves and their families from persons of diverse cultures. And **transcendentists** believe that race, gender, and ethnicity reflect our unified humanity. Where do you fit? Speculate on how these lenses might apply to human needs, emotions, and attitudes. How do you look at persons of other races, nationalities, genders, sexual preference, or ethnicities? If you want to explore Williams's work further, pick up his book and take his "ten lenses survey," or go online to Weblink 7.7 and explore its home page options.

Notice that the various options in the ELM depend on whether you have the motivation to process a persuasive message. You must want to investigate a given product, candidate, or cause or the elaboration process is short-circuited. If they are motivated to process an offer, appeal, or claim, persuadees must also possess the ability to complete the processing. Thereafter, the nature of the attitude change depends on which path is followed. If the peripheral path is used, the attitude change will be weak, short-lived, and less likely to yield behavior. If the central processing path is used, attitude change will be potent, long-lived, and likely to lead to behavior.

Each path has its strengths and weaknesses. Most researchers agree that attitudes have something to do with behavior, that attitudes can be altered by persuasion, and that the suggested behavior usually follows a change in attitude. What does all this mean to us as persuadees who live in a world concerned with diversity and ethics? What can we do to uncover persuaders' intentions toward and beliefs about the diverse audiences? Being aware of attitudes helps us to pinpoint what persuaders think of us and others. Identifying the attitudes that persuaders assume we

have makes us more critical receivers, and so we judge persuasive attempts as ethical or unethical. We also become conscious of our attitudes, and as a result, we anticipate how persuaders use them to get us to follow their advice. However, few situations involve a single attitude. Most situations involve several attitudes, which lead to a need for consistency among those attitudes. (See Box 7.5.)

CONSISTENCY: THE FOURTH PROCESS PREMISE

We looked at balance theory in Chapter 4. It posits that we feel comfortable when the world lives up to (or operates consistently with) our perceptions or our predictions of it. By **consistency** we mean that our expectations about future events, the behaviors of other persons, and so on, ought to live up to or be consistent with what we expect. When that is not the case, we feel what we earlier called "imbalance" or psychic discomfort, and will tend to doubt the expected relationship and evidence related to it. Further, when this consistency doesn't happen, we try to change either ourselves or our interpretations of events to bring about a balanced state. As a result, persuaders offer a strategy or means (usually a product, service, or action) to return to balance and psychological comfort. If you want to change attitudes toward health care, for instance, then try to create imbalance in health care users. You might say, "With an HMO, you can't go to the best surgeon."

We all seek out psychological equilibrium, so as receivers we need to identify what puts us into states of imbalance or inconsistency, thus making us vulnerable to persuasion. If psychological equilibrium is our goal, we need to feel comfortable and look for persuasion that reinforces attitudes. As Eiser (1987) pointed out, defining the "existing frame of reference" is a critical factor in predicting attitude shifts. Once we identify the receiver's current frame of reference, we create the kind of inconsistency that prompts psychological uneasiness, which leads to attitude change.

Cognitive Dissonance Theory

A problem with balance theory is that it doesn't relate to the degree of difference between the two people or the two instances judged. Instead it looks at the kinds of differences—positive or negative—that exist in the comparisons of persons or instances. In other words, the theory accounts for *qualitative* differences between judgments but it doesn't deal with *quantitative* differences. That may seem like a minor problem, but major differences might exist between persons or concepts regarding controversial topics such as abortion, school prayer, or patriotism, so it's important to determine how far persons and their issue positions are from one another on a topic. Leon Festinger's cognitive dissonance theory (1962) addressed this problem of quantitative and qualitative differences between persons and ideas.

Unlike balance theory, **cognitive dissonance theory** predicts that when we experience psychological tension, or dissonance, we try to reduce it in some

way instead of totally resolving the tension. Tension reduction has a quantitative dimension. We can change our attitudes a little, a moderate amount, a lot, or not at all. The tension caused by dissonance grows out of our psychological belief system, whereas balance theory relies more on logical inconsistencies. Festinger defined dissonance as a feeling resulting from the existence of two unfitting or contrasting pieces of knowledge about the world. As in balance theory, there are times when things fit or go together and times when they do not (see Figure 7.23).

For Festinger, the opposite of dissonance, or "consonance," exists when two pieces of information do fit together, and hence reinforce one another. Some persons change dissonant cognitions by moving their beliefs closer to one another. Others rationalize the problem away or discredit the source of the information. Others reduce dissonance by selective perception, selective retention, or selective exposure; they choose not to receive or perceive the dissonance, they forget about it, or they choose not to be exposed to conflicting information.

Recently, dissonance theory helped explain the new sense of uneasiness affecting sexually active individuals who have multiple partners. Most of us know that the main causes of infection by the AIDS virus are unsafe sex practices, the sharing of needles among drug users, and sometimes from blood transfusions or accidental exposure to the blood of AIDS earners. What can sexually active people do to reduce the uneasiness or dissonance they feel regarding their own sexually activity? They can do one or all of the following:

1. Devalue their beliefs about the most effective methods of birth control and use condoms.

2. Devalue AIDS information, telling themselves that this is just a scare tactic to cut down on the promiscuity of the younger generation.

3. Selectively perceive the information and choose to believe that *their* sex partners don't have the AIDS virus.

4. Try to forget the information about AIDS through the process of selective retention.

FIGURE 7.23   What about this image might produce dissonance?

SOURCE: 12manage.com.

5. Try to rationalize the problem away by believing that a cure for AIDS is just around the corner.

6. Become celibate or have fewer partners.

Although Festinger mainly dealt with the notion of dissonance, it seems clear that we seek its opposite, consonance, to reinforce our existing attitudes. We listen to the candidates of our choice and avoid listening to their opponents. Conservatives read conservative newspapers, and liberal people read liberal ones. We seek information that confirms our position and reinforces our beliefs.

Several actions build consonance in this way. We can again do one or more of the following:

1. Revalue our initial beliefs, making them stronger.

2. Revalue the source of the information input by giving it more credibility than it deserves.

3. Perceive the information as stronger than it actually is.

4. Remember the most positive parts of the information and highlight them.

5. Seek out even more supporting information.

Creating consonance strengthens and reinforces attitudes, increases credibility, and probably induces action. Persuaders probably use consonance at least as frequently as dissonance. They often want to reinforce people's opinions, attitudes, beliefs, or behavior.

In many cases, dissonance theory oversimplifies the human situation. Recently, researchers in communication, psychology, and sociology have looked at a variety of other factors that affect feelings of dissonance. Wood (2000) points out that social factors play a role in reducing dissonance. People want to fit in with significant reference groups and engage in normative behavior to do so. Internal states determine the outcome of persuasion as much as do the source's skill at designing the dissonance- or consonance-producing messages.

Sources of Dissonance

What causes you to feel imbalance or dissonance? Some factors are unique to you, but many of them are similar for large groups of people. These more universal factors are useful for persuaders because they are potent first premises in enthymemes. Descriptions of a few common ones follow.

Loss of Group Prestige. This relates to the pride felt by members of a well-respected reference group, profession, or organization that has fallen on bad times and no longer is as highly respected. For instance, Martha Stewart was highly respected by many people who identified with her because they felt that they also had her class and good taste. They wanted to emulate her, to try her recipes, and to have a flower garden like hers. One of her fans said, "We put a copy of Martha Stewart's *Living* magazine on a coffee table. It's the prettiest thing in the living room." Another said, "We want a little of what she's got—a scant teaspoon in Marthaspeak—of her taste and talent" (Rowell, 2002, p. 16). After she suffered a financial scandal and served jail time, her sheen dimmed a bit. A former fan observed, "There's nothing in her magazine that even hints at her virtue"

(Rowell, 2002, p. 16). Ultimately, however, Martha regained some of her previous sheen. The loss of group prestige affects small and large groups alike—from a sorority to an entire profession such as lawyers, or a region of the country such as the East Coast.

Economic Loss. When we feel that our economic value is in danger of being reduced, we experience dissonance. We deal with the obvious dissonance of losing a job in a number of ways. After the dot-com bubble burst, many displaced workers chose to take early retirement, others returned to school or accepted jobs with much lower salaries, and others started their own businesses. (See Figure 7.24.)

Loss of Personal Prestige. Ads promoting hair restorers or weight reduction plans play on one's loss of personal prestige resulting from physical appearance. Being passed over for a promotion at work also leads to a loss of personal prestige. Other fears relating to loss of prestige include the loss of youth, the loss of health, and the loss of self-respect.

Uncertainty of Prediction. Whenever we move, change schools, take a new job, or break up with a spouse or significant other, we feel uncomfortable because we can no longer predict probable outcomes. Products that promise to protect us from some negative circumstance (illness, job loss, financial difficulties) use the inability to predict as a "hook" to persuade us. Events like the nuclear disaster in Japan due to a tsunami wave created uncertainty about the safety of nuclear facilities around the world.

Sources of Consonance

On the other side of the coin, some appeals give receivers a sense of consonance, and reinforce beliefs, attitudes, or behaviors and activate receivers.

Reassurance of Security. Today, police stations, airports, courthouses, schools, and other public buildings are protected with metal detectors and even armed guards. We want to feel secure in public places, and these preventatives provide that sense of

IF WE CAN'T MOVE IT, WE CAN'T MAKE IT.

If our transportation system can't move our goods and services, it can't support our economy. Adequate transportation infrastructure capacity and reliable and cost-effective transportation services are essential to create jobs, spur economic growth, increase productivity, and maintain competitiveness.

FasterBetterSafer.org
AMERICANS FOR TRANSPORTATION MOBILITY

Congress: Our transportation system is broken, and American businesses and workers are paying the price. Now is the time to invest in transportation by advancing a long-term, robust highway and public transportation bill.

www.uschamber.com

FIGURE 7.24

The traffic jam was on following the surge for jobs.

SOURCE: chamberpost.com.

security. Promises of job security are powerful persuaders for persons making career choices, and IRA and Keogh accounts offer retirement security. The UK'S Nuclear Security Agency repeatedly tried to reassure people after Japan's 2011 nuclear disaster.

Demonstration of Predictability. Consonance happens when the world operates in predictable ways. Manufacturers rely on the appeal to predictability by offering guarantees or warranties. And everyone likes to know what to expect at work, at home, and in the community.

The Use of Rewards. Rewards or positive reinforcements increase feelings of consonance and the probability that a behavior will be repeated. Persuaders often use positive and complimentary statements to reinforce behavior. In his best-selling book, *How to Win Friends and Influence People*, Dale Carnegie (1952) advised his readers to "try to figure out the other man's good points … and people will cherish your words and treasure them and repeat them over a lifetime" (p. 38). Carnegie put his finger on ways to make audiences feel good about themselves. This is still good advice for persuading audiences or influencing people. Successful supervisors seem adept at giving rewards rather than offering criticisms.

REVIEW AND CONCLUSION

We are searching for various kinds of unstated and widely held major premises that can serve in persuasive enthymemes. One is the process or emotional premise, which appeals to our needs, emotions, attitudes, and the psychological processes of dissonance and consonance operating daily in each of us. We can see needs and wants operating in Maslow's hierarchy of needs, Packard's compelling human needs, and Feig's hot buttons. Although some of these models have been around for a long time, they still have applicability for us as their multitude of rejuvenations demonstrate.

A second kind of process premise involves our emotions. Persuaders target our emotional states and get at us through fear, guilt, and anger or by appeals to more positive emotions such as happiness, joy, or pride. A third kind of process premise involves attitudes, beliefs, and opinions. If persuaders change our attitudes about fuel efficiency, they predispose us to buy fuel-efficient autos, furnaces, and water heaters. If persuaders want us to continue voting for a certain party, they reinforce our existing beliefs and attitudes about that party.

Both of these persuasive types can be used with either attitudes toward objects and issues or attitudes toward situations. It may be important for persuaders to reinforce or change our behavioral intentions. Attitudes also affect important and not so important purchase, voting, joining, or donating decisions, as depicted in the ELM.

The fourth kind of process premise is the human desire for psychological consonance, in which we seek a world where our predictions are verified, and in which people we like approve of the same things we do. If we feel a lack of balance, or dissonance, we actively seek ways to bring our world into congruity by reducing psychological tensions. If we perceive balance or consonance to exist, we experience a sense of ease and can be easily motivated to continue to act as we have been. Persuaders try to create dissonance affect want us to change our behavior, and they create consonance if they want us to maintain our behavior. Process premises are important in the ways we persuade others and the ways in which we are persuaded.

KEY TERMS

After reading this chapter, you should be able to identify, explain, and give an example of the following key terms or concepts:

process or emotional premises or appeals	compelling needs	reassurance of worth	sense of power or strength
motivation research	hot buttons	ego gratification	need for roots
hidden needs	emotional security	creative outlets	line extensions
	symbols	love objects	

prepotency	self-actualization needs	comprehension	affective function
basic needs	physiological dimension	retention	behavioral intention
need for security	cognitive dimension	action	consistency
belongingness or affiliation needs	intention to behave	attitudes	cognitive dissonance theory
love and esteem needs	attention	opinions	

APPLICATION OF ETHICS

It is finals week at a state university. A professor of communication gets an e-mail from a student in one of his classes in which the student expresses a fear of failing the final exam. The two previous exams were so difficult that she was only able to get low "D" grades on them, and since the final counts double, she is in danger of failing the class. She tells the professor that she is already on probation and will be dismissed if she fails the class. Her parents have already given her an ultimatum: "Get off probation or support yourself through the remaining two years of schooling!" By chance, the professor runs into the student in the library and tells her that he is not about to cater to students who don't study enough and chides her for even sending the e-mail. She denies having sent the message and says that she suspects someone has stolen her password and sent a forgery to embarrass her. The professor convinces the manager of the university e-mail system to track down the source of the message, and indeed it had not been sent from the student's computer but from the male teaching assistant for the class. The professor suspects that the teaching assistant wants to use the e-mail to sexually harass the female student. There are emotional issues involved. Has the teaching assistant used a fear appeal? Is that ethical, given the professor's suspicions? What should the professor do?

QUESTIONS FOR FURTHER THOUGHT

1. What is a process premise? Explain.
2. What is the difference between an attitude and a need? Give examples.
3. What did Maslow mean when he called his hierarchy of needs "prepotent"?
4. Which needs described by Packard are the most ego involving or personal in nature?
5. What is an example of the need for emotional security?
6. What is an example of how advertisers use the need for ego gratification?
7. What is an example of the need for a sense of power?
8. What emotions are being used when persuaders alert us to the possibility of job loss or identity theft?
9. What emotions are being used when a persuader tells us that we have been cheated by an auto repair shop?
10. What are three functions of an attitude?
11. What is the difference between an attitude and an opinion?
12. What is the difference between a behavior and a behavioral intention?
13. According to the ELM, which decision path will be used when purchasing ice cream?

14. According to the ELM, what happens if the audience isn't motivated to vote?

15. According to the ELM, what happens to a decision if the audience can't respond?

16. Using the elaboration likelihood model in Figure 7.22, explain the flow of information regarding a current issue.

17. What are some sources of dissonance?

18. What are some sources of consonance?

19. What ethical standards should we apply when using processing in regard to the economy? The involvement of the United States in the uprisings in Egypt, Tunisia, and Libya?

 You can access your online resources at the companion website for *Persuasion*. Log in at **http://www.cengagebrain.com**.

8

Content or Logical Premises in Persuasion

LEARNING GOALS

After reading this chapter, you should be able to:

1. Give everyday examples such as ads or speeches that rely on logical versus emotional appeals.

2. Find everyday examples of each of the types of evidence discussed.

3. Explain the difference between the two types of analogy and when they might be appropriate.

4. Find everyday examples of the three types of syllogisms and explain them to the class.

5. Explain the three major elements and the three substantiating elements in the Toulmin model.

6. Identify examples of logical fallacies in ads, newspaper editorials, and letters to the editor in a news weekly like *Time* or *Newsweek*.

7. Identify logical fallacies used in sensational publications like the *National Enquirer*—our nation's largest circulation "newspaper."

8. Explain the various types of reasoning (e.g., reasoning from symptoms).

Chapter 7 looked at premises based on psychological processes or emotions. Another type of premise frequently operating in enthymemes is based on people's ability to think logically or rationally. The elaboration likelihood model (ELM) suggests that this kind of persuasion uses the central information-processing route and entails considerable analysis and intellectual activity. The advocacy face of persuasion relies heavily on this kind of premise while the propaganda face tends to rely on the process or emotional premise discussed in Chapter 7. Premises relying on logical and analytical abilities are called **content premises** because they do not rely on psychological processes and/or emotions as process premises do. Many content premises such as "causes have effects" are perceived as valid and true by large segments of the audience almost automatically on first glance, so persuaders can use them as major premises in enthymemes. (See Figure 8.1.)

Some persuasion theorists call these premises **arguments** or propositions while marketers might call them brand benefits or offers. In fact, argumentation scholars and professors Lunsford and Ruszkiewicz (2004) claim that everything is an argument,

including stained glass windows, the presidential seal, and most bumper stickers. Aristotle defined an argument as a statement that is supported by some kind of proof. The dictionary defines it as "a discussion in which disagreement is expressed for some point" (*American Heritage Dictionary,* 1985). Most theorists agree that argument contains a controversial claim (that is, there are at least two sides), which should be debatable and be able to be supported by evidence (Lunsford and Ruszkiewicz, 2004). They make the case that an argument seeks to discover the truth in order to win conviction, while persuasion seeks to apply the known truth in order to prompt others to action. Whatever the label—premise, argument, proposition, offer, or claim—this chapter looks at persuasion that uses the receiver's logical, reasoning, rational, and intellectual abilities, and which is therefore processed through the central route of the ELM.

Of course it is also persuasion that reflects one or more of the elements of intensification and downplaying discussed in Chapter 1. For example, suppose I want to persuade you to support a system of regional national presidential primary elections to select presidential nominees instead of the present mixture of caucuses, winner take all primaries, super delegates, and proportional delegate primaries. What would you consider good and

Every cigarette we smoke makes
fatty deposits stick in our arteries.

We'll help you give up before you clog up completely.   bhf.org.uk

FIGURE 8.1

Cause and Effect
Advertisement

The obvious and logical
conclusion to this ad is
that you either get your cholesterol
tested or die.

SOURCE: Image Courtesy of The Advertising
Archives.

sufficient reasons for supporting the idea? For some people, there aren't any good (let alone sufficient) reasons for such a policy, so there would be no way to persuade those folks. For others, the policy seems so sensible on the face of it that you don't need to persuade them either. But what about those who neither approve nor disapprove—the undecided members of the audience? They require more information, evidence, discussion, and debate before taking a side. In other words, they are asking for good and sufficient reasons for supporting the proposition. You might tell them about past elections, when the truly popular person was not nominated because of super delegate influence or because of proportional versus "winner take all" primaries. And you might point out that such instances have led to subsequent election problems. The success or failure of any of these arguments, claims, or propositions relies on beliefs already held by the audience. They already believe that

tax revenues are needed and that criminal elements in any activity are undesirable. Those widely held beliefs serve as major or minor premises in persuasive enthymemes, and all of them are subject to the various distortions we have discussed thus far.

We have all encountered and learned logical patterns from our earliest years. Most of us believe, for example, that causes have predictable effects. When certain things occur, other things invariably follow. Problems have causes, but their removal resolves the problems. Infants learn quickly that crying brings parental relief of various kinds of discomfort—hunger, thirst, wetness, and so on. Crying becomes the cause, and relief is the welcomed effect. This pattern of rational and intellectual reasoning is called **cause-effect reasoning**. Huglen and Clark (2004) define it as "linking some cause and effect to prove their existence" (p. 23). This makes sense, because if you have no effect(s), there obviously would be no cause, and vice versa. The

FIGURE 8.2

Faulty Cause-and-Effect Reasoning

This ad uses faulty cause-and-effect reasoning. What is faulty?

SOURCE: Sky Bonillo/PhotoEdit.

two have to exist together. For instance, a certain baseball team's pitching staff had experienced many training camp injuries. A logical effect of this cause would be that the team ends the season with a poor record. It's not necessary to convince anyone that injuries lead to losses. You just need to list the various injuries and rely on the cause-effect premise already at work in the audience's mind. The end of the season results may not be a losing record, but, as this example shows, the cause-effect pattern is a potent first premise in a persuasive enthymeme. Politicians and government officials, the courts, businesses, and advertisers all use cause-effect reasoning. Content premises persuade because they rely on widely held patterns of logical reasoning.

Our goal in this chapter is to identify some of these patterns. Recognizing them will make you a more critical receiver. (See Figure 8.2.)

WHAT IS PROOF?

Basically, content or logical premises consist of two elements—proof and reasoning. **Proof** is defined as enough evidence connected through reasoning to lead the majority of typical receivers to take or believe the persuader's advice. For example, one claim given to justify going to war in Iraq was that Iraq had chemical, biological, and nuclear weapons, and that these were a threat to stability in the region. What evidence would be needed to prove this claim? For some, satellite photos of supposed weapons sites sufficed. For others, physical evidence was needed—they wanted to see the actual weapons. Others required the actual weapons and evidence that Iraq intended to use them. In hindsight, we learned that there were no weapons of mass destruction (WMD), but that there was an intention on the part of Iraqi leadership to develop such weapons. Therefore, the case for invasion would not have been as strong as it first seemed, and maybe support for that policy would not have been so strong. This example tells us that "proof" varies from person to person and from situation to situation. For example, in 2008, the administration claimed that cutting certain taxes (especially for the very wealthy, the top 2 or 3 percent of income earners) and sending almost everyone a rebate of some other taxes would spur economic growth (the effect) and thus avoid a recession. Their evidence convinced some people but not others. When the economy did

not improve after the tax cuts and rebates, many of the believers in the actions were disappointed and blamed the government for doing too little too late. Other economists argued that cuts in the estate tax, taxes on dividends, and capitol gains would spur growth in the economy; the taxes were cut (the cause), but growth didn't follow (the effect) so the actions were judged to be faulty. (See Figure 8.3.)

Most contemporary theorists agree that proof is composed of two facets: **reasoning** and **evidence**. The dictionary definition of reasoning is "the use of reason especially to form conclusions, inferences, or judgments." Evidence is defined as "the data on which a conclusion or judgment may be based; something that furnishes proof" (*American Heritage Dictionary,* 1985). In the proper mix, these two elements lead persuadees to adopt or believe in the changes a persuader advocates. There are several ways to look at evidence and reasoning. First, by examining how persuaders operate, we can infer their motives and discover what they are up to. For example, suppose I want to persuade you that

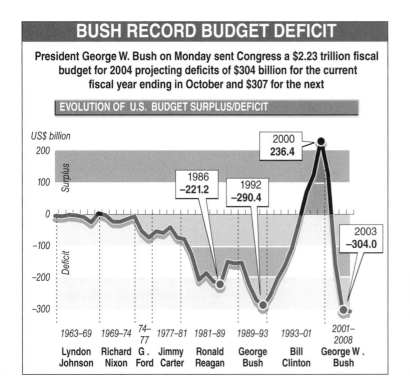

FIGURE 8.3

What is proof? Examine this graph. What is it supposed to prove? Does it prove that to you?

SOURCE: Reuters.

an unrequested kiss on the lips between a male and a female was *NOT* a cause for a charge of sexual harassment. In terms of finding proof, Lunsford and Ruszkiewicz advise asking four questions: (1) Did something happen? (2) What is its nature? (3) What is its quality? (4) What action should be taken? In this case there was an unrequested kiss on the lips, witnesses observed it, and the female objected to it. Usually, unwanted kisses on the lips are considered harassment. In this case the answer to the third question—"What is its quality?"—provided the proof because both participants were six years old, and "most people don't consider six year olds as sexually culpable" (pp. 16–17).

Another way to look at evidence and reasoning is to investigate how specific the evidence is in relation to the reasoning it supports or the conclusion that most persons draw. Before the advent of electronic media, modern advertising, and contemporary propaganda, audiences were accustomed to receiving very specific and verifiable evidence. For example, if a person gave testimony to prove a point, it was critical to tell the audience why that person qualified to give the testimony. Audiences were also suspicious of some kinds of evidence such as analogies. Today, however, we accept the testimony of professional athletes when they endorse an investment plan even though they don't qualify as experts on finance. And we frequently do accept visual or other nonverbal analogies as evidence, such as animated automobile tires depicted as having tigers' claws to grip the road better than other brands.

Other kinds of premises and evidence convince us through the central information-processing channel that a certain brand is superior. For example, if a neutral rating agency, such as "Good Housekeeping Seal of Approval," gives its imprimatur to a brand, that may constitute proof to some persons. Politicians offer us evidence in support of a policy. Brands give us various kinds of proof—testimonials, test results, past history, and so forth—to prove that their features and benefits are worth buying. Economists and financial advisors give us reasons for investing in certain things (for example, the likelihood that future energy prices will increase, so invest in biofuels). And parents supply what they

think are good reasons for not living with someone of the opposite gender prior to being married. Underlying these examples is the pattern of "enough evidence with reasoning results in proof."

TYPES OF EVIDENCE

Evidence varies in persuasive power depending on the context in which it is used. In some situations, for instance, statistics have a powerful effect while in other situations, pictorial evidence persuades; in yet others, vicarious or retold experience convinces us. Experiential evidence relies on the assumption that people learn about and act on information gained indirectly, and this is why stories about the experiences of others are so persuasive. Advertisers use testimonials from both ordinary people and celebrities to endorse products, assuming that consumers vicariously absorb the experiences and buy the product. Demonstrations can also logically persuade us, as so many TV direct marketing ads for food preparation devices show. (See Figure 8.4.)

But even when we do not learn from or become swayed by the experiences of others, our own experience is usually enough to cause us to change. The Lakota were aware of this. As a Lakota baby crawled close to the campfire, no one pulled it away with shouts of, "Hot! Stay away, baby! Hot!" as we would do in our culture. Instead, they watched the baby's progress very closely and allowed the baby to reach into the fire and touch a hot coal, burning itself mildly. They then quickly pulled the baby away and treated the burn. The experience persuaded the child to be careful with fire.

Suppose a professor explains to you his or her very stringent attendance policy for a television production class, but you take the policy with a grain of salt and fail the class, necessitating taking it over. You hear the same lecture on attendance on the first day of the class the next semester. If experience persuades, you won't miss a class this semester. Or remember your first auto accident and what you did, who you called, and so on? Chances are

Help him revitalise his skin advertisement for Wilkinson Sword Hydro

FIGURE 8.4

Demonstration Ads

Is this demonstration ad persuasive to you? Through which channel of the ELM? Why? Using which technique discussed by Rank in Chapter 1? Why?

SOURCE: Image Courtesy of The Advertising Archives.

that you took away several lessons that you will use in your next accident (don't worry, you will have one).

There are three broad forms of evidence: (1) **direct experience**, (2) **dramatic or vicarious experience**, and (3) **rationally processed evidence**. The first two usually are processed via the peripheral information-processing route of the ELM without much forethought, whereas rationally processed evidence usually follows the central information-processing route. Direct experience demonstrates the major premise that actions have consequences. All can be used ethically or unethically via SNM, but dramatic evidence works better at capturing audience attention and holding audience interest. Dramatic evidence relies on the human tendency to structure our lives in narrative or story form. Rational evidence relies on our innate ability to reason using logic and evidence. In previous chapters, we looked at some theorists who present the case for dramatic evidence convincingly. Burke (1985), for example, discusses the power of dramatic or narrative evidence. Let us briefly examine these three broad categories of evidence in more depth.

Direct Experience

Direct experience is probably the most powerful kind of proof or evidence there is and usually remains a part of one's memory for one's lifetime, being referred to repeatedly as a way to make a point or determine one's own actions. As I write these words, the Chicago area television news channels are reviewing the tragic events of Valentine's Day 2008 on the NIU campus. On that day a former graduate student walked into a lecture hall with a 12-gauge shotgun and three pistols and opened fire, shooting 54 times, injuring 21, and killing 6 students before killing himself. The students who were in that class will never forget that event and may always feel uncomfortable in lecture-hall-type situations. Public responses to the event ranged from conclusions pro and con regarding gun control, to gated campuses, to arming volunteer student security forces, to inviting Jesus into one's life. Most direct experience is far more mundane and leads to far less extreme responses. For example, most parents of more than one child tell of their one kid who always had to learn the hard way by experiencing the "actions have consequences" principle. Most of us learn the power of this principle after only a few experiences, but some seem never to catch on. Probably each of us has been in an auto accident, and as a result we have learned to call the police, family, and insurance agent, in that order. You also learned that even a minor accident can take up an inordinate amount of time, paperwork, and effort. You can probably identify some direct experiences in your life that provided a powerful form of evidence for you, but even if you have no direct experience with a violent massacre, you can be persuaded by other related forms of proof or evidence such as dramatic or vicarious experience related to you by others or via the media.

Dramatic or Vicarious Experience

All of us have learned or been persuaded by hearing about the experiences of others—that is, by vicarious experience. There are a variety of types of vicarious experience, most of them dramatic in nature. Very frequently, advocates or propagandists use dramatic experience to capture your attention. Hearing a story or narrative that relates to you or your life in some way is likely to get your attention, so such persuaders either relate real experiences that they or others have had or they create fictional ones.

Narratives.   A good way to use dramatic evidence is through the narrative or the story of an event recounted to you by others or enacted in some way (e.g., a documentary, media news report, sermon). People have always been fascinated by stories, including myths, legends, and ballads handed down in oral/aural cultures, and are often persuaded by them. Literacy brought other forms of the narrative (plays, poetry, novels, and short stories). Technology has brought us still other forms such as movies, cartoons, video games, documentaries, ads, talk shows, and broadcasts of athletic events—all having roots in storytelling. Evidence that is dramatic invites our vicarious involvement as it attempts to persuade us to a course of action. (See Figure 8.5.)

It relies on the human ability to project ourselves into the situation described by the persuader and to co-create proof. The results are powerful and long lasting, though probably not as shattering as the direct experience of witnessing a stranger aiming and shooting a shotgun at you.

In his book *People of the Lie: The Hope for Healing Human Evil,* noted author and psychotherapist M. Scott Peck (1983) related "The Case of Bobby and His Parents." The narrative began with Bobby, who had been admitted to the hospital emergency room the night before for depression. The admitting physician's notes read as follows:

> Bobby's older brother Stuart, 16, committed suicide this past June, shooting himself in the head with his .22 caliber rifle. Bobby initially seemed to handle his

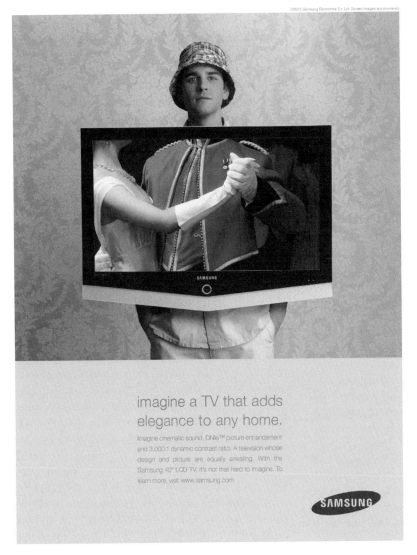

imagine a TV that adds
elegance to any home.

Imagine cinematic sound, DNIe™ picture enhancement
and 3,000:1 dynamic contrast ratio. A television whose
design and picture are equally arresting. With the
Samsung 40" LCD TV, it's not that hard to imagine. To
learn more, visit www.samsung.com

FIGURE 8.5

**Narrative
Advertisement**

What narrative is being
told here in this
advertisement?

Is advertising necessarily
global? Is it multicultural?
Where is it processed in
the ELM? Is it ethical?

SOURCE: Photo by Business Wire via
Getty Images.

sibling's death rather well. But from the beginning of school in September, his academic performance has been poor. Once a "B" student, he is now failing all his courses. By Thanksgiving he had become obviously depressed. His parents, who seem very concerned, tried to talk to him, but he has become more and more uncommunicative, particularly since Christmas. Although there is no previous record of antisocial behavior, yesterday Bobby stole a car by himself and crashed it (he had never driven before), and was apprehended by the police.... Because of his age, he was released into his parents' custody, and they were advised to seek immediate psychiatric evaluation for him (p. 48).

Peck went on to observe that, although Bobby appeared to be a typical 15-year-old, he stared at the floor and kept picking at several small sores on the back of his hand. When Peck asked Bobby if he felt nervous being in the hospital, he got no answer:

"Bobby was really digging into that sore. Inwardly I winced at the damage he was doing to his flesh" (note how little details lend drama and credibility to the narrative). After reassuring Bobby that the hospital was a safe place to be, Peck tried to draw Bobby out in conversation, but nothing seemed to work. Peck got: "No reaction. Except that maybe he dug a little deeper into one of the sores on his forearm." Bobby admitted that he had hurt his parents by stealing the car; he said he knew that he had hurt them because they yelled at him. When asked what they yelled at him about, he replied, "I don't know." Peck noted, "Bobby was feverishly picking at his sores now and … I felt it would be best if I steered my questions to more neutral subjects" (p. 50). They discussed the family pet, which Bobby took care of but didn't play with because she was his father's dog. Peck then turned the conversation to Christmas, asking what sorts of gifts Bobby had gotten.

BOBBY: "Nothing much."

PECK: "Your parents must have given you something. What did they give you?"

BOBBY: "A gun."

PECK: "A gun?"

BOBBY: "Yes."

PECK: "What kind of a gun?"

BOBBY: "A 22."

PECK: "A 22 pistol?"

BOBBY: "No, a 22 rifle."

PECK: "I understand that it was with a 22 rifle that your brother killed himself."

BOBBY: "Yes."

PECK: "Was that what you asked for, for Christmas?"

BOBBY: "No."

PECK: "What did you ask for?"

BOBBY: "A tennis racket."

PECK: "But you got the gun instead?"

BOBBY: "Yes."

PECK: "How did you feel, getting the same kind of gun that your brother had?"

BOBBY: "It wasn't the same kind of gun."

PECK: (Peck's notes: *I began to feel better. Maybe I was just confused.*) "I'm sorry, I thought they were the same kind of gun."

BOBBY: "It wasn't the same kind of gun—it was the same gun."

PECK: "You mean it was your brother's gun?" (*I wanted to go home very badly now.*) "You mean your parents gave you your brother's gun for Christmas—the one he shot himself with?"

BOBBY: "Yes."

PECK: "How did it make you feel getting your brother's gun for Christmas?"

BOBBY: "I don't know."

PECK: (*I almost regretted the question: How could he know? How could he answer such a thing?*) "No, I don't expect you could know" (p. 52).

Peck then brought the parents in for counseling. However, they seemed unable to realize what message they had sent their remaining son by giving him his brother's suicide weapon. Bobby continued therapy until he was sent to live with a favorite aunt. When I first read this dramatic example, I literally gasped as I learned about the Christmas gift, and I was totally dumbstruck to learn that it was *the* gun. When I read this dialogue aloud in class, I always hear gasps from around the room. Although the story was emotionally charged, we would be hard put to call it "illogical." In fact, it is probably totally logical to conclude that the parents' behavior was harmful, perhaps even evil. If the evidence is dramatic enough or emotional enough, persuadees will not ask for more. Again, is the narrative or dramatic evidence persuasive? Globally? Multiculturally? In which channel of the ELM? Is it ethical? Try using the story of Bobby via an SNM. Spread it as far as possible virally by sending to your various contact lists and try to gauge the effectiveness of narrative and that of viral dramatic evidence on SNM.

Most great preachers, orators, and politicians are also great storytellers. They use the narrative to capture the audience's attention and to draw them into the topic. This effect is reinforced with other evidence, and more narratives might be worked in to keep the audience interested. Chances are that you have heard speeches or sermons in which the narrative was skillfully used. Such speeches seem to have the most impact and to be remembered the longest. As a professor of mine, Dr. Ralph G. Nichols, once said, "The narrative will carry more persuasive freight than any other form of evidence."

Testimony.   Testimony of a person who has seen, heard, and experienced events also is persuasive. The persuader might read aloud an eyewitness account or simply recount his or her personal experience. If the issue is unemployment, receivers might be swayed by hearing from people who are out of work. The humiliation of waiting in line for an unemployment check, the embarrassment of accepting government surplus foodstuffs, and other experiences of the unemployed will probably have dramatic persuasive power. As receivers, we vicariously live through what others experienced when we hear their direct testimony. Although eyewitness testimony is potent, studies have shown that it is often unreliable and even incorrect (Loftus, 1980). In many cases, as has been documented, persons have been wrongfully imprisoned on the basis of eyewitness testimony (Loftus, 1984). As Figure 8.6 illustrates, witnesses often see and hear what they want to see and hear, and give testimony from their idiosyncratic points of view.

As receivers, we need to carefully examine the testimony used to persuade us. We need to ask questions like these: Was the witness in a position to see what is claimed? Could the witness be mistaken in any way? Does the witness have a bias that might cloud his or her testimony? Might the witness have a motive for giving the testimony? Is the witness being paid for giving the testimony? What might he or she have to gain from testifying? Has the 24/7 media-saturated world colored the testimony? Is it advocacy, propaganda, or something else? And we should remember that there are several other kinds of narrative proof or evidence that

can persuade such as anecdotes, jokes, demonstrations, quotes, and so forth.

Anecdotes.   Anecdotes are short narratives that make a point in a hurry—maybe in only a sentence or two. For example, there is the anecdote of the optimist who was asked to describe his philosophy: "That's simple. I'm nostalgic about the future." Anecdotes are often funny and are frequently hypothetical, so they are quite different from actual testimony. The key thing about anecdotes is that, unlike testimony, we rarely take them as truth. Instead, we tend to process anecdotes as if they are the exclamation points of persuasion—the core of an obvious truth. Consider the anecdote about Abraham Lincoln being asked why he had pardoned a Union deserter during the Civil War; he quipped, "I thought he could do us more good above the ground than under it" (Moore, 1909).

Participation and Demonstration.   There are several other ways in which persuaders can dramatize evidence. At an antismoking presentation, for instance, audiovisual materials can show cancerous lung tissue. Smokers can participate by exhaling cigarette smoke through a clean white tissue and observing the nicotine stains left behind. Sometimes persuaders dramatize a point by using visual aids to demonstrate the problem and solution. The demonstrations that form the core of most direct marketing on television (e.g., kitchen devices, exercise equipment, weight loss formulas) also use participation in that the viewer is asked to visualize himself or herself using the device and is repeatedly urged to call the 1-800 number to place an order, which is usually sweetened with some "extra" bonus for acting "now." The viewer sees the greaseless grill, the guaranteed bass bait, or the shapely persons using the Bowflex, and imagines what it would be like to use the product, and then he or she takes direct action by phoning and placing the order. The direct marketing industry is able to fine-tune its persuasive demonstrations using these immediate response behaviors and to test various bonus gifts against one another, selecting the most effective one for prompting purchase behaviors.

FIGURE 8.6

Witnesses see events or persons from their own point of view.

SOURCE: Reprinted by permission of John Jonik.

Rationally Processed Evidence

Not all evidence is dramatic. Sometimes evidence appeals to our logical processes in nondramatic and intellectually oriented and rational ways. For instance, newspaper editorials frequently use evidence that appeals to readers' logical processes, as do other persuasive messages such as legal argument, political discourse, and some advertising. Look at Figure 8.7. As you can see the ad is very simple and includes testimonial evidence from a celebrity.

It urges readers to speak out on the topic of breast cancer and help save lives. Presumably it is urging you to advise women to do a self examination of their breasts and to follow up with a mammogram if they find unusual new lumps. The ad also urges the reader to make a donation so it does recommend at least two kinds of action steps. Where in the ELM is the ad processed? Which of Rank's intensify or downplay techniques is used? Could the ad be used to persuade using an SNM? Is it an ethical ad?

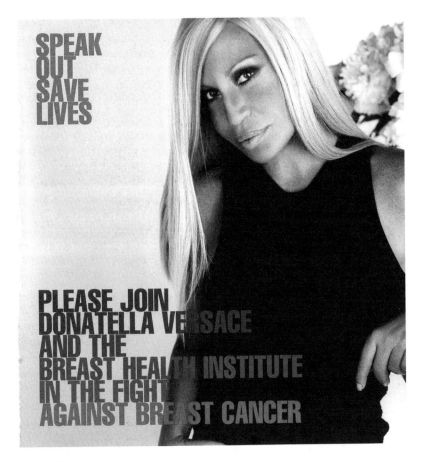

SPEAK
OUT
SAVE
LIVES

PLEASE JOIN
DONATELLA VERSACE
AND THE
BREAST HEALTH INSTITUTE
IN THE FIGHT
AGAINST BREAST CANCER

BREAST HEALTH
INSTITUTE
CATALYST TO A CURE FOR CANCER
Company registered in Breast Health International, Ltd. Registered charity No. 1169838

TOGETHER
LET'S MAKE
THE DIFFERENCE
FOR DONATION: 0800-0284347
WWW.BREASTHEALTHINSTITUTE.ORG

FIGURE 8.7

Breast Examination

As you can see, this ad makes several logical appeals using the technique of testimonial and in this case the advice is made more powerful by its celebrity speaker.

SOURCE: Image Courtesy of The Advertising Archives.

TYPES OF REASONING

Recall our definition of proof as "enough evidence connected with reasoning to lead an audience to believe or act on a persuader's advice." We now explore the second step in the process of logical persuasion, which is the connecting of pieces of evidence using some kind of logical reasoning. Several patterns of reasoning seem to be deeply ingrained in our culture and often differ from those of the many other cultures coexisting in our world of persuasion. When people violate these accepted deep structures of such logical reasoning, they are often labeled "off the wall" or "out in left field." Perhaps the student classroom shooter referred to earlier acted on Valentine's Day because he had been jilted by a female student in the class and thought that shooting at her and her fellow classmates was justified. At this point we may never know, but while not "sane," there is a line of reasoning there. Or perhaps he was angry at the lecture hall since he had often attended classes there. There is obviously much less of an insane line of plausible reasoning there. Sometimes a logical deep structure is violated, and tragedy or humor results. Sometimes, such violations make a potential persuader sound like a lunatic.

What follows is a more mundane example of such reasoning in a letter to the editor of a local newspaper that discussed alternatives for removing nuisance deer from public parks in the area (Scott, 1989). The author pointed out what it had cost for other alternatives used to remove such deer from other parks (e.g., trapping them, using trained sharpshooters to kill them, chemically induced birth control) and he pointed out the advantages and logic to opening the areas to controlled hunting—as well as to the taxes hunters pay on ammunition and guns—and how removal costs were cut at another park by allowing controlled hunting at the park. So far, so good. He begins with what appears to be an inductive line of argument using **effect-to-cause reasoning**, which is defined as citing a set of effects and then concluding by identifying their cause. We anticipate that he is about to claim something like, "Therefore, hunters are positive persons and deserve to hunt in a highly controlled environment to reduce the numbers of nuisance deer in the park." But what does the author conclude? Take a look.

> If you were an animal, would you prefer to live ten years free, even if you died a slow death, or would you want to live it penned up, sleeping in your own manure? I think most Americans would want to be free. That's also the way God wanted it. That's why he said it is a good thing to be a hunter. For Jesus Christ is alive and well, but Bambi never was (n.p.).

The conclusion is wacky. It seems unrelated to the evidence. Remember that we are looking for content premises—logical patterns that serve as the first premises in enthymemes. The deeply ingrained logical preferences serve in this way. We believe and act on what we perceive to be logical arguments backed by good and sufficient evidence that is well presented to us. Fishbein and Ajzen's (1975, 1980) theory of reasoned action (TRA) is one such deeply ingrained logical structure. The theory predicts that actions are the effects of behavioral intentions. Behavioral intentions, in turn, are the results of people's attitudes on issues and on the social norms that they hold in high esteem and which they use as guides to action. For example, if we

were trying to persuade people to stop buying SUVs and to consider purchasing one of the new hybrid automobiles or totally electric ones, we might compare the hybrid's performance with the poor mileage of most SUVs, and note that four-wheel drive isn't really necessary for most people's needs in the average climate, and back that up with a quote: "Critics claim that 95 percent of SUVs never venture off road" (Lunsford and Ruszkiewicz, p. 28). This might change peoples' attitude toward SUVs. Then we could point out that the hybrid owners are opinion leaders, tend to be better educated, to have better jobs, to earn more, and to be more socially conscious. According to TRA, if our audience believes that these traits are ones to be emulated, then the shift in attitudes toward SUVs and the audience's changing respect for hybrid or totally electric users will lead to a behavioral intention—the audience will consider buying a hybrid or electric instead of an SUV or perhaps a compromise option of a hybrid SUV. Communication scholar S. Sutton (1998) points out, however, that intentions are subject to change over time and are provisional in nature. Several researchers have found the predictive power of behavioral intentions to be either weak or negative as time passes. Let us now turn to some other traditional forms of reasoning.

Cause-to-Effect Reasoning

We've already seen that **cause-to-effect reasoning** is also powerful in our culture, and even our language depends on it. For example, we rarely say, "The ball was thrown, and the window was broken." Instead, we put the cause out front and let it "create" the effect. We say, "Johnny threw the ball and broke the window, and his parents punished him severely." This active-voice sentence tells us that Johnny caused the ball to fly through the air, resulting in the broken window, which in turn resulted in the punishment. It gives us much more information: It tells us who did what and with what effect.

Persuaders frequently use cause-to-effect reasoning to identify events, trends, or facts that have resulted in certain effects. They tell us that if a cause (e.g., a powerful earthquake) is present, we can expect certain effects (damage to buildings and infrastructure or even a tsunami) to follow. If these effects are bad, and we want to do something about them, we usually try to remove the cause. For instance, we are using too much carbon-based fuel, and the result or effect has increased global warming and further destruction of the environment, resulting in potentially dangerous climate changes. We should therefore take action to reduce the use of carbon-based fuels. Or, if you are carrying too much credit card debt, some suggest that you should get rid of all but one of your credit cards to avoid the resulting effects of poor credit and possible bankruptcy. This argument assumes that cutting up all but one credit card (cause) will reduce your ability to accumulate consumer debt (effect). This effect then becomes a new cause resulting in positive effects like good credit ratings. Both examples make sense, and that is why cause-to-effect has such persuasive power.

There are three kinds of causal reasoning: (1) a cause is identified, and you seek out its effects; (2) an effect is identified, and you try to trace it back to its cause; and (3) as we have seen above, a series of cause-effect relationships lead to a final effect (Lunsford and Ruszkiewicz, p. 207). Advertising frequently uses the first strategy, as in an ad for a cellulite-reducing complex. It identifies the cause—a weak skin support system—and its undesirable effect—ugly cellulite in body cells. Regular use of the product strengthens the skin support system, thus removing the cause and its effects. In the second strategy, the effect is identified. We look at the effect—global warming—and try to identify its possible causes (e.g., carbon dioxide from the burning of fossil fuels, the greenhouse

effect). Or take the case of food poisoning. Only those who ate the dishes that contained mayonnaise became ill. Conclusion? They probably were ill from salmonella, a kind of food poisoning that occurs when mayonnaise is not properly refrigerated. In the third strategy, we trace a series of cause-and-effect relationships: the persuader says sulfur dioxide emissions from power plants cause acid rain, which in turn causes hydro-plant life to die, which in turn reduces plankton, which in turn causes stunted fish populations. Conclusion? Stop using high sulfur energy sources because there are multiple negative effects. In law courts, establishing a motive for the crime is sometimes seen as the same thing as identifying its cause. We speculated about a romantic cause or motive for the student deaths on the NIU campus. But the fact that the shooter had stopped taking his medication might have been the best cause for his tragic behavior. So here can be varying causes for a given effect. There may be twisted kinds of reasoning (see Interactive Box 8.1).

Effect-to-Cause Reasoning

Another type of reasoning that is less frequently used (and sometimes flawed) is called effect-to-cause reasoning. Mistaken sources of food poisoning, for example, are sometimes identified this way. In another example, many auto accidents are attributed to the driver using a cell phone while driving. There is a problem here with the possibility of an intervening cause due to whom the driver is talking to, or what the topic of the conversation is, or what the

---

BOX 8.1   Interactive Reasoning in Wonderland

Go to Weblink 8.1 and explore the many logic games, conference announcements, interactive activities, and more. (You can access this and all of the other Chapter 8 weblinks through your companion website for *Persuasion*, Chapter 8 resources.) Lewis Carroll is of course most famous for his children's stories, such as *Through the Looking Glass* and *Alice in Wonderland*, and his poetry,

such as "Jabberwocky." However, few realize that he was a professional logician and that he worked with many elements of logic, reasoning, and fallacy throughout his fiction. A great example of illogical reasoning occurs when the Queen of Hearts insists that she must sentence Alice before, not after the verdict. And the Cheshire Cat is a whole different case.

traffic conditions were at the time of the call. Suppose that further investigation shows that in a high percentage of these accidents the drivers were arguing with their spouses about family matters. Is the cell phone the cause of the accidents, or is the discussion of family problems the intervening cause?

Reasoning from Symptoms

Persuaders sometimes identify a series of symptoms or signs and then try to conclude something from them. For example, politicians cite how much worse things are now than they were when their opponent took office. Unemployment is up, the stock and bond markets have been ravaged, and foreclosure rates on family homes are skyrocketing. Additionally, recent polls show that people have lost faith in their ability to control their own destinies and fear losing their jobs. The hope is that the voters will blame the incumbent for all of these the

troubles even though he or she is totally unrelated to any of these symptoms. In a results-oriented world of advocacy/propaganda with multicultural sets of values, this line of reasoning may be extremely persuasive. Many advertisements present receivers with a set of symptoms that indicate there is a real or potential problem for them. Receivers have lost their job, can't pay the bills, are faced with foreclosure, and therefore need to contact a financial advisor. Interpersonal persuasion is frequently laced with **reasoning from symptoms**, especially when laying blame. (See Figure 8.8.)

Criteria-to-Application Reasoning

Sometimes persuaders establish a reasonable set of criteria for purchasing a product, voting for a candidate, or supporting a cause and then offer their product, candidate, or cause as one that fits these criteria. For example, when a credit card company makes an offer

FIGURE 8.8

Laying Blame/
Reasoning from
Symptoms Sometimes small symptoms logically lead to major conclusions.

SOURCE: Maxim Godkin/Shutterstock.

to you, you probably have several criteria in mind that the card must meet before you will take the offer. There must be no annual fee. There must be free balance transfers and an introductory rate of 0.0 percent and a reasonable rate thereafter. The initial 0.0 percent must hold for at least a year, and the company must give you frequent traveler points on any airlines plus discounts on other travel services. These are your criteria for accepting the offer and unless the card meets your criteria, you apply these criteria and reject the offer. Remember the student who cut classes and flunked because of his absences, only to have to retake the class and maintain perfect attendance, thus earning a passing grade? Reasoning from criteria to application persuaded him.

Reasoning from Analogy or by Comparison

Sometimes persuaders use figurative or real analogies as their logical reason for some conclusion. In this form of reasoning, the persuader analyzes and describes an issue, and an analogy is made comparing this issue with an example of a similar one or a figurative one. In a real-case analogy on the war in Iraq, opponents to the war compared it to the war in Vietnam because in both cases we were losing by fighting an indigenous population that was very different from us culturally, both sets of terrain were not conducive to traditional warfare, and we did not have United Nations cooperation. The conclusion was that we should not invade Iraq. In the figurative analogy, comparisons are done through a figure of speech, usually a simile or a metaphor. Returning to the Iraq War, some opponents compared the war to walking through heavy mud with the next step gaining little ground and further exhausting one's physical strength while the progress

made by one's footprints is quickly wiped away as the mud flows back to result in the initial situation. Therefore, either don't go into the war or get out before you exhaust your physical and financial resources. Or consider the following figurative analogy: "War is like a boxing match in which the opponents are evenly matched and there's no referee. Rarely does anyone throw a single knockout punch. It's slugging it out in round after round until you get the other guy on the ropes, and his managers admit defeat." This was certainly the case in the revolution against Moammar Khadafi in Libya in 2011.

We frequently see argument by comparison in real analogies in advertising, with competing products compared in realistic terms of cost, effectiveness, safety, and so on. For instance, the big battle over the light beer market largely relies on reasoning from comparison, with one brand claiming fewer calories and better taste than others. The same thing is seen in ads for low-tar and low-nicotine cigarettes. And the Energizer rabbit uses comparison to make the point that the Energizer brand is much longer lasting than, say, Duracell, by using the figurative analogy of the mechanical rabbit, one of the most effective and long-lived figurative analogies. (See Figure 8.9.)

Deductive Reasoning

A familiar form of appeal to logic is **deductive reasoning**, which is reasoning from the general to the specific. For example, in a legislative body a persuader might support a bill or a motion by saying something like, "The legislation before us is desperately needed to prevent the state budget from going into a deficit situation," and then

FIGURE 8.9

What is the figurative analogy here?

SOURCE: Aaron Johnson.

providing the specifics that support or "prove" the conclusion. An editorial might begin, "Sycamore needs to pass this school bond referendum to save its extracurricular sports, its music and art programs, its newspaper, and its drama program," or "We need to cut the rapidly increasing costs of medical care or the Medicare program will bankrupt the nation," and then go on to describe the details. One of the problems with the deductive approach is that receivers who feel negatively about the persuader's general point may quickly lose interest, not pay attention to the specifics that are at the heart of the issue, and simply dismiss the entire argument or tune it out. That is what happened to the debate about national health care in 2011—people simply tuned out, and the funding issue remained unresolved.

Inductive Reasoning

Inductive reasoning gets the specifics out on the table before bringing up the generalized conclusion. For example, in the school bond case, the persuader might begin this way: "Many of you know that it costs over $60,000 just to run the athletic program. The budget for the marching band is over $12,000 for travel, instruction, and uniforms. I was surprised to learn that it cost over $2,000 just to pay the royalties for the spring musical. We have cut and cut until there is nothing left to cut. The last referendum increase was 14 years ago—inflation has risen over 200 percent since then. Unless we pass the referendum, the district now faces elimination of these valuable extracurricular programs." With the specific evidence apparent, the generalization flows logically from it.

MISUSES OF REASONING
AND EVIDENCE

Of course, logical persuasion is vulnerable to intentional or unintentional misuse of either evidence or reasoning, or both. Let's look at some examples of the misuse of reasoning and evidence so that we can spot it when it occurs.

Statistics

One of the mainstays of logical persuasion is the use of **statistics**. We tend to believe statistics without questioning them simply because they seem specific and well researched. But we ought to ask several questions when statistical evidence is offered. First, "Is the sample from which the statistics are drawn a representative one?" In other words, is the sample selected in a way that might bias the results? Or is it a reliable representation of the larger population? We might want to know how the sample was selected. Perhaps the researchers took names from the phone directory. But not everyone has a telephone number listed, some people have several, and others only use cell phones for which there is no directory. Perhaps the subjects were approached at a shopping mall versus on campus and given a survey there. But, again, mall shoppers might not be representative of the campus population at large. Maybe the subjects were intercepted in front of the student union late in the evening. Would we find any different results if we interviewed them early in the morning rather than in the evening when most students are studying? These and other questions should be asked of any statistical proof used by the persuader. Another misuse of statistical evidence is the use of a single instance as an example of all instances. Thus, we hear of an enormously wealthy person who pays no taxes and are led to believe that other enormously wealthy persons pay no taxes. Or we read of a hammer costing $50 when purchased by the Department of Defense. Still another misuse of statistics is biased sampling, which occurs when a nonrepresentative portion of the population is sampled. Responses from a sample drawn from subscribers to *Newsweek* will be very different from one drawn from subscribers to *Horticulture* or *The Organic Gardener*.

The mode of presentation can also misrepresent statistics. For example, the graph in Figure 8.10 was used to demonstrate the degree to which homosexuality exists in the general population. The shaded portion indicates persons who have had at least one homosexual encounter; the unshaded portion of the graph indicates heterosexual persons.

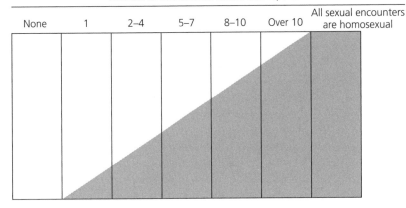

Number of homosexual encounters reported

| None | 1 | 2–4 | 5–7 | 8–10 | Over 10 | All sexual encounters are homosexual |

FIGURE 8.10

This graph is misleading because it implies that half the population is homosexual when the statistics being represented are much lower than that.

SOURCE: © Cengage Learning 2013.

The graph suggests that the proportion of the population that is homosexual is at least 50 percent when actual research indicates that it is far smaller—around 2 percent (Guttmacher, 1993). Clearly, the graph visually misrepresents the actual case and distorts the meaning of the statistics. What the graph fails to provide is information about the size of the sample in each segment.

Testimony

One problem with the use of testimonials is that the person testifying might not be providing accurate information. In fact, eyewitness testimony is frequently erroneous. In the Valentine's Day killings, students in the lecture hall at the time differed on the color of the killer's hat when his entire outfit was clearly black. Also, seemingly insignificant shifts in wording can lead witnesses to certain answers. Most of the time, we don't have the opportunity to cross-examine the person giving the testimonial. Instead, when we see or hear a person endorsing a product, a candidate, or an organization, we are forced to make up our minds right away about whether the person is qualified to give the testimonial. When testimonials are used to persuade, we need to ask whether the person giving the testimonial is an authority on the subject, and if so, how reliable he or she is. Was the person close enough to have witnessed what he or she is testifying about?

Is it possible that the person giving the testimonial is biased, and if so, in what direction? For example, in Chicago, a violinist was recently awarded nearly $30 million from METRA, the commuter train conglomerate. Her $500,000 violin got caught in the train doors, and when she tried to save it her leg was torn off. She testified at the trial, offering "dramatic detailed testimony … as she painfully recalled for jurors the winter day in 1995 when she became pinned against the doors of a commuter train and was dragged more than 360 feet before she fell under its wheels," (Deardorf & Finan, 1999, p. 1). Could her testimony have been biased? How much of it was used to build sympathy and thus boost the size of the award? How well could you remember what happened if you were in that situation? Was she partially responsible for putting herself at risk? These and other questions are the kinds of issues to be raised when the testimonial is being offered as evidence.

As persuadees, we need to be alert to the ways in which testimonials can be distorted or misused. We know that in many cases the testimonial is being given only because the sponsor has paid the person to give it. So, the next time you see a sports personality endorsing a product, don't assume that he or she uses it on a daily basis. By law, they only have to have tried it one time. And try to determine the degree of authority the person has about the product.

COMMON FALLACIES USED IN PERSUASION

Merriam-Webster's Collegiate Dictionary defines **fallacy** as "deceptive appearance … a false or mistaken idea … an often plausible argument using false or invalid inference." It is this last definition that concerns us here: believable arguments or premises that are based on invalid reasoning. Keep in mind that a logical fallacy is not necessarily false, but its process of inference can be invalid. In spite of the fact that these fallacies have been identified for centuries, they still pop up frequently in advertisements, political persuasion, interpersonal persuasion, and other arenas. Briefly, here are some of the common fallacies we encounter almost daily.

Post Hoc, Ergo Propter Hoc

Post hoc, ergo propter hoc, commonly called **the "post hoc" fallacy**, derives from the Latin meaning "after this, therefore because of this." As the translation implies, because one event follows another, the first event is assumed to be the cause of the second. One sometimes sees this in the world of sports where the acquisition of a new player or coach is seen as the cause for a winning or losing season. Views on history sometimes argue that a particular event or organization is the cause for subsequent results (e.g., the birth control pill came before the decline in morals and was therefore the cause of the decline). We constantly run into this fallacy in the world of advertising. After using the diet pill, Jane lost 40 pounds. Maybe she just got more exercise. Citizens might charge that the reason the school system is out of money is that the superintendent and school board wasted all the money from the referendum eight years ago on unneeded frills, but it is not necessarily so.

Ad Hominem

The Latin term *ad hominem*, meaning "to or at the person," refers to any attack against an individual instead of against her or his position on the issues.

The purpose is to lead the audience to take certain actions simply because of an alleged character quirk or other flaw in the person presenting the opposite viewpoint. The cartoons in Figure 8.11 are good examples of the ad hominem argument being used against your author when he was the faculty president of the policy-making body on our college campus. "Mudslinging" in politics is a frequent platform for the ad hominem. This tactic is not usually used in advertising because products, not people, are being promoted. However, it is frequently used in ideological persuasion such as in the abortion debate where the argument is aimed at the abortionist, not the law. Whenever attacks are made on a person's character instead of on his or her stand on issues, be aware that the *ad hominem* fallacy is probably at work. If persuaders have nothing to debate, they frequently resort to attacking the personality of the opponent.

Ad Populum

As its name implies, the *ad populum* **fallacy** relies on whatever happens to be popular at that time. It is aimed at or to the populace or public opinion. In fact, public figures frequently attack the polls or claim them as proof positive for supporting or opposing public policy. There are many historical examples of *ad populum* arguments—some important, some tragic, and some trivial. For example, consider just a few popular notions that justified themselves using the logic of the *ad populum*: Prohibition (in which drinking was evidence for loose living), the baby boom (which was blamed for all the faults of the "boomer" generation from birth on until old age), rock 'n' roll (which caused juvenile delinquency and free sex), and the suburbs of the 1950s and later (which caused global warming by commuters driving so much). Appeals using the *ad populum* also abound in the worlds of fashion and popular culture—for example, wearing one's baseball cap backward or askew, getting one's body pierced, tattoos, and short skirts (which encouraged fornication). Encouragement to "follow the crowd" clues us in to the *ad populum* fallacy in operation.

FIGURE 8.11 These cartoons use the ad hominem fallacy. They are aimed at the person, not the issue.

SOURCE: Kevin Craver.

The Undistributed Middle

The fallacy of the **undistributed middle** can be defined as "inferring that because an individual, group, or philosophy shares some aspects or attributes with another, it shares all other aspects or attributes." It occurs in most cases of what we call "guilt by association." For example, "Gut Malloy is a member of Tappa Kanna Bru fraternity, and fraternity boys are heavy drinkers, so he must be a heavy drinker, too." Common sense tells us that there is something missing here. The heart of the fallacy is in the phrase "fraternity boys are heavy drinkers," which is used to suggest that all fraternity members share all attributes beyond group membership. In other words, the argument assumes that heavy drinking is equally distributed among all members of fraternities when some are moderate drinkers or don't drink at all (Jensen, 1981). Of course, this example is trivial, but persuaders use the undistributed middle principle to sway opinion and alter behavior in significant ways. For example, because someone serves on the school board, many critics assume that the person must favor all the board's decisions. This example appeared in a small town newspaper recently:

> Consider these facts: The Japanese eat very little fat and suffer fewer heart attacks than the British or the Americans. On the other hand, the French eat a lot of fat and suffer fewer heart attacks than the British or the Americans. The Italians drink excessive amounts of red wine and also suffer fewer heart attacks than the British or Americans. Therefore eat and drink what you like. It's speaking English that kills you (*Consider the Facts,* 2002, p. 10).

This fallacy also underlies any appeal suggesting that using a certain popular brand will make us like others who use it.

The Straw Man

The **straw man fallacy** sets up a weak, or "straw man," case that can be easily defeated. The persuader represents this case as the position of the other side in the debate, and then brings out key evidence and reasoning to defeat the bogus case, along with the opposition or opposing candidate. Political persuasion is riddled with this tactic. For instance, Candidate A might charge that Candidate B's position on defense spending is reliance on conventional weapons. This is an easy position to demolish. Candidate A promptly shows how wrong the straw man position is by presenting impressive statistics and examples to the contrary. In the world of advertising, we occasionally see, read, or hear a straw man case. A good example is the TV ad in which the announcer says something like, "Some think this Chevy pickup truck can't climb this tough mountain carrying a Dodge pickup on its back." Then we see the Chevy climb the mountain with the Dodge on its back. Of course, if the Chevy couldn't do the job, they would never have aired the ad. Most comparative advertising depends on the straw man fallacy. In the cola and burger wars, for instance, the opposition is often set up as a straw man waiting to be overcome by the advertiser's brand. The straw man fallacy is also commonly used in ideological arguments. Antiabortion advocates frequently argue that abortion is an inhumane form of birth control and should thus be outlawed. However, pro-choice advocates have never recommended abortion as a means of birth control—that claim is a straw man argument that will naturally be demolished by pro-life advocates.

Other Common Fallacies

Another type of fallacious reasoning uses partial or distorted facts (such as telling only one side of the story or quoting out of context) or specious reasoning. My dean once explained the reason for me not receiving a $3,000 raise for promotion to full professor by comparing me to other full professors with lesser records by saying: "Yes, Charles, but you are younger than them and can work longer." Other fallacies include substituting ridicule or humor for argument (such as depicting the opposition candidate as "a slow-dancing bureaucrat"), using prejudices or stereotypes, appealing to tradition, begging the question or evading the issue ("National health care is nothing less than socialism!"), using a non sequitur (a thought that doesn't logically follow from the preceding one), or creating a false dilemma ("either outlaw deficit spending or declare the country bankrupt") (Kahane, 1992; Thompson, 1971).

LOGICAL SYLLOGISMS

A form of logical argument that goes back to the ancients is called the syllogism. **Syllogisms** are forms of reasoning with three parts: a major premise, a minor premise, and a conclusion. They typify content premise persuasion and can be of three types: conditional syllogisms, disjunctive syllogisms, and categorical syllogisms.

Conditional Syllogisms

Conditional syllogisms are defined as arguments using "if/then" reasoning. Like other syllogisms, they have a major premise, a minor premise, and a conclusion. The major premise states a logical relationship that is presumed to exist in the world and that receivers are to accept. The minor premise states the existence of one element in the relationship, and the conclusion is then drawn between the relationship and the existence of one element in it. Here is a conditional syllogism in classical form:

> If the U.S. government can't control terrorism with the present laws, then we need to give it new laws that are tough enough to stop terrorism (major premise).
> The World Trade Center bombings and the events of 9/11 are proof that the government can't control terrorism with the present laws (minor premise).
> Therefore, we need to give the government tougher laws to stop terrorism (conclusion).

The first element, or the "if" part in the major premise, is called the antecedent, and the second element is called the consequent. Affirming the antecedent, which we did in the minor premise by referring to the attacks, we can draw a valid conclusion that tougher laws are needed. Note that the syllogism is valid, but the premises are not necessarily true. **Validity** refers to how well the syllogism conforms to the general rules of reasoning, and not to the true or false nature of the premises. The other valid way of affirming a part of the conditional syllogism is to deny the existence of the element in the major premise. Using the same example, we could state, "Since 9/11, there have been no major terrorist acts in the United States (minor premise). Therefore, there is no need for new laws (conclusion)."

Advertisers frequently make perfectly valid arguments using false premises. A good example is this statement on a package of Trilene fishing line: "If you are seeking a world record, you should use one of the pound tests coded in the chart at right." You can detect the "if … then …" format in the sentence. We all know that using the right line—Trilene—won't assure anyone of a world record fish, but receivers tend to accept it as logical and buy the line. There are two valid ways to draw a conclusion in a conditional syllogism. First, we can affirm the "if" part of the major premise and accept the "then" part of the major premise. For example, if we affirm the first portion of the premise ("If you are seeking…") we can affirm the second half about using Trilene line. The other valid combination begins by stating something about the first part of the initial premise. For example, we might say, "smaller fish taste better," and then reject the advice on using Trilene line. A related but invalid procedure is to deny the antecedent and conclude that the consequent has also been denied. In the Trilene example we might state, "you don't want a ranker," and conclude that therefore you shouldn't use Trilene. The fallacy becomes apparent immediately—you might still want to use Trilene for another reason—perhaps because of its warranty.

In a related but also invalid procedure, suppose in the terrorism example we had denied the consequent in the minor premise by saying: "We have not given enough tough new powers to the U.S. government"; and then concluded, "Therefore, the U.S. government will not be able to control terrorism." The fallacy is less apparent but is still there—the lack of tough laws doesn't necessarily indicate an inability to control terrorism. Again, there could be intervening causes. Although invalid, this form of syllogism is frequently used in advertisements. For instance, a romance is "saved" by a certain mouthwash or shampoo. Be alert to this trap. Persuaders can use a logically valid syllogism to camouflage untrue premises. Ask yourself whether the premises are true and whether the argument is valid. The conditional syllogism is similar to the cause-effect linkage described earlier.

Disjunctive Syllogisms

The **disjunctive syllogism** uses an "either/or" format. Consider this major premise of a disjunctive syllogism: "Either we reduce the deficit or we increase taxes." The premise is usually accompanied by some proof or evidence in the minor premise, and the conclusion is then drawn. For example, a school board threatens, "Either we vote to increase property taxes or you lose all extracurricular activities." The voters would provide the minor premise of the syllogism through their votes—if they vote to increase taxes, the board denies the need to eliminate the activities. A second valid conclusion comes about if the voters vote down the tax increase and the board eliminates the activities. This strategy works if the issue is clear-cut.

However, few situations have a clear "either/or" dichotomy, even in extreme cases such as the Terri Schiavo case in 2005. She had been in a comatose state for several years, and her husband wanted to remove her feeding and water tubes, but her parents objected and the issue went into the courts. Ultimately, the U.S. Congress voted on the right to life aspects of the case. The central issue revolved around the disjunctive syllogism "either she is alive or she is dead." The real question should have been: "Will she ever recover?" This argument would still exemplify a disjunctive syllogism—either she will recover or she will not—but the controversy would not have been as extreme. Strict either/or logic cannot take into account other belief systems or more than two alternatives in a situation. Examine persuasion framed in the either/or mode to search for other alternatives or belief systems under which the disjunctive model will not work.

Categorical Syllogisms

Categorical syllogisms deal with parts and wholes, or sets and subsets, of events in which the major and minor premises both involve membership or nonmembership in one of two categories. The conclusion relates the clusters of both premises into a new finding or result, as shown in the following classic categorical syllogism:

All men are included in the class of mortal beings (major premise).
Socrates is included in the class of men (minor premise).
Therefore, Socrates is a mortal being (conclusion).

Although this example is frequently used to demonstrate the categorical syllogism, it is not one that you will find many opportunities to use. Its format, however, is frequently seen, read, or heard in various kinds of persuasion. Take, for example, the U.S. Marines' recruiting slogan: "We're looking for a few good men." The implied categorical syllogism is as follows:

All U.S. Marines are included in the class of good men (major premise).
You are a good man (minor premise).
Therefore, you should become a Marine (conclusion).

Because you are a member of one category, it is assumed that you must or should be a member of another.

When you really think about it, human beings often do much of their everyday reasoning via categorical thinking. For example, consider what we all do when we first meet a person, or encounter a new event, or sense the presence of a certain logical system in the way things work, or decide how you will act in certain situations. You and I probably try to compare and then group these unfamiliar persons, events, systems of logic, or potential plans of action into categories that we have learned from past experiences. In the case of new persons: He's an athlete or a nerd, or a hale hearty and well-met jokester, or a griper and a pain in the sitter while she's a blabbermouth, a demure and shy girl, an organizer-librarian type, or a party girl. In the case of events, the new one calls for certain actions because it is a formal parliamentary procedure-type one versus a casual mixer "meet-and-be-met" type, or it is a combative event in which you can practically feel the tension and combat just beneath the surface event versus a "pitch in and get the job done" type of event. In terms of systems of logic, we quickly

---

BOX 8.2   **Fallacies as a Tool of Propaganda: The Illusion of Logic**

Propagandists wish their prospective converts in the audience to believe that they are converting to the cause for "good and sufficient reasons." The keyword here is "reasons," which naturally leads to the reasoning process. One way to make their arguments appear to be logical is by creating the illusion of logical reasoning through the use of fallacies such as the few discussed above. Go to Weblink 8.2 where you will find a list of links to over 40 separate fallacies that can be used in propaganda, including those discussed above but going well beyond with such fascinating fallacies as "appeal

to spite," "burden of proof," "appeal to novelty," and "slippery slope," all accompanied by clear and concise definitions and good examples. (You can access this and all of the other Chapter 8 weblinks through your companion website for *Persuasion,* Chapter 8 resources.) Another good site that could provide you with a multitude of good term paper topics with links to excellent sources and examples is Weblink 8.3. Each topic is loaded with links, resources, and examples and again would be an excellent starting point for a paper on propaganda, logical fallacies, or logic.

---

categorize them into highly authoritarian, laissez faire, autocratic, or democratic systems of thinking and as a result we should act accordingly—submissive to authority and the "chain of command" or free to do what you feel like doing versus acting like a "yes, sir," subservient-type person. Mostly we infer categories into which to fit these people, events, ways of thinking, or appropriate actions. At the base of these inferences are categorical syllogistic patterns described long ago and which seem to have remained valid across the centuries.

IBM used this technique when it ran a two-page public relations ad that features two pairs of baby booties, one pink and one blue, and the question, "Guess which one will grow up to be the engineer?" The question implies a cultural gender stereotype—women are poor at math and science. One underlying premise concerns engineers. It is: "Persons encouraged to excel in math and science are likely to become engineers" (major premise). The next step is: "Males are encouraged to excel in math and science" (minor premise). Thus we infer that "Males are likely to become engineers" (conclusion). On another level, the ad creates good public relations by implying that "Good companies encourage women to excel" (major premise); "IBM encourages women to excel" (minor premise); "IBM is therefore a good company" (conclusion). Although the first syllogism is valid (and probably true as well), the second is invalid. IBM uses the illusion of a valid syllogism to make its case that good companies encourage women to excel, but simply doing that does not necessarily guarantee that a company is "good." And in our 24/7, media-

saturated and multicultural world of advocacy/propaganda such syllogisms can make great differences, so responsible receivers will carefully consider all of the premises leading to a conclusion. For other examples of such cultural biases see Box 8.2, where nonverbal patterns and different ways of considering time and space are part of the cultural stereotype involved in the syllogism.

This tendency to use categorical reasoning usually serves us well and allows for a great deal of flexibility as we encounter many new people and events, but occasionally a miscue or faulty conclusion using categorical reasoning can lead people, groups, and even nations to make disastrous, even tragically flawed decisions. For example, ever since the 9/11 terrorist attacks on NYC and Washington, DC, U.S. foreign policy has operated on the categorical premise that democracy is the best weapon against terrorism. If we can just democratize the rest of the world, terrorism will cease to be used to influence national issues. Unfortunately, the facts don't seem to justify this premise. In fact, they seem to prove the opposite— authoritarian and autocratic militaristic regimes seem to be the best preventative against terrorism. Across a decade, India had over 400 terrorist incidents while China had only 18; Russia saw an increase in terrorism once the old Soviet system collapsed in 1990; and the shining star of democracy—the United States—has had more terrorism than Cuba, North Korea, or many other autocratic regimes. Why did we draw the conclusion that democracy was best? Because we've been propagandized to believe that? Partly. It is more likely we came to that conclusion/premise based on categories developed from our past experience in world events where other nations sought to emulate us and our system of government in dealing with national issues other than terrorism, and therein likes the potential flaw in categorical thinking—our familiar logical flaw—Gut Malloy or the problem of the undistributed middle. Events aren't necessarily shared by both (or all) categories under consideration. So our watchword when dealing with categorical (and other) syllogistic reasoning is to avoid placing too much faith in any logical system no matter how venerable and seemingly attractive, but to continue to be critical and skeptical receivers of persuasion.

THE TOULMIN FORMAT

Most of us do not encounter persuasion that is overtly syllogistic—conditional, disjunctive, or categorical. Instead, the syllogism often is just the underlying and basic structure in persuasive arguments. British philosopher Stephen Toulmin (1964) developed a model that identifies the kinds of logical persuasion we encounter in everyday events. According to Toulmin, any argument aimed at our logical reasoning processes is divided into three basic parts: the claim, the data, and the warrant.

Basic Elements

The **claim** is the proposition or premise that the persuader hopes will be believed, adopted, or followed by the audience. But claims usually need to be supported by **data**, the second part of the model, which is more simply stated as "evidence." Data give the receivers plausible reasons for following the advice of the claim. The **warrant** is the reasoning that demonstrates that the data do indeed support the claim; it explains the relationship between them. These three elements become clear as we examine persuasion at work in our everyday affairs—deciding which brand to choose, which policy to adopt, whom to believe or reject, which path to follow to satisfy our goals and desires (without costing us or others too much). Most of these decisions are benign and not very momentous, but the overall process of persuasion seems to

follow a series of very rational and economical steps. For example, if there is reason to believe that receivers will accept the claim on its face, there is no need for the persuader to continue. However, if the persuader expects receivers to doubt the claim, then data must be presented. If the data are anticipated to be strong and hence likely to be accepted, thus agreeing with the claim, again there is no need to proceed further. However, if the persuader anticipates some doubt about the claim now supported by data, then it will be necessary to present a warrant that explains the reasoning by which the data support the claim. This pattern of moving the logical argument from claim to data to warrant, and the resulting three kinds of responses (agree, disagree, and uncertain), are typical of almost every reasoned argument in the everyday marketplace of ideas. Figure 8.12 uses the claim that the United States must become a "globo-cop" to show how the flow of argument goes in the **Toulmin system**. Trace the stages of argument in the figure. (See also Box 8.3.)

Substantiating Elements

Toulmin's system has a number of secondary terms. For example, a claim may be modified by a qualifier—usually a simple word or phrase such as "in most cases," or "probably," or "it is likely that." Conceding that the claim is not necessarily universal qualifies or limits the claim. In our globo-cop example, the persuader might alter the claim to state, "In most cases, the United States should become an international peacekeeper in world crises." **Qualifiers** limit the claim, thus allowing for the possibility that this is not a simple case of the either/or argument. Another minor term in the model is the **reservation**, defined as a statement that specifies the conditions under which the war rant is valid. The reservation features words like "unless" or "only if there is a reason to believe that." In the globo-cop case, suppose the warrant stated, "Except in the case of revolutions, the United States is the only remaining superpower capable of establishing and maintaining world stability." Another reservation is expressed with the word "unless," in which case the warrant might state, "Unless the United States

Claim: The United States should become an international peacekeeper using military intervention and other assistance in world crises.

Option 1. Accept the persuader's claim, and the United States becomes globo-cop.

Option 2. Reject the persuader's claim and rely on other means of solving global crises.

Option 3. Request evidence to support the claim.

Data: Past crises have escalated into full-scale warfare and its resulting loss of life and property (Vietnam, Kuwait, Somalia).

Option 1. Accept the claim now supported by the data and work to institute global police power for the United States.

Option 2. Reject the claim as unsupported by the data—work to keep the United States out of international conflicts.

Option 3. Request an explanation of how and why the data support the claim.

Warrant: The United States is the only remaining superpower capable of maintaining stability in a world that would otherwise lapse into total war, suffering, death, disease, and so on.

Option 1. Accept the claim now supported by the data and explained by the warrant.

Option 2. Reject the claim as unsupported by the data and the warrant.

Option 3. Ask the persuader to refine the claim, back up the data, or provide for possible exceptions in the warrant.

FIGURE 8.12 Toulmin's basic elements of an argument, applied to the example of U.S. intervention in world crises.

SOURCE: © Cengage Learning 2013.

BOX 8.3 **The Logic of Cultural Transformation**

In his book *Communication and Cultural Transformation: Cultural Diversity, Globalization and Cultural Convergence,* Stephan Dahl (2000) draws a distinction between "high culture" (the opera or symphony, art museums, live theatre) and mass or popular culture (MTV, sports events, newspapers), which emerged in the mid-nineteenth century. He argues that it is popular culture that really is affected by diversity issues. Some of the diversity issues he lists include social groupings, language, nonverbal communication, values, concepts of time and space, perception, and national character. For example, he maintains that in Western culture, time is thought of as linear, while in Eastern cultures time is thought of as being circular in nature. Or take our nonverbal signal for "A-Okay," which is the thumb and forefinger forming the letter O. In other cultures or subcultures, the same signal has sexual implications. What kinds of differences in persuasive meaning might follow from these ways of viewing time and space? Various nonverbal gestures? Which of his other diversity issues can you see operating in your everyday life? You may want to do a web search to view a copy of Dahl's book and his other publications. (You can access the Chapter 8 weblinks through your companion website for *Persuasion,* Chapter 8 resources.)

is not the only remaining superpower capable of establishing and maintaining world stability."

Both persuaders and persuadees often overlook the use of the reservation to cite circumstances in which the claim should not be accepted. They assume that both parties begin from the same point, from the same frame of reference. We must begin at the same point or make allowances (such as reservations) to make real progress in any persuasive transaction. Coupled with the qualifier, the reservation allows for great flexibility in persuasion because both encourage dialogue; both provide the persuadee with an opportunity to object or agree to part but not all of the persuasion.

Advertisers are clever with the use of qualifiers. For example, the label on Cascade dishwasher detergent says that it will make your dishes, not spotless, but "virtually spotless." Who can say whether one spot or three spots or twelve qualifies as being "virtually spotless"? Thus, we need to be aware of two problems connected with qualifiers and reservations: (1) their absence, which can lock us into one course of action or belief; and (2) the use of vague qualifiers, which allows persuaders to wriggle out of any

commitment to a product, action, person, or idea. Persuaders may still try to interpret the qualifiers to their advantage, but it is more difficult when more details are given. The final element in Toulmin's system for showing the tactics of argument is the **backing** for the warrant, which is information that establishes the credibility of the reasoning or connection between data and claim.

We can now see that the tactics of persuasion are not usually simple syllogisms. Instead, persuaders make claims that persuadees can respond to by (1) accepting them outright, (2) rejecting them outright, or (3) asking for proof. Persuaders then can provide data, which receivers can accept, reject, or question. If the persuadee continues to request more proof, the persuader ultimately must provide the warrant, or reason, for linking the proof to the request. Given enough time, three other elements may enter into the persuasive appeal: the qualifier, the reservation, and the backing. What matters is that persuadees be aware, critical, and systematic as they are exposed to persuasion. Toulmin's system provides us with a simple tool that operates well with many kinds of persuasion.

REVIEW AND CONCLUSION

Content or logical premises don't rely on the internal states of persuaders, as do process or emotional premises. Instead, they rely more on universally agreed-upon norms or rules. Evidence tends to be either dramatically oriented, intellectually oriented, or experiential/participative in nature. Users of dramatic evidence lead persuadees to a "logical" conclusion by creating a dramatic scene and then inviting the audience to join in the drama. Persuadees thus "prove" the validity of the premise to themselves. Users of intellectually oriented evidence lead their persuadees to "logical" conclusions by presenting them with a set of data in support of a certain claim or content premise. The persuadees provide the connection between these data and the claim in the form of a warrant. And experiential or participative evidence may prove to be the most persuasive because of persuadees' personal involvement with

the evidence and its sometimes interactive nature. All three types of evidence rely on self-persuasion on the part of the persuadee, and all three kinds of evidence appear prominently in our 24/7, media-saturated and advocacy/propagandistic, and results-oriented multicultural world. Also, persuadees participate in some way in their own persuasion, whether the evidence is intellectual, dramatic, or experiential/participative. When we engage in self-persuasion, even if it runs counter to our own beliefs, the effect of the participation is powerful.

The traditional syllogism usually forms the skeletal structure of arguments or content premises. Within this structure, the tactics or particular arguments or premises are represented by claims supported by data. Claims and data are linked through warrants.

Finally, of the types of evidence available to the persuader, several seem more important than others. Most important, probably, are those that support the three major linkages: cause-effect, symptoms, and comparisons. Also, evidence that provides a perspective for the audience is probably more effective than evidence that does not. We focused on two particularly effective methods of providing this perspective: the use of analogy, which provides a comparative perspective; and the use of narrative, which has the same ability to provide a perspective within a dramatic frame of reference. Both are also "artistic" in the sense that neither merely presents information; rather, both depict evidence in dramatic or visual formats. In sum, we are most effectively persuaded by experiences—real, vicarious, or imagined. Successful persuaders try to shape content premises—their linkages, claims, data, and warrants—in terms of the audience's experience. If persuaders invite audiences to participate in drawing conclusions, audiences will share in their own persuasion.

KEY TERMS

After reading this chapter, you should be able to identify, explain, and give an example of the following key terms or concepts:

content premises

arguments

cause-effect reasoning

proof

reasoning

evidence

direct experience

dramatic or vicarious experience

rationally processed evidence

participation and demonstration

effect-to-cause reasoning

cause-to-effect reasoning

reasoning from symptoms

criteria-to-application reasoning

reasoning from analogy or by comparison

deductive reasoning

inductive reasoning

statistics

fallacy

the "post hoc" fallacy

ad hominem

ad populum fallacy

undistributed middle

straw man fallacy

syllogisms

conditional syllogisms

validity

disjunctive syllogism

categorical syllogisms

claim

data

warrant

Toulmin system

qualifier

reservation

backing

APPLICATION OF ETHICS

Two logical opposites in decision making are (1) conflict of interests and (2) compatibility of interests. In conflicts of interest, a person in a position to have inside information might be able to influence decisions so that she or he might personally benefit, as in the case of most corporate scandals. When compatibility of interests exists, persons with an inside position and information make decisions that benefit both themselves and all others with the same interests. For example, a company is having production problems that may lead to layoffs. The CEO decides to bring in efficiency experts to analyze the problem. They do so and cut costs, returning the company to profitability, and removing the layoff option. Apply both of the options to the following example: A CEO at a major automobile corporation sees the prices for energy rising at increasing rates and a resulting drop in sales of SUVs. The executive has several choices. One is to provide incentives for buying SUVs (e.g., "Now you can buy an SUV at employee discount rates"). Another option is to develop hybrid models, which will result in higher costs of the vehicles because of the research and development needed. Still another option is to "cook the books," which will jack up the stock value, at which point the CEO can sell off his stock at a profit. Which option should the CEO choose?

QUESTIONS FOR FURTHER THOUGHT

1. What are the three types of syllogisms discussed in this chapter? Give examples of each from advertisements, political speeches, or some other source of persuasion.

2. Define proof. What constitutes adequate proof for you? Does it change from issue to issue? If so, in what ways?

3. Review some magazine commentary concerning a particular issue, and attempt to identify the data offered. What kinds of evidence are they? Are they dramatic? If so, in what ways? If not, are they persuasive? Why or why not? What is the underlying syllogistic structure inherent in the discussions of the issue?

4. What is the difference between intellectually oriented evidence and emotionally oriented evidence? Give examples and explain how they differ.

5. Give examples from your own experience of (a) opinion, (b) attitudes, (c) beliefs, and (d) values that affect behavior. Give examples that do not affect behavior. How do they differ?

6. Why was "The Case of Bobby and His Parents" so persuasive? Was logic involved? Was the example an illogical one to prove the point Peck wanted to make?

7. What is the difference between a figurative and a literal analogy? Which is being used when a political campaign is compared to a horse race?

8. What are some of the ways in which statistics can be misused? Give examples.

9. What are some of the ways in which testimony can be misused? Give examples.

10. What is a *post hoc* fallacy? Give an example.

11. What is an *ad hominem* fallacy? Give an example.

12. How has the *ad hominem* been used in recent elections?

13. What are some contemporary examples of the *ad populum* being used in advertising?

14. How does the undistributed middle fallacy operate? Give examples.

15. How does the straw man fallacy operate? Give examples.

16. What is the false dilemma fallacy? How does it operate? Give examples.

17. How does the ELM help to explain the differences between content and process premises?

18. How do content premises occur in your use of SNM?

19. Why is the route of the ELM used to process information relate to the idea of content premises?

You can access your online resources at the companion website for *Persuasion*.
Log in at **http://www.cengagebrain.com**.

Cultural Premises in Persuasion

After reading this chapter, you should be able to:

1. Identify and explain what cultural patterns are.

2. Recognize how you are affected by cultural training and societal pressures.

3. Recognize in persuasive messages the cultural myths of the wisdom of the rustic, the possibility of success, the coming of a messiah, conspiracy, the value of challenge, and the myth of the eternal return.

4. Identify, explain, and give examples of Reich's cultural parables in advertisements, editorials, or political speeches.

5. Identify messages that appeal to the myths of the man's man and the woman's woman.

6. Discuss image and charisma as cultural premises and explain their three central elements.

7. Identify Redding and Steele's core American values, giving contemporary examples of each.

8. Relate the values, myths and cultural patterns discussed here to how persuasion seems to operate.

9. Understand how cultural premises can impact messages sent via SNM.

10. Understand which channels of the ELM are used in most cultural premises and why.

11. Understand why it is difficult to apply standards of ethics to cultural premises

THE MULTICULTURAL FACES OF PERSUASION

We are all prisoners of our own culture. As a result, we often overlook patterns of behavior that influence us and by which we are persuaded, and yet a major facet of persuasion discussed in Chapter 1 and continuing on through Chapter 8 is on that list—our "multicultural world of shared values" that typifies persuasion today. Anyone who has visited another culture (even a similar or related culture) immediately becomes aware of significant differences between our patterns of behavior and language, and those of the foreign culture. Not only are values, languages, and customs different, but hundreds of little things are also different. Bus passengers line up in orderly fashion in England, whereas Americans usually crowd around the bus door. In the United States, skiers line up in orderly fashion to wait their turn to use the lift, but in France, locals walk over others' skis to get ahead in the line. In a more significant example of cultural differences, one third of the world's people eat using knife, fork, and spoon; another

third eat with chopsticks; and the rest use their fingers.

I visited several formerly communist countries in Eastern Europe in the 1990s following the fall of the Soviet Union, and quickly understood the immense difference between hard currency and soft currency. Hard currency has real worth, but soft currency is widely overvalued, so people don't want to accept it. The hotel I stayed at in Prague refused to accept its own "soft" Czech currency but was more than willing to accept hard currencies like the U.S. dollar or the German mark and, more recently, the euro. It has been that way for so many years that it became a cultural habit in the former Czechoslovakia to trade currency on the black market even though trading at above the official rates had been outlawed there for more than 50 years. I was told that the best exchange rate one could get in Czechoslovakia was from any priest. That's something that would never occur to someone from America.

At that time, customers in Eastern European countries carried their own net shopping bag just in case they found something available to buy. In fact, the slang term for such a shopping bag was a "perhaps." People at that time didn't buy something because they needed it, but because it was available. Usually store shelves were nearly empty of any goods, and as a result hoarding was common—an idea that would rarely cross an American's mind, and carrying one's own cloth or net shopping bag indicates a societal awareness of potential global climate change.

Although many aspects of any given culture are relatively permanent (such as ways of doing business, religious patterns and dress, and national pride, as can be seen from the example of "People of the Deer" in Box 9.1), cultures are also subject to constant change. In the United States and elsewhere, for example, the constant influx of different ethnic groups and minorities is reflected in the culture in a variety of ways, and diversity and multiculturalism are apparent everywhere. For instance, in our supermarkets the shelves are always loaded, which astounded many visitors from Eastern Europe during the last 20 years. In addition, you will usually find ingredients for foreign dishes that weren't available just a decade ago. So increasing diversity is changing our shopping options. Many schools have sought the help of translators and interpreters to assist them in communicating with the immigrant parents of their newest students. In such small things we can see the continual changes in U.S. culture.

CULTURAL PATTERNS

Cultural patterns are defined as the "socially transmitted values, beliefs, institutions, behavioral patterns, and all other products and thought patterns of a society" (*American Heritage Dictionary,* 1985). These are instilled in us from early childhood through our language, the myths and the tales we hear, and our observations of the behavior of those around us. These become cultural patterns, or the activities, beliefs, and values that typify a culture. Women in Muslim countries have a cultural pattern of dress which obscures all but the upper face and covers the head, whereas American women go to great lengths to decorate and call

---

BOX 9.1   People of the Deer

Consider the following instance of cultural patterning. Suppose you are a member of a tribe whose sole food supply is caribou. When the animals make their fall migration south, the tribe kills enough to supply it with food until spring, when the animals migrate north to follow their food supply. The custom is to kill and preserve these deer in a period of a week or two. You have just finished the fall hunt, only to discover that you face a severe winter without having killed enough caribou to last until the spring migration north. Death is certain without sufficient supplies of protein and fat. You attend a council of elders called by the chief to address the crisis and to solicit input and ideas. What would you do? For many years, students in my persuasion classes have brainstormed solutions to this problem and come up with the following suggestions, usually in this approximate order:

■ Follow the deer and kill more of them, thus increasing the supply.

■ Seek an alternative food supply—we can eat berries or fish or birds.

■ Send a band of the young and healthy to get help.

■ Ration food to make it last longer.

■ Eat all the parts of the caribou—skin, horns, everything—to increase the supply.

■ Send some of the people away to another place where food is more plentiful and thus decrease demand.

■ Kill some members of the tribe to decrease demand.

■ Kill the most useless persons—the old first, and the very young next to decrease demand.

■ Resort to cannibalism; let's eat those we kill.

The most practical solutions emerge first, and then the ideas become increasingly desperate. The actual tribe does nothing. They eat the food at their regular rates, knowing that it will not last through the winter. Then they sit and wait for death. They accept the situation, whereas Americans try to find solutions for all problems, even though some are probably insoluble. In all the years of using this example, not a single one of my students has suggested doing nothing. Do you think it is good to be solution oriented? Why or why not?

attention to their faces, shape, and hair. In fact, France tried to limit Muslim cultural values by outlawing this type of dress. In Japan professional "packers" stuff as many persons as possible into their subways, while in American subways there is always room for a street entertainer to try to earn some money. Most persons from the United States would view sardine packing as unacceptable, and Japanese wouldn't allow the entertainer to have enough room to display his or her talents. Cultural training or patterning is the basis for some of the widely held premises we have discussed in earlier chapters.

These cultural preferences, myths, and values which we embrace can all serve as major premises in enthymemes. Persuasion that builds on cultural premises occurs at a low level of awareness and is usually processed in the peripheral information-processing channel of the ELM. Thus, we often react subconsciously to various stimuli based on our cultural training. Robert Cialdini (2008) calls these reactions fixed action patterns or shortcuts, which are automatic and instantaneous. Cialdini observes that "you and I exist in an extraordinarily complicated environment, easily the most rapidly moving and complex that has ever existed on this planet. To deal with it, we need shortcuts. As the stimuli saturating our lives continue to grow more intricate and variable, we will have to depend increasingly on our shortcuts to handle them all" (p. 7). And cultural patterning and cultural premises are just such shortcuts to being persuaded.

A major cultural pattern for most Americans is the value of individualism. We like the idea of pulling ourselves up by the bootstraps. There is a flip side to this individualism, as Robert Bellah and his associates (1985) pointed out in *Habits of the Heart: Individualism and Commitment in American Life*. Bellah and his colleagues did in-depth interviews with more than 200 Americans from various walks of life, and described the core American values and beliefs as "habits of the heart." Key among them was the value of the individual. Bellah and his coauthors point out:

> The central problem of our book concerned the American individualism that Tocqueville described with a mixture of

admiration and anxiety. It seems to us it is individualism and not equality, as Tocqueville thought, that has marched inexorably throughout our history. We are concerned that this individualism may have grown cancerous (p. viii).

What they meant by "cancerous" is that until very recently, individualism equaled me-ism, with emphasis on the individual and not the community, thus drawing people into themselves and forgetting others. Many other observers have echoed this theme. Recall that the initial student responses to the dilemma of too few caribou are positive and action oriented, reflecting the good side of the American value of individualism. The middle responses are more reflective of a sense of community and cooperation, but the last three reflect the bad or cancerous side of American individualism. Why for instance is the income tax rate for the very wealthy—billionaires for example—so low in our culture (in the mid 30 percent level or much less—zero percent for some) and so high in other Western democracies (as high as the 90 percent level)? Perhaps in difficult times, we are returning more to the idea of the individual in community, but how do we identify these patterns of cultural values? Where do they come from? How do persuaders appeal to them? To see how these premises relate to persuasion in general, we look first at how we get them—through cultural training and societal pressure. Then we look at two kinds of cultural premises: (1) **cultural images and myths**, which are defined as real or imagined narratives that illustrate a society's values, and (2) our value system, which is defined as the hierarchical network of beliefs and values that typify a culture. Bear in mind that a value is an idea of the good or the desirable that we use as a standard for judging people's actions or motivations. Examples of American values are honesty, justice, beauty, efficiency, safety, and progress. Because our value system is a major source of persuasive leverage, you may be interested in discovering how persuaders link proposals and arguments to such values. Cultural training forms the core of our values, which then become rules for governing ourselves. Persuaders appeal to and believe these premises and expect their audiences to do so too.

CULTURAL IMAGES AND MYTHS

Every culture has its own myths and heroic figures which/who do things valued by the culture, and many of these myths are borrowed from other cultures, particularly European cultures. An example that Greek society developed centuries ago was a series of myths surrounding the sin of pride. The hero of their tragedies was almost always guilty of this sin and wore purple to indicate his or her hubris. We have similar beliefs. You know that the overly proud student won't be elected or chosen as team captain. The more humble person will be picked. What are some of the myths or legends or images underlying American culture and society, and how do persuaders use them? Can these images be changed, and if so, how? Are they being changed at present, and if so, how? Stereotypes and proverbs are indicators of cultural myths. Let us consider a few.

The Wisdom of the Rustic

One of the legends in American lore that has great persuasive appeal is the **wisdom of the rustic**. No matter how devious the opposition, the simple common-sense wisdom of the backwoods hero or heroine wins out. Numerous folktales rely on this rustic image, including the Daniel Boone tales and many Abraham Lincoln stories about his humble beginnings and meager education. We believe in humble beginnings, and we believe that difficulty teaches even the most uneducated to be wise and worldly. Thus, politicians throughout American history have emphasized their humble origins. For example, Ronald Reagan emphasized his humble origin in Dixon, Illinois, and Bill Clinton let it be known that he was born in a small house in the tiny town of Hope, Arkansas. President Obama has emphasized his African-American and multicultural origins. Neither President Bush (father nor son)

emphasized that they came from privileged origins. If the politician cannot claim humble beginnings, he or she finds some substitute, usually hardship or suffering, such as having been a POW or suffering from some disability. In the campaign of 2008 several candidates referred to their humble beginnings. For example, Barack Obama referred to the fact that he was multiracial and that his father had left the family; Mike Huckabee, whose name even suggests the rustic image, referred to his humble Arkansas backwoods roots; and John McCain referred to his years as a POW to indicate his humility. Others who came from better circumstances skipped discussing this issue (e.g., Hillary Clinton and Mitt Romney) and instead emphasized experience or accomplishments.

Products are frequently marketed using a rustic as the spokesperson. Actor Wilfred Brimley, for instance, was a spokesperson for AARP, and served as a rustic when he endorsed the value of good old-fashioned Quaker Oats—and the smiling Quaker man on the package reinforces the rustic image (see Figure 9.1).

Nothing could be more rustic conveying common sense about basic survival issues than a caveman—right? Well, Geico Insurance must think so since they used him as their spokesperson, giving advice on a fairly complex product like insurance. In fact, his rustic nature even led to a regular television series. It failed, but the wisdom of the rustic myth upon which it was based is with us today. Even as we value the simple, common-sense rustic, our culture tends to devalue the intellectual or the educated. Persuaders often use this reverse side of our faith in the wisdom of the rustic: The intellectual or egghead is the brunt of jokes, and the rustic wins out over the smart, educated, and sophisticated person.

The Possibility of Success

The **possibility of success** myth is easily seen in the numerous television series where desperate housewives, wimpy lawyers, ugly Betty, and bumbling home repair figures achieve their individual goals of success by the end of each episode. These all reflect the power of our hopes for the American dream of success. It was probably most powerfully

Waist not, want not.

If you're watching your waistline, why in the world should you eat good old stick-to-your-ribs Quaker Oats for breakfast? Because good old stick-to-your-ribs Quaker Oats is one of the leanest, most sensible foods you can include in your diet. Whether you're on a diet or not.

A bowl of Quaker Oats has surprisingly few calories. Just over a hundred. Only two more calories than a bowl of corn-flakes. And what's more, the cal-ories in oatmeal are pure warmth and satisfaction. Very important ingredients if you're going to get through the whole rest of the day on a little cottage cheese and melba toast.

Quaker Oats is a beautifully balanced food, absolutely loaded with good protein. And this slow-burning protein is balanced by fast-release nourishers and energizers. You not only feel satisfied first thing in the morning. Quaker Oats can help keep you feeling satisfied right up until it's time for lunch.

A steaming, smiling bowl of oatmeal fills you up and fuels you up. Without fattening you up. So with Quaker Oats you can be weighed in the balance. And not found wanting.

FIGURE 9.1 **Quaker Oats and Wisdom of the Rustic**

Though the Quaker man has changed a little over 100 years, he still represents the values and wisdom of the rustic.

SOURCE: Barbara Singer/Hulton Archive; Image Courtesy of The Advertising Archives; Jerry Arcieri/Corbis.

introduced to our culture within the numerous novels on the topic, written mainly for boys, in the early twentieth century by Horatio Alger, including titles like *Ragged Dick, Tattered Tom,* and *Pluck and Luck.* The protagonist of these novels was invariably a young man who, through hard work, sincerity, honesty, law-abiding behavior, and faith in the future, was able to make good. He might even rise to the top and own his own company, have a beautiful wife, live a fine life, and be able to do good for others. The possibility of success myth appealed to immigrants, the poor, and the downtrodden. They passed it on to their children, and today's immigrants still do this, admonishing their children to work hard to achieve success. The myth has been generalized to include women and minorities, and has great appeal for new groups of immigrants—particularly those from Third World countries, who often share living quarters to save money or go into business for themselves, and all members are expected to help provide for the family. The myth of possible success is as alive today as it was when immigrants came mainly from Europe. Again, this myth was observed by Tocqueville (1965):

> No Americans are devoid of a yearning desire to rise…. All are constantly seeking to acquire property, power, and reputation…. What chiefly diverts the men of democracies from lofty ambition is not the scantiness of their fortunes, but the vehemence of the exertions they daily make to improve them…. The same observation is applicable to the sons of such men … their parents were humble; they have grown up amidst feelings and notions which they cannot afterwards easily get rid of … (pp. 156–158).

You may recognize your grandparents in this description if they or their parents immigrated to the United States. You may also see yourself in it at times. Isn't that why you are in college? You want to be as successful as your parents and grandparents or preferably exceed their levels of achievement.

Naturally, we are receptive to persuasion that promises the possibility of success. Self-help programs and products and services are marketed promising success for the entire family. Ads promoting success are powerful and persuasive. Consider the street signs in Figure 9.2.

The Coming of a Messiah

A cultural myth related to the possibility of success myth is the **coming of a messiah**. Whenever our society is approaching disaster or is already in a terrible mess (economic, religious, or political); or we are in a period of great uncertainty and pessimism; or when things are chaotic, confusing, and frightening, such as those things we face in the

FIGURE 9.2

Which Word is Foremost in Your Mind?

Politicians promise a bright future for voters who support a common-sense approach to problems. Whether it is a pyramid marketing scheme, the lottery, or a weight-loss club, the carrot is always the same—try and you will succeed.

SOURCE: Andy Dean/Istockphoto.com.

second decade of the new millennium, we believe someone or something will save us. We want to be rescued from the chaos and danger of bankruptcy, unemployment, war, and other disasters by some great leader who projects a sense of confidence and who can turn things around, or by a new technology that will solve our problems (e.g., the fuel cell or coal gasification). Many past leaders filled this role. For example, Abraham Lincoln emerged from semi-obscurity to save the Union. Franklin Roosevelt used his patrician education and background to lead the common people of United States out of the Great Depression and to victory in WWII. Ronald Reagan delivered us from 18 percent interest rates and unbelievable inflation. And Barack Obama was seen as someone who could save the world from a global depression. And maybe he did—we were on the edge of one when he followed through on George W. Bush's TARP program of financial bailouts for various companies like the auto industry and the banking and financial communities as a whole. Products can also be messiahs of a sort; ethanol or the low energy light bulb are depicted by some as ways to free us from foreign energy. Policies are also frequently put forward as messiahs to save us from vexing problems, such as carbon dioxide caps for corporations. The future will no doubt bring us other problems, and you can rest assured that there will be someone or something which will emerge in the role of a messiah.

What makes us so receptive to the messianic? First, we are action-oriented, as we noted earlier. We live in a results-oriented world of persuasion in which efficacy and efficiency are what really count, we decide by looking at the bottom line, and we want our saviors to be doers, not just idealistic dreamers. Second, we want their solutions to be simple and practical. Thus, as a persuadee, be aware of the advocates and propagandists who promise a messianic figure, policy, product or idea to solve the problems we face. These appeals can come at you from persons, products, organizations, and so forth; and they will always be attractive and easy to believe in, which is what makes them so potentially persuasive—and treacherous.

Presence of a Conspiracy

Another cultural premise is the belief that when we face enormous, almost overwhelming problems, the only plausible explanation is that a powerful and conspiratorial group must be behind them. This pattern is called the **paranoid style** and is defined as using conspiracies as explanations for otherwise unanswerable dilemmas (Hofstadter, 1963). Probably the best examples are the various conspiracy theories concerning the assassination of John F. Kennedy, which are said to have been hatched in a variety of possible places depending on who is making the argument (e.g., the mob or the CIA). Many other conspiracy arguments have recurred throughout our recent history, such as those about the Masons and Knights Templar, conspiracies that lent credence to the recent novel and film, *The Da Vinci Code,* and other papal conspiracy theories. Most recently, the conspiracy argument was used to explain the 9/11 bombing and the Jihadist terrorism of our times. Some people believe that Muslim groups are presently conspiring to overthrow governments in the Middle East and build nuclear weapons. Some feel that the Iranian government is already in the hands of international conspirators including radical fundamentalist Muslim leaders and Russian co-conspirators. A conspiracy theory regarding terrorism apparently prompted the Bush administration to illegally wiretap phone calls to American citizens without obtaining warrants, even when such warrants are granted as a matter of course. This in turn led to a conspiracy theory about the administration's disregard of constitutional rights.

When it comes to persuasive communication, and if Hofstadter is right, we can expect to hear conspiracy offered as an explanation for problems any time three factors are operating for the audience members:

1. They have something of value to lose—power, property, or privilege.

2. They feel in danger of losing this power or property, or they have already lost some of it.

3. They see themselves as helpless to prevent the loss.

FIGURE 9.3   **Russian Propaganda**

This is an example of a local political propaganda billboard in Russia.

SOURCE: © Smirnov Vladimir/ITAR-TASS Photo/Corbis.

It is easy to see how belief in a conspiracy could give rise to a messiah as well (see Figure 9.3). Only a messiah can defeat evil conspirators and save us. One of the dangers of this myth is that it invites mass hysteria and the rise of charismatic leaders, who seem to be heroes but who may be just the opposite. And once again products use this myth to promote their brand while demoting the competition.

The Value of Challenge

The myth of the **value of challenge** is fairly simple and parallels tribal tests of strength and character. It suggests that a kind of wisdom can be gained only through rigorous testing and suffering, and that some rite of passage or initiation gives us power, character, and knowledge. You are probably now going

through such a test in attending college. People say that going to college is more a test of endurance than training for a specific job. By graduating, you show that you can meet a challenge and handle it, that you have matured, and that you have learned how to learn. Job training comes after that. The challenges that are offered by persuaders are myriad. Boot camp offers another example of belief in the value of overcoming difficulty and meeting challenges. The "outward bound" program rests on the value of challenge myth. It says the most problematic children will be restored to good behavior if they get through a mountain-climbing expedition, a rafting trip down the Colorado river, or a wilderness canoe trip. Even corporate America believes in this concept and often sends its executives on such outward Bound types of experiences to shape them up and build unity. Brands also offer you this in some form, with something like

"The Chevy Challenge," and many ideological groups challenge you to step up and join.

Political persuaders frequently offer voters a dramatic challenge to be met by their election. For instance, John F. Kennedy said that with his election a torch had been passed to a new generation and that the light from the torch would "light the world." The candidates for the 2008 elections all promised changes that were really challenges to be met—in fact "change" was a key word to almost every candidate's campaign. Product appeals frequently present consumers with a challenge: "Use the Soloflex machine regularly and lose 20 pounds in 30 days!" "Get your MBA at Olivet College by attending one Saturday a month!" Both rely on the value of challenge. The value of challenge suggests that suffering could be good, or that nothing was ever accomplished without pain. Second, the myth suggests that suffering begets maturity, humility, and wisdom. Individuals learn and grow as they meet challenges and surmount them. Finally, all great leaders became so because they were tested and found equal to the challenge. Thus, defeats and failures are both just tests that prepare you for the future. As you begin to catalog the persuasion

aimed at you, you will find the value of challenge used frequently, whether for products, candidates, or ideologies (see Figure 9.4).

The Eternal Return

Mercia Eliade (1971), a French professor of history and cultural myth, identified a historical myth persistent not only in Western culture but in other cultures as well. He called it the **myth of the eternal return**, and defined it as a rejection of concrete historical time or things as they actually happened, and substitutes a return to an interpretation of history as we wish it might have been accompanied by a yearning for and reenactment of a "periodical return to the mythical time of the beginning of things, to the 'Great Time.'" American culture embraces this myth, perhaps because our beginnings are so recent. As you are aware, America was conceived as a "second Eden," a chance to start anew with no historical baggage to clutter up its purpose. This was a key element in Barack Obama's campaign in 2008. Many immigrants of the past and present want this chance to start over at a time when things were perfect and harmonious, when events

FIGURE 9.4
The Value of Challenge
Challenge that offers growth and maturation.

SOURCE: Courtesy of The Association for Experiential Education.

could be shaped or molded as they were meant to be. This time of creation is usually associated with a specific geographical center where things are assumed to have begun. In the United States, this center is probably Philadelphia, where the Continental Congress signed the Declaration of Independence and where the Liberty Bell is housed. Another potential symbolic center is Washington, DC, where our great historical documents are enshrined in the National Archives. At the creation there were great heroes (George Washington, Benjamin Franklin, Paul Revere, John Hancock, and others) and there were villains (King George, the colonial governors, Redcoats, and Tories). After suffering indignities, the heroes enacted some critical feat that was redemptive, and it released them and the people from their former enslavement and permitted them to create the "Great Time" or the "Golden Age." The Boston Tea Party is a familiar example. The now famous right wing fringe "Tea Party" drew its 2009 inspiration from this dumping of overtaxed English tea into Boston Harbor. Included in the myth and the real event is the notion that society has lost sight of its archetypal beginning and must find its way back if we are to rid ourselves of the corruption and confusion that have developed since then. We often accomplish this through reenactments of the original feat in a ritual, usually held at the center where everything began. For today's "Tea Party," this started by throwing useless investment derivatives into Lake Michigan. Its name stands for **t**axed **e**nough **a**lready and spread rapidly until tea bags were being dumped into lakes and rivers and the party endorsed national political candidates like Sarah Palin. This periodic return to the origins of our beliefs reestablishes our values for us and redeems the culture. The ritual freezes us in a mystical time that has power to transform us. As Eliade noted, "Time, too, like space is neither homogeneous nor continuous. On the one hand there are the intervals of a sacred time, the time of festivals and on the other hand there is profane time, ordinary temporal duration" (Beane and Doty, 1975, p. 33). We believe in and talk about the cyclical nature of things in the two types of time. For example, when we say, "What goes around comes around," or "History repeats itself," we really mean, "This will come back to haunt you," or "What ye sow, so shall ye reap." We have a reverence for certain

sacred times like historical holidays, ritualistic meals such as Thanksgiving or Passover, and national rites such as the Inaugural Address, the Oath of Office, or the State of the Union Address. The ad for Danner boots in Figure 9.5 demonstrates this appeal of the myth of the eternal return.

Commercial persuaders are aware of the importance of sacred time. They have invented special sales on historical holidays—a "Hatchet Days Sale" on Washington's birthday, an "Independence Day Sale" on the Fourth of July, and, in recent years, a "Super Bowl Sale" in mid-January. And every four years, the Olympics provide numerous instances of sacred time being celebrated. At the same time, we disdain persons who waste time, who are just passing the time, or who are "couch potatoes" living through profane time. Recessions are profane times, as are losing seasons for athletic teams. Politicians are skilled at challenging us to return to an earlier time to reestablish and renew ourselves. Not only is this apparent in their speeches, but also in the inaugural ceremonies themselves, which are acts of renewal that promise to return us to the untainted past.

In ideological campaigns and mass movements, the return-and-renewal theme is also persistent. Martin Luther King, Jr., used it in his "I Have a Dream" speech. We hear strains of the myth referring to profane times in the pro-life, antiabortion movement. One pro-life leader said, "People are going to look back on this era the way they look back on Nazi Germany. They'll say 'Thank God there were a few sane people'" ("America's Abortion Dilemma," 1985). This profane time was echoed by a "moral majority" leader who said of abortion: "This criminal activity … sets us back to the Stone Age" (p. 22).

Even in product ads we can detect appeals to the new beginnings or to the return and renewal myth. NEC Corporation says, "The new information age is built on the merging of computers and communication … you deserve no less. NEC, the way it will be." Mercedes-Benz reminds us, "This Year, as for 99 Years, the Automobiles of Mercedes-Benz are Like no Other Cars in the World." This myth of the eternal return is a powerful tool that persuaders use in a variety of circumstances. It is reflected in a set of cultural myths or parables described next.

It was cold. It was wet. And losing your life was as easy as falling off a log.

Among early loggers in the Northwest, the boot that earned the highest praise—"Skookum tough"—was the one made by W.B. Danner. All leather, it had caulked soles to give "river pigs" a grip on shifting logs. A pair weighed about 6 lbs.

Nowadays Danner makes boots for every kind of outdoorsman. We use the same full-grain 5½ oz. leather, but we chrome tan it to repel water and reduce weight (to about 3½ lbs.).

For the inside we invented the Gore-Tex™ bootie. Water cannot penetrate its 9 billion pores per square inch, but perspiration can evaporate to the outside. The boots are guaranteed waterproof.

Gore-Tex is a trademark of W.L. Gore & Assoc., Inc. Thinsulate™ is a registered trademark of 3M. Cordura® is a registered trademark of Dupont.

We use Thinsulate™ Thermal Insulation. One forest ranger said the insulation was so good he couldn't tell his boots were on fire. He asked for one of our uninsulated models.

In any case, with a cushioned insole, neoprene and EVA midsoles, and Vibram® outsole, your feet are well protected from the primary source of cold, the ground.

For even lighter weight, we use Cordura® nylon in our fabric and leather boots. Originally used as tire cord, it has ten times the scuff resistance of leather and can bring the weight of a boot down

to 24 oz. So there's a lot that's new in a Danner boot.

But it still takes 72 square feet of material to make a pair. And it still involves 250 separate operations, most of them by hand (we're about the only manufacturer that bothers with double lasting).

If you'd like a boot that's good enough to go back for resoling, we should be your bootmaker. We got our feet wet a long time ago.

Danner

Call us for a free brochure or the name of your nearest Danner retailer. 1-800-345-0430.

CORDURA® GORE-TEX® Thinsulate

FIGURE 9.5

Lasts Forever

This ad by Danner boots appeals to the myth of the eternal return with its reference to a "Golden Age" when men were men and their boots stood the test of time.

SOURCE: Danner Boots.

REICH'S CULTURAL PARABLES

In his book *Tales of a New America,* Robert Reich (1987) contends that the future appears chaotic for a variety of reasons: rapidly advancing technology, rising expectations for prosperity throughout the world, and general confusion about where we are headed as a nation, what is happening to human values, the environment, and the dangers of global warming. Reich and his Harvard colleagues have identified what they call basic cultural parables for the United States. These parables convey lessons about the how and why of life through metaphor, which may be a basic human trait, a universal characteristic of our intermittently rational, deeply emotional, and meaning-seeking species. In America, the vehicles of public myth include the biographies of famous citizens, popular fiction, films, and music, and feature stories about people who do good things. They anchor our political understandings. What gives them force is their capacity to make sense of, and bring coherence to, common experience. The lessons ring true, even if the illustration is fanciful (p. 7). Reich's work often echoes what has been emphasized earlier in our study of persuasion: Human beings are fascinated with and driven by the power of the dramatic.

Reich's parables are manifest in the following story about a man named George, the son of immigrant parents who worked hard to provide a good home for his family and a good community for his friends and neighbors. He did well in school and worked long hours as a young man to bring home a few dollars for the family. He was good in sports although he didn't have much time to participate. He never picked a fight, but on one occasion he did step in to stop the town bully and banker's son, Albert Wade, from beating up on the smallest kid in class. He let Albert have the first swing and then decked him with a single punch. George went off to fight in Europe in World War II and saved his squad by single-handedly destroying a machine gun nest, but he was too humble to wear or display the medal he received for bravery. After the war, he returned to his hometown, married his childhood sweetheart, and built a successful construction business. He gave his spare time to good causes and lived modestly. George kept to himself until his old nemesis, Albert Wade, inherited his father's bank and began to squander the depositors' savings by making shady loans to his buddies and buying himself into the office of mayor. The only person to stand up and challenge the corrupt election was George. Then Wade's bank refused to loan any money on houses built by George. In a showdown town meeting, one of Wade's corrupt councilmen finally broke down under George's accusatory gaze and spilled the beans on Wade, who ended up in jail while George went back to his modest life. It is the American morality play, according to Reich. This brief story has been told over and over again in many versions, including Horatio Alger novels, and biographies of famous Americans. It contains Reich's

basic cultural parables that have remained current for generations. We see it every Christmas in the classic *It's a Wonderful Life,* with Jimmy Stewart as its George. As you read about this and other parables, look for the similarities between them and the following cultural myths.

The Mob at the Gates

The basic idea in this parable is that America stands alone as the last, best hope for a good, moral, and affluent life in a world filled with perilous possibilities and awesome problems. This parable creates an "us versus them" mentality or mind-set. The **mob at the gates** may be drug traffickers, illegal aliens, terrorists, Jihadists, the pro-choice movement, or it may be environmental polluters, the militia movement, or foreign or slave labor that can provide goods at lower prices than American companies charge. The mob may also be the greedy corporate executives who exploit workers through insider trading, outrageous salaries and perks, outright cheating, and moving their companies offshore. The mob may be secular humanists, minorities, tree-huggers, and do-gooders. Those who see themselves as heroes may defy the mob at the gates on some issue, such as foreign competition, global warming alarmists, or tax and spend politicians; but on other issues, the mob may be acceptable for one side but not for the other. For instance, most liberals see illegal aliens as less threatening than conservatives do.

Reich (1987) cites several persuasive events of central importance to our nation that rested on the mob at the gates parable. One is the "rotten apple" metaphor. Several rotten leaders or countries can ruin the "whole barrel" of free nations. The rotten apples at the top of corporate America have ruined the trust and confidence so essential for a healthy and growing economy. We also have seen this myth applied to George W. Bush's condemnation of "rogue nations" that he said formed an "axis of evil" that condoned, supported, and even trained terrorists. Note how the language used frames the issues for us. "Rogue" nations don't play by the "rules," defined by Bush as American ways of behaving; and the "axis of evil" is reminiscent of the German, Italian, and Japanese "Axis" of WWII, thus equating those nations with fascist tyrannies. Interestingly, a few years after Bush's speech, our invasion of one of these rogue nations resulted in thousands of deaths and injuries, and an enormously enlarged national debt, all accompanied with a growth in the recruitment of terrorists by al Qaida and others—the very thing the invasion was sure to eliminate. So the mob at the gates may not be the real cause of our problems. Nonetheless, this parable has attractive appeal and allows us to easily lay blame. (See Figure 9.6.)

Advertisers base many of their ads for products on this parable. Millions of germs are lying in wait to infect you, but if you use Listerine mouthwash, you'll knock them for a loop. Hordes of mosquitoes will ruin your picnic unless you are vigilant enough to spray the area with long-lasting Raid insect fog. The mob myth is a natural for ideological campaigns as well. For example, the secular humanists are supposedly tainting America's moral fiber, so it is absolutely essential to join the Born Again group. And, of course, politicians use the image in a variety of ways: The mob may be the other party, the homeless, or tax-and-spend politicians. Not to worry—the "good guys" will save the day.

The Triumphant Individual

The **triumphant individual** parable has as its subject the humble person who works hard, takes risks but has faith in himself or herself, and eventually reaches or even exceeds goals of fame, honor, and financial success. It is the story of the self-made man or woman who demonstrates what hard work and determination, combined with a gutsy approach to problems and a spunky style, can do. Usually, the individual is a loner (sometimes even a maverick) who is willing to challenge the establishment and try to do something on a shoestring. A modern example is Bill Gates, the inventor of Microsoft, and now a major philanthropist donating more than $20 million to worthy causes. Another was the late Steve Jobs, who invented the Apple computer and built the Apple empire, beginning in his garage. Both Gates and Jobs were self-reliant and hardworking, and they believed in themselves. Another example from the fairly recent past is Lee Iacocca, the maverick at Ford who bucked the odds and the office politics, and finally persuaded the company to bring out its most successful product ever—the Mustang. He took over the nearly bankrupt Chrysler Corporation and turned the company around, paying off a $1.2-billion government bailout loan early; innovating with front wheel drive, the minivan, airbags, customer rebates, a 70,000-mile warranty, and a return of the convertible—all affordable for the common man.

The triumphant individual myth strikes the same chord as several cultural myths mentioned earlier, such as the wisdom of the rustic. We frequently see the triumphant individual in a variety of persuasive arenas. In politics, self-made men or women are the ones to put your money on. They made it this far on guts and a belief in themselves,

FIGURE 9.6 Skinhead Mobs in Action

Neo-Nazi mobs are becoming more prevalent as the world economy declines.

SOURCE: Jim West/Alamy.

FIGURE 9.7

Bill Gates—The Triumphant Individual Triumphant individuals are attractive because our culture is fond of cheering on an underdog.

SOURCE: Shutterstock, 2009/Used under license from Shutterstock.com.

and as a result, they will come out winners on election day as well (see Figure 9.7).

Companies that are willing to take risks on new technologies, small teams who get into the final four, fringe religions that attract large congregations after finding the right preacher, and new products that overcome the competition, all can become the equivalent of triumphant individuals. Sometimes these triumphant individuals become spokespersons for certain brands, ideological causes, or political interests.

The Benevolent Community

The myth or parable of the **benevolent community** reflects the essential goodness of people and their willingness to help out the other guy in time of need. A magazine story once portrayed this myth in action. A small, dying town, Greensburg, Kansas, was struck by a tornado that demolished several homes, businesses, and nearby farms. But the men and women of surrounding communities joined forces and within weeks had nearly rebuilt all that had been destroyed. It was all done in environmentally sound ways—better insulation, sounder foundations, and so on, thus justifying its name. During devastating floods and storms, students, neighbors, and others volunteer to fill sand bags, build levies, and help out the victims. And the hurricane-ravaged Gulf states received billions of dollars in relief from donations by ordinary citizens of the "benevolent community." And of course following Japan's 9+ earthquake, tsunami, 10,000 deaths, and nuclear

disaster, the entire world became the "benevolent community."

Though recent events have soured our trust in CEOs, corporate America regularly enhances its image after various disasters by advertising that it has donated money and products to the victims, and thus the corporation becomes part of the benevolent community. The U.S. Marines are a part of the benevolent community with their annual Toys for Tots campaign around the holidays. We find this cultural parable recurring throughout our history in struggles like abolition, women's suffrage, the civil rights movement, past and current anti-war movements, and pro-life or pro-choice demonstrations. As Reich notes, "The story celebrates America's tradition of civic improvement, philanthropy, and local boosterism" (p. 10). Persuaders will continue to use the lesson of this parable to market products, candidates, and ideologies.

Rot at the Top

The **rot at the top** parable or myth has conspiratorial aspects and revolves around a number of sub-themes such as corruption, a lack of morals or ethics, decadence, greed, and the malevolence of persons in high places. Like the **presence of conspiracy** myth, it allows us to lay blame easily and always seems to follow a cyclical pattern, which Reich calls "cycles of righteous fulmination." First, we trust the elite, but then we find them lacking in trust or goodwill, and finally, we end up unseating them and "throwing the rascals out!" Almost every presidential administration leads to scandals as it nears its end—feathering the financial nests of its friends, losing moral direction, lying about important issues or events, and so on. Reich traces the myth to the founding fathers' sensitivity to the abuse of power experienced under King George and his colonial governors. Abuses of power by elites who buy their positions of power with money and favors (as Albert Wade did) or who have been corrupted by power always existed. Our history features numerous and varied types of rot at the top; but Reich believes that the myth usually has one of two main targets: political corruption or economic exploitation. Politically, we have seen it in Teapot Dome in the 1920s (the damages of which continue on even today, as seen in the film *There Will Be Blood*). We saw it in Watergate during the 1970s with the scandal reaching to the highest levels of government, in Bill Clinton's sex scandals in the 1990s, the fiscal scandals in corporate America, and the financial scandals associated with military cost overruns and over-charging in Iraq in the new millennium. And you can bet that we will soon be uncovering the misdeeds of those in charge in the first decade of the new millennium, as has already happened in Illinois, where the governor apparently tried to sell the U.S. Senate seat vacated by Barack Obama when he became president. The enormous amounts of money spent "off budget" on the two longest wars in U.S. history would have been too tempting for the "greedy guts" in government during those years. Put that together with the outlandish freedom given to banks and other financial institutions during those years and you have to know that the "thieves" were in charge. We often hear that big business has exploited the common man, and we still see Wall Street scandals based on insider trading by "stock market jackals" and "corporate barracudas." All of these are examples of rot at the top. The lesson of this myth is simple: Power corrupts; privilege perverts. Writer Michael Parenti (1994) identifies several other myths that are fairly self-explanatory: "You can't fight city hall," "Our leaders know best," "You can't legislate morality," and "All politicians are the same" (pp. 2–13) are all examples. Communication scholar D. Hahn (1998) identified

several other political myths, such as the myth of progress, the myth of youth, and the myth of love and openness (pp. 128–129).

Taken together, Reich's cultural parables provide fertile ground for persuaders whether they be politicians, ideologues, business interests, or religious leaders. As a receiver, you should be armed against such appeals and as you encounter them, examine them carefully. Try to see if there are flaws in the plot, weaknesses in its heroes, deception in its outcomes, and so on.

THE MAN'S MAN AND THE WOMAN'S WOMAN

Another popular cultural myth for many Americans is that for a male to be a success, he must be a macho **man's man**. Schools, family, and television tell children that important males are those who do macho things: compete in manly activities, use colognes with names like "Iron," get involved in sports, talk tough, own guns, and drive SUVs. They never show their emotions, and they die with their boots on. In contrast, the ideal **woman's woman** is soft-spoken, kind, and nurturing, but also practical and competent. She may work, but she is also the perfect wife and mother and is always immaculately groomed. However, she may also be vain, rarely has meaningful thoughts, and never wastes time talking about serious things.

These myths, of course, affect the way we treat our children, valuing certain things they do and devaluing others. Until recently, it was unfeminine for females to engage in any sport except tennis, golf, gymnastics, figure skating, or swimming. Today they are cheered on in basketball, lacrosse, field hockey, and many other sports. On the other side of the coin, it was not masculine for males to take up gourmet cooking, needlepoint, or flower gardening (vegetables were okay). Further, males weren't very nurturing or emotional, and they talked about big things like jobs, the economy, cars, and sports.

However, this myth of the distinctions between the sexes is obviously changing beyond the arena of competitive sports. Female executives are now featured in ads for business hotels boxing, and playing hockey. Female pilots are shown using deodorant, and we see female champs at poker and billiards (two activities that used to be reserved for men only). At the same time, men are now expected to contribute their fair share of housework, and they can be affectionate to their wives and children, not just their bird dogs. Old myths do not die easily, however, and we still see many examples of the stereotypical macho man and the perfectly feminine woman. Beer ads feature retired athletes engaged in a man's world, bragging to one another over beers or testifying to the effectiveness of potency and erection enhancers. One look at any magazine shows ads pitching their products at people who buy into these images of men and women.

Although gender-bound and stereotypical representations of men and women are changing, these images still have persuasive power and are still used to advertise products and promote ideas. Despite reductions in gender differences in job and political candidacy and in gender-related language use, the old stereotypes are still potent persuaders. The major change in attitude towards gender-related issues has occurred in young, college-educated, upper-middle-class, nonminority populations. But the far greater proportion of our population still seems to buy into the man's man and woman's woman myths. We still see ads for SUVs, assault weapons, and chain saws, all geared toward men; and we continue to see "women's" ads for Victoria's Secret, *Elle* magazine, and many beauty products. All of these examples still promote gender stereotypes. Count the number of women's features or ads in a single issue of a magazine like *Elle* or *Marie Claire*. Consider a few of the following feature titles from the cover of a single issue of *Cosmopolitan:* "Super Sensual Sex—Teach Him Tricks," "A Man's Body Craves Certain Strokes, Caresses and Pressure. Here's Your Hands-On Guide," or "28 Romantic Rituals to Do With Your Man." They all promote gender stereotypes and the woman's woman is not only good at work and home, but she is also skilled at lovemaking. They are just a few appeals to the woman's woman myth we encounter every day. Persuaders will adapt as Americans shift their values regarding gender and other

human characteristics, such as age, single parenthood, and economic status, but their persuasion will reflect the premises that the audience believes. Persuasion is more often a reflection of a culture's values than a shaper of them (see Figures 9.8 and 9.9).

IMAGE AS A CULTURAL PREMISE

Sometimes persuaders are successful because of their **image or charisma**. Somehow they seem to have a special presence, and they command the public's attention. We believe them because their presentations are convincing and dynamic, or because they have a reputation for being truthful or knowledgeable. Barack Obama seemed to have this kind of charisma during the 2008 primary campaigns but lost some of it when Democrats lost the House in 2010. As we noted earlier, Aristotle called this kind of credibility *ethos*, or ethical proof. More recently, researchers have worked at identifying exactly what causes or creates high ethos in some persons and low ethos in others. In other cultures, the elderly are revered even if they are not articulate, and the most effective leaders are not necessarily the most articulate—though being articulate always seems to help. One research technique to measure the effectiveness or presence of such charisma is to have audiences rate speakers on a variety of scales that have sets of opposing adjectives at either end. For example, the scales may have words like "fast/slow." On one end of the scale is the number 1 and on the other end is the number 5. Other word pairs include strong/weak, hot/cool, or active/inactive. Researchers see where the ratings cluster and infer that those items with positive loadings are important to credibility, image, charisma, or ethos. The choices tend to cluster around the three traits or dimensions of source credibility: expertise, trustworthiness or sincerity, and dynamism or charisma. Together, they accounted for more persuasive success than all the rest of the dimensions. For example, the dynamism ratings were associated with words like "active," "fast," "hot," and "strong." Let us explore these dimensions of source credibility more fully.

FIGURE 9.8 Here are examples of the myth of the "man's man" done tongue in cheek.

FIGURE 9.9 The myth of the man's man has always revolved around sexual potency, as can be seen in this Big Stinky cartoon.

SOURCE: Nick Jeffries.

BOX 9.2 Diversity and Media Literacy

There is growing concern over media literacy, particularly as we enter the global community. For instance, if you don't know how to get on the Internet, are you truly literate in today's global community? How much information are you missing if you are not media literate? Do people of diverse ethnicities need different kinds of training in media literacy?

Go to Weblink 9.1, which is a website that explores these and other issues. (You can access this and all of the other Chapter 9 weblinks through your companion website for *Persuasion*, Chapter 9 resources.) Go to the home page and explore some of the materials/articles there. From Issue 45, I particularly recommend the items on the virtual school.

Expertise

The **expertise** dimension of source credibility means that highly credible sources are perceived as having knowledge and especially experience regarding the topic they address and therefore are credible. Hillary Clinton expressed this in the 2008 run for the presidency, but then regained it as she handled the corrupt and twisted foreign policies and foreign leaders around the world as Secretary of State later. Trusting those with experience and common sense makes sense because we tend to put more store in ideas and advice that come from experts than in those that come from non-experts. To whom would you go for advice on gourmet cooking—Emeril or the cook at the local cafe? The clustering of words such as

"competent," "experienced," and "professional" relate to the expertise dimension and have been verified by experiments in which a variety of groups listened to the same audio tape of a speaker giving the same speech. The speaker was introduced to some of the groups as the surgeon general while to others the speaker was introduced as a college senior. The listeners found the "expert" much more credible than the nonexpert. This same kind of respect and credibility applies to a person's media literacy as seen in Box 9.2. When President Bush said that a person could look for maps on "The Google" during a 2007 CNBC news interview, he betrayed his lack of media literacy by putting the word "the" in front of "Google" and thus embarrassed himself and members of his staff and probably lost some credibility as well. Many advertisements use expert testimony from doctors, financial advisors, and scientists because they are deemed to be credible, and consumers feel that they can rely on these experts' advice. Over 35 years ago, researchers reported that three believability factors emerging from audience-generated words describing credible sources were safety, qualification, and dynamism (Berlo, Lemmert, and Davis, 1969). Qualification is similar to expertise. This dimension seems to be one of the more stable factors in determining whether we believe someone.

Trustworthiness or Sincerity

Another dimension that recurs in studies of image, credibility, or charisma is **trustworthiness** or **sincerity**. Early persuasion researchers at Yale first identified this factor in their attitude studies, concluding that the credibility of any source is tied to "trust and confidence" (Hovland, Janis, and Kelley, 1953). This dimension emerged in numerous other studies over the years, and has sometimes been called "safety" or "personal integrity" (Baudhin and Davis, 1972). An interesting indicator of trustworthiness occurs in situations in which a biased source testifies against his or her own self-interest or bias. This may give us a clue to what is really involved in the trust dimension. Psychology researchers Herbert Kelman and Carl Hovland (1953) wanted to know who would be believed in the following situation: a message promoting the need for stiffer penalties for juvenile delinquents that was attributed in one case to a juvenile court judge and in another case to a reformed drug-pushing juvenile delinquent. The audience believed the judge because of his expertise in dealing with juvenile cases, but their belief in the delinquent came from their trust that his sincere testimony was obviously against the speaker's image. Trust or sincerity requires us to analyze speakers' motives or hidden agendas. The etymology of the word "sincerity" gives us some insights. It comes from the Latin *sincerus,* which literally means "without wax." This referred to a practice of unethical

pillar carvers, who used wax to cover up blemishes in an otherwise perfect pillar that had been ruined by the carver's mistakes. Only after decades of weathering did the wax fall out and reveal the deception. So a sincere person was without wax or not camouflaged.

Audiences believe speakers who are sincere and trustworthy. These speakers maintain good eye contact, don't shift back and forth on their feet, and lack a tremor in their voices. Or audiences judge sincerity from speakers' reputations—offices they have held, accomplishments, and what others say about them. Trustworthiness has been repeatedly demonstrated in research studies as a key component of credibility. Although its effects vary from situation to situation, receivers believe persons they trust, whether because of their reputation, delivery, or motivation.

Dynamism

A final dimension of credibility that has been demonstrated through experimental research is not as easy to define or even describe. This factor has been labeled **dynamism**, charisma, or image by various researchers. It is the degree to which the audience admires and identifies with the source's attractiveness, power, forcefulness, and energy. The following word pairs have been used in the testing referred to above searching for the dynamism factor: "aggressive/meek'," "emphatic/hesitant," "frank/reserved," "bold/passive," "energetic/tired," and "fast/slow." The ratings clustered around the first word in each pair. Dynamism equates with charisma, and although it is influenced by a speaker's attractiveness, unattractive persons can be charismatic or dynamic. Dynamic speakers don't necessarily move about or wave their arms to give off dynamism cues. They simply seem to take up a lot of psychological space. They enter a room and people expect them to be in charge. Their voices seem to be assured and confident. They are eloquent and sometimes border on being poetic. They seem to know just what to say in tough or even tragic moments, and the audience lingers on their words. Dynamic persuaders populate important occasions and crisis events across American history. Researchers have investigated other dimensions of source credibility. A tall speaker, for example, is generally more likely to be believed than a short one. Timid or shy and reserved persons are likely to have low credibility, whereas authoritative and self-assured ones have high credibility. Bossy and egotistical persuaders lose credibility, whereas pleasant and warm persuaders do not. These and many other dimensions of source credibility interact and affect the three fundamental dimensions of credibility—trust/sincerity, expertise, and dynamism/potency.

These elements of source credibility are not shared by all cultures. In cultures in which the baksheesh (bribe) is the order of the day, people actually are admired for being untrustworthy. The popularity of haggling over prices in bazaars is based on insincerity, not sincerity. So credibility has cultural differences, too.

THE AMERICAN VALUE SYSTEM

The myths and parables we have examined are actually fantasy forms of deep and enduring values held by most Americans. They are expressed in myths in order to simplify them. For example, Americans have a belief or value that all persons are to be treated equally and that in the eyes of the law, they are equal. This value has been debated for more than two centuries in the context of such issues as slavery, women's suffrage, civil rights, desegregation, and affirmative action. It is acted out or dramatized in the possibility of success myth. We see the myth portrayed in print and TV ads. For example, a recent print ad for the DuPont Chemical Company featured a man who was still able to play basketball even though he had lost both legs in Vietnam. This was thanks to DuPont, who sold the raw materials for making the artificial limbs that enable the man to succeed in the world of amateur sports (see Figure 9.10).

One of the early speech communication studies that explored American core values was conducted by Edward Steele and W. Charles Redding (1962). They looked at the communication used in several prior presidential election campaigns and tried to extract core and secondary values. Their work has

been replicated numerous times since then with very similar outcomes, suggesting that these core American values have great durability and persistence. They seem to be the core values appealed to in the rhetoric of our most recent presidential campaign, which testifies to the validity of the original research that identified them. These values are frequently articulated by the media as the values that relate to various social issues (Kosicki, 2002). You will be able to see them if you look around. The following are descriptions of the core values observed by Steele and Redding and since verified by other communication researchers.

Puritan and Pioneer Morality

The **puritan and pioneer morality** value is our tendency to cast the world into categories of right and wrong, good and evil, ethical and unethical, and so forth. Although we tend to think of this value as outdated, it has merely been reworded. Persons on the political right and left frequently make judgments based on it. The advocates and foes of marijuana laws and of legal abortion both call on moral values such as just/unjust, right/wrong, and moral/immoral to make their cases. The injustice of terrorism, whether perpetrated against us or against others, is viewed as morally inexcusable, and the resulting loss of innocent lives leads Americans and others to see it as having major moral dimensions. The decision by the Bush administration in 2004 not to fund new stem cell research was viewed by both sides as a morality issue. For those who favored the research, Bush's decision was viewed negatively because stem cell research might have provided cures for many diseases like diabetes and cancer. For those on the other side, they saw the good of not harming embryos that hypothetically could become living persons.

We saw John McCain become a presidential nominee in 2008, in part because of his stand on the morality of abortion. Other politicians argued over the morality of invading Iraq and its resulting human and material costs and depicted their stands as highly moral.

For Bill Demby, the difference means getting another shot.

When Bill Demby was in Vietnam, he used to dream of coming home and playing a little basketball with the guys.

A dream that all but died when he lost both his legs to a Viet Cong rocket.

But then, a group of researchers discovered that a remarkable DuPont plastic could help make artificial limbs that were more resilient, more flexible, more like life itself.

Thanks to these efforts, Bill Demby is back. And some say, he hasn't lost a step.

At DuPont, we make the things that make a difference.

Better things for better living.

REG. U.S. PAT & TM OFF

FIGURE 9.10   This ad enhances DuPont's ethos by implying that the company is responsible for Bill Demby's "getting another shot" at an active life.

SOURCE: DuPont Company photograph. Used by permission of DuPont.

The Value of the Individual

This value ranks the rights and welfare of the individual above those of the government or other groups. It is encapsulated in many of our historical documents—the Declaration of Independence, the Constitution, the Emancipation Proclamation, and others. All politicians claim to be interested in the value of the individual, and our laws ensure and protect individual rights over all others. Further, each person has the right to succeed or fail on his or her own. Although no one is an island, no one is tied to the will of the majority, either. This value was called into question by our government following the 9/11 attacks. The right to privacy was repeatedly violated by our government as it unlawfully jailed individuals, wiretapped their phone conversations, and suspended the writ of habeas corpus, in addition to the government's subordination of appointments to the judicial bench. We have yet to see the results of these offenses, but they will be a kind of testimony to the continuing validity of this longstanding cultural value. In the more mundane world of advertising, most products are marketed with the individual in mind. Cosmetics, according to this value, are also made "especially for you," and Burger King lets you "have it your way." And if the bottom line is the measure, it seems that attention to the individual consumer pays off for most businesses and most of them find that it is profitable to trumpet their interest in the value of the individual throughout their advertising of the brand. In politics and government the real power of a democracy lies within each individual, as we hear politician after politician testify to in election after election. It meshes with the parable of the triumphant individual. In the presidential campaign of 2008, candidate John McCain profited in many ways from being literally on the bottom during the primaries, having to carry his own luggage and to fly commercial airlines when his funds ran out, and yet winning the nomination in the end. And most good causes target both the individual recipient of aid, and especially the individual donor, as individuals who are "making a difference" without whom the cause could not advance. In a multicultural and media-saturated world where the bottom line cause is what counts, it is essential for government, religion, business, and human charity to depend on the value of the individual. And that makes for good persuasion.

Achievement and Success

Achievement and success entails the accumulation of education, power, status, wealth, and property by triumphant individuals from any and all of the multicultural parts of our society. It is the successes and achievements of individuals that make up the history and myths/parables of our times at whatever point in our history one looks. During the anti-Vietnam War years, many young Americans rejected these values, favoring communal living and refusing to dress up for job interviews. That phase soon faded with most of the participants becoming conventional, achievement-oriented, and hopefully successful individuals. Many of those same young people are now upwardly mobile, achievement-oriented, and graying muppies (mature urban professionals). Many of these former renegades now evaluate others by the symbols or emblems of success they own—whether a BMW or Mercedes-Benz, a Rolex watch, or a Mont Blanc pen. Persuaders frequently appeal to our need for achievement or success. Most military recruitment advertisements and slogans promise that by starting a career in the Army, Navy, Air Force, Marines, or Coast Guard you will be able to climb the ladder to success faster. If you read the *Wall Street Journal,* success and status will be yours. First impressions count, so be sure to "dress for success" by shopping at Nordstrom, and don't wear pierced jewelry to the interview. Self-help books and programs will help you to be an achiever and will contribute to your success. The achievement and success value, like the cultural myths, seems to ebb and flow with time. Thus, self-improvement will continue to be marketed even when the values of achievement and success seem most dormant.

Change and Progress

The **change and progress** value is typified by the belief that change of almost any kind will lead to progress and that progress is inherently good for us. This is the appeal of any product that is "new" or "new and improved." It was the ever present theme of the 2008 political campaigns at all levels—national, state, and local. Product life-cycle theory, which you may have studied in a marketing class, almost dictates that change and progress in the form of improvement must recur repeatedly to delay a decline of brand sales,

We cannot go Back and make a new start, But we can start now to make a new ending.

FIGURE 9.11

A Thought About Change and Its Values

Few would disagree with this thought about the idea of the change and progress value.

SOURCE: fancy/www.shutterstock.com.

and the phrase "new and improved" is the life preserver for many a brand. From a legal point, the producer of a laundry product, for example, can claim that its product is "new and improved" merely by changing the color of the beads of bleach in it or by slightly altering the ratio of ingredients or offering a new pouring spout. General Electric once had as its slogan: "At GE, Progress Is Our Most Important Product." The word "new" is one of the most powerful words in advertising, almost equaling the champion "free" in fostering brand switching. Indeed, many changes across time obviously have been beneficial, such as the downsizing of the American automobile and the increase in its fuel efficiency. And few would disagree on the value of the new generations of home and business computers, or digital audio and video, or many new medical technologies. The Internet has made an enormous quantity of information on any and every topic available to almost everyone as well as making communication with people all over the globe instantaneous. Change is everywhere and blasting at us with breathtaking speed.

At the same time, certain products and brands intentionally have built-in obsolescence. While annual models make sense for automobiles where styling is the watchword, many other products bring in new models year after year when change isn't really called for and advertisements tell the world about, which is probably also unnecessary.

The new and improved Whirlpool dryer may just have a new coating on its tumbler or a new latch on its door, but does that justify a major advertising effort? Yet every year manufacturers bring out new models of their product or brands that really aren't changed that much. Nonetheless, the value of change and progress continues to be a powerful first premise in many enthymemes we encounter. If you don't change and make progress, you are falling behind in life. It certainly isn't a very exciting claim that you're the same as the last guy or that your 2010 model is identical to your 2009 offer. Instead we are persuaded when we feel progress and change is in the mix.

Ethical Equality

The **ethical equality** value reflects the belief that all persons ought to be treated equally. They should have an equal opportunity to get an education, to work and be paid a fair wage, to live where they choose, and to hold political office. But we all know that, although this value may be laudable, the reality is that not everyone is born equal, nor do they all have an equal opportunity for jobs, education, or decent housing. Nonetheless, since the nation's founding, through the abolition, women's suffrage, civil rights, and other movements, attempts to create a situation of equality have been a part of the American cultural landscape. The words from the Declaration of Independence, "All men are created equal," best illustrate the power of this value.

Effort and Optimism

The **effort and optimism** value expresses the belief that even the most unattainable goals can be reached if one just works hard enough and "keeps smilin'." The myths of the triumphant individual and the possibility of success are examples of these values in action. And in today's business world, it is important to be a "striver" or a "self-starter." Nuggets of folk wisdom such as: "Every cloud must have a silver lining," "If at first you don't succeed, try, try again," "Keep on the sunny side," and "Lighten up" serve as cultural metaphors of the value we place on effort and optimism. And phrases such as "a hard worker" and "the eternal optimist" reflect how we much we believe in the value of effort and optimism. If you don't let the world get you down and keep plugging away, things will work out. This value motivates many of our life decisions. Our literature and popular culture emphasize this value repeatedly in our entertainment channels, our politics, and in the pep talks of corporations, religions, good causes, and the professions.

Efficiency, Practicality, and Pragmatism

The **efficiency, practicality, and pragmatism** value is based on our need for solutions. It is persuasion in a results-oriented world. What counts is what is most efficient and effective in getting to the final goal. The key question often asked of any piece of legislation is: "Will it work?" This is true whether it be a new set of tax revisions, a new cabinet office such as the Office of Homeland Security, or new immigration statutes. This value extends to other parts of our lives, too. Years ago, my family was among the first purchasers of a microwave oven, which cost $400 then. Before making the purchase, we wanted to know whether a microwave oven would be energy efficient, practical, and handy, and not merely another fad. And, of course, we now know that they are energy efficient, handy, and practical; but now they are available for less than $100. And the same pattern occurred in technological innovation after innovation—the PC, DVDs, and the digital world. On another issue, we want to be certain that an advanced education will lead to a rewarding job. We are fascinated by questions of efficiency—fuel efficiency in our cars, energy efficiency in our appliances, and efficiency of movement on the production line. And we go for practical solutions, whether it is the most efficient way to lose weight, to get in good shape, or to be able to buy one's first home. In other words, we value what is quick, workable, and practical.

Even though these values were cataloged more than 40 years ago, they still have a great deal of relevance. We find them recurring in every national election and in advertising year after year. And the fact that they are held in high regard by liberals and conservatives speaks for their credibility and for the conviction that they are indeed "core" American values. Our culture is effective in instilling these values in nearly all its members; radicals, moderates, and reactionaries may believe in the same values, but they tend to apply them quite differently. The power of a social system or culture to train its members is immense—even though people do not often realize it, they react to the dictates deeply ingrained in them. Does this mean that values remain essentially static and cannot be changed? Not necessarily. It means only that they are so deeply ingrained in a culture that its members often forget how strong they are, as shown in the different responses likely to be given to the Canadian harvest of Harp seal pups discussed in Box 9.3. They are probably processed in the peripheral channel of the ELM.

FIGURE 9.12

Ultimate Optimism

Optimism is a powerful cultural value in our culture.

SOURCE: OLIVIER DOULIERY/MCT/ Landov

BOX 9.3 **Propaganda, Harp Seals, and Canadian vs. U.S. Cultural Values**

Most U.S. citizens are horrified by the Canadian harvest of baby Harp seals by clubbing them to death as the newborn seal pups climb onto the ice to unite with their mothers who are resting on the ice following giving birth. Recall that this was visualized in an anti-hunt ad back in Chapter 1. The average American is likely to ask: "How can Canadian citizens possibly tolerate such a brutal and heartless slaughter?" The Canadian answer is: "It's for their pelts." The U.S. questioners are likely to gasp in surprise at the mindset that could believe this after seeing pictures and videos of the harvest.

Go to Weblink 9.2 and visit the page entitled "The Politics and Propaganda of the Seal Hunt," which addresses both sides of the issue. (You can access this and all of the other Chapter 9 weblinks through your companion website for *Persuasion,* Chapter 9 resources.) Use the "Quick Links" in the right hand margin to trace the debate and explore the rest of the site. Keep in mind that while the site is discussing propaganda, it is itself a kind of propaganda based on the cultural differences between Canadians and Americans— groups one would assume to be very similar.

REVIEW AND CONCLUSION

By this time, you know that the world of the persuadee in a diverse and interactive, media-saturated and multicultural information age is not a simple one. There are so many things to be aware of: the persuader's self-revelation in the language used and their style, the internal or process premises operating within each of us, and the interactive rules for content or logical premises. In addition, societal and cultural predispositions for persuasion can and do act as premises in persuasive arguments. Persuaders instinctively appeal to values that rely on the societal training in the target audience. On separate levels, this training has an effect on each of us—in the cultural myths, images, or parables to which we respond, in the sets of values we consciously articulate. And in an increasingly diverse world, both persuaders and receivers need to be aware that the cultural premises of today may not be the only way to see the world.

KEY TERMS

After reading this chapter, you should be able to identify, explain, and give an example of the following key terms or concepts:

cultural patterns	mob at the gates	trustworthiness	ethical equality
cultural images and myths	triumphant individual	sincerity	effort and optimism
wisdom of the rustic	benevolent community	dynamism	efficiency, practicality, and pragmatism
possibility of success	rot at the top	Puritan and pioneer morality	
coming of a messiah	presence of conspiracy	value of the individual	
paranoid style	man's man	achievement and success	
value of challenge	woman's woman	change and progress	
myth of the eternal return	image or charisma		
	expertise		

APPLICATION OF ETHICS

Dr. L. teaches a course in "Research Methods in Mass Communication," which is a difficult course for most communication majors, especially the quantitative topics like inferential statistics. A female student who is a member of a minority has been absent from classes frequently and has done poorly on all the tests. Dr. L. calls her in to discuss the problem and discovers that she is a single mother who is putting herself through school by holding down several part-time jobs. She is getting good grades in all of her other communication courses and expects to graduate at the end of the semester. Furthermore, she has been promised an excellent job as an anchor newsperson and in all likelihood will never need to know statistics or research methods in order to report on upcoming changes. The Affirmative Action Office has issued a memo stating that students who are members of a protected minority (including females) should be given special consideration and help. What should Dr. L. do? (1) Give the student a "D" grade so she can graduate. (2) Give the student an Incomplete to be made up when the semester is over. (3) Give the student a failing grade. (4) Offer to give the student private tutoring in statistics—something Dr. L has not done before and is not doing for other students in a similar situation.

QUESTIONS FOR FURTHER THOUGHT

1. What are the three types of culturally or socially learned predispositions for persuasion? Give examples of each from your own experience.

2. How does a culture or society train its members? Give examples from your own experience.

3. How do you rank the core values mentioned in this chapter? How do you put them into practice? Are there other values in your value system not mentioned here? What are they? Are they restatements of the core values? If so, how? If not, how do they differ?

4. Considering today's headlines, is there a mob at the gates presently? Explain.

5. To what degree can you identify a benevolent community in your life? Explain.

6. In the popular Harrison Ford film, *Patriot Games*, there clearly is rot at the top. At what critical moment does the "narrator" of the film discover the "rot"? What does he do about it?

7. Explain the ethos of the hosts of the various TV talk shows. How does each host's ethos differ from the others'—for example, does Jay Leno seem more or less sincere, expert, or dynamic than David Letterman?

8. How have the core values described by Steele and Redding operated on your campus? In your own life?

9. How have American values changed since September 11, 2001? What examples can you give?

10. The slogan "These Colors Don't Run" that appeared in many places following the events of 9/11 clearly articulate an American value. What is it?

11. How do SNM reflect the cultural premises offered here?

12. In which channel of the ELM are persuasive proposals processed? Give examples.

 You can access your online resources at the companion website for *Persuasion.* Log in at **http://www.cengagebrain.com**.

Nonverbal Messages in Persuasion

After reading this chapter, you should be able to:

1. Differentiate and give examples of the various channels of nonverbal communication.

2. Explain what various tactics of nonverbal communication can indicate.

3. Recognize nonverbal messages in your everyday life (e.g., in interpersonal relations, advertising, entertainment, and other communication situations).

4. Alter your own nonverbal communication behaviors and determine the differences in meaning they cause (e.g., look puzzled when someone is trying to explain something to you, and see if that causes them to elaborate).

5. Identify and explain what various gestures communicate (e.g., Allstate's bowl gesture).

6. Discuss the ethical issues involved in manipulating nonverbal behavior.

7. Identify how and where nonverbal messages interact with the ELM.

8. Identify how even nonverbal messages have impact on SNM.

INTRODUCTION

Videotapes of persons shopping in stores during a devastating earthquake in San Francisco show that the first thing people did during the quake to check the environment was to see whether objects fell from shelves, windows broke, and walls cracked. The next thing they did was to check out the nonverbal behavior of the people around them and in the same scene and circumstances. They looked for facial expressions, movement, and other cues of impending danger. During the Gulf War of the 1990s, Saddam Hussein tried to win worldwide public approval for his invasion of Kuwait by being photographed and filmed talking with young Western children who were being "detained" (or held hostage) in Iraq (see Figure 10.1—interestingly enough this image is no longer available for public uses such as this one). During his interviews, he touched the children in a parental way, prompting widespread criticism and even outrage, especially because armed guards stood at attention in the background and the children appeared frightened and looked past Saddam, perhaps at more armed guards behind him. This photo was part of our 24/7 world of mediated persuasion and was seen and processed by millions accurately or inaccurately in the peripheral channel of the ELM, thus changing world opinion about the dictator. What do you think it communicated about the dictator at that time? What about as it is viewed today? In another example of how revealing nonverbal premises can be, consider fictional hero Jason Bourne, in Robert Ludlum's best sellers and popular films. In *The Bourne Ultimatum,* Bourne is able to identify the disguised assassin and terrorist Carlos the Jackal by recognizing the Jackal's walk. Later books and films in the series revealed even more ways the hero used nonverbal communication to get him into and out of various crises. Can you name any? We also know that advertising researchers now can observe and record the dilation of the pupil of the eye as it travels a predictable path across a print advertisement. We know, for example, that it travels clockwise beginning at the upper left corner, pausing at the lower right slightly before it moves to 10 percent below the center of the page. This makes the lower right corner the most fertile or useful for ad messages (such as coupons, the words "Free!" or "Save!," and other calls to action). It is followed by the upper left corner. Guess where advertisers put their logos, slogans, pictures of the package, and coupons?

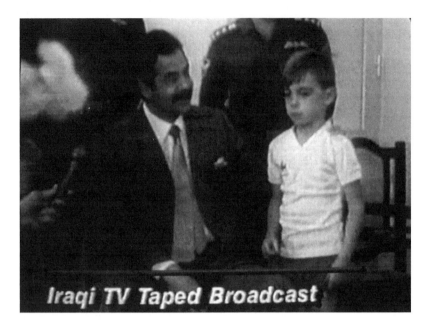

FIGURE 10.1

What kinds of meaning do you derive from this photograph? How is the meaning communicated? In which channel of the ELM? Is the young boy looking at Saddam Hussein or past him? How does the presence of uniformed guards standing at attention in the background affect the kindly, concerned, and grandfatherly image that Saddam wanted to convey?

SOURCE: Getty Images.

The fallow corners are the upper right and lower left. Guess where the tobacco companies put the surgeon general's warning against their use for health reasons?

These are a few examples of nonverbal communication that occur every day, and which we process unconsciously. We process thousands of such nonverbal messages daily. In fact, researcher Albert Mehrabian (1971) long ago (and prior to the new media of SNM, cellular phones, Twitter and so on) estimated that nonverbal communication accounts for over 80 percent of the meaning transferred between people. Others agree with him (Burgoon, Bufler, and Woodall, 1996; Knapp and Hall, 2002; Guerrero, DeVito, and Hecht, 1999; Archer, 2010). Nonverbal messages also accompany most persuasive appeals we process. Do they help or do they hinder persuasion? Nonverbal premises in persuasion resemble cultural premises in that both are taught by our cultures and learned by us from infancy onward via processes of reinforcement. Remember that everything is some kind of reinforcement. When a baby smiles and gets cuddles,

it is being reinforced in a positive manner just as a dog that jumps up on you is reinforced when you scratch it behind the ears or under the chin—the likelihood of future jumping up on people is reinforced. The baby's smile and the dog's jumping will recur more often as a result of the reinforcement. So people smile when meeting both familiar persons and strangers. A difference between cultural and nonverbal premises is that nonverbal ones seldom are carefully analyzed while verbally expressed ones are more carefully considered. We may sense that a certain persuader seems dishonest, and that it has something to do with his or her shifty eyes. However, we rarely dissect the interaction to find out exactly what causes us to distrust the other person.

Another difference is that nonverbal premises usually occur at a very low level of awareness and so aren't readily apparent. We almost certainly process them in the peripheral route of the elaboration likelihood model (ELM). We need to sensitize ourselves to some of the nonverbal factors that enter into persuasion. This sensitization serves two purposes: (1) It increases the information on which we can base our decisions and (2) it can tip us off to persuaders' hidden agendas, favorite tactics, and ultimate goals.

Communication researcher Donald Orban (1999) points out the power of these nonverbal "tip-offs" when he wonders if, "When a person glares at you, forms a fist, invades your space, [or] uses a harsh and loud voice to accompany a verbal argument demanding that you do it his way instead of your way, are you intimidated? Are you more likely to be influenced by the manner of the argument behavior or the validity of the argument?" (n.p.) Most nonverbal communication occurs almost instinctively or automatically. It is hard to fake, and even then, the persuader intent seems to "leak" true meaning through his or her nonverbal channels. Ekman (1999) points out that some persons (such as law enforcement officers and psychologists) can detect liars from their nonverbal behaviors. These liars leak nonverbal cues that indicate that they are lying.

NONVERBAL CHANNELS

There are several channels through which we can communicate nonverbal meaning. Communication researchers J. K. Burgoon, N. E. Dunbar, and C. Segrin (2002) have identified three classes of nonverbal appeals: (1) appeals to attractiveness, similarity, intimacy, and trust; (2) dominance and power displays; and (3) expectancy signaling and expectancy violations. With regard to appeals to attraction and similarity, we have long been aware that physical attractiveness is strongly correlated with persuasiveness, regardless of the expertise, sincerity, or trustworthiness of the persuader. And we have also long known that the degree of similarity between persuader and persuadee is a powerful predictor of attractiveness and hence of persuasiveness. Remember that Heider's balance theory indicates that people like and believe in persons who hold opinions similar to their own and may

find those individuals attractive for this reason. Since Heider's time, a variety of other persuasion theories have confirmed his predictions. For instance, cognitive valence theory (CVT), proposed by P.A. Andersen (1999), predicts that the nonverbal immediacy of the persuader leads to what he calls arousal, which, in turn, leads to relational nearness or closeness between the two. Another theory, proposed by H. Giles, N. Coupland, and J. Coupland (1991), is called communication accommodation theory (CAT). It predicts that people respond more positively to persuaders whose nonverbal style is similar to their own. This is particularly true when their vocal qualities are similar (tone of voice, articulation, volume, and so on) although other nonverbal channels have influence as well. Both theories link similarity and attractiveness with persuasiveness because acting and thinking like a physically attractive source is seen as socially rewarding.

This theory accounts for various fads in clothing and communicating that are patterned after a famous or attractive person. For example, until rock music stars and film idols began piercing body parts, few thought these nonverbal messages were of much value. It turns out that bodily piercing is a real turn-off in job interviews, so some nonverbal messages may boomerang on us. Both theories recognize the various channels or cues of attractiveness and similarity. They include physical movements, or **kinesics**; the use of interpersonal space, or **proxemics**; touch and texture, or **haptics**; the way one looks, or **physical appearance**; use of time, or **chronemics**; and the use of symbolic objects, or **artifactual communication**.

Communication researcher Dale G. Leathers (1986) identified seven **nonverbal channels**, including facial expression, eye behavior, bodily communication, proxemics, personal appearance, vocal factors, and haptics, or the sense of touch. Communication researchers Mark Knapp and J. Hall (2002) identified eight channels: environment (including architecture and furniture), proxemics and territoriality, physical appearance and dress, physical behavior and movement, touching another person, facial expression, eye behavior, and vocal cues. Orban (1999) identified nine channels that affect argumentation. They are eye contact, facial expression, gesture, and bodily movement (of which there are five types: emblems, illustrators, regulators, affect displays, and adaptors). So you can see that even among the experts there are broad areas of agreement as to what nonverbal channels (and hence premises) are involved in any act of persuasion. Some researchers study nonverbal cues of deception and the nonverbal behavior of liars (Knapp and Comendena, 1985). And remember that in our 24/7, media-saturated and multicultural world, the multiple factors make nonverbal communication even more perplexing. We can't begin to examine all these, but we can focus on some of them, especially those that affect persuasion, beginning with Orban's and Leathers's categories.

Facial Expression and Eye Behavior

Leathers's (1986) first two nonverbal channels are **facial expression** (affect displays) and **eye behavior**. According to Leathers, the face is "the most important source of nonverbal information" (p. 19). Facial expression is familiar and readily noticed, and subtle nuances in facial expression can greatly alter perceived meaning. Orban (1999) defines eye contact as "visual interaction with the eyes of listeners" and facial expression as "variations of facial muscles that convey perceptual stimuli to listeners." He claims that these two channels can combine to "create emotional and credibility cues that can ignite or diffuse argument potential" (n.p.). Naturally, credibility is essential to persuasion, so persuaders can enhance their communication credibility via the nonverbal channel. We notice this not only in interpersonal interactions but in the interactions we observe in our media-saturated world of advocacy/propaganda.

Knapp and Hall (2002) noted that people often use the face as a measure of personality, which frequently determines persuasiveness. Leathers also identified ten general classes or categories of facial expression which include: disgust, happiness, interest, sadness, bewilderment, contempt, surprise,

anger, determination, and fear. Among his more specific kinds of expressions, Leathers also included rage, amazement, terror, hate, arrogance, astonishment, stupidity, amusement, pensiveness, and belligerence. Any of these could help or hinder persuasion. It's quite a list—I didn't know I was capable of them all. Leathers (1986) also identified six functions that the eyes serve. One is the attention function indicated by mutual gazing. (See Figure 10.2.) Some persons at parties or other social events continually look over your shoulder and past you as if they are looking for more interesting conversational possibilities. Would you believe persuasion coming from them? Other eye behavior serves a regulatory function by indicating when a conversation is to begin or stop.

When speakers look back at a person or audience and drop their chins, this is a signal for listeners to take their turn. Naturally, being able to express one's opinion to the source would build that source's credibility and persuasiveness, especially in interpersonal settings. Eyes can serve a power function as well, as when a leader stares at an audience. Observers noted that this was the case with Adolf Hitler and

FIGURE 10.2
Eye Contact and Online Dating
Find out why eye contact in online

pictures used in dating services is effective at source website.

SOURCE: micro10x/Shutterstock.

cult leader Charles Manson. When you next see an image of either man, look at his eyes. Can you think of any other persons with such "gaze power?"

Eye behavior also serves an affective function by indicating positive and negative emotions. When your parents' eyes look like they are angry with you, do you listen to their persuasion? Further, eyes function in impression formation, as when persons first meet and communicate a winning image or high self-esteem. Finally, Leathers noted the persuasive function of eye behavior. We rate speakers who maintain eye contact as more credible, and we are suspicious of those whose gaze is continually shifting. If people avert their eyes when talking to us, we assume that they are either shy or hiding something. This may help explain some of the problems real estate representatives had when communicating with Asian or Indian prospects as discussed in Box 10.1. Orban (1999) puts it this way: "Through our eyes we reflect cognitive and emotional behavior. We project impressions of penetrating thought, confusion, and inattentiveness. We show our emotions of fear, anger, happiness, and sadness. We do not realize the hidden messages eye contact reveals" (n.p.).

Bodily Communication

Bodily communication has several dimensions, one of which is kinesics, or physical movements of the body, such as how a person holds her or his body (tense or relaxed), and whether the person is moving about or gesturing with the shoulders, hands, or head. Persuaders indicate power by seeming to be physically or perceptually above their audiences.

They demonstrate a relaxed but erect posture (not slouching), dynamic gestures, good eye contact, and variations in their speaking rate and inflection. Powerless persuaders, in contrast, behave more submissively and exhibit lots of body tension, little direct eye contact, closed postures with legs and arms crossed, and use few gestures.

Knapp and Hall (2002) identified several head movements that convey meaning, including cocking, tilting, nodding, and shaking the head, as well as thrusting out the jaw. And, of course, other bodily movements convey meaning, such as clenching a fist, putting hands on hips, and standing in an open stance with legs spread apart. These movements can indicate anger, intensity, and degree of commitment or dedication, all of which can help or hinder persuasion. In some cases, gestures and bodily movements are emblematic—they stand for a particular meaning. For example, in U.S. culture, stroking the index finger while pointing it at someone indicates "shame on you," crossed fingers indicate "good luck," and the hitchhiker's closed fist and extended thumb are emblematic of wanting a ride. Orban (1999) points out several others, including the A-OK sign (but it conveys the same meaning as "flipping the bird" to Latin Americans, so persuaders need to consider who is in the audience before using that one). Some emblems perform a regulatory function (index finger on lips means "shush"); communicate positive, negative, or neutral values (thumbs up, thumbs down, or shoulder shrugging); or provide an evaluation (as in the thumbs up or the A-OK gesture in the United States). Most obscene gestures can quickly provoke anger and usually reduce the

---

© Cengage Learning 2013

BOX 10.1 **Interactive Media and Nonverbal Communication**

Go to Weblink 10.1 and explore topics such as reading female body language, nonverbal communication and intimacy, how to listen with your eyes, how to be a subject in national research on nonverbal communication, how nonverbal communication operates in real estate transactions involving Asians and buyers from India, and other research

reports on the power of nonverbal communication in the process of persuasion. (You can access this and all of the other Chapter 10 weblinks through your companion website for *Persuasion*, Chapter 10 resources.) Search for other interesting sites where you can test your ability to "read" nonverbal messages.

source's credibility, depending on the cultural background of the receiver, and in a multicultural society, persuaders must always keep this in mind.

Proxemics

Proxemics, or the use of physical space, is the fourth nonverbal channel in Leathers's system. You have undoubtedly noticed, for example, how most people fall silent and don't look at one another when they are in crowded elevators or public restrooms. Try facing the passengers in an elevator and perhaps try to strike up a conversation. You'll be surprised at the results. Report them back to the class. Edward T. Hall identified several kinds of space in his best-selling book *The Silent Language* (1959), which have been confirmed by numerous researchers since then. They are discussed below.

Public distance. **Public distance** is often found in public speaking settings in which speakers are 15 to 25 feet or more from their audiences. Informal persuasion probably will not work in here, and persuaders who try to be informal in a formal situation don't usually meet success.

Social or formal distance. **Social or formal distance** is used in formal but nonpublic situations, such as job interviews or committee meetings. Persuaders in these situations are formal but not oratorical. Formal distance ranges from about 7 to 12 feet between persuader and persuadee. Persuaders never become chummy in this context, but they do not deliver a speech, either. You probably select this distance when you go to your professor's office for a conference and sit across the desk in the guest chair. You can see some handy ways to estimate proxemics distances in Figure 10.3.

Personal or informal distance. Two colleagues might use **personal or informal distance** when discussing a matter of mutual concern—such as roommates discussing a problem they share. Here, communication is less structured, and both persuader and persuadee relax and interact with one another, bringing up and questioning evidence or asking for clarification. In U.S. culture, informal distance is about 3 to 4 feet—the eye-to-eye distance when sitting at the corner of a teacher's desk as opposed to the formal distance created when you sit across the desk. You use informal distance when you sit around a banquet table or in an informal meeting.

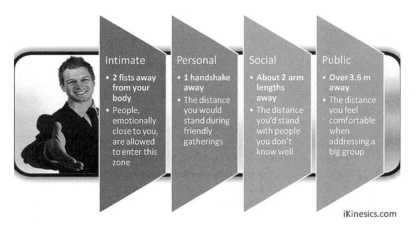

iKinesics Guide To...

Proxemics
The distances between two or more individuals.

Intimate
- 2 fists away from your body
- People, emotionally close to you, are allowed to enter this zone

Personal
- 1 handshake away
- The distance you would stand during friendly gatherings

Social
- About 2 arm lengths away
- The distance you'd stand with people you don't know well

Public
- Over 3.6 m away
- The distance you feel comfortable when addressing a big group

iKinesics.com

FIGURE 10.3

Distances in Proxemic Communication

E.T. Hall's Four Levels of Proxemic Communication.

SOURCE: ikinesics.com

Intimate distance. People use **intimate distance** when they whisper messages they do not want others to overhear or when they are involved in a conspiratorial, intimate, or other secret conversation. Persuasion may or may not occur in these instances. Usually, the message is one that will not be questioned by the receiver. He or she will nod in agreement, follow the suggestion given, or respond to the question asked. When two communicators are in this kind of close relationship, they probably have similar aims. The distance ranges from 6 to 18 inches and probably communicates as much to those observing the intimate pair as is communicated to the pair. When forced into intimate distance (e.g., sitting next to someone in a bus), we usually do not communicate face-to-face but instead lean away from the person while talking. In an elevator we create informal distance by speaking toward the door instead of to fellow passengers.

How do persuaders use these distance boundaries? Are we vulnerable to persuasion using proxemics? Actual examples of such persuasion often escape our notice because nonverbal communication is transmitted at such a low level of awareness. Take automobile sales. When customers come into a showroom, imagine the results if the salesperson rushes over to them and, within personal or even intimate distance, asks something like, "What can I do for you folks today?" The customers will probably flee totally or at least distance themselves from the salesperson, saying something like, "Well, we're just looking around." Clever salespeople stay within public distance of customers until they perceive an indication of interest or a verbal or nonverbal signal that the customers want help, such as catching the salesperson's eyes, raised eyebrows, and so on. Only then will they move into formal or even informal distance. If they are overly personal, they may even move into intimate distance. What should persuadees do in such a case? Probably the best thing to do is to signal disinterest or only faint interest as noted above and move back into formal distance, perhaps by moving around the car and putting it between you and the salesperson.

Look at the advertisements in any popular magazine, and you will notice the use of proxemics as a persuasive device (see Figure 10.4). The young adults who "go for it" in beer ads are having fun and enjoying one another in personal or intimate space. Recently, people in the real estate profession have become interested in the communicative power of the strategic use of space. Industry publications have discussed such questions as how close a real estate agent should be to prospective buyers during a tour of a home and whether the agent should lead or follow the buyers. In many other contexts—offices, hospitals, banks, prisons, and factories—serious consideration is given to the use of space as a communicative device or a communication facilitator. There are cultural differences in the use of space.

Try to be alert to the uses of space in your life. How have you arranged the furniture in your room or apartment? Does the arrangement facilitate or deter communication and persuasion? How do various people whom you know use space? Do persons from other cultures use space differently than you do? Observe how other people use space and discover how this nonverbal channel affects persuasion.

Physical Appearance

It's always easy to guess what's going on toward the middle of the spring semester when my students come to class dressed to kill. It is job interview time on campus, and everyone knows that appearance sends a message to interviewers. As noted above, pierced body parts are deadly. But physical appearance involves much more than simply good grooming and proper attire. Leathers (1986) claimed that larger-than-normal facial features (nose, ears, and lips) are generally considered unattractive. Knapp (2002) reports other findings regarding physical appearance. For instance, first-born females who are attractive are likely to sit toward the front of the class, make more comments during class, and get good grades. Attractive females are also more likely to persuade male audiences than are unattractive females. You may wonder what is meant by "attractive" in these cases. In one study, the same female subject appeared in

FIGURE 10.4

Which of Hall's four types of communication distance seems to be operating in this ad? Why do you suppose this distance was chosen?

SOURCE: Hotel Intercontinental.

both the attractive and unattractive conditions. In the unattractive condition, she wore loose-fitting clothes, wore no makeup, had messy hair, and was generally poorly groomed (p. 155). In the attractive condition she wore tailored clothes, used makeup, was coiffed, and well groomed. The attractive condition resulted in more persuasion.

Another element in physical appearance is bodily attractiveness, according to Leathers (1986). Specifically, slenderness is considered attractive in females, whereas larger-waisted and hippier females are perceived as being heavier and thus less attractive. A fashion trend called "heroin chic" featured attractive but emaciated-appearing female models who looked like they should be immediately taken to an all-you-can-eat buffet. They are neither attractive nor persuasive to the average audience member. For males, broad shoulders, a muscled body, and a tapering upper trunk result in high attractiveness ratings. Leathers found that self-image also has a lot to do with ratings of attractiveness. If you feel good about yourself, you will probably practice good grooming and keep in good physical condition. Clothing and adornments such as jewelry also contribute to people's physical appearance (see Figure 10.5). With regard to jewelry, think of the different evaluations you might make of a person wearing a Rolex as opposed to a Timex or the degree to which heavy gold jewelry attracts your attention. Or think about what one's "bling" can communicate of being overdone or underdone. Yet, the evidence shows that regardless of what nature has given us, good grooming and taste and a sensitivity to the occasion can all add up to a more attractive and hence a more persuasive self.

Artifacts

Artifacts are physical objects that are used in construction, display, and decoration of oneself or of a setting. Birds feather their nests with bits of string, straw, and lint. We humans feather our nests for highly symbolic and persuasive reasons. Look at your work area or at that of a roommate or friend. You will find that it is arranged not only for work but for other reasons as well, and is usually decorated with things that symbolize the owner's sense of self, such as posters, pictures, a favorite coffee mug, and so on. **Artifactual communication**, or the messages others get from the objects we choose to display, decorate, or wear, is also symbolic. Culture teaches us how to react to the artifacts of others and the way they are used. These patterns of response form premises for persuasion. A common type of artifactual communication is revealed in the objects surrounding a political persuader in a public speech—the banners, bunting, persons, and flags all contribute to the ultimate success or failure of the persuasive attempt. Clothing is another type of artifact. What people wear sends

signals about what they are like and what they believe or represent (e.g., a clerical collar or a nurse's or army officer's uniform). During the 2008 presidential primary campaigns for the Democratic nomination, candidate Hillary Clinton almost always wore pantsuits. What did that communicate? In an earlier period female agents of the F.B.I. were permitted to wear pantsuits but not slacks and a blouse or sweater. What do you suppose that directive communicated? Another type of artifact is exemplified in the personal objects surrounding persuaders. Consider how you feel when you go into a doctor's or professor's office that only has diplomas on the walls—no art, no pictures of the family, one's pet, or of one's hobby. What kind of person is the doctor or professor likely to be? Will he or she be more or less persuasive? Compare that with the feeling you have when you enter the doctor's or prof's office that has posters, family photos, children's art, bowling trophies, and art reproductions. These artifacts cue the kind of persuasion you are likely to hear. In the "diplomas only" case, it will probably be concrete, formal, and prescriptive whereas in the posters and family photo office, it will be abstract and informal, and empathic.

Large objects like furniture also send signals. We expect a certain kind of persuasion when we are told to sit down at a table and the persuader sits on the opposite side. Persuaders who put a lectern between themselves and the audience will engage in formal communication. If they step out from behind the lectern or walk around while talking, they will come across as more informal. Which approach seems more persuasive? Types of furniture can also symbolize certain characteristics. What kinds of persuasion and persons do you associate with French provincial versus early American furniture? What kind of persuasion is likely to occur in a room with metal office furniture versus one with wooden desks and leather chairs? In many ad agencies, the creative floor differs dramatically in decor from the other floors of the agency. Instead of desks and cubicles, the creative floor has futons, pinball machines, video games, and conversation pits. What do these kinds of furnishings

Put on a Highlight trouser suit and take over the company.

You can imagine them all in your power when you wear a success like this in **Courtelle.** Immaculate trouser suit, with separate toning shirt. A brilliant investment for washing and keeping in shape. Start at the top in big-deal colours of burgundy, purple, midnight, black, dark brown. The suit from about 12 gns., the shirt about £3.15.0.

Or how to succeed in business without trying at all.

RCG 17

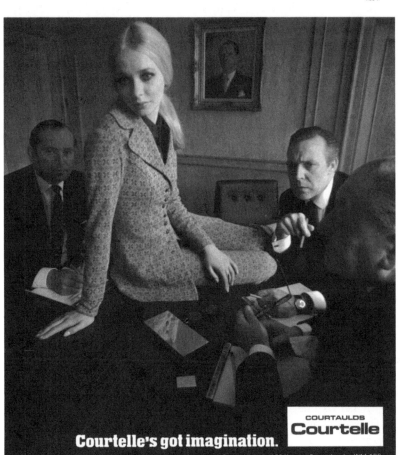

Courtelle's got imagination.

COURTAULDS
Courtelle

Courtaulds Limited 22 Hanover Square London W1A 1BS

FIGURE 10.5

Clothing is used to communicate. What message is being communicated in this ad?

SOURCE: Courtesy of Advertising Archives.

communicate about the activities likely to occur? Consider how artifactual communication is discussed by the characters in Figure 10.6. Artifactual messages vary among cultures and even subcultures. They make the difference between successful and unsuccessful persuasion. Try to identify the most effective kinds of artifacts for persuading you and for persuading others. Try to see what kinds persuade you.

Vocal Features

Each of us has had the experience of answering the phone and not being able to figure out who is calling. We are embarrassed and so we listen carefully and ask innocuous questions until something the person says triggers recognition of his or her **vocal features**. Then we breathe a sigh of relief, say to ourselves, "Oh, so it's you! I should have

FIGURE 10.6

What message(s) are sent by altering one's hair color? What about piercing parts of one's body?

SOURCE: Nick Jeffries.

known," and carry on as if we knew who was calling all along. Leathers (1986) notes that a semantics of sound—or the meanings we deduce from the sound of a voice or other sounds like hesitation or heavy breathing—can affect the way we respond to persuaders' messages. The factors in each voice include volume or loudness, pitch, rate, vocal quality, clarity of pronunciation, intonation pattern, breathiness, and the use of silence. They influence whether you are persuaded by a given source, and they frequently indicate a lot about persuaders and their emotions, goals, and sincerity. So in interpersonal persuasion, the recognition of a personality from their voice seems important.

Monotonic persuaders are boring and lose most of their persuasiveness. High-pitched voices can indicate excitement while low-pitched but tense voices indicate anger; and rate of speech can indicate nervousness or confidence. Vocal quality communicates a number of things. Breathy voices in females communicate a stereotype of simple-mindedness and shallowness, whereas breathy voices in males may indicate that the speaker is effeminate. Screeching or tense voices indicate stress and concern, and nasality is often associated with arrogance. Persons who articulate poorly, mispronounce words, or have a speech impediment generally lose some of their credibility and effectiveness (see Figure 10.7).

Knapp (2002) reported on research indicating that people can fairly reliably identify certain stereotypes from vocal cues. These stereotypes include such characteristics as masculinity or femininity, age, enthusiasm or apathy, and activeness or laziness.

Knapp also reported on research that identified the following correlations: (1) breathiness in males indicates youthfulness and an artistic nature; (2) a thin voice in females indicated social, physical, and emotional insecurity; (3) vocal flatness indicated sluggishness for both males and females; and (4) nasality was associated with snobbishness. Knapp noted that most listeners are sensitive to vocal cues in the communication coming from persuaders.

Tactile Communication and Haptics

Some of the more important nonverbal message carriers are the ways in which and the degree to which people touch one another or sense things communicated by the sense of touch. This is called **tactile communication**. We know that infants need to be touched and cuddled. We also know that this need doesn't diminish as the child matures. However, in American culture the number, type, and duration of touches the growing child gets are greatly reduced as the child gets older. They may get more touching in other cultures and hence will behave differently in response to persuasion that involves touching. In fact, they may feel more or less comfortable with persuasive messages (e.g., ads or speeches) that involve heavy amounts of touching than in ones with less. Children (and others) may substitute other kinds of physical contact for the touches they received from their parents—they might sock or shove someone, for instance, or use tickling a pal, holding hands, and so on. Leathers (1986) observes that we live in a non-contact society,

FIGURE 10.7   Here Malaprop Man demonstrates how mispronunciation can damage credibility and persuasive effectiveness.

SOURCE: Frank and Ernest/United Feature Syndicate, Inc.

with touch absent in public places, particularly between males. We probably would not accept the male vice president of the United States hugging and kissing the male president on his return from abroad, yet such behavior is perfectly acceptable in many cultures.

These Western norms for the use of touch, Leathers notes, usually relate to two general factors: (1) the part of the body being touched; and (2) the demographic characteristics of the persons interacting, such as age, gender, social class, race, and status. The head, shoulders, and arms are the most frequently touched parts of the body, with other parts being more or less off limits to public touch. Touching is also more frequent among minorities, and persuaders who touch persuadees are the most successful (Kotulak, 1985). Persuaders who touch too much probably offend. Credibility can be drastically undermined if persuaders misread a relationship and touch or respond to touch inappropriately. Touch also conveys special kinds of emotional

persuasion like empathy, warmth, and reassurance. Touching or hugging is frequent at wakes and weddings. Among male firefighters, about the only acceptable touch off the job, from another male, is a handshake or backslap. However, firefighters on the job must sometimes calm frantic men, women, and children to save them, and they often use touch to facilitate that. So willingness to touch varies depending on the situation and the persons involved. In some religions, the laying on of hands signifies ordination and is often given credit for religious conversions or faith healing.

Touch can be extremely important in facilitating certain kinds of communication. Terminal cancer patients, for example, need more touch than less ill patients. Touch expresses sympathy for someone who has been fired or who failed in some other way. In another study, strangers were asked for information by a researcher posing as an ordinary citizen. In half the cases, the researcher lightly touched the stranger on the shoulder before saying,

"Excuse me, but I'm sort of lost. Can you tell me where the nearest bus stop is located?" The researcher got much more information and even conversation when using the light touch than when not using it. How does touch affect you in communication associations? What if the touching person is from another culture? Would you feel more or less comfortable? Depending on the situation and culture involved, some touches are taboo, such as the touching of strangers for no reason. Other taboo touches include touching that inflicts pain (touching a wound); touching that interferes with another's activities or conversation; touching that moves others aside; playful touching that is too aggressive, as in mock wrestling, tickling, or pinching; and double-whammy touching used to emphasize a negative point, as in touching someone's belly when mentioning that they have put on weight (Kotulak, 1985). Receivers as well as persuaders need to become aware of the communicative impact of touching.

As you continue to improve your abilities as a receiver, one of the nonverbal channels of communication to observe closely is the use of touch, whether it occurs at a first meeting with a stranger, or punctuates the closing of a business deal, expresses empathic sensitivity toward another person, or provides the assurance to help move people out of dangerous situations. For example, firefighters often need to use touch to guide trapped persons in a fire to safety. Grief is often affected by touch, and touching someone during a wake is often therapeutic. Tactile communication says many things.

Haptics relates to touch, but not between persons. Instead it is what is communicated by the texture or the feel of objects or other things in the situation—temperature, humidity, and so on. And it usually communicates something to the receiver, either accidentally or intentionally. Velvet communicates different things than does silk; rough-hewn lumber walls communicate something different than plaster, which communicates something different than concrete. My hunting dog is a Vizsla, the royal dog of Hungary. His coat is silky and short haired, quite unlike the shaggy hair of a Chesapeake Retriever. While people are friendly and pet other dogs, they can't resist stroking my dog's coat over and over and as a result, he is extraordinarily friendly to strangers and those with whom he already knows. Sometimes he's a pest, the way he begs for stroking and nuzzling. I've concluded that it's a matter of mutual haptic attraction.

Chronemics

Chronemics is the way we use time, such as being prompt, late, or long-winded. Indeed, the use and misuse of time can communicate many messages to others. It too is changing in our 24/7, multicultural world of persuasion. Different cultures have different chronemic behaviors, and now that we are media-saturated every day and all day, we no longer use or even think of time in the ways we used to use or think about it. The computer makes time practically disappear when we are involved with it. We may even become impatient when it operates too slowly. However, there are still some widely held chronemic patterns—like showing up for professional or formal appointments. For example, few of us anticipate being showed right in to the examination room when we show up on time for a doctor's appointment, but we don't mind being a few minutes late or even unannounced for an appointment with a professor, and we are okay with not getting right in.

Suppose you have set a time and reserved a place for the meeting of a work group. Because you set up the meeting, you show up ten minutes early to make sure things are in order. A few minutes before the meeting is to start, two members of the group arrive and begin to chat. Right on time, to the minute, in comes another group member. Now only two people are missing. You probably suggest waiting a few minutes. After five minutes, one of your missing members shows up, so you start the meeting. Nearly half an hour later, the final member arrives. What messages were sent by each member of the group? In U.S. culture, it is permissible to arrive at a meeting five minutes late, but arrive much later than that, and you'd better have a good excuse such as a flat tire, impossible traffic jam, a stalled elevator, or a speeding ticket. By coming late, you communicate to the others that you don't care about the appointment or that you are a thoughtless person and a "prima donna." I always showed up a little early for my physical therapy appointments because I was aware that the office charged $75 for each 15 minute segment of the appointment, but I didn't mind arriving a little late for choir practice. However, if you are invited to a party, be sure to show up at least 15 minutes late if it is a dinner party and 45 minutes late if it is a college bash. If you arrive on time, the hosts might still be grooming themselves or putting the final touches on the place settings.

If you really want to put people in their place, make sure they have to wait to get to see you. This is a favorite trick of some police officers, corporate executives, and even some college professors who make you wait in the hall. However, in other cultures, students might feel honored if the professor saw them at all, thus demonstrating that there are important cultural factors related to chronemics. One of the most familiar of these is the way time is handled by African-Americans, which has come to be called "CPT," or colored people's time, even by African-Americans. In a scene in the 1999 play *OO BLA DEE,* the story of an all-black women's jazz band during the 1940s, the members of the band discuss CPT. One character traces the concept to the emancipation from slavery. Before that, she says, slaves had to work from "cain't" until "cain't" six days a week, or from when you "cain't" yet see the sunrise until you "cain't" see the sunset because it's already set. Freedom from this grueling schedule, she goes on to say, made flexibility of time use one of the prime features of the new-found freedom, and the idea carried on across generations. Begin to observe how time works in your culture or subculture, but don't be surprised if it doesn't operate the same way in other cultures. And don't forget that our 24/7 world has reset many person's time clocks. On an individual basis, time use may also reflect our results-oriented world. I, personally, cannot stand meetings where nothing is accomplished and have to bite my tongue as one or two members of the committee carry on and on and on, thus "wasting"

the time of the rest of us. Other cultures are more tolerant of long-winded consideration of issues.

GENDER DIFFERENCES IN NONVERBAL COMMUNICATION

Researchers have investigated **gender differences** in nonverbal communication. For example, in a 1989 study of attitudes toward the use of touch, researchers found that women are significantly more comfortable with touch than are men, have higher levels of touch comfort than men, and that the touches are signs of a greater level of socialization (Fromme et al., 1989). Communication scholar Brenda Major (1984) noted significant gender differences in the way individuals touch others and receive such touches. While men tend to initiate touching in cross-gender encounters, they are less likely to initiate touch in same-gender encounters. Women are more comfortable about touching other women and about touching in general. Although touch often expresses warmth and intimacy, especially among women, it can also communicate power or status relationships. Men touch more frequently if they perceive themselves to be superior to the person they touch. They also initiated cross-gender touch in public places more often than women. Researchers thought that this was to signal dominance and control (Singley, 2004).

In terms of reactions to touch, Major noted that if the toucher is of the same status as the touchee, women react more positively and men more negatively, particularly if the toucher is a woman. Major concluded that, overall, women tend to react more positively to touch than do men and that this probably stems from the fact that girls are touched more frequently from birth on. They also use more facial expression and speak in softer tones (Fay, 2006).

There are other gender-related differences in the use of touch as well. The average U.S. woman touches someone else about twelve times per day, but the average man touches someone only eight times a day (Kotulak, 1985). Touches by both males and females in the United States are more likely to involve a person of the opposite gender (see Figure 10.8), which is the

FIGURE 10.9

Men and Women in Social Relationships

Men spend less time in social relationships and then it is usually job related. They also use SNM less frequently than women.

SOURCE: Tribalium/Shutterstock.com.

FIGURE 10.8 Male and Female Touching

Women are more "touchy" than men.

SOURCE: © Kenn Wislander/iStockphoto.com.

reverse of what occurs in some other cultures. In Western culture, touch between men generally is limited to shaking hands or backslapping—with the occasional manly hug, especially in sporting events. In some cultures, it is not uncommon for males to walk down the street hand in hand.

Use of time also differs between the genders. Males tend to spend more time in leisure activities than do females, who tend to interact in social activities and conversations not related to entertainment more than males (e.g., family, friends) (See Figure 10.9.). Research also shows that family time tends to reduce the risk of substance abuse and sexual activity while peer time promotes such activities in both genders (Barnes et al., 2007). And among adolescents, females spend more time in interpersonal relationships than do males. They also put more time into social relationships and use SNM more than men do. That is, unless sports or business is involved (Smith, 1997). Scholars N. Porter and F. Geis (1984) wondered if gender and nonverbal communication were

related to leadership in small groups. They found that, in both all-male and all-female groups, physical placement at the head of the table is the best predictor of who gets to be the leader. But in mixed-gender groups, males emerge as the leader if they sit in the leadership position, but women do not. Researchers S. Ellyson, J. Dovidio, and B. J. Fehr (1984) investigated dominance in men and women as it relates to visual behavior. They found that dominance is usually indicated by what they called "look/speak" rather than "look/listen" behavior. Look/speak attempts to indicate dominance by speaking rather than by listening when catching the eyes of others. If women use the look/speak strategy, they are just as likely to be evaluated as dominant as are men who use the same strategy. Communication scholar Judy Hall (1984) found that women have more expressive faces than men and smile and laugh more often than men, especially when they are in all-female groups. She speculated that smiling and laughing may be seen as immasculine, which tends to discourage males from exhibiting these behaviors.

Regarding gaze and gaze holding, Hall found that women tend to gaze more at other persons than do men and that they are more uncomfortable than men when they cannot see the person to whom they are speaking. They also seem to be gazed at more frequently than men. Hall hinted that gaze differences between men and women exist because females are perceived as having more warmth than males

FIGURE 10.10

Mother, Child and Gaze Holding

We begin to learn the importance of gaze holding and love as infants.

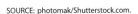

SOURCE: photomak/Shutterstock.com.

(see Figure 10.10). Also, males avoid the gazes of other males to avoid the potential sexual implications of such behavior.

Hall also observed that men maintain greater distances from others when in conversation and that women are approached more closely than men are. Women tend to face more directly toward the person with whom they are interacting. When given the choice of sitting adjacent to or across from others, men tend to occupy the across position, whereas women prefer the adjacent position. Finally, females are more approachable than males. She also found that women initiate touching more than men. Hall speculated that this may be due to women's appreciation for being touched more and that there may be gender-related differences for various kinds of touch,

such as where on the body and how emphatic the touch happens to be.

Hall found little research on which to base generalizations regarding body movements and positions. However, it does appear that men are more relaxed and more physically expansive—spreading their arms and legs and leaning back in chairs with their legs forward—and are more restless than women, fidgeting, playing with objects, and shifting their bodies in various ways. Another difference is that, while women tend to carry things in front of them, men carry things at their side. Hall also reported several gender-related differences in the use of the voice. Men are less fluent than women, make more verbal errors, and use more vocalized pauses such as "uh" or "um." Women's voices tend to have higher pitches even though their

FIGURE 10.11   There are some verbal gender differences in this cartoon, but notice some of the nonverbal differences, including facial expressions or affect displays, the use of touch, and the use of proxemics.

SOURCE: Reprinted by permission of Todd Michaels.

vocal mechanisms permit them to use lower ones. Women's voices have more variability in pitch, are more musical, and are more expressive than men's voices. Women's voices are also softer than men's and are judged to be more positive, pleasant, honest, meek, respectful, delicate, enthusiastic, and anxious and less confident, domineering, and awkward. Men's voices tend to be demanding, blunt, forceful, and militant (see Figure 10.11).

So there are important gender differences in nonverbal communication beyond dress and vocal features, and successful persuaders as well as skeptical persuadees are aware of these and use and respond to them when attempting to persuade or when being persuaded.

DIALECT

Dialect, or patterns and styles of pronunciation and usage, is also culture bound and often indicates an individual's socioeconomic or regional background. We learn dialect culturally. It communicates many things about us. Many of my students come from Chicago or its suburbs. South Siders cheer for the Sox but also get angry with me when I tell some of them to stop using factory talk. They do not hear themselves saying "dis" for "this" and "dat" for "that" and "dem"

for "them." Yet they will be discriminated against if they keep their dialect. Students from the North Side cheer for the Cubs, and some have another dialect that may cause equal problems for them. They say "Dubbie" for "Debbie," "Shovie" for "Chevy," and "new-ahth" for "north." And it would be easy to document the kind of discrimination that occurs when African-American or Latino dialects are used. Be aware of your responses to various dialects, and see whether people respond to your dialect in certain ways. I have a sing-songy Minnesota dialect and get certain responses because of my frequent use of "yup," "Don't cha know?" and "you betcha." People look for hayseeds in my hair.

THE USE OF NONVERBAL TACTICS

Nonverbal message carriers can be manipulated by persuaders in a process that scholar Ervin Goffman (1959) called "impression management." This means using powerful verbal and nonverbal signals to convince the audience that the source is a certain kind of person. One candidate for the presidential nomination wore red-and-black checked lumberjack shirts when he campaigned in New Hampshire and hip boots when his opponents began to engage in mudslinging.

BOX 10.2 Diversity and Nonverbal Communication

It is fascinating how members of diverse groups react differently to nonverbal messages. In low-context cultures like the United States, and Canada, there is less emphasis on the nonverbal aspects of communication than in high-context cultures like Japan or Colombia. The nonverbal messages are there for both contexts but are not paid attention to by persons in low-context cultures. Gender is another diversity factor in expressing nonverbal behavior like facial expression. In the United States it is acceptable for women to show fear in their facial expression but not anger. The opposite is true for males. North Americans need and occupy more space than persons in Europe, who occupy more space than persons in Japan or China. And while some facial expressions are consistent across cultures, such as enjoyment, anger, fear, sadness, disgust, and surprise, there are major differences between diverse groups as to when and where it is appropriate to display such emotions. Laughter can

communicate nervousness or fear in some cultures. Differences occur over how members of various cultures respond to the placement or movement of furniture. One German corporate executive working in the United States became so upset about visitors to his office moving the "guest chair" that he had it bolted down. Some mediators in conflict resolution meetings spend more time getting the furniture arrangement just right than they do in preparing for the agenda. To learn more about these examples and many others, go to Weblink 10.2 and scroll down to the section on nonverbal communication. (You can access this and all of the other Chapter 10 weblinks through your companion website for *Persuasion,* Chapter 10 resources.) Be sure to visit some of the links there and learn how nonverbal communication works in such diverse groups as Jewish and Arab Israelis, Angolans, and blacks and whites and in Islamic cultures. Listen to participants in Beyond Intractibility experiments.

Bill Clinton managed our impressions of him by wearing jogging suits and other casual clothing in the White House. Obama does much the same when "pressing the flesh." Or consider the use of timing discussed in Box 10.2 when used by then President Bush to announce "victory" or "Mission Accomplished" in Iraq. This misuse of timing continued to be used as criticism of his handling of the war long after the end of his term five years later—the longest war in American history. He wore a pilot's uniform and landed on an aircraft carrier announcing "Mission Accomplished!" in Iraq the day after the initial invasion in 2003, even though he was not a pilot, never landed the airplane and the mission was not close to being accomplished as the next more than 3,000 days of conflict and casualties demonstrated.

The use of artifacts of clothing to communicate nonverbally in impression management is a popular topic in the corporate world. In her book, *The Power of Dress,* Jacqueline Murray (1989) provides a number of case studies to demonstrate the persuasive use of dress. For example, at Electronic Data Systems, everyone has a military look, with clean-shaven faces, shiny, black, plain-toed shoes, white shirts, dark suits,

and army-style haircuts for men. Murray identifies three categories of business dress: (1) "corporate dress," which is used by bankers, attorneys, and executives; (2) "communication dress," which is used by persons in sales, marketing, education, personnel, and high-tech industries; and (3) "creative dress," which is used by interior decorators, commercial artists, persons in advertising, boutique owners, and entrepreneurs. Corporate dress is simple in line, shape, and design, tends to be tailored, and features gray and blue colors for suits, and off-white or light blue for shirts and blouses. Corporate dress also uses fabrics such as silks, herringbones, tweeds, and flannels in suits or dresses, and plain cottons, wools, or linens in shirts and blouses. Communication dress features suits and dresses that are practical, relaxed, and semi-traditional, and includes blazers and sports coats. It also includes a mix of colors for the blouses and shirts, featuring stripes or relaxed prints, and fabrics such as knits and loose or bulky weaves. Creative dress tends to be loose-fitting, with elongated lines and exaggerated design in both suits and dresses and blouses and shirts. The preferred colors in this category are striking, dramatic hues, as well as understated taupes, peaches, and basics. Although some may question Murray's conclusions, few would argue

Top view

Triad A

Triad B

FIGURE 10.12

Notice the difference between the body positions of the persons in each triad. Which is involved in "blocking" behavior?

with her premise that dress is important as a nonverbal channel of communication. (See Box 10.2.)

We rely on the visual medium for a large percentage of our impressions of others. In cyberspace, the research shows that people make impressions of how others look without many visual cues, and these impressions often vary from offline reality (Jacobson, 1999). When you consider that fact with the multicultural aspect of our 24/7 world, you need to take virtual impressions gained without the visual medium with a grain of salt. And we even use non-verbal communication in cyberspace—the open or closed parentheses are often used as happy or unhappy faces.

OTHER NONVERBAL MESSAGES

Eye movements and other movements of the head can also communicate. We are all aware of the negative impression we have of persons whose eyes are continuously darting about or who can't look us in the eye for more than a brief moment. Completely different meaning can come from what is called "gaze holding," or maintaining eye contact. Albert Scheflen (1973) found that when a psychiatrist uses the "bowl gesture," patients often open up and reveal more about themselves and their problems. This gesture in used in persuasion and is the logo for the Allstate company. As Box 10.3 demonstrates, many things including

music, art, and even cooking styles can have meanings—even propagandistic meanings.

People also use their bodies to invite or inhibit communication. This is termed **blocking behavior**. Notice the two configurations in Figure 10.12. In triad A, the body positions of the three persons would inhibit a fourth person from joining in the conversation, whereas in triad B, the body positions invite participation.

Another way to block communication is using objects such as furniture or piles of books on a library table to obstruct it. Research shows that lifting or lowering the chin at the ends of sentences serves as a signal that the person intends to continue to speak or that he or she is finished speaking and someone else can join in. And, of course, we are all aware of the communicative power of head nodding, winking, and various obscene gestures, which vary in meaning from culture to culture. Orban (1999) and others call these nonverbal indicators "regulators." Among the regulators are those that involve turn taking, turn requesting, and turn yielding or "back channeling," where the listener encourages the speaker to continue instead of taking his or her turn. Orban says back channeling indicates a listener's full attention and interest, which means back-channeled persuaders will advocate longer and with more enthusiasm. As you begin to observe the nonverbal messages occurring around you, you will discover an almost infinite number

BOX 10.3   Nonverbal Propaganda

When you think about the many kinds of things besides words than can convey meaning, you soon realize that the list is going to get quite long. For example, there's the old reliable propaganda poster. Then there are famous propaganda films like *Triumph of the Will* from the WWII era and more recent films like *Fahrenheit 9/11* and *Sicko* (both by Michael Moore) or *An Inconvenient Truth* by Al Gore, all of which carry ideological messages. And many propaganda experts claim that even music, art, architecture, jewelry, dance, drama, perfume, automobiles (after all, what did owning a Rolls-Royce "mean" if not that being a capitalist was a good life model?), clothing, furniture, and even many simple crafts like cooking can be used for propaganda purposes—don't you think gourmet cooking promotes a

certain lifestyle or that the vegan lifestyle has propaganda implications? Go to any search engine and enter the word "propaganda" and any of the examples noted above (i.e., "music," "architecture," "cartoons," "perfume," etc.) and visit some of the sites you find there. For a real insight into the works of a modern propagandist, go to Weblink 10.3 and explore the many links and sublinks that employ nonverbal messages, or view a DVD of some of his films. (You can access this and all of the other Chapter 10 weblinks through your companion website for *Persuasion,* Chapter 10 resources.) Report back to the class what you find (or perhaps even prepare a brief PowerPoint presentation that imports some of these nonverbal examples of propaganda) to show how ubiquitous propaganda is, and use it in place of a term paper.

of potential nonverbal message carriers. Who reaches for the check at a restaurant first? What do nervous gestures or twitches, volume, tone, and pauses communicate? How do you interpret curious habits such as cracking one's knuckles or doodling, which could communicate subconscious tensions?

Even the sense of smell seems to be an important carrier of information. We are all aware, for example, of the person who uses too much perfume, cologne, or after-shave lotion or of the person with body odor. Apparently, we can detect more subtle odors as well. For instance, some persons claim to be able to smell hostility or tension in the air upon entering a room. Many homes have unique and characteristic odors caused by the kinds of food cooked in them, the kinds of cleaning solutions used, the presence of pets, or the kinds of wood used in their construction or furnishings. The fragrance of a new car is now available in aerosol cans to spray in used cars, thus making them seem newer and "fresher."

REVIEW AND CONCLUSION

By this time, you know that the world of the persuadee in an information age is not an easy one. You need to be aware of so many things, including the persuader's self-revelation via language choices and the internal or process premises operating for each of us. The responsible receiver recognizes the variety of nonverbal channels, including facial expression, eye behavior, and bodily communication. You need to be aware of the ways in which gestures and posture, proxemics, physical appearance, and artifacts can communicate. You also need to realize that vocal communication, tactile communication, haptics,

chronemics, and gender all send messages. These premises do not make receivers' tasks any easier, given that they operate at particularly low levels of awareness, and we often overlook them as we analyze persuasion. That's probably because they are processed in the peripheral channel of the ELM where we don't really do much analysis. You will have to train yourself to be more sensitive to nonverbal elements in the persuasive process, so you can skillfully use these channels in your own communication, but, more importantly, so you can accurately decode the real meaning of the messages aimed at you every day.

KEY TERMS

After reading this chapter, you should be able to identify, explain, and give an example of the following key terms or concepts:

kinesics

proxemics

haptics

physical appearance

chronemics

artifactual communication

nonverbal channels

facial expression

eye behavior

bodily communication

public distance

social or formal distance

personal or informal distance

intimate distance

vocal features

tactile communication

gender differences

dialect

blocking behavior

APPLICATION OF ETHICS

You are in charge of nurse/patient relations at a small-town hospital, and recently you have hired nurses from other cultures. You are just beginning to realize that there are great cultural differences in the way nurses view their work and interact with patients. For example, in the United States nurses value individualism and reliance, while 70 percent of the rest of the world's nurses value collectivism over individualism. This is exemplified by two contrary philosophies regarding health care: (1) to each person according to what is available in a free market; and (2) to each patient according to their need. Your hospital has limited resources and diverse patients, nurses, doctors, and staff working together, often on the same patients. How will you go about training the various diversities to cooperate, especially when their philosophies on health care are so different? Your options are (1) have an open free-for-all discussion of the issues; (2) conduct individual counseling with nurses, doctors, and staff who must work together but disagree about the two opposing philosophies; (3) hire a professional consulting group specializing in diversity and nursing to conduct a series of diversity seminars; or (4) handle the conflicts on a case-by-case basis.

QUESTIONS FOR FURTHER THOUGHT

1. What are some of the facial expressions you find easiest to identify? Which is most difficult?

2. What is kinesics? Give some examples, and explain how and what they communicate.

3. Which one of your friends uses gestures most effectively? What does he or she do that makes the gestures so effective?

4. What are some examples of how physical appearance sends messages in your world? What are some examples of the way physical appearance identifies a contemporary musical artist or group?

5. With what artifacts do you surround yourself? What do they mean to you? (Some students have reported that the first thing they do after

unpacking for dormitory living is to purchase "conversation pieces" or artifacts that symbolize themselves.) What about your roommate? What artifacts does he or she use? What do they symbolize about him or her? What about your family members' artifacts?

6. How often do you touch others? Try to increase the number of touches you use, and observe the responses of others. Does the increase have any effect? If so, what?

7. What are some examples of how chronemics operates in your life—on campus, in the dorm, in the classroom, and at home?

8. What are some of the gender differences in nonverbal communication as they appear in contemporary advertising?

9. What is the predominant dialect where you live? Are there any other dialects that you can identify in your community? What effects do they have on people's attitudes and behaviors?

10. What is "blocking" behavior? Give examples from your everyday life.

11. What are some ways you respond to texture or haptics?

12. What are some cultural differences in nonverbal communication?

13. Would it be ethical to manipulate your nonverbal behavior to affect persuasive outcomes?

14. How could you use nonverbal communication through SNM?

15. In which channel of the ELM are nonverbal elements of a message perceived?

16. Is it ethical to knowingly alter the nonverbal message elements you send?

17. How do ethics operate in communication via SNM? Can you lie there? Can you misrepresent your identity?

18. Which channel of the ELM is likely to be used in processing nonverbal messages? Give an example.

You can access your online resources at the companion website for *Persuasion*. Log in at **http://www.cengagebrain.com**.

Applications of Persuasive Premises

11

The Persuasive Campaign or Movement

After reading this chapter, you should be able to:

1. Compare and contrast campaigns and single-shot persuasion.

2. Explain why campaigns are communication systems.

3. Differentiate among the three types of campaigns and give examples of each.

4. Demonstrate how campaign goals, strategies, and tactics are used in campaigns.

5. Identify and explain the five stages of the Yale campaign model.

6. Explain the hierarchy of effects model.

7. Differentiate between social movements and other types of campaigns.

8. Discuss symbolic convergence and show how it is used in persuasive campaigns for products, persons, and ideas.

9. Identify and discuss various kinds of campaign communication including buzz marketing.

10. Identify how SNM are used in campaigns or mass/social movements.

11. Determine which paths or routes of information processing of the ELM work most frequently in the campaign, and/or mass/social movement.

12. Understand why and how the social movements of our times occur (e.g., the Middle East).

For many years, the study of persuasion focused mainly on the public speech and "single-shot" or "hypodermic needle" perspective on persuasive communication. This model placed a receiver at a certain position on an issue prior to an injection or "shot" of persuasion. Following the persuasion, the researcher either speculated about or tried to statistically measure any changes that might have occurred in the receiver. This approach makes for simple models for persuasion, but it hardly matches reality. After all, instances in which a single persuasive message changed the outcome of events are rare indeed. Most persuasion is incremental and cumulative instead, and this is especially true in a media-saturated world. For instance, if you were considering whether to buy a new technology, vote for a candidate for office, give money to a charity, or join a cause, your decision would not be instantaneous. Rather, it would be the result of a series of messages. Some would be processed in the peripheral path of the elaboration likelihood model (ELM),

such as the ads for the new technology, the candidate's appearance, your history with the charity, or the stirring words of the leader of the movement or cause. Other elements in your persuasion would be processed via the central route. These might include what *Consumer Reports* says about the technology, or what editorials say about the candidate, statistics, donation administrative costs, and more.

Until the 1990s, marketing, advertising, and public relations campaign planning were dominated by the single-shot approach. Ad and public relations campaigns were both seen as periods of time during which many messages were being sent, but it was still assumed that a single ad or news release could sell a product, candidate, or cause. Then a new term came into vogue—**integrated marketing communication** (IMC)—which refers to more carefully coordinated activities of marketing, advertising, public relations, sales promotion, packaging, personal selling, websites, branding, brand contacts, and event staging. Each element works with the others and leads to synergies that make the whole far greater than the sum of the parts. For a long time, political scientists also ignored the communication dimensions of political campaigns, with the possible exception of research on campaign financing and public opinion polling. They remained focused on the nature and structure of government and ignored the electoral process as "mere politics." Meanwhile, most of the research done on campaigns occurred in advertising or marketing departments and was proprietary, meaning that it belonged to the client, candidate, or cause leader who paid for it, and therefore seldom was made public. The fact that candidates used focus groups to determine their dress or hairstyle was the best-kept secret in town. Remember the politician who changed her style of dress and mode of transportation to a motorcycle when she shifted from a GOP women's luncheon audience to a college campus? No doubt her campaign committee wished the revelation hadn't ever become public.

Campaign and movement theory has come a long way since those days, and this is appropriate, given that the persuasive campaign is probably the most prevalent form of persuasion today. In this chapter, we look at three general types of persuasive campaigns: **product-oriented**, **person- or candidate-oriented**, and **idea- or ideologically-oriented**. We shouldn't underestimate the impact of advancing technology and research on persuasion and especially on the strategy considerations of persuasive campaigns—multi-mediated, psychologically constructed, interactive, and highly sophisticated SNM messages that don't occur "all at once," but over time. They are targeted at specifically designated campaign or market "segments," and lead the persuadee through a series of steps to the final campaign goal; whether it be adoption of a new practice (such as recycling), a new product type (e.g., a pharmaceutical), a specific brand (Viagra), or a particular candidate or organization. The Internet, interactive media, digital audio, video, and graphics all can and do convey powerfully persuasive messages in such campaigns that interact with one another and with receivers for overall effect. In the future, the number and sophistication of persuasive campaigns will increase exponentially as we increase the use of the Internet, digital technologies such as Wii dual-digital, air wave broadcasting, computer/television interfaces, and many others. Market segmentation will be much easier to accomplish. Experts predict that soon most campaigns will be aimed at a segment of one: You will be in one separate segment receiving a tailored set of messages specifically designed with *you* in mind; and everyone else will receive a similar—but individually tailored—appeal, sort of in a "Big Brother is watching you" approach. In a way, it is too immense and frightening to consider. We're talking about accounting for our uniform reactions, votes, purchases, and so forth by using individually focused and strategically planned bits of persuasion, layered to come together in the end with near-identical behaviors—all perhaps designed from bits of information about yourself that you don't even know you have revealed to anyone. These bits of information have been gathered and analyzed by persuaders through your use of the Internet, the characteristics of your Facebook friends, your responses to prior ads and appeals, and perhaps you have even been secretly videotaped while you used an SNM.

CAMPAIGNS VERSUS SINGLE-SHOT PERSUASIVE MESSAGES

As noted above, campaigns are not merely a series of messages sent to audiences, although they once were thought of that way. Political campaigns used to always start on Labor Day and end on the day of the election. Now they might begin years in advance and will surely encompass much more than just debates over specific issues, position papers, attack and support television spots, and so on. Campaigns have and will continue to differ from single shots of persuasion or from collections of persuasive messages delivered over time in several ways.

1. Campaigns create "positions" in the audience's minds for the product, candidate, or idea. So, for instance, "mountain grown coffee" is the position occupied by Folgers (even though all coffees are grown in mountains), and Maxwell house occupies the "reheatable" position as promoted in its memorable slogan, "Good to the Very Last Drop."

2. Campaigns are intentionally designed to develop over time. They have stages for getting the audience's attention, preparing them to act, and, finally calling the audience to action. Politicians announce their candidacy, then appoint their staff, then agree to debates, then begin to produce commercials, and so on with each step following the other like the acts and scenes in a drama. The same is the case with mass movement campaigns. The persuaders first get their audience's attention: "The Arctic and Antarctic ice caps are melting, the earth is experiencing the beginning of a great climate change, and we're facing global warming. We must do something!"

3. Campaigns dramatize the product, candidate, idea, or ideology for the audience, inviting members to participate with the campaign and its goal(s) in real or symbolic ways. We want our brand to have a personality, so we say that Pepsi is a younger person's drink, and "GetSoClean" detergent is engaged in continual warfare with germs and dirt—all cast in the dramatic mode. In the mass movement persuaders show the retreat of glaciers: "Glacier Park only has about five years of glaciers left! Polar bears are moving south!"

4. Campaigns use sophisticated communication technologies to reach target prospects. Computers, films like *An Inconvenient Truth*, and television specials demonstrate a threat, and SNM pass the message onto those who do not know or realize the threat.

Starting in the late 1980s, computers began to store large amounts of information about potential voters, customers, donors, and joiners. These technological advances led to what is called "data-based marketing," which allows the persuader to gather information about prospective voters, customers, donors, or joiners to be used in future campaigns long before they are actually put to use. Since that time, the techniques have become more and more sophisticated, and technological devices like cellular phones, various digital devices, and systems like Facebook, Twitter, and others have made most humans willing to participate in providing and identifying these data. Movements and campaigns now have the tools and systems to pinpoint the individual members/targets of their aims. If technology continues to increase in sophistication and power/memory in the next decade as it has in the past, it's frightening to think of how we might be manipulated. Furthermore, more of you are reading fewer books and are relying on less genuine news, thus becoming "isolatos" from the world around you and non-discussants of issues that will determine the future. Conversation is nearly dead, and meanwhile the technology for killing it and manipulating you is becoming more powerful, compact, and specific in targeting you for persuasion and in invading your individual and independent selves—reason than ever for being skeptical and responsible receivers.

Following movements or campaigns is like watching a TV series. Although the episodes can stand alone (each has its own beginning, middle, and end), together they form a collage of messages that meld together until an entire image with its own overall beginning, middle, and end (also known as the big picture) of the campaign is perceived and stored. If it is well-designed, large segments of the population will have been exposed to enough "episodes" that most will come away with a similar image of the product, candidate, or idea. And they will influence one another through highly credible testimonials about the truth of the messages being sent via personal and interpersonal communication, which spreads like a virus and at minimal cost to the persuaders out there.

SIMILARITIES AMONG THE TYPES OF CAMPAIGNS

The three campaign types (product, person, and idea or ideology) share some similarities. All of them occur over time. Most are targeted and use mass media to accomplish their goals. Several high profile individuals are usually present in person and idea and propaganda campaigns, but not necessarily in product-oriented campaigns. In the person-oriented political campaign, the focus is on an individual's name and the purpose associated with the name. For politicians, this focus is always election to office or nomination to office. However, in other person-oriented campaigns the focus may be on donating to pay for an operation, helping to save the person's home, or engaging in action to further a cause (such as in righting a wrong done to someone in the past—for example, an unjust conviction). The slogan might feature the person's name, whether a candidate—"Be sure to vote for John Countryman"—or someone needing financial support—"Dollars for Jimmy, Our County's Liver Transplant Candidate." In issue or cause-oriented campaigns the slogan or theme usually features the cause—"Think Globally; Act Locally," "Stop Smoking Now," or "Stop Importation of Foreign-Made Toys." The image depicted in Figure 11.1 illustrates many of the characteristics of the ideological campaign, such as simplified ideas, unusual logical

connections between premises (e.g., in this case Congress equals the slave owner or taxpayer), use of patriotic colors and symbols, and so on. Most try to use professional-looking signs with correct spellings.

Political campaigns might focus on a cause or issue such as stem cell research policy, terrorism, or school vouchers. There are also some differences among the three types of campaign, which we'll discuss later in this chapter. All campaigns, of course, use mass media to further their goals and strategies, and employ mass-media-driven tactics in our media-saturated, 24/7 networked world.

GOALS, STRATEGIES, AND TACTICS IN CAMPAIGNS

Campaigns don't sell anything, but they do deliver a prospective consumer, voter, donor, or joiner to the point of buying, donating, voting, joining, or visiting a website of the good cause where further persuasion occurs. The successful campaign must also educate and prepare the consumer, voter, or joiner to take action. To accomplish this task, campaigns must (1) zero in on well-defined goals, (2) create appropriate strategies to accomplish the goals, and then (3) use various tactics to put the strategy into action. This pattern of goals leading to strategies, which in turn lead to tactics, applies to all three types of campaigns.

A recent goal for a Claussen's pickles campaign was to increase sales in specified test markets by 10 percent. Claussen's differs from its competition because its pickles are much crispier and crunchier since they are refrigerated, not cooked and canned like other brands. Usually in product campaigns, product/brand features are tied to consumer benefits. In this campaign for Claussen, this kind of feature/benefit linkage was that refrigerated (the feature) means crunchier (the benefit). The campaign staff then works out a promising strategy to demonstrate the feature/benefit equation. For Claussen's, the strategy was to use TV spots to show the unique features and benefits of the brand. As noted, the product is refrigerated rather than cooked, so the pickles are crisper and crunchier than the competition. Previously, Claussen's had only used print ads, which can't show crispy and crunchy very well. To implement the TV strategy, Claussen's used the tactic of comparative advertising, matching Claussen's against Vlasic's in the TV spots. The tactic was to show Vlasic's cooked pickle being bent in half and not breaking, while Claussen's pickle was bent and snapped in two, giving off a spray of brine accompanied by a crunchy sound effect.

In a political example, the goal in primary election campaigns is to win the party's nomination from opposing candidates. Strategies for achieving this include ignoring the opposition, taking the high road on the issues, simply letting the candidates attack one another, or again stressing the feature/benefit linkage. Such a linkage might be that the candidate had opposed the costly and foolish decision to go to war in Iraq. The benefit was obviously that he or she would make wise decisions in the future and thus avoid costly wars. A tactic for implementing the strategy might be to stage a debate against several empty chairs, each labeled with the name of one of the opponents who had voted to go to war. The campaign models highlighted in the following discussion demonstrate similarities and differences among campaign types. Your task is to use the models to help you make decisions about purchasing, voting, joining, or supporting causes.

DEVELOPMENTAL STAGES IN CAMPAIGNS

All three types of campaigns pass through a series of predictable stages as they grow, mature, and adapt to audience feedback along the way to the competition, the issues, and the demands of the persuasive situation. One campaign goal of a new product, candidate, or idea is to establish itself in the

audience's consciousness. A variety of strategies can accomplish this identification. For instance, a company might give out free samples or hire a celebrity to be associated with the brand, a candidate might announce his or her candidacy, or a group might stage a dramatic protest against a policy in an idea-oriented campaign. This initial message helps the campaigner learn about the audience. Perhaps prospects buy the brand because of its warranty and not its price. Maybe the voters don't favor increasing taxes on gasoline but do respond to the issue of deficit reduction. Animal rights supporters may respond to some issues but not others. So, in all three types of campaigns, strategies are tried and kept, altered, or dropped as the campaign develops, and based always on audience response to the persuasion beginning with its goals and moving to its strategies and tactics.

The Yale Five-Stage Developmental Model

Most campaigns include one or more of the stages of a model developed by researchers at Yale University (Binder, 1971). The **Yale five-stage developmental model** is highly applicable to product, person, and ideological campaigns and has been used to analyze hundreds of campaigns since it was first put forward. The five functional stages noted by the researchers are identification, legitimacy, participation, penetration, and distribution.

Identification. Identification is defined as establishing a position in the minds of consumers, voters, and potential converts. Many products and causes use logos to create audience identification. The well-established logo of the Goodyear Tire and Rubber Company, shown in Figure 11.2, has the winged foot of Mercury inserted between the two syllables of Goodyear, to suggest that the company's products are swift and safe. The lower case "e" used to identify the environmental movement was inserted inside the capital letter "C" to create the logo of the Commonwealth Edison electric company, suggesting that the company is

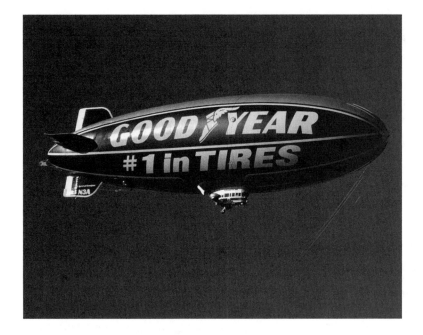

FIGURE 11.2

Many devices are used to establish product, person, or idea identification in campaigns. Logos such as this are one kind of identification device. Why is the winged foot of Mercury used? What does it communicate? Why put it between "GOOD" and "YEAR"? Answers to these questions help explain how product image or identification develops.

SOURCE: Goodyear/Getty Images.

environmentally conscientious—a good position for an energy monopoly. A series of arrows in a triangle with the point of each arrow bent to point at the base of the next arrow is the logo for any kind of recycling. The name associated with the product, candidate, or cause is also critical and closely related to the logo. The cold and flu medicine, Theraflu, is a good example because it suggests that it is a good therapy against the two sicknesses. It is a much better name than Smith Brothers Cold and Flu Syrup.

The name *Newsweek* is a good example too. It suggests that it contains the news of the past week (much more descriptive than competitor *Time)*. The name of Cadillac's "Escalade" SUV is meant to suggest good taste, classiness, and European distinction, since the brand's name is similar to the French term for a walking path. Candidates for office may label themselves the "people's candidate" or "the candidate for true change" or a similar term to create identification. In the abortion controversy, anti-abortion advocates chose "pro-life" for their cause. It "framed" the issue by suggesting that advocates are in favor of life. Who would disagree? It also implies that opponents of the movement are either anti-life or pro-death. Upstaged

by the "pro-life" framing label, abortion rights advocates had to settle for the far less effective "pro-choice." So choosing the best name for your idea or ideological campaign is also critical. Why did the Christian conservative "new right" choose the name "the Tea Party" as their identification device? One can think of a few obvious reasons, such as the reminder of the Boston Tea Party during pre-revolutionary times, and the party's originator said it stood for **T**axed **E**nough **A**lready, but was it a good name for identification of their true nature? It had some disadvantages. The sexual practice known as "tea bagging" is one, especially since one of their rallies involved crowds of members tossing tea bags into the Charles River in Boston.

To demonstrate the potency of a good name, ask a sample of people to name three brands of frozen turkey. Butterball will be on everyone's list while many competitors' names will not. Then ask what the key benefit of a Butterball turkey is, and they will tell you that it is the moistest brand. Why? Consider the name again and you will soon see why "Butterball" is a far better choice than Armour or Jenni-O. Figure 11.3 shows an ad for NameLab, a company that designs and tests various names to

MAKING NAMES

A leading name development firm since 1981, NameLab has created brand and company names like Acura, Acuvue, Aeron, American Century, Compaq, CompUSA, Luxor, Olive Garden, Renova, simplehuman, Slice and Viactiv. We quote costs accurately in advance and complete most projects within 4 weeks.

NAMELAB®

San Francisco, CA
415-517-0803 www.namelab.com info@namelab.com

FIGURE 11.3   The name of a product, political entity, or cause is part of the mix of factors that create identification for the brand.

SOURCE: Used by permission of NameLab.

help organizations establish an identity for a product, political entity, or cause.

Another device that helps create identification is the use of consistent color coding and typefaces on all printed or televised promotional items for the brand, candidate, or cause. These things create what are called "brand contacts" in the advertising business. The campaigner picks a color code and uses it in packaging, advertising, letterheads, and perhaps uniforms. For instance, UPS carriers wear dark brown uniforms, and their trucks are painted dark brown. Political candidates usually select some combination of red, white, and blue. The successful "Stop ERA" movement to defeat the Equal Rights Amendment adopted the color red, used signs shaped like stop signs, and had movement supporters wear red and white clothes when they demonstrated. On my campus, the university accepted $8 million a year for its general scholarship fund in return for naming Pepsi products as its official soft drink company. Now all napkins, soft drink cups, and so on have the Pepsi name, colors, and typeface on them. This not only rivets the brand name into student's minds but builds brand loyalty in them. It is between the ages of 18 and 34 that loyalty is most likely to be developed.

Slogans can also promote identification: "Folgers—The Mountain Grown Coffee," "When You Care Enough to Send the Very Best," "You're in Good Hands with Allstate," and "Smart. Very Smart" are all successful examples of identification-gaining tactics. Consider how coordinated and successful the campaign for State Farm Insurance Company has been over the years. The slogan and jingle "Like a Good Neighbor, State

Farm Is There" is the central theme, as is the red and white color code and the unique typeface. Agents are urged to live in the community they serve, to join civic organizations there, and to be visible and active in their communities. All ads must include the slogan, colors, and the agents' pictures. Agents are advised to send congratulatory cards to customers and their families on important days. National advertising usually includes a feature on a specific agent who was there when needed. Finally, jingles, uniforms, salutes, and all sorts of campaign paraphernalia like balloons or buttons help establish name and purpose identification in all three types of campaigns. The State Farm and Allstate insurance slogans are good examples— most of you can name them (see Figure 11.4).

Legitimacy. The second stage in the Yale model is the establishment of **legitimacy**, which is defined as being considered a worthy, believable, and trustworthy brand, candidate, or cause. Candidates usually achieve legitimacy by gaining endorsements or by winning primaries. Legitimacy can also serve as a power base from which to get financial and other support. Candidates demonstrate their power by holding rallies; appearing with well-known supporters or celebrities; being photographed with symbols of legitimacy, such as the U.S. Capitol building, the Lincoln Memorial, or the White House; or having ads currently being seen on TV, and distributing many visible signs, bumper stickers, buttons, and so on—all "brand contacts" in political propaganda. For incumbents, legitimacy also derives powerfully from holding

WE SEE YOUR NEED FOR
LIFE INSURANCE GROWING EVERY DAY.
WE LIVE WHERE YOU LIVE.™

As your family grows, so does your need for protection. From whole life insurance to
term insurance, nobody helps you provide that protection like State Farm.® We're there to help
you with your investment needs too, with State Farm Mutual Funds.™

LIKE A GOOD NEIGHBOR   STATE FARM IS THERE.™

Call your State Farm agent or visit us at statefarm.com.®

FIGURE 11.4   State Farm's
slogan, "Like a Good Neighbor, State
Farm is there," is classic and builds legitimacy.

SOURCE: Image Courtesy of The Advertising Archives.

office. In my congressional district, the incumbent
retired and a run-off for the remaining six months
of his term was held. Winning this campaign was
almost more important than winning the true general election six months hence because of the legitimacy obtained from incumbency. A favorite tactic
for both incumbents and challengers is getting
endorsed by local newspapers, politicians, and
well-known and respected citizens. Another is to
list one's experience in government or community
groups, church affiliations, family accomplishments,
and so on. Expertise, sincerity, and dynamism or
charisma are also elements in establishing candidate
legitimacy. A candidate's personal life can reduce
legitimacy, as demonstrated in Figure 11.5.

Product campaigns sometimes gain legitimacy
by demonstrating the product in use—a favorite
tactic in the television marketing of exercise
machines and kitchen gadgets. Professional athletes
wear Nikes to demonstrate the legitimacy of the

shoes and may offer a testimonial for the product.
Established endorsers like the Underwriter's Laboratory and *Good Housekeeping* seals of approval also
create legitimacy. Brands also develop legitimacy by
associating themselves with good causes, or by
sponsoring sports events, such as the Virginia
Slims Tennis Tournament, or by getting testimonials on their behalf by well-known celebrities,
such as athletes or movie stars. They might also

FIGURE 11.5   **Candidate**
Legitimacy and Newt Gingrich.
Candidate Gingrich lost some of
his credibility when he had an affair with an aide while his wife
was hospitalized for cancer, and he further weakened it when
he ultimately followed that with two divorces. How has this
impacted his future political ambition to become president?

SOURCES: AP Photo/John Raoux.

use endorsements by experts. For example, Promise (who makes a margarine), spread claims that in a study of 326 cardiologists, 9 out of 10 endorsed the brand and even printed the words "Cardiologist Endorsed" on their packaging.

In ideological campaigns such as supporting the U.S. Olympic swim team, well known personages and products are often teamed for the purpose of giving legitimacy to the idea of support. As shown in Figure 11.6, this is the case in the ad featuring eight-time Olympic gold medal winner Michael Phelps and the Planet Ocean Chronograph by Omega—they legitimize one another. Newspaper ads with the names of known supporters who endorse the movement also help establish legitimacy—even in seemingly minor causes like adding on to the local library. Large numbers of angry citizens show up at council meetings, and these events turn up on the evening news. In one high school, students protested their school lunch program and showed their legitimacy using nonviolent protest tactics. One day, hundreds of students boycotted the hot lunch, leaving the school with tons of leftovers. The next day, all students bought the hot lunch, leaving the school short of supplies. The following day, everyone paid with a large bill, running the cashiers out of change. The next day, they paid in pennies, creating havoc in the checkout lines as cashiers had to count pennies. On the fifth day, the school met with students about improving the lunches.

Participation.   The legitimacy stage of campaigns usually blends so smoothly with the **participation** stage that it is almost impossible to tell when one ends and the next begins. The participation stage is defined as the recruitment and involvement of previously uncommitted persons. In the legitimacy stage, the participants are considered known supporters who are not actively involved in the campaign. In the participation stage, the leaders seek to show their clout by getting these inactive persons actively involved in real or symbolic ways. There are many techniques for doing this. Some require effort by potential participants, such as marching at a protest or standing in a candlelight vigil, while others require minimal or only symbolic

participation, such as signing a petition or wearing a button. Customer rebates are another form of participation in product-oriented campaigns. The customer picks up, fills out, and clips the UPC code and mails it and the rebate form to get money—all steps requiring effort. And of those who pick up the rebate form or clip it out, only a small percentage actually follow through. But even the small act of participation of picking up the rebate form and clipping the UPC code gets the person involved. All these items encourage real and/or symbolic participation with the brand. Customers even advertise the brand by wearing clothing imprinted with the brand logo. Coupon offers are another way to promote participation—clipping the coupon is a behavioral intention and symbolic participation.

A movement may also urge participation in real or symbolic ways. People wear armbands or badges, yell slogans at rallies, put signs on their lawns or auto bumpers, or distribute leaflets. Or they sign an online petition or make a written statement to their "friends" on Facebook or another SNM. Candidates running for student body president may ask others to canvass dormitory floors or student groups. These kinds of activity get people involved in the campaign or movement and guarantee further active support. Sometimes new ad technologies are used to encourage participation. Examples of this kind of participation may include holograms and scratch-and-sniff perfume strips, or free music downloads as part of the ad. We see participation also in the uses of interactive media where prospective customers can "try out" the brand in virtual ways and thus become "presold" on the ultimate purchase of the brand.

During the nominating process and primaries of the presidential campaign of 2004, Governor Howard Dean used the participative interactivity of the Internet to generate previously unheard-of amounts of donations to his candidacy. He used the Internet and a website to generate funds. Remember this was less than 10 years ago and was considered revolutionary at the time. President Barack Obama then used viral marketing to raise funds for his 2008 run for the presidency (Tumulty, 2007). We can anticipate that both parties will be replicating his efforts for the 2012 campaign, and that as

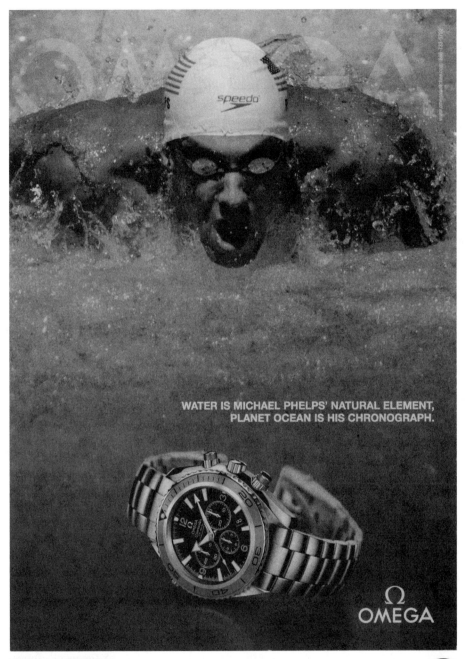

WATER IS MICHAEL PHELPS' NATURAL ELEMENT,
PLANET OCEAN IS HIS CHRONOGRAPH.

Ω
OMEGA

F I G U R E 11.6   Legitimacy is built both for the product and for the U.S. Olympic swim team in this ad featuring the Omega Planet Ocean Chronograph and record-setting swimmer Michael Phelps.

SOURCE: Image Courtesy of The Advertising Archives.

head of the party he will be their guru and model. If you are taking this class during an election year, visit the websites of some of the candidates looking for new uses of interactivity to generate candidate support—financial or other kinds of help. All these participative devices are designed to get the audience involved with the product, candidate, or cause, and even symbolic behavior represents both commitment and participation. Participation fits nicely with the idea of persuasion as a process of co-creation, as discussed in Chapter 1 and elsewhere. As Figure 11.7 demonstrates, participation can include interacting with an advertisement. Box 11.1 demonstrates how one can interact with other commercial messages on media to the point where you can design your own automobile.

Penetration. The **penetration** stage can be defined as the point at which a person, product, or idea has earned a meaningful share of the market, electorate, or other constituency. "Meaningful" might be defined as enough to be noticed by the opposition brand, candidate, or cause. For products, gaining a significant market share is enough to achieve the penetration stage. Chrysler's various innovations, including front-wheel drive, the mini-van, and the 7-year/70,000-mile warranty, enabled it to penetrate the auto market. The market share that these captured forced the competition to follow suit. Later, cars that you can communicate with, that have TV cameras to assist in backing up, and so on, were similar innovations that forced the competition to follow suit. That is a sure sign that a campaign has reached the penetration stage. The old idea that imitation is the most sincere kind of compliment one can get applies here. A successful penetration stage in campaigns for products usually prompts a response from the competition.

Early in the primary campaign season, candidates don't have to win the most delegates to establish penetration. Running third or even unexpectedly strong might be enough. Other indications of political penetration include higher ratings in opinion polls, increases in financial contributions, increases in the number of persons volunteering to help, and larger crowds showing up for campaign events. This was surely the case

with Barack Obama in 2007 and 2008. Following his unexpected win in the Iowa caucuses (the "kick-off" to the traditional primary campaign season), the Hillary Clinton campaign sat up and took notice, and responded to him and his messages, and as his crowds continued to grow it became even clearer that he was a true contender until he finally exceeded Clinton's delegate count. The Clinton campaign responded more and more negatively, even criticizing the remarks of his childhood minister to show Obama's weakness—clear proof that he had penetrated the primary electorate's consciousness. Communication scholar T. A. Borchers (2005) reports that one key to Jesse Ventura becoming governor was his use of e-mail and his website to turn out large crowds on short notice—700 people in the small town of Willmar, Minnesota within an hour.

In ideology-oriented campaigns, penetration is achieved when those in power find that they are barraged by mail or have to repeatedly answer questions about the campaign topic. Other indicators of penetration in these campaigns include large rally crowds that inconvenience supporters of the status quo and increased financial and volunteer support.

Distribution. The fifth and final stage of development, **distribution**, is defined as the campaign or movement's succeeding and rewarding supporters in some way. The candidates now live up to their promises. They signal their supporters that social change is going to occur. Patronage or government jobs are given to supporters to help distribute the rewards won by the campaign. In movement campaigns, persons on the campaign staff or in leadership are appointed to office or positions of power. One problem with ideological and political campaigns is that sometimes the persuaders don't live up to their promises, and this is often the case with propagandistic movements such as Nazism and many of the militant and Jihadist propaganda campaigns like those conducted by Al Qaida. No one got any real rewards following the bombings, unless one considers the promise of life in paradise for the suicide bombers. The potential recruits or lower level supporters of the terror only got internal rewards such as feelings of revenge.

1. Glue page to heavy construction paper and let dry before cutting.

slot
fold
C
fold
fold
slot

2. Fold, slide tabs into slots. Slide wing section into fuselage section.

C
fold
C
A
B
D
E
fold
D
E
fold

A
B
D
E

3. Insert lettered tabs into matching lettered slots.

One of two ways to get your hands on an F-16.

If you think you're too young to fly, cut it out.

Fold. Assemble. And prepare for take-off.

While your paper airplane may not quite reach the speed of sound, use it as a reminder of just how fast the Air National Guard can help you get your future off the ground.

And we're not just talking about a military career. Air Guard training can prepare you for a civilian career in over 200 fields of technical expertise. Every-thing from meteorology to security. Tele-communications to computer technology.

We'll even pay part of your college tuition. What's more, you'll have the chance to take part in exciting adventures that can lead you around the world.

All you have to do is serve as little as two days a month and two weeks a year.

Want to learn more? Call your local recruiter. And find out if you're cut out for the Air National Guard.

AIR NATIONAL GUARD

Americans At Their Best.

88-501

FIGURE 11.7

This ad for the Air National Guard encourages real, not symbolic, participation by cutting out the model F-16 and gluing it together, or by joining the Air National Guard.

SOURCE: Courtesy Air National Guard.

Distributors and users of products can also par-ticipate in the distribution stage by sharing some of the profits from the products, free supplies of the brands that they can turn around and sell, or some kind of symbolic acknowledgment like being named salesperson of the month. Stores are paid

> **BOX 11.1** **Interactive Media and Campaign Participation**
>
>
>
> Mitsubishi recently launched an interactive Internet campaign in which an Eclipse drives from one Mitsubishi banner ad on the screen to another. Then the viewer can take over the car and drive it around the screen. Following the test drive, viewers are invited to play the "Thrill Ride Challenge" game and drive around one of four race courses. Depending on their score, they could win a Mitsubishi flat-screen TV or an Apple iPod. The company
>
> hopes to harvest 20,000 dealer leads from the campaign. Viewers are also directed to a link where they can build their own Eclipse—including options, color, and so forth—and get a price quote (Morrissey, 2005). To see how interactive media can be used to sell products, go to Weblink 11.1. (You can access this and all of the other Chapter 11 weblinks through your companion website for *Persuasion*, Chapter 11 resources.)

"slotting allowances" for devoting some of their shelf space for special offers for the brand. They can get extra discounts for pushing certain products. Dealers also are urged to participate in contests to win prizes and luxury vacation trips by increasing monthly sales. The retailers are given "dealer loaders" or free valuable display containers like wheelbarrows or garden carts in which to display the brand of garden glove and which are theirs to keep or offer as mini-sweepstake prizes for their local customer base. And both dealers and customers can earn prized items such as an NBA Championship warm-up jacket. Devices such as rebates, money-back coupons, and other purchase incentives act as kinds of distribution to customers.

Product-Focused Models

Some campaign models help to describe all three types of campaign, and other models focus on one type of campaign. Let's examine models that are appropriate for and focused on product-oriented campaigns.

The Hierarchy of Effects Model. Advertising and marketing experts Robert Lavidge and Gary Steiner (1961) suggested a model that for many decades has set goals in marketing and advertising agencies. This model assumes that potential customers must pass through a series of stages beginning with initial lack of **brand awareness** and ending with ultimate purchase. The **hierarchy of effects**

model remains as valid today as it was when first suggested (Schultz and Barnes, 1999).

The model has seven distinct stages and employs various communication, advertising, research, and promotional strategies and techniques at each stage. In the first stage, consumers are completely unaware of the product, brand, or service being promoted or of the promised benefits. So the persuader's first task is to identify current patterns of use of similar products, brands, or services using focus groups, surveys, and other research methods, and then to build prospect awareness of their own brand as a superior competitor. (See Figure 11.8.)

In a hypothetical example, suppose the makers of Oreo cookies want to add a new product to the Oreo and Double Stuffs line. They do research using focus groups and observing people eating the regular Oreos and the Double Stuffs. Most people start eating the cookies by splitting the cookie layers in two, licking off the filling, then eating the cookie portion—behavior that had originally inspired Double Stuffs (Fortini-Campbell, 1992). Consumers rate the filling as the best part of Oreos/Double Stuffs and say that a cookie stuffed with a different flavored filling would sell. So they introduce the Double Chocolate Stuff by Oreo. With a consumer-driven product like cookies, the hierarchy of effects model suggests creating consumer awareness of the product and then developing consumer knowledge about it. The brand gets a name, a slogan, and a jingle, and public relations sends invitations to the media for the premiere taste-testing press conference. Then "teaser ads"

FIGURE 11.8   Olcay Gulsen is a Dutch media specialist in building brand awareness in the fashion industry and a former model.

SOURCES: Rick Pushinsky/eyevine/Redux Pictures.

communicate that "Double Chocolate Stuffs are coming soon!" Various promotional devices are used, such as free samples, events, and coupons. As the awareness stage merges with the developing knowledge stage, the ads teach consumers about the brand, and researchers use tests to discover consumers' knowledge level using surveys, mall intercepts, and unaided and aided recall.

In the fourth and fifth steps—liking and preferring—the advertiser uses "image ads" that communicate that status and glamour are associated with the brand by using such tactics as celebrity testimonials. If the brand has competition, the advertiser might use comparative ads or contests with taste tests that demonstrate that Double Chocolate Stuffs are better than the competition's single lemon-filled cookies. Consumers are now aware of the brand and have reason to like and even prefer it. The only task remaining is to convince them to try it. A goal of many persuasive campaigns is to induce trial, and this occurs in the final two stages of the hierarchy or the conviction and purchase stages, where consumers are convinced that the brand deserves a try and then go out and purchase it. Lavidge and Steiner's hierarchy of effects model is but one model that helps us understand the **goals**, **strategies**, and **tactics** of product-oriented campaigns. Let's continue with some others.

The Positioning Model. In their best-selling books, *Positioning: The Battle for Your Mind* (Trout and Ries, 1986) and *The New Positioning* (Trout, 1995), marketing experts Jack Trout and Al Ries offer their **positioning model** as a way to attract prospects. The definition of positioning is to get the brand, candidate, or idea/ideology into top of mind awareness (TOMA) among consumers, voters, or joiners. Having top of mind awareness is defined as being in the consumer's top seven plus or minus two (or five to nine) identifiable brands, depending on the complexity of the product. Trout and Ries advise searching for unoccupied "niches" in the marketplace and then positioning the brand in that psychological space. These niches and appeals to them are almost always processed in the peripheral channel of the ELM. You will find some ways to position a brand in the marketplace at Weblink 11.2. (You can access this and all of the other Chapter 11 weblinks through your companion website for *Persuasion,* Chapter 11 resources.)

Be the First. The first brand to appear in a product class has the natural advantage of being the pioneer in that product class. Lunchables by Oscar Mayer, now a 20-year success story, are such a brand and were initially positioned in the "first" niche in 1990 and continued to stress their "first" position throughout their introductory and subsequent campaigns. Other snack-pack brands followed, but none could claim pioneer status. Lunchables were subsequently able to offer line extensions, or new and improved versions of the product/brand such as Lunchables with a dijon mustard packet and a chocolate mint dessert and later a pizza lunch and a "wrap" version of the brand. Another example of being first, but in this case losing that position, is Blockbuster. It was the first national brand to provide rentals of videotapes and later DVDs, but it neglected to stay ahead of the curve and ignored changes in technology and consumer wants, and thus lost out to Netflix, Redbox, and others. Blockbuster, once a national leader, filed for bankruptcy protection in September of 2010. It now sells for $.08 a share. (Once again, see Weblink 11.2.)

Be the Best. Consumers shop for quality and are usually willing to pay a reasonable price for high-quality brands. This niche is filled by the brand that can claim to be the best in the product category. Swift's Butterball turkey, noted earlier, is one of the most expensive brands, and claims to be best because a full pound of butter is injected into each turkey, resulting in butter-basting during cooking, a feature which leads to the benefits of moistness and good taste. Research shows that Butterball consumers spend more time in the supermarket and buy more premium condiments and desserts, like cranberry relishes or bakery pies, than other brand consumers. As a result, retailers are glad to more prominently advertise and display the brand to extend purchases like these, which usually have a higher profit ratio. Over the years, several imported car brands have tried to claim the best position. Once, Mercedes-Benz seemed to be the permanent "number one." Later, other brands such as Jaguar and BMW also claimed to be best, resulting in more advertising by all three that focused on various features and benefits, all trying to prove that they were "the best!"

Be the Least Expensive. Besides shopping for quality, consumers often shop for price, so being able to claim that one's brand is the least expensive is a definite advantage. A good example is the burger and cola wars which continued until everyone offered a 99-cent menu version of their brand—now slightly inflated. Another is Walmart's "Every Day Low Prices," which eventually included eye examinations, bank services, and $4 prescriptions. Even with high-ticket items such as cars, computers, and camcorders, price wars proliferate. The Geo, Hyundai, KIA, and other brands compete to offer the best value. The airline industry goes through regular cycles of fare wars. Various banks and credit cards engage in price wars related to annual fees, low initial finance rates, and loyalty programs with "points." My credit card/bank no longer charges interest; it pays me 4 percent interest if I use the card 12 times or more per month.

Be the Most Expensive. Status is always critical to some buyers and frequently important to others, and they demonstrate their status by buying the most expensive brand on the market. Coco Chanel, the renowned French clothing designer and perfumer, insisted on marketing only the most expensive brand, never mind if the fragrance was best. We see this trend in the worlds of fashion, jewelry, home decorating, wines, and even gourmet cooking.

Tell What You're Not. Another position for gaining TOMA is telling consumers what the brand is not, thus differentiating it from the competition. On the brink of bankruptcy, 7-Up was saved by claiming that the soft drink was the "Uncola." Dr. Pepper imitated this strategy and also captured a portion of the cola market. Given recent interest in various health issues, numerous brands claim to be fat free or to have no carbs. Pharmaceuticals sometimes advertise that they do not make you sleepy. Some candidates focus on what they are not as well.

Position by Gender.   Many brands target only one gender by positioning themselves as the woman's brand or the man's brand. Virginia Slims and Eve cigarettes are examples. After learning that pro football players and many outdoor workers wear pantyhose in cold weather for warmth, one company considered marketing a male version of pantyhose. Among its strategies were naming the brand Mach-Hose, getting testimonials from outdoor construction workers and firemen, offering it in camouflage colors, and selling it in six packs. Calvin Klein's Obsession for Men and the magazine, *Gentleman's Quarterly,* are obviously positioned by gender, as is the ad for Lincoln Financing Company shown in Figure 11.9. Communication researcher A. N. Valdivia (1997) analyzed product advertising for women's lingerie and discovered both gender and class positioning of competing brands. After looking at catalogs for Victoria's Secret and Frederick's of Hollywood, she concluded that Victoria's is targeted at the female upper middle class while Frederick's is targeted at the male and female lower middle class. Victoria's Secret sounds discreet and Victorian, whereas Frederick's of Hollywood sounds male dominated, voyeuristic, and glitzy. Victoria's address is "London" and a prerecorded English voice answers when you place a telephone order. Frederick's models are unknowns and usually are photographed against simple fabric backdrops. Victoria's models are well-known and usually are photographed in indoor and old-world settings suggesting elegance and class.

Position by Age.   Advertisers often target a given cohort as the most likely prospect for a product or brand. Cohorts can be defined either as those born in the same year or those born in a certain set of years, like Baby Boomers or Generation Xers. Targeting a specific set of potential consumers has many advantages because you can custom-tailor all aspects of advertising and other appeals for that specific cohort. For example, one of the most targeted cohorts is the Baby Boom generation, or persons born between 1946 and 1964, and subsequently their children or the "mini-boomers." The American Association of Retired Persons (AARP) chose a brilliant name to appeal to this cohort and marketed itself based on the benefits of features like lobbying efforts on behalf of retirees, discounts on certain products, group activities like low rates on travel, and information about topics like retirement planning, inexpensive health insurance, and exercise equipment. People are invited to join AARP at age 45 instead of 65, and they receive a subscription to *Modern Maturity* magazine (an aptly named publication). It has the largest circulation in the country, making it an ideal magazine for targeting this affluent and growing cohort. You see the words "retired persons" carry little if any negative connotation. They don't say that you're old or decrepit or anything like that. You're only retired or soon to be and isn't that the thing we are supposed to look forward to? Imagine how the targeting of cohorts by age affects packaging, slogans, message strategies, and media buys. And in an age of advocacy, propaganda, and SNM, it is nice to have someone working for you. In which channel of the ELM are such messages likely to be processed?

Politically Oriented Campaign Models

Although they share some characteristics with product-oriented campaigns, politically oriented campaigns differ in many ways from the marketing of products or brands. For example, there is only limited research data available to candidates, and

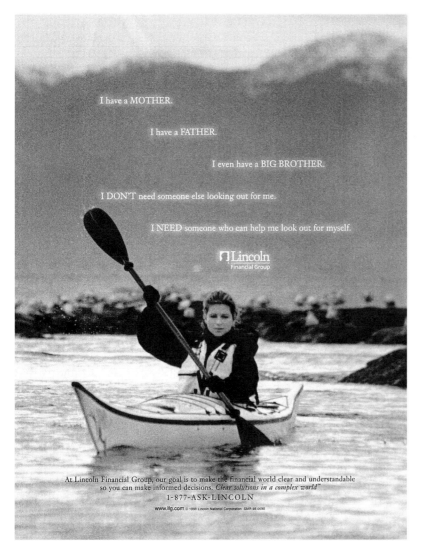

I have a MOTHER.

I have a FATHER.

I even have a BIG BROTHER.

I DON'T need someone else looking out for me.

I NEED someone who can help me look out for myself.

Lincoln
Financial Group

At Lincoln Financial Group, our goal is to make the financial world clear and understandable
so you can make informed decisions. *Clear solutions in a complex world*"
1-877-ASK-LINCOLN
www.lfg.com © 1998 Lincoln National Corporation SMR 98-0690

FIGURE 11.9

In this ad, Lincoln Financial promotes its product by appealing to the independent woman, thus positioning Lincoln's services by gender. Considering the increased number of women in the labor force and in various kinds of investment plans, the strategy seems to be a good one.

SOURCE: Used by permission of the Lincoln Financial Group.

politically oriented campaigns usually must communicate much more sophisticated information than product/brand campaigns, and they have a definite end day—the election—which doesn't happen to products or most idea-oriented campaigns. Let us now turn to developmental models that help explain political campaigns.

The Communicative Functions Model. Communication researchers Judith Trent and Robert Friedenberg (2007) describe four stages that a political campaign must achieve if it is to be successful.

They call their approach the **communicative functions model**. In the first stage, the candidate makes a formal announcement of candidacy and lays some groundwork by mapping out the district, organizing financial committees, developing contacts in key areas of the district, and so on. This stage is called the "surfacing" stage. The main campaign themes are floated and focused, and the candidate's image is tested and promoted. Issues are addressed, position papers are issued, and, with luck, adequate funds are raised. In presidential politics, this process may begin as early as the day after the most recent presidential election. In stage two of this model, the "winnowing" stage, the primary election campaigns serve to narrow or winnow the field of candidates and to focus issues. In 2008, the initial fields of candidates for both Democratic and Republican parties were crowded and support for each was thus spread out. But as more people get involved (as in the participation stage of the Yale model) some of these withdraw or are forced out because of lack of money or appeal. The newcomer supporters or shifters from other candidates may pass out leaflets, attend rallies, sponsor fund-raisers, or perform some activity that gets them involved and this puts pressure on the remaining candidates. In presidential politics, this stage is extremely expensive, even with the matching funds the government gives to candidates. Fifty million dollars or more can be spent in just pursuing a presidential nomination (National Public Radio, 1999). Of course, the costs are smaller with lower offices, but even U.S. Senate primaries cost millions of dollars. This is a dangerous stage for candidates because they might make promises that they later can't fulfill, or they might reveal plans that come back to haunt them. They also might make mistakes, misstatements, or "gaffes" that undermine their legitimacy. A problem for the GOP for the 2012 election was that no one really had surfaced by June of 2011 except Newt Gingrich, who had run and lost earlier and discredited himself by his personal life. By this time in a presidential cycle (about a year from nomination time) there are a usually a whole crowd of surfaced candidates making themselves heard. What did this silence mean? No one thought they could win? Obama was unbeatable? The world was in such bad shape no one wanted the job?

During stage three, the "nomination" stage, the candidate is legitimized in the eyes of the media and potential voters, as are the party's platform and themes. The final stage, the "election stage," is that period between nomination and election day when candidates hectically go from state to state and crowd to crowd saying basically the same thing, over and over again. Here, the use of the press is critical in paid-for political promotions like billboards, signs, bumper stickers, buttons, TV ads,

radio spots, or newspaper ads. Unpaid media coverage such as interview programs or short sound bites on the evening news can be critical. Candidates also use purchased media spots aimed at the right target audience at the right time, in the right way, and in a cost-efficient manner. In 2008, this stage occurred quite early (though informally) for candidate John McCain, and he was able to use the extra time to raise a huge war chest for the general election and could afford lots of media time, signs, travel, and so forth. It all went for naught. The electorate was sick of wars in faraway lands and a rising recession caused in part by them, sick of tax cuts for the rich, and a crooked and largely unregulated banking and mortgage loan industry doing its will, by unmet foreign competition, and by a huge "TARP" bail-out loan program for major financial and manufacturing (i.e., automobile) industries initiated by the Bush administration. Who could run against that eight-year mess?

The advent of the Internet in national politics during the 1996 presidential primaries means that future candidates at all levels must use this method of communicating with their constituencies. This interactive and highly personal medium will only increase in importance in campaigns in the future. Both candidates for mayor of my small town (population 17,000) had webpages with multiple links back in 2000. As we will see in Chapter 13, this use of media is sophisticated and complex. Political campaign messages are probably processed in both paths of information-processing of the ELM. Issue-oriented messages probably follow the central path and require rational thinking and preparation. Image-oriented messages, though they may be rationally thought out, are probably processed peripherally.

In the third edition of *Political Communication in America,* Robert Denton and Gary Woodward (1998) focus on the strategies and tactics used in political campaigns. They say that strategies are the various plans a campaigner forms in hopes of achieving the campaign goal or goals; tactics are the means used to implement the strategies or to put them into action. In political campaigns, of course, there is but one goal— to win election to office—but several strategies could be used to meet that goal, such as winning a primary, raising money, or getting favorable voters registered. Referring to R. Faucheux (1998), Denton and Woodward identify four strategy types that occur in any political campaign. The first is a "message sequence strategy" that addresses the order in which various campaign messages should be sent out. These could be messages about issues, the candidate or the opponent, qualifications for office, and personal beliefs. Second, a "timing and intensity strategy" suggests when messages should go out, and how much effort, money, and other resources should be dedicated to that phase of the campaign. Third, a "mobilization and persuasion strategy" focuses on reaching and convincing groups of voters who might be favorable to the candidate, such as first-time voters, homeowners, minority voters, and the party faithful. Finally, an "opportunity strategy" allows the campaign to respond to the unexpected events, opportunities, or threats that inevitably arise. Examples include revelation of the amount of spending and its source, negative advertising, a candidate's key misstatement, or a scandal involving the candidate or his or her opponent. Several message sequence strategies are possible. The "ignore the opposition" strategy usually means being positive in speeches, news releases, interviews, and comments from the beginning of the campaign until election day and rarely or never referring to the opponent. The "aggressive message sequence" strategy begins the campaign on a positive note but then quickly turns to negative campaigning focused on the opponent's shortcomings. In the final days of the campaign, this strategy is implemented by using a dual-track approach with both positive and negative or comparative appeals.

With the "frontal attack strategy," as can be seen in Figure 11.10, the candidate begins with negative and comparative ads focusing on the opponent's shortcomings, turns positive in the middle portions of the campaign, and then closes using the same dual-track approach as in the "aggressive" strategy.

Several message timing and intensity strategies are available as well. With the "tortoise strategy," the candidate begins slowly, communicating and spending only modestly, and then builds momentum until election day, when a message and spending blitz happens. The "bookend strategy" uses a big, flashy, and expensive opening with a steady buildup and the same blitz strategy used to close the campaign the day before election day. With the "Pearl Harbor strategy," the candidate starts very slowly and is barely noticeable. This is intended to lull the opposition into underestimating the candidate's strength, which then allows him or her to sneak-attack the opponent at an opportune moment.

Opportunity strategies might include "setting a trap," whereby the candidate attacks the opponent over a minor shortfall to set the opponent up to respond in such a way as to lead to much more criticism. For instance, the candidate might accuse the opponent of being financed by an enormously rich father who is trying to buy the election for his spoiled son or daughter. The opponent responds by saying that it is no sin to be successful and to spend money on what one truly believes. Then the candidate springs the trap by revealing that dear old Dad amassed his fortune by exploiting slave labor in China. The "technological advantage strategy" was used in the 1996 presidential campaign by numerous candidates who were aware of the newly emerging Internet and put up sophisticated webpages, which surprised their uninformed opponents.

"Three's a crowd" is a strategy that takes advantage of a crowded field by financing a minor third or fourth opponent who will siphon off votes from the real opponent. The "lightning rod strategy" gets a controversial person to endorse the opponent or introduces a controversial issue to which the opponent can only respond in a negative, controversial, and highly visible way.

Persuasion and mobilization strategies relate to how the candidate deals with voter groups—the party faithful, undecided voters, and those favoring the opponent. Candidates identify their voter base and the undecided voters and then reinforce them with messages and turn them out to vote.

Idea/Ideological Campaigns

In the idea or ideological campaign, neither a product nor a person nor a candidate is promoted. Instead, the persuader wants the audience to engage in or change some behavior or to embrace some

FIGURE 11.10 **Aggressive Message Strategy**
Here the ad strategy is for the candidate to attack the
positions taken by the incumbent Rick Perry thus reducing his/her credibility.
SOURCE: AP Photo/Eric Gay.

religion or other ideology. In the change of behavior option, campaigns might promote preventive measures that individuals might take to avoid contracting STDs. Other campaigns solicit donations to various not-for-profit churches, charities, or other good causes. Idea campaigns urge people to help the environment by recycling aluminum, glass, tin cans, and plastic containers or to practice factory safety or defensive driving. A protest campaign might persuade people to wear black armbands on a certain day to indicate their displeasure with a policy or law. In early 2003, the group Women Against Military Madness (WAMM) protested the

saber-rattling rhetoric of various members of the second Bush administration directed toward Iraq. They held rallies, sold yard signs and bumper stickers reading "Say No! to War with Iraq," and used other tactics to implement their strategies for avoiding a U.S. invasion of Iraq, which we now know happened with disastrous results both economically and in terms of casualties, despite their efforts. Any of the elements in the Yale model help explain the strategies of such campaigns, and some elements of the product/person campaign models can also apply. But other models specifically explain idea/ideological campaigns or social movements.

The Social Movements Model. Communication researchers Charles J. Stewart, Craig A. Smith, and Robert E. Denton, Jr. (2007) define and describe the **social movement model** of idea/ideological campaigns. They maintain that social movements have seven unique characteristics that set them apart from product- or person-oriented campaigns. First, social movements are organized groups of people, with leaders who usually act as spokespersons for the movement. Second, although they are organized, social movements are not institutionalized or recognized by those in power. Third, they attract large numbers of persons and are large in scope either geographically or historically. Thus, pro-lifers would qualify as a social movement, whereas promoting radon-free drinking water probably wouldn't because of its limited scope. Fourth, social movements either promote or oppose social change. There are three subtypes of groups promoting or opposing change. The "innovative movement" wants to totally replace existing social values and norms, and includes movements like gay liberation or radical feminism. The "revivalistic movement" seeks only partial change in society and a return to past values. The "resistance movement" seeks to block instead of favor change. For example, the pro-choice movement wants to keep *Roe* v. *Wade* in effect, and the NRA opposes limitations on the right to own handguns. Fifth, social movements are moralistic, preaching about good versus evil, right versus wrong, or patriotism versus opposition to the government policy. Sixth, social movements encounter opposition from those in power. The power may be held by formal groups such as the military, police, or a regulatory body. This opposition often leads to symbolic and then real violence, as has happened in a number of dramatic cases. For their part, those promoting change might begin by shouting slogans, then move to violence against property, and ultimately against people. Finally, persuasion is the essential tool for attracting new converts, changing people's minds, and ultimately motivating members to take action. The persuasion, verbal or nonverbal, may attempt to use mass media, and it usually includes a call to action on the part of the persuadee.

Social movements also have their own set of developmental stages. Stewart, Smith, and Denton's model of a social movement outlines five stages: "genesis," "social unrest," "enthusiastic mobilization," "maintenance," and "termination" stages. In the "genesis stage," ideologues preach about perceived shortcomings or injustices. These early prophets might go unheard for a long time as they did throughout the Middle East in the second decade of this millennium, but finally, like-minded persons are drawn to these prophets, and the first stage creates a core of devoted supporters. Then, usually, a dramatic event such as a mass rally in the middle of the capitol catapults the issue into the public spotlight. In the "social unrest" stage, growing numbers of people identify with the movement practically daily, and now are agitated by the identification of the devils and gods of the movement, such as the longtime dictatorial president of 30 years. This leads to the third stage of "enthusiastic mobilization" when the true believers begin to convert more and more people and continue to encounter opposition from those in power. These converts are now activists, not merely persons who identify with the movement. Fourth, in the "maintenance" stage the movement adopts a lower profile as the media attention turns to other events, and some success is perceived by converts. These successes dull enthusiasm for and drain energy from the movement, so it must bide its time until a significant event occurs to rekindle enthusiasm. In some instances, as was the case in Tunisia, Libya, and Egypt in 2011, the movement achieves its goal(s), or it may merely wither and die in the "termination" stage. Perhaps supporters lose faith and patience, or the movement becomes outmoded, or its leaders are assimilated into the establishment, or it becomes irrelevant.

The Agitation and Control Model. In their book, *The Rhetoric of Agitation and Control,* John Bowers, Donovan Ochs, R. J. Jensen, and D. P. Schultz (2010) describe several stages in ideological movements that must occur before the movements ultimately fail or succeed. In the first stage, the "petition stage," agitators petition the sources of power such as the government, a corporation, or a school district, making demands or "requests" that slightly exceed what the power source will give up. The power source thus appears unreasonable. The agitators now initiate the "promulgation stage" or the marketing of the movement. Using handbills, leaflets, and rallies, the agitators develop their movement by informing outsiders of the unreasonableness of the power source. At this stage, the movement leaders hope to gain recruits and get publicity that will attract even more recruits, as was the case in 2005 when the American Civil Liberties Union and other free speech groups objected to illegal surveillance of American citizens by the Bush administration and a nationally publicized social movement was born. If promulgation succeeds, the movement moves into the "solidification stage." Now the newly recruited members are hyped up through rallies, marches, and protest songs like "We Shall Overcome" or "We Shall Not Be Moved." They may use salutes and symbols or uniforms. In the "polarization stage," the movement leaders target the uncommitted population. They do this by focusing on a flag issue or person. The reason they are called flag issues or persons is that they epitomize the ultimate enemy or are the most easily recognized symbol of what the movement or ideology objects to or hates. Past flag issues have been the aborting of fetuses, the use of napalm on civilians, the mistreatment of refugees, illegal surveillance of citizens, and the bombing of civilian targets. Flag persons personify the issue. Past flag persons have included President Lyndon Johnson, Saddam Hussein, and President George W. Bush. In local politics, flag persons might include mayors, councilpersons, senators, representatives, or others depicted as the root of the problem. The polarization stage forces the onlookers to choose between us and them.

In the fifth stage, the "nonviolent resistance stage," such tactics as name-calling or rent strikes are used. For instance, police call in sick with the "blue flu," or students occupy a building and claim that they have liberated it. These and other devices call attention to the movement and usually bring some sort of response from the power source,

such as calling out the army or police. Usually, the media will cover the confrontation. Then agitators claim repression or Gestapo tactics. Usually, this leads to the "escalation stage," which increases tensions in the power source. Perhaps threats are made, such as rumors of planted bombs or public displays of weapons. Perhaps some violent act occurs, such as a strike with brickbats and fistfights, a killing or kidnapping, or the bombing of an important building or landmark like the Twin Towers. If the power source represses the movement at this time, there usually is a split within the movement between those who favor violence and those who favor nonviolence. Bowers, Ochs, Jensen and Smith call this the "Gandhi versus guerrilla stage." Usually, the nonviolent segment goes to the power source and argues that, unless they give in, the guerrillas will take over. Violence will escalate, as was the case in Operation Iraqi Freedom when the numbers of bombings by insurgents increased radically as the occupation wore on. Depending on the power source's response, the final stage may or may not emerge.

This last stage—the "revolution stage"—rarely happens, but social movements using the rhetoric of agitation and control have led to revolutions in a variety of places in the Middle East in recent decades. With the world focused on global terrorism and the United States engaged in costly wars, we will very likely continue to see such agitation and control tactics used as objection to the actions of various governments increase. The ability of the agitation and control model to describe, explain, and even predict stages in movements across time testifies to both its validity and its reliability.

The Diffusion of Innovation Model. Some idea campaigns hope to induce people to adopt new practices or change their behaviors, such as following safer procedures in a factory, reducing their intake of red meats and fats, conserving energy, or adopting new technologies like SNM. Everett Rogers (1962) studied the stages through which people approach the adoption of any new technology such as computers, cell phones, e-mail, the Internet, or one's BlackBerry. The stages also occur with adopting new practices such as recycling or changing values such as favoring the hybrid automobile. Rogers's **diffusion of innovation model** also has some applicability to product and person-oriented campaigns. He outlined four stages on the way to adopting change. In the first stage, the "information/knowledge stage," the potential adopter acquires or actively seeks information about the innovation. How does an SNM work? What are its features and benefits? How much will it cost? How have other adopters rated it? How do I adopt it? When people first became aware of the practice of recycling, which was a time-consuming activity with little direct payoff, few persons rushed out and got containers for aluminum, glass, tin cans, newspaper, and mixed paper.

However, being made aware of recycling drew people's attention to various pieces of information like the life expectancy of local landfills and the effects of deforestation on the climate. In the second stage, the "persuasion stage," the potential adopter processes information aimed at inducing him or her to actually try the new product or practice. Those advocating the change might use testimonials from well-known persons who have adopted this product or practice. In the third stage, the "decision, adoption, and trial stage," the potential adopters decide to try the new practice. They get the recycling containers, or they order prescriptions, groceries, books, or other items via the Internet. Then they use the new technology, product, or practice. Sometimes, marketers request that new users respond to the product/brand/practice by completing a rating survey. This technique moves potential adopters into the final stage, the "confirmation and evaluation stage," in which they reconsider the adoption and measure its performance against their expectations. They ask if it delivered what it promised, and was it worth their time and costs. If they continue usage, they then search for information that confirms the adoption.

The Rogers model is helpful in considering campaigns that offer new and innovative practices to consumers and can be especially helpful in persuading culturally diverse audiences as discussed in Box 11.2. With the rate of change accelerating in our information age, we will undoubtedly go through these stages repeatedly. Knowing what is happening in such situations helps put decisions to adopt new practices into a clearer perspective, resulting in wiser choices. Besides these developmental models of campaigns, several other theories help explain the success or failure of a given product-oriented, person-oriented, or idea/ideological campaign.

Symbolic Convergence Theory

Most of us like to affiliate with people with whom we agree and who are like us in Burke's "substantial"

BOX 11.2 **Cultural Diversity in Campaigns**

In 2005, three media and advertising professional organizations sponsored the first National Expo of Ethnic Media to identify how best to target campaigns to the over 50 million ethnic Americans. Soon the number of ethnic consumers, voters, joiners, and donors will outnumber nonethnic ones, thus representing an enormously powerful market segment. Take just one part of this huge segment—Hispanics and/or Latinos. They presently represent an advertising expenditure of $3.5 billion per year, but they are changing. Why? Because by 2020, only 34 percent of Hispanics/Latinos in the United States will be from the first-born generation. The newer generations will be more acculturated, be better educated, will speak English, and probably will be more affluent, according to the Pew Hispanic Center. Today, 88 percent of Hispanics/Latinos under the age of 18 are foreign born. When you combine the Hispanic/Latino minorities with other culturally diverse groups, you get a "New American Mainstream," according to Guy Garcia (2005) in his best-selling book of the same name. What are the implications for politicians, advertisers, and idea/ideological persuaders? What do these numbers imply for other culturally diverse minorities?

ways, and we seek to find communities of agreement or groups of people who share our basic values and lifestyles. This usually requires the merging of my meanings for events and values with your meanings for those same things. Having similar values and lifestyles identifies us as a particular audience to whom advertisers, politicians, and ideologues try to appeal. How do such "communities of agreement" develop?

The first clues to the power inherent in the social creation of meaning came from the work of Robert F. Bales (1970), a professor of sociology at Harvard. His initial interest was in identifying the kinds of verbal interactions in small, task-oriented groups. He noticed that in one category of interaction, group tension was released through the telling of stories. Bales called this category "dramatizes." He began to describe the way these stories or mini-dramas seemed to develop or, as he put it, "**chain outs**" in the group, resulting in what he called **fantasy themes**. At this point, Bales's work caught the attention of E. G. Bormann and his students and colleagues. They had also noticed fantasy sharing in task-oriented small groups and thought that the process of small-group building of reality had a wider application. This wider application of fantasy sharing was ultimately developed by Bormann (1985), his students, and other researchers, and it helps explain how shared meanings begin, develop, continue, and finally motivate us to action. This is known as "**symbolic convergence theory**," and its technique of analysis is called **fantasy theme analysis**. This theory was initially applied to small-group communication. After witnessing the power of the theory and methodology in the analysis and explanation of group communication, Bormann and his followers applied them to interpersonal, corporate, institutional, creative, and organizational communication. For our purposes as students of persuasion, the theory and methodology are ideal for doing audience analysis for product, idea, and political campaigns. When combined with focus group interviews and research techniques like surveys and Q-sort analysis, the theory and method have great power for analyzing the kinds of dramas to which specified groups of consumers and voters respond (Cragan and Shields, 1994, 1995).

A basic premise of symbolic convergence theory is that reality is socially based and symbolically constructed. That means that each of us perceives the world as a result of our interactions with others and our adoption of and addition to the meanings of these interactions using symbols. Second, many of these interactions include stories or narratives, a pattern we have noted in earlier chapters. As we initially hear these stories or fantasies, we ignore them, embrace them, or participate in them. It is in the participative behavior that we create social reality and come together in symbolic convergence. That is, we share common symbols, meanings, and cues to them. A brief example might help here. At the halftime show of the 2005 Super Bowl, Janet Jackson either intentionally or unintentionally exposed her naked breast. The incident got instant and widespread media coverage and triggered thousands of group discussions among the massive audience. One person says, "Well, that family's been messed up since they were kids." Another person chimes in, "Right, just look at her brother molesting kids." A third says, "His goofiness started with that moonwalk thing." The story or fantasy is beginning to chain out or become a shared version of reality. Media reports added to the fire, and when Janet's brother Michael was acquitted of ten molestation charges, another set of "reality links" and "**fantasy links**" probably chained out. The fantasy continued even into subsequent Super Bowl halftime shows with people wondering if the starring celebrity would try to stage some similar stunt. When aided by media coverage, enough of these group fantasies resemble one another and symbolic convergence has occurred.

Borman called these composite fantasies a **rhetorical vision**, which he maintained could become the national purpose of an entire country. Past rhetorical visions in our time include a Cold War between the Soviet Union and the United States, a worldwide terrorism conspiracy, exploitation of the little guy by big oil, and global warming. It doesn't matter what the truth or reality about the event is, it is what people participate in and come to believe that forms our social reality. While there were many who said global warming was just part of the natural cycle of things (including then-president George W. Bush) the rhetorical vision became cemented into reality in an unusual way—through the film/documentary, *An Inconvenient Truth,* by former Vice President Al Gore, who won international recognition and an Oscar. Because we share our inputs and interpretations with others in our social groups, we come to believe them even more devotedly than if we got them from a respected authority. People might ask one another if they have seen Gore's film. Others may discuss it at church choir, bowling league, or fraternity/sorority meetings. If the story becomes widely believed, we have a national rhetorical vision that can motivate nations to take drastic action. We saw this with Nazism, Communism, and terrorism.

In thousands of studies, Bormann, his students, colleagues, and followers identified the operation of symbolic convergence in political and other campaigns, including those using the techniques of propaganda as described in Box 11.3.

This pattern replicated itself in studies of purchasing and joining behavior. The technique was used to generate plot ideas for a popular prime-time comedy series. In political campaigns, fantasy types, favorite topics, themes, or images emerge. Reporters cover the campaigns and develop their own rhetorical vision in which they "dig out the real truth" (Bormann, 1985). One fantasy theme is that of the "frontrunner," or the candidate with the early legitimacy who is focused on by the media, which covers such issues as whether the candidate is showing signs of stumbling, is hiding something, or is acting as a stalking horse for other candidates. Another political campaign fantasy theme is that of the baseball game, with the candidates being in the "early or final innings" or unable to "get to first base" with the electorate. Another theme makes use of boxing images, with candidates being "on the ropes" or "delivering knockout blows" to the opposition, who is just a "lightweight" and not a real "contender." In political and product-oriented advertising, the ad agency puts "spin" on the product by issuing press releases about it, by getting press coverage" for giving the product away to some worthy group, or by emphasizing the product's astounding benefits. Bert Metter (1990), chairman of the J. Walter Thompson USA advertising agency, puts it this way:

> We are in the age of spin. The art and science of creating images is out of the closet.... As spin becomes more common...we've got to deliver more effectiveness.... The agencies with the answers will succeed. Others will have a lot of spinning to do (p. 36).

In product-related campaigns, Cragan and Shields (1995) found various types of individuals who have differing principles and beliefs. Their symbolic convergence tends to happen on one of three "planes" or philosophies. They are the "**pragmatic (or practical) plane**," the "**righteous (or highly principled) plane**," and the "**social (or interactive) plane**." Suppose you want to sell growth-enhancing ingredients to livestock growers, and you

BOX 11.3 **Propaganda and Campaigns**

It is not surprising that campaigns of various types—political, product-oriented, and ideological—might use some of the classic propaganda techniques. Remember that propaganda does several things, like telling one side of the story, stereotyping, and repeating the "big lie" over and over. It uses the mass media and conceals either the source, the source's intent, the technique(s) used, its goal, or the results if successful, and it circumvents the logical process. Enter "People for the American Way" in a search engine. The organization focuses on how Coral Ridge Ministries and others are trying to affect political outcomes in this country. Explore its many and varied links and see how many of the characteristics of propaganda listed in Chapter 1 apply to the work of Right Wing Watch in the links in the right hand column—Politics. There you will find video footage of candidates responding to their tactics. To see how propaganda campaigns for nonpolitical reasons or causes, go to Weblink 11.3.

want to reach those growers on each plane. For the pragmatic cattle growers, you would stress the practical statistics on cost, effectiveness, and increased yield and profits. For the righteous cattle growers, you would stress that the enhancer is totally natural and does not violate any USDA regulations. For the social cattle growers, you would want to use testimonials from other cattle growers to the effect that just about everybody in the know is using the enhancer. Cragan and Shields have used this model to help sell products ranging from livestock estrogen and drugs, to increasing enrollment in private schools, and to training programs for firefighters. Then briefly survey the kinds of activities and beliefs you like or hold dear and discover whether you are a pragmatic, righteous, or social type of consumer. Cragan and Shields also related how such spin operated in idea or ideological campaigns. Symbolic convergence "spin" was used to convince the Iowa legislature to permit riverboat casinos, to recruit physicians to small towns, and to help train firefighter instructors.

We shouldn't forget that symbolic convergence is not limited to political campaigns. Following the train, bus, and subway bombings in London and Spain by various groups of terrorists, the public meaning of the word "terrorism" took on new dimensions. Terrorism was associated with a series of small cells of individuals around the world and not a worldwide organization, which meant no country was safe, not even neutral ones. Perhaps the cells were coordinated by Osama Bin Laden and the leadership of other "rogue nations" that formed an "axis of evil," which justified a "War on Terrorism." Those key words got picked up by the press and soon by the public also, and ultimately emerged into a global rhetorical vision.

REVIEW AND CONCLUSION

All persuasion involves self-persuasion. We must agree to be persuaded and then find good reasons for deciding. Many of these good reasons are already embedded in our conscious or subconscious memory. Clever persuaders identify ways to cue these memories and connect them to a product, candidate, or idea or ideology. Persuaders tune persuadees' ears to the kinds of messages that will be communicated in campaigns seeking new buyers, new voters, or new joiners. The formal and functional characteristics of campaigns that we have explored seem to persist over time, forming permanent patterns. The ever-shifting issues and increasingly sophisticated technologies of product testing, public opinion polling, media production, and direct marketing are a few of the elements of change.

Among the recurring aspects of campaigns is the establishment of formal goals, strategies, and tactics, and the creation of a position or niche in the audience's mind all communicated not by single messages but by a series of messages. There are also stages through which most campaigns must pass, which usually involve a participatory dramatization of the product, candidate, or idea/ideology in which the audience is involved in real or symbolic ways. Then there are the kinds of appeals that unify and recruit zealots for the mass movement and the "chaining out" of rhetorical visions in campaigns/ social movements that ultimately involve mass audiences.

You need to become a critical receiver who makes responsible decisions about which product to buy, which candidate to vote for, and which ideas or ideologies to endorse. These decisions are appropriate only after thorough analysis of the campaigns. Ask yourself how the campaign responds to feedback and what its objectives, strategies, and tactics are. Ask how the campaign positions the product, person, or idea and what developmental stages emerge during the campaign and in what kind of drama you are being invited to participate. When you have answered these questions, you will be ready to make a responsible decision.

KEY TERMS

After reading this chapter, you should be able to identify, explain, and give an example of the following key terms or concepts:

integrated marketing communication

product-oriented

person- or candidate-oriented

idea- or ideologically-oriented

Yale five-stage developmental model

identification

legitimacy

participation

penetration

distribution

brand awareness

hierarchy of effects model

goals

strategies

tactics

positioning model

communicative functions model

social movement model

diffusion of innovation model

chain outs

fantasy themes

symbolic convergence theory

fantasy theme analysis

fantasy links

rhetorical vision

pragmatic (or practical) plane

righteous (or highly principled) plane

social (or interactive) plane

APPLICATION OF ETHICS

A rapidly growing approach to campaign persuasion, whether for product, person, or idea/ideological campaigns, is known as "stealth marketing" or "buzz marketing." It is based on the old adage that the best kind of advertising is word of mouth and is a response to increasing consumer, voter, and joiner skepticism about traditional advertising and to the increasing use of TiVo technology and remote controls to zap television ads. Buzz marketing hires people to engage in "word of mouth" advertising without informing the potential consumer that they (the sources or testifiers) are being paid for telling the consumer positive things about the product/brand, person, or cause being promoted (Ahuja, 2005). It has changed the whole landscape of the marketing and advertising industries. Take a look at examples at Weblink 11.4. (You can access this and all of the other Chapter 11 weblinks through your companion website for *Persuasion,* Chapter 11 resources.)

One of the most vulnerable market segments for this approach is teens, and the "buzz agents" being hired are usually between the ages of 13 and 19. In addition to promoting the brand or service, these agents also do consumer research by asking those they buzz about the competition, their preferences, and so on. Sometimes they give out free samples. Tremor Inc., which is a subsidiary of Procter and Gamble, employs over 280,000 such agents. The parents are informed prior to recruitment that their lucky child has been selected to influence family and friends by joining the "Tremor Crew" and getting paid at the same time. This gets around the parental consent issue. Tremor Inc. has been very successful in marketing the Toyota Matrix, Coca Cola, Cover Girl makeup, and movies like *My Big Fat Greek Wedding*. What are the ethical implications of this type of "honest deception" marketing (Ahuja, 2005)? What are some of the critical issues? Is the practice fair if the consumer doesn't know the word of mouth is paid for? If you were asked to become a part of a Tremor Crew, would you? Why or why not?

QUESTIONS FOR FURTHER THOUGHT

1. Choose a current campaign for a product, person, or idea/ideology. What appear to be its objectives, strategies, and tactics?

2. Define each of the Yale developmental terms. Can you identify examples of the first three stages in a magazine or newspaper campaign?

3. In the agitation/control model, what stage of a campaign or movement is represented when we vote for or against a particular candidate or proposition? Why?

4. What are some ways now being used to position products you use? Candidates running for office? Idea campaigns requesting your active or financial support? Mass movements seeking converts?

5. Identify a social movement that is either going on or seems to be developing. Use the social movements model and agitation/control model to trace its development. Which most accurately describes what is happening?

6. Using Bormann's symbolic convergence theory, explain the same social movement identified in question 5. Which of the methods seems most message-oriented? Which is most audience-related?

7. Which plane or philosophy fits you—pragmatic, righteous, or social? How do you know?

8. Identify several fantasy types in a campaign for a product made popular in the previous decade. Are they similar to those for today's products?

9. Using the diffusion of innovation model, study the development of a new product in the marketplace.

10. Enter the words "buzz marketing" into a search engine and peruse the sites offered there. What do you think of this method? Would you be influenced by it? Why?

11. How might SNM be used in viral or buzz marketing?

12. In which channel of the ELM is buzz marketing processed?

You can access your online resources at the companion website for *Persuasion.*
Log in at **http://www.cengagebrain.com.**

12

Becoming a Persuader

LEARNING GOALS

After reading this chapter, you should be able to:

1. Conduct an analysis of a hypothetical audience using demographics and identifying their needs.

2. Organize the same speech via the three formats of space, topic, and chronology.

3. Identify, explain, and give examples of stock issues used in considering a policy issue such as randomly assigned registration dates being debated on campus.

4. Give a speech using the motivated sequence format and exhibiting good delivery techniques and persuasive language.

5. Explain how you can improve your own credibility.

6. Identify various forms of proof statement in the mass media.

7. Explain the critical effects that the choice of channel can have on persuasion.

8. Explain some of the ways one can persuade better using an SNM.

INTRODUCTION

Thus far, we have focused on receiver skills: how to be a critical, responsible, and ethical consumer of persuasion as the title of this book implies. Aside from lawyers, teachers, politicians, ministers, and a few other professions, few of us are regularly asked to deliver a speech, sermon, or lecture. However, sometimes, we must become persuaders. Luckily, we can take the knowledge we gained about being receivers of persuasion, and apply it to our own targets of persuasion. We can use tactics of intensification and/or downplaying; we can mold our persuasion using process, content, cultural, and nonverbal premises; and we can apply our knowledge of what is ethical in persuasion and what is not. In earlier editions of this text, this chapter has focused on you now becoming a persuader giving a public presentation in the form of a speech. Most of you have already studied some of these principles in a basic communication course. You likely learned to make a persuasive speech and an informative one.

Few, if any of you, have learned much about using social networks to persuade, yet we know the use and growth of these media have been phenomenal since the publication of the twelfth edition of this book. Assuming most of you have had a basic communication course, we will not repeat the principles of creating the basic speech, but will focus instead on using SNM in persuasion. Right now, little is known about how or why or even if these media work in persuading others. We do know they have been influential in raising money for political campaigns and in fostering revolutions in countries where other kinds of communication is under strict government control or censorship (e.g., Tunisia, Libya and Egypt). So let's move forward under a slimmed-down version of persuading using the public speech and move on to what is known at present about persuasion and SNM.

Persuading Via the Public Speech— A Slimmed-Down Version

As a persuader, you'll take your first steps in preparing your message by learning about your audience and shaping your message. Few do this while using an SNM. People may have hundreds of "friends" on Facebook but that is deceiving. Rather than having 50 "friends," someone may have 50 acquaintances, but that's it. Remember that your audience is regularly dealing with a 24/7, networked, and ethically challenged world of advocacy and/or propaganda, so you must be well-prepared, interesting, and above all persuasive, but advocacy and propaganda can happen on an SNM, too. Most persons don't actually stop and plan their messages on an SNM. They usually respond to another person's statement(s) quickly and without much thought, though to be a successful persuader, they probably should follow some of the advice given for preparing a persuasive speech.

There are some differences from the face-to-face persuasive situation. You won't need to choose how to go about delivering your message, which includes choosing the channel (face-to-face, radio, TV, Internet, e-mail, memo, etc.); you also will not need to think about your voice and posture, making eye contact with your audience, gestures, and so on. The lack of such cues makes careful scrutiny of our messages even more important to prevent misunderstandings. Yet you will want to be aware of some common persuasive tactics and how they vary from culture to culture and audience to audience, topics which we will cover in this chapter. Throughout this entire process, you need to ask whether what you are doing is ethical in terms of the models presented by Richard Johannesen in Chapter 2. Sometimes, you need to ask questions about the lasting, larger issues in life—not just how to make the next sale, convince the professor that your answer to the test item is justified, or persuade your friend to accompany you to some activity, and so on. One such question is, "Is what I am being persuasive about likely to have a more negative or more positive effect on my listener's lives? For that matter, will it make for a better or worse world?" Being an ethical persuader means being part of a community larger than yourself in which your persuasion has a potentially positive effect on relationships in the community with which you interact with via SNM.

AUDIENCE ANALYSIS: KNOWING YOUR AUDIENCE

It is easy to assert that persuaders should always know as much as possible about their audience, but it is not always so easy to prescribe specific ways you can get to know them. It should be easier on an SNM since the audience asked to be "friends" with you, and you probably have mutual "friends" about whom you know at least something. One of the best ways to learn about an audience is to listen to them when they persuade, because they will probably use tactics in their persuasion that would seem convincing to them in the persuasion they receive. For example, you may have noticed that I often use narratives and life examples in this book to get you to take my advice or at least pay attention to it. I rarely use statistics or charts and graphs. I am not a numbers person—in fact I have problems balancing my checkbook. Most communication majors are like that. If you want to persuade me, you should probably lace your message with narratives, anecdotes, and examples—not with numbers and charts. I am a "stories" person—I have loads of jokes and stories on hand but no numbers or statistics. So listening to your audience when doing audience analysis is an essential idea. When doing **audience analysis**, I also look at my audience's patterns of processing information in terms of the elaboration likelihood model (ELM). I want to use the central information-processing route when that is appropriate (usually when detailed reasoning is called for), and I want to allow the audience to use the peripheral information-processing route when that is called for (when their responses are more likely to be emotionally prompted from their memory and don't need lots of thought or elaboration).

In other words, you and I will need to do some audience analysis—which is defined as learning as much as possible about the projected audience and what is likely to motivate them. So we'll need to know some basic things like their ages, their majors, the gender split in the audience, their attitudes on the topic, and many other things. We will want to think about what their needs and wants are and what might most effectively move them to belief or action. Study your audience members, observe them, listen to them, and analyze what they say and how they say it. When your parents try to persuade, how do they go about it? What kinds of evidence do they use? What kind of reasoning—elaborate or peripheral? Some people, for example, are most easily persuaded when they think they are the ones who came up with the idea for change. It is best to give such persons several alternatives and let them make the choice—a tactic sometimes called "putting it up to you" or "don't ask if, ask which" by some theorists. In either case, the thing that makes this tactic really effective is that the audience feels as if it "owns" the idea or innovation and is therefore highly motivated to take action or change belief in accord with their "own" ideas. Others are most satisfied with a decision if they see that significant others (perhaps friends, authority figures or experts) have made or are making the same or similar decisions. Bestselling author Robert Cialdini (2007) calls this tool of influence "social proof," which means viewing a behavior or decision as correct "to the degree that we see others performing it" (p. 100). Knowing how your target audience—parents, teachers, your boss, friends, coworkers, and others—persuade will give you a clue as to how to persuade them. This is pretty obvious when you think about it. After all, most people tend to desire to be like others and to go along with what others, maybe the majority of others, are doing. None of your "friends" on Facebook are totally unlike you in all probability. It's why fads catch on or why a candidate for political office gets what is called "momentum" on the road to victory and why some brands seem to be adopted by nearly everyone.

They identify with them. Remember identification from our definition of persuasion in Chapter 1? But is it ethical for the persuader to use such "social proof" to win the day? That depends on the issue, the costs to you and others, and the potential benefits for you and them for following the decisions, actions, or the benefits of the outcome. It is far more important for us as receivers of a message (sensing that a persuader is using social proof to convince us) to ask ourselves whether we should decide or act simply because others have acted in a certain way. The ancients called this tactic *ad populum* or appeal to the populace or the popular. Sometimes the masses are wrong, and we need to forge a different path. Thus, the ethical issue reverts back to where it

should be—with receivers of persuasion. It is certainly true that persuaders ought to be ethical, but unfortunately that is not always the case. We need to be on guard for unethical persuaders and not be fooled by affinity appeals or social proof, which may lead us to follow the advice of persons who only seem to be like us but in reality are not. Recognizing ethical and unethical appeals aimed at us as receivers also helps us to practice good ethical persuasion when we are in the persuader's role.

AUDIENCE DEMOGRAPHICS

When persuasion is aimed at large audiences—in the hundreds, thousands, or more—professional persuaders like advertisers or politicians can use professionally gathered demographics to analyze the audience. In less formal situations like that described in Figure 12.1, one may or even must do a more casual analysis. **Demographics** describe people in quantifiable terms of their shared attributes—their likes, dislikes, and habits, as well as age, gender, education, religious beliefs (if any), and income. If you subscribe to *Outdoor Life*, *Field and Stream*, and *Sports Illustrated*, you likely differ from the person who subscribes to *The Atlantic Monthly*, *Horticulture*, *Organic Gardening*, and *Bon Appetit*.

Both of you would be good bets for catalogs featuring outdoor clothing. Probably neither of you is interested in rock music or MTV. Your affiliations (church, fraternal, or community groups) are another demographic index. (See Figure 12.2.)

Some marketing firms specialize in doing such demographic research and it is sometimes readily available online or in a library. Among the professional databases, census data, state government records such as driver's and fishing licenses, returned warranty cards, and many other sources, are sources in which all of us have been identified demographically in great depth, and some of it easily available even though we are unaware of its existence, as exemplified in Box 12.1. Most of us don't do this kind of in-depth and elaborate analysis of a potential audience, but we can do a lot even with limited

FIGURE 12.1

The subscriber to outdoor magazines is a likely prospect for a Timex Expedition watch.

SOURCE: Image Courtesy of The Advertising Archives.

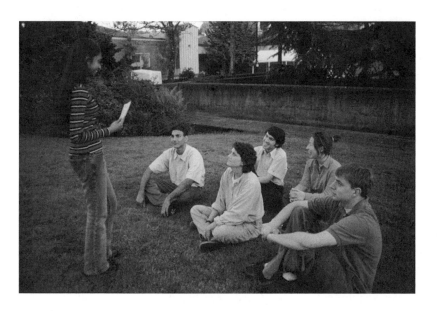

FIGURE 12.2

If you were preparing to speak in an informal situation such as this, how would you do your audience analysis?

SOURCE: © Cengage Learning 2013.

time and resources, as the online advice given above indicates.

Not all demographic or psychological audience factors make a critical difference, so you need to look at them carefully. Age is important if you are discussing tax planning for retirement, but not if your topic is recycling. Other factors such as level of income, political affiliations, and many other factors may be more or less relevant in some situations than others, so spend some time thinking these through.

Once you know some of these key demographic factors for your group/topic/context, the next stage is to explore them in further detail. Sometimes, merely talking to one or two typical members of a group before you attempt to persuade can be helpful in getting to know the audience.

BOX 12.1   **Interactive Demographic Research**

Try entering a word or two describing your audience (e.g., "demographics" and "my space") into any search engine and review the results that appear. You will discover that many users of "MySpace" are between the ages of 16 and 34, are high school but not college graduates, and tend to be enlistees in the Armed Services rather than officers. There are lots of "MySpace" users who have important interests in music and popular culture and are ideal

customers for those products and brands. What other things do you find about them? Now enter the words "Facebook" and "demographics" and see what differences there are between MySpace and Facebook users. Why do you think MySpace asked to be re-categorized from a social network to an "entertainment destination"? Try using the words that describe your audience and explore the results. What do you find about them?

BOX 12.2   **YouTube and Interactive Audience Analysis**

We are all aware of the presence of e-mail spam. Why do you think some spammers pick on you and others don't? How do they know to what you might respond? To get an idea of how detailed audience analysis has become in the interactive age, type the words "audience analysis spam" into the search engine and peruse the many items which appear. Go to Weblink 12.1 and view the three-minute video

there and find out how a group of recent college grads turned out as judged by the groups they fell into while in school. (You can access this and all of the other Chapter 12 weblinks through your companion website for *Persuasion*, Chapter 12 resources.) View some of the other videos available there. How might you use sites like these when you need to do audience analysis?

Any characteristics they share as a group can be useful in shaping your message for that audience. Would it be ethical for you to do demographic research for your presentation? (See Box 12.2.)

Determining Audience Needs

Some audience touchstones are emotional, some logical, some cultural, and some nonverbal. We can do some fairly sophisticated analysis of our target to determine **audience needs**. We might focus on the responsibility of all universities to protect the health of students, faculty, and visitors to sell the idea of no smoking in dorms. Or we could talk about the need of university decision makers to constantly keep up to date with social and environmental issues. Most of the "hot buttons" that help persuade others can be traced back to emotions, memories, and experiences that are common to large percentages of the population.

All audiences have some sets of shared experiences—familiar chords. Most drivers remember taking their first test to get a driver's license (I failed the first time and was too embarrassed to tell anyone). Most of you remember your first visit to the campus where you now go to school and not knowing where the various buildings were located. You all remember hearing about the death of feared terrorist Osama Bin Laden and wondering why those older than you were so much more relieved than you. Stored memories like these can be persuasive building blocks. The next time you need to persuade someone, try to list the experiences he or she likely has had for yourself and see if any of them can be tied into your message. Tony Schwartz (1973) identified what he called the "task-oriented" approach to persuading, which is also useful for audience analysis. He said that it was useless to tell your audience to do something if the circumstances didn't permit them to do it fairly easily. If you want audience members to communicate with their governmental representatives, make it easy for them and have a sample e-mail message ready for them to cut and paste. Try to find out the state of mind of your audience—the board, the sales force, or the job interviewer. What is their likely mood? Will they be relaxed? Will they have doubts? Take these things into account, and design your message accordingly. In other words, ask yourself: "What job do I want this message to successfully complete?" and then sculpt your message to fit the job. Once you know something about your target group and how its members feel about your topic, you can shape the message. People are more likely to recall messages that are well organized, so you need to consider the various forms of organization available to you. This is especially so on SNM like Twitter, since messages must be so short. The volume of messages on Facebook can also make a poorly organized message more likely to be neglected or forgotten.

FORMS OF ORGANIZATION

There are a number of ways to organize messages to make sure they are memorable and persuasive. We will look at five such formats here: (1) the **topic format**, (2) the **space format**, (3) the **chronological format**, (4) the **stock-issues format**, and (5) the **motivated sequence format**. For the first three of these formats, we will use the following example: A student group on my campus wanted to bring back a highly successful filmmaker (a former student) as a guest speaker to discuss the challenges of film production as a potential job opportunity—how to get a job, what kind of pay to expect, and so on. The speaker was even willing to donate his honorarium to the sponsoring student group to be used for field trips, travel to national conferences, and funding for a career day. The persuasive challenge was to convince the Student Association to budget several thousand dollars to pay for the expenses of the visit, such as speaker's airfare, the honorarium (which was being donated to the student group as noted above), his housing and meals, receptions, and so forth. Below are several methods the student group considered for its presentation, which was both in public speaking and written formats.

Organization by Topic

Organizing by topic is most useful when the message you want to convey covers several topics or issues. Here is a list of topics the student group might present in the filmmaker alumni example:

1. His fame and success as a reason to bring him to campus.
2. The kind of role model he would provide.
3. The special opportunity to preview his latest film.
4. The degree to which he is in demand on the speaking circuit.
5. His generosity in donating his fee to the student group in the department.
6. The other benefits to be derived from his presence on campus: publicity for the school, the added programming made possible by his donation, and the career counseling he might be able to give to aspiring student filmmakers.

By presenting these topics with supporting evidence, you give the student government a variety of good reasons to fund the speaker. The topic format is a good choice when presenting specific reasons for some suggested action.

Organization by Space

Organizing by space is a good choice when you want to compare your topic to some larger picture. In the filmmaker example, you might compare the relative cost of the desired speaker to that of speakers invited by other groups. The filmmaker's fee was less than half of that asked by another student group for a less well-known speaker. Further, his fee represented only 5 percent of the total guest speaker budget for the semester, while majors in film programs in several departments represented a higher percent of the student population; thus the fee was a fair use of student fees. Moreover, the student group was only one of more than 20 similar groups in the university; so the fee was not out of line. In the spatial format, you might draw several pie graphs. In one, you could visually depict your speaker's fee as one-twentieth of the pie and label the remainder "Other Speaker Fees." A second graph might show your 5 percent share as only a fraction of the funds allocated to other student groups. Another might show share of speaker fees requested by major. In all these examples, you are using space as an organizing principle.

Organization by Chronology

Sometimes, the essential message in persuasive communication is best relayed by taking the audience through the issues in historical sequence or organizing by chronology so that it is sort of a narrative or story—both of which are very persuasive forms. You might relate the filmmaker's career as follows:

1. In 1975, he became a major in our department and took his first media classes there.

2. Two years later, he transferred to the USC film school, but he still values the basics of filmmaking he learned while he was with us.

3. He made his first picture as an independent writer/producer a year later.

4. It was released the next June, and as a minor summer hit, it recaptured the initial investment plus a small profit.

5. Later that year, the film got several "honorable mentions" at film festivals, and he then signed a contract to make pictures for one of the largest film studios.

6. In the next few years, he turned out several moneymakers and prize winners.

7. Then, in 1982, he made his first blockbuster, and went on to win the Oscar for writing and directing and has followed that up with several more prize-winning blockbusters.

8. He is now one of the best-known writer/producers in Hollywood.

9. His family still lives in the area and his speaking visit might allow him to visit them and for them to attend the presentation, perhaps enlarging the audience with friends of his from his youth, neighborhood, and old friends in general.

As a result of these facts, the committee backed the proposal and provided funding.

Organization by Stock Issues

The stock-issues organizational format is most useful for persuaders who are proposing a change in policy, such as changing the present system of registering for classes to a random one. The name **"stock issues"** refers to the fact that there are three universal (stock) issues that must be addressed when major policy changes are considered. They are sort of like the stock characters in melodrama: the villain, the hero, the heroine, the hero's helper, and so on. Anytime there is a policy change under consideration the stock issues will be discussed. These stock issues are the **need for change**, a **plan to solve the need**, and your proof statements showing that the **plan meets the need** or removes the problem(s) you have raised and recognized. We frequently see stock issues used as content premises in the world of politics and business, and in other policy-making forums as well. As a persuader attempting to bring about a change in policy, you need to begin by demonstrating a strong need for altering the status quo. You have the **burden of proof**. As a receiver, you should also be aware of the stock issues. Anytime you are the target of persuasion focused on policy change, identify which side of the debate is suggesting change. That will tell you who has the burden of proof. In the case of the random method for class registration, the side promoting it has the burden of proof. They would need to establish the need for change by citing symptoms of the problem, such as some transfer students getting no requested classes in their first semester. You should research specific instances that demonstrate to the audience that students are suffering something unfairly, are losing something, or are in danger of losing it. In terms of the FUD (fear, uncertainty, and doubt) model mentioned in Chapter 4, you should create fear, uncertainty, and/or doubt in your audience's mind regarding the unfairness of present registration policy in order to establish a need for change. Tie the symptoms of the problem being considered to a cause that, if removed and replaced, will solve the problem. For instance, you might state that there is a need to ensure fairness for transfer students in order to encourage future transfers to select your school. Next, present a reasonable alternative or plan to the status quo—the plan or the new policy. You are suggesting a totally random basis for class registrations, but what will that do to those expecting to graduate on time? One way to do this is to show that the plan has been successful in other places. Perhaps a random registration policy has been adopted at a neighboring university with great success. Again, use the Internet to help you find examples. This is called "arguing from precedent," and it is a powerful tool to the persuader. Still another way is to use expert testimony to the effect that the plan for change has a reasonable chance of succeeding and in fact increasing patronage or profit. At each stage in the stock-issues organization, you can usually expect a rebuttal. In some cases, it will be openly stated, as in a policy debate within your student government. If you are giving a speech covering all three stock issues—need, plan, and plan meets need—anticipate such rebuttals and be ready to counter them in your own question-and-answer period. You might also short-circuit anticipated rebuttals by presenting a two-sided message in which you state the anticipated rebuttals and answer them then and there, prior to them even being brought up. This deprives the opposition of an opportunity to impress the audience with its rebuttal and shows you to be a fair persuader at the same time.

Organization by the Motivated Sequence

Another organizational pattern, one that resembles the stock-issues approach, is the motivated sequence format, suggested by communication scholars Alan Monroe, Douglas Ehninger, Bruce Gronbeck, and R.E. McKerrow (2000). This format uses five steps to get persuadees to attend to the message, to feel a need to follow the persuader's advice, and, most importantly, to take action related to the advice. The motivated sequence is an especially successful pattern when used in sales, recruitment, politics, and many other contexts where one needs audience members to take a specific action such as making purchases, joining, or donating. The first step—the attention step—aims at capturing the attention of the audience. If you don't get your audience interested at the beginning, you'll never get them to pay attention to the rest of the message. You could begin your message with a question, a startling statistic, or a fear appeal. Or you could use a quotation, a joke, or an anecdote—a brief incident or cliché that makes the point. A good example of the anecdote relates to the umpire who was asked if he called strikes and balls the way he saw them or the way they were. He responded, "They ain't nothing until I calls 'em." That story could make a good beginning to many issues where the judgment of others (umpires of a sort) is critical.

Other approaches are to make an important announcement in the first few moments of the message, begin with a narrative or story, or use a visual aid. The audience may process the attention gaining emotionally or in the peripheral channel of the ELM, but you want listeners to process more of your claims centrally. In the second step of the motivated sequence, you try to convince the audience that they are losing something, are about to lose something, or could be gaining something they are missing. This is the need step (as in the stock issues approach), and it can be tied to the attention-getter.

Steps 3 and 4 are the visualization and satisfaction steps. Here you give examples that tie directly to the audience and make them feel as if this issue will affect their lives. Here is a good place to use individual data such as testimony from persons like themselves, or some other form of proof to induce the audience to visualize what life will be like for them if they follow your advice. For instance, if they invest part of their student loan in inexpensive student housing such as a mobile home, they will be able to build up a nest egg for the future from the savings over a fraternal, dorm or apartment for their college days. Alternatively, you might take the opposite tack by pointing out what life will be like if they don't invest in the mobile home and instead graduate with the burden of student loans at high rates of interest that may take years to repay. As a consequence, they will graduate without the experience of having been in business for themselves, and, most importantly, without a nest egg to build their future on. Following this visualization step, you can then offer some way to satisfy the positive need or to avoid some negative consequences—for example, showing them how easy getting a student loan is, how little is needed for a down payment on mobile homes, and how little initial upkeep is needed.

Finally, the persuader needs to ask the audience to take a definite, specific, and realistic action step. It probably will do little to no good to ask audience members to alter their attitudes on the topic. They must show that they have changed their attitudes by doing something. Asking for change is different from providing good reasons for changing an attitude. Attitudes are fickle—it is hard to know whether an audience has really changed their behavior. It is far better to give the audience specific action-type things to do, such as flossing to avoid tooth decay or saving energy by turning down the thermostat. Point out to them that making a wise real estate investment, and graduating with no debt and a handsome nest egg is easy; the first step is to apply for the student loan and consult a mobile home park about costs and their own eligibility for owning one. In one research study, people given a booklet with specific action steps to cut electricity consumption registered less use of electricity on their meters in the following two weeks than did those not given the specific action steps (Cantola, Syme, and Campbell, 1985). Again, if you want the audience to write to their elected representative, it is a good idea to have a petition on hand that members can sign or to announce the phone number and e-mail address of the legislator's local office and perhaps a sample e-mail or note. After all, phoning or e-mailing is much easier

than writing a letter, especially if you have to start by finding an address. Of course, most politicians have a Facebook site where you can also visit and voice your opinion on issues. This would probably be very effective since most of their "friends" are likely supporter/voters.

A related model for making a persuasive appeal is called the **AIDA** approach—short for attention, interest, desire, action. In this model (as in the motivated sequence), the first step is to capture the audience's attention using any of the tactics cited earlier (i.e., startling examples or statistics, narratives, or quotations). In the second step, the persuader's goal is to heighten the audience's interest in his or her topic or proposal. This might be done using a satisfaction or a visualization process, as in the motivated sequence. Or the persuader might tell how many persons have already tried the product or procedure and found it to be useful, or point out unforeseen problems with continuing the present practice, or note the increased revenues, votes, or other signs of success. Once attention and interest have been gained, the next task is to create a desire or need in the receivers to purchase the product or service, vote for the candidate, take the action, or follow the advice. In product-related persuasion, this usually is done by providing some product benefit or product promise. For example, Chrysler was the first auto company to advertise built-in air bags for the front seat and side doors. The obvious benefit of this feature was that it could save lives in an accident. In its action step, Chrysler asked the customer to go to the nearest Chrysler dealer to learn more about the air bag and to take a test drive. Of course, the purpose of the visit and test drive was to expose the prospect to the product and to let the salesperson try to make the ultimate sale (which usually follows a test drive).

Rank's Desire-Stimulating Model

Hugh Rank (1982) (whose intensify/downplay model was introduced in Chapter 1) has offered a simple four-part model for creating the kind of audience desire needed to cause the audience to take the requested action step that is part of all of the forms of organization noted above. His techniques are not a method of organizing a presentation. Instead, his techniques and examples relate to product promotion, but they can be easily adapted and used in other kinds of persuasion such as you might face in the future and as discussed in all of the forms of organization addressed in the preceding section. Rank says that persuaders can use four kinds of desire-stimulating tactics with this model (see Figure 12.3). First, they can promise the audience's security or protection by demonstrating that their advice will allow the audience to do one of two things: **keep a good** they already have but might be in danger of losing, or gain the possibility of **getting a good**. Politicians frequently point out all the funding they have brought to their home districts (e.g., road funds, increased security programs), each of which is considered a "good," and then claim that their reelection will mean keeping this good flow of positive programs. The other approach to motivating persons is to make them aware they are not taking advantage of an available good. It might be an inexpensive online account for buying and selling stocks and mutual funds, or something as simple as trying Jell-O's No-Bake Cheesecake—the ideal dessert to take along on a backpacking or wilderness canoe trip. If audience members have not tried the new, then telling them about it might motivate them to acquire it.

If you notify them via an SNM, they are likely to act since you will have similar interests.

A third desire-stimulating tactic relates to either **avoiding a bad** (or preventing an uncomfortable situation, problem, symptom, or feeling), or by following the persuader's advice on how to **get rid of a bad**, or experience relief from it. For example, you probably would consider reducing credit card debt a good thing to do, but at the same time it is good advice to never get the credit card debt in the first place. Rank called these approaches the "prevention" and "relief" appeals. Advertisers often promise that their products will prevent the embarrassments of bad breath, body odor, or dandruff; or they will provide relief or help avoid headaches, heartburn, flyaway hair, acne, and other problems. Such "scare and sell" approaches can also be used in non-product persuasion. Recently, universities and school districts have had to reassure both students and parents that their campuses, including all school buildings and grounds, are safe and secure because of the presence of security devices and increased security personnel on duty and in a variety of ways (e.g., bicycle patrols and metal detectors). The idea is that these precautions will prevent killings, such as occurred on my campus on Valentine's Day, 2008, and elsewhere in the nation's colleges, universities, and even in the public schools. These actions demonstrate that the school board or university trustees are responsible and credible and are genuinely concerned with student welfare; therefore, that university or school is a good place to send one's kids. In other words, sending them there is a good way to "avoid a bad" that seems to be becoming ever more prevalent.

The other kind of advice is involved when we already have a problem and we want to get rid of it, as in the case of reducing credit card debt. The persuader might advise converting all of one's credit card debt into a single card (watch for the zero balance offers and then pay at least the minimum but on time) and then cutting up all other cards and placing a reminder strip of duct tape on the card to "tickle" your guilt at ever using the card. Or they might advise taking out a relatively low interest account from one's credit union (if you're not already a member, it's easy to join one) and using

To keep a "good" (protection)	To get rid of a "bad" (relief)
To get a "good" (acquisition)	To avoid a "bad" (prevention)

FIGURE 12.3 Rank's model for ways to create desire in audiences.

SOURCE: © Cengage Learning 2013.

the loan to pay off credit cards while retaining only one for emergency and needed purchases. You can easily think of bad things that most persons would want to get rid of in most situations, occupations, and circumstances, and these can form excellent topics for persuasive speeches or presentations. Remember to do careful audience analysis and to organize your presentation in such a way as to prompt the desired action step.

FORMS OF PROOF

People want good reasons for changing their attitudes, beliefs, decisions, and especially their behaviors or actions. The proofs required for taking action steps, even good ones, are always the most demanding and your audience will be no different. You must convince them that your suggestions or proposals make good sense and are at least worth considering. Let's look at the forms of proof available to persuaders like you and discuss how you can use them to prompt audiences to change attitudes or take action.

Statistical Evidence

Sometimes the most effective proof or support is convincing **statistical evidence**. For instance, an important goal of some potential car buyers is to get a model that gets good gas mileage. In this case, EPA data will probably help persuade them to choose a car model more effectively than will a salesperson's reassurances that the car is a real gas saver. Statistics also persuade best when they are simple and easy to understand.

When you decide to use statistics, make them clear and provide a reference point for the numbers. For instance, if you are warning persuaders about the severity of the U.S. national debt, make it real to them. Don't just tell them how much the debt is. Tell them that interest on the debt amounts to more than $100,000 for every man, woman, and child in the

country. Or tell them that the debt has doubled or tripled since the last administration. In other words, make the statistics really mean something in relative terms. Give them some measure against which to compare or evaluate the impact of your statistics.

In recent years, there has been much concern about the proliferation of the use of plastic containers (especially for drinking water, which is readily available from drinking fountains in most instances, and most of which simply comes from the public water supply). In fact, some cities have put a tax on such bottles to prevent them being discarded in landfills (reducing their life expectancies) or tossed away creating dangerous pollution—particularly in our oceans. If persuading on this topic using statistics, make them meaningful: "It will take a more than two years to clear the Pacific Ocean of algae-gathering, aquatic life-destroying empty plastic water bottles that are being thrown away each year;" or "We are falling ever more behind in cleaning our precious natural resources of these useless containers and we are fouling the future. After all, more than 90 percent of plastic water bottles contain nothing but tap water, so refill yours at the nearest water fountain and help save the planet!"

Narratives and Anecdotes

Earlier, we noted the power of drama, stories, and jokes. **Narratives** make examples come alive and real and also make them easy to recall, relevant in personal terms, and easy to relate to. The story of a person rising from rags to riches probably persuades more people than any set of statistics of the percentages of successful start-ups or franchise operations ever could. A former professor of mine used to observe that an effective narrative can carry a lot of persuasive freight. In order to persuade my advertising students of the power of the one word, "free!" in advertising (and hence to keep it in mind when advising future advertising clients), I use a simple narrative. I tell about how the Cabela family and its widely distributed outdoors catalog and several retail outlets became so successful by simply using the word "free" wisely. Mr. Cabela began in the 1950s by purchasing hand-tied trout flies from Japan at a fraction of a penny each. He advertised them in newspapers in trout country using an initial offer of: "Five Hand-Tied Trout Flies—Only $0.25!!! Free Shipping and Handling," and he got some orders. Notice that "free" was offered for shipping and handling—things that no one can touch, feel, see, hear, or taste. But the venture didn't really take off until Mr. Cabela changed his ad to attach "free" to touchable things—the flies. The new ad read, "Five Hand-Tied Trout Flies—Absolutely Free!!! Shipping and Handling—only $0.25." The offer was really the same except for the way the word "free" was used. This narrative not only persuades my students but also persuaded several of my advertising clients to include the word "free" in their ads.

Testimony

We usually suspect people who attempt to persuade us using only their own feelings or opinions. They could easily be simply biased in one direction or another. This is why the **testimony** of another or secondary witness (or more) is valuable. Of course, expert testimony is the best kind, but even unqualified testimony, delivered sincerely, has powerful impacts on receivers. As you plan your presentation, go back to your original audience analysis and try to determine what kind of testimony your audience will most appreciate and believe. Ask yourself who or what kind of people would they most likely believe. In other words, since testimonials act as a kind of social proof (to use Cialdini's term), pick the kind of person whom the audience would most likely feel attracted to and would feel as if they were friends with or could become friends with. We tend to believe people who are like us socially, intellectually, and in terms of lifestyle. Most ads that use testimonials will use persons or celebrities whom they (the audience) would like to be friends with in real life. Choose your testimony with the same kind of things in mind—"birds of a feather flock together" is a good rule of thumb. When using testimony on SNM, remember who your readers are and select accordingly.

Visual Evidence

Walk into any store where a salesperson or a videotape is demonstrating a food processor, a pasta machine, or a recipe for using some unusual kind of vegetable, and you will see the power of **visual evidence**. The many television offers for various cooking gadgets also testify to the power of the demonstration. Ron Popeil has made millions of dollars using the technique, beginning with his Pocket Fisherman, continuing with his Veg-o-matic, Ronco glass and bottle cutter, and various other unlikely kitchen devices, such as his current rotary oven. Much of the information offered in the demonstration is processed in the peripheral channel of the ELM. "Seeing is believing" is the cliché that is proof of this fact.

Visual persuasion also can be used—and misused—in political news coverage and all kinds of advertising—especially where we see before/after formats (Simons, 2001). You can probably come up with visual aids of your own (e.g., posters, charts, graphs), and you may have presentational skills that can use computerized visual aids like PowerPoint. A critical thing to remember with all visual aids that you use in persuasion is this—the visual always draws attention from what you are saying, so plan to reveal your visuals as you use them and do not—repeat DO NOT—show or distribute them prior to when you are going to talk about them—do it during or afterward instead. If you do it before, you will lose your audience immediately. I can't tell you how many PowerPoint presentations I have seen where the speaker reveals the point he or she is trying to make prior to trying to make that point, and as a result they lose the audience's attention. After all, why pay much attention to what the speaker is saying if you have already read what he or she is going to say? Instead, reveal your visuals—graphs, pictures, PowerPoint slides, or whatever, slightly after or during the point you want to make. That way you keep the audience focused on you (where it should be after all) and not on the visual evidence, which is just to make things easier to remember or to take notes on. The visual evidence then becomes reinforcement of what it is that you have just said.

Of course, actual demonstrations of products are not always feasible, but persuaders can develop various kinds of visual evidence (one student brought a backpack and gear to demonstrate how to pack for a canoe trip) to help the audience understand the problem. Visuals should be large enough that everyone can see them (e.g., a postage stamp would be too little!). They should also be simple, because complex charts will only confuse the audience. For example, a student successfully promoted a trip to Jamaica sponsored by the student association by using simple travel posters, large pictures of local cuisine, easily seen cutouts of sandy beaches, and other images of tropical life to motivate her audience.

Keep visual evidence simple or unobtrusive. Don't let it overtake the audience, as it did when one student brought in his entire sets of camping, canoeing, and fishing gear for a speech. It might be better to use drawings or only a few examples of the gear.

Another student wanted to tell about how to fend off an attacking dog. She actually brought her dog to class and had it pretend to attack while demonstrating how to fend it off, but the dog unfortunately had an "accident" during the speech, thus ruining all of her careful preparation. As noted above, if you plan to use graphs, charts, and/or informational handouts in your presentation, be sure to hold the handouts until the end or they will get all of the audience's attention and you will have none, thus destroying the effect of all of your work (go to Weblink 12.2). (You can access this and all of the other Chapter 12 weblinks through your companion website for *Persuasion,* Chapter 12 resources.)

Comparison and Contrast

Sometimes it is difficult to put problems in perspective, but we know that **comparison and contrast** work from thousands of "before/after" ads and presentations we have seen or heard. People tend to see issues from single viewpoints and then judge them inaccurately. For instance, how big is the problem of disposing of your old cell phone or other small batteries in landfills? Most people simply toss them into wastebaskets or dumpsters. They don't know how this small disposal compares with the problem of the disposal of auto or flashlight batteries. It is a little difficult to fully understand, so persuaders should provide something with which to compare or contrast their point about small battery disposal, like comparing the quantity of pollution from one discarded cell phone battery compared with one discarded flashlight battery, compared with a dry cell. As another example, it doesn't help the audience much to know that OPEC decided to increase crude oil production by 550,000 barrels per day. It will be more meaningful to mention that this is an increase of 20 percent over previous production level. Or tell your audience that the increased production will reduce the price of a gallon of gas by as much as 25 percent—that will mean even more to them than the number of barrels of oil. Or compare the gas mileage of the new gasoline/electric-powered hybrids with that of other fuel-efficient car models.

BUILDING YOUR CREDIBILITY

All the evidence in the world, organized perfectly and delivered well, will not persuade if listeners do not trust the persuader. In matters such as persuading the boss to give us a raise, **credibility** is a key factor. What makes some people credible and others not? How can we build our own credibility before and during persuasion? In Chapter 1 and elsewhere, we discussed the idea of credibility using Aristotle's ideas about the reputation of the speaker, the speaker's delivery during the speech, and the audience's response to the speaker's image.

In more modern times, ethos or credibility has translated into several dimensions. We roughly equate reputation with the known expertise or knowledge level of the speaker. For example, when in research studies an identical speech is attributed to clearly labeled experts in some cases and to novices in others, the "expert's" speech is always rated as more persuasive than the "novice's." Effective delivery is related to sincerity, dynamism, and charisma and these dimensions of credibility rely on your delivery in large measure. We don't believe speakers who cannot maintain eye contact or those who are sloppily groomed, and tall speakers have more persuasive potential than do short ones. Further, speakers with an animated delivery persuade more effectively than do speakers who are frozen at the podium. Exciting language usually helps make the speech more credible, and a relaxed but firm posture is more credible than a stiff or sloppy one. Most of these points seem obvious, yet they are overlooked daily by sales reps, politicians, spouses, teachers, students, and parents. Here are some examples from everyday life in which the elements of credibility can be used.

Trust

We **trust** people for many reasons. We trust them because they have been trustworthy in the past, because they have made direct eye contact, and because they have a calm voice. We also try to give off trust cues. We look at our persuadees directly; we try to sound sincere; we remind our audience of our past record for trust; and we refer to times when it would have been easy to break that trust. You might, for example, remind your boss of the many times when she was out of town and you could have slacked off but didn't. Or you might remind your parents of the many opportunities you had to party but studied instead. All these devices help build credibility. Take a minute and make a list of why the audience should believe you and then mention those reasons at the very outset of your presentation. Here is a simple example: "I have taken over

a dozen classes in this major and had an internship at a prestigious ad agency over the summer, so I learned a lot about the ad industry that might be of interest to you."

Expertise

How do we know whether someone is a true expert on something? Generally, we look for **expertise** in past success at a task—at their record. If a person was a good treasurer for the fraternity or sorority, he or she will probably be a good treasurer for the student government. You can also signal expertise by being well-prepared and by demonstrating knowledge about the topic. Being willing to engage in question-and-answer sessions when you have finished speaking also communicates knowledge and expertise. Even if you do not have direct expertise on a given topic, you can "borrow" it by referring to known experts in your presentation. It is always useful and ethical to refer to your sources' background so receivers can judge the credibility of their testimony.

Dynamism

Dynamism is an elusive quality. It is sometimes related to physical appearance, in that attractive people tend to hold attention better than less attractive persons. Attractiveness or charisma probably cannot be developed much. However, many people who aren't particularly attractive are nonetheless persuasive and dynamic. Dynamic speakers seem to take up a lot of psychic space—they have stage presence. You can project a dynamic image in several ways. One is to speak with authority—project your voice, maintain appropriate volume, and choose words that indicate certainty. Try speaking a little more rapidly than you do in normal conversations—about 125 words per minute instead of 90—and you'll be able to cover more information as well. Good posture and good grooming also signal dynamism, as do appropriate gestures, facial expressions, bodily movement instead of being riveted to one spot, and direct eye contact with various areas of the audience and not a point at the center back of the room just above their heads.

WORDING YOUR MESSAGE

Stylistic speeches and exciting language choices persuade better than dull speeches. How do persuaders develop style in their presentations? What kinds of factors make some speeches, advertisements, or other persuasion memorable while other presentations are quickly forgotten or even ignored? At the very least, use the thesaurus function on your computer and work at developing a varied and interesting vocabulary.

Varied Vocabulary

Most of us need to improve our vocabularies. You should try to rewrite your speeches using word variety to make them livelier, flashier, more dramatic, or more humorous. It helps to develop an interest in puns and other wordplay, as they can help you get the attention and earn the goodwill of your audience. Study the eloquence of great speakers from the past. Pay attention to the language used in government news releases, by politicians, and in advertisements. Try to learn a new word a day and, as noted above, use the thesaurus feature on your computer.

Figures of Speech, Alliteration, and Assonance

Enhance your style by using appropriate **figures of speech** at the right time. We discussed several in Chapters 5 and 6. Metaphors and similes help your audience visualize a point. The audience ties the information to the metaphorical structure and then remembers the information better as a result. Alliteration, the repetition of consonant sounds, and assonance, the repetition of vowel sounds, also enliven style. Both create a kind of internal rhythm in the message, which makes it more lively and memorable. We see both alliteration and assonance in "A portable phone system? Gee! No, GTE." Both devices help improve your style.

Vivid Language

Choose **vivid language** to catch your audience's interest. Although vividness can be overdone, it is more frequently overlooked in favor of dull and uninteresting language. Which of the following is more vivid?

> I'm offended by your representation of lutefisk. It is not rubbery!

> Lutefisk may be "a rubbery and repulsive ethnic dish" to the socially deprived, but to the properly initiated, it is the nearest thing to ambrosia this earth has ever produced.

While this may not be the most "vivid" language, Box 12.3 may lead you to websites that will help you discover vivid language to use in your persuasive efforts.

BOX 12.3   **Vivid Language and Propaganda**

Go to Weblink 12.3 and learn about the many figures of speech, tropes, and other types of vivid language and how they've been used and continue to be used in various kinds of communication including propaganda, copywriting, and more. (You can access this and all of the other Chapter 12 weblinks through your companion website for *Persuasion*, Chapter 12 resources.) To learn how vivid terms like "shock and awe" were related to a poetry conference promoted by the First Lady, Laura Bush, and how the poets became a force of propaganda themselves, go to Weblink 12.4. Increasing your vocabulary of vivid language will help make you a more convincing and interesting persuader. You don't need to become a propagandist—you can just be an effective advocate for worthy causes. Vivid and colorful language helps make a persuasive presentation memorable and effective. Developing your vocabulary arms you with more vivid and persuasive language. Familiarize yourself with famous quotations, which you can find by a subject search on any Internet search engine. Just enter the words "famous quotations" and you will find what you're looking for. There are also websites dedicated to listing quotations by category.

Concise Language

A good way to ensure that you are using compact and **concise language** in your presentation is to script it. Then go back over it and pretend you are paying 50 cents per word to send it by telegraph; see how much excess baggage you can cut. Don't try to memorize it and deliver it word for word, but try to boil it down and "tell" it rather than "read" it to your audience. You can come up with more concise language that way. Straightforward statements are usually the most effective ones for your audience to absorb. Make your major point as a concise assertion or frame it in a provoking question; for example, "We need to put a tax on all plastic water bottles to encourage their proper recycling or reuse." Then follow up with elaboration: "Most plastic water bottles are discarded into landfills, thus cutting the life of the facility and costing us all more now and in the future." If you try to say everything in the opening sentence, you will confuse your audience. The use of concise language also will help build your credibility and will improve the organization of your presentation.

Parallel Structure

Parallel structure uses similar or even identical wording or sentence structure to make a presentation memorable. For example, in a speech to the American Legion, former president Bill Clinton once said, "I am not the only American whose life has been made better by your continuing service here at home. From baseball to Boy Scouts; from keeping veterans hospitals open to keeping kids off drugs; from addressing homelessness to preventing child abuse to instilling a deep sense of patriotism into still another generation of Americans, a grateful nation owes you a debt of gratitude." His repeated use of the "from ... to ..." format provides parallel structure and symmetry in the speech. The idea behind parallel structure is to build audience expectations. For example, Cicero once said, "Ask not what your country can do for you: rather ask what you can do for your country." President John F. Kennedy used almost exactly the same words in his inaugural speech in 1960.

Imagery

Imagery appeals to our senses. Perhaps you can't bring the smell, taste, touch, sight, or sound of something to the audience, but you can use words that conjure up sensuous memories. It might be of a "tall, cool glass of chilled beer dripping with beads of perspiration" or the "fragrant smell of Mom's pot roast, ready to fall apart, with its juices making a savory gravy that starts your mouth watering." A famous salesman once said, "Don't try to sell the steak; sell the sizzle." Think about the sensory experiences your audience has had that relate to your topic and that you can evoke. See Box 12.4 on using interactive sites to improve your sensory language. For example, "I'm sure that all of you have seen what a mess discarded plastic water bottles make. But you can't

---

BOX 12.4   **Interactive Exercises for Language Improvement**

Want to try fun and easy ways to improve your vocabulary? Once again, the Internet is the tool of first choice. Initially, go to Weblink 12.5 where you will find a wide variety of multiple choice exercises on the proper word(s) to use in various business situations. (You can access this and all of the other Chapter 12 weblinks through your companion website for *Persuasion*, Chapter 12 resources.) Even if you are planning on a nonbusiness occupation, working your way through exercises on word variety for emotions like "anger" or "happy" can help improve your language variety. They'll even put you on a weekly e-mail short course to help you improve further. For more advanced vocabulary building, go to Weblink 12.6 where you will find a host of interactive word puzzles, learn Latin roots so you can decipher new words, and see numerous videos hosted by current television personalities.

BOX 12.5   **Interactivity and Developing Humorous Examples**

If you have been asked to or have volunteered to make a public speech or other kind of persuasive presentation and want to use a few humorous examples to liven up your presentation, go to any search engine and enter the word "humor" and the topic of your speech. Keep surfing until you find what you want. If you have difficulty, think of a synonym for your topic and enter it. I tried it with the topic "bad breath" and found a number of humorous lines (e.g., "It was the onion dip, wasn't it?") as well as visuals (e.g., two elephants fighting head to head with the caption "Hey Joe! Did you ever try mouthwash?"). Using humor loosens your audience and gets your audience involved in your topic. It's memorable, too.

FIGURE 12.4

The trapeze artists seen in the cartoon face broken expectation, which accounts for the humor in the cartoon, along with the surprised looks on their faces.

SOURCE: FlowingData.

imagine the stink they create when simply left to stand partially filled in a landfill or floating and covered with slimy algae in our oceans." A good way to develop this skill is to take a given product and try to restate its appeals in terms of the various senses. For instance, Campbell's soups are "Mmm, mmm, good" (taste). How might they be described using the sense of sight? Of smell? Of the other senses?

Humor

The use of **humor** in persuasion is an obvious stylistic asset if handled properly, and it can build credibility as well. A word of warning is necessary here: If a persuader uses humor that is inappropriate, in bad taste, or just plain not funny, it will likely backfire and actually destroy credibility and persuasiveness. If you are going to use humor in your persuasion, test it out with friends and relatives.

How can you develop humorous examples, comparisons, anecdotes, and stories?

People who regularly engage in public speaking usually have a ready supply of humorous material with which to embellish their speeches (see Box 12.5). They develop the humorous aspects as they work up other materials for their speeches. Humor sometimes relies on the breaking of expectations as can be seen in Figure 12.4. If you can never remember a story or joke, keep a file of stories or jokes or just punch lines. When you need the material, the file will trigger your memory. Late night television can provide you with humorous examples, as can your daily newspaper, *Reader's Digest*, and friends who frequently tell jokes. Don't forget the Internet. Just enter your subject and the word "humor," and have some fun while building a successful and entertaining presentation. You can also use visual humor such as cartoons, perhaps by using PowerPoint.

DELIVERING YOUR MESSAGE

Usually, we think of delivery as relating just to the source or speaker. But other factors can affect the delivery of your message, including the channel and the means of audience involvement. Persuaders often overlook these. For example, consider the sample propagandistic sources referred to in the video clips noted in Box 12.6. In the following section, we will look at all these factors.

The Persuader

Among the factors that persuaders adjust before and during delivery are their posture, eye contact, body movement and gesture, articulation, dress, grooming, and vocal quality. Other factors under the speaker's control are the use of visual aids and other nonverbal cues. Some persuaders are so nervous that they cannot stop pacing back and forth. When they do stop, they stand stiffly, looking as if they might freeze into statues. Other speakers are so relaxed that they seem uninterested in their own messages. They slouch over the podium or slide down into their chairs during a meeting. What does the posture of the speaker in Figure 12.5 suggest?

Clearly, the persuader's posture can signal the audience that you are either nervous or too relaxed. Observe persuaders in differing contexts—interviews, speeches, arguments—and you will see that

---

BOX 12.6 **Propaganda Speakers, Then and Now**

The oldest media for carrying propaganda are the public speech and the propaganda poster, of which we have seen several throughout this text. To see and listen to some of these propagandistic speeches and/or speakers go to Weblink 12.7 where you will see clips from examples ranging from WWII Nazi propaganda to Tom Cruise on behalf of Scientology, and Iraqi warlord speeches to 1935 anti-drug propaganda used to dramatize the classic "Reefer Madness" film with the speaker as the audio track to animated speakers. (You can access this and all of the other Chapter 12 weblinks through your companion website for *Persuasion*, Chapter 12 resources.)

FIGURE 12.5 Posture is important in giving a persuasive message. Is this speaker's posture appropriate for the formal situation seen here?

SOURCE: Used with permission of Doug Walker.

the effective ones avoid both extremes. The ideal posture lies somewhere in between. You should be alert and erect, and your shoulders should not tense or slump. Your posture should communicate confidence. You will be more believable if you maintain eye contact with your audience. You don't need to look at everyone individually (unless you are speaking to only one person). Instead, look at various areas in the room. Politicians look directly into the TV camera and so seem to make eye contact with each viewer. In meetings, establish eye contact with as many participants as possible. Body movement and gestures liven up a speech, as long as they don't distract. Using gestures during a speech keeps audience attention. However, it is a mistake to over-rehearse gestures, body movements, and facial expressions.

These nonverbal elements in delivery must appear natural, not staged, to have a positive effect. We all use gestures every day without thinking about them. Let your natural impulses guide you in your use of gestures in formal and interpersonal exchanges. Nothing can add more to your message than a natural gesture, movement, or facial expression (Scheflen, 1964). But rehearsed gestures usually backfire so let them come naturally—do what feels right. Articulation and vocal quality also affect your delivery. Everyone has heard people who pronounce words incorrectly; as a result, the audience focuses on the error and not on the message. Successful persuaders work on articulation, pronunciation, and vocal quality. Listening to yourself on tape will help you pinpoint your mistakes and focus on your vocal quality. As Box 12.7 demonstrates, the successful persuader will also examine the speech in view of the ethnicity of the audience and the ethnicity issue in general. The mistake in using the word "oriental" (which refers to rugs or a type of cuisine as opposed to the ethnicity of a person or persons) is a classic example. Listening to yourself on tape will help you pinpoint your mistakes and focus on your vocal quality. Some persons, especially females, think that a breathy or "thin" voice makes them sound sexier, but just the opposite is true. If you are

---

BOX 12.7   **Honoring Diversity in Public Speaking**

Lenora Billings-Harris is an internationally known public speaker working on diversity issues with Fortune 500 companies, and she offers the following advice for public speakers wanting to be diversity conscious. First, select your language carefully. One ill-chosen word can undo you in an instant. For example, saying "Hey guys ..." in a mixed gender group can offend some. Pointing to your "flip chart" can offend any Filipinos in the audience—refer to your easel instead. Research your audience first—who will be there? Be careful about using humor even if it is self-deprecating. Whenever possible use people's names, especially during question-and-answer sessions, and don't refer to someone as "the tall guy in the back." If you do refer to ethnicity make sure that you've got the right word. Some Latinos resent being referred to as "Hispanic" since that term groups together persons from Cuba, Mexico, Latin and South America, and Puerto Rico. (The word was invented by the U.S. Census Bureau more than 35 years ago to categorize people who spoke only Spanish.)

One way around this potential trap is to use the words "Americans of (blank) heritage." When speaking of persons from the Orient, use the adjective "Asian." If a member of the audience uses a potentially insensitive word, don't call attention to it in public unless it is truly offensive; instead talk to the person privately after the presentation. If the word is truly offensive, point that out by saying something like, "Most people consider that usage offensive and using it reduces your credibility." Billings-Harris notes some potentially offensive usages and offers acceptable alternatives. Use "outcasts" instead of "black sheep." Refer to occupations in non-gendered ways—"postal workers" not "postmen." Can you think of other examples of embracing diversity in your public speaking? For further study, explore the work of Billings-Harris at Weblink 12.8 and the many other interesting links on public speaking. (You can access this and all of the other Chapter 12 weblinks through your companion website for *Persuasion*, Chapter 12 resources.)

interested in persuading others, spend some time working on your voice and your articulation.

The Channel

Choosing the correct channel for sending your message is another key element in delivery. In one rural political campaign for the U.S. House of Representatives on which I worked, the candidates put most of their money into billboard space—which was rather surprising in this electronic media age. In this case, however, the candidate's district was large, stretching nearly half the length of the state, and no single TV network or cable channel reached all of it. Using TV would have meant having to pay a huge amount to get a single message across—the candidate's name and a brief statement of his goal. Because the district was so large, all residents had to drive to shop, do business, socialize, worship, and farm. Thus, the billboard was the one channel that could touch nearly all voters in the district.

Recent presidents have returned to using radio for regular Saturday persuasive talks, which are then responded to by representatives of the opposing party—sort of mini-debates. Why is radio such an appropriate channel for political persuasion? It is because we use much more radio than we imagine—almost as much as we use television. It is estimated that Americans listen to the radio an average of four hours a day, and more than half listen at work, especially females (Russell and Lane, 2005). People also use their iPods to listen to the radio while they are doing something else—driving, reading, commuting, exercising, and so on. By choosing the relatively inexpensive medium of daytime radio, politicians can reach people they otherwise might not, and at a reasonable price.

On a more personal level, ask yourself what is the best way to inform your boss that you will look for another job if you don't get a raise or promotion. Perhaps tapping into the channel of the grapevine might be best (usually done by identifying the group's gossip and letting them know that they shouldn't "pass this along, but I have a job

interview scheduled next week"), or maybe sending a straightforward memo, or asking her to be a reference so she will not get an out-of-the-blue inquiry about you from another firm. At the same time, you are letting her know that you are looking.

In general, start by listing all the potential channels that could be used to send your message. Then try to match them with your audience. If your audience uses a particular channel over others, then that is probably a good one to use. Sometimes the correct channel will give persuaders a chance to encourage audience participation, which in turn can increase audience energy, interest, motivation and activity. Get your audience involved by asking direct open-ended questions (ones that can't be answered by a simple "yes" or "no" but that need elaboration instead), and don't forget to address people by name if at all possible (if not possible, then by pointing and describing their dress or some other distinguishing characteristic such as if they have a briefcase or some other object). Or leave a sentence incomplete and let listeners finish it. One speaker got audience involvement right away by asking everyone to stand up before he even began his speech. He then asked them to become aware of the muscles they were using in their feet, ankles, calves, and thighs at that moment and tied this awareness to his topic—the need to develop communication awareness on the job. One word of caution: Don't distribute any printed material until the end of the speech. Audiences start reading right away, and you will lose them.

COMMON TACTICS OF PERSUASION

We mentioned some persuasive tactics that are used frequently and even are emphasized in public speaking and sales short courses. Let's consider some of the more common ones.

The Foot in the Door or Door in the Face

Robert Cialdini (2008) describes several persuasive tactics, including the **foot-in-the-door** and the

door-in-the face techniques. The foot-in-the-door technique relies on getting a potential customer, joiner, donor, or convert to make a small initial commitment that starts what will become a long-term relationship resulting in ever larger sales, contributions, and commitments. To illustrate, some time ago I signed a protest petition from the Citizens' Utility Board (CUB), which promised to use the petition to prevent price increases by several Illinois utilities. Soon after, I received a newsletter explaining that CUB had stopped one of the utilities from instituting a 15 percent price increase. The battle was far from over because the utility was appealing. Could I donate $50, $25, or even just $10 to help carry on the fight? I donated $10. Next, a letter from CUB informed me of another victory, but warned that the other utilities were suing CUB, and asked that I become a full-fledged, dues-paying member of the organization for only $25. My signature on the petition was merely a foot in the door, and I continue to receive requests for donations.

In the retail field, this technique might mean getting a prospective retailer to agree to carry one item in a product line. That commitment becomes the foot in the door to the retailer's finally agreeing to carry the entire product line. As Cialdini puts it, "You can use small commitments to manipulate a person's self-image; you can turn citizens into 'public servants,' prospects into 'customers,' prisoners into 'collaborators'" (p. 67). Cialdini relates how the same technique is used by the highly successful Amway Corporation. Staff members are asked to set specific sales goals and then to write them down: "There is something magical about writing things down. So set a goal and write it down. When you reach that goal, set another and write that down. You'll be off and running" (p. 71). The written commitment somehow translates into motivation and action.

The door-in-the-face tactic is what a persuader uses when turned down on a request for a significant commitment, and then settles for an initial small commitment or engages in what Cialdini calls the **rejection-then-retreat** strategy. In other words, if a salesperson tries to get the prospect to go for the top-of-the-line or "loaded" version of the brand but is rejected, he or she can always retreat by offering a stripped-down version of the brand. Cialdini attributes the effectiveness of this strategy to feelings of responsibility and satisfaction on the part of customers, joiners, or donors. By agreeing to the lower commitment, they can feel as if they are in control of the situation and have "dictated" the deal. This satisfaction makes them happier with their decisions. So try to think of simple or partial commitments to your proposal that your audience can take and which can then be upgraded to more significant actions.

A related persuasive approach is to "sell up" after retreating to a position of concession. Thus, once you've signed the contract to buy the new car, a good salesperson will offer you the extras— the undercoating and soundproofing, the extended warranty, the upholstery fabric protection, and so on. Others have suggested similar tactics using somewhat different terms. The following are some tactics suggested by Drs. William Howell and Ernest Bormann (1988). They may overlap with some of the other techniques discussed previously. Examine your world of persuasion for examples of these tactics in action.

The Yes-Yes Technique

A common tactic in sales and other persuasive appeals is called **yes-yes**. The source attempts to get the target group or person to respond positively to several parts of the appeal, withholding the key request until last. Having agreed to most parts of the appeal, the persuadee is likely to say yes to the key and final request. For example, suppose you are trying to sell a lawn service. You might ask the homeowner, "You would like to have a beautiful lawn, wouldn't you?" The answer is going to be yes. Then you ask, "And you'd like to get rid of the weeds?" Another yes is likely. "And wouldn't it be nice if these things could be effort-free?" A yes answer is likely again. Now that the homeowner has accepted all your points in favor of the service, it is nearly impossible to respond with a "no" to "Then you'll want to sign up for our lawn service, won't you?" By accepting the yes pattern, the buyer accedes to your final request. At another university close to mine, the topic "Hate Speech Should Be Outlawed on Campus" is being debated by some classes. The "yes-yes" tactic could be incorporated here. For example, the pro advocate might begin by saying, "You'd like to avoid racial and ethnic confrontation on our campus, wouldn't you?" The audience is most likely to agree—yes. The advocate could then go on by asking, "And it would be good, wouldn't it, if this could be done by each of us simply trying not to use language that is offensive to various minorities?" Again, the audience is likely to agree. And the advocate could continue asking questions resulting in yes answers that led to the logical conclusion that outlawing hate speech was a good idea. The same technique is useful in a meeting in which a persuader gets the participants to agree to all but the final point in favor of, say, a change in work schedules. They agree that flexibility is good, that more free time for workers is good, that changing schedules would relieve boredom, and so on. They are then likely to agree that the change is a good one.

The Tactic of Asking Not "If" but "Which"

It is easier to make a choice between two alternatives than from among many. This is the strategy behind the "**don't ask if, ask which**" persuasive tactic. I learned as a parent of young children that the worst thing to ask on Saturday mornings was, "What would you like Dad to make for breakfast today?" It was better to say, "Which would you like for breakfast today—Dad's blueberry pancakes or Dad's blueberry coffee-cake?" The same thing applies in persuasion. Don't ask your audience to choose from too many options; ask them to choose from only a few or only two, as in the following use of the technique by a car salesperson: "Would you rather have us undercoat your new car, or do you want to take it elsewhere?" Another employment example might be "Would you rather meet on your promotion this week or next?" It comes down to "Do you want guns or butter?"—a favorite tactic of many propagandists. It was the basis for the initial approval for the war in Iraq. The real question posed by the Bush administration was:

"Do we attack them now and in their own country, or do we wait for them to attack us again—maybe in more terrible ways and here at home?" Although this tactic can be manipulative and is frequently used that way, and hence can be used unethically, it has the distinct advantage and value of forcing some decision or action when buyers, voters, or others are stubbornly trying to avoid it. You might use such a technique in a speech on stopping global warming by starting with questions that are going to be answered "yes" in the audiences' mind (e.g., "We all want to slow down global warming don't we?") and then adding others until you have a pattern of yes responses. Then you can ask for a key commitment (e.g., "So why not try changing all the light bulbs in your home or apartment to the low-energy, fluorescent-coiled ones—you'll save money in the long run as well!").

A Question for a Question

A tactic some people in audiences use to throw others off guard is to ask an embarrassing or tough question. Asking someone a question in the first place puts the ball in their court. But if you find yourself in this situation, a good tactic is putting the ball back into their court by asking them a question in return instead of answering their original question. It buys you time as well. For example, if asked, "Wouldn't you like to sign up for the National Guard?" or " Would you like to pledge Tappa Kanna Bru tonight and join our pledge class?" you might say, "Why do you think I would want to do that?" or "What gave you that idea?" Responding with a question, or asking the person to repeat or even to elaborate on the question, also gives you time to think.

Answering a question with a question puts the ball back in the other person's court. People who question you sometimes are trying to discredit or annoy you. Turn the tables—answer with another question. Suppose a prospect for advertising services asks, "Who else has used your services? Maybe I could check with them before deciding to go with your agency." A good response is, "I can bring you written testimonials about how successful we are in generating qualified leads" or "I can give you names and phone numbers for local businesses that might be slightly different than yours, and you can call. Which would you prefer?" Now the other person has to make a commitment, which puts them somewhat in debt to you, even if only in a tiny way.

The Partial Commitment

The **partial commitment** tactic resembles the door-in-the-face or rejection-then-retreat strategy discussed above, but uses acts instead of words to lead the prospect to the final request. Once you are partially committed, you are a good prospect for full commitment. Trying a sample of a product in the store represents a partial commitment, as does clipping a coupon. The smart auto salesperson won't ask you to sign a sales agreement right off the bat. Instead, he or she will suggest that you look around and see whether you find anything that appeals to you and then suggests that you take it for a test drive. Merely by looking around, you are partially committing to the sales pitch, and the test drive is usually the clincher.

Of course, other kinds of commitment are used to persuade. When a politician asks you to sign a petition to put his or her name on the ballot, your signature is a form of partial commitment to that politician, and research shows that you are more likely to vote for him or her when you get to the ballot box. A favorite way to generate "qualified leads" in the marketing of some products is to run a sweepstakes. Anyone who submits an entry for the free version of the product has already made a partial commitment to buy it and thus is a good sales lead to follow up. You can use this tactic in your presentations by asking for an almost insignificant action—raising one's hand, for example. Then having got agreement to your initial proposition—say buying a season ticket for athletic events—you can ask for more significant steps for supporting the school's athletic program such as joining the Huskie Club or buying a Huskie Club hoodie and then pledging to go to as many games as possible.

Planting

Memory responds best, it seems, to messages that have sensory data as raw material. The tactic of **planting** uses one or more of the five senses to open a channel to the audience's memory of how they experienced the product, idea, or candidate. Recall that the five senses we have are smell, taste, touch, hearing, and seeing. Earlier we asked you to describe Campbell's soup using each of these senses and not the obvious one of taste—"Mmm, mmm good." This kind of use of the sensual memory is almost certainly processed in the peripheral information-processing channel of the ELM. Restaurant ads often appeal to several senses at once, and not just the obvious sense of taste. They describe the "crisp and crunchy garden salad" to appeal to the sense of touch. They offer "sizzling hot steaks seared on a grill" to appeal to the sense of hearing. They describe the "thick red tomato sauce" to appeal to the sense of vision, and use the words "a steaming fragrance of garlic and spices" to appeal to the sense of smell.

In a classic case of invoking the sense of touch in an ad campaign, Charmin toilet paper was successfully marketed as an uncommonly soft bathroom tissue in TV ads because the grocer, a nerdy fellow named Mr. Whipple, was always caught squeezing the packages of the stuff when he thought no one was looking, and he was always getting caught and scolded for it. Of course the humor of the spots caught and maintained audience attention, but the squeeze he always gave the package was a sensual reminder that the brand was supposed to be unusually soft. No other of our five senses could have communicated that concept more successfully than touch or feel. An ad for a new automobile might have someone slam the door or trunk lid so audience members hear the solid "thunk" and mentally compare it with experiential memories of the sounds and rattles of their own five-year-old car when doors or trunk lids are slammed. No other of our senses could have communicated the aging of the owner's present car than that of sound (other than perhaps sight). Tie persuasion to the senses of sight, sound, touch, taste, and smell if at all possible using this technique of planting, and the audience will recall your message better and longer. In other words, "Don't sell the steak; sell the sizzle."

The IOU

Sometimes called the reciprocity tactic, the **IOU technique** gets listeners to feel they owe you something. For instance, the insurance salesperson spends several hours doing a complex assets-and-debts analysis to prove to the prospect that he or she needs more insurance. The sales rep then spends several more hours explaining the figures to the spouse, perhaps taking the couple out to lunch or dinner. By the end of all the special treatment, the couple may feel that they really ought to buy something even though they may not need it or cannot afford it. They respond to the obligation—the IOU—that was created by the salesperson's effort. After observing how reciprocity works in various cultures, Cialdini (2008) notes that the need to reciprocate—the IOU—transcends "great cultural differences, long distances, acute famine, many years, and self interest" (p. 21). Persuaders find this tactic useful when it is hard to make a first contact with buyers, voters, or joiners. You can place your audience in your debt by giving them free samples or offers of help. As a listener, you may want to remember that "There's no such thing as a free lunch."

REVIEW AND CONCLUSION

We all have to persuade at some point. To be effective, we need to analyze the audience before planning how our format will affect the message. To do that, we need to remember that they, like us, are living and processing information in the same world. We must also control factors in delivery. We need to use source factors, such as posture, convincing eye contact, and appropriate appearance in a world filled with scams and deceptions. Start your planning by assuming that your audience will not believe you initially and then work to build your credibility through the various techniques we have discussed here.

Remember that even channel factors are subject to our control as well. Receiver factors can be used to get the target group involved in its own persuasion through techniques such as "yes-yes" or "putting it up to you" or "don't ask if, ask which" and others. As you are called on to persuade, use these skills in preparing. Rely on the audience analysis and demographics that the receiver-oriented approach teaches—listen to your audience. Get messages out of them, not into them.

KEY TERMS

After reading this chapter, you should be able to identify, explain, and give an example of the following key terms or concepts:

audience analysis	audience needs	space format	stock-issues format
demographics	topic format	chronological format	motivated sequence format

stock issues	get rid of a bad	expertise	door-in-the face
need for change	statistical evidence	dynamism	rejection-then-retreat
plan to solve the need	narratives	figures of speech	yes-yes
plan meets the need	testimony	vivid language	don't ask if, ask which
burden of proof	visual evidence	concise language	answering a question with a question
AIDA	comparison and contrast	parallel structure	partial commitment
keep a good		imagery	planting
getting a good	credibility	humor	IOU technique
avoiding a bad	trust	foot-in-the-door	

APPLICATION OF ETHICS

A fellow student in your public speaking class gives a speech on the dangers to freedom of speech posed by renewing the Patriot Act. After listening to the speech, you realize that your classmate has made inaccurate claims based on inadequate research. Apparently the rest of your classmates are enthusiastic about her speech. You also know that she has stage fright and just getting through the speech has been a victory for her. There is a question and answer period where you could point out her inaccuracies. Should you remain silent, hoping that no harm will come to the class from hearing the speech? Or should you approach her privately and tell her that her claims are inaccurate and her research is inadequate? Or should you inform the instructor about the inaccuracies and research shortcomings?

QUESTIONS FOR FURTHER THOUGHT

1. What demographic clusters can you identify for the people in your class? In your dorm? In a club? Elsewhere? How might the Internet help you?

2. What is a task-oriented message? Give examples from ads in which persuaders used this technique effectively. Give other examples from ads in which they failed.

3. What are the forms of organization? How do they differ from the forms of support? What might be other ways to organize a message?

4. What is AIDA, and how does it differ from the motivated sequence?

5. What are Rank's desire-building tactics? How do they work?

6. What are the factors that make up a speaker's credibility? Give examples of people who have them. Find ads that rely on each factor.

7. Where does humor fit into the persuasion process? Give examples of sources that use humor. Does it relate to the audience? How? How might the Internet help you develop humor for a specific topic?

8. How can a persuader get his or her audience more involved? What are some examples you

have seen or heard recently? What techniques mentioned here might help?

9. What is the difference between the forms of proof discussed here and those discussed in Chapter 8?

10. How does "planting" work? What about "getting an IOU"? Can you restate a proposition using all five senses?

11. How does persuasion work differently via SNM?

You can access your online resources at the companion website for *Persuasion*. Log in at **http://www.cengagebrain.com**.

Modern Media and Persuasion

After reading this chapter, you should be able to:

1. Appreciate societal changes that followed the introduction of the spoken, written, printed, electronic, and interactive words.

2. Show how the interactive and SNM worlds have already begun to change global society.

3. Explain the resonance principle and how it relates to Schwartz's theory of evoked recall.

4. Explain and give examples of what Schwartz means by "experiential meaning."

5. Explain Marshall McLuhan's concepts of hot and cool media.

6. Explain and give examples of the various reasons people use media, as discussed in Uses and

Gratifications Theory, and judge which information processing path of ELM they use.

7. Explain and give examples of news manipulation and Agenda-Setting Theory.

8. Explain and give examples of Social Learning and Cultivation Theories.

9. Demonstrate familiarity with the wide variety of information available on the Internet.

10. Apply ethical standards to Internet communication.

11. Explain the challenges of the Internet, security, and SNM.

LANGUAGE AND MEDIA
DEVELOPMENT

Back in Chapter 5, we discussed the development and various aspects and theories of language and language development. We learned for example that language—especially English—was a powerful development in human history. We also learned that language use was a creative and symbolic act. And author Richard Lederer (1991) reminded us that:

> The boundary between human and animal—between the most primitive savage and the highest ape—is the language line. The birth of language is the dawn of humanity; in our beginning was the word. We have always been endowed with language because before we had words, we were not human beings. [Words] tell us that we must never take for granted the miracle of language (p. 3).

Kenneth Burke suggested there that most language, regardless of media used, is dramatic while it

is symbolic, and it can be used and, more importantly, it can be *misused*. With the advent of each new kind of media or kind of "word" (i.e., spoken, written, printed, electronic, or interactive words) language can be misused, and we have seen both the Internet and SNM misused outrageously in the recent past. As a result, our present study of "Media and Persuasion" seems more important now than in previous editions. As we shall also see, more and more of the meaning of persuasive messages is being conveyed via the peripheral channel of the ELM.

Since the development of spoken language, basically four other major media of communication have developed and gradually each has superseded its predecessor in important ways; each of them has made communication and hence persuasion easier (but also more complex), more prevalent and enduring, and enormously more far-reaching and effective. Each of these media innovations has changed the scale and pace of human life in breathtaking ways that we can only vaguely imagine. This has become the case most recently with Internet and SNM communication. For example, take the case of "Wiki Leaks." The entire concept of private communication has been dissolved when anyone can steal or "hack" their way into our personal information. How can we have a truly private or "secret" communication life anymore? And if we examine the number of hours spent using the "Interactive Word," including SNM, we will soon conclude that humans are becoming "isolatos" and also "revealatos," isolated from our receivers and utterly "open" to those would see and perhaps use us. It is just a grown-up version of "You show me yours, and I'll show you mine!." We freely and naively give away important data and other information about ourselves and our affairs—public, private, and even intimate data and information. We would also probably conclude that what used to be called "the art of conversation" is slowly dying. What impacts will such changes have on the scale and pace of human life in the future? Think about that in comparison to the other communication/media innovations of human history and the impacts they produced on human activity and values.

Imagine, if you can, what it would have been like to try to comprehend the affects of writing (the "Written Word") when we previously only had speaking with which to communicate? It must have been breathtaking, and we had centuries to absorb it rather than just decades, which has been the case with electronic and interactive words. The same must have been true for those first realizing the potentials of printing or the telegraph, telephones, and radio (as was just pointed out with reference to tank warfare in the previous chapter). And today we are being introduced to new and interactive media at what might be called "supersonic" speed, although that is too ancient a word to accurately describe the changes we face. Let's set the stage for the almost unimaginable change that we face in the almost instantaneous future by a brief examination of the history of five major human communication innovations and the changes they have had on human persuasion.

MEDIA INNOVATIONS

Each of the five major human communication innovations was tied to the development of a new medium or technology, and all have shaped and changed the world and the way we see it, and how we persuade using the innovation. These innovations or technologies are: (1) the spoken word, (2) the written word, (3) the printed word, (4) the electronic word, and (5) the interactive and digital word. And it is this fifth and final media innovation that we have most seen, experienced, and probably adopted and used in the past decade; and we will continue to see new developments in future decades, all relating to the remarkable changes facing us—in the ways in which humans communicate with others and themselves and how technology affects them. These devices and activities will change forever the structure of human life as we know it, and we are already beginning to feel that great shift in human life with devices like iPods; cell phones that text, photograph, link to the Internet, and function as GPS devices; digital television and radio; and activities like texting, Hogging, tweeting; and a host of others yet to come. In a way we are expanding our roles as both sources and receivers of persuasive communication by many, many fold.

The Spoken Word

The first communication innovation in human history was the ability to speak and to symbolize. As Lederer pointed out in Chapter 5, prior to language we were not truly human beings. We were just grunting, mating, killing, and consuming sorts of creatures. We sense the reverence for the **spoken word** in many avenues of human activity. In religion, for instance, the Judeo-Christian story of the creation in the book of *Genesis* indicates that the first and major creative act was accomplished by God using the spoken word (i.e., "And God **SAID** 'Let there be light', and there was light—the first night and the first day'"). *John 1:1*

The Word Made Flesh

1 In the beginning was the Word, and the Word was with God, and the Word was God.

2 The same was in the beginning with God....

3 And the Word was made flesh, and dwelt among us, (and we beheld his glory, the glory as of the only begotten of the Father,) full of grace and truth. (*John 1:1*)

In our daily social life, this reverent attitude toward the spoken word continues even today. We must, for example, be sworn in to testify, or to *speak* to the court, and, except in unusual cases such as if the defendant is deaf, the judge must *speak* the sentence before the convicted person can be taken to prison. We rely "on a person's *word*," actions "speak for themselves," and we look for "the final *word*" on various issues. We swear in political officials with the spoken word, and we require new citizens to *take a spoken oath* of loyalty. The spoken word permitted humans to become social animals and to work together for the common good. It allowed one generation passing down the history and knowledge of the tribe in myths, ballads, or legends, and thus progress could occur. The wheel didn't have to be reinvented each generation. Rules didn't have to be re-instituted (though they could be altered *via the spoken word*—kept by "*men of words*").

They were largely the province of the leaders—chiefs and medicine men (see Box 13.1). In the oral/aural world, and even after, the spoken word was experiential—an event that was felt and witnessed in real time—after which it disappeared. It also occupied time and not space and had to be thought over rather quickly before it was easily forgotten. It was ephemeral—the beginning of the word was gone before its end was uttered. Its only permanence was in the human mind, memory, and sometimes encapsulated in stories and legends, so people re-experienced it only by re-uttering it. One couldn't have real history with the spoken word—only a dramatic narrative of events that could be somewhat accurately recalled when the spoken event or the word was gone. It was a primitive world, but it produced many beautiful things and much wisdom, and still does in some oral/aural cultures that exist in the world today.

The Written Word

The next major communication innovation was the development of the phonetic alphabet, which unlike the pictographs of the ancient Egyptian or Chinese languages, is tied to speech sounds. With this alphabet, people could collect knowledge and store it for long periods of time—far longer and more reliable than history in the old spoken word. Advances of various kinds could be based on these stored records of what others had tried to do and how. The **written word** allowed societies to develop complex sets of knowledge, legal systems (you could write down laws and not have to recall them from memory), behavior patterns and customs to assign or deed land and other possessions, and to declare behaviors illegal by common definition.

BOX 13.1 **Knowledge and the "Old One"**

And the spoken word led to the organization of information that could be shared by everyone—the tanning of hides, the preservation of meats and vegetables, birthing, death. In oral/aural cultures, information or knowledge is most fully held by the old; thus, age became and remained valued and honored until recently. For example, among the Lakota, every newly married couple was given an "Old One" to live in the couple's tepee for tending fires, comforting the babies, and giving advice. This helped the couple learn the lessons of parenting, marriage, and family as well, and the practice provided the Old One with a home and sustenance for life. There were no homeless ladies among the Lakota or any "nursing homes" in which to warehouse them. The spoken word still exists, of course, but not in the same way it did in an oral/aural world where it was the only means of communication (Ong, 1982).

Unlike knowledge stored in the spoken word, information in writing can be recalled very precisely—there is no reliance on the fallibility of memory for the information is truly palpable. For centuries, however, few people were literate, and thus only the rich and powerful could read and write (or afford scribes if they couldn't), so knowledge stored in writing was hoarded by them. Knowledge and information (and hence power) could be and was obtained and centralized by those who controlled the written word—kings, emperors, feudal lords, and church leaders. Information became individual property (scrolls, books, etc.) that could be owned and certainly not widely shared. The great ancient libraries, like the one at Alexandria, Egypt, were the repositories of society's knowledge and information, but they didn't loan out scrolls or "books" to just anyone. That would have to wait until Benjamin Franklin invented the remarkably generous concept of a lending library back in the mid-1700s. Therefore, not everyone had access to the gathered knowledge or information of the culture, and without it the average person remained ignorant and at the bottom of the social order, as peasants—it was in the Dark Ages. Once writing made the ownership of knowledge possible in Europe, Asia, and elsewhere, this concept was applied to other property besides knowledge encapsulated in writing—things like land, cattle, horses, jewelry, and buildings could also be owned; whereas in the oral/aural culture those things belonged to the tribe. It made sense

that if you could own knowledge, you could own other things that symbolized, created, and ensured power. No such concept existed in the oral/aural cultures of Native North Americans, to whom the claims to land treaties, which they signed with a simple mark, were written down and kept by those in power to be used later to prove ownership of the land. To these oral/aural people, the treaties were "worthless scraps of paper" that could be destroyed by tearing them up or casting them into a fire, but to the designers of the treaties (who kept copies) they were the law.

The written word in the treaties took up space, was not ephemeral, didn't disappear, and unlike spoken agreements could be seen and touched time and again and lasted across generations (Ong, 1967). This permanence made people not only rely on written records for the "last word" on an issue, but to respect written words. Indeed, the written word came to be thought of as far more trustworthy than the spoken word (even "holy" in a sense), as seen in the ways we preserve and honor written documents like our Declaration of Independence. Even those who couldn't read insisted regularly on seeing the documents in writing before they would believe them and placed a high reverence in them. Even as recently as my mother's youth (about the time of WWI) people from her Scandinavian village would come to her uncle's house simply to see (not borrow and read) his single book (of course it was printed, not handwritten, but the point remains). (See Box 13.2.)

© Cengage Learning 2013

BOX 13.2   I'm Rich, But I Can't Read or Write

As Ong (1967) observed:

> Ancient Hebrews and Christians knew not only the spoken word but the alphabet as well…. But for them and all men of early times, the word, even when written, was much closer to the spoken word than it normally is for … technological man. Today we have often to labor to regain the awareness that the word is still always at root the spoken word. Early man had no such problem: he felt the word, even when written, as primarily an event in sound (p. ix).

So with the written word, humans experienced an enormous change in life—especially in terms of knowledge, ownership, and power. No longer did the entire village or tribe own knowledge, but only an elite few did, and they were the ones who came to great power and ruled over the others, whether in the church, in government, or throughout the rest of society. If they happened to already have power and wealth but couldn't read or write, they hired scribes. So knowledge and information became—and remains—the equivalent of power, and even today with the advancements of print and electronic record keeping, information equals power.

BOX 13.3 Print = Spread of Power and Knowledge

The effects of spreading this power of the **printed word** to more and more "average" people were immense, creating widespread literacy (of course that also took centuries and is still going on), the emergence of a middle class of merchants and tradesmen, and spurring such intellectual revolutions in Europe as the Renaissance and the Reformation. Because information could be spread and shared fairly inexpensively, the "New Science" developed rapidly. Scientists could read about one another's work and experiments and build on what they had done and on the theories they proposed. Musical scores could be cheaply duplicated and sent to others, including composers who could learn and adapt the newly composed works. The same phenomenon occurred in other areas such as philosophy, commerce, and religion. People could read the writings of Martin Luther, and his objections to the Church, and they were printed and distributed widely.

Imagine what would happen if all the electronic records or information of our society were wiped out in an instant (a military strategy related to the so-called "Star Wars" theory). No bank records, no laws, no permanence. Perhaps the "hard copies" of the past (writing and printing) are still critical to us today. A film entitled *The Net* (1995) starring Sandra Bullock works off this premise—all knowledge is being "stolen" by a conspiracy of persons known as "the Praetorians" who are using a computer security company called "Gateway" to steal, own, and use the information supposedly secured by Gateway. Bullock's character, who also works for the company, discovers the enormity of the theft (mankind's knowledge base) accidentally by trying to track a virus in a video game also owned by the company. After her discovery, the film is basically a "chase" plot with bad guy Praetorians trying to catch and/or kill Bullock, but she ultimately saves all computer information for use by the public and not the villains.

The Printed Word

The third communication innovation came with Johannes Gutenberg's moveable type and the printing press in the late 1400s. Of course, it was just a way of duplicating its predecessor, the written word, but it could do this repeatedly and much more cheaply. This made knowledge less expensive, more portable, and far more easily available to more and more people who were not associated with the official church or government of the times. Hence print was an enormously liberating and democratic communication innovation even though it took centuries for its use to spread (see Box 13.3).

It was basically a very slow SNM in which most information was being processed in the central information processing channel of the ELM, unlike most of the "information" communicated by today's versions of SNM (e.g., MySpace, Facebook, Twitter, etc.) where the information being communicated is gossipy and inane. With the advent of the printed word, the notions of serfdom were superseded by the idea of individual ownership of land or a business. And governments weren't unaware of this diffusion of knowledge— *such a thing could be dangerous!* As a defensive measure, soon most of them set up censorship policies to help them control this potentially dangerous, rapid, and inexpensive spread of information. Not until John Peter Zenger was tried for sedition for printing a tract criticizing a British colonial governor did the notion of freedom of the press come into being. Curiously, Zenger was tried not for writing the criticism but for printing or spreading it, just as happened recently in Middle Eastern countries where revolutions overthrew dictatorships during the early years of the new millennium. They also tried censorship, but the availability of the means of spreading "*The Word*" was widespread (personal computers and the Internet) and thus almost impossible to control, and it was inexpensive.

Imagine what things would be like today if governments held each of us legally responsible for everything that was sent by our personal computer. Think of that in comparison to the "print age" of the British government, which held all printers responsible for what they published, in effect making every printer an unofficial censor.

Like the power of the spoken and written words, the power of the printed word has diminished; yet it still remains potent, as any illiterate person trying to read a job application will tell you. Although the number of newspapers published in the United States has actually increased since the advent of television, readership of both newspapers and news is down (sometimes to as little as eight minutes a day), and the average age of newspaper readers is becoming older and older—few persons younger than 35 read one regularly, and only a small portion subscribe. Besides your student paper, what others do you read? Besides your assigned text and other readings, how many books do you read for general knowledge and entertainment?

Remember that more than 22 percent of the U.S. population is functionally illiterate today, meaning that they can't read such simple things as menus, directions for operating appliances, labels, and street signs. In the nineteenth century, the literacy rate was nearly 90 percent for similar everyday purposes (Kaplan, Wingert, and Chideya, 1993). Some estimates indicate that even those who do read newspapers today devote their time to only special sections of interest to them and not to important "issue" pages like the editorial or business pages.

Yes, the printed word brought about a veritable revolution in many areas of human accomplishment. Musical scores, scientific theories, and artistic images were readily exchanged among scientists, composers, and artists across national boundaries, and those who read or saw these items learned from one another's works. In terms of persuasion, the printed word ultimately gave us widespread literacy, and greatly influenced the way people formulated and shared their thoughts. Literacy in the Western world led to a new view of humans as unique individuals and led to great discoveries and inventions in Europe, America, and elsewhere. In a way, it was a kind of mini SNM, yet not as instantaneous as that we are now experiencing. Instead of it taking only microseconds for new information to be transferred, it took a few months or years.

Literacy also resulted from shared knowledge via print. Interestingly enough, literacy perhaps made childhood necessary (and surely extended it) by making protracted formal education and literacy both possible and essential if one were to have a chance to succeed in business or civic life. SNM use can be learned in a few minutes if one is literate, but you need to be mature enough to avoid its pitfalls (like giving your real birthdate on your profile—identity thieves can use it to get your real Social Security number as well as your identity). Prior to the printed word, children were considered to be just like tiny adults and were sent to work in the coal mines, city streets, or farm fields. Eventually the emerging middle class realized that it was essential for their children to learn to read and write and so set aside a time of life for the kids to learn to do those things so they could get a good job and earn enough to have an identity worth stealing. My emigrant parents did not go past sixth grade, but they were tremendously advantaged over other illiterate immigrants when it came to getting jobs, moving up in society, and training their children to achieve even more than they themselves had. And of course the many new immigrants we have today feel the same way and honor the printed word in similar ways.

The Electronic Word

The **electronic word** came into being in 1844 with the invention of the telegraph. Of course, it didn't supersede books, for it couldn't rapidly transmit books or even lengthy messages; but it could transmit dots and dashes which, when decoded, communicated words and, thus, short messages with meaning. But more far-reaching and truly communicative inventions utilizing electricity were soon on the way in numerous forms of the electronic word. The successor to the telegraph—the "wireless" or radio, which also transformed dots and dashes—was ultimately to translate the electrical impulses into spoken words via electronically produced sound waves; and not long afterward it was actually sending human speech through the airwaves to homes across the globe—to most it must have seemed remarkable. It is possible to get a glimmering of the effect these inventions had from a quaint example. While the Pony Express got a written message across the country in just 10 days, people could telegraph the message in minutes. In a sense, the electronic word wiped out not only space but time as well. People now could learn almost immediately about election results, sports events, catastrophes, stock and commodity prices, and joyous and sad family events. At age eight I recall getting a black-bordered telegram from Sweden with words on a strip of paper glued to it that announced the death of my grandmother.

In 1876 came the first SNM but it could only network to two or three persons. It was the telephone, transforming the spoken word into electronic impulses that could be transmitted long distances via wires and could be understood as words and complete messages, thus almost eliminating space. The "distance" between New York and Boston could be measured in microseconds, not miles, as far as communication distance was concerned. I recall telephoning Sweden at Christmas each year to talk to my grandparents (and then for only ten total minutes for the whole family). We had to reserve time on the transoceanic Atlantic Cable Network of wires weeks in advance.

Other channels of the electronic word—television, computers, video games, cell phones, VCRs, DVDs, CDs, and a host of others—are now bringing similarly remarkable changes to society as a whole, and as a result, we are undergoing awesome changes in our individual lives. Some critics claim that this explosion of electronic media adversely affects us and may soon make us incapable of interacting with others on any truly face-to-face level, but only via a machine, thus creating a nation of isolates cocooned in front of computer screens. There may be some truth to that. For example, few of us ever write a letter to another person anymore; we rely instead on e-mail. Imagine what kind of history can be recovered in the future from your e-mails versus the history retrieved from the extensive correspondences that persons in past times exchanged across years, even lifetimes. In those days, many people set aside special times of the day to carry on these correspondences. People are also concerned about the amount of screen time being watched by the average U.S. child and the effects this is having on all kinds of human behavior including violence, development of the brain, human relationships, and so on (Larson, 2009).

We live in a world in which electronic and print messages literally surround us—on billboards and in newsletters, magazines, catalogs, signs on shopping carts (some of which can speak to you as you pass the shelves), Internet banners, unwanted spam and pop-ups, telemarketing, electronic kiosks in airport terminals, demonstration videos in supermarkets, ads in restrooms and more. Despite even newer technologies like TiVo that allow viewers to bypass ads, electronic mass media are still the most effective channels to persuade us to buy products, to vote for candidates, and to take up or join and donate to causes, sometimes without giving the actions much serious thought. One reason is that these electronic messages are inherently oral/aural in nature. That is, in the same way that spoken words are ephemeral or fleeting, electronic signals or images are also fleeting and ephemeral unless we choose to record them in some way, such as saving them electronically or printing them. We *experience* them more than we logically think them through. And, of course, there is a multitude of other information one could bring up in regard to the quickly emerging and changing world of electronic media aimed at us as receivers. But there is a new kind of electronic word impinging on our lives—the interactive word.

The Interactive Word

As I understand it, with the newest communication innovation of recent times—interactive media—messages speed up; have higher "definition," to use McLuhan's term, or greater fidelity in more colloquial terms, and as a result, become more numerous and ultimately less expensive to send and receive. And receivers can get much more into the act than with earlier electronic media like radio, film, or television, where receivers were simply passive sponges. In a way we are reverting to an aural/oral world, but now it is with the experience and knowledge of print technology, literacy, and the electronic word. That is, we are rapidly becoming more able to be both source and receiver, even though we don't always use spoken words to do that. We are just beginning to deal with this new and highly dynamic communication channel, and we don't know quite what to make of it yet. It can be used in a variety of ways. Interaction via texting, for example, aids in cheating on tests and also bypasses most eavesdropping. Many persons today pay more attention to cell phones than they do to land lines or, of course, traffic; and Wii is becoming an important therapy in hospitals, nursing homes, and assisted-living facilities instead of being considered a new kind of video game. Wii is a kind of therapy, not only psychiatrically but physically as well—90-something old folks are using Wii to play virtual tennis and getting physical exercise, too. The **interactive word** is more ephemeral than either the written or the spoken word even though we can retrieve it—at least out of the trash, the "C" drive, or some other device if needed.

To date, the electronic word has affected us mostly as receivers—we have been consuming more messages from these media than we have produced messages for them. Few of us produce broadcast television messages, and all of us consume them, but we can and do use interactive media to produce on-screen video that we can "narrowcast" to our friends and others via electronic and interactive media like YouTube. You can also reach sizable and persuadable audiences by YouTube using easy-to-find and mostly free images and video clips to make your own video as seen in Figure 13.1.

We can enter into chat groups and interact with persons we do not and never will "know" in the traditional sense. Advertising can invite us to "enter" it and "play" with ads in ways the old advertising could never accommodate. And multiple other examples of various kinds of interactivity could be mentioned now or are soon on the way. So, while the real audience is far smaller than in previous times, the interactive word has encouraged us to not only interact more often with others by geometric degrees, but it has also let us become skilled at producing effective persuasive messages to convince and challenge those virtual audiences.

Yes, with newly emerging interactive media, we are becoming more and more both producers as well as consumers of messages. Consider just one of these interactive media—at one time widely scoffed at—virtual reality technology, for example. At first, it was considered another sort of video war game that was entertaining because it had 360-degree surround sound and vision, but it was not considered of much true commercial use. But new and impressive uses have resulted from this technology of electronic interactivity. For example, surgeons now conduct virtual surgery for training purposes long before the actual highly technical and remote operation happens. Following enough "perfect" replications of the actual operation, the robotic laser scalpels are programmed, using the virtual operation, to perform the actual physical cutting and suturing. And most of the sorties flown in the 1990s wars in Iraq and Afghanistan and in today's wars, there and elsewhere, were and are "rehearsed" in virtual reality, and the planes are drones flown in virtual reality. Many predict that virtual reality will soon replace the showroom floor or retail outlet in stores for "virtual shopping," and then what will we do with all those strip malls? More than 20 years ago, Charles Madigan (1993) was criticized and laughed off the stage when he described a hypothetical virtual purchase this way:

A customer in his or her own living room facing a bigger-than-life fully digitized television screen will say, "Shop Ralph Lauren." After a pause of only a few

FIGURE 13.1

YouTube Image

Available for Use

Thousands of images are available for making your own video on search engines like Google.

SOURCE: SAUL LOEB/AFP/Getty Images; Central Press/Getty Images.

seconds, the image of Ralph Lauren will come, smiling to life on the screen…. Ralph will ask for some particulars…. Perhaps price will be discussed…. It won't really be Ralph Lauren…. More accurately, it will be virtual Ralph having a virtual conversation. He'll ask about your size, your color preferences and so on, an exact version of it will appear on screen (p. 14).

It was funny then, but a reality now (see Figure 13.2). Already you can try on items of clothing in "virtual reality" and on the screen alter the color schemes, accessories, sizes, and so on, and add or subtract what you wish (see Figure 13.2). Other possible uses for virtual reality technology include such things as virtual golf lessons, perhaps taught by a virtual Tiger Woods using Wii. And think about what the pornography industry might do with this new and disengaged interactive technology. One hesitates to imagine the possibilities—especially since there are already over eight million pornographic websites available for the average voyeur. The military is particularly interested in this interactive media and how it can be used to measure the endurance of its troops under certain conditions (e.g., heat, humidity, freezing temps, carrying various weights of "stuff") (see Box 13.4). One only needs to stop and think of the possible applications of the interactive word to find that they too are

breathtaking. This is one of the reasons we have included at least one interactive box in each chapter of this book—to remind you of the possibilities. Of course, many of them are merely "fun," but then warfare on the interactive screen might be labeled "fun" by some persons as well. In a way, the interactive world involves the print, audio/video, and computer industries all at the same time.

According to Stewart Brand's (1987) description, these three industries realized over 25 years

FIGURE 13.2 **Virtual Changing Room**

You can also "try on" your preferred fashions using interactive media.

SOURCE: WU CHING-TENG/Xinhua/Landov.

BOX 13.4 Interactive Media and "Department Store" Shopping

Most of us already shop for some things online, such as books and clothing, but what about an interactive site with a mega-menu that tops most major department stores? Go to Weblink 13.1 and surf through the multitude of options there, ranging from 11,000 baseball cards with price comparisons from over 20 sources or an online college degree in interactive media or interactive branding. (You can access this and all of the other Chapter 13 weblinks through your companion website for *Persuasion*, Chapter 13 resources.) Enter whatever you are shopping for at the top of the page and select from the categories in the next space. Click the "find" button and explore the interactive mega-market, which could run to thousands of options. What might sites like this do to traditional in-store, television, and catalog shopping? How might a political candidate use a similar site to compare positions on various issues, to solicit voter input, or to raise money? Check out Weblink 13.2 and see how the shopping cart in your local supermarket will be interacting with you to remind you of special offers, and so on. Or search the web and discover how to get a custom-tailored suit in more than 1,000 styles and many more colors where your measurements are taken and clothing is custom-made electronically. Imagine how else this technology will impact our individual and isolated personal lives in the future.

ago that phenomenal changes in communication technology were inevitable and that the ability to develop them effectively and prudently was far improved by pooling their resources. So the Media Lab at MIT was invented and funded, sought out the brightest and best media researchers, and asked them to literally "invent the future" in the various communications industries. The three industries were already beginning to converge before the Media Lab was instituted, as shown in Figure 13.3. Some examples of this convergence or overlapping of media include print that is computer typeset and enhanced visually by digital video technology, or computer-generated and produced video graphics, and electronic mail, faxes, and digital audio. Even some print ads, like birthday greeting cards, contain a chip that plays a song like "Happy Birthday" when opened, and no one is surprised anymore. Some observers foresee a much broader convergence of the three technologies.

Look at Brand's predicted new configuration, which he made 25 years ago, and consider how the convergence has become even more unified in recent times as seen in Figure 13.4.

FIGURE 13.3 The convergence of the print, film/video/audio, and computer industries and technology in the 1990s.

SOURCE: © Cengage Learning 2013.

FIGURE 13.4 The convergence of the print, film/video/audio, and computer industries and technology today and in the future.

SOURCE: © Cengage Learning 2013.

| BOX 13.5 | **Two Pioneers in Media Theory** | |

The work of these two important media theory pioneers—Tony Schwartz and Marshall McLuhan—can help us understand the experiential nature of the current electronic interactive technology and how and why it is so very effective in the process of persuasion. Thus, we can begin to prepare for the nearly unbelievable developments we have been encountering in the recent times and get ready for the many more that we will have to encounter in the years ahead. Their theories can help us to become accustomed to the changing world of the resulting persuasion and to use and be persuaded by those media. For both of them, validity of their theories, like proof, is "in the pudding" or in the degree to which what they predicted early on in the electronic age has come true and persists in the persuasion each of us faces today.

A brief example demonstrates this point. Over 30 years ago, Brand predicted, "Twenty years from now your TV set will probably have 50 megabytes of random access memory and run at 40 to 50 MIPS [millions of information pieces per second]. It'll basically be a Cray computer" (Brand, 1987, pp. 77–78). While we're not there yet, we have come a long way and are closing in on Brand's predictions. In England, it is now possible to order goods and services directly over your television using an upgraded type of remote control. Did all this change just suddenly appear or were there some who predicted that it would come and how it might be used to persuade us? Of course, the answer is "yes," and we will focus on the work of two of the most insightful of these innovative theorists who dared to imagine the future. They are both widely recognized as true pioneers in the study of media effects. One theorized more about the content of these amazing new media and how the messages sent via them would persuade; and the other theorized more about the media themselves and how the physics of their signals pattern our habits of being persuaded, both physiologically and psychologically, and how they ultimately shape our entire culture, as explained in Box 13.5.

Since the writing of the eleventh edition of this book, much has changed. Then, the most obvious change was that almost every student on campus had a cellular phone and spent almost every hour checking with their friends about nothing—meaningless topics like "Hi! How ya' doing? Yeah, I'm doin' about the same. When's your next class? In DuSable? Yeah, me too," and so on. Then when that 12th edition came out, these same students decided to keep doing it while class was going on and they were supposed to be listening, taking notes, or working on a project. Things have gone downhill since then. Now students don't check their e-mail. They check Facebook or Twitter, or they text something meaningless. They have become handcuffed to their cell phones, isolated from others, and rarely communicate with another person face to face. Now it's an iPhone that'll tell them what the score on the game is, where they are on the globe, and what the constellations are in the sky in the current month—all virtual information that is next to irrelevant to the lives they are leading (see Box 13.6).

| BOX 13.6 | **Interactive Ralph Lauren** | |

Madigan's prediction, now nearly 20 years old, seemed like a fantasy. To see how his imagination matches up with today's reality, look at the similarity between what he described then and what is operating in our interactive world now by going to Weblink 13.3. Read about his new kind of "window shopping" on Madison Avenue. (You can access this and all of the other Chapter 13 weblinks through your companion website for *Persuasion*, Chapter 13 resources.)

SCHWARTZ'S PERSPECTIVES
ON MEDIA USE

The ideas in Tony Schwartz's book *The Responsive Chord* (1973, 1983) have been used by sources ranging from presidential media staffs to business firms and ad agencies selling everything from baby powder to booze. Since its publication and until his recent death, Schwartz has consulted with politicians, industry, the mass media, and the government. In 2007, the Library of Congress decided to archive a complete compilation of his work from 1947 to 1999 as a resource for scholars wanting to study the growth of modern audio, television, and electronic communication technologies (Library of Congress, 2007). Schwartz's original interest was in radio (the understanding of which he believes is basic and essential for understanding all electronic communication) and how radio is able to create emotional and highly involving effects in its listeners. Later he came to believe his theory also explained the effects of television—especially commercials—and other electronic communication technologies. One of his most famous commercials called "Daisy" is a classic in negative political campaigning. He produced over 30,000 radio and TV spots for candidates, corporations, and non-profits. He also demonstrated how citizens who feel neglected by the electronic media can use it in irregular and surprising ways, called "guerilla advertising" by some. With his death in 2008, the Library of Congress has archived over 30,000 of his radio and television commercials, his books and articles, and much of his personal notes and correspondence.

His theory compares two competing models for explaining the way radio and television media work to persuade us: (1) the **evoked recall** (or "resonance") model and (2) the transportation model, which is also called a "teaching" model. The outcome in the first approach is a highly emotional and motivating (almost physiological) recollection of past memories which move us to action, while the second relies on a belief that receivers are more logical and that they learn and believe in good reasons for why they should act as directed.

Schwartz favored the first approach and offered reasons related to how we remember and learn at least some of the lessons of life. He has been called a "media guru," a "media muscleman," and a "media genius," and the tobacco industry voluntarily agreed to stop their advertising on radio and television after viewing one of his anti-smoking commercials. (See Weblink 13.4 for many resources—audio and video—in which he explains or demonstrates his theory in action. You can access this and all of the other Chapter 13 weblinks through your companion website for *Persuasion*, Chapter 13 resources.)

Resonance and Experiential Meaning

As Kathleen Hall Jamieson, Dean of the Annenberg School of Communication notes, Schwartz's theory closely resembles a concept put forth by Aristotle called "empathematic" communication, which means that the receiver becomes essential in creating meaning. This fits nicely with the definition of persuasion put forth in Chapter 1. Schwartz labeled his ideas the "evoked recall model" of communication, which rests on the "resonance principle," which is defined as using messages or message elements that almost unconsciously cue out meanings that receivers already have stored in their conscious or unconscious minds and which combine with the source's cues to create emotional and/or logical meaning. This recollection of past memories connects with present-day events and circumstances, resulting in a harmony or a "resonance" between source, message, and receiver. The basic idea is that it is better to get "messages out of receivers" that will motivate them to action than to try to put, plant, or teach information into their memories, which they will then hopefully recall accurately when the time comes for action. In other words, the resonance principle relies on the sets of experiences and memories that people already have stored inside their heads. This set of past experiences can be cued to produce what Schwartz called "**experiential meaning**" via the resonance principle. It's as if the receiver says, "I've been there," after getting the message, and thus the source's reference to the stored experience resonates with the audience in the same way that notes of music resonate or harmonize with one another.

Using this approach, persuaders might address the problems people have, such as a stalled car, a stolen identity, a problematic child, or paying back a student loan. The potential buyer of a AAA membership knows what a stalled auto is like, and the source can use that experience (or "experiential meaning," to use Schwartz's term) to build a persuasive message around those feelings that will convince you to join AAA even though you might never have given it any previous consideration. Actors in the ad might show frustration exactly like yours at having your car stall just at the most inconvenient time. Their verbal and nonverbal cues, coupled with the proper musical score, might signal the anxiety motorists have felt when they knew a stall would make them miss the commuter train, the important appointment, or meeting the critical person, and thus prevent them from accomplishing important things at work, or in their personal lives. As noted, technical effects like the music or score can heighten those fears by using suspenseful sounds as the stall slowly becomes apparent to the motorist and perhaps stressful clanging as the appointment "emerges" in his or her mind. The voice-over might then say soothingly, "When you've got to be there, AAA gets you there." And we can then observe our now relaxed motorist cell-phoning AAA accompanied by serene music as the driver starts to daydream about how successful his or her meeting will be. Schwartz observed that most experiential meanings such as those depicted in the ad are not usually cued with words in one's conscious memory because the experience and feelings are not really stored in words. Instead, they are stored as a physiological feeling in the pit of our stomach or a sense of ease or uneasiness when problems disappear or emerge in our daily lives. We all know what it feels like to

be embarrassed, and our recollection of that can be cued out of us in ways similar to the AAA ad described above.

The same is true for other emotions, such as those discussed in Chapter 7. And they are coming at us more and more dramatically in our 24/7, networked world of deceptive and dangerous persuasion, and for this we must be prepared. In all likelihood these cues are processed in the peripheral channel of the ELM. The surest way to cue such powerful and emotional feelings out of most receivers is via dramatic enactments (or the narrative), the importance of which we have discussed at length elsewhere. The source's message dramatizes the feeling in the receiver's unconscious memory through music, color, sound effects, the actors' facial expressions or tone of voice, the acoustics, or some other nonverbal and usually visual or auditory image or message—all communicated electronically. This experiential cue creates actual physical feelings in us, according to Schwartz, and results in the kind of co-created meaning discussed in Chapter 1.

One of Schwartz's most famous and critical examples is the iconic "Daisy" ad mentioned above. It was used in the 1964 Presidential campaign at a time when the country greatly feared nuclear war with the U.S.S.R. They had seen the destruction of Hiroshima and numerous televised nuclear tests. In the commercial, the viewer processes the sounds and sights of a little girl counting the petals she pulls off a daisy which then merge with the countdown 10...9...8...7 and so on of a nuclear test—something with which viewers of that time would have been very familiar. This is finally accompanied by the mushroom cloud of a nuclear bomb, followed by a voice-over asking which candidate you want in charge. The images and sounds made viewers feel threatened and emotionally insecure—afraid in the pits of their stomachs—and the ad re-created those experiences and those feelings of fear and insecurity as the voice-over identified nuclear weapons with candidate Barry Goldwater, who had previously suggested using nuclear weapons. We saw a Hillary Clinton commercial in the 2008 presidential primaries that was quite similar. It featured a sleeping child and the visual of a ringing and flashing of the White House "nuclear hotline," after which the voice-over asked a similar question. It apparently did not have the same impact of the 1964 ad, which many at the time thought had swung the entire election to LBJ. In terms of Schwartz's resonance theory, this makes perfect sense. Viewers in 2008 did not have the same experiential fears about nuclear war in their memories. They had probably never seen televised nuclear tests, demolished buildings, vaporized test dummies, and so on and had never been through a nuclear drill at school, or been unable to go to sleep for worrying over the possibility of such an attack. In other words, the ad had no resonance with the modern receivers.

What are some stored experiences and emotions that are common to large numbers of people today, and how can an electronic media interact with internal experiential memories in receivers to cue a recall of them? The job of persuaders is to try to catalog and use these experiential memories in their persuasive arsenals and be ready to pull them out when encountering a set of persuadees for whom these experiential meanings are stored, meaningful, and critical. Then the persuaders must design persuasion to tap those feelings and experiences. We've looked at the stalled car example already. Some others might include: (1) forgetting an important anniversary or event, (2) a plugged toilet or sink, (3) missing out on a great sale or important event, or (4) losing one's wallet or car keys. Any event or situation—everyday or extraordinary—which we have experienced and to which people respond by saying something like, "You're getting awfully close to home," probably is evoking experiential meaning in those receivers. Mass media persuaders, especially advertisers, cue out these resonating experiences using electronic and/or interactive media in most cases. As you examine the media persuasion aimed at you in magazine ads, TV and radio spots, billboards, the Internet, or in interactive media, try to identify the common experiences being targeted in your experiential storehouse and the storehouses of others in the

greater audience. In all likelihood, we process such experiential meanings in the peripheral channel of the ELM without much intellectual evaluation or introspection. Instead, they simply "feel right," and we let them pass through the peripheral channel, taking them in at face value. In other words, they are resonating in a **responsive chord** that "rings true" to us and leads to co-created persuasion that causes purchase, joining, or voting behavior—all of which are critical in the results-oriented world of the Seven Faces of Persuasion. There are several "scripts" that can cue out these powerful meanings, especially now with virtual reality (e.g., the smell or olfactory script as in scratch-and-sniff ads, or the use of various cues to the senses in 4-D movies now available at many theme parks) that can cue out these meanings, thus implementing Schwartz's resonance principle and resulting evoked recall.

We shall discuss three of them that are most familiar to the broader population. They are the verbal script, the visual script, and the auditory script. Depending on future technological developments, other scripts related to the physical senses will certainly emerge. Let us explore these three familiar scripts to discover how clever persuaders are using our experiential memories to convince us by strumming on our "responsive chords" and our experiential memory sets. Schwartz's suggestions seem to be even truer today than when he first wrote about them in those pioneer days of mass media research. You can think of the channels through which evoked recall can be prompted as the verbal, auditory, and visual "scripts" for, as media are being produced, their originators must look at all three.

The Verbal Script

Schwartz's ideas run counter to what many ad agencies practice in developing and testing commercials and to much persuasion theory, which emphasizes specificity, logic, and word choice in building and more importantly in testing the headlines and copy for most ads. Those ads and theories test such things as recall of specific statements, the logic of them, and the effects of the language of the copywriters, in prompting the desired behavior—purchase, donation, or commitment, for example. In Schwartz's opposing view, the **verbal script** is the message in words that we see or hear, but more importantly this script is more than the mere information of the words that are remembered. It includes the emotional feelings that they evoke in the receiver. When most ad agencies test their ads, they usually ask people to look at various ads and then to recall the words, images, statistics, and names in the ad. Rarely are respondents asked about their feelings or experiences, or about relating to the characters in the ads, which is what Schwartz does when he tests ads. For him, if the verbal script resonates and cues experiences from the audience, powerful results usually occur and remain long after the ephemeral words of the ad are gone. For example, a recent radio ad for a brokerage firm cued the experience of being trapped by an automated telephone answering system and its menu. The ad said, "If you want to check your balance, press 1 now. If you want to get a quote, press 2 now. If you want to talk to a real financial advisor, press 8 now and start over. Or try calling Financial Expertise at 1-800-MONEYAID." This message is probably processed in the peripheral channel of the ELM; because of its experiential nature, we all listen to the ad (and probably chuckle) because we've all had the experience of having to wait through similar irritating automated menus and despise them. That feeling is what makes the ad work, and it helps us remember the easily recalled phone number and how we despise the menu after menu of prerecorded messages.

The Auditory Script

The typical TV spot also has an **auditory or sound script**, which are the things you hear that are not words. They are the "language" of sound—sizzles, pops, grinds, clunks, plops, and buzzes—that can often cue powerful, unconscious emotions like those Schwartz describes and which he credits for the most powerful and persuasive message elements or "responsive chords" to which we are likely to respond. For instance, good feelings about parties could be cued by the sounds of beer being poured in mugs rather than by words that talk about the party. Of course, the advertiser usually simply adds some words to reinforce the powerful feeling that the sounds have already called up: "We've got beer in a can that's as good as beer from a keg—Hamm's draft in the new pop-top aluminum can." This auditory script is then further reinforced by the positive musical score and more evocative sound effects such as laughing or beer-chugging sounds.

We have all had experiences cued out of our collective storehouses of auditory memories. For example, take a prize-winning classic ad for Diet Coke that was targeted at working women ages 18 to 34 a few years back. These women are the typical drinkers of diet cola but more importantly are in the age group when powerful brand loyalty is developed. We see and hear the murmurings of a group of attractive women starting to gather at the drinking fountain at break time, and we sense that something important is about to happen. They are laughing and joking with one another even though we don't hear their words. Soon they are all looking out the window, and one says something like, "Okay, it's time" (the only words spoken in the action portion of the ad or its verbal script). The camera cuts to a handsome muscular male construction worker across the street as he peels off his T-shirt revealing the body of a muscle builder (the visual script). The women sigh (again not words but sounds or the auditory script) as he pops open a Diet Coke and swigs it down. (Hint: go to Weblink 13.5 or what is known as the Coke "Hunk v. Bloke" ad. You can access this and all of the other Chapter 13 weblinks through your companion website for *Persuasion*, Chapter 13 resources.)

Words are practically nonexistent and irrelevant because it is the sounds of the women murmuring and sighing coupled with the sight of the male worker stripping off his shirt to reveal his physique that together made the ad work. These sounds and sights act as cues for the experience of voyeuristic lusting in the minds of the women in the ad, probably of the women watching it, and perhaps providing general viewers with at least a touch of humor watching the reality of female sexuality being dramatically revealed. There is nothing logical about the ad or in the responses it cues from viewers. There is little an advertising researcher could test regarding the actual copy used in the ad—it has only a few words. It works for reasons other than clever words—again, in Schwartz's terms, it "resonates" with the audience. The same kinds of experiences can be cued out of receivers in a variety of media contexts—an entertainment program, a radio spot ad, or a print ad containing a musical chip playing "Jingle Bells" while advertising the ideal Christmas gift. They would all rely on stored experiential memories associated with a particular auditory cue like a sound effect or a musical score. Each (or taken together) would lead to a co-created or "empathematic" meaning.

The Sight or Visual Script

The **sight or visual script** also serves as an important source of experiential cues. Several cues happen in the Diet Coke ad—the male's muscles, his sweaty T-shirt being peeled off, and so on. In another example, we see (and hear) Liquid-Plumr clearing an impossibly plugged kitchen sink as the yucky water whirlpools out of the plugged drain with a slurping sound. Another way the sight script cues feelings is by using various camera angles and movement as well as skillful visual editing—all things most beginning film students are taught. A low angle distorts size somewhat and says that this person is someone to be looked up to, is a cut above most people, and is probably a leader who is to be trusted and believed—or a larger-than-life and fearful villain or monster. Quick-cut edits of new cars coming out of a tight S curve can convey a sense of action, power, and control. A snowmobile cuts through a huge snowdrift, suggesting action and excitement. The view then cuts quickly to downhill racers carving their way through a tough slalom course and bouncing through tough moguls, and then a

final quick cut shows ice-boat racers zooming across a frozen lake, skidding around the iceboat race course, and skidding to a stop at the finish line. Not until the end of the ad does the verbal script say, "Warm Up Winter This Year. Come to the Winter Wonderland of Lake Geneva." The ad then closes by showing an attractive couple snuggling in front of the fireplace in the ski lodge, and we all know that it's the end of a perfect day without a single word being spoken. An experiential feeling (e.g., the satisfaction we feel at the end of a taxing but remarkably enjoying day) is again cued out of receivers with only a few words being spoken if at all. The visual script does most of the work here. It builds the excitement and cues experiential meanings from the audience's subconscious. The verbal script tagged at the end of the spot merely tells viewers that Lake Geneva is where experiences like these happen and where memories can be brought to life.

Other aspects of the sight script include the set, costumes, props, and other objects that continue the job of evoking experiential responses from us and thus resonating and resulting in co-created meaning. For example, many newscasts convey a "busy newsroom atmosphere" using a visual script that shows machines churning out copy for fast-breaking news stories while people rush around the set carrying pieces of paper meant to be news flashes; it looks like the anchorperson is engulfed in a functional and hectically busy newsroom. The actual anchors who read the news stories are in another room in front of a blue screen, which is simply superimposed on the staged newsroom that is meant to give the visual impression that they are in the middle of the hustle and bustle. Similarly, the background shots for political candidates can cue nuances of meaning. If candidates are standing in front of the Lincoln Memorial with the president, they must be devoted to issues of equality and justice. If they gather with a bunch of bowlers or drinkers at a local watering hole, they must be regular "guys." And though it's hackneyed for politicians to be shown kissing babies during parades, it also probably cues out experiential memories in many people. The visual script, especially when taken with the auditory script, may be far more powerful, persuasive, and memorable than the words that accompany the sights and sounds.

The titles of Schwartz's books, *The Responsive Chord* and *Media: The Second God*, both reflect the relationship between the audience and the message that is cued out by advertisements, the articles printed in magazines, banners on the Internet, or the programs we see on TV or the films we watch. Think of any of the familiar chase scenes in most thrillers—no words, just sights and sounds—and we all end up on the edge of our seats, perhaps with adrenalin pumping through our veins. Schwartz also noted that the issue of truth is irrelevant in examining this kind of persuasion. In fact, that is what makes his principle and its accompanying scripts the raw material of contemporary propaganda. Today, we see print ads with little or no copy that present a potentially dramatic script that could be brought to life on a television screen using the resonance principle and few words, relying instead on sights and sounds. You will see this principle being used by advertisers in the storyboard of an Acura Integra ad, shown in Figure 13.5. The ad aims at graying baby boomers who recall the experience of playing with a toy called "Hot Wheels" when they were kids. You may have played with a similar toy in your youth and could be a target for a similarly designed ad in the future. The script resonates with these experiences stored in the target's conscious or unconscious mind and uses the visual and auditory scripts to cue out experiential meanings shared by the intended receivers. Of course, the ad intends to use experiential memories to prompt receivers to purchase the car. Persuaders identify such common experiences and then design print or electronic ads that prompt audiences to recall the experience while also mentioning the brand, candidate, or cause.

As it is used in contemporary advertising, Schwartz's resonance principle presents receivers of persuasion with several challenges. They need to identify common experiences that the persuasion aims to prompt out of them. They may need to analyze persuasive messages that plant such experiences to be triggered later at the point of purchase, voting, or donating. They also need to be aware of relationships between the verbal, auditory, and visual elements in any persuasion. (See Box 13.7.)

McLUHAN'S PERSPECTIVES ON MEDIA USE

The Modern Media Revolution

Marshall McLuhan (1963) has been called the "first father and leading prophet of the electronic age" and the "high priest of pop culture" (Kappelman, 2008). Like Schwartz, he was a pioneer of the electronic age (Press, 1995). He was the author of 36 widely acclaimed books on electronic media. Also like Schwartz, he was remarkably accurate in anticipating media effects. As a result, his 40-year-old predictions, such as the development of a "global village," the Internet, virtual reality, and other prophesies related to the media of modern times, have become far more than the simplistic messages that they carry. He also called Tony Schwartz his "disciple" with 20 years of experience. The accuracy of his predictions can be partially realized by reading Box 13.8.

We might take the ubiquitous cell phone as an example of this global village. For example, not that many years ago you could only call Europe using a land line and sometimes only through an operator. Today you can make the same call from your car and for pennies compared to what it cost back then, thus fulfilling McLuhan's prediction of the global village and modern media's ability to "destroy space." On a proportional basis, very few truly essential messages are transmitted using cell phones, but who could live without one nowadays? Certainly none of my students can.

30 Second Television Commercial
COMMERCIAL TITLE: "Hot Wheels"
COMMERCIAL NO: HAAI 3358
PRODUCT: 1994 Acura Integra
Sports Coupe & Sedan

MUSIC AND SFX THROUGHOUT

Introducing the new 1994
Acura Integra.

Not since Hot Wheels...

have cars been this much
fun.

Track sold separately.

© 1993 Acura Division of American Honda Motor Co. Inc. Acura and Integra are registered trademarks of
Honda Motor Co. Ltd. VTEC is a trademark of Honda Motor Co. Ltd. Make an intelligent decision. Buckle up.

FIGURE 13.5

This ad for the Acura
Integra taps into the
experience of having played with a
Hot Wheels racetrack, thus resonating with the experiences of its target audience—male baby boomers
and others who enjoyed the toy.

SOURCE: Reprinted by permission of American
Honda Motor Co., Inc.

BOX 13.7   Resonance and Today's Propaganda

In a collection of quotations from propaganda experts, Kenneth Warren and John Guscott (2000) cite many examples of
the resonance principle being used in propaganda. Go to
Weblink 13.6 and read a few examples and maybe report
them back to the class. There is also an interesting

discussion of how resonance worked in helping bring about
the propaganda leading to the war in Iraq at Weblink 13.7 as
well as video images and examples. (You can access this and
all of the other Chapter 13 weblinks through your companion website for *Persuasion*, Chapter 13 resources.)

BOX 13.8 **Interactivity with Marshall McLuhan**

If you want a quick and somewhat personal interaction with McLuhan and what he might have said about YouTube, go to Weblink 13.8 where you will find video footage of him discussing media as extensions of our senses and bodies. Other short videos of him discussing such topics as cyberspace, the Internet, the "medium is the message," and other interesting parts of his theories are available. For a quick but excellent overview of his work go to Weblink 13.9. (You can access this and all of the other Chapter 13 weblinks through your companion website for *Persuasion*, Chapter 13 resources.)

Cell phones have become devices that I must outlaw being on during exams (because answers to test items can be easily texted to one's friends in the class, and because the exams themselves can easily be photographed and quickly put into fraternity files). The destruction of space and other predictions by McLuhan predictions are just now coming to pass. We saw the global village in action when nearly 100 countries around the world sent help to the victims of Hurricane Katrina in late 2005 and the tsunami in Japan in 2010. A recent book by one of his critics is entitled *The Virtual McLuhan* (Theall, 2002), and his popularity is experiencing an enormous rebirth. Once again he is being labeled the "guru of new media," and most of his works are being reissued due to the relevance of his work. His work is being examined from the perspective of the new media, including interactive ones. As we said, he predicted virtual reality, cyberspace, the Internet, and that information would become the crucial commodity of the future—and all 40 years ago and long before any of the needed technology was even invented.

McLuhan thought that most people were looking at the present through a "rearview mirror," viewing the past instead of the future and trying to use history as a guide to decisions and actions of the future. That's probably how we are looking at the mushrooming of terrorist organizations and their actions—we assume their past actions will be repeated and then we go about taking actions and enacting laws designed to prevent similar actions in the future. In reality, the past actions will probably not be repeated and new (and

perhaps deadlier) tactics will be employed—who would have predicted that someone would use a shoe for hiding an explosive device on airplanes? Or that an eight-year-old would be wired with dynamite? Yet, you and I have to take off our shoes every time we want to get on a plane. And who would have predicted that Wii technology would be used not so much as an entertaining video game but as a therapeutic technique in assisted-living facilities? Who would have predicted 40 years ago that we could shop online? Or that information would become the prime product of our culture today, with millions of websites from which to choose, and with the information readily available simply by entering a few key words into a search engine. And virtual reality is here for real—it's not just another video game, but the place where many things will be invented, designed, engineered, marketed, and accomplished in the future.

Yes, McLuhan had much to tell us—especially about persuasion and being persuaded in an electronic and interactive age.

If you type the words "Marshall McLuhan" into any search engine, you will find that his work has taken on new relevance in an interactive media age. Four years ago I found over 50,000 entries. Today, I found 1,140,000. His relevance is immediate, cogent, and still prophetic. McLuhan's most often quoted idea was that "the medium is the message," by which he meant that the effect any new medium has on culture is much greater than the actual messages it carries. The invention of print is a good example, as we noted above. The Renaissance was much more important than the books that were printed at the time. It became a whole new way of thinking, acting, and organizing. Television as a medium was much more important for its impact on modern life than any television programming has been. We were entertained by *I Love Lucy*, but we were not really informed by the program. Instead, we were introduced to a new way of life. Your parents and grandparents had to learn a whole new way of family living and learning. We got live news on TV instead of yesterday's news in tomorrow's newspaper, and now we can get it 24/7. People used to wait impatiently for the delivery of the day's newspaper to get the latest stock reports, weather predictions, fast-breaking news stories, and more. Today fewer and fewer subscribe to a newspaper, especially if they are under age 35, and fewer yet read more than a few pages, and then usually in favorite sections like sports. Now, we can overdose on the news to the degree that it almost seems as if there is nothing that is really "new" news anymore—just the same re-runs of the 20-minute news cycle we hear on all news radio stations, and it doesn't matter if you watch FOX, CNN, MSNBC, or any of the 24/7 news sources. You will see pretty much the same footage and hear the same interviews. Most students believe they are getting their political news from the monologues on late night television shows like The Daily Show, their Facebook or MySpace site, or from blogs. The "real" news that you might see locally or read about in a news weekly magazine is much more in-depth, of course; but it is much less dramatic, much less visually interesting, and much more work for you as a receiver. So television as a medium has also changed the nature of our news since the introduction of the 24/7 news networks. Of course, there isn't enough real news to fill all that time, so "fillers" have had to be invented to round out all that excess "news" time. These have usually been in the form of talk television and radio or political humor shows from commentators like Bill O'Reilly and Rush Limbaugh or shows like "The Colbert Report."

Another good example that demonstrates how the medium has become the message is professional football. In order to work an extra timeout into each game (and thus squeeze in more money-making commercials), some decades ago television induced the leagues to insert a two-minute warning just before each half ended. This in turn led to the two-minute drill, which changed football from a running game to a short passing game with lots of quick plays being called in a short amount of time. This changed the game into one in which the great percentage of contests get decided by a few points scored in the last two minutes. So McLuhan's fans can argue that TV gave us an entirely new sport—virtual pro football. There is the joke about the guy who lost $10,000 on the games and another $20,000 on the instant replays. Of course, while television gave us some good things, it also cost us others like long family talks at the evening dinner table and actual conversation in our leisure. In fact, the art of conversation is barely still alive except among old folks like your author

McLuhan's ideas resemble Schwartz's in many ways, and the two worked together at one time. McLuhan believed that we relate to media in two ways. First, he said that every medium is an extension of one of our senses or body parts. For example, print is an extension of our eyes—it allows us to see and absorb much more information than we could prior to its invention.

Speech speed is far slower than reading speed, so we can cover much more information than we ever could during the age of the spoken word by learning to read. Radio and the telephone were an extension of our ears, so we could hear many more things from much farther away than we could without those media. Television is an extension of our eyes and our ears, so we can see and hear far more and from farther away than we ever could without it. And McLuhan predicted that the computer would become an extension of our brain, which is potentially frightening when you think of it. It allows us to think of much more than we could prior to its presence. What has that led to? Just think about all the new jobs, the new ways we do business, identity theft, blogging, Hogging, the elimination of almost all written personal communication and correspondence (on which much of our written history has been based) other than via e-mail (which can be easily misunderstood, leading to various arguments and miscues and that seems to be dying through neglect by today's users of SNM).

Media also can change our way of thinking about our world. For example, as noted earlier, when the telegraph gave people the ability to communicate quickly across great distances (thus "destroying" space) we began to think of our country as much smaller than we had before. We could now predict the future better. We could know the price of wheat at the Chicago markets in seconds, even way off in Kansas where the stuff was actually grown. In fact, the power to predict may have led to what we now call the "futures market," in which we buy and sell wheat that hasn't yet been planted. TV also gave us new ways of organizing our lives around its programming, such as the six o'clock or ten o'clock news at night, *The Today Show* and its clones in the morning, and *Sesame Street* and other children's programming in the afternoon. In fact, most people schedule their lives to some degree around TV programming.

Television has surely altered our sense of community and belonging as well. Following the devastating submerging of New Orleans and other parts of the Gulf coast, millions of people altered their views about a variety of things like donating aid, and what it was like to be black and poor. Public opinion of the president took a nosedive after he did a "flyover" not until some days after the disaster. People also probably altered their viewing habits by watching 24/7 news channels and the Weather Channel during those days. And with TVs on more than seven hours a day in the average American home, there simply is not enough time for the socializing and family life that occurred prior to its existence. Imagine the possibilities that can emerge from the fact that 65 percent of children the age of eight or above have a television set in their bedrooms (and probably a computer as well, and possibly a cell phone), thus further fracturing family relations (Kaiser Family Foundation, 1999) making child pornography and child stalking much easier in the new millennium than could ever have been imagined.

This media explosion has created what one critic labeled "the lonely crowd," in which people in neighborhoods and apartment complexes rarely know one another, and persons tend not to come to the aid of their neighbors like they used to do. A recent trend in Chicago that is causing some members of the population to always stay home are the attacks, robberies, and murders committed by young gangs at L stops and fast food restaurants, all resembling terrorist attacks—though on a smaller scale—all attributed to the televised reports of such attacks. Contrast that to some developing countries where the only television set in the village is owned by the entire community and brings people together daily to interact and discuss things of which they were formerly unaware—world events, propaganda, crops, visions of prosperity in other countries, and so on. And we must remember that television also has an easy **access code**, which means we don't have to learn to watch it in the same way we had to learn to read, calculate, or write, so the poorest peasant in the most wretched of circumstances can see how you and I live. Is it any wonder that others are jealous of America and that we have low ratings and are hated as a people by many across the world? As a result, living in contemporary times can be both positively and negatively affected by what we learn via TV, the Internet, and other media. MTV, for example, clearly altered American pop culture, and many believe it provided new and disturbing role models for the actions and emerging values of young people like yourselves—things like violence, sexual role models, and the denigration of women. What has TV and the computer taught us about the treatment of minorities, children, and women? MTV was so concerned about these possibilities that the network partnered with the American Psychological Association to develop a warning system that gave indications of the link. Prisoners at a minimal security facility in Minnesota used the Internet to access local small-town newspapers. There they harvested the names of young children whose parents or grandparents put birthday greetings into the newspaper along with a picture of the child. The harvested pictures and names were then collected into a sort of "catalog" and sold presumably to at least some, if not most, persons who were pedophiles (Larson, 2008).

In a curious and unexpected surprise to most readers, McLuhan distinguished the difference between the **signal** used by a medium (sounds that activated the ear drum or visual dots on a television screen that triggered nerves in the eyes to send information to the central nervous system) and the messages that the signal conveyed via the radio or television program. The signal is what stimulates our information-processing receptors, so print stimulates our eyes, radio stimulates our ears, and television stimulates both, and the computer stimulates our brain waves via one or more of the senses. The message is the meaning intended and conveyed by the signal. McLuhan felt that some signals come to us in what he called a complete (or high fidelity) form, while others come to us in an incomplete (or low fidelity) form. He further speculated that **high-fidelity forms**, such as radio with its complete words, sentences, and music (see Figure 13.6), or film, with its series of complete 35-mm visual pictures (interrupted by brief spaces of no light to give the illusion of movement). They require little effort from information-processing receptors like our eyes or ears. They only send high-definition signals that we then intellectually assemble into complete message that have meaning to us.

Low-fidelity forms, on the other hand (e.g., the telegraph, whose electronic impulses or dots and dashes had to be translated into letters and then into words, cartoons, or television where only a few lines of resolution or pixels are processed by the central nervous system) require much more effort (as seen

FIGURE 13.6   **Family Radio Listening was a Hot Media with Little Social Networking**

Radio as a "hot" media was not useful for social networking.

SOURCE: Daily Herald Archive/SSPL/Getty Images.

in Figures 13.7 and 13.8) before meaning can be derived. These low-fidelity media signals may only consist of lighted dots on a lighted screen (and in analog TV far less than half of the lines of resolution are showing at any given instant, as seen in Figure 13.8), and they require us to stretch our senses to convert the incomplete signals into complete

1366 Pixels

768 Pixels

FIGURE 13.7   **HDTV**

A View of "Pixels" or Basics of HDTV

SOURCE: © Cengage Learning 2013.

FIGURE 13.8

Half-Lit Lines of Resolution of Analog TV

We really only see half of the picture at any given instant on analog TV.

SOURCE: Yaruta Igor/www.shutterstock.com.

signals before assembling them into meaningful messages or images. So, though its content may be insipid, the television signal is complex. According to McLuhan, the same message content (e.g., a news flash or headline) differs when sent via the two forms—one high-fidelity like printed headlines and the other low-fidelity like a news flash on TV. The high-fidelity forms, such as film, result in little physiological or **sensory involvement** in decoding the signal, and it doesn't take much physiological effort to process these completed signals into the meaningful message. The low-fidelity form is quite the opposite. It requires much more physiological participation in order to decode the signal and assemble its parts into meaningful elements. This results in high physiological or **sensory participation** according to McLuhan. He called the high-fidelity or complete message signals like film "hot" media and the low-fidelity or incomplete ones like the TV screen "cool" media (see Table 13.1).

TABLE 13.1 Hot and Cool Media

Medium	Source of Information	Definition	Participation	Type of Medium
Television	Lighted dots	Low	High	Cool
Books	Completed letters	High	Low	Hot
Cartoons	Dots on paper	Low	High	Cool
Photographs	Image on film	High	Low	Hot
Telephone	Low-fidelity sound wave	Low	High	Cool
Movies	Moving image on film	High	Low	Hot
Telegraph	Dots and dashes in sound	Low	High	Cool
Digital audio	High-fidelity sound wave	High	Low	Hot
Personal computer and Internet	Lighted dots	Low	High	Cool

© Cengage Learning 2013

Hot Media

Hot media rely on signals having high-fidelity, completeness, or **definition**, as McLuhan called it. Hot media include film (but not TV, which was cool since only partially lighted pixels or lines of resolution had to be completed by the central nervous system), digital music (but not analog music for the same reasons), photos (but not cartoons—ditto), and books (but not comic books—ditto again). McLuhan considered them hot because, unlike cool media such as television or the computer screen, they do not require much effort from our sensory receptors to communicate complete signals with which the central nervous system finally arrives at meaning. Hot media, conversely, have complete or fully defined high-fidelity or "finished" signals. As noted earlier, films used to be made up of sequential photographs (usually 35-mm "slides" filling the whole screen and separated by a brief blackout to create the illusion of motion), while television "pictures" are quite incomplete, in comparison, since not all pixels or all lines of resolution glow on the screen at any one instant. In fact only half of the lines of resolution are lit at the same time in analog TV. As a result, there is only an incomplete signal being processed to the central nervous system where it must be assembled to yield meaning.

Cool Media

As noted, the signals we perceive and process in **cool media** have low-fidelity definition, or completeness, so we must work harder to physiologically process them. Cool media include television, the telephone, and the computer screen. Consider the telephone. It does not have a high-fidelity speaker in the earpiece. If you really want to know what the fidelity of its speaker is, just hold it away from your ear by a foot or two. This poorer quality of the speaker is why it is sometimes difficult to determine who is calling us. In fact, if we don't recognize who is speaking, we fake it until we pick up a cue that allows us to correctly identify who it is that is calling us. And the fidelity is worse with cellular phones, which are really only greatly improved walkie talkies. Similarly, we had to

imagine both high and good sound quality with the old wind-up phonograph and even with the early electronic phonographs, though they had much greater fidelity in their sound. To be decoded, these cool media require far greater physiological and later psychological effort on our part in order to decode the signals and assemble the meaning of the messages they carry to us. For example, a cartoon's signal consists of simple line drawings that are far less complete than a photograph. Charlie Brown's head and face consist of a round ball with two dots, a sidewise letter "u" for a nose, a wiggle line for a mouth, two bumps for ears, and a squiggle of hair—almost nothing to put together. A photograph of the young boy who may have served as Charles Schultz's model for Charlie Brown would be far more complete—in fact, a near replica. So the cartoon is cool while the photo is hot.

What kinds of messages are best for cool media? McLuhan said that cool media breed cool messages. More than a decade early, he predicted that someday a cool person—perhaps a movie star—would be elected president, and 16 years later, that's what happened. Today, the politicians who catch on are easy-going and cool, like Bill Clinton, George W. Bush, and perhaps Barack Obama. They are informal, relaxed, personable, and sometimes even ambiguous in their style and messages. They might differ widely on policies, but they will be very similar in communication styles. Likewise, we see more and more TV commercials relying less and less on specific and concrete words or scripts, and more and more on the creation of a mood or feeling using Schwartz's visual and auditory scripts. Viewers add to or subtract from such commercials and arrive at their own final meanings. Think of the spots that create a sense of anticipation through the use of music, sets, or lighting. For example, we hear the sounds of a love ballad. Then we see a well-dressed couple slowly walking down the stairs of the fancy restaurant. The man gives the valet the keys to get his car. Up drives a Volkswagen Passat. Only then does the voice-over tell us (and then only with a few words) that the "Passat is in good taste anytime, anywhere." The specific content of the message (the words spoken) is almost as incomplete as the signals used—the visual and auditory scripts—and so the message matches the cool quality of the TV signal.

It is interesting to apply some of McLuhan's ideas about hot and cool media to recent communication technologies that have become widespread since his death. As cellular technology increases, for instance, we have processed more and more cool digital signals such as digital photographic and digital televised images. And you have probably experienced how cool these messages are—the photos need re-touching, the already cool signal from a cell phone breaks up, the flat screen television seems to have lines that divide it into quadrants, and it breaks up into tiny bits. What we experience is the further cooling of signals sent by a cool medium. It may get so cool that both cell phone parties agree to hang up and try again later. And those who use texting don't even use complete words. McLuhan also accurately predicted a great increase in the use of cool media, resulting in increased audience participation. And he predicted that when coupled with satellite transmission of TV, radio, telephone, and computer messages, these cool media would lead to his global village, in which everybody would be interested in everybody else's business. The iPhone is very cool and you must work your senses very hard to decode its many applications. One app now in testing stages with rabbits consists of contact lenses with sensors that are able to pick up data of various kinds—the visual scenes that you are in, their temperature, actions taking place in them, things that you recognize (e.g., other people's faces), and sends them to your iPhone, which will analyze and file these data for later use ("Fresh Air," NPR, July 14, 2011).

We are now beginning to experience that global village in many forms--the Internet, chat groups, blogs, Twitter, e-mail, and of course SNM—all of which are highly participative and involving, as his theory predicted. However, the global village is not very peaceful because everyone's business is somehow affecting everyone else's business, so conflict becomes more and more likely. Most of us have had the experience of being almost totally misunderstood when using e-mail and losing track of real-life cues (e.g., facial expression, tone of voice, etc.), and the same can be the case when having an argument via cell phone. And taken together with Schwartz's idea of resonance, the involving and participatory trend and coupled with evoked emotional experiences that are prompted by mini-cues allow people to add their own meanings, which provides a powerful set of tools in the hands of creative and insightful persuaders. In addition to the highly philosophical, predictive, and almost rhetorical theories of both Schwartz and McLuhan, the study of media and media effects on people and culture have been enriched by several other more "scientific" theories developed by social scientists versus philosophers, and they continue to be enriched by other theories meant to explain human behavior in terms of the effects of the mass media of our times. Let us examine some of them now. In one way or another, they all involve both of the paths of the ELM and the power of SNM.

USES AND GRATIFICATION THEORY

Uses and gratification theory is another approach to studying the effects of mass media, and it focuses on how receivers use media to gratify, meet, or satisfy their individual needs. It assumes that we all have differing primary, secondary, and even tertiary needs for various types of information in our complex and sometimes confusing world. In order to make sense of our lives, to help us make decisions about the various circumstances we meet in a 24/7, potentially dangerous world, to learn or to simply avoid boredom, it has become essential for us to use various media at different times and in different situations to get highly critical as well as inconsequential information (Blumler, 1979; Rubin, 2002). As we observe ourselves using various media, we can easily identify that there are four basic or primary needs and many secondary or even tertiary ones for which information is needed and for which we turn to mass media to gather.

The first need is **surveillance**, or the need to keep track of our daily physical and human environment—the events that can impinge on our lives like the price of gasoline, the likely candidates for political office, the economy, new brands, our favorite sports team, community events, and of course, the weather. There is too much happening for us to keep track of all the events and persons and things affecting our daily lives, so we usually turn to the media to keep up to date, and we use that information to decide which items to focus on and attend to in order to maintain order and to avoid trying to multi-task with what amounts to information overload and total chaos.

The second need is **curiosity**, or the need to discover and learn about previously unknown information that is not necessarily critical to our interests and daily lives but which could possibly be important someday and that also simply interests us. Topics might include the upcoming TV season of a favorite series, the latest celebrity gossip that might come up in conversation, the upcoming elections, scandals, new technologies that we might adopt, world events that could affect our lives, new developments in medicine, or the details of a direct mail or direct television sales offer. News tabloids have always traded on this curiosity need, and it is no surprise that the *National Enquirer* claims to be the newspaper with the largest circulation in the country. No one really believes in Elvis sightings, or 40-pound babies being born, but people continue to buy the tabloids that publicize out of curiosity these unlikely and unbelievable events. Our curiosity is piqued by the sensationalist headlines (I even pick them up sometimes while waiting in the checkout line), and the paper regularly sells out. And, of course, there are far more intelligent and "truer" sources that deal with topics that pique our curiosity, as seen in Figure 13.9 where there are at least nine curiosity "teasers." Just on the cover.

We view them on some television channels like A&E and the History Channel, public television, and news specials, or we read about them in specialized publications like news weeklies and special interest magazines *(Golf, Tennis, Family Circle, Architecture,* and *National Geographic)*.

The third need we experience and use media to gratify is **diversion**, or relief from boredom, which is a problem for many if not most persons at one time or another. For example, we watch movies or sporting events on TV, read newspapers or magazines, play video games, attend films or watch DVDs of them, listen to the radio or our iPod while we drive, or read novels for pleasure. We do all these things and many others in order to gratify our need to relax and to avoid being bored, according to the uses and gratifications theory. Media are used in these cases to fill time, but not really to gather information that we believe we must know or that will impact our daily lives.

The fourth need is for **personal identity**. We are all uncertain about our identities, our life goals, and the impact of certain events in an ever-changing and networked world, so we turn to media to help us discover who we are, what we stand for, what we should strive for, what will make us feel satisfied with ourselves, and how we are living out our lives. To fill this need we might read about places we have never visited, watch The Learning Channel, or learn what we believe regarding political issues and government policies by listening to or watching radio and television talk shows. We also learn what we are *not* by watching "trash TV" shows such as the *Jerry Springer Show, Judge Judy,* or other similar programming, or by reading about current events or the lives of other persons whom we admire, or by paying attention to cultural issues featured on or in other media. Interestingly enough, persons who are more self-assured and outgoing fill personal identity needs by reading, whereas less self-assured and outgoing persons rely on television to fill this need.

Other lesser or secondary needs (e.g., the need for mastery and control) are served in simple and complex ways by media. We want to feel competent at things so we reassure ourselves of our competence by watching or reading about carpentry, auto

FIGURE 13.9

Satisfying the Curiosity Need

The *National Enquirer* maintains its top national circulation through the curiosity need.

SOURCE: NC1 services only, and do not, nor are they intended to, convey to the user any ownership of Copyright or License in the material. By publishing this material, the user expressly agrees to indemnify and to hold WENN harmless from any claims, demands, or cause/Newscom

mechanics, gourmet cooking, home decorating, for example. There are even tertiary competence needs that we gratify by watching game shows to see if we know more than the contestants, playing video games and challenging others at them, listening to nostalgic music of the past, attending revivals of old Broadway hits like *South Pacific* or *Oklahoma*, or by gambling online to see if we can beat the odds. Our primary, secondary, or tertiary social needs can be gratified by entering into and participating with others in chat groups to compare accomplishments, discuss issues,

learn about the latest fad, and exchange knowledge with and from our chat "partners."

All these primary needs, as well as some secondary and tertiary ones, frequently can serve as attention-getting devices in persuasion and even in some cases as first premises in enthymemes. They appeal to us to keep up with the world around us, not to miss out on the latest technology, and above all to avoid becoming just another bored loser. Knowing how people are using media to gratify needs can help us plan targeted persuasion.

As receivers, we need to monitor our own uses of media and what are we turning to media for to gratify our personal needs for persuaders—politicians, marketers, ideologues, etc.—who often target their messages at our needs and use various media to gratify them.

AGENDA SETTING

Another explanation of the ways mass media persuade us relates to their **agenda-setting** function (McCombs & Shaw, 1972). According to this theory, the public's agenda of what is important and needs our attention includes the kinds of issues people discuss, think and worry about, and the emotions and data that these issues involve. Further, the theory holds that this public agenda is powerfully shaped and directed by what the news media choose to highlight and report on repeatedly, as well as what they choose to downplay, dismiss, or ignore (as shown in Figure 13.10).

This is especially important since the concentration of media ownership has increased with mega-media giants like Rupert Murdoch, Time Warner, Disney, General Electric, or Viacom, all of which own and control multiple information outlets and feed us much of what we read, see, hear, and "think" we know and ultimately believe. The main point about agenda setting is that *mass media do not tell us what to think; but they* **DO** *tell us what to think about* and ultimately believe and act upon. How many persons would have stayed glued to their TVs during the O.J. Simpson trial or the Japanese tsunami and resulting nuclear disaster if the media hadn't reported on them daily? Would we be thinking about the war on terrorism if the media hadn't run stories about various bombings around the world *after* September 11th? After all, few ever heard of Osama bin Laden or Al Qaeda prior to then. The decisions about what to focus on and, equally important, what *not* to focus on in reporting the day's events fall to a small number of persons.

Agenda-setting theory calls such persons "gatekeepers," and they include people like reporters for the wire services, editors, news photographers, and others. They are called gatekeepers because they decide what gets covered in the news and what doesn't; which pictures of a crime scene are televised and which ones are not; which victim interviews get used and which are discarded. In other words, they decide what gets past the "gate" or the finite space and/or time used for print or electronic news. This agenda setting can be seen in the propaganda conveyed.

FIGURE 13.10

A Model of How Agenda Setting Occurs

SOURCE: Prof. Frank Brettschneider, University Höhenheim, Germany.

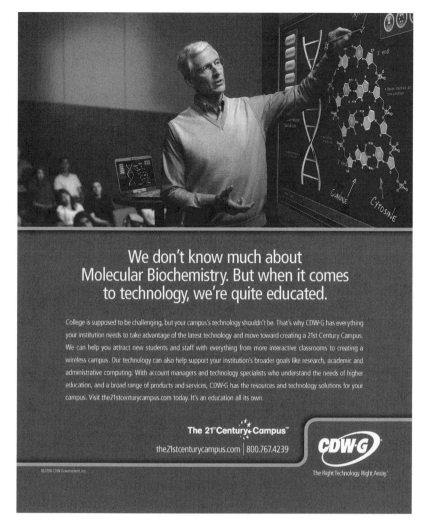

FIGURE 13.11 **CDW Shares Technology with Colleges** CDW Government, Inc., in addition to offering its regular products, are now working to share technology with college campuses. It should increase student access and convenience to Internet resources.

SOURCE: Courtesy of CDW. All Rights Reserved. Visit www.cdwg.com.

The gatekeepers have access to more news than they can ever possibly report on, and so they must choose what stories to run, which way to point their cameras, what illustrations to use, whom to interview, and what point of view to use in reporting the events of the day. How do they make program decisions, and by what criteria? Why, during the 2008 primary elections, did they focus on Barack Obama's former pastor and some of his inflammatory sermons but not on some other issue, such as what Obama himself believed in

terms of religious issues? Why didn't they give Hillary Clinton's pastor similar attention?

Not much is exactly known about the process gatekeepers go through and what criteria goes into making such decisions, but there are some hints as to how and why the decisions are made. Media scholar J. Meyrowitz (1985) refers to one criterion called "least objectionable programming," which he defines as "… a program that is least likely to be turned off, rather than a program viewers will actively seek out" (p. 73). Some media critics note that, although media advertisements purportedly sell products to viewers, the real economic design of the mass media industry is to sell *audiences* to advertisers. With TV, for example, we think of programs as products for which we pay a price in that we have to watch ads from the programs' sponsors. In reality, *we are the products*, and *we are being sold to the advertisers.* That's why "Sweeps Week" is so critical. The amount a network can charge for a commercial during a program that gets high ratings during Sweeps Week is much higher than for a low-rated one, so it all comes down to what advertisers are willing to pay for the real product—you and me! Thus, according to Meyrowitz, the media's agenda-setting goal is to design programming that will capture, hold the attention, inform, educate, etc., the largest number of people, but the media aims for the most likely segment of people who might purchase, vote, and/or join and whom advertisers and policymakers want to reach as a result (e.g., upscale spenders, gourmet cooks, sports fans, or college students willing to adopt a credit card).

One criterion for determining what news to present is the nature of the audience (sometimes called the "target" or the "prospect" by marketing experts). Persons who read *U.S. News & World Report* or who watch *The O'Reilly Factor* will be more conservative than those who read *Newsweek* and who watch *The Colbert Report* or public television news. Gatekeepers frequently select stories that put a conservative slant on an issue, thus setting a different agenda for the conservative viewers, listeners, or readers than for the liberal ones. Another criterion for deciding what is to be broadcast or printed is whether it can be delivered as a 20- to 30-second sound "bite" on TV or told simply and quickly in a magazine story or a television news report to sufficiently answer the journalist's five key questions—what, when, where, how and why. Communication scholars Hall Jamieson and Kohrs-Campbell (1996) define such reportage as a **news bite** or a piece of news "less than 35 seconds long, delivered by a credible source in an energetic way." If the first story in the broadcast is an unexciting news bite, then it hasn't been an important news day. However, if the first story is a fascinating news bite of a national or international tragedy like the cyclone that killed 100,000, or a breaking scandal about Rupert Murdoch's employees hacking into Queen Elizabeth's cell phone, which will be followed up on later in the broadcast, viewers know that an in-depth report will follow. Because they provide us with yesterday's news tomorrow, newspapers and news weeklies are practically compelled to run a version of the stories that TV news programmers ran the day before. In a sense, television sets the agenda for print versions of the news, and together they set the public agenda of things that must be taken care of or attended to. Try to keep track of this progression—see what the top story on the television evening news is and see if that isn't tomorrow's headline or front page item in your newspaper and the focus of the news weeklies later in the week. Both the newspaper and the news weekly can do in-depth coverage of issues, but fewer and fewer people are reading them and for less and less time.

Another criterion used by gatekeepers to determine what gets reported and what does not is the expressiveness or dramatic quality of both the audio and video in the story (Meyrowitz, 1985). The old chestnut about "man bites dog!" being more interesting and newsworthy than if the dog bit the man applies here. Newsworthy stories include the instantaneous reactions of parents who just heard that their children have been killed in an auto accident. The camera zooms up to their faces, and the audience supposedly experiences how they must feel. Or if the lead story on the 10 o'clock television news is "Washington, D.C., Madam Commits Suicide in Trailer Park!" watch for a front page feature on her history. Another criterion that may or may not have important implications for the larger question of agenda setting is the degree to which today's citizenry is getting part or most of their daily news from Internet sources like YouTube, MySpace, Facebook, various search engines, the blogosphere,

---

BOX 13.9   **Agenda Setting and Propaganda**

For a good review of the agenda setting research, go to Weblink 13.10. An important implication to the theory of agenda setting is how this characteristic of media can be used to create propaganda. The media focus on the topic of "weapons of mass destruction in Iraq" helped set the agenda for the U.S. invasion and the mammoth expenditures in lives and materials that resulted and that may be preparing the

United States for a war with Iran. See Weblink 13.11 for a complete analysis of how this happened. A very complete catalog of both print and video propaganda flowing out of agenda setting can be found at Weblink 13.12. (You can access this and all of the other Chapter 13 weblinks through your companion website for *Persuasion*, Chapter 13 resources.)

---

and so on. A recent example may give us a hint. In the spring of 2008, actress, dancer, celebrity, and judge on *American Idol*, Paula Abdul, made an on-air blunder by reading her critique of one of the contestants before the contestant had performed. It was fairly obvious she was reading her critique from a script (due perhaps to her being treated with a "pain patch" for a back ailment). Naturally, the mistake was noted by the usual news sources but it was the number one topic on YouTube the next day, indicating that that's where the news was and is really happening! In fact, many college instructors no longer use e-mail addresses to send class notices to their students, but instead request their Facebook addresses since the students check them far more frequently than they check their e-mail. Perhaps we are seeing an entire revolution in the news industry—it is the receiver who is *really* reporting the news and not the standard news media sources.

How can ordinary receivers like you and me protect ourselves from these agenda-setting and gatekeeping functions of the standard media sources and get at least a sense of what is "really" important in today's news world? Critical receivers of persuasion need to diversify their reading of, listening to, and viewing of news and information to expose themselves to as many divergent sources as possible. Try listening to the news as reported on public television stations or National Public Radio. Watch several television news programs, including your local one. Try to read at least one news magazine per week. Above all, don't let one medium so

dominate your awareness of the world that you overlook other sources of news and information. Even if you watch as much television as others, vary your sources of information.

Agenda setting tells us what to think about in terms of the public agenda, but what about our private agendas? What kind of persons do we want to be? How should a good employee behave in the workplace? What is good parenting? The answers to these questions used to be learned when people lived in nuclear families and in small communities by observing how persons they knew behaved (see Box 13.9). How do we learn these things now? Let us turn to two other media theories that may shed a little light on the potentially disturbing answers to these questions.

LEARNING FROM THE MEDIA
AND PERSUASION

Since most of us no longer live in nuclear families containing three living generations, and rarely live in insular or very small communities, how do we learn the proper behavior for acceptable members of our societies? Further, in a constantly changing world of values and norms, what can we expect of various situations, occupations, personal encounters, and situations that we will meet up with in the future? Remember that new and unexpected occasions and behaviors can occur wherever and whenever you live, whether in cities, suburbs, gated communities, or "rurban" (or rural/urban) locales, and we need to learn what is okay and what is not. These questions are the focus of two theories about how and what we learn regarding events and behaviors from the media of our time and that relate to the process of being a responsible receiver—the goal of this book. These theories are called the social learning and cultivation theories, and of course they are not the only other theories about media effects and persuasion. A good way to remember which is which is that **social learning theory** tells us what to think and do with ourselves and how to behave in given situations (Bandura, 1994). **Cultivation theory**, on the other hand, teaches us what to expect in future possible situations or, to think of it in another way, we learn what to prepare for in future situations (Signorelli and Morgan, 1990).

Social learning theory it is the difference between how to enact violence or when to expect it and maybe how to respond to it in certain situations, as well as the degree to which we can expect to experience violence in our lives in the future. For example, heavy watchers of television, especially violent programming, believe in a much more violent world out there and expect to encounter violence sometime in their lives. This learning can greatly impact us in persuasive ways and can influence how we are persuaded by politicians, advertisers, propagandists, and others. A few examples might help here. You can learn from a television news show (or perhaps a fictional program) that it is possible to smuggle a gun into a classroom or a school in a backpack, or a guitar case, or something similar, and you can learn that you can use it to intimidate someone who is bullying you by threatening them with violence. In other words, you can learn how to commit the crime known as "assault" (which means threatening someone with harm). That's one kind of social learning—you learn how to behave in unpleasant ways as well as pleasant ones. Of course, you can learn many good things as well, such as how to be polite, how to interview for a job, how to ask for a

date, or how to behave when asking your professor about your grade. On the other hand, you can also learn from the same news or fictional programming just how likely a violent event is to occur in your future, at your school, on your job, or at home. A more benign example might help here. Suppose you are a female school student who is regularly watching a daytime soap opera that features teenage moms as characters. Social learning theory would tell you how such moms behave (e.g., how they dress, what they talk like, how they interact with others, how they care for their children). For example, you might learn that such moms use profanity around their children all the time, that that they frequently are antagonistic to authority figures like the school counselor or their parents and neighbors, and that belonging to a gang will help one feel like a part of something.

Cultivation theory, on the other hand, resembles what we called the surveillance need in our discussion of uses and gratification theory. In other words, cultivation theory tells us what is happening in the world around us and what kinds of things we can expect to happen, when, where, and how often. In other words, it "grows" or "cultivates" expectations about the world in which we live. It would tell the same viewers of the sitcom involving teenage single moms about what kind of lives they could expect to live in the future. It might teach them that as a teenage single mom, they can expect lots of boyfriends, extensive wardrobes, exciting times, good jobs, and babies that never cry or are sick. In a very real sense, both theories *persuade* media users about how to behave and what to expect from life. Those views or expectations might range from totally or partially accurate to totally or partially inaccurate, but nonetheless, the viewers tend to believe them and as a result to expect a certain lifestyle.

`In fact, the theory's developer, George Gerbner, felt that television watching dramatically affected viewer's beliefs about what the world outside of television was really like. Furthermore, he thought that these views developed slowly and with repeated viewings and that they were cumulative. In other words, if you watched a lot of television, and particularly similar types of programming, your views of the world "out there" would "build up" until you came to sincerely believe—almost fervently—in their reality. These views of the world didn't necessarily tell you how to behave (as with social learning theory), but instead led you to develop a mindset or a worldview that affected your attitudes about what to expect from teen motherhood, or violence in the streets, or going to college, rather than learning what to do.

Recall what we said back in Chapter 7 about the difference between attitudes and behavior. Attitudes are much easier to change than behaviors—they are fickle in a way. This is probably why cultivation theory predicts changes only after *extended viewing* and even then over repeated times. The theory also holds that these worldviews aren't invented by those who articulate them or demonstrate them through television programming and other media. Rather, they lie dormant in the culture—such as the likelihood of violence happening to you—and are "cultivated" by media exposures to various forms of them. Further, the theory holds that media exposure only has a *tendency* to help them grow and then primarily with heavy viewers who are more likely to overestimate the amount of violence in our culture, rather than light media-viewers whose beliefs are more realistic (Gerbner et al., 1986). This worldview can also be magnified when the viewer actually does experience events that are similar to the media events. (Most students at my school who were in that lecture hall, when the shooter opened fire, killing six and injuring dozens, dreaded ever going back to the room or any large lecture hall. The room never again was used as a lecture hall and many wanted it totally destroyed.) Most important, for our purposes here, is that both kinds of beliefs—those growing out of the "how to" school of social learning theory and the worldviews/mindsets growing out of cultivation theory frequently serve as major premises in persuasion that is highly effective in persuading us (see Chapter 8).

Both theories can be traced back to the Surgeon General's report on violence of over 40 years ago (Baker & Ball, 1969). The report was commissioned back then to look at why the 1960s had been so violent, and why violence had increased, particularly in terms of protest movements over civil rights and the war in Vietnam that ultimately spawned violent acts. The statistics of the times (and more recently) showed increasing violence in the streets, at home, in schools, and elsewhere. Naturally, the interest and research into the media violence grew in the decades following. Most recently, this interest has heightened because of incidents like the shooting and killing of students in schools (e.g., Columbine High School, on our campus, at Virginia Tech in 2007–2008, and elsewhere). Later, other major and minor incidents such as bathroom graffiti forced officials to close schools and to institute severe security procedures (e.g., metal detectors at school entrances, strip searches, and armed security officers) and caused officials and scholars to look to media messages as the underlying causes of this increase in violence. This interest persists but, as in the hypothetical example of teenage moms, the media effects on human behavior of all sorts have been scrutinized using these two "learning theories."

Critical receivers need to ask themselves, "What things have I learned, not from direct observation or experience, but from media sources ranging from television to video games to the Internet, and from SNM?" "How have they implanted major premises in my conscious and unconscious mind that might be used in persuasive arguments to get me to engage in behaviors that I otherwise might have avoided?" "In which information processing path of the ELM have I processed them?" Further, "What expectations do I have about the future world that I may have absorbed from seeing images or ideas via media and not from any reality or direct experience?" and "How might they be used as major premises of arguments to me about preparing for or avoiding such expected circumstances?" After all, in a 24/7 world that is inundated with media of various sorts that bombard us daily, no one should be surprised that persuasion of various kinds—deceptive and accurate, advocacy and propaganda, and the bottom line—is occurring constantly and that receivers should be prepared for it; otherwise, they risk being scammed, deceived, and misled. In past times we could usually rely on newspapers, magazines, radio news, and television news to keep us prepared for this onslaught of persuasion; with the growing monopolization and centralization of our news services, this is no longer necessarily the case. For example, Time Warner now owns CNN, HBO, Cinemax, the Cartoon Network, TBS, TNT, America Online, MapQuest, Movie tone, Netscape, Warner Bros., and over 150 magazines like *Time, People*, and others. These many outlets also have implications for the possibility of propaganda being used against our citizenry, by convincing viewers that just because we have more news media outlets reporting 24/7, we are necessarily getting the news we need.

NEWS MANIPULATION
AND PERSUASION

The news industry is a business, a very centralized and profitable industry, as just mentioned; and the news media stand to profit from the success of their advertiser clients and customers. As a result, no one should be surprised to learn that they don't always print the whole truth and nothing but the whole truth, particularly when it involves their clients—the advertisers—and not us, the consumers of the news. Consider the discussion in Box 13.10 as you struggle as receivers to make decisions about everything ranging from which brand to buy, to which candidate to vote for, to what is the appropriate governmental policy to promote—we need to ask ourselves if the news we get is as truly unbiased as it claims to be. Do the media ever manipulate the news, as some critics suggest? If so, how often? By how much? In what ways? If we have reason to suspect biased news reporting, we ought to acquaint ourselves with the possible tactics that can make or unmake the news. This knowledge will allow us an extra safeguard against possible hidden persuasion in news programs that can affect us as receivers as we try to make decisions that can affect us in major or minor ways.

Key News Sources and Conglomerates

Three major wire services (AP, UPI, and Reuters) used to supply most of the news we see, hear, and read. There was/is nothing wrong with that small number of sources, as long as the news is accurate and as long as the key news items get printed or broadcast. But today even with the numerous and continuous news networks like FOX, CNN,

---

BOX 13.10   **News Manipulation and Propaganda**

We often hear words like "spin" and "junk news" when people discuss what is happening in their daily lives as related to the news in part. They may wonder how high the price of gasoline can go (it actually went to an unbelievable $5/gallon in Chicago in 2011), if we are really "making progress" in Iraq, and just what can be done about global warming? And the news conglomerates play to these issues because they know that such news can draw audiences, increase ratings, and improve advertising revenue. To get a feel for the various facets of this problem, go to

Weblink 13.13 and follow a few of the links, especially the one entitled "Why Big Media is Mum About Its Propaganda Habit," and be sure to watch and listen to some of the video and audio presentations, such as "Stop Big Media—Before the Shot Clock Runs Out." (You can access this and all of the other Chapter 13 weblinks through your companion website for *Persuasion*, Chapter 13 resources.) Also try the articles on why some media outlets choose to consider Paris Hilton to be "big news." There's more here than you can cover, but it's a real eye-opener and interesting besides.

MSNBC, and others, key items don't always get prominent coverage, and it can't all be blamed on gatekeepers any longer. Even your local half-hour 10 p.m. TV news programs contain only 22 minutes of news, or about 3000 total words. The average 400-words-per-minute reader can cover that in only 7 to 8 minutes, and that, in fact, is about the average time spent per day by newspaper subscribers on reading their newspapers. So we miss a lot of important information if we rely on only one electronic media for news; and surfing between them doesn't always do much good either—they all seem to be reporting the same things at the same time and they even use much of the same footage—some of which, of course, is to be blamed on the old wire service system, but much more of which is related to the massive media conglomerates we have mentioned. When you are trying to gain a certain segment of the market (which is what news broadcasts must do to earn profits for the corporate networks and their shareholders) the temptation is to manipulate the news to make it more dramatic, interesting, sexy, sensational, and/or entertaining, so that's why we get the most coverage of sensational or controversial topics. More recently this need for controversy and drama has led to programming that has a certain political bias with programs like *The O'Reilly Factor* and broadcast demagogues like Rush Limbaugh (Larson, 1997). As electronic news pioneer Edward R. Murrow put it: "One of the basic troubles with radio and television news is that both instruments have grown up as an incompatible combination of show business, advertising, and news. Each of the three is a rather bizarre and demanding profession, and when you get all three under one tent, the dust never settles" (Matusow, 1983, p. 304). The show-business aspects of today's news distort electronic news more than ever and can easily let us fall prey to some of the traps in clever persuasion. What are some specific ways news can be manipulated that we should be watching out for as receivers? Perhaps we should investigate reworking our "free for all" model for something more like the BBC or CBC models of state supported media.

Methods of Manipulation

Ignoring. One way gatekeepers and media moguls who control news conglomerates can distort the news is by simply **ignoring** and not ever reporting it, or by minimizing it by giving something else a larger portion of the news space and time than the topic really deserves (e.g., Paris Hilton), or by giving it a bad position in the newspaper, magazine, or television news time. For example, news media initially ignored the danger of global warming and not until former Vice President Al Gore produced a feature film entitled *An Inconvenient Truth*, which also won an Academy Award, did any news source really give the topic the space or time it deserved. Following the film and its awards, numerous specials on various aspects of the problem began appearing on the news media and on special programming on channels like A&E. Until a decade ago, few persons in the United States could say where Afghanistan was located, and fewer knew who Osama bin Laden was and why he mattered to them in any way. And many important political issues are initially ignored because they don't seem interesting or sensational enough.

Favoring the Sponsor. Because every commercial news program has several sponsors, news reporters and editors may soft-pedal any negative news about these sponsors (**favoring the sponsor**). In an old but classic example, it took years to pass a law forcing broadcasters to refuse advertising from cigarette manufacturers. But remember, it pays to "fight fire with fire" and only when Tony Schwartz crafted his devastating anti-smoking ad and the industry saw the damage that could result when taken on by a true expert, did they voluntarily withdraw their ads. Tobacco's newest challenge relates to another element of marketing—packaging. The most recent legislation will require packages to carry pictures of cancerous body parts and warnings depicted with a skull and crossbones, pointing out the dangers of smoking.

How much news time/space is devoted to the profits of the big oil companies even though we all know that the profits are obscene? It is always wise to ask who the sponsor is for a newscast, and getting our news from several sources helps us to avoid sponsor-favoring editing. This is getting even harder to do as news conglomerates continue to grow and slant the news their way. Sometimes, broadcasters have even previewed the news story for advertisers to make certain there is no objection. There is a practice in some television news of distancing advertisers' commercials from the place in the program that could result in negative publicity.

The Pseudo-event. Although there is an overabundance of news each day, not all of it is interesting or entertaining, so news reporters are often drawn to highly dramatic or bizarre events. Historian Daniel Boorstin (1961) called these **pseudo-events** or "planned news." A more modern term is "hyper reality" which sounds like "virtual reality" (and indeed can use virtual reality) but is different. It is a supposedly newsworthy event or story that is carefully scripted and rehearsed. French philosopher and critic Jean Baudrillard defined it as "the simulation of something which never really existed." Umberto Eco called it "the authentic fake." Basically, it is the reportage of an event that has been totally planned in advance and hence isn't really news at all—like a hot dog eating contest or "polar bear" swimming by humans in mid-January.

Such stories fall somewhere between public relations and soft news, such as reporting on a sports celebrity like Michael Jordan deciding to play minor league baseball or coming out of retirement to play basketball again. Various mass movements hold fully planned marches, rallies, or vigils, or use violent tactics such as bomb scares to get media attention. A bomb scare is not a natural or ordinary event. It had to be planned and executed, hence the prefix "pseudo" in "pseudo-event" denoting an unreal event. Numerous pranksters are getting exams and even school canceled by leaving cryptic graffiti threatening bombs or shootings on restroom walls at the schools, thus forcing administrators to be overly cautious out of necessity.

Bias: Verbal and Nonverbal Cues. A skillful interviewer can make an interviewee seem to be quite different from his or her real self. Politicians complain about being misrepresented by the news industry all the time. For example, during the 2008 Democratic primary contests, candidate Barack Obama appeared nervous when questioned about his pastor Jeremiah Wright's comments during a sermon that Obama hadn't even attended or heard about. Wright had said "God damn America!" during the sermon, thus raising the audience's emotions and anger and enraging elements of the viewing audience, especially among religious, working class, families—one of Obama's hoped for constituencies. And Obama's nonverbal discomfort when questioned by the reporter was mentioned as part of the coverage of the news event on my local television evening news report. Naturally, the news reporter nearly "raised an eyebrow" as he commented on the item, and later Obama had to ultimately renounce his pastor, which of course again made a big news item on both local and national network and cable news programs for several days—due at least in part to nonverbal cues. News reporters can make a candidate seem controversial by dubbing an audio track of booing on a video track showing people cheering and then having the announcer say, with a frown on his or her face, that the candidate faces opposition from left and right. Or editors might superimpose two or more conflicting images such as angry housewives complaining about higher food prices and farmers and grain dealers trying to explain why ethanol production was causing higher food prices. The news sources select who is featured, choosing only pro or only con advocates or ones that can be expected to make emotional and exciting quotes. How can we protect ourselves from all these ways of manipulating what we are to believe?

You and I can't possibly look at and listen to all the print and electronic news available out there to combat this sort of bias, but we all can diversify our exposure to news and especially the sources from which we get it. Recognize that much of the news we see, hear, and read is at least somewhat emotional and biased and must be taken with a grain of salt. Again, try reading at least part of a newspaper and news weekly magazine regularly. Listen to the news on a public radio station instead of one that relies on commercial sponsors. If you have to rely on cable all-news stations, try to vary the ones that you choose—don't just watch FOX or CNN or MSNBC—vary your selections. And above all, don't assume that all the news you are getting is the most important, the most accurate and reliable, or the most unbiased.

In reality, most of you don't regularly do any of the above. Maybe you're ignorant of news manipulation or just plain lazy. Across my 40+ years of teaching I've also found that fewer and fewer of you have a good grounding in the history of our country or of the last century or even of the last decade. I fear for you and the country. In fact, most of you are now relying on the MSN home page, Facebook, MySpace, various blogs, SNM, Twitter, and other Internet sources to find out what you will believe is happening in the world and what is *truly* important to you. But at least keep in mind that the news can be manipulated there as well, and its reliability is difficult to determine. I urge you as a critical receiver, gather all the information you have time to get, but judge all of it with a critical eye. Let us now turn briefly to the newest entrant in not only the news industry but more importantly the advertising and related persuasion industries—the Internet.

THE INTERNET AND PERSUASION

A recent editorial in the *Chicago Tribune* noted that early in its life (i.e., the 1980s), the Internet was unregulated and reliant upon the good will of its "Netizens," or citizens of the net. But there was a dark side: "Then came the hackers, the viruses, the worms, spyware, phishing and spam... A handful of groups are now looking into whether the entire Internet needs an overhaul.... With more than a billion Internet users ... a structural overhaul is not an outlandish idea" (*Chicago Tribune*, July 4, 2005). Considering what is discussed in Box 13.11, do you think such an overhaul will ever happen?

At this stage, it is pretty obvious that there will be no such structural overhaul, so we must deal with what we now have. With the bursting of the dot-com bubble and falling Internet advertising revenue, many dismissed the importance of the Internet as a persuasive channel, and some countries like China even forbade its citizens to log on to many sites. Early in the spring of 2011, several Middle Eastern countries facing near-revolutions did the same in the face of public demonstrations demanding that their governments resign. Yet even

---

BOX 13.11   **Diversity and the Media**

The Freeman Institute, found at Weblink 13.14, is an educational resource that celebrates cultural diversity in a number of ways, such as providing training in dealing with diversity and books and videos on the topic and many other issues. (You can access this and all of the other Chapter 13 weblinks through your companion website for *Persuasion*, Chapter 13 resources.) Their slogan is "Dealing with People Who Drive You Crazy." Go to their webpage and explore the links that direct you to a number of diverse communities. Select from among the options that deal with the diversity groups and media and explore their content. For example, regarding Latinos, you might want to select the "Electric Mercado" link and discover how media are now advertising to the $331 billion global Latino retail markets and the $3.2 trillion business-to-business markets. Or you might want to try some of the Black, Native American, or Asian-American sites. Or watch "The Value of Mutual Respect" as well as many other interesting links.

such heavy-handed actions could not stop the citizens of countries like Egypt, Tunisia, Syria, Libya, and others from communicating with one another via cellular and social networking media to plan and execute these revolutions. The same thing happened when the communication innovation of the printed word allowed more persons (e.g., Tom Paine) to communicate with the many instead of the few. And while we can trace the number of hits a certain site gets, we don't yet really know very well yet whether people actually read what is there or whether they process it at all or in the central or peripheral routes of the ELM. Most importantly, we remain unsure that it actually persuades them, but the trend is beginning to emerge that this is so. The Internet not only engages people, it does indeed persuade them and in important ways. Those "in the know" point to the sweeping effects the Internet continues to have on such things as the global economy, world politics, international relations, and a host of other important issues. It is clear that the Internet is changing the structure of persuasion as perhaps no other medium has since television, and it will probably continue to change persuasion by much more than television ever did. It is a major technological revolution that is changing the structure of our communication practices, and it has democratized the voice of the individual and turned receivers into potential sources with yet-to-be-determined audiences. There are now new ways for persuasion to be delivered (e.g., the viral persuasion mentioned earlier at Weblink 13.15 sponsored by Burger King to market its chicken offerings) and "Guerilla marketing" (see articles for hundreds of related strategies, tactics and sites) in which students like yourselves and other persons are paid to spread what used to be called "word of mouth" advertising. The Internet is also changing the persuasive process by altering the power structure of its participants, which now includes a huge percentage of the U.S. population. Let's review how the Internet is changing the way we persuade and are persuaded. (You can access this and all of the other Chapter 13 weblinks through your companion website for *Persuasion*, Chapter 13 resources.)

Changes in the Information Power Structure

When we considered the massive changes resulting from the printed word earlier, we noted that the biggest change was the redistribution of information as it represented power. When information was difficult to obtain, people could easily be taken advantage of and scammed. But when this information became easier to obtain because of the printing press, a middle class of merchants and tradesmen emerged and soon began to accumulate various kinds of power—economic, political, and philosophical. Imagine that kind of change multiplied many, many times—that's what the access to information via the Internet means.

It isn't hyperbolic to say that the two most significant contributions of the Internet are the redistribution of the control of information, and the democratizing of individual voices in the persuasion process. A tiny example might help. Automobile salespersons do not like the Internet because dealer costs for vehicles are available online to potential customers, who can then solicit competitive bids from various dealers via the Internet thus avoiding travel and time and learning what the various dealers stand to make on the sale. In other words, the consumer access to that information allows them to bargain for the best price, interest rate, rebate offer, and so on. The "shoe is on the other foot" until dealers find a way to switch tactics (e.g., sticker price vs. invoice price vs. dealer price or some other euphemism (see Chapter 8 for a reminder).

What a great tool for the persuadee! Or take travel agents who were previously the major source of information for long-distance trips, airfares, and reservations for accommodations. Now, travel agencies are closing their doors in droves due to competition from the Internet. As you well know, reservations can be made without direct human assistance, and some carriers provide additional incentives for using the Internet, such as special fares online and preferred member programs. Southwest Airlines, the most profitable airline over the past decade, uses the Internet as its *primary source* of booking trips and no longer pays commissions to travel agents. Its new discount service called DING, described at Weblink 13.16, might interest those of you interested in saving money on travel. (You can access this and all of the other Chapter 13 weblinks through your companion website for *Persuasion*, Chapter 13 resources.)

Companies such as Priceline and Travelocity also enable consumers to find bargain fares. So the Internet is changing the travel and lodging industries as well, and that is just one small example in the great multitude of businesses now being affected by Internet commerce, not to mention the many new start-up businesses that have emerged as a result of the Internet and its ability to make information available to the masses. As noted above, the Internet is also a democratizing technology. For example, it is a marvelous boon to small individually owned bed-and-breakfasts, enabling them to publicize their presence very inexpensively. Prior to Internet advertising, they had to rely on road signs, the Yellow Pages (which few consulted and which were pricey), or relatively expensive advertisements in their local town tourist magazine and elsewhere (ditto). Imagine the impact of Internet information on local and even larger newspaper classified advertising—traditionally the "cash cow" for most dailies. The Internet now offers free classified ads, run in thousands of free sites, and e-mail "blasted" to over 5 million targeted customers. How does any newspaper compete with that? The critical receiver will ask, "How many read them?" or "Does it work?" or "How do they make any money doing that?" Yes, the Internet democratizes small voices, but it can't guarantee an audience that pays attention.

The challenge for persuaders is to frame persuasion in ways that draw visitors to their sites and not those of their competitors, and then to draw the customers into reading (and that requires literacy that 30 percent don't have), and more importantly, to ensure that the customers carefully consider what is being offered for what is being given. In other words, the consumer must ask what the costs and benefits are, if he or she decides to read and process this information. And this is where critical reception comes in once again. Are there a significant number of audience members paying any attention to the millions of bloggers, chat groups, MySpace, and Facebook members out there? If not, then we are possibly facing an electronic "cage" where crowds of persons and/or businesses are communicating with an insignificant minority of possibly bored participants. We may be like a cage full of chimpanzees chirping at one another to no effect.

Of course, television had the same problem in its infancy when only 100,000 persons owned a set and programming sometimes consisted of a "test pattern" or simple puppet shows, and critics labeled it a temporary gimmick. Yet look how it changed our lives. So the democratization of the individual may, in the end, not add up to as much as hoped for, even though it has made information readily available and the opinion of others is ubiquitous. On the other hand, it may prove to be more beneficial than was Guttenberg's printing press, and look what that brought.

Information on Demand

A major selling point of the Internet is its ability to deliver information (especially advertising and other persuasive messages) immediately to a 24/7, potentially enormous global audience as we noted earlier. As one critic put it, "the gold rush is on" for advertising revenues. (See Weblink 13.17 for a few insights. You can access this and all of the other Chapter 13 weblinks through your companion website for *Persuasion*, Chapter 13 resources.) Of course, while traditional businesses still struggle to find hours to accommodate customers across time zones in just our nation, the Internet has already "seen it overtake newspaper and magazine revenue with TV in its sights" (Walters, 2007). The Internet provides and collects information worldwide regardless of the hour. Of course, in complex situations that involve many issues, it's still preferable to deal with a person than a machine. However, many routine transactions are well suited to the Internet, just as automatic teller machines can handle most of our banking needs.

Whether we like it or not, the Internet does provide advertising information to consumers like you and me on this 24/7 basis so we must learn to respond to it. The task for persuaders promoting products and brands is how to attract potential customers to their sites to harvest the information, and in terms of persons like yourselves—aged 18 to 34—keep in mind that advertising vendors didn't pay over $2 billion for ads on YouTube and MySpace on a whim. They know that you receivers out there in the blogosphere are looking for all that free information/power that is so easily available. Know also that you are in your most impressionable years (18–24), just when you are developing your deepest brand loyalties (Walters, 2007), so be prepared to critically process and respond to the persuasion you will continue to face. We are only in the first stages of experimenting with the Internet advertising challenge. In the meantime, while the Internet allows persuadees to easily research available information on candidates, brands, donating to, or joining a particular organization, remember that Internet ads also create what are called "brand impressions" or instants when the name of the brand is processed by one of your senses into your central nervous system to be stored and recalled (as both Schwartz and McLuhan predicted) and is processed in either the peripheral or central paths of the ELM when making an important decision. Be ready to exercise your critical skills.

Direct-to-Consumer Markets without Geographic Boundaries

Naturally, the direct marketing industry discovered the Internet very early on. But even starting so early, at present over 30 percent of their revenues is being reaped from online consumers, and this is in a time when most of them are basically niche marketers targeting very small audiences with specialized needs. In a way, that is very good. Consumers who previously were ignored by giant industries are now getting services they never had. The Internet also provides direct market access to people around the globe, whereas earlier direct marketing was geographically limited. Direct marketers doing business online are also much more able to provide more and better customer service, and they avoid one of the basic costs of doing business previously—postal charges for direct mailing a catalog. And remember that they are also able to more carefully test variables—the price they ask, the extras they include, the subject line in the message, the signature, and so on—and they get results on each variable change almost immediately. This allows them to fine-tune and craft their messages and offers, again making the receiver more and more vulnerable to such appeals—BUT WAIT! Once again the receiver needs to hone critical skills—BUT WAIT! The power of Internet information goes further than exploiting catalog customers; it can aid small businesses that were previously cut out of the marketplace. Small, independent organic coffee growers now possess the means to sell their crops internationally for better prices by cutting out the middleman—a process called **disintermediation**—BUT WAIT! And in the arts, many fine artists now use the Internet's direct-to-consumer capability to sell their art and avoid paying commissions—BUT WAIT!! People can use eBay, Craigslist, and other networks to buy and sell across international boundaries and thus avoid taxes and regulations and re-sell merchandise to their own benefit—and always tell the truth. For persuadees, the Internet can make price, quality, quantity, and selection available before they have to make a purchase decision, as was the case with auto buyers armed with accurate information about the real costs of the brand. It seems highly probable that site evaluation or rating systems will soon emerge for each and every category of product, cause, candidate for office, religious philosophy, and a host more. The receivers will have to be aware of such developments in order to continue to be critical processors of the most important information available from among all the options. And then there are the dating/matching services for all tastes. And who knows what comes next?

Increased Access and Convenience

As shown in Figure 13.11, CDW-G is dedicated to improving the technological efficiency and capabilities of college campuses. That could translate to more time instructors can spend with students and less time being hampered by outmoded technology. Outside the working world, increased Internet access and technological innovations offer instructors and students (and all consumers) the opportunity to spend more time with their families and friends, more time on commitments, and more time to enjoy activities and pursue other interests.

Consumers may now choose online purchase opportunities such as that found at Weblink 13.18, and can consider many more choices than are generally available locally to save time, travel costs, parking, waiting in line, and other troubles having to do with real-time shopping. (You can access this and all of the other Chapter 13 weblinks through your companion website for *Persuasion*, Chapter 13 resources.) This option is changing the retail industry in favor of persuadees, as is niche marketing via the Internet, and this can accrue advantages and convenience for consumers with special needs. For example, people with very narrow or very wide feet have more shoe options via the Internet than at the shoe store in the mall. This tactic, with the help of the Internet, will result in many more new and successful start-up home businesses. Persuaders who wish to focus on niche or specialty markets can now do so far more easily and cheaper than ever before. But an old-fashioned word of consumer caution is needed—"Let the Buyer Beware." BUT WAIT!!!

Ethical Behavior on the Internet

To this point, ethical use of the Internet has mainly focused on using the Internet for research, but many newer and more critical issues are emerging daily, and codes of Internet ethics are emerging covering many different issues like student use of e-mail, health care, pornography, privacy issues, financial issues, Internet counseling, legal issues, and a host more. (I find over 177,000 Web sites on this topic right now.) The Internet's potentially unseemly underbelly brings opportunities to exploit others, and critical receivers again need to be prepared for these and how they can affect our communities and our quality of life. As with mail-order houses, consumers must always question whether a persuader on the Internet is trustworthy.

A key issue for persuaders on the Internet involves establishing their credibility, and for persuadees, their task is to search out credible sources. Again, rating systems may help. Many merchants and persons doing business on the Internet are forming associations that provide some level of assurance of trustworthiness. The best advice we can give to Internet users—whether senders or receivers—is to give careful thought to what might or might not be ethical regarding the issue, brand, candidate, or other commodity you are dealing with, and ironically, you can get advice simply by entering the words "Internet" and "ethics" and a word or words describing the topic or issue about which you are unsure.

REVIEW AND CONCLUSION

The average college freshman has watched tens of thousands of hours of television and hundreds of thousands of commercials by the time he or she comes to school. And TV is just one media channel being used for persuasion. Billboards, films, magazines, and newspapers affect most of us. Labels, bumper stickers, t-shirts, and other paraphernalia persuade us. And most recently we opened the potential Pandora's box of the Internet. Positive and negative things beyond our imaginations will come from it. All in all, we live in a highly persuasive, media-rich environment, and we need to be aware of how media affect us, especially in regard to persuasion—BUT WAIT!!

New media have effected great changes in how we were persuaded in the past and how we are being persuaded in the present. We have looked at the major communication innovations over time and how they changed persuasion and society forever after their introduction. We need to be persuaded about some things, and media persuasion is sometimes the best way to get information about alternatives. You can protect yourself from unscrupulous persuasive attempts made by various media by looking beneath the surface. Look for the responsive chords being plucked via the verbal, visual, and auditory scripts, and whether the messages that elicit them are hot or cool. Examine how the introduction of a new medium extends one of your senses or body parts. Consider whether "the medium is the message" and what the implications of that concept are as you are targeted by persuaders. In public affairs, look for the agendas being set by the media, what you are being forced to think about, and how that can affect you as a persuadee.

You also need to examine your own patterns of behavior in media use. Why do you turn to media, and to which media do you turn? What needs do they meet for you? What do you learn from them? Also consider the immense changes we are facing because of the development of new communications media (Gumpert and Drucker, 2002; Larson, 2002; Postman, 1996; Zettl, 1996). Establishing trustworthiness remains important across all of these media innovations, but it is particularly important with regard to the Internet. To restate previous advice—"Let the Receiver Beware."

KEY TERMS

After reading this chapter, you should be able to identify, explain, and give an example of the following key terms or concepts:

spoken word	auditory or sound script	definition	news bite
written word	sight or visual script	cool media	social learning theory
printed word	access code	uses and gratification theory	cultivation theory
electronic word	signal	surveillance needs	ignoring
interactive word	high-fidelity forms	curiosity needs	favoring the sponsor
evoked recall	low-fidelity forms	diversion needs	pseudo-events
experiential meaning	sensory involvement	personal identity needs	disintermediation
responsive chord	sensory participation	agenda-setting	
verbal script	hot media		

APPLICATION OF ETHICS

On April 2, 2004, editors at two newspapers decided to publish a controversial front-page picture of the dismembered and charred remains of four American civilian contractors with their body parts hanging from a bridge. A crowd of Iraqis were cheering the sight in the foreground. The editors had to consider a number of ethical issues before deciding to publish the complete photo. Should the picture have been published at all? From the "Letters to the Editor" in the days following, publication opinion ran from "outlandish" to "necessary for the public to see" to one suggesting the papers get a Pulitzer Prize for poor taste. What if the bodies were of soldiers? What if the bodies were Iraqi? What if they hadn't been dismembered or charred? What if they had been of women and/or children? Could running the photo affect public opinion about the war? Would you run the picture on the front page? Inside? Would you warn readers of the graphic nature of the photos? Why or why not? It also ran on various television news reports. Would it be ethical to display the event on an Internet site?

QUESTIONS FOR FURTHER THOUGHT

1. What are some similarities between primitive oral/aural cultures and the electronic culture in which we now live?

2. Why is information associated with power? Give examples.

3. How was the concept of ownership associated with the development of writing? Print? Television and radio? The Internet?

4. What changes in literacy resulted from the development of print?

5. How did literacy both free us and enslave us?

6. What are some of the developments at the Media Lab at MIT? How will they affect us in the future?

7. Which media type—hot or cool—dominates our times?

8. What are some examples of the criteria gatekeepers may be using to determine what to put on the evening news?

9. What are the implications of an unregulated Internet? What are we doing about it?

10. What should the ethics of Internet communication include?

11. What are the implications of the exploding presence of interactive media?

12. How does cultural diversity affect the many media of our times?

13. What are the implications of the many potentially propagandistic appeals being made on the Internet?

14. How can receivers possibly navigate the many options on the Internet when choosing to shop, vote, join, and donate, and so on?

15. How might SNM be used unethically? How ethically?

16. In which channel of the ELM—peripheral or central—are most messages sent via SNM processed?

17. What are the implications of "BUT WAIT!!"

14

The Use of Persuasive Premises in Advertising and IMC

After reading this chapter, you should be able to:

1. Describe, explain, and give examples of the various tasks that advertising can accomplish and the tactics that are used to achieve them.

2. Explain the difference between advertising and integrated marketing communication (IMC).

3. Differentiate among the various elements of IMC, such as consumer advertising, sales promotion, PR, event planning, and others.

4. Explain the functions of demographic, sociographic, psychographic, and ethnographic advertising research.

5. Identify and explain various techniques for positioning a brand and name some of those positions, and discuss repositioning a brand.

6. Recognize weasel words used in advertising, explain and give examples of them.

7. Apply Rank's 30-second-spot quiz to several television spots.

8. Differentiate between obvious, sophisticated, and subliminal sexual appeals in advertising.

9. Explain in which channel of the ELM a variety of ads are likely to be processed.

10. Identify SNM that are and can be used for advertising.

11. Explain viral marketing, guerilla, and other epidemical ad theories.

INTRODUCTION

We referred earlier to many examples of advertising that effectively persuade receivers. Of course, advertising is rooted in a results-oriented perspective that will improve the "bottom line" of the company or organization and yield "profit" to someone or some group in the forms of purchases, votes, donations, and so on. In this chapter we will examine in more detail the almost constant, insistent, and sometimes annoying world of commercial advertising on behalf of brands, persons, or ideas. We will look in-depth at the several jobs it can do or tasks it can accomplish, as well as what tactics it uses to do them. We will also examine how it works with other forms of marketing persuasion, and how ad researchers analyze and target the audiences most likely to purchase. This will include how they position or reposition their brands against the competition, how ad agents develop persuasive advertising strategies and tactics, and especially how they use language in the ads—sometimes accurately, but sometimes deceptively. We will also

explore the many recent changes in advertising and their implications for the future, especially concerning SNM and the two information processing channels posited by the ELM. Additionally, we will explore the increasingly controversial topic of sexual appeals in advertising and the possibility of subliminal persuasion.

Advertising is a fascinating kind of persuasion to study, especially in a rapidly changing culture such as ours. Just mention the word "advertising" in almost any group and a lively conversation will follow—everyone has an opinion on it. Since the inception of modern brand advertising in the late 1900s, it has had dramatic impact on our purchasing, voting, donating, joining, and other decisions since at least the time of widely distributed newspapers and magazines. It affects our identification with brands, our forming of attitudes toward them, our evaluations and adoption or rejection of them, and even our choosing of a preferred lifestyle that promises us certain amenities associated with the brand. In previous chapters, we discussed various approaches to direct and interactive marketing, Internet ads, market segmentation, and other examples of what is sometimes called the "marketing mix." A more recent term for this varied array of persuasive techniques is called **integrated marketing communication**, or **IMC**, and it is a new and unique way to promote brands, persons, and ideas using more than the traditional consumer advertising and promotional forms of persuasion on behalf of brands used in the past. A major goal of IMC is to build a one-to-one dialogue or a unified and personalized "relationship" between brands and consumers using various kinds of persuasion. It uses advertising as its major component most of the time, but IMC also includes direct marketing, public relations, event planning, sales promotion, packaging, personal selling tactics, and interactive and Internet communication of various kinds to name a few. All of these operate together to create a unified message with unique appeal about most brands. Using highly sophisticated research data, these ads are "customized" for certain "slices" or segments of the consumer market. In the case of IMC, this customization results in the whole being greater than the sum of its parts. This means that the advertising is reinforced by the public relations, which in turn strengthens the brand's use of direct marketing, sales promotion, public relations, and so on. As a result, each tactic of persuasion makes every other tactic stronger and more effective than it would have been alone, and so the whole package becomes highly persuasive.

There are various new emerging trends in advertising. The need to respond to the increasing diversity in our society and new technologies that are being adapted to advertising will come into play and be noted as a part in our considerations. For example, take advertising targeted at Latinos in the United States, whose portion of the economy continues to grow. At 13 percent of the U.S. population, they are the largest ethnic minority. In fact, McDonald's devotes 10 percent of its general market ads to Spanish-language spots (Wentz and Cuneo, 2002). At the same time, the fastest growing and most affluent ethnic group in the country is Asians from a variety of countries, while the fastest growing market segment is consumers who are aged 50+ years and who are also usually affluent. And these segmentations are only part of the ever changing industry.

At this point let's distinguish between a "brand" and a "product," since many people use those terms interchangeably, as in "Downy is the best *product* for softening clothes," when they mean it is the best *brand*. There are many brands in each product category, and the role of advertising is to distinguish among them (often they are near clones of one another) and then to get as many consumers as possible to favor and purchase one particular brand from among the many others. To do this, companies use the elements of IMC and especially advertising to accomplish one or more of the several "tasks" or jobs necessary in order to move the brand off the shelves, into the shopping baskets, and ultimately to their homes or places of business. Let us now briefly examine some of those tasks and the persuasive tactics they use.

THE TASKS OF ADVERTISING AND THEIR TACTICS

It is obvious that the underlying task of all advertising is to increase sales and profits—to increase or "lift" sales of the brand—but there are many ways that advertising can help do this. One basic model that we discussed back in Chapter 11 is the "Hierarchy of Effects" model, which sets out several sequential stages of persuasion (in this case advertising) that occur on the way to the purchase of a brand, a vote for a candidate, a donation to a good cause, or the adoption of an ideology or a practice such as recycling. Most consumers, voters, and donors begin by being totally unaware of the brand, candidate, or idea that is being promoted, so the first task of advertising is to create:

Stage 1. *Awareness* of the product category and brands, which then leads to...

Stage 2. *Increased knowledge* about the brand before...

Stage 3. *Preference* will develop. Once the brand is known, this preference for the brand is usually based on its advertising or word of mouth from friends. If it is disliked, of course, the persuasion and the brand fail. But if it is liked, based on its ads and/or word of mouth, advertising may even lead to the consumers becoming...

Stage 4. *Convinced* of its superiority. Of course, they will never know if this is true unless they can be induced to try it, so another task of advertising is to lead to...

Stage 5. *Prompting of trial* of the brand. If the trial goes well, they will ultimately...

Stage 6. *Evaluate* the brand positively and finally move to the hoped-for...

Stage 7. *Development of brand loyalty* and will thus repurchase it many times over. Marketing experts refer to this brand loyalty as "the lifetime value of the customer" which, as you can imagine, can be enormous.

And now with the Internet and interactive advertising increasing, the job of the copywriter in achieving any of these tasks is more challenging. A few tips that will help can be discovered by following up on suggestions given in Box 14.1.

We will discuss this concept in more depth later. In any case, moving consumers through those stages is the prime task of all advertising. Now, what advertising strategies and appropriate tactics might be used to get consumers moving into and through those stages? Let's look at a few.

Promote Brand Features and Benefits

Every successful brand has some *perceived benefit* in the consumer's mind. That particular benefit makes them choose the brand time after time. Usually, the benefit comes from some *feature of the brand*. For example, Cheerios, traditionally a children's brand but losing market share to sugared cereals, responded to concerns older Americans have about the amount of fiber in their diets. Cheerios now advertises that the brand contains 100 percent oat bran as a feature, as opposed to being a "fun" cereal. It always did have bran or whole oats in it, but children saw no benefit in that, and it gave them no reason to ask their parents to buy it. The perceived benefit of 100 percent oat bran for older folks is that bran has lots of fiber, resulting in a healthier and fiber-full diet.

A common feature of electronically operated devices (whose benefit is obviously the saving of money and time) is to advertise "Batteries Included" when selling these battery-powered toys or appliances. "Open 24 hours" is another feature, and it yields a convenience benefit for the consumer. Another good way to show benefits is to actually demonstrate them to consumers, and TV is an excellent medium for demonstrations, which is why we see so many TV ads that use the tactic (for example, the BowFlex or other exercise machine, or various gourmet cooking devices like the revolving oven or special knives and food processors). Promoting a brand's features and the resulting benefits is one task that advertising can achieve using several tactics of persuasion—testimonials, statistics, examples, demonstrations, and others.

BOX 14.1   **Interactive Short Course on Ad Copy**

For an informative and fun short course on developing ad copy go to Weblink 14.1. There, you will find a discussion of five steps or questions a copywriter should ask when trying to develop copy for an ad—captivating headlines, features, benefits, unique selling propositions, and calls to action.

(You can access this and all of the other Chapter 14 weblinks through your companion website for *Persuasion*, Chapter 14 resources.) For a few chuckles go to the link at Weblink 14.2 where you will find mock ads and mock steps for copywriters.

Generate Traffic

In order for consumers to make most purchases, they have to be in the retail store, reading the catalog or direct mail offer, watching the right TV channel at the right time, listening to the radio ad, reading their Facebook page or some other SNM while they have a cell phone handy to place the order, or visiting the correct website. The act of getting consumers to the point of making a purchase can therefore be a tricky one. You are probably most familiar with how this is done in grocery ads. They usually do this by offering some familiar and staple goods like milk or eggs at below cost. These items are called "loss leaders" because they lead consumers to the store by taking a loss. These special prices draw consumers to the store or POP ("Point Of Purchase") where they then will make many other purchases. In fact, some estimates say that as many as 60 percent of the items in the shopping cart at the checkout counter are purchased on impulse, even if the customer brings a shopping list with them to the store.

Another proven tactic for generating store traffic is a "free" offer. Consumers come in for the free item and stay to purchase other things. Sweepstakes work this way also. Folks come in to try the key they got in the mail to see if it opens the prize—a new SUV, and if it does, they win it. Naturally if their key doesn't fit, they can look around at other models. Money off on the first purchase from a catalog also works, as does "pay per click," in which the Internet advertiser pays search engines for placing them early in the log of relevant sites. Yet another tactic for generating traffic is to offer some service or advice for "free" if the consumer comes in—checking the battery in your watch, for example. Internet free offers include things like "install a free screensaver on your laptop!" or "free music downloads now!" and all of them have worked in the past. As we noted earlier, "free" is probably the most powerful word in advertising.

Another way to get traffic is to have some special attraction or event. The event might be a celebrity who is signing autographs at the store, attention-getting giant balloons or blimps flying over the store, sweepstakes where the customer must come in to enter, or a "kiddie carnival" in the store's parking lot; all have been used to generate store traffic. More recently, creating traffic for websites has become a major issue and the use of ad or e-mail "blasting" and using advertising on eBay and Craigslist have also been successfully used to generate traffic and thus increase sales. More are being invented all the time. Go to Weblink 14.3 for a tour of how extreme videos have been used to create traffic and have some fun at the same time. (You can access this and all of the other Chapter 14 weblinks through your companion website for *Persuasion*, Chapter 14 resources.)

Make Brand Comparisons

To be truly successful, all brands need to be perceived as superior to the competition in the minds of consumers. Comparative advertising is one way to convince them that Brand X is superior to the others. Comparative advertising is defined as advertising in which there is mention of a *specific competing brand* (not just "the competition" or "other brands") and some sort of comparison that must be stated or implied to show why the competitor is inferior. Consider a Duracell ad in which a "bunny" operating on a Duracell outlasts a "bunny" running on a no-brand black battery. The end of the ad makes the claim that cheaper batteries wear out faster, and the implication is that since Eveready batteries are cheaper, they won't last as long as Duracells. Naturally, the competition is likely to cry "foul," so the FTC has had to establish a number of regulations (e.g., full disclosure, complete substantiation, improper disparagement) regulating comparative advertising. That's why the vague "other brands" and "Brand X" are so frequently used to avoid noncompliance with the FTC regulations. Advertisers want consumers to believe that their brand or candidate is better than the opposition's, especially in regard to price, quality, and performance. These kinds of comparison ads are especially good ways to do this; and of course, guarantees, warranties, and demonstrations are also excellent ways to make comparisons. So again, TV is frequently used, but according to the FTC, the demonstrations may not be deceptive in any way. Comparison lists of statistics, specifications, or ingredients are also good ways to show superiority, using such things as different mileage or interest rates, costs, standards, performance, and quotations from users or rating services. Usually the basis of most ad comparisons relates to the way features produce consumer benefits. Taste tests are also a tactic to make comparisons using actual consumers to do the comparing. The consumer tastes both Pepsi and Coke and then rates them; and if the advertiser's brand wins, the results are ballyhooed far and wide. The tactic has been used to compare numerous products including pet foods, organically grown vegetables and fruits, garden plants, and "healthy" snacks for teenagers. One potential drawback to comparison advertising is that there is always the danger that simply mentioning the competition's name will increase and reinforce that competing brand's memorability at the POP. The old advice of making sure the persuader is not comparing "apples to oranges" is always good advice for receivers when comparisons are being made in ads or when confronting demonstrations of competing brands.

Induce Trial

One of the most difficult stages to get one's prospects to reach consumers is actually trying the brand or idea, and this is especially true if the brand is a new introduction on the market, expensive, or complex to use. The task is made more difficult because many brands are nearly identical in contents, features, and benefits. A good example

is "Sure" versus "Secret" deodorants. Their list of ingredients is identical, as are their sizes and recommended price, so how does the advertiser get consumers to try one of them over the other? Free samples are a favorite tactic to persuade consumers to try the brand, but another way is to come up with an ad slogan and copy that tells the brand story. Secret's long-lasting winner, "Strong Enough for a Man. But Made for a Woman," according to research, targets the key audience—insecure females, aged 12 to 24 with uncertainty about gender identity. (See Weblink 14.4 for a more detailed analysis. You can access this and all of the other Chapter 14 weblinks through your companion website for *Persuasion*, Chapter 14 resources.) The slogan sounds kind of daring as well. A more familiar example of the free sample being used to induce trial is seen in supermarkets all the time—especially on Saturdays when one can "graze" through the store on free samples. The free sample is usually accompanied by a coupon for the brand, thus giving the consumer two reasons to make the purchase—the free taste and the monetary savings.

A favorite way that car dealers have used for many decades to induce trial is to urge the prospect to "take'er out for a test drive." And the prospect usually notices the difference between the demonstrator and their existing car, which often helps make the sale. Using an ingenious tactic, one auto company sold many of its models at greatly reduced prices to auto rental companies, convinced that if only the potential customers drove the vehicles, they would prefer, and hopefully, finally buy the brand. In this way, renting one of the models induced trial, and it worked to lift sales. Of course, discounts such as coupons and rebates can also induce trial. In the final analysis, however, the product must perform as promised or even in a superior way.

Generate Qualified Leads

Some product types (especially high-priced and complex ones) are difficult to sell using traditional

Website Visitors

Leads

Customers

FIGURE 14.1 This ad for a website-producing company explains what lead generation is and how it works. Obviously anyone going to the website at the top is interested in the product category and so is a good prospect for the brand being advertised.

SOURCE: © Cengage Learning 2013.

methods (e.g., energy efficient-furnaces, home theatre systems). They are hard to demonstrate, even on television, and are expensive to demonstrate in a home for a single trial purpose (given the salesperson's time and wages plus the risk of damaging the system during set-up and take-down). While the trial works well in finally getting the sale (and is sometimes possible onsite), advertisers want their sales personnel to spend time and resources on only those prospects who are most likely to ultimately buy the product type, as seen in Figure 14.1.

Good prospects usually already like the product type and are shopping for the best brand; with the proper sales technique, they will buy the demonstrator's brand. What the advertiser wants to do is to identify those persons who most likely want or need the product category and then promote their brand of that product to them. One of the ways to do this is to focus on the knowledge stage of the hierarchy of effects. In other words, the advertiser needs to educate the potential

buyer not only about the product category (which they already want to purchase) but also about their brand and its strengths (and especially against the competition and its flaws). As noted, it's hard to do a demonstration of a furnace or a complete home theatre system on a short 30-second or even longer television commercial or to stage a live demonstration in the home. Therefore, many advertisers rely on television, direct mail, or another medium to offer further free information about the product type and the brand in the form of booklets, DVDs, extended free trials, or trips to the factory, as tactics to induce the prospect to become educated about the product type and more importantly, the brand.

Sometimes interactive advertising can do the trick. If a consumer is researching something like a furnace, he or she might use the Internet as a resource, and "pay per click" advertising may be the most economical way to get users involved, particularly if a clever "hook" is used to get the prospect to make the click to go into the brand's website and see an extended video demonstration of the brand. In some cases, prospective consumers can request to see an even longer and more detailed video. This technique is called "permission advertising." (see Weblink 14.5 to watch an interesting video on this method. You can access this and all of the other Chapter 14 weblinks through your companion website for *Persuasion*, Chapter 14 resources.) Casinos frequently get potential customers to try the games of chance by giving then an initial "stake" or free spins of the wheel, and even children's versions of some gaming get them "hooked" early, thus assuring a greater "lifetime value of the customer."

Prompt Purchase. Most salespersons will tell you that the hardest part of a sale is "closing" or "asking for the order," as it is sometimes called. Most advertisers want consumers to make on-the-spot purchase decisions, but there is a lot of customer resistance to making the decision too quickly. While all consumers make some impulse purchases, the usual strategy is for the advertiser to create some sense of *urgency* or the need to take prompt action, warning that they will lose the opportunity by waiting to decide. Urgency can be communicated by setting a time limit that the consumer must meet in order to get the special promoted price, so expiration dates work well on some devices (e.g., coupons, rebates) as do phrases like "13-hour sale!" or "Only a few left at this price!" "Supplies limited!" or the old reliable "Act now!"

Promising quick action for a service is also a good way to trigger the purchase of a service such as plumbing. "We'll be there in 15 minutes or you can reduce the price 25 percent!" is a clever promise, especially since the consumer doesn't know what the price was initially. When the issue is prompt payment of bills, the offer of a reduction if paid within 10 days or less often works. Offering a bonus or even a "surprise bonus" is another tactic. We often see this on direct television pitches. The original offer is made, but if you call the 1-800 number in the next 15 minutes, they'll send you

not one, not two, but three of the kitchen food processors, and then there is usually another offer tagged on—"Plus, if you act now …" or "But wait!!" to get you to make the call, place the order, and get the added bonus blade sharpener. Prompt ordering is always increased by making it easy for the consumer to respond. That's why the "inbound" 1-800 telephone numbers and plastic credit have both been boons to these advertisers, and they regularly succeed. Besides, they give the well-trained operator/salesperson who answer your call the chance to "up-sell" and get you to buy the two pair of wool socks to go with the hunting boots that were all you really intended to purchase.

Building the Brand

"Building the brand" has been a major task of advertising since the inception of early print advertising, as seen in Figure 14.2 for Nabisco saltines using the brand name "Uneeda Biscuit" (later to be re-named Nabisco Saltines) and a logo (the boy in the yellow slicker with the box of crackers under his arms).

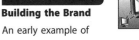

FIGURE 14.2

Building the Brand

An early example of "building the brand."

SOURCE: Courtesy of The Advertising Archives.

Branded goods back in the late 19th century were new and some products were generic, as was the case for Nabisco, but the type of ad seen in Figure 14.2 changed all that. Soon everyone was branding, and it is even more of a byword in today's ad industry. Initially, people bought unbranded soda crackers from a barrel by the bagful at the general store, and they varied in quality and freshness. Then in the late 1890s, the National Biscuit Company branded and advertised its version of soda crackers as "Uneeda Biscuit" and packaged them in a protective and well-sealed tin box, thus reducing breakage and avoiding staleness. Furthermore, the package itself was useful for storing things like nuts and bolts when the crackers were gone. So advertising and packaging began to help build the brand and the rest is history for Nabisco and its many "line extensions" (e.g., Ritz Crackers, Barnum's Animal Crackers, and Oreos).

There are many strategies and tactics used to build brands, but none is more familiar than simple repetition done through a combination of advertising, packaging, logos, jingles, slogans, brand names, and the use of multiple media types to assure that the brand name is repeatedly picked up by one or more of the consumer's physical senses (see "Planting" in Chapter 12). One kind of brand-building ad tactic is the testimonial given by a satisfied user who seems trustworthy and gives you the details from his or her point of view. Weight loss and special diet products frequently use this combined with before-and-after pictures—both coach Don Shula and his wife lost noticeable pounds on Nutri-System. Another brand-building device is the use of powerful images, music, and words in the advertising and packaging, examples of which we all can recall (e.g., "Wheaties—the Breakfast of Champions" accompanied by pictures of a famous athlete on the package). Another way is to make the advertising of the brand entertaining and memorable—Tony the Tiger is but one enduring example, as are Geico's caveman or gecko and "rhetorical question" campaign which asks, "Is it really true that you can save 15 percent on car insurance when you choose Geico? Did the third little piggy cry 'Wee, wee, wee....'" Some advertisers choose to tell the "story"

of the brand. Others may target new market segments like minorities and gays, or use a gender focus. Still others make their brand into a symbol of a lifestyle that target individuals want to emulate (e.g., Rolex, Victoria's Secret).

Advertisers may associate the brand with certain experiences like world travel, whitewater rafting, or kayaking. Some suggest new uses or recipes for the brand so that consumers try the new applications and thus increase use and repurchase. Avon's "Skin So Soft" claims to have over 80 uses, including use as an insect repellant and as a lubricant. Interestingly enough, coupons associated with recipes succeed better than the coupon alone, and coupons with a dotted border work even better. If there is a pair of tiny scissors on the dotted line, redemption rates will increase even more …Duh! In a way, clipping a coupon is a behavioral intention (see Chapter 7). When we clip a coupon, we intend to purchase the brand, wherein lies its selling power. There are many other tactics for building the brand (for example, contests where entrants must write a slogan for the brand, sweepstakes, free prizes, clothing with the brand name imprinted on it), but regardless of which ones are used, the basic goal is to create brand awareness, preference, and ultimately brand loyalty because it is the repeat purchase or the number of sales that really counts—the focus is on the "lifetime value of the customer." Building the brand involves IMC and all of its dimensions, repeated exposures over long periods of time, and clever advertising copy and design coordinated with memorable packaging and tempting sales promotion.

Adapting to Change

The advertising industry is constantly changing, with many new forces—especially technology like SNM—coming into play. If the most powerful word in advertising is "free," certainly the word "new" must rank nearly as high. We are a culture that is fascinated by the new, the entertaining, and the different; and this is reflected in advertising as well. So advertisers and their receivers must be constantly aware that new and innovative ways are always being tried on consumers to "get the sale." No change has affected advertising in the last decades more than the Internet and digital technologies. MSN sponsored an extended study entitled "The Consumer in Control," whose results indicate that power in advertising today has shifted from the various media to the consumers who now have many more options for purchasing goods, much more convenience in doing so, and who are becoming more and more empowered and savvy in their media use decisions. As a result, "future advertising needs to be more engaging, interactive, and relevant if it is to succeed," says Joanne Oates of Brand Republic. The report notes that the days of the 30-second television commercial are over. In large measure, these changes are due to digital technology plus the extraordinary fragmentation in the number and type of media choices available, the fragmentation of the audiences into ever more discreet segments, and the proliferation of brands within all product categories. The future promises to bring the consumer the opportunity to be rewarded for watching or reading advertisements. These rewards may come through free music downloads, interactive games, things like airships with 30-by 70 foot interactive "billboards" floating overhead, new techniques by Nielsen ratings to measure audiences, new applications for search engines that show advertisers how to buy ad time during the "upfront" season (due in part to a writer's strike that crippled Sweeps Week), and a host of others yet to be introduced. Some ad experts have characterized our contemporary era as a "sea change" in the world of advertising with the main problem for advertisers being that of trying to anticipate where that change will most likely occur—via the Internet, interactive advertising, stealth advertising, viral advertising, or other new techniques, all of which have come into being only recently. As receivers, we need to attend carefully to these changes as they catch on and hone our critical skills to be ready to meet the new ad challenges facing us. And well we should—look at how advertising dominates the culture of our modern times. While we excel at many things, we Americans produce

more popular culture than all of the rest of the world taken together. Americans are also the world's biggest and best producers, as well as consumers, of the kind of pop culture known as advertising. Consider the following surprising statistics:

- The average per capita expenditure on advertising in the United States is now well over $1,000/year.
- The average American sees or hears between 2,000 to 5,000 advertisements per day, according to various estimates.

Compare those numbers with what the rest of the world spends on advertising, including the Western democracies such as the United Kingdom, Canada, the rest of "old" Europe, Japan, and increasingly India and China. They spend less than $100/year per person. No wonder the many newcomers to the United States cannot believe that anyone can process all that advertising—radio, television, papers, magazines, billboards, signs, T-shirts, spaces to print on, buses, airports, the Internet. And that's reason enough for consumers to learn about this form of highly persuasive communication.

Some advertising ranks as pop art and is creative and entertaining, and some of it is simply junk. Our goal in this chapter, however, is not to evaluate the creative side of the industry (take an advertising design class for that) but to learn how advertising affects human society and behavior, how it works, where it is likely to go in the future (here and throughout the emerging global economy), and especially how it persuades us. We need to discover whether those effects are bad or good for us in particular and for humanity in general, as well as how understanding advertising can help us understand ourselves as consumers. Marxist critics see advertising as a tool of the upper classes used to exploit the lower classes because it creates wants for unneeded goods and thus tempts people to waste their "wage slave" earnings on them. Advertising executives see ads as a way to beat the competition while making big bucks. And consumers see them as either just so much clutter or as a silly kind of entertainment. Often advertisements intend not only to persuade but also to inform us, and that is one of the values put forward by ad executives for the industry—in addition to the claim that by creating competition there will ultimately be a reduction in prices, they help consumers decide what to buy.

Consider how the introduction of the Internet has changed our lives and how it has changed our purchasing and voting behavior. The Internet is also changing the face of advertising enormously, and it will play a major role in the future by all predictions (Cuneo, 2002). "All Things Considered" reported early in 2006 that more and more traditional advertising efforts (e.g., television spots, print ads) are being replaced with Internet ads and banners (NPR, January 3, 2006). As noted above, the Internet is also being used for what is called "permission advertising," where the consumer actually asks to receive an extended ad on behalf of the brand—perhaps as much as 20 minutes of informative material to help them make decisions about a variety of brands, candidates, and other issues. ("All Things Considered," January 3, 2006). That's remarkable if you think of it—consumers actually *requesting* advertising! Research shows that 92 percent of the large audience of mainly affluent teens is online and seeing advertising all the while. Frito-Lay devotes 9 percent of its marketing budget to Internet ads (Thompson, 2002). A Frito-Lay promotion with Microsoft's

Xbox prompted 700,000 new customer registrations at a website where you can also get a form to enter a sweepstakes. The world of advertising is in flux like everything else, and persuadees need to be ready for its new forms, strategies, and tactics.

ADVERTISING, SALES PROMOTION, AND POSITIONING

As we just noted in our discussion of the tasks of advertising and the advertisers' tactics, we all are targets of this form of persuasion in multiple ways that perhaps we never consciously thought of, or considered in detail. With increasing exposure to advocacy and propaganda (Box 14.2), making sensible decisions is becoming more difficult. This is especially true in regard to various national policies—even more critical for receivers to consider.

There are multiple factors that go into the advertising we see, hear, read, and feel, so let's begin with some basic principles of modern advertising. Some have been with us for a long time and will probably persist a lot longer, while some are of more modern vintage and may change the market in major ways; all can be used in modern propaganda to further political, economic, and ideological agendas. Let's explore some of these in Box 14.2.

BOX 14.2   **Persuasion, Manipulation, Advertising, and Propaganda**

"All propaganda must be so popular and on such an intellectual level that even the most stupid of those to whom it is directed will understand it" (Adolf Hitler from *Mein Kampf*, Chapter IV).

The propaganda that Hitler used was so heavy handed and obvious that today's sophisticated audiences nearly laugh it off the page. While the word "propaganda" had such a disagreeable connotation after the fall of the Soviet Union that an entire chapter on the topic was removed from subsequent editions of this book, propaganda is still with us. It is becoming more sophisticated than ever. This is particularly true as it appears in popular culture—in things like advertising. For a good tour of the history of modern propaganda and how it has manipulated

us through advertising and other means of persuasion, go to Weblink 14.6 where you will find examples of propaganda old and new. (You can access this and all of the other Chapter 14 weblinks through your companion website for *Persuasion*, Chapter 14 resources.) These examples deal with propaganda as it occurs in political advertising as well as propaganda as it has occurred and continues to do so in popular product advertising, and how it influences such topics as the war in Iraq, the fast food industry, toxic chemical waste, media ownership, obesity and brainwashing. This is a good site to use for beginning a term paper on propaganda. To get a sense of advertising as propaganda used in nations emerging from third-world status go to Weblink 14.7.

Branding, Brand Names, Slogans, Jingles, and Logos

As noted in reference to Nabisco crackers, contemporary advertising grew out of the development of packaged goods in the late nineteenth and the early twentieth centuries. Producers needed to differentiate their version of a product type from the competition in order to promote brand recognition, influence purchase decisions, and ensure brand loyalty in consumers' eyes. Earlier consumers bought generic and unbranded products from barrels, sacks, countertop jars, and other containers at a general store. One way to differentiate your kind of coffee was to give it a name or brand; for example, Folgers's slogan, "It's Mountain Grown." All coffees are mountain grown, but it's no use for competitors no use for them to claim that; they must differentiate themselves from Folgers. So it became Maxwell House—Good to the Last Drop." It's probably never wise to name your brand after yourself as Hills Brothers did—it communicates little about the brand, its features, benefits, or comparisons with the competition. Yet that's how many brand names came into being in those early days—Maytag, Hamm's, Pillsbury, Disney, Sears, and Ford are a few examples. More recent brand names usually try to use some benefit or words that describe it—Taster's Choice or Lunchables are examples.

A definition of the term "brand" might read as follows: **Brands** are the names given to a certain manufacturer's version of a **product** type. Different brands of coffees compete with one another, but they also compete with teas, cocoa, and spiced ciders in the "hot drink" product category and with soft drinks, juice, bottled water, and others in the "beverage" category; thus, brands compete not only within but across product categories. Advertising slogans and especially jingles really became part of the popular culture and branding with the advent of radio and radio advertising in the 1920s and 1930s. Advertisers wanted to remind consumers of their brand in short, easy to remember, and interesting ways. **Slogans** are defined as such catch phrases that express a brand name, its

benefits, and its "personality "as seen in the M & M's famous "Melts in your Mouth; Not in Your Hands!" which dates to WWII. Its originator had seen pictures of chocolate bars melting in the hands of soldiers during the Spanish American War.

In another example, Gatorade has a different personality than Gulp, which is different from Snapple or Blast. **Jingles** are usually a musical version of the slogan combined with lyrics that tell the "story" of the brand. Television emerged in the 1950s and permitted advertisers to not only talk and write about the brand, but also to demonstrate it using print, visuals, special effects, animation, mood music, sound effects, and various other audio and video techniques. Several strategies to market the brand and to make it stand out more effectively emerged in those early years of modern advertising. For instance, the name of the brand made a big difference in the way it was perceived and embedded in consumers' minds. LifeSavers was a good early brand name because it described how the brand looked, and since it was the first hard candy to be branded, it needed to look different from generic hard candies in a jar at the general store. It got its Lifesaver shape as an identifier—almost a logo. One of the early facial soaps was called "Palmolive," suggesting that the product contained a combination of coconut and olive oils.

Another way to differentiate a brand from the competition is to make an attractive offer. Consider Cracker Jacks, which originated at the Chicago's 1893 World's Fair and were popularized in 1908 with the song "Take Me Out to the Ball Game." The company came up with a novel offer in 1912 to differentiate itself from other popcorn snacks. Each package offered consumers a "free prize" inside. And in 100 years, there has probably never been a worthwhile prize, yet consumers go for the prize before they go for the caramel corn and nuts. Note that they do not offer a "free gift" but a "free prize" in every box. What is the difference between these two very similar words? Which is more powerful? Why? Netflix differentiates itself from the competition by offering a "free trial" period in addition to "no late fees," which relieves fears of consumers that they're being outfoxed.

Packaging is another way to differentiate a brand. Coors and Coors Light now come in unbreakable 16-ounce plastic bottles rather than glass ones or aluminum cans, making them useful on backpacking, canoeing, and other outdoor trips where breakage is more likely. Some brands came in a reusable container that is hard to throw away, like Nabisco tin boxes or L'eggs plastic eggs, which were saved by many—such as my Aunt Nancy, who made awful Christmas ornaments of them. (You can guess what awful items she made of a used furnace filter). Consider other brand names to see whether they differentiate the brand from the competition and if so, in what ways. In the frozen turkey market, one brand excels as we observed earlier. Guess which brand? Ask people to name a brand of frozen turkey, and few if any will say Armour or Jennie-O. Most will say "Butterball," the brand with the greatest name recognition. The name is memorable and says something about the brand's attributes and benefits. Butterball turkeys have the reputation of being the moistest brand because they are supposedly pre-basted with a pound of butter before being packaged. Furthermore, Butterball purchasers stay in the store longer and buy more expensive condiments for their Thanksgiving dinner. That kind of statistic will convince the grocer to devote more shelf or freezer space and more advertising to the brand (Dollas, 1986). Consider a few other brand names that demonstrate their benefits, such as Sears DieHard batteries, Easy-Off oven cleaner, No Pest Strip insect repellant, Jiffy Lube oil changes, Taster's Choice instant coffee, Fruitopia fruit drinks, and many more.

A good brand name describes product benefits, fits with company image, and is memorable. It should also be easy to pronounce and promote, suited to the product packaging, contemporary, and persuasive. Naturally, there will be exceptions like Snapple, which describes nothing about the brand and may be why it took so long for it to gain market share. Research on shopping lists shows that consumers often list brands and not product types on their shopping reminder lists (Rothschild, 1987). Another key tip is to create a persona for the brand. Rice Krispies, for example have the characters "Snap, Crackle & Pop" associated with a favorite childhood treat—the "Rice Krispie Treat" known to every child. Closely related to the brand name is the brand's slogan and **logo** or its corporate emblem. You all probably know which brand of coffee is "good to the last drop" by its slogan and logo. Maxwell House wins with its "last drop" slogan and its unique logo of a coffee cup with the last drop about to fall out of the cup. Starbucks' name is an anomaly since it doesn't communicate much about the brand or its benefits, but it has an identity as an upscale young person's coffee house specialty brand, probably gained from word of mouth advertising, which is also very effective. Consumer advertising aims at getting "word of mouths," which is a too-clever way of saying many persons respond by giving word of mouth testimony. And as noted, Folgers's is the "mountain grown" coffee even though that's where all coffees are grown. So one of the multiple factors that go into promoting a brand is its use of easy and fun names, slogans, and later musical jingles that may incorporate the slogan. The idea is to imprint the slogan and brand name on the consumer's unconscious mind so that it is evoked in a recall when he or she is ready to make a purchase, voting, or joining decision, just as Tony Schwartz predicted in his "resonance theory" discussed in Chapter 13. Again "Rice Krispie Treats" is a winner—the brand name is in the treat's name and in its recipe!

Packaging

Packaging is defined as the container or wrapping that protects and identifies the product, reinforces the brand name, and builds **brand equity** (or easy brand recognition), and it can have value as a promotional device—it's cute, contemporary, can be a toy, and so forth. By law, packaging must provide information about the brand's contents in the order of their proportion in the brand and should inform consumers about its functions, features, benefits, and methods of use. From an advertising perspective, the package should also make the brand attractive, recognizable, and easy to see and stock on store shelves and displays.

Showing the package in ads helps consumers recall the product's advertised characteristics and benefits at the point of purchase. This is usually in the retail store, but as noted there are other ways to purchase goods nowadays, such as by phone, from a catalog, or online where a picture of a well-designed and distinctive package can also increase sales just as it does on store shelves. The package can also carry a sales promotion, such as a coupon or a free travel size of the brand, and it can seem valuable in and of itself as was the Nabisco package mentioned earlier. Another example is the Grolsch beer bottle, which has a ceramic stopper and can be used to store other liquids once the beer is gone. Others kept the L'eggs plastic "egg" container for storage, crafts, and containers for jelly beans in Easter baskets, as well as serving as the package for hosiery. L'eggs was also the first hosiery to be sold in supermarkets (thus also occupying a "being first" niche or position in the market).

Packages make a brand impression, especially when used in the strategy of package/brand placement in movies and television programming. There, characters/actors make conspicuous use of familiar brands like Coke, Sweet Success Foods, Toyota, Procter and Gamble, and GM. But is it effective in leading to sales increases? Communication scholar T. Borchers (2002) reports that sales of Red Stripe beer jumped 50 percent after Tom Cruise sipped from a can of the brew in the popular film *Top Gun*. As a critical consumer, try to identify the effects of branding, packaging, and labeling and how they interact with brand advertising (e.g., look at the packaging of Mrs. Butterworth's and Log Cabin syrups). We consumers tend to disregard the effects package design have on our brand perceptions.

Sales Promotion

Sales promotion is defined as "… temporary inducements used to encourage immediate purchase." This marketing tactic has grown greatly in the past two decades due to the overbuilding of retail strip malls, catalogs, 1-800, online ordering of goods and services, telemarketing, eBay and Craigslist shopping, "Groupons" and imitations, and SNM/words of mouth(s), all of which make for greater competition for the consumer's discretionary income. Every marketer wants to induce the consumer to spend this discretionary money in their store, on their brand, in their catalog, and they use gimmicks to prompt purchase—some of them are aimed at consumers and some are aimed at the trade (i.e., wholesalers and retailers) to get them to "push" the brand onto store shelves. Consumer-targeted sales promotions include special sale pricing like "two for the price of one" and short-term price reductions like "special six-hour sales." Basically, they are designed to move the goods off the shelves and into consumer's hands. Other more familiar sales promotion tactics include coupons, rebates (key word = "save"), extra product in the package (keyword = "more"), travel sizes that go with the main package (keyword = "handy"), contests (keyword = "win"), premiums (keyword = "free"), sweepstakes (keyword = "win"), recipes (keyword = "great taste"), and bonus packs (keyword = "extra").

These advertising tactics have the same goal—all sales promotional offers are designed to increase demand. They try to "pull" the brand through the supply pipeline using artificially pumped-up consumer demand for the brand. They do so by using techniques such as temporary price reductions or contest possibilities (as the "carrot"), and short-term exclusions such as expiration dates or limited supplies, or minimum purchase levels (as the "stick") to prompt quick purchase. As far as the trade is concerned, sales promotions can motivate sales staff through bonuses, such as winning a free trip to Alaska for topping the previous sales records for the period. Sales promotions also alert retailers to upcoming increases in demand and therefore the need to stock up. If wholesalers know coupons or rebates are coming out and are going to be accompanied by a large advertising campaign, they will advise their retail customers that the demand is about to increase sufficiently and the retail managers will order extra supplies and thus have been "pulled" into moving the brand onto store shelves. An interesting example is Jell-o, which was virtually unknown when introduced and only came in only two flavors from the slaughterhouse—"meat" or "hooves and bones." An adroit entrepreneur purchased the formula and then it evolved into the product we know today (see Weblink 14.8). (You can access this and all of the other Chapter 14 weblinks through your companion website for *Persuasion*, Chapter 14 resources.) "First came team-drawn wagons, to be followed by smart auto-cars. Pictures, posters, and billboards over the American landscape, as well as page ads in magazines, carried the Jell-O Girl and the six delicious flavors...." (see Weblink 14.8). Then came a wide distribution of recipe books urging wives to consult their local grocer (thus creating demand) and offering the merchant cases of the stuff ("comes in 6 delicious flavors!") each on consignment. The rest is history. What once had been the dessert of the wealthy (because of the labor involved in making gelatin from scratch—just try it!) became the cheapest dessert to serve a family during the Depression. It was now available for a dime a box with servings for four. People tried it and then added anything imaginable to it—fruit, nuts, 7-Up, etc. The managers, in turn, probably used "push" tactics like special pricing, discounts, and store displays, as well as the nationally advertised coupons or rebates to move the brand off store shelves. All these sales promotions work hand-in-hand with brand advertising, brand naming, packaging, PR, the Jell-O jingle and other clever word tricks (e.g., "Follow the Jell-O Brick Road!"), and other sales promotion practices to form the IMC that persuades us to buy certain brands right now before it's too late.

TOMA and Positioning

We live in a world filled with too many of almost everything—too many television channels, too many product categories, too many media options, and too many brands in most categories to ever remember, yet alone to purchase. Research shows that we can only recall a finite number of brands in each product category, depending on the product category complexity. Actually they speculate that this "top of mind awareness," or **TOMA** as it is called, is limited to categories other than products or brands. That's probably why your car radio has only about 5 or 6 buttons to set for favorite radio stations—after all, that's probably about the number that you regularly tune into. And TOMA applies to favorite TV channels, recipes, car brands, and so forth. For complex product categories such as computers or cell phones, most consumers usually can recall only about 5 brands, whereas they recall as many as 9 brands in less complex categories such as beer or breakfast foods. As a result, a brand needs to stand out so it will be remembered at the point of purchase when TOMA most significantly affects purchase behavior. TOMA is most likely created through information processed in the peripheral channel of the ELM—through repeated things like slogans, jingles, mood music, logos, and packaging. Most contemporary professionals in the field agree that advertising as a tool of marketing has changed the whole structure of bringing products to market. In other words, companies don't usually come up with a product and then try to sell it to consumers using advertising messages anymore. That strategy is known as an "outside-in" strategy, which means beginning with the product type or brand approach. Instead, today's most successful marketer begins with the minds of consumers, and tries to identify their potentially unmet or unsolved needs or problems. Then the R&D department designs a brand (or redefines an existing brand) to fill the consumer's perceived needs or problems. That is an "inside-out" strategy. This approach of beginning with consumers was made popular by Al Ries and Jack Trout. In their bestselling books, *Positioning: The Battle for Your Mind* (Ries and Trout, 1986), *The New Positioning* (Trout, 1995), and *Focus: The Future of Your Company Depends on It* (Ries, 1996), they deal with the concepts of positioning and repositioning, which are strategies for finding an empty niche in the consumer's mind—a perceived need or problem—that a given brand might fill, and then targeting that niche with advertising that stresses the need-meeting or problem-solving features and benefits of the brand. For example, the designers of a new snack chip asked

---

BOX 14.3   Interactive Media and Consumers—Mainly Kids

Over 16 million children had Internet access in 2000, and the number increases every year. In 2011, 80 percent of kids between 0 and 5 years of age use the Internet in some way. Most of the time parents don't monitor their children's online activity except to block pornographic sites using the V-chip. A proposal is now under consideration to turn the V-chip into an A-chip that would block interactive advertising as well as pornographic websites. In its Spring, 2005 issue, *Children Now* raised a number of questions regarding interactive advertising and how it might be used in the coming digital age. It said that soon the Internet will be accessible from your digital television set, and kids will be able to make purchases using a remote control and a parent's credit card. The most advertised product types aimed at children today are breakfast cereals, soda pop, and fast foods. Critics attribute the 300 percent increase in childhood obesity in part to advertising these product categories. Some predict an average shortening of the life expectancy of today's children of about five years as a result of such ads.

Many companies also create websites (and soon TV sites) that attract children into them by making video games available for free and then promoting the brand via the game. Examples include the Kool-Aid Mad Scientists "Mix it Up" game, Kraft's "TooMuchFun.com" and "Chips Ahoy! Cookie Guys' Housewarming Party" at Weblink 14.9. (You can access this and all of the other Chapter 14 weblinks through your companion website for *Persuasion*, Chapter 14 resources.) This strategy of offering free games laced with advertising for the brand is called "advergaming" and is a part of "T-commerce," or television commerce, and defined as the ability to purchase goods using your digital television and its remote control. It is now in operation in the United Kingdom, and Domino's Pizza is using it very successfully there to take orders (Espejo and Romano, 2005). To explore the implications of these innovations, go to Weblink 14.10. You can also go to "advergaming" on any search engine to learn more about how companies are advertising to adults and children via interactive media in sophisticated games like "Second Life." Do these tactics seem ethical? Why or why not?

---

consumers to open bags of potato chips, pour them into serving dishes, eat a few, and discuss what each of their five senses processed. Customers in these "focus groups" then were asked to comment on the chips and tell what they liked and disliked about them, and how they would use them in entertaining. They said the chips were hard to store, and sometimes they were burned or had parts of the green peel on them—can't serve those to guests. They also smelled and felt greasy and broke easily, leaving small pieces that no one wanted to serve or take—they were the discards left at the end of the party. In response, the company designed an alternative—which was, of course, Pringles. They were easy to store, were never burned, weren't greasy because they were baked, not fried, were all the same size and shape, and rarely broke because of their protective packaging. Pringles were positioned as the easiest (and classiest) chip to store and serve.

Once a position has been established for a product, advertising prepares customers for trial, ultimate purchase, and hopefully repeat purchases. Advertising lays the groundwork for sales by increasing brand awareness using repeated slogans, jingles, memorable packaging, and by communicating and improving the brand's attributes, features, and benefits. And this is done especially with interactive advertising, as seen in Box 14.3. What is needed is advertising that makes an attractive offer that will move consumers to the point of purchase. Once consumers are at the POP, sales promotion and personal selling take over to close the deal. What a change from early branding attempts!

PROBLEMS OF AN OVER-COMMUNICATED SOCIETY

One of Ries and Trout's main points is that we live in an **over-communicated society**. There is simply too much communication for the average person to even hope to process. They claim that, in response, the average consumer develops an over-simplified mind, which largely ignores or tries to forget most of the information to which it is exposed. This oversimplification leads to the "positions" in the average person's TOMA. People select the brands they think are good and then stick with those preferences because it makes shopping easier. We call these preferences brand loyalty. Brand loyalty makes it easier to live in an over-communicated society because you never have to change your mind, and you can easily ignore all the ads for competing brands. Furthermore, you can rely on those brands no matter where in the country you happen to reside. Interestingly, brand loyalty is most strongly developed in consumers like yourselves who are between the ages of 18 and 24. Brands are portable. You can take them with you wherever you go—it's like taking part of home with you when you move, and in a mobile society like ours, you will move many times. Research shows that most college grads move a dozen or so times in the first decade after graduation. Nationally, 20 percent of the population is on the move every year, which averages out to a move every five years. It's why most retailers, and professionals like dentists and doctors, must continually seek to add to their customer base to replace those who are moving away. Also, brand loyalty helps consumers predict quality and value from place to place. This is appealing to those in the early years of their careers, and those who face frequent job or location changes.

Advertising agencies often face the criticism that they sell people unnecessary products or brands that might even be harmful, like tobacco, alcohol, and foods high in sodium or fat. As Michael Schudson notes (1984), they defend themselves by claiming that their aim is "not to change people's product choices but to change their brand choices. Advertising … is a competitive war against commercial rivals for a share of a market" (p. 54). To break through the cluttered media landscape and get into oversimplified minds, advertisers must find something that is already in the audience's mind and then tie it to their brand. This is similar to Schwartz's evoked recall model, which identifies critical experiential information in consumer's minds and then gets messages out of

audiences, not into them. Ries and Trout suggest that the best way to do so is to use an oversimplified message. They report the results of a name recognition survey in which only 44 percent of people recognized a photo of the then-current vice president of the United States, while 93 percent of them quickly recognized Mr. Clean—he was a much simpler message. The over-communication problem is also exacerbated by what Ries and Trout call the "media explosion" that we looked at in Chapter 13. In the near future it includes potential doubling of TV, cable, satellite, and radio options due to digital programming. We are also likely to witness an increase in newspapers, news weeklies, magazines, catalogs, direct mail, billboards, and other kinds of "out-of-home" ads, bus signs, interactive media, and signage in public restrooms. And that doesn't even take into account the ever increasing use of the Internet for advertising purposes. There are other message carriers at work as well (see Figure 14.3). Not only do we have too many messages coming at us, as Figure 14.3 demonstrates, but now they are everywhere. Even the human body carries trademarks like Calvin Klein, Gucci, Benetton, and Guess. Retailers like McDonald's and Subway insist that their staff members become branded by wearing the brand logo on their uniforms, adding on buttons for the latest special offers, and more.

Ries and Trout also call attention to the "product explosion." For example, there are mega-supermarkets (mainly in Europe and the United States) that contain more than 60,000 items from which to choose, compared to the 12,000 to 20,000 we find in the usual supermarket. Each year 25,000 new trademarks are registered at the U.S. Patent Office, with "hundreds of thousands of products and brands being sold without trademarks" (Ries and Trout, 1986, p. 14; Trout, 1995; Ries, 1996). Not only is there an increase in the volume of brand advertising, but unlike in the past, ads are now used to promote professionals and non-profits like lawyers, doctors, universities, pharmaceutical companies, and hospitals—institutions that rarely if ever used to feel the need to advertise to potential clients. As a result, brands must seek to gain a unique position or niche in the consumer's mind. We have

aochsner@northernstar.info

FIGURE 14.3   One of the major problems for advertisers today is what Ries and Trout call the "advertising explosion," by which they mean not only the increased volume of advertising but also the new advertising vehicles, surfaces, or places where advertising can appear.

SOURCE: Used with permission of Al Ochsner.

discussed Ries and Trout's traditional forms of positioning earlier (see Chapter 11) and once again, its need seems due to too much competition. No wonder brand loyalty develops early and persists for many years—how else are we to choose from among the many alternatives? Positioning became one way to break through all the brand, media, and advertising proliferation and resulting advertising clutter. Let's take a closer look.

Positioning, Repositioning, and Breaking Through the Clutter

How do advertisers overcome the triple whammy of burgeoning media, products, and advertisements? In other words, how do they break through all of this clutter? The technique known as **positioning** provides one way to do so. We encountered some of these tactics back in Chapter 11, which covered market segmentation in persuasive campaigns. Here are some of them again. "Being first" among the alternatives in a product category helped many products to be recalled by the consumer—products such as Jell-O, Kleenex, and Xerox copiers didn't have to break the clutter because initially, there was none. They were the only show in town and, being exclusive, they were permanently implanted in consumers' minds right away. These brand names and more recent "first" additions like Lunchables

are now virtually generic terms for the product category and are therefore known as **master brands** in the ad industry. Not only was the Apple Personal Computer the first in the PC market, but it was also the first user-friendly PC. This let Apple get the jump on IBM, which had deferred going into the consumer computer market, preferring to focus on business computers costing millions. Later, when IBM and other brands entered the consumer market, Apple lost its competitive edge to these other brands that offered new, better, and more universally adopted, user-friendly software such as Windows by Microsoft. Being first doesn't always guarantee that you will remain in that position or that you will become a master brand someday.

For brands not first in the market, positioning becomes even more important and complex. They don't want to be "me too" brands by saying that they were "grown in the mountains too" or that they were good to the "next to the last drop." In earlier advertising eras (the brand benefit or the unique selling proposition) and in the "brand image" era, the competition wasn't nearly as fierce as it is today; there wasn't as much competing clutter to overcome or break through. With more and more "me too" versions on the market including things like house brands and generics, neither product benefits nor image ads work as well as they used to work. Brands have to be unique in the marketplace, and they should be perceived as having a high-quality image (e.g., like Bayer aspirin used to and may still be perceived), but this is no longer enough. Now price, selection, and equivalence, plus simple but distinctive ad copy are all needed to make a brand break through and communicate their similarities to the more expensive high-image brands; and those brands have to face the advantages of the less expensive but nearly equivalent options for the consumer. The "poetry of product benefits" can still work as can be seen by the many enduring brands that have been around for 75 years or more. Folgers's "Mountain Grown" and Maxwell's "Good to the Last Drop" still have brand loyalty and are readily recalled by consumers, but they are the exception and not the rule.

Circumstances can also change for a brand. Take the example of Ivory Soap, whose slogan "99 and 44/100% Pure—It Floats" was among the earliest product benefit ads; its slogan is still often recalled. Interestingly enough, the "It Floats" benefit was the result of a factory worker who accidentally pumped too much air into the soap, making it buoyant. Not long after that, consumers asked for the floating version of Ivory because it was easier to find in the bathtub. It has now dropped from being the leader in the bar soap product category down to being the number six selling soap. Why? Not because of poor advertising, but because circumstances changed—more people now take showers and finding the bar of soap isn't a major problem anymore (Parente, 2004). Other examples of positioning to break through the clutter include convincing ad benefit copy such as: "At Ford, Quality Is Job #1," "Introducing the Smell of Luxury," and "Dermatologist Recommended." We still encounter colorful poetic ad copy, as Figure 14.4 demonstrates.

A variety of techniques can make a product seem to be the only, the sexiest, or the most exciting one on the market. A relatively new position is the environmentalist or "green" niche or positioning oneself as the "greenest" brand in the product category, which convinces consumers of the brand with a certain desirable and socially responsible benefit. Other niches we have discussed earlier include positioning by age (AARP), positioning by gender

(Virginia Slims), being the best (Mercedes), being the most expensive (Rolex), being the least expensive (Hyundai), and being "user friendly" (Microsoft Windows). There aren't many new niches or positions in a given product category, so if competitors are firmly entrenched in the audience's mind as "first" or as a "master brand" for example, what can be done? One possibility is to go up against one of them with comparative advertising, which we discussed in depth earlier. Ries and Trout give an example of this approach in the Avis Rent-a-Car campaign, whose slogan was "Avis is Number 2 in Rent-a-Cars, so We Try Harder", and can be seen in Figure 14.5.

What was the result of this comparison? After 13 years of losing money, Avis made $1.2 million the first year after it admitted to being second. Interestingly enough, the "We Try Harder" ads didn't really hurt the market leader, Hertz. Instead, the campaign took business away from other brands in the market like National and Budget. Consumers must have perceived that Avis tried harder than them but not that much harder than Hertz. Another way a brand can break through clutter is to reposition itself (Trout, 1995) by telling consumers "what we're not." The soft drink 7-Up was near bankruptcy when its advertising agency, J. Walter Thompson, came up with one of the most successful "what we're not" brand turnarounds in advertising history with the invention of the word "un-cola," which they then used in very creative ways. For example, the brand advertised itself was being delivered by the "man from uncola," which was a take-off on the title of a popular television series of the time—a spy thriller called *The Man from U.N.C.L.E.* Other humorous ads were also part of the campaign, so the humor acted as a tactic to put the "what we're not" strategy to work. The campaign not only saved the company from bankruptcy, but it ultimately positioned 7-Up as third in the soft drink category, right behind Coke and Pepsi. Another approach to positioning a brand is to take advantage of an existing brand image or reputation, and build on it by bringing new product categories on the market, which also carry the original brand name. For example, Arm & Hammer has always produced its well-known baking soda, but more

ther clutter breakers noted above and also in
er 11 are positioning by gender or age. One
ct occupying the age niche in a major way is
Maturity magazine, which has the leading
ne circulation in the country and is aimed at
s aged 45 years or older who have joined
. Naturally, brands such as high-fiber or
dium foods, cholesterol and arthritis reme-
upplemental health care, erectile dysfunction
tions, and retirement planning advertise
Consider the marketing of such products and
s as iPods, Zappos, the BlackBerry, or resume
g companies, all of which position by age to
the younger consumer who is looking for
technologies, a better appearance or job
unities.

stribution and packaging can also break
. We have already mentioned L'eggs as using
aped packaging to increase sales, but it was also
st hosiery to be distributed in supermarkets—
w position "available in supermarkets" really
d. That fact *and* its packaging gave it a unique
n in the hosiery market and raised its market
incredibly, while saving the manufacturer
ring costs (Ries and Trout, 1986). In contrast
nary envelope hosiery packaging that needs to
ded and packed by hand, the L'Eggs hosiery
simply be stuffed into the container by
ne, thus eliminating labor costs and reducing
both positioning the *brand* as a unique one.
gg-shaped container was also used by consu-
or storage as we noted above (Dollas, 1986).
tisers can also break through the clutter by
itioning an existing brand, as was the earlier
ith 7-Up. A more recent repositioning is the
ng of Cheerios from a children's brand to an
one by stressing its high-fiber content (Trout,
The brand always had high fiber, but ads
mentioned that until recently, probably
e Cheerios was losing its children's market
nt to sweetened brands like Fruit Loops or
s. Choosing the right name for a brand not
uts through the clutter but can also create a
n for the brand. A powerful bathroom
r named itself "The Works," which fits
he idea of trying the ultimate—consumers

were urged to "Give It The Works!" All these
clutter-breaking techniques grow out of various
ad research on ways to get into consumers' heads
and create ads that will "resonate," to use
Schwartz's term (1973). The major way advertisers
get into consumer's experiential and other memories is via one of four kinds of research, which
allows them to target specific markets by studying
consumer behavior.

GETTING INTO THE CONSUMER'S HEAD: ADVERTISING RESEARCH

Four kinds of advertising or integrated marketing
research can be used to get consumer data that
reveals much about how and why consumers
purchase. They are (1) demographics, (2) psychographics, (3) **geographies** or socio-graphics, and
(4) ethnography (O'Guinn, Allen, and Semenik,
2006). Sometimes one, two, three, or all four
kinds are used. Specific ways of conducting these
kinds of research include gathering information
that comes from public archives like census data,
conducting surveys among users and non-users,
questionnaires used with shoppers in malls and elsewhere, warranty cards that require the giving of
purchase information, state and local government
archives such as hunting and fishing licenses, the
department of motor vehicles and state and local
tax records, focus group interviews where typical
users discuss the brand and its ads, the pupilometer
(which tracks the eye as it scans a printed ad), the
tachistoscope (which measures how quickly the
human eye can read the words on a sign or a
page), and many others. All attempt to identify
Feig's (1997) consumer "hot buttons" and "cold
buttons," the idea being to design ads that press
those buttons and thus help to break through the
cluttered marketplace of brands, ads, and media.

Demographics

Demographics identify specific market segments
on the basis of data—usually numerical—like

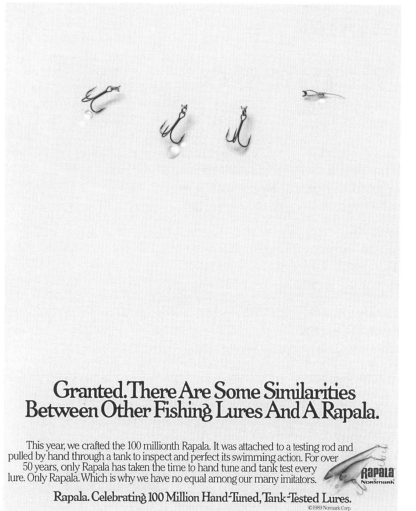

FIGURE 14.4

How did this hard-hitting product ad by Rapala break through the clutter?

SOURCE: Reprinted by permission of Normark Corp.

recently it began to make and sell the stuff in bulk to
cattle farms to aid in digestion and the resulting
increases in weight gain. Arm & Hammer also positioned its added categories to its product line by carrying the parent company name; we now have Arm
& Hammer laundry detergent, carpet cleaner, toothpaste, and so on. This practice of bringing new brand
products to market under the parent company's
name is called **line extension** and relies on one's
reputation or brand equity to break through the clutter. Inventing *new uses* for a brand also helps to reposition it. Again, Arm & Hammer's traditional baking
soda provides a great example of this tactic. The

brand has an unaided recognition of 97 percent and
can be found in almost 100 percent of kitchen cup-
boards, so there was no need to increase brand awareness. It just wasn't being used very much. It only takes
a small amount for a batch of chocolate chip cookies
or to pour on an acid-covered battery connection,
and few persons use it in their baths or as a substitute
for toothpaste. In 1972, the company decided to
advertise a previously mentioned but not heavily
promoted alternate use for the brand. They reposi-
tioned it as a "deodorant" for your refrigerator. The
baking soda had always been used to clean refrigera-
tors. The usual result is gross discoveries and

No. 2ism.
The Avis Manifesto.

We are in the rent a car business, playing second fiddle to a giant.

Above all, we've had to learn how to stay alive.

In the struggle, we've also learned the basic difference between the No. 1's and No. 2's of the world.

The No. 1 attitude is: "Don't do the wrong thing. Don't make mistakes and you'll be O.K."

The No. 2 attitude is: "Do the right thing. Look for new ways. Try harder."

No. 2ism is the Avis doctrine. And it works.

The Avis customer rents a clean, new Plymouth, with wipers wiping, ashtrays empty, gas tank full, from an Avis girl with smile firmly in place.

And Avis itself has come out of the red into the black.

Avis didn't invent No. 2ism. Anyone is free to use it.

No. 2's of the world, arise!

FIGURE 14.5

Avis "We Try Harder" Strategy Ad.

SOURCE: Image Courtesy of The Advertising Archives.

disgusting smells which the consumer feels ashamed of. Clever ads used embarrassing visuals and gross odors coming out of the refrigerator, which were then "absorbed" by the box of Arm & Hammer baking soda put there for exactly that purpose. Sales increased 72 percent in less than two years (Honomichl, 1984). Analysts attributed the increase to consumers who felt "refrigerator guilt" because they weren't as diligent at cleaning as their mothers, who used to clean the fridge once a month. But they could relieve their guilt by putting a box of baking soda into the refrigerator to absorb the smells. Later sales increases were accomplished by hitch hiking on this idea and urging consumers to put a box in the freezer compartment, in the refrigerator of their camper in and picnic coolers. The ultimate pitch warned consumers that the odor-absorbing quality of the soda got weaker in a few months but could still be of use if you put it down the garbage disposal, getting rid of bad odors there, too. This assured the

company of ongoing demand for its "new use" for the Arm & Hammer product.

Another strategy used by many "me too" brands is the claim to be better than old standbys in some way and thus to break clutter. The problem is that it's hard to convince consumers that a brand is better than an old favorite. Sometimes a minor improvement such as

a new ingredient—beads of blea brand available in a new form— spray bottle!"—can reposition the another clutter breaker. A produ priced niche, such as that filled Focus, or it can find a high-price and BMWs (see Figure 14.6).

Take me to your husband.

Tell him you want him to test-drive me. The BMW 2000. Let him take the wheel. And watch him fall.

I was made for a man like yours – I respond to his slightest command. I am fast. In fact, I can cruise at 108 mph. Hour after hour with ease. Which is great for those continental holidays. But in a tight situation, it's good to have an engine that delivers so much power.

And my BMW suspension. Independent on all four wheels. I'm proud of how it enables me to hold the road no matter how fast I run.

You'll notice that I am elegantly styled.

I'm roomy. I have reclining seats. With space for five adults and plenty of luggage. But the best thing about me: I'm fun to drive for the man who enjoys driving.

So, go ahead and take me to your husband. What if he *does* fall in love? It's better than having him fall for another woman. *2000 brief specification – 4 cylinder 1990 c.c. overhead camshaft. 113 bhp (SAE) at 5,800 rpm. Price: £2,199. Price shown is recommended retail price incl. P.T.*

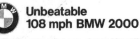

Unbeatable 108 mph BMW 2000

For the man who can please himself

Other models include: 106 mph BMW 1600 £1648. – 113 mph BMW 2000 £1874. – 106 mph BMW 1800 £1796-97. 121 mph BMW 2500 £2999. – 125 mph BMW 2800 £3499. – 130 mph BMW 2800 CS £4996-98.

BMW Concessionaires GB Ltd., BMW House, Chiswick High Road, London W.4. Telephone: 01-995 4651 · London Showroom, N.A.T.O. Diplomatic and Export Office· 56 Park Lane, London W.1. Tel: 01-499 8881.

29

FIGURE 1

This clever ad pla husband/wife/au triad and makes that the BMW is upscale consume her husband as w the entire high-pr tion is engineered vehicle).

SOURCE: Image courtes Archives.

annual family income, religious affiliation, political preferences, age, family size, gender, purchase patterns, or any combination of such factors (O'Guinn, Allen, and Semenik, 2009). Most of such data is available from the U.S. Census, state and local governments, warranty cards, and other sources. Based on these data, advertisers design ads that feature certain kinds of characters and spokespersons or that have certain settings or props. One demographic pattern involves the growing number of DINKs (or folks with Double Incomes and No Kids). DINKs actually comprise two separate subgroups: (1) those who intentionally have no children, are largely self-indulgent, and usually have lots of discretionary income to spend on the extras; and (2) those whose children have left home and are now independent, and who finally have some discretionary income. The first group tends to be younger and loves spending their discretionary income on things like travel, club memberships, fashion, and upscale autos for themselves. The second group is the now-aging front edge of the baby boom, whose members are retiring in increasing numbers, and who spend their discretionary income in different ways—on travel, grandchildren, health, and retirement savings.

Aging boomers are increasing at the rate of more than 2 million new consumers a year. Advertisers need to appeal to these subgroups in very different ways, and demographic data helps advertisers know a lot about them. For example, there are about 157 women for every 102 men in this age group, and their rate of divorce is three times the national rate. They tend to get up earlier in the day and retire earlier at night. They spend lots on grandchildren, recreation, medications, organically grown foods, and travel. Now, you play advertising executive with these data and tell when, where, and how you would appeal to this market segment and for what kinds of brands. Your product is a nationwide network of health clubs that can be used anywhere in the country while traveling. Would you advertise in *Modern Maturity*, with the world's largest subscription base with lots of **reach** (defined as the number of persons who see or hear the ad) but not much **frequency** (defined as how often they see the ad)? Or would you make your appeal during local evening news shows that most of them watch on a regular basis—mainly for the weather forecast and local interest? These programs have a much smaller reach but greater frequency and are far less expensive. How about using the History Channel, which also shows a higher age demographic? Would you use direct mail to persons over the age of 60 in the states where many older citizens retire, such as Florida, Arizona, or Nevada? Whom would you pick to be your spokesperson—Lauren Hutton, Mike Ditka, Suzanne Sommers, Tina Turner, or someone under the age of 30? As you can see, demographics help target segments, and can also help design effective ad copy and make wise choices about which media to use, suitable spokespersons, and even the time of day to run the ads. What about another similar cluster known in the Chicago area as DITKAS, which stands for "Double Incomes with Two Kids Away at School"? How would you target them? Whom would you choose for a spokesperson?

Psychographics

Psychographics is the study of consumers' lifestyles, attitudes, and interests, and how they feel about a product or brand—that is, what happens to them emotionally when they hear the name of a brand (Amft, 2004). Again Schwartz's theory comes into play because what psychographics really aims to find out is how a brand resonates with audiences. This information can help customize ads. Psychographics also provides data about how consumers spend their time and money, what activities they engage in, what interests them, and what their opinions and attitudes are on various brand-related issues (O'Guinn, Allen, and Semenik, 2009). Frequently, this research method measures such things by cataloging people's values, attitudes, and their preferred lifestyles using a variety of research techniques—attitude polls, mall intercepts, focus group interviews, telephone surveys, and analysis of leisure time.

Activities, Interests, and Opinions. Examples of activities are work, social events, vacations, hobbies, entertainment, club memberships, church, sports, and community activities. The subcategory of "good-life activities" includes cultural events, gourmet cooking, investing, travel, wine tasting, and collections. Advertisers could look at outdoor activities like skeet shooting, fly fishing, RVing, or motorcycling. In each of these subcategories, consumer advertising needs to be tailored to fit the way target groups spend at least some of their time. The golfer interested in gourmet cooking, skeet shooting, and digital photography is different from the bowler who is focused on the same things. Each needs to receive personalized advertising messages for maximum effect, and that is the ultimate goal of consumer research—to customize advertising messages to fit every individual having similar (but not identical) activities. This is known as "one-to-one" segmentation, "personalized advertising," or iMEDIA (which stands for "interactive media" such as SNM).

Examples of an individual's interests include the family and home, church, achievements, health issues, investing, recreation, fashion, technology, food, and media use patterns. You can easily imagine the differences between a person interested in family, fashion, and technology who reads *Cosmopolitan* and *Elle* and watches *Oprah*, and those of someone interested in achievements, health, orchids, and gourmet cooking and who reads *Organic Gardening, Gourmet*, and *Southwest Living*, and who watches the Food and Home and Garden cable channels. They are obviously different and would respond positively to customized ad messages that included references to their personal interests. Using consumers' interests can also help advertisers pick spokespersons and appropriate media when making their targeting decisions, just as other elements in ad research can. Opinions relate to oneself; international, social, and political issues (e.g., global terrorism, energy alternatives, global warming); business and economics (e.g., the rate of inflation, the home mortgage or credit crisis); religion and culture; education; film; and the future (e.g., interactive television, virtual reality). Remember, as we said in Chapter 7, opinions are weaker than attitudes and can easily change almost overnight. You often see this fickleness in the public opinion polls about politicians and candidates; however, they aren't particularly strong predictors of actual behavior. You could profile two very different persons with differing opinions and make appropriate advertising decisions for each of them. This would be especially true with issues like politics and propaganda, as seen in Box 14.4.

BOX 14.4   **Hidden Propaganda—the New Camouflage**

Ever since 9/11, we have seen increasing amounts of governmental propaganda characterizing enemies such as terrorists, Jihadists, and others. But what about more subtle and disguised forms of propaganda that remains invisible at first glance? Many critics are concerned by such camouflaged propagandistic appeals that address social and political values. Take the "Letters to the Editor" portion of a daily newspaper. It is assumed that these opinions are coming from everyday citizens just like you or your neighbors. Do a web search to learn how both the John Kerry and George W. Bush presidential campaigns of 2004 used this seemingly harmless form to create hundreds of false letters to the editor by using simple cut-and-paste technology to pepper the letters section of daily papers with bogus letters. In a more surprising example, learn how Warner Brothers' holiday dancing-penguins film *Happy Feet* was interpreted by critics as propaganda espousing ecological issues like pollution, human over-consumption, and environmental exploitation in the film (Weblink 14.11). Other critics were carrying the propaganda idea a bit far when they reasoned that because the penguins danced with one another, the film was propaganda for homosexuality. (You can access this and all of the other Chapter 14 weblinks through your companion website for *Persuasion*, Chapter 14 resources.)

As you can imagine from the invented profiles of "typical" individuals noted above, taken together with attitudes, activities, and interests, opinions can spawn an almost infinite number of such profiles and an equally huge number and complicated mix of media decisions and advertising appeals. Such a goal is out of our reach at present, but with emerging technologies and the means of measuring the elements in psychographics, advertisers are coming closer every day to the goal of a single-person market—segments with individually customized ads aimed at each of our individual prejudices, quirks, activities, opinions, and interests. Psychographics also asks people to respond to questions about their activities, attitudes, interests, and opinions but in a different way, by asking about specific brands. Advertisers then infer the respondents' lifestyles and how they are likely to respond to a brand and its advertising package. Claussen's pickles are a good example. The brand is not cooked like its competitors' brands and therefore must be refrigerated, and the pickles are significantly more expensive than the competition. They are also much crunchier and "gourmet" tasting, and you won't find them on the canned goods shelves but in the refrigerator case. They are the kind of pickle you "used to" find in barrels. They are associated with upscale consumers who don't shop for price and who want to be perceived of as persons of good taste. Knowing these things allows the advertiser to tell how well a particular brand or ad for that brand will "fit" that particular kind of consumer and about how this information can be used to promote the brand to similar-minded individuals with the proper spokesperson, setting, script, music, and so on. Initially, Claussen's were sold in a plastic quart jar, but that packaging decision proved to be a poor one. Think about it. When you reach for a jar of some product category in the refrigerator case, you want it to feel cold. Plastic doesn't transfer temperature nearly as well as glass, and it somehow seems "chintzy" and downscale. As a result the company switched to packaging the brand in glass jars. Consumers wanted to not only taste how expensive their chosen brand was, but they wanted to physically feel its refrigerated quality.

In another example, a study determined what type of consumer would be likely to bring a malpractice suit against their doctor (perhaps useful information for the doctor, his malpractice insurance programs, and even our government). Items in the survey included some like these:

1. I have a great deal of confidence in my own doctor.
2. Many physicians are out of date.
3. Physicians are overpaid.
4. Malpractice is hard to prove.
5. You are your own best doctor.

Responses ranged from "strongly agree" to "strongly disagree." Trends in responses were then correlated to persons actually bringing malpractice suits. Conclusions were drawn about what kind of malpractice insurance the doctor should buy, and given what they know about their own patient base, which individuals should be referred to another doctor or specialist in order to reduce the likelihood of having a suit brought.

In yet another example, persons strongly agreeing with the following items are highly likely to use Listerine mouthwash rather than Listermint mouthwash:

1. I do not feel clean without a daily bath.
2. Everyone should use a deodorant.
3. A house should be dusted three times a week.
4. Odors in the house embarrass me.
5. The kind of dirt you can't see is worse than the kind you can see.
6. I am a very neat person.
7. Dirty dishes should be washed after every meal.
8. It is very important for people to wash their hands before eating each meal.
9. I use one or more household disinfectants.

Effective ads based on this data and the result-ing trends included appeals to the germ-killing and antiseptic qualities in Listerine ads, such as "Clean Doesn't Mean 'Good Tasting' in Mouthwashes—Use Listerine Today!"

Interestingly enough, Listerine was not initially marketed as a mouthwash but as an antiseptic cleaner to be used on sterilized operating room floors. Only when mouth freshness emerged as a consumer need did the company go into the mouthwash category. Of course the above psycho-graphic information would be useful for brands in other product categories—household floor cleaners, bathroom cleansers, and so forth, so psychographics is a powerful way to get into the consumer's head and can be applied in ads promoting various brands and product categories.

Socio-graphics

Socio-graphics refer to an individual's social grouping, where they live (i.e., what kinds of neighborhoods with what characteristics) and other sociological factors such as their life stage (e.g., single, married without kids, married with kids, divorced) ethnicity, affiliations, and so on. If one were to define it in one sentence, it would be "Birds of a feather flock together." Generally, this means they live in identical or adjacent zip codes or in similar and usually nearby geographic areas. People choose to live with or near persons similar to themselves. Socio-graphics or geographies is a combination of the places peo-ple live, their demographics (the clusterings of variables associated with them), and their psycho-graphics (O'Guinn, Allen, and Semenik, 2006). Research on all of these data is done by sampling persons from a zip code area or areas that resemble the kind of neighborhood the advertiser believes will be attracted to the brand. Then the ad agency's creative staff designs messages around the consumer-generated copy points. Socio-graphics

also show media-use patterns and program prefer-ences for persons in these "typical" zip codes as well as a wealth of other data related to them (e.g., most recent financial transactions).

This makes sense. We choose to buy or rent in neighborhoods that house persons like ourselves, or who are in a similar life stage. We like to belong to groups that reflect ourselves and our ideals, atti-tudes, and values. For example, many people prefer to live in "gated" communities, but others would hate living there. If we're single, we'd like to live in an apartment complex with persons our age, one that has a party room and health facility and neigh-bors who are interested in the things that interest us. If we have children, we'd prefer to live in a community that has lots of families with kids—especially children near the age of our own kids. If our children have grown, we'd probably prefer not to live in a neighborhood with lots of pre-school kids or lots of teens.

A related system is PRIZM, which is mar-keted by the Claritas Corporation. The system has identified 62 distinct psychographic and socio-graphic neighborhood types or what it calls "clusters." It uses catchy names that suggest what the neighborhood is like. For example, one is called "two more rungs," for the young emulators on their way up. "Shotguns and pickups" are high school educated or non-grads, blue-collar belonger-workers who live in mobile homes, have a flat screen TV, a dusty pickup, drink generic brands of sugared soft drinks, and have a lot of consumer debt. They are frequently over-weight and often go to fast food or all-you-can-eat buffet restaurants. Claritas knows an amazing amount about "town and gown," or typical col-lege towns like the one where you might be going to school. The "town and gown" zip codes are populated largely by white single college students or recent grads. They tend to vote Republican, are overweight, and jog. They use ATM machines, bounce checks frequently (fines for this are a major income stream for the banks), and are unlikely to have a van, a toy-sized dog, mutual funds, or burglar alarm systems. However, they do have personal loans, like to water ski and snow ski, and drive Subaru DL4s, Toyota Tercels, Hyundai Excels, or Volkswagen Passats. They like David Letterman and Jay Leno but hate Sunday morning interview programs like *Meet the Press*.

Ethnographics

A research technique called **ethnographics** depends on the researcher going out into the field and observing how consumers select and use brands. For example, they might watch shoppers in the supermarket and receive permission to see and photograph the shopper's refrigerator, freezer, pantry, and cookbooks. Based on the results, the researchers go to their R&D department and either develop a new brand or reposition an old one (e.g., Cheerios) to fit the consumers' reported habits and needs. A good recent example was the development of Gillette's Sensor 3 disposable razor. It is specifically designed for women (Parente, 2004) and was based on the differences between the ways men and women shave. For example, researchers noted that when men cut themselves while shaving, they blamed the shaver. When women cut themselves when shaving their legs, they blamed themselves. When interviewed, men said they wanted a sharper razor, whereas women wanted a duller one. After asking more probing questions, researchers found that women used a razor with the handle pointing up while men shaved with the handle pointing down. This makes sense since men usually shave their faces while standing at a sink, while women usually shave their legs by bending over while showering. Armed with this research, designers created the Sensor 3 for women with three spring-loaded blades, protective micro fins, and an ergonomically styled, thicker, rubber-coated handle with grip-holding ridges. The men's Sensor had two razor blades with a similar handle but with a smaller head to shave hard-to-reach places around the nose and mouth. Both razors got high marks, and Gillette launched a successful nationwide rollout in 2002. Taken together with demographic, psychographic, and socio-graphic research, ethnographies assure that marketers are well-prepared to design products and brands as well as ads that appeal to consumers like yourself.

FROM RESEARCH TO COPY: THE LANGUAGES OF ADVERTISING

Research results next go to the agency's creative staff for conversion into attention-getting and memorable ad and PR copy. It must be believable but should also sell the brand amidst the clutter. John O'Toole (1985), past president of the American Association of Advertising Agencies, made some interesting observations about reaching the audience. He believes the consumer should be at the center of the process, and that the only kind of language—verbal and/or nonverbal—that effectively persuades targets the consumer as an individual. The first task with a new brand is to develop a personal profile of the consumer and then to custom design personal language and copy, especially using the word "you," which makes the message feel personalized, such as, "Aren't you glad you use Dial? Don't you wish everybody did?" or the Sears DieHard battery ad copy that follows a demonstration of the battery in action and has copy targeting the individual: "The DieHard. Starts Your Car When Most Other Batteries Won't." Consumers recognize their experiences (*see* Schwartz) in the words and visuals of the ad. We could cite many other examples, but consumers and critical receivers need to be ready for a set of usually misleading language that one ad executive, Carl Wrighter, calls "weasel words." Let's examine some of his examples.

WEASEL WORDS IN ADVERTISING

Carl Wrighter's classic book, *I Can Sell You Anything* (1972), focuses on some of the key words used to deceive us. He calls them "weasel words" because they allow persuaders to seem to say something without really saying anything. These "bogus" words can allow sources to neatly slide their way out of the brand's apparent promises. Politicians facing some sort of political blunder often say, "Mistakes were made," and in doing so, they seem to be taking the blame, but look more carefully—what kinds of mistakes? With what intent? These are the critical types of queries that responsible receivers need to raise in such situations. Otherwise the comment is just so much spin. For you, they are key tip-offs to the kind of pitch to guard against, and you will discover that they are frequently used in today's advertisements and how up-to-date his predictions are. Let's investigate a few of them, and if you find them interesting, enter "weasel words" into any search engine, and you will find that we have barely touched the surface in this discussion.

Helps

The word "helps" seems to offer aid, relief, or perhaps even a solution to a consumer's problem but in reality promises nothing very concrete. For example, take the slogan "Listerine mouthwash helps prevent colds." What is the promise here? Can you expect that you will feel better in a few days if you use Listerine? If you did, was your improvement from the help Listerine gave or was it because you drank lots of fluids and got lots of rest? The word "helps" has lots of "wiggle room" and lets the brand escape from being held to its supposed promise.

Like

Another weasel is the word "like." A tennis star says, "Driving a Nissan Maxima is like driving an expensive European model." The house brand is "just like" the expensive name brands. You can easily see the deception with a word that has as many loopholes as "like." It only means that something seems to resemble something else that is supposedly superior—and even that resemblance may be a stretch. A jug wine tastes *like* the expensive French brands. When you encounter the word "like," ask yourself if there are any ways that the advertised brand *differs* from the superior one and if those ways are beneficial or detrimental to you.

Virtually

The weasel word "virtually" resembles "like," except that it seems to make an even more genuine and concrete promise. The new cotton chamois shirts are "virtually indestructible." Leatherette feels "virtually" like hand-buffed cowhide. Cascade leaves your dishes and glassware "virtually spotless." The promises seem so specific, yet there is a tiny loophole—does one or two spots on a glass qualify as "virtually" spotless? What about three or five? If the product truly did the job it promises to do, the word "virtually" would be irrelevant. So don't expect 100 percent fulfillment of the benefit promised in the advertisement. Or moving from product sales to foreign/military policy, consider the story of Pat Tillman, the Cardinals pro-football safety who turned down a multimillion dollar contract to fight in Afghanistan and then was killed by "friendly fire." Enter his name in any search engine to find out whether we are "virtually" winning or losing that war and whether he was "virtually" a victim of U.S. military incompetence or just another "accident" or "collateral damage," as the military likes to put it.

Faster or Better

Some products need to be fast acting, such as over-the-counter medication for intense physical symptoms or products related to personal safety and promising to give you a faster response time to dangerous events. The brands in this product category frequently use the weasel word "faster" to sell the brand. Goodyear tires stop faster. Faster than what? Another brand? Than a donut? They give no basis for comparison. When you encounter the weasel words "faster" or "better," start making comparisons with the competition and make sure the conditions under which the faster or better response happens are really the same. Are the advertisers comparing the incomparable; are they simply comparing apples to oranges? Consider the ad featuring the sexy female smoking a cigarette in Figure 14.7, which really argues a "better than" claim.

As Much As

This weasel phrase seems to offer high performance or savings but only to up to a point. You may save nothing, a little, or maybe 50 percent, but there are no guarantees on the supposed 50 percent savings. When you see the words "**as much as**" or "up to," try to find out the regular everyday price; then make the true comparison.

DECEPTIVE CLAIMS IN ADVERTISING

Wrighter also identified another kind of deception in ads—the claims that brands often make about themselves. Clever promoters use deceptive claims or promises to attract our attention and to prompt us to buy, to vote for candidates, or to adopt certain practices, but they promise little.

The Irrelevant Claim

Some ads make claims that sound impressive but are irrelevant if you really look at them closely. The basic tactic is to make a truthful claim that has little to do with the benefits of the brand. Then the claim is dramatized in such a way as to link the claim with the product, candidate, or movement and to expound on its superiority. For example, J&B Scotch claims to be "rare" and "natural." That sounds good, doesn't it? Faced with claims like this one, receivers need to probe and ask questions like, "Are other scotch whiskeys unnatural?" If you can't find an answer to your question, you have identified an irrelevant claim. Wrigley's new "Green Apple Extra" chewing

FIGURE 14.7

Faster or Better—the E-cigarette

The claim here is that the E-cigarette is safer and hence better than the "real thing."

SOURCE: Image Courtesy of The Advertising Archive.

gum has a scratch-and-sniff feature, but that's also irrelevant. You chew gum, you don't scratch it. And you usually buy it for its flavor, not its aroma. The Ford Escape is "built for the road." Well, so are all brands and models. The old Ivory claim about being able to float is probably 99 and 44/100 percent irrelevant now that few folks take sit-down baths. Shell Oil recently ran an ad with the claim that they "Don't Throw Anything Away—There Is No Away" and went on to claim that they were a "pro-environmental" corporation because they were concerned with recycling. "Biodegradable" is another such green term and is meant to suggest that the brand is the only one which is biodegradable, but that's not true—all detergents have to be biodegradable today. The "pro-green" image is just a new position, but "green" is a clever position claim that receivers need to watch for in ads today.

The Question Claim

Wrighter also noted a kind of claim that asks a question. By asking a question, the advertiser puts the ball in the receiver's court and often there is no answer, leaving the consumer wondering. For example, take the question claim of Prestone antifreeze. "If you can't trust Prestone, who can you trust?" Well, I'd trust my friends who maybe recommended another brand, or my parents who always used a different one. But beginning the ad with a question puts the receivers on the defensive—feeling like they need to come up with an answer. Consider these question claims: "Why not buy the original?" "Would a bunch of guys really go at it this hard just for a Michelob?" and "Why not catch a lunker—with Stren monofilament?" How can receivers answer them? All examples of the question claim can have differing answers without there being any quibbles or real difference. Sure, I'd like to catch a lunker, and I'd love it with any brand of line—just so long as it's a lunker; and I know other brands can catch and land them, too. Some guys I know go at

it even harder, and they do it for a cheap brand like Old Milwaukee. Notice that the product advantage is only implied. Trusting one's anti-freeze is okay, but the question implies that dependability is to be found *only* in Prestone. Why buy the overpriced original? Maybe the Michelob is just an afterthought to the hard work-out and not the *only* reason for playing hard. Will using Stren guarantee that you'll get a big one? Not likely. When receivers see a question mark, they should ask for details and guarantees.

The Advantage Claim

Wrighter noted some claims that seem to offer a unique advantage for the brand. For example, Mother's Noodles claim to be made with 100 percent semolina wheat, which seems to be a unique advantage to the brand, but so are all the other brands of noodles, including the generics. Besides, what the heck is semolina wheat compared to Russian Red? These are advantages that aren't advantages at all. Most generics have the same or similar advantages or additives. Politicians often claim to have humble origins; this is supposed to be an advantage, but it may in fact be a real disadvantage. People who had humble beginnings might be very insecure and even greedy. They might also have limited educations, weak social skills, and an inability to communicate with persons from higher social strata. So the claim to an advantage might be a disadvantage in reality, and receivers need to probe deeper when they hear a brand, politician, or idea claim to have some sort of advantage. Whenever you are faced with a person, product, or idea that claims some significant advantage, ask if it is real and if it is exclusive to that brand, candidate, or cause.

The Hazy Claim

The hazy claim is designed to confuse the buyer, voter, donor, or joiner. While the claim seems to be related to the evidence presented and the logic involved, closer examination usually reveals that this is not so. Early ads for Dannon Yogurt used examples of persons from Soviet Georgia who ate yogurt regularly and lived to be over a hundred years old. The ads then went on to recommend that everyone should eat yogurt because "It couldn't hurt!" That is among the haziest claims I have ever read. Hazy claims are also widely used in the world of politics. For example, a politician says that she would not vote to raise the U.S. debt ceiling because that will cut government deficit spending and thus create jobs. Those two things could be mutually exclusive or even diametrically opposed.

The Mysterious or Magic
Ingredient Claim

Wrighter says that some claims refer to a magical or mysterious ingredient that supposedly makes their brand better. Noxzema sells a brand called Acne 12, which they say contains a secret ingredient dermatologists prescribe most—it may be one that all creams contain, such as alcohol or lanolin. Oxy-Clean contains "a powerful yet gentle medication no ordinary cleanser has." What is this powerful and gentle stuff, anyway? And let's not forget that Zantrex-3 claims to have a highly scientific sounding and confusing ingredient—bifurcated compounds—that can increase weight loss by 546 percent when compared to pills having ephedrine. That mysterious or magic ingredient claim would be difficult to track down, let alone truly test.

CHANGES IN OUR WORLD:
IMPLICATIONS FOR ADVERTISING

Recall the trends noted at the beginning of this chapter. Markets are becoming more global, fragmented, and diverse. More families than ever now rely on two or more incomes per household and are often strapped for time. These types of families are the prime targets of ads promising convenience and the saving of time, but the receiver also needs to ask who the actual beneficiary is. Working spouses? Widows and widowers? Single persons? Divorced persons? Workers earning overtime? Or the company making extra profit? To some extent all of these benefit, because busy two-income families and kids who have increased activities aren't the only ones who need convenience and time-saving brands. But some of these consumers can't afford to pay for the convenience or the savings in time, and in some cases all of these people can benefit from convenience and time savings. Meals are no longer the traditional family around the dinner table. Families and singles in today's world are both dining out more (one of every two meals), bringing home meals, or having home delivery of dinner. Another change has been the emphasis on another kind of convenience for these same consumers. Since the introduction of 1-800 dialing, it is easier to purchase anything, from clothing to baseball tickets. Time is a commodity for most two-income families and should be spent carefully, so mail-order and online purchasing not only saves time but allows you to avoid the inconvenience of finding a parking spot, walking to the store, shopping for what you want, and then waiting in line to check out and walking back to the car. The marketing of convenience and the saving of time are also new changes in the marketplace. The direct marketing industry, which concentrates on convenience and saving of time, now accounts for about 20 percent of all advertising dollars spent in the United States. In fact, many strip malls and even mega-malls have "space for lease" because we now face a very competitive marketplace, especially given the amount of income spent using catalogs, the Internet, shopping channels, and other direct-marketed outlets; nobody wants to take the time to drive to the mall, park and wait. As a result, another change in today's marketplace is the rush to get to the consumer's discretionary dollars before the competition can grab it. Today we see pre-Christmas sales right after Halloween as well as the traditional post-Christmas sales. We start selling back-to-school stuff right after the Fourth of July. Retailers want to get a jump on the competition. Large discount chains have increased as well, so advertising had to increase to beat the competition. In the years to come, there will be still more clutter for us to try to sift through, and we are only on the front edge of interactive and Internet advertising.

Creating Interest, Desire, and Conviction

Advertising consultants Vestergaard and Schroeder advise getting attention for an ad by asking a question that consumers cannot answer. This provokes curiosity and leads the audience to interact with the ad. Other examples include scratch-and-sniff ads, recipes in ads that use the brand as an ingredient, and ads including a true/false quiz for the reader to answer. An ad by General Motors asks, "Do you know where your next fender is coming from?" Then they satisfy the reader's curiosity by answering, "America's body shops are being flooded with imitation parts. Look-alike doors. Copycat hoods. Imitation bumpers, grills, fenders, and more.... Insist on genuine GM parts." This ad copy not only answers the attention-getting question in the headline, but it also creates interest, desire, and conviction in the consumer via product benefits and at the same time creates fears that they might not get the genuine article. Notice the frequent use of sentence fragments in the ad—"look-alike doors" and "copycat hoods." These give the advertiser extra shots at the reader in less time and space.

Advertisers also need to avoid looking like "me too" imitations of the original. All dog food looks pretty much the same—either like gravel if it is dry or like glop if it is canned. But look at what Gaines Burger did. In the first place, the name sounds like and the product looks like hamburger—the all-American food. Of course, its redness is not natural. It's just iron oxide, and

it won't hurt your dog, but it will cause your mind to make a link with hamburgers on the grill. Another tactic used to create interest, desire, and conviction for a "me too" brand is to stress its high quality. For example, Solar Power SPF-20 face powder is marketed by a company named Physicians Formula. Now if a physician formulated the powder, it must be good. But the name may not describe who actually formulated the brand. Its slogan is "Your eyes won't believe your face." If they claim that the brand has the best quality for the price, they are not likely to be asked to prove the claim. Another approach is to appeal to anything scientific by including some scientific-sounding ingredient such as got2b, DZM-21, or Adidas' "aluminum free deodorant with cotton TECH that absorbs wetness." An advertiser can also make a scientific claim like "Contains the pain reliever recommended most by doctors and hospitals." That ingredient is aspirin. Or someone wearing a white lab smock tells us about the features and benefits of the brand. And so we seriously consider buying and trying it.

Getting Action

As we have noted several times, the hardest thing to do in sales is to "close the sale" or to "ask for the order" or, in other words, prompt or get action. Vestergaard and Schroeder also speak to this goal. They note that while "Buy now!" would seem to be the most direct call to action, there are other ways to say "buy" without using the word "buy," which can turn many prospects off. For example, "act now," "phone now," "try now," and "send now" say the same thing but avoid the potentially negative word "buy." Other urgency-stressing words stress Cialdini's scarcity principle to **prompt action**, as in "offer good until," "24-hour sale," or "only a few left at this price." Of the many ads studied by Vestergaard and Schroeder, 32 percent used this kind of directive language. Directive language falls into one of several categories.

1. The imperative clause, which gives an order. "Get one today" is one example. Another example is in an ad for a fishing lure supposedly in short supply—the Shadrap. The ad copy for it implied that the company was only able to send a limited quantity to the United States and then added, "That's enough for every serious fisherman … as long as they take only one—if you see one, grab it!" Interestingly, the company publicized that at that time they were only available *to rent* the lures and then only for a limited time in Ely, Minnesota.

2. Other less directive and more suggestive language encouraging purchase, or asking questions like "Isn't it time you tried Dial?" or "Why not try Dial?" or "Dial is worth a try."

3. Directive language inviting the reader/viewer to send for details, use the trial sample, or remember the product. These appeals might get a sale, but more often, they create what we earlier labeled "qualified leads" that can be followed up on later. For example, if consumers send in for a free pamphlet on energy saving, they are probably good prospects for storm windows, aluminum siding, insulation, energy efficient furnaces and air conditioners, or solar panels. Vestergaard and Schroeder recommend seventeen verbs than can be used instead of the word "buy." They are "try," "ask for," "take," "send for," "call," "make," "come on," "hurry," "come," "see," "give," "remember," "discover," "serve," "introduce," and "choose."

SEXUAL APPEALS AND SUBLIMINAL PERSUASION IN ADVERTISING

The use of sexual appeals (and for some subliminal persuasion) in advertising is not new and has always been credited with success, but it is sometimes very controversial in today's changing marketplace. For example, feminists are concerned about the use of sexual images in advertising as being an exploitation of the female body. Others, like parents, school officials, and physicians, are concerned about increases in STDs in today's youth and wonder if all the sexual appeals in advertising might be the cause. They question very much the ethics of subliminal appeals—sexual or otherwise. And the gay market has objections as well, which is where cultural diversity becomes an issue and is reflected in Box 14.5. Sexual appeals in ads range from the blatant ones promising sexual success and satisfaction with use of the brand (e.g., Viagra or Cialis) to more sophisticated and symbolic appeals that only *suggest* sexual success if the brand is used (e.g., Victoria's Secret). There are also possibly subliminal ads that strongly suggest sexual success if the product is used or given as a gift, but that target the unconscious or subliminal level of sexual drives and needs.

Freud maintained that the sexual and procreative urges are among the most powerful motivators of human motivation and behavior, even if not overtly apparent. They frequently lead to some symbolic behaviors such as fathers passing out cigars on the birth of a new child. These symbolic actions often give sexual meanings to objects and actions. Freud saw cylindrical or rod-like objects such as pens, cigarettes, and guns as symbols of male genitalia, and round or open objects such as goblets or open windows and doors as symbols of female genitalia. To him all sorts of ordinary, everyday activities such as smoking a cigarette, cupping the hands, or fiddling with one's pen unconsciously symbolized various kinds of sexual activities. His work was ridiculed by many, but it was and is still taken very seriously by many people in the field of advertising. Whatever the case, simple observation makes it clear that sexual appeals abound in ads, and you won't have to look very long to identify objects that exemplify Freud's phallic and vaginal symbols.

Let's examine some *obvious* and overt uses of sex in ads; some *more sophisticated* and not so obvious ones; and some *possibly subliminal* uses of sexual

BOX 14.5   Cultural Diversity and Advertising

The fastest growing and most fascinating segments of the ad industry are the multicultural and diversity markets. A variety of agencies specializing in diverse and multicultural advertising have mushroomed in the past decade. A prime example is the Associated Content Corporation located online at Weblink 14.12. (You can access this and all of the other Chapter 14 weblinks through your companion website for *Persuasion*, Chapter 14 resources.) Just consider a few of the services it offers for advertisers to target various cultures and ethnic segments: public relations, media planning, direct marketing, media design and placement, event planning, web design, multimedia productions, mailing lists, ethnic radio and television, and translation. Visit its website, and you will be amazed at the depth and breadth of the kinds of skills and services now emerging to address the advertising needs of our increasingly diverse and multicultural country and world.

appeals in print and electronic ads. It is quite certain that three of these kinds of appeals are probably processed in the peripheral channel of the ELM without much conscious thought or evaluation.

In a revealing analysis, researcher A.N. Valdivia (1997) deconstructed two very different kinds of sexual appeals in lingerie catalogs. The merchandise was priced almost the same, but the quality was quite different, and the ad appeals for the two different brands were not nearly equivalent. For example, the name of one company, Victoria's Secret, connotes an old-world class that seems almost prudish. On the other hand, the other catalog, Frederick's of Hollywood, connotes a kind of leering glitziness. The settings in Victoria's Secret ads connote wealth, leisure, class, and an English country house atmosphere—a genteel lifestyle. In Frederick's of Hollywood, the photos are mostly shot against fabric backdrops, and the only items of furniture in them are beds, couches, and poolside lounge chairs—implying quite a different lifestyle. Victoria's Secret models appear demure and look away from the camera. Frederick's of Hollywood models leer at the camera, hands on hips, eyes closed, and jaws clenched. The Victoria's Secret catalog is published every month and costs $3 (although no one really pays for it), the company's home address is in London, their telephone operators speak with an English accent, and the catalog is mailed from England. So the range from sophisticated sexual appeals to more blatant and obvious appeals is clear in the difference between these two lingerie catalogs.

Blatant Sexual Appeals

Blatant sexual appeals usually *overtly promise* sexual success or satisfaction to the user in both the verbal and the nonverbal channels. It's as if the advertiser was standing behind the ad just winking at the reader.

Ads for any of the male brands designed to "cure" or aid in reducing ED or erectile dysfunction abound in media and use macho spokespersons like pro-football stars and coaches in ads for these types of products and brands. They are relatively new in the field of advertising. They are not exactly blatant, but they do fit the definition of promising sexual satisfaction to the user and are usually accompanied by a nude couple nuzzling or lying in twin bathtubs gazing at a sunset with wine glasses in hand.

More Sophisticated Sexual Appeal

More **sophisticated sexual appeals** only *hint* at sexual satisfaction if a consumer uses the brand—no promises here. Such appeals contain subtle cues (some perhaps Freudian) to indicate sexual prowess and satisfaction.

Subliminal Appeals

Subliminal appeals are a highly controversial topic (Phillips and Goodkin, 1983). In fact, many people doubt their very existence while others swear that not only does subliminal appeal exist, but it works to prompt sales and votes.

There have been some uses of subliminal appeals in national presidential campaigns. Why should this topic stir up so much controversy? It does so because it runs counter to the idea that human beings are by nature logical, not emotional, especially in making political decisions. And it would be highly unethical if they were motivated by subliminal appeals. So subliminal appeals are not limited to sexual ones. Then, too, **subliminal persuasion** smacks of sensationalism, beginning with its first reportage ages ago in the 1950s when it was claimed that during a movie, the word "popcorn" was flashed instantaneously on the screen several times resulting in a huge reported increase in sales. Most dismissed the report as mere fantasy. Let us examine the arguments of those who claim that subliminal messages do indeed exist and the controversy over whether the technique actually works. Box 14.6 should inform you fully of the controversy.

Support for the Existence of Subliminal Messages. The basic premise underlying subliminal persuasion rests on the notion of the unconscious mind and that its impulses are so powerful that they must be enacted in conscious life, even if in only symbolic ways. Freud believed that the unconscious mind is constantly at work processing information that the conscious mind simply ignores. Those who believe in the existence of subliminal appeals maintain that such appeals are sometimes so short-lived and disguised that the conscious mind ignores them, yet at the subconscious level, they are extremely powerful and highly motivating. As noted, the technique was dismissed when first publicized in the 1950s, but it was and still is barred from use in the electronic

media by the FCC because of fears that the report might be accurate. However, their ruling did not cover the print, film, and video media, and we know that blatant pornography is readily available in those media. But from a non-porn perspective, we also know that over a dozen commercial research firms in Chicago and New York still offer services in producing subliminal messages for advertisers. So there remains concern that subliminal persuasion, particularly using sexual appeals, is "secretly" being used in advertising, and that possibility is disturbing to some. The issue re-emerged in the presidential campaign of 2000 when the aforementioned negative television "RATS" ad was commissioned by the Republican National Committee to criticize Al Gore's prescription drug proposal, and some at the time credited the ad with Gore's defeat. At the same time, there were many other irregularities over the election which finally had to be determined by the U.S. Supreme Court, leaving the RATS episode unresolved. Also, it is known that the CIA has an ongoing interest in subliminal persuasion in intelligence work, espionage, and counterespionage, which tends to give one pause as to the presence and effectiveness of subliminal cues in persuasion—especially in advertising (Goodkin and Phillips, 1983).

Researcher and professor of advertising. Wilson Bryan Key (noted in Box 14.6) popularized and sensationalized the issue of subliminal sexual appeals in his books *Subliminal Seduction* (1973), *Media Sexploitation* (1977), and *Clambake Orgy* (1980). All the books claimed that subliminal and erotic cues were "embedded" or airbrushed into magazine ads that were appealing to subconscious and repressed sex drives. These **embeds** were faintly airbrushed into many liquor ads in the final stages of production, Key claimed, and they were supposedly then subconsciously remembered later when cued by a store display to buy the brand. Key was originally struck by the need to retouch photos in most liquor ads by airbrushing

BOX 14.6   **Subliminal Sexual Appeals**

As noted, this topic has always been controversial, with one side claiming to see or hear subliminal appeals, "embedded" sexually suggestive words, images, actions, and so on practically everywhere in print and video advertising, and the other side claiming that those folks must be some sort of perverts who only think about sex and therefore interpret everything as sexually suggestive. For an excellent analysis of the topic (and some fascinating examples—both visual and verbal) go to Weblink 14.13 where you will find an in-depth discussion of the topic including controversial titles, references, books, and examples on the topic ranging from scientific reports on subliminal perception to top sellers like *Subliminal Seduction* by Wilson Bryan Key, who created a big media stir over the topic in the 1970s. (You can access this and all of the other Chapter 14 weblinks through your

companion website for *Persuasion*, Chapter 14 resources.) This background is followed by a tour of the "easy to identify" examples (those that we are calling "blatant") to the "harder to notice" examples (those that we are calling "more sophisticated") to those that are "hardest to identify" examples (those that we call "subliminal" appeals). The site also discusses and gives examples of non-sexual but still subliminal appeals or claims. A seven-minute video discussion of the topic by Derren Brown and two employees of an English ad agency with videos of subliminal ads on behalf of brands ranging from McDonald's to The Food Network can be found at Weblink 14.14. Enter the words "subliminal advertising" into any search engine if you want to explore both sides of the controversy further. This also provides an interesting topic for a term paper.

in images of ice cubes in the glasses—real ice cubes melted under the hot lights needed for magazine-quality photos. Since the persuaders were airbrushing in the ice cubes, he reasoned that they might consider airbrushing in a subtle message such as the words "sex," "buy," or "good" in the cubes. Key showed 1,000 persons such an ad and asked them to describe the feelings they had while looking at them when the word "sex" was embedded in the ice cube. Although 38 percent didn't respond, 62 percent reported that the ad made them feel sensual, aroused, romantic, and sexy. Key says that he replicated the test with several different ads and other audiences with similar results.

More recently, Kevin Hogan (2005) observed that subliminal perception has been back on the front burner since 1990. His research and that of others show that subliminal *audio* messages do not work—with the exception of "priming" and "stealth marketing." The story is much different with visual or video subliminal messages. Hogan contends that the visual cortex does not respond to stimuli in conscious awareness and instead, takes unseen or unperceived information and shares it with other parts of the brain, causing actions to be taken. He reports an experiment on paying for

drinking water conducted by Piotr Winkleman, a psychology professor at the University of California at San Diego in 2004. Testing undergraduate students there, Winkelman used thirst, amount of consumption, and the price that a person was willing to pay for a glass of water as dependent or outcome variables. Subjects would be offered a glass of water in two conditions—one after seeing a happy face and the other after seeing an angry face. Thirsty subjects drank twice as much after being exposed to the happy face versus an angry one and were willing to pay $0.38 versus only $0.10 after the angry face. At present the whole subliminal issue is unclear and may or may not be just so much overly active imagining. Let's look at several ads which use sexual appeals and try to determine where the line between simply sexually oriented advertising and subliminally in sexually oriented advertising may or may not exist.

Some Possible Subliminal Ads.   Let's explore some definitions of advertisements that indeed use subliminal or near-subliminal persuasion. "Near subliminal" is used here because in these ads, someone usually has to point out the subliminal stimuli to the casual observer. This is similar to the picture puzzles where someone points out both the old woman and the young woman. It's a case where one's perception of a visual stimuli shifts (sometimes called a "gestalt shift"), and the viewer can see two very different images when they are pointed out. In all example ads used here, the advertising appeals seem to promise sexual prowess, success, and satisfaction, and one can only infer if their use is subliminal or not. If the cues must be pointed out to the observer, then they come close to being labeled subliminal. If they are even fairly obvious and don't require such help, they are not.

Consider the two perfume ads in Figures 14.8 and 14.9. The first ad is called "The Promise Made," and the second is called "The Promise

"The Promise Made"

FIGURE 14.8

What kind of promise is being made?

"The Promise Kept"

FIGURE 14.9

What differences imply that the promise was kept?

Kept." The difference in titles immediately and quite obviously suggests that some sort of change has occurred, especially since on first glance, the ads appear to be nearly identical except for their headlines. They were run side by side or on consecutive pages. Their sponsor, Lanvin Parfums Inc., admitted to your author by telephone that the changes were intentional and was quite surprised that anyone would question them. Observe what has changed between "The Promise Made" and "The Promise Kept." For instance, in "The Promise Kept," the champagne bottle is empty, the phone is off the hook, the fire has died down, the woman's shoes and perfume atomizer are now on the dais, the flowers on the left seem to have "blossomed" and "opened" in the heat, and the woman's earrings are off, as is her stole. Now that these changes have been called to your attention, you will naturally infer the answers to what has happened in the time period between the two ads. You might also notice other changes that are far more subtle and likely to be overlooked. For example, what subtle sexual messages do you find in the nonverbal differences between the two ads? (See Chapter 10 on nonverbal communication.) For example, consider the expression on the woman's face. In which ad does she smile more? In which does her body language seem more tense or relaxed? In which ad is more of her body revealed? In which ad does her hair seem more or less coiffed? In which ad do the lights seem brightest? What about the fire? What has happened to the pillow on the couch? And so on. Do these changes and the headlines imply any dual meanings?

Are Subliminals Effective? If subliminal messages such as those apparently visible above are intentionally used in ads, the next question to be asked is if they are effective in persuasion. In other words, do they sell the brand or are they just amusing tomfoolery? Most information (sales statistics, brand recognition, etc.) from the brands and the ad agencies for all advertising is called "proprietary information," which means that they are held in confidence and can't be released unless both parties agree to reveal these data. As a result, few to no direct message/purchase linkages are possible to quote or otherwise demonstrate, so we must operate on inference, admittedly a weak form of reasoning. Also, another question that arises is, "Are the embeds intentional or merely accidental?" Since they are almost always re-touched, embeds are always possible, and few advertisers are as forthcoming as Lanvin in the above ads.

Are they caused perhaps by the melting of the ice cubes or a slip of the air brusher's hands? Key notes that when such photos are taken in a studio lit with hot lights, the ice cubes do melt and very quickly which is why, he says, they have to be air-brushed in after the photo shoot is completed, and wouldn't the clever artist dream up the idea of brushing words and images into the cubes? The ad agencies reply that they would never think of using such a sullied and unethical technique just to sell the brand, but would they admit to doing it even if that was their purpose? Here's what the past president of the American Psychology Association's Division of Consumer Psychology says about the existence of subliminal cues in ads: "Absolutely.... The controversy has always been over changing people's attitudes. That you can't do. What you can do is trigger a prior attitude or predisposition" (Lander, 1981, p. 45). So perhaps the embeds act as unconscious "triggers" for purchase behavior. That statement reflects what we have been talking about all along—the most effective persuasion taps information that receivers already possess—such as images of sexual satisfaction, and similar fantasies such as conflict or violence could be embedded as Key claimed. As we have repeatedly observed, effective persuaders get messages out of their audiences, not into them, so while the ad people deny using the technique as noted, there's room for doubt as to the veracity of their denials. We do know that subliminal self-help tapes have become a multibillion-dollar business to which their creators openly admit, and many users of the tapes are true believers in the methods and testify to their usefulness in learning languages, quitting smoking, and so on. Of course, certain ads that use sex aren't at all subliminal about their messages. The Calvin Klein ads promoting Obsession for Men are good examples. Others only border on the subliminal like the blatant examples shown above. Their message is hazy but clear enough to give you a linkage between the brand and the "imagined" or "subliminal" and "embedded" images the advertiser wants you to perceive and process.

REVIEW AND CONCLUSION

As noted earlier, we live in a world exploding with new products, brands, and media that are even more cluttered with ads for those products and brands. This trend is sure to continue with more and more surfaces being used to imprint with ad messages (and to embed)—carpeting in a store, "free" T-shirts, the giant digital TV screens now being used on the sides of balloons and blimps flown over high attendance events, the backs of doors in public bathroom stalls, interactive websites, and a host of others. Advertisers want to capture our attention and try to educate us about their brand's features, benefits, and advantages. They use clever cues and sales promotions to prompt us to buy at the point of purchase.

These ads and sales promotions are but two elements in what is now termed IMC, which integrates several elements with advertising to make "brand impressions" or "brand contacts" on or with consumers. These elements include public relations, packaging, imprinted items (such as clothing, napkins, wrapping paper, and soft drink cups), and special events that feature the brand (such as the Pepsi Challenge or the Virginia Slims Tennis Tournament), consumer trade sales promotions like coupons, sweepstakes, rebates and many others; and increasingly the direct marketing industry is becoming more and more sophisticated not only in creating motivating offers and ad packages but at developing highly sophisticated data bases to target only their most promising prospects in ever smaller and highly defined segments. IMC specialists use sophisticated kinds of research, including demographics, socio-graphics, psychographics, and ethnographics to target narrower and narrower segments of the general audience. Based on this research, they develop products (e.g., Pringles and the Sensor 3 disposable razors), ad copy, layouts, music, and scripts to appeal to various needs and desires.

Ads often use misleading and even deceptive weasel words and misleading claims. And advertisers sometimes use blatant, sophisticated, and subliminal sexual appeals to hype their brands. As consumers, we need to be on guard, for there is an ethical dimension to advertising, and ads, which if violated, can easily be detrimental instead of being informative.

According to John Chaffee (1998), the positive side of advertising is that it provides consumers with valuable information about brand benefits in important areas like safety, health, nutrition, and cleanliness, as well as about more mundane issues like being attractive, sexy, and successful. He also argues that advertising as a tool of competition inevitably leads to lower prices, which is inherently advantageous for consumers. At the same time, author Russ Baker (1997) points to more questionable practices such as brand manufacturers trying to manipulate the editorial content of the media in which their advertising appears. They warn media executives that they intend to withhold advertising if editorial content is critical of the brand or even of the product category. They have been successful in censoring programming and articles to their benefit, and in some cases, they have managed to spike certain programs or articles. Recently, the Bush White House was discovered paying supposedly neutral news media personalities to slant news stones in favor of the president's words and actions. You might want to take a look at advocates on both sides of the issues in A. Alexander and J. Hanson's (2003) provocative book, *Taking Sides: Clashing Views on Controversial Issues in Mass Media and Society*. In any case, whether you as a consumer are encountering advertising, public relations, special events, sales promotions, brand contacts, and so on you need to be vigilant and critical of what you choose to reject and what you choose to process and evaluate before making purchase, voting, donating, or joining decisions.

KEY TERMS

After reading this chapter, you should be able to identify, explain, and give an example of the following key terms or concepts:

integrated marketing communication (IMC)	sales promotion	demographics	prompt action
brands	TOMA	reach	blatant sexual appeals
product	over-communicated society	frequency	sophisticated sexual appeals
slogans	positioning	psychographics	subliminal appeals
jingles	master brands	socio-graphics	subliminal persuasion
logo	line extension	ethnographics	embeds
packaging	repositioning	faster	
brand equity	geographies	as much as	

APPLICATION OF ETHICS

You work for East/West Medical Corporation, which performs medical testing. It has purchased ad time on television news programs to announce that consumers can get a "free" test kit for melanoma screening at the local Kroger supermarket. The ads masquerade as informational news items using the same anchorperson as the news program uses. A question concerning the ads has been raised. Critics ask, "Is it ethical to make an ad appear to be a news item?" The screening kit is free, and the consumer simply sends it into East/West and gets results back in a week or so for a small processing fee. The fee is mentioned in the directions for use of the kit but not in the ad. Some say that if it saves lives, it cannot be unethical. Others say that society relies on news journalists to present the truth, the whole truth, and nothing but the truth, and the "ad as news" violates the social contract between viewers and journalists. There are several options open to East/West. They could label the TV commercial as an advertisement at the outset of the spot, thus alerting the viewer. They could label it at the end of the ad after it has been processed by viewers. They could change their appeal by not emphasizing the "free" aspect of the offer and telling the viewer that there will be a processing charge. They could stop using the news program as an envelope for the ad. Which option would you choose and why?

QUESTIONS FOR FURTHER THOUGHT

1. How much money is spent for advertising in the United States per person compared with that spent in other countries?

2. How might advertising reflect the values and norms of a culture?

3. What might a Marxist critic say about the purpose of advertising?

4. What is "positioning," and how does it relate to the term "niche"?

5. What product features can serve as niches?

6. What are some of the problems of an "over-communicated society"?

7. What is the "product explosion," and how does it affect us?

8. What does "breaking through the clutter" mean?

9. Why is "American-made" an example of positioning?

10. What are the differences between demo-graphics, socio-graphics, and psychographics?

11. What is a DINK?

12. What are focus groups, and what is their purpose?

13. What are some of the languages of advertising? Give examples.

14. How does advertising research lead to adver-tising copy? Give examples.

15. What are weasel words? Give examples.

16. What are some deceptive claims? Give examples.

17. What differentiates blatant sexual appeals in advertising from sophisticated ones? Give examples.

18. How are subliminals used in advertising? How effective do you think they are?

References

Chapter 1

All Things Considered, April 11, 2005.

Brembeck, W., and Howell, W. S. (1952). *Persuasion: A means of social control.* Englewood Cliffs, NJ: Prentice-Hall.

Brembeck, W. L., & Howell, W. S. (1975). *Persuasion: A means of social influence* (2nd ed.). Englewood Cliffs, NJ: Prentice-Hall.

Brembeck, W., and Howell, W. S. (1976). *Persuasion: A means of social control* (2nd ed.). Englewood Cliffs, NJ: Prentice-Hall.

Burke, K. (1970). *A grammar of motives.* Berkeley: University of California Press.

Burke, K. (1970). *A rhetoric of motives.* Berkeley: University of California Press.

Callahan, D. (2004). *The cheating culture.* New York: Harcourt.

Campbell, J. (1991). *Transformations of myth through time.* New York: Harper and Row.

Campbell, J. (1972). *The hero with a thousand faces.* Princeton: Princeton University Press.

Cialdini, R. B. (2008). *Influence: Science and practice.* Boston: Allyn and Bacon.

Cook, P. (1996). *The winner take all society.* New York: Martin Kessler Books.

Donaldson, D. and Wamberg, S. (2001). *Pinocchio nation: Embracing truth in a culture of lies.* Colorado Springs: Pinion Press.

Ekman, P. (1999). A few can catch a liar. *Psychological Science*, 10, 3.

Fishbein, M. and Ajzen, I. (1980). *Understanding attitudes and predicting social behavior.* Englewood Cliffs, N. J.: Prentice Hall Inc.

Fishbein, M. and Ajzen, J. (1991). The theory of planned behavior. *Organizational behavior and human decision processes*, vol. 50, pp. 179–211.

Fisher, W. F. (1987). *Human communication as narration: Toward a philosophy of reason, value and action.* Columbia: University of South Carolina Press.

Hall Jamieson, K. (1992). *Dirty politics: Deception, distraction and democracy.* New York: Oxford University Press.

Huxley, A. (1932). *Brave New World.* London, UK: Chatto and Windus.

Keyes, R. (2004). *The post-truth era: Dishonesty and deception in contemporary life.* New York: St. Martin's Press.

Klein, J. (2007) *Newsweek.* October 8. Inflating a little man, p. 30.

Larson, C. U. (2010). *Persuasion: Reception and responsibility.* Belmont: Thomson.

Levy, S. (2007). *Newsweek.* November 26. The future of reading, pp. 56–64.

Levy, S. (2007). *Newsweek.* October 8. The technologist, p. 20.

News Record (2005), Gillette, Wyoming, May 10.

Obama, B. (2006). *The audacity of hope: Thoughts on reclaiming the American dream.* New York: Crown Publishers.

Obama, B. (2007). *Dreams from my father: A story or race and harmony.* New York: Crown Publishers.

Petty, R. E., and Cacioppo, J. T. (1986). The elaboration likelihood model of persuasion. In L. Berkowitz (Ed.), *Advances in experimental social psychology* (vol. 19, pp. 123–205).

Rank, H. (1976). Teaching about public persuasion. In D. Dieterich (Ed.), *Teaching and doublespeak.* Urbana, IL: National Council of Teachers of English.

Roberts, R. (1924). *The works of Aristotle.* Oxford: Clarendon.

Shannon, C. E., and Weaver, W. (1949). *The mathematical theory of communication.* Urbana: University of Illinois Press.

Simons, H. W. (1986). *Persuasion: Understanding, practice, and analysis.* Reading, New York: Random House.

Simons, H. W., Deems, M., and Kamrath, C. (2010). *Persuasion in Society.* Thousand Oaks: Sage, Inc.

Tumulty, K. (2007). http://www.time.com/time/ magazine/article/0,9171,1640402,00.html (detailed discussion of Obama's viral marketing campaign).

Chapter 2

Adam, A. (2005). *Gender, ethics, and information technology.* New York: Palgrave Macmillan.

Bailey, R. W. (1984). George Orwell and the English language. In E. J. Jensen (Ed.), *The future of nineteen eighty-four* (pp. 23–46). Ann Arbor: University of Michigan Press.

Baker, S., and Martinson, D. L. (2001). The TARES test: Five principles for ethical persuasion. *Journal of Mass Media Ethics*, vol. 16, pp. 148–175.

Bate, B. (1992). *Communication and the sexes.* (Reissue). Prospect Heights, IL: Waveland Press.

Bennett, M. J. (1979). Overcoming the golden rule: Sympathy and empathy. In D. Nimmo (Ed.), *Communication yearbook 3* (pp. 407–422). New Brunswick, NJ: Transaction Books.

Berkman, R. I., and Shumway, C. A. (2003). *Digital dilemmas: Ethical issues for online media professionals.* Ames, IA: Blackwell Publishing.

Black, J. (2009). The ethics of propaganda and the propaganda of ethics. In L. Wilkins and C. Christians (Eds.), *The Handbook of Mass Media Ethics* (pp. 130–148). New York: Routledge.

Blood, R. (2002). *The weblog handbook.* Cambridge, MA: Perseus.

Bok, S. (1979). *Lying: Moral Choice in Public and Private Life.* New York: Vintage.

Booth, W. C. (2004). *The rhetoric of RHETORIC: The quest for effective communication.* Malden, MA: Blackwell Publishing.

Bosmajian, H. (1983). *The language of oppression* (rpt. ed.). Lanham, MD: University Press of America.

Bovee, W. G. (1991). The end can justify the means— but rarely. *Journal of Mass Media Ethics*, vol. 6, pp. 135–145.

Callahan, D. (2004). *The cheating culture: Why more Americans are doing wrong to get ahead.* New York: Harcourt.

Cavalier, R. J. (Ed.). (2005). *The impact of the Internet on our moral lives.* Albany: State University of New York Press.

Cunningham, S. B. (2002). *The idea of propaganda.* Westport, CT: Praeger.

DeGeorge, R. (1999). *Business ethics* (5th ed.). New York: Prentice-Hall.

Eldeib, D. (2010). Web site brings out the bullies: Formspring proves popular with teens and their tormentors. *Chicago Tribune*, December 3, sec. 1, pp. 1, 13.

Ermann, D. M., Williams, M. B., and Shauf, M. S. (1997). *Computers, ethics, and society* (2nd ed.). New York: Oxford University Press.

Foss, S. K., and Griffin, C. (1995). Beyond persuasion: A proposal for an invitational rhetoric. *Communication Monographs*, vol. 62, pp. 2–18.

Freund, L. (1960). Responsibility: Definitions, distinctions, and applications. In J. Friedrich (Ed.), *Nomos III: Responsibility* (pp. 28–42). New York: Liberal Arts Press.

Froman, L. A. (1966). A realistic approach to campaign strategies and tactics. In M. K. Jennings and L. H. Ziegler (Eds.), *The electoral process.* Englewood Cliffs, NJ: Prentice-Hall.

Gorsevski, E. W. (2004). *Peaceful persuasion: The geopolitics of nonviolent rhetoric.* Albany: The State University of New York Press.

Hamelink, C. J. (2000). *The ethics of cyberspace.* London: Sage.

Hatzfeld, J. (2005). *Machete season: The killers in Rwanda speak.* Trans. Linda Coverdale. New York: Farrar, Straus, and Giroux.

Hauerwas, S. (1977). *Truthfulness and tragedy.* Notre Dame, IN: University of Notre Dame Press.

Horsey. (2007). The speech Mitt Romney should give. *Chicago Tribune*, December 10, sec. 1, p. 20.

Johannesen, R. L. (1971). The emerging concept of communication as dialogue. *Quarterly Journal of Speech*, vol. 57, pp. 373–382.

Johannesen, R. L. (1991). Virtue ethics, character, and political communication. In R. E. Denton, Jr. (Ed.), *Ethical dimensions of political communication* (pp. 69–90). New York: Praeger.

Johannesen, R. L. (1997). Diversity, freedom, and responsibility. In J. Makau and R. C. Arnett (Eds.), *Communication ethics in an age of diversity* (pp. 155–186). Champaign: University of Illinois Press.

Johannesen, R. L., Valde, K. S., and Whedbee, K. E. (2008). *Ethics in human communication* (6th ed.). Long Grove, IL: Waveland Press.

Johnson, D. G. (2001). *Computer ethics* (3rd ed.). Upper Saddle River, NJ: Prentice-Hall.

Kane, R. (1994). *Through the moral maze: Searching for absolute values in a pluralistic world.* New York: Paragon.

Klaidman, S., and Beauchamp, T. L. (1987). *The virtuous journalist.* New York: Oxford University Press.

Knapp, M. (2008). *Lying and Deception in Human Interaction.* Boston: Pearson/Allyn and Bacon.

Lebacqz, K. (1985). *Professional ethics.* Nashville, TN: Abingdon.

Lesher, S. (1972). The new image of George Wallace. *Chicago Tribune*, January 2, sec. 1A, p.1.

McCammond, D. B. (2004). Critical incidents: The practical side of ethics. In D. Lattimore et al., *Public relations: The profession and the practice* (5th ed.) (pp. 84–85). New York: McGraw Hill.

Meiklejohn, A. (1948; 1960). *Political freedom.* New York: Harper and Brothers.

Miller, C., and Swift, K. (1981). *The handbook of nonsexist writing.* New York: Barnes and Noble.

Niebuhr, H. R. (1963). *The responsible self.* New York: Harper and Row.

Opotow, S. (1990). Moral exclusion and injustice: An introduction. *Journal of Social Issues*, vol. 46, pp. 1–20.

Pennock, J. R. (1960). The problem of responsibility. In C. J. Friedrich (Ed.), *Nomos III: Responsibility* (pp. 3–27). New York: Liberal Arts Press.

Pincoffs, E. L. (1975). On being responsible for what one says. Paper presented at Speech Communication Association convention, Houston, TX, Dec. 1975.

Primer: Blogs and blogging. (2005). *Media Ethics* (Spring), vol. 16, pp. 14–16.

Ramirez, M. (2008). *Everyone has the right to my opinion.* Hoboken: NJ: John Wiley and Sons.

Samovar, L. A., Porter, R. E., and Stefani, L. A. (1998). *Communication between cultures* (3rd ed.). Belmont, CA: Wadsworth.

Sellers, M. (2004). Ideals of public discourse. In C. T. Sistare (ed.), *Civility and its discontents* (Ch. 1). Lawrence: University Press of Kansas.

Singer, M. G. (1963). The golden rule. *Philosophy*, 38, 293–314.

Singer, M. G. (1967). The golden rule. In P. Edwards (Ed.), *Encyclopedia of philosophy*, vol. 3 (pp. 365–366). New York: MacMillan.

Spence, E. H., and Van Heekeren, B. (2005). *Advertising ethics.* Upper Saddle River, NJ: Pearson/Prentice Hall.

Steuter, E. and Willis, D. (2008). *At war with metaphor: Media, propaganda, and racism in the war on terror.* Lanham, MD: Lexington Books.

Stewart, J., and Zediker, K. (2000). Dialogue as tensional, ethical practice. *Southern Communication Journal*, vol. 65, pp. 224–242.

Strangelove, M. (2010). *Watching YouTube.* Toronto: University of Toronto Press.

Toulmin, S. (1950). *An examination of the place of reason in ethics.* Cambridge: Cambridge University Press.

Williams, H. M. (1974). What do we do now, boss? Marketing and advertising. *Vital Speeches of the Day*, vol. 40, pp. 285–288.

Wolf, M. J. P. (Ed.). (2003). *Virtual morality: Morals, ethics, and the new media.* New York: Peter Lang.

Wood, J. T. (1994). *Gendered lives: Communication, gender, and culture.* Belmont, CA: Wadsworth.

Chapter 3

Andrews, J. (1980). History and theory in the study of the rhetoric of social movements. *Central States Speech Journal*, 31, 274–281.

Aristotle. (1984). *Rhetoric.* (W. R. Roberts, Trans.). New York: Modern Library.

Ashcraft, K. L. (2005). Resistance through consent?: Occupational identity, organizational form, and the maintenance of masculinity among commercial airline pilots. *Management Communication Quarterly*, 19, pp. 67–90.

Blair, J. A. (2004). The rhetoric of visual arguments. In C. A. Hill and M. Helmers (Eds.), *Defining Visual Rhetorics* (pp. 41–61). Mahwah, New Jersey: Lawrence Earlbaum Associates.

Bowers, J. W., & Ochs, D. J. (1971). *The rhetoric of agitation and control*. Reading, MA: Addison-Wesley.

Bowers, J. W., Ochs, D. J., Jesen, R. J. and Schulz, D. P. (2010). *The rhetoric of agitation and control* (3d ed.). Long Grove, IL: Waveland Press.

Burke, K. (1969). A rhetoric of motives. Berkley: University of California Press (originally published in 1950).

Burns, S. (1990). *Social movements of the 1960s: Searching for democracy*. Boston: Twayne.

California Milk Processor Board (2011a). Got Milk? Retrieved February 14, 2011 from http://www.gotmilk.com.

California Milk Processor Board (2011b). Get the glass. Retrieved February 14, 2011 from http://www.gettheglass.com/index2.html.

Cloud, D. (2001). Laboring under the sign of the new: Cultural studies, organizational communication, and the fallacy of the new economy. *Management Communication Quarterly*, vol. 15, pp. 268–278.

Cox, R. (2010). *Environmental Communication and the Public Sphere* (2nd ed.). Thousand Oaks: Sage Publications.

Decker, K. (September, 2007). How photographs of war impact public opinion. Retrieved February 13, 2011 from http://www.associatedcontent.com/article/364635/how_photographs_of_war_impact_public_pg9.html?cat=37.

Dylan, B. (January, 1964). The times they are a-changin. Columbia Records.

Fisher, W. R. (1978). Toward a logic of good reasons. *Quarterly Journal of Speech*, 64, 376–384.

Fisher, W. R. (1984). Narration as a human communication paradigm: The case of public moral argument. *Communication Monographs*, 51, 1–22.

Fisher, W. R. (1987). *Human communication as narration: Toward a philosophy of reason, value, and action*. Columbia: University of South Carolina Press.

Foss, Sonja K. (1994) A rhetorical schema for the evaluation of visual imagery. *Communication Studies*, 45, pp. 213–224.

Lester, P. M. (1995). *Visual communication: Images with messages*. Belmont, CA: Wadsworth Publishing Company.

Pezzullo, P. C. (2007). *Toxic tourism: Rhetorics of pollution, travel, and environmental justice*. Tuscaloosa: The University of Alabama Press.

Picture power. (May 9, 2005). BBC News report. Retrieved February 13, 2011 from http://news.bbc.co.uk/2/hi/4517597.stm.

Plato. (1937). *The dialogues of Plato* (Vol. 1). (B. Jowett, Trans.). New York: Random House.

Rowland, R. C. (1989). On limiting the narrative paradigm: Three case studies. *Communication Monographs*, 56, 39–54.

Scott, R. L. (1993). Rhetoric is epistemic: What difference does that make? In T. Enos & S. C. Brown (Eds.), *Defining the new rhetoric* (pp. 120–136). Mahwah, NJ: Erlbaum.

Story behind a picture. (June 5, 2007). Retrieved February 13, 2011 from http://www.militaryphotos.net/forums/showthread.php?113527-REQ-story-behind-a-picture.

Warnick, Barbara. (1987). The narrative paradigm: Another story. *Quarterly Journal of Speech*, 73, 172–182.

Chapter 4

Allen, M. (1998). Comparing the persuasive effectiveness of one and two-sided messages. In M. Allen & R. W. Preiss (Eds.), *Persuasion: Advances through meta-analysis* (pp. 87–98). Cresskill, NJ: Hampton Press.

Allen, M., & Stiff, J. (1998). The sleeper effect. In M. Allen & R. W. Preiss (Eds.), *Persuasion: Advances through meta-analysis* (pp. 175–188). Cresskill, NJ: Hampton Press.

Anderson, A. G., and Lavallee, D. (2008). Applying the theories of reasoned action and planned behavior to athlete training adherence behavior. *Applied Psychology*, 57, pp. 304–312.

Ajzen, I. (2001). Nature and operation of attitudes. *Annual Review of Psychology*, 52, 27–58.

Ajzen, I. (2010). Frequently asked questions. Retrieved February 21, 2011 from website of Icek Ajzen at http://www.people.umass.edu/aizen/faq.html.

Ajzen, J. (1991). The theory of planned behavior. *Organizational behavior and human decision processes*, 50, 179–211.

Armitage, C. J., & Christian, J. (2003). From attitudes to behavior: Basic and applied research on the theory of planned behavior. *Current Psychology*, 22, 187–195.

Bamberg, S., Ajzen, I., Schmidt, P. (2003). Choice of travel mode in the theory of planned behavior: the roles of past behavior, habit, and reasoned action. *Basic and Applied Social Psychology*, vol. 25, pp. 175–187.

Bandura, A. (1977). Self-efficacy: Toward a unifying theory of behavioral change. *Psychological Review*, 84, pp. 191–215.

Bandura, A. (1993). Perceived self-efficacy in cognitive development and functioning. *Educational Psychologist*, 28, pp. 117–148.

Bless, H., & Schwarz, N. (1999). Sufficient and necessary conditions in dual-process models. In S. Chaiken & Y. Trope (Eds.), *Dual-process theories in social psychology* (pp. 423–440). New York: Guilford Press.

Bornstein, R. F. (1989). Exposure and affect: Overview and meta-analysis of research, 1968–1987. *Psychological Bulletin*, 106, 265–289.

Capner, M., Scarcia, M., Graham, D. (2007). Establishing the psychometric properties of measures of implicit memory. *Australian Journal of Psychology*, 59, pp. 51–62.

Chaiken, S., Giner-Sorolla, R., & Chen, S. (1996). Beyond accuracy: Defense and impression motives in heuristic and systematic information processing. In P. M. Gollwitzer & J. A. Bargh (Eds.), *The psychology of action: Linking cognitions and motivation to behavior* (pp. 553–578). New York: Guilford Press.

Chaiken, S., & Trope, Y. (Eds.). (1999). *Dual process theories in social psychology*. New York: Guilford Press.

Dahl, D. W., Frankenberger, K. D., & Manchanda, R. V. (2003). Does it pay to shock? Reactions to shocking and nonshocking advertising content among university students. *Journal of Advertising Research*, 43, 268–280.

DeSteno, D., Petty, R. E., Rucker, D. D., Wegener, D. T., & Braverman, J. (2004). Discrete emotions and persuasion: The role of emotion-induced expectancies. *Journal of Personality and Social Psychology*, 86, 43–56.

Fazio, R. H. (1989). On the power and functionality of attitudes: The role of attitude accessibility. In A. R. Pratkanis, S. J. Breckler, & A. G. Greenwald (Eds.), *Attitude structure and function* (pp. 153–179). Hillsdale, NJ: Erlbaum.

Fazio, R. H., and Olson, M. A. (2003). Implicit measures in social cognition research: Their meaning and use. *Annual Review of Psychology*, vol. 54, pp. 297–327.

Fishbein, M., & Ajzen, I. (1975). *Belief, attitude, intention, and behavior: An introduction to theory and research*. Reading, MA: Addison-Wesley.

Fishbein, M., & Ajzen, I. (1981). Acceptance, yielding and impact: Cognitive processes in persuasion. In R. E. Petty, T. M. Ostrom, & T. C. Brock (Eds.), *Cognitive responses in persuasion* (pp. 339–359). Hillsdale, NJ: Erlbaum.

Fishbein, M., and Ajzen, I. (2010). *Predicting and changing behavior: The reasoned action approach*. New York: Psychology Press.

Frey, K. P., & Eagly, A. (1993). Vividness can undermine the persuasiveness of messages. *Journal of Personality & Social Psychology*, 65, 32–44.

FUD-Counter. (2001, November 1). How does FUD relate to Linux? Retrieved December 17, 2002 from http://fud-counter.nl.linux.org/rationale.html.

Goei, R., Boyson, A. R., Lyon-Callo, S. K., Schott, C., Wasilevich, E., Cannarile, S. (2010). An examination of EPPM predictions when threat is perceived externally: An asthma intervention with school workers. *Health Communication*, 25, pp. 333–344.

Greene, K., Campo, S., and Banerjee, C. (2010). Comparing normative, anecdotal, and statistical risk evidence to discourage tanning bed use. *Communication Quarterly*, 58, pp. 111–132.

Grush, J. E., McKeough, K. L., & Ahlering, R. F. (1978). Extrapolating laboratory exposure research to actual political elections. *Journal of Personality and Social Psychology, 36,* 257–270.

Hartenstein, M. (January 12, 2011). Giffords shooting causes gun sales to skyrocket in Arizona, some buyers looking to stock up. NYDailyNews.com. Retrieved on February 27, 2011 from http://www.nydailynews.com/news/2011/01/12/2011-01-12_giffords_shooting_causes_gun_sales_to_skyrocket_in_arizona_some_buyers_looking_t.html

Hovland, C. I. (1957). *The order of presentation in persuasion.* New Haven, CT: Yale University Press.

Hovland, C. I., Janis, I. L., & Kelley, H. H. (1953). *Communication and persuasion.* New Haven, CT: Yale University Press.

Janis, I. R., & Feshbach, S. (1953). Effects of fear arousing communications. *Journal of Abnormal Social Psychology, 48,* 78–92.

Janis, I. L. (1967). Effects of fear arousal on attitude change: Recent developments in theory and experimental research. In L. Berkowitz (Ed.), *Advances in experimental social psychology* (Vol. 3, pp. 166–224). New York: Academic Press.

Kang, Y., Cappella, J. N., and Fishbein, M. (2009). The effect of marijuana scenes in anti-marijuana public service announcements on adolescents' evaluation of ad effectiveness. *Health Communication, 24,* pp. 483–493.

Kruglanski, A. W. and Thompson, E. P. (1999). Persuasion by a single route: A view from the unimodel. *Psychological Inquiry, 10,* pp. 83–109.

Kumkale, G. T., & Albarracin, D. (2004). The sleeper effect in persuasion: A meta-analytic review. *Psychological Bulletin, 130,* 143–171.

Lavine, H. (1999). Types of Evidence and Routes to Persuasion: The Unimodel Versus Dual-Process Models. *Psychological Inquiry, 10,* 141–144.

Lavine, H., Thomsen, C. J., Zanna, M. P., & Borgida, E. (1998). On the primacy of affect in the determination of attitudes and behavior: The moderating role of affective-cognitive ambivalence. *Journal of Experimental Social Psychology, 34,* 398–421.

Leventhal, H. (1970). Findings and theory in the study of fear communications. In L. Berkowitz (Ed.), *Advances in experimental social psychology* (Vol. 5, pp. 119–186). New York: Academic Press.

Lund, F. H. (1925). The psychology of belief, IV: The law of primacy in persuasion. *Journal of Abnormal Social Psychology, 20,* 183–191.

Mackie, D. L., & Worth, L. T. (1989). Cognitive deficits and the mediation of positive affect in persuasion. *Journal of Personality and Social Psychology, 57,* 27–40.

Manstead, A. S. R. and van der Pligt, J. (1999). One process or two? Quantitative and qualitative distinctions in models of persuasion. *Psychological Inquiry, 10,* pp. 144–149.

March, J. G. and Simon, H. A. (1958). *Organizations.* New York: Wiley and Sons, Inc.

Miller, G. A. (1956). The Magical Number Seven, Plus or Minus Two: Some Limits on our Capacity for Processing Information. *Psychological Review, 63,* pp. 81–97.

Mitchell, M. M., Brown, K. M., Morris-Villagran, M., & Villagran, P. D. (2001). The effects of anger, sadness, and happiness on persuasive message processing: A test of the negative state relief model. *Communication Monographs, 68,* 347–359.

Mongeau, P. A. (1998). Another look at fear arousing persuasive appeals. In M. Allen & R. W. Preiss (Eds.), *Persuasion: Advances through meta-analysis* (pp. 53–68). Cresskill, NJ: Hampton Press.

Munoz-Silva, A., Sanchez-Garcia, M., Nunes, G. and Martins, A. (2007). Gender differences in condom use prediction with theory of reasoned action and planned behavior: The role of self-efficacy and control. *Aids Care, 19,* pp. 1177–1181.

Nabi, R. L. (2002). Anger, fear, uncertainty, and attitudes: A test of the cognitive-functional model. *Communication Monographs, 69,* 204–216.

Olson, M. A., and Fazio, R. H. (2001). Implicit attitude formation through classical conditioning. *Psychological Science, 12,* pp. 413–417.

Olson, M. A., and Fazio, R. H. (2009). Implicit and explicit measures of attitudes: The perspective of the MODE model. In R. E. Petty, R. H. Fazio, and P. Briñol (Eds.), *Attitudes: Insights from the new implicit measures* (pp. 19–63). New York, NY: Psychology Press.

Petty, R. E., & Cacioppo, J. T. (1979). Effects of forewarning of persuasive intent and involvement on cognitive responses and persuasion. *Journal of Personality and Social Psychology, 37,* 1915–1926.

Petty, R. E., & Cacioppo, J. T. (1986). *Communication and persuasion: Central and peripheral routes to attitude change.* New York: Springer-Verlag.

Petty, R. E., Wegener, D. T., & Fabrigar, L. R. (1997). Attitudes and attitude change. *Annual Review of Psychology*, 48, 609–647.

Petty, R. E., & Wegener, D .T. (1999). The elaboration likelihood model: Current status and controversies. In S. Chaiken & Y. Trope (Eds.), *Dual-process theories in social psychology* (pp. 41–72). New York: Guilford Press.

Petty, R. E., Wheeler, S. C., Bizer, G. Y. (1999). Is there one persuasion process or more? Lumping versus splitting in attitude change theories. *Psychological Inquiry*, 10, pp. 156–163.

Pfau, M., Szabo, E. A., Anderson, J., Norrill, J., Zubric, J. C., & Wan, H. (2001). The role and impact of affect in the process of resistance to persuasion. *Human Communication Research*, 27, 216–252.

Pornpitakpan, C. (2004). The persuasiveness of source credibility: A critical review of five decades' evidence. *Journal of Applied Social Psychology*, 34, 243–281.

Rogers, R. W. (1975). A protection motivation theory of fear appeals and attitude change. *Journal of Psychology*, 91, 93–114.

Roskos-Ewoldsen, D. R., and Fazio, R. H. (1992). On the orienting value of attitudes: Attitude accessibility as a determinant of an object's attraction of visual attention. *Journal of Personality and Social Psychology*, 92, pp. 198–211.

Roskos-Ewoldsen, D., Yu, J., Rhodes, N. (2004). Fear appeal messages affect accessibility of attitudes toward the threat and adaptive behaviors. *Communication Monographs*, 71, 49–69.

Sauer, Abe (February, 2011). Announcing the Brandcameo Product Placement Award Winners. Retrieved February 22, 2011 from BrandChannel website at http://www.brandchannel.com/home/post/2011/02/22/2010-Brandcameo-Product-Placement-Awards.aspx.

Sherif, M., & Hovland, C. I. (1961). *Social judgment: Assimilation and contrast effects in communication and attitude change.* New Haven, CT: Yale University Press.

Thomson, D. R., Milliken, B. Smilek, D. (2010). Long-term conceptual implicit memory: A decade of evidence. *Memory & Cognition*, 38, pp. 42–46.

Wegener, D. T., Petty, R. E., & Smith, S. M. (1995). Positive mood can increase or decrease message scrutiny: The hedonic contingency view of mood and message processing. *Journal of Personality and Social Psychology*, 69, 5–15.

Witte, K. (1992). Putting the fear back into fear appeals: The extended parallel process model. *Communication Monographs*, 59, 329–349.

Witte, K., & Allen, M. (2000). A meta-analysis of fear appeals: Implications for effective public health campaigns. *Health Education & Behavior*, 27, 591–615.

Yzer, M. (2010). The impact of the work of Martin Fishbein on health issues in the world. *Health Communication*, 25, pp. 625–627.

Zajonc, R. B. (1968). Attitudinal effects of mere exposure. *Journal of Personality and Social Psychology*, 9, 1–27.

Chapter 5

American Heritage Dictionary (1985). Boston: Houghton Mifflin.

The American Heritage Dictionary Second College Edition, (2005). Boston: Houghton Mifflin.

Berger, A. A. (1989). *Signs in contemporary society: An introduction to semiotics.* Salem, WI: Sheffield.

Burke, K. (1966). *Language as symbolic action: Essays on life, literature, and method.* Berkeley: University of California Press.

Burke, K. (1986). *Language as symbolic action.* Berkeley: University of California Press.

Burke, K. (1970). *A grammar of motives.* Berkeley: University of California Press.

Burke, K. (1970). *A rhetoric of motives.* Berkeley: University of California Press.

Campbell & Jamieson. (1990). *Deeds done in words: Presidential rhetoric and the genres of governance.* Chicago, IL: University of Chicago Press.

Deeds Done in Words: Presidential Rhetoric and the Genres of Governance (1990). Chicago: University of Chicago Press.

Feig, B. (1997). *Marketing straight to the heart: From product to positioning to advertising.* Chicago: American Management Association.

Hahn, D. (1998). *Political communication: Rhetoric, government and citizens.* State College, PA: Strata.

Hildebrandt, G. Co-author of parts of the official report to Hitler on the 1936 Olympics.

Korzybski, A. (1947). *Science and sanity.* Lakeville, CT: Non-Aristotelian Library.

Langer, S. K. (1951). *Philosophy in a new key.* New York: New American Library.

Langer, S. K. (1957). *Philosophy in a New Key.* New York: New American Library.

Lederer, R. (1991). *The miracle of language.* New York: Pocket Books.

National Public Radio. (1999). *Morning Edition,* Feb. 3.

O'Harrow, R. (2005). *No place to hide.* New York: Simon and Schuster.

Postman, N. (1992). *Technopoly: The surrender of culture to technology.* New York: Vintage Books.

Solove, D. (2005). *The Digital Person: Technology and Privacy in the Information Age.* New York: NYU Press.

Sopory, P., and Dillard, J. (2002). Figurative language and persuasion. In Dillard and Pfau (Eds.), *The persuasion handbook: Developments in theory and practice.* Thousand Oaks, CA: Sage.

Suplee, C. (1987). Semiotics: In search of more perfect persuasion. *Washington Post,* Jan. 18, Outposts sec., pp. 1–3.

Chapter 6

American Heritage Dictionary. (1985). Boston: Houghton Mifflin.

Andrews, L. A. (1984). Exhibit A: Language. *Psychology Today,* Feb., p. 30.

Berger, A. (1984). *Signs in contemporary culture.* New York: Longman.

Berger, A. A. (2005). *Media analysis techniques* (3rd ed.). Thousand Oaks, CA: Sage.

Black Elk. (1971). *Touch the earth.* New York: Outerbridge and Dienstfrey.

Broder, D. (1984). The great American values test. *Psychology Today,* Nov., p. 41.

Buissac, P. (1976). *Circus and culture: A semiotic approach.* Bloomington: Indiana University Press.

Burke, K. (1960). *A grammar of motives.* Berkeley: University of California Press.

Chicago Daily News. (November 24, 1972). Fed up? It may lead to an ulcer.

Cialdini, R. (2008). *Influence: Science and practice.* Boston: Allyn and Bacon.

Dillard, J. P., and Pfau, M. (2002). *The persuasion handbook: Developments in theory and practice.* Thousand Oaks, CA: Sage.

Domzal, T., and Kernan, J. (1993). Mirror, mirror: Some postmodern reflections on global marketing. *Journal of Advertising,* Dec., p. 20.

Eco, U. (1979). *The role of the reader.* Bloomington: Indiana University Press.

Eco, U. (1984). *Semiotics and the philosophy of language.* London: Macmillan.

Eisenberg, E. M. (1984). Ambiguity as a strategy in organizational communication. *Communication monographs,* 51, pp. 227–242.

Gozzi, R., Jr. (1999). *The Power of metaphor in the age of electronic media.* Cresskill, NJ: Hampton Press.

Hahn, D. (1998). *Political communication: Rhetoric, government and citizens.* State College, PA: Strata.

Hosman, L. H. (2002). Language and persuasion. In J. P. Dillard and M. Pfau (Eds.), *The persuasion handbook: Developments in theory and practice.* Thousand Oaks, CA: Sage.

Koenig, P. (1972). Death doth defer. *Psychology Today,* Nov., p. 83.

Larson, C. U. (1982). Media metaphors: Two models for rhetorically criticizing the political spot advertisement. *Central States Speech Journal* (Winter). pp. 533–546.

Larson, C. U. (2010). Persuasion: reception and responsibility. Belmont: Thomson.

Lederer, R. (1991). *The miracle of language.* New York: Pocket Books.

Lewis, H., and Lewis, M. (1972). *Psychosomatics: How your emotions can damage your health.* New York: Viking Press.

Messaris, P. *Visual persuasion: The role of images in advertising.* Thousand Oaks, CA: Sage Publications, 1997.

Osborn, M. (1967). Archetypal metaphors in rhetoric: The light-dark family. *Quarterly Journal of Speech*, April, pp. 115–126.

Seigel, B. (1989). *The healing power of communicating with your body.* New York: Weider.

Sopory, P., & Dillard, J. (2002). Figurative language and persuasion. In J. P. Dillard & M. Pfau (Eds.), *The persuasion handbook: Developments in theory and practice.* Thousand Oaks, CA: Sage.

Swanson, S. L. (1981). Sensory language in the courtroom. *Trial Diplomacy Journal*, Winter, pp. 37–43.

Weaver, R. (1953). *The ethics of rhetoric.* Chicago: Regnery.

Chapter 7

Austin, N. (2002). The power of the pyramid: The foundation of human psychology, and thereby motivation; Maslow's hierarchy is one powerful pyramid. *Incentive*, July, p. 10.

Bellah, R. N., Madsen, R., Sullivan, W. M., Swoder, A., and Tipton, S. M. (1985). *Habits of the heart: Individualism and commitment in American life.* New York: Harper and Row.

Booth, E. (1999). Getting inside a shopper's mind: Direct marketers are working out how and why consumers arrive at decisions, in order to satisfy their needs. *Marketing*, June 3, p. 32.

Booth-Butterfield, S., and Welbourne, J. (2002). The elaboration likelihood model: Its impact on persuasion theory and research. In J. P. Dillard and M.Pfau (Eds.), *The persuasion handbook: Developments in theory and practice* (pp. 155–173). Thousand Oaks, CA: Sage.

Borchers, T. A. (2005). *Persuasion in the media age* (2nd ed.). Boston: McGraw-Hill.

Carnegie, D. (1952). *How to win friends and influence people.* New York: Simon and Schuster.

Colley, R. H. (1961). *Defining advertising goals for measured attitude results.* New York: Association of National Advertisers.

De Bono, K. G., and Harnish, R. (1988). Source expertise, source attractiveness, and the processing of persuasive information. *Journal of Personality and Social Psychology*, 55, p. 541–546.

Egley, A. H., and Chaiken, S. (1993). *The psychology of attitudes.* New York: Harcourt Brace Jovanovich.

Eiser, R. J. (1987). *The expression of attitude.* New York: Springer-Verlag.

Feig, B. (1997). *Marketing straight to the heart: From product to positioning to advertising–how smart companies use the power of emotion to win loyal customers.* New York: American Marketing Association.

Festinger, L. (1962). *A theory of cognitive dissonance.* Stanford, CA: Stanford University Press.

Fishbein, M., and Ajzen, I. (1975). *Belief, attitude, intention, and behavior: An introduction to theory and research.* Reading, MA: Addison-Wesley.

Fonda, J. (2005). *My life so far.* New York: Random House.

Freedman, D. H. (1988). Why you watch some commercials—whether you want to or not. *TV Guide*, Feb. 20.

Hoveland, C.I. and others (1953). *Communication and persuasion: Psychological studies of opinion change.* New Haven: Yale University Press.

Lafavore, R. (1995). From here to eternity: Men's desire for immortality. *Men's Health*, Nov., p. 74.

Lears, T. J. J. (1983). From salvation to self realization: Advertising and the therapeutic roots of the consumer culture. In *The culture of consumption: Critical essays in American culture, 1880–1980.* New York: Pantheon Books.

Levitt, S., and Dubner, S. (2005). *Freakonomics: A rogue economist explores the hidden side of everything.* New York: Harper Collins.

Maslow, A. (1954). *Motivation and personality.* New York: Harper and Row.

Nabi, R. L. (2002). Discrete emotions and persuasion. In J. P. Dillard and M. Pfau (Eds.), *The persuasion handbook: Developments in theory and practice* (pp. 289–309). Thousand Oaks, CA: Sage.

National Public Radio. (2002). *All things considered*, Aug. 30.

Nelson, R. (2001). On the shape of verbal networks in organizations. *Organization Studies*, Sept.–Oct., p. 797.

Packard, V. (1964). *The hidden persuaders.* New York: Pocket Books.

Petty, R., and Cacioppo, J. (1986). *Communication and persuasion.* New York: Springer-Verlag.

Petty, R. E., and Wegener, D. T. (1998). Attitude change: Multiple roles for persuasion variables.

In D. T. Gilbert, S. T. Fiske, and G. Lindsay (Eds.), *Handbook of social psychology*. Boston: McGraw-Hill.

Pinsky, M. S. (2002). Houston minister views Gospel according to the Sopranos. *Orlando Sentinel*, Sept. 4, 2000.

Porter, R., and Samovar, L. (1998). *Intercultural communication: A reader*. Belmont, CA: Wadsworth Publishing Co.

Putnam, R. D. (1995). Bowling alone: America's declining social capital. *Journal of Democracy*, vol. 6, p. 65–68.

Putnam, R. D. (2000). *Bowling alone: The collapse and revival of American community*. New York: Simon and Schuster.

Rokeach, M. (1968). *Beliefs, attitudes, and values: A theory of organization and change*. San Francisco: Jossey-Bass.

Rowan, J. (1998). Maslow amended. *The Journal of Humanistic Psychology*, Winter, p. 84.

Rowell, R. (2002). Martha's taste, not her ethics lures fans. *Knight Ridder/Business News*, Oct. 2.

Schiffman, L., and Kanuk, L. (1997). *Consumer behavior*. Upper Saddle River, NJ: Prentice Hall.

Schrader, D. C. (1999). Goal complexity and the perceived competence of interpersonal influence messages. *Communication Studies*, Fall, p. 188.

Shavitt, S. (1990). The role of attitude objects in attitude functions. *Journal of Experimental Psychology*, vol. 26, p. 124–148.

Sibley, K. (1997). The e-mail dilemma: To spy or not to spy. *Computing Canada*, March 31, p. 14.

Staal, S. (2001). Warning: living together may ruin your relationship. *Cosmopolitan*, Sept., p. 286.

Williams, M. A. (2001). *The ten lenses: Your guide to living and working in a multicultural world*. Herndon, VA: Capitol Books.

Wood, W. (2000). Attitude change: Persuasion and social influence. *Annual Review of Psychology*, p. 9.

Zemke, R. (1998). Maslow for a new millennium. *Training*, Dec., p. 54.

Zimbardo, P. G., Ebbesen, E. E., and Maslach, C. (1976). *Influencing attitudes and changing behavior*. Reading, MA: Addison-Wesley.

Zimbardo, P. G., and Leippe, M. R. (1991). *The psychology of attitude change and social influence*. New York: McGraw-Hill.

Chapter 8

American Heritage Dictionary (1985). Boston: Houghton Mifflin.

Burke, K. (1985). Dramatism and logology. *Communication Quarterly*, vol. 33, p. 89–93.

Consider the facts. (2002). *Pine County Courier*, July 25, p. 10.

Dahl, S. (2000) *Communications and cultural transformation: Cultural diversity, globalization, and cultural convergence*. London: E.C.E.

Deardorf, J., and Finan, E. (1999). Barton wins $29.6 million. *Chicago Tribune*, March 2, p. 1.

Fishbein, M., and Ajzen, I. (1975). *Beliefs, attitude, intention and behavior: An introduction to theory and research*. Reading, MA: Addison-Wesley.

Fishbein, M., and Ajzen, I. (1980). Predicting and understanding consumer behavior: Attitude behavior correspondence. In I. Ajzen and M. Fishbein (Eds.), *Understanding attitudes and predicting social behavior*. Englewood Cliffs, NJ: Prentice-Hall.

Guttmacher, A. (1993). Social science and the citizen. *Society*, July–Aug., p. 2.

Huglen, M, and Clark, N. (2004). *Argument strategies from Aristotle*. Belmont: Thomson Learning.

Jensen, J. V. (1981). *Argumentation: Reasoning in communication*. New York: Van Nostrand.

Kahane, H. (1992). *Logic and contemporary rhetoric: The use of reason in everyday life*. Belmont, CA: Wadsworth.

Loftus, E. F. (1980). *Eyewitness testimony*. Cambridge, MA: Harvard University Press.

Loftus, E. F. (1984). Eyewitness testimony. *Psychology Today*, Feb., p. 25.

Lunsford, A., and Ruszkiewicz, J. (2004). *Everything's an argument*. Boston: Bedford/St. Martins Press.

Moore, C. (1909). *A short life of Abraham Lincoln*. Chicago: Houghton Mifflin.

Peck, M. S. (1983). *People of the lie: The hope for healing human evil*. New York: Simon and Schuster.

Scott, B. (1989). *Rockford Register Star*, Nov. 8, editorial page.

Sutton, S. (1998). *The Persuasion Handbook: Developments in Theory and Practice*. Eds. James Dillard and Michael Pfau, Thousand Oaks, CA: Sage Publications. p. 264.

Thompson, W. N. (1971). *Modern argumentation and debate: Principles and practices*. New York: Harper and Row.

Toulmin, S. (1964). *The uses of argument*. Cambridge: Cambridge University Press.

Chapter 9

American Heritage Dictionary (1985). Boston: Houghton Mifflin.

America's abortion dilemma. (1985). *Newsweek*, Jan. 14, pp. 20–23.

Baudhin, S., and Davis, M. (1972). Scales for the measurement of ethos: Another attempt. *Speech Monographs*, vol. 39, pp. 296–301.

Beane, W. C., and Doty, W. G. (1975). *Myths, rites, and symbols: A Mercia Eliade reader*. New York: Harper Colophon.

Bellah, R. N., Madsen, R., Sullivan, W. M., Swidler, A., and Tipton, S. M. (1985). *Habits of the heart: Individualism and commitment in American life*. New York: Harper and Row.

Berlo, D., Lemmert, J., and Davis, M. (1969). Dimensions for evaluating the acceptability of message sources. *Public Opinion Quarterly*, vol. 33, pp. 563–576.

Cialdini, R. (2008). *Influence: Science and practice* (5th ed.). Needham Heights, MA: Allyn and Bacon.

Edelman, M. (1967). Myths, metaphors and political conformity. *Psychiatry*, vol. 30, pp. 217–228.

Eliade, M. (1971). *The myth of the eternal return: Of cosmos and history*. Princeton, NJ: Princeton University Press.

Hahn, D. (1998). *Political communication: Rhetoric, government, and citizens*. State College, PA: Strata.

Hofstadter, R. (1963). *Anti-intellectualism in America*. New York: Knopf.

Hovland, C., Janis, I., and Kelley, H. (1953). *Communication and persuasion*. New Haven, CT: Yale University Press.

Kelman, H., and Hovland, C. (1953). Reinstatement of the communicator: Delayed measurement of opinion changes. *Journal of Abnormal and Social Psychology*, vol. 48, pp. 327–335.

Kosicki, G. M. (2002). The media priming effect: News media and considerations affecting political judgments. In J. P. Dillard and M. Pfau (Eds.), *The persuasion handbook: Developments in theory and practice* (pp. 63–82). Thousand Oaks, CA: Sage.

Parenti, M. (1994). *Land of idols: Political mythology in America*. New York: St. Martin's Press.

Reich, R. (1987). *Tales of a new America*. New York: Times Books.

Steele, E. D., and Redding, W. C. (1962). The American value system: Premises for persuasion. *Western Speech*, vol. 26, pp. 83–91.

Tocqueville, A. de (1965). *Democracy in America*. New York: Mentor.

Chapter 10

Andersen, P. A. (1999). *Nonverbal communication: Forms and functions*. Mountain View, CA: Mayfield.

Barnes, G. et al. (2007). Adolescents time use: Effects on substance use, delinquency, and sexual activity. *Journal of Youth and Adolescence*, vol. 36. July, 2007.

Burgoon, J., Bufler, D., and Woodall, W. (1996). *Nonverbal communication: The unspoken dialog* (2nd ed.). New York: McGraw Hill.

Burgoon, J. K., Dunbar, N. E., and Segrin, C. (2002). Nonverbal influences. In J. P. Dillard and M. Pfau (Eds.), *The persuasion handbook: Developments in theory and practice* (pp. 445–473). Thousand Oaks, CA: Sage.

Ekman, P. (1999). A few can catch a liar. *Psychological Science*, vol. 10, p. 3.

Ellyson, S., Dovidio, J., and Fehr, B. J. (1984). Visual behavior and dominance in men and women. In C. Mayo and N. Henley (Eds.), *Gender and nonverbal behavior*. New York: Springer-Verlag.

Fay, P. (2006). Gender differences in non verbal communication. Retrieved from ehow.com/list/Family.

Fromme, D., Jaynes, W., Taylor, D., Hanhold, E., Daniell, J., Rountree, R., and Fromme, M. (1989). Nonverbal behavior and attitude toward touch. *Journal of Nonverbal Behavior*, vol. 13, pp. 3–13.

Giles, H., Coupland, N., and Coupland, J. (1991). Accommodation theory: Communication, context, and consequence. In H. Giles, J. Coupland, and N. Coupland (Eds.), *Contexts of accommodation: Developments in applied sociolinguistics* (pp. 1–68). Cambridge: Cambridge University Press.

Goffman, E. (1959). *The presentation of self in everyday life*. New York: Doubleday.

Guerrero, L., DeVito, J., and Hecht, M. (1999). *The nonverbal communication reader: Classic and contemporary readings.* Mt. Prospect, IL: Waveland Press.

Hall, E. T. (1959). *The silent language.* Garden City, NY: Doubleday.

Hall, J. A. (1984). *Nonverbal sexual differences: Communication accuracy and expressive style.* Baltimore, MD: Johns Hopkins University Press.

Jacobson, D. (1999). Impression formation in cyberspace: Online expectations and offline experiences in text-based virtual communities. *Journal of Computer-mediated Communication.* September, 1999.

Knapp, M. and Hall, J. (2002). *Nonverbal communication in human behavior.* 5th edition. Belmont CA: Wadsworth/Thomson Publishing Company.

Knapp, M. L., and Comendena, M. E. (1985). Telling it like it isn't: A review of theory and research on deceptive communication. *Human Communication Research,* vol. 5, pp. 270–285.

Knapp, M. L., and Hall, J. (2002). *Nonverbal communication in human interaction* (5th ed.). Belmont, CA: Wadsworth.

Kotulak, R. (1985). Researchers decipher a powerful 'language.' *Chicago Tribune,* April 7, sec. 6.

Leathers, D. (1986). *Successful nonverbal communication: Principles and applications.* New York: Macmillan.

Major, B. (1984). Gender patterns in touching behavior. In C. Mayo and N. Henley (Eds.), *Gender and nonverbal behavior.* New York: Springer-Verlag.

Mehrabian, A. (1971). *Silent messages.* Belmont, CA: Wadsworth.

Murray, J. (1989). *The power of dress.* Minneapolis, MN: Semiotics.

Orban, D. K. (1999). The integrative nature of argument and non-verbal communication in different communication contexts. Unpublished paper delivered to Midwest Basic Course Directors Conference, Feb., pp. 4–6.

Packard, V. (1964). *The hidden persuaders.* New York: Pocket Books.

Porter, N., and Geis, F. (1984). Women and nonverbal leadership cues: When seeing is not believing. In C. Mayo and N. Henley (Eds.), *Gender and nonverbal behavior.* New York: Springer–Verlag.

Scheflen, A. (1973). *Communicational structure: Analysis of a psychotherapy session.* Bloomington: Indiana University Press.

Singley, K. (2004). Touching behavior. *Hohonu,* vol. 2, no. 2.

Smith, T. (1997). Adolescent gender differences in time alone and time devoted to conversation. *Adolescence,* vol. 32.

Chapter 11

Ahuja, B. (2005). *Buzz marketing: Honest deception.* www.commercialfreechildhood.org/articles/4thsummit/ahuja.

Bales, R. F. (1970). *Personality and interpersonal behavior.* New York: Holt, Rinehart and Winston.

Binder, L. (1971). *Crisis and sequence in political development.* Princeton, NJ: Princeton University Press.

Borchers, T. A. (2005). *Persuasion in the media age* (2nd ed.). Boston: McGraw-Hill.

Bormann, E. G. (1985). *The force of fantasy.* Carbondale and Edwardsville: Southern Illinois University Press.

Bowers, J. W., Ochs, D. J., Jensen, R. J., and Schultz, D. P. (2010). *The rhetoric of agitation and control* (3rd ed.). Prospect Heights, IL: Waveland Press.

Cragan, J. F., and Shields, D. C. (1994). *Applied communication research: A dramatistic approach.* Annandale, VA: Speech Communication Association and Creskill, NJ: Hampton Press.

Cragan, J. F., and Shields, D. C. (1995). *Symbolic theories in applied communication research: Bormann, Burke, and Fisher.* Cresskill, NJ: Hampton Press.

Denton, R., and Woodward, D. (1998). *Political communication in America* (3rd ed.). Westport, CT: Praeger.

Faucheux, R. (1998). Strategies that win! *Campaigns and Elections,* Jan., pp. 24–32.

Fortini-Campbell, K. (1992). *The consumer insight book.* Chicago: Copy Workshop.

Garcia, G. (2005). *American mainstream: How the multicultural consumer is transforming American business.* New York: Harper Collins/Rayo.

Lavidge, R. J., and Steiner, G. A. (1961). A model for predictive measurements of advertising effectiveness. *Journal of Marketing,* vol. 24, pp. 59–62.

Metter, B. (1990). Advertising in the age of spin. *Advertising Age,* Sept. 17, p. 36.

Morrissey, B. (2005). Mitsubishi issues web 'Thrill ride challenge.' *Adweek*, June 8, 2005.

National Public Radio. (1999). *All things considered*, April 2.

Rogers, E. (1962). *The diffusion of innovation*. New York: Free Press.

Schultz, D. E., and Barnes, B. (1999). *Strategic advertising campaigns* (4th ed.). Lincolnwood, IL: N.T.C. Business Books.

Stewart, C. J., Smith, C. A., and Denton, R. E., Jr. (2007). *Persuasion and social movements* (5th ed.). Prospect Heights, IL: Waveland Press.

Trent, J. S., and Friedenberg, R. V. (2007). *Political campaign communication* (6th ed.). New York and London: Praeger.

Trout, J. (1995). *The new positioning: The latest on the world's # 1 business strategy*. New York: McGraw Hill.

Trout, J. and Ries, A. (1986). *Positioning: The battle for your mind*. New York: Harper and Row.

Tumulty, K. (2007). Obama's Viral Marketing Campaign. *Time Magazine*, July 5, 2007, p. 1.

Valdivia, A. N. (1997). The secret of my desire: Gender, class, and sexuality in lingerie catalogs. In K. T. Frith (Ed.), *Undressing the ad: Reading culture in advertising*. New York: Peter Lang.

Warren, K., and Guscott, J. (2000). Wild ideas Lecture Series. *The battle for your mind: Proaganda, PR, and Psyops*. http://www.lkwdpl.org/wildideas/propaganda.html.

Chapter 12

Cantola, S. J., Syme, G. I., and Campbell, N. A. (1985). Creating conflict to conserve energy. *Psychology Today*, Feb., p. 14.

Cialdini, R. (2007). *Influence: Science and practice*, 5th edition. Boston: Allyn & Bacon.

Cialdini, R. B. (2008). *Influence: Science and Practice* (5th ed.). Englewood Cliffs, NJ: Prentice Hall.

Howell, W. S., and Bormann, E. G. (1988). *The process of presentational speaking*. New York: Harper and Row.

Monroe, A., Ehninger, D., Gronbeck, B., McKerrow R. E., (2000). *Principles and types of speech communication*. Chicago: Scott, Foresman.

Rank, H. (1982). *The pitch*. Park Forest, IL: Counter Propaganda Press.

Russell, J. T., & Lane, W. R. (1999). *Kleppner's advertising procedure* (14th ed.). Upper Saddle River, NJ: Prentice-Hall.

Russell, J. T., and Lane, W. R. (2005). *Kleppner's advertising procedure*, 16th edition. Upper Saddle River, NJ: Prentice-Hall.

Scheflen, A. E. (1964). The significance of posture in communication systems. *Psychiatry*, vol. 27, pp. 316–331.

Schwartz, T. (1973). *The responsive chord*. Garden City, NY: Anchor.

Simons, H. (2001). *Persuasion in society*. Thousand Oaks, CA: Sage.

Chapter 13

Baker, R. K., and Ball, S. K. (1969). *Violence and the media: A staff report to the national commission on the causes and prevention of violence*. Volume 9a. Washington: U.S. Government.

Bandura, A. (1994). Social cognitive theory of mass communication. In J. Bryant and D. Zillman, eds. *Media effects: Advances in Theory and Research*. Hillsdale N.J.: Erlbaum.

Blumler, J. (1979). The role of theory in uses and gratifications studies. *Communication Studies*, 6, pp. 9–34.

Boorstin, D. (1961). *The image: A guide to pseudo-events in America*. New York: Harper & Row.

Brand, S. (1987). *The media lab: Inventing the future at M.I.T.* New York: Viking Penguin Books.

Chicago Tribune. (2005). Time to explode the Internet? July 4, 2005, editorial page.

Gerbner, G., Gross, L., Morgan, M., and Signorelli, N. (1986). Living with television: The dynamics of the cultivation process. In J. Bryant and D. Zillman, (Eds.), *Perspectives on media effects*. Hillsdale: N.J. Erlbaum.

Gumpert, G., and Drucker, S. J. (2002). From locomotion to telecommunication, or paths of safety, streets of gore. In L. Strate, R. Jacobson, and S. J. Gibson (Eds.), *Communication in cyberspace: Social interaction in an electronic environment* (2nd ed.). Cresskill, NJ: Hampton Press.

Hall Jamieson, K., and Kohrs-Campbell, K. (1996). *The interplay of influence* (4th ed.). Belmont, CA: Wadsworth.

Kaiser Family Foundation. (1999). *Kids and media at the new millennium*. Menlo Park, CA: Author.

Kaplan, D., Wingert, P., and Chideya, F. (1993). Dumber than we thought. *Newsweek*, Sept. 20, pp. 44–45.

Kappelman, T. (2008). Marshall McLuhan: The medium is the message www.leaderu.com/orgs/probe/docs/mcluhan.html

Larson, C. U. (2002). Dramatism and virtual reality: Implications and predictions. In S. Gibson, R. Jacobson, and K. Strate (Eds.), *Communication and Cyberspace*. N.Y. Fordham: University Press.

Larson, M. (1997). Rush Limbaugh: Broadcast demagogue. *Journal of Radio Studies*, IV, 1997.

Larson, M. S. (2009). *Watch it: What parents need to know to raise media literate kids*. Highland City, FL: Rainbow Press.

Lederer, R. (1991). *The miracle of language*. New York: Pocket Books.

Library of Congress (2007). Library of Congress acquires media pioneer's collection. *News from the Library of Congress* (News Release, August 2, 2007) Washington, D.C.

Madigan, C. M. (1993). Going with the flow. *Chicago Tribune Magazine*, May 2, pp. 14–26.

Matusow, B. (1983). *The evening stars: The making of a network news anchor*. New York: Ballantine Books.

McCombs, M., and Shaw, D. (1972). The agenda setting function of the media. *Public Opinion Quarterly*, vol. 36, pp. 176–187.

McLuhan, M. (1963). *Understanding media: The extensions of man*. New York: Signet.

Meyrowitz, J. (1985). *No sense of place: The impact of electronic media on social behavior*. New York: Oxford University Press.

National Public Radio. (2011). Fresh Air, July 14.

Ong, W. S. (1967). *The presence of the word*. New Haven, CT: Yale University Press.

Ong, W. S. (1977). *Interfaces of the word*. Ithaca, NY: Cornell University Press.

Ong, W. S. (1982). *Orality and literacy: The technologizing of the word*. London: Metheun.

Postman, N. (1996). Cyberspace, schmyberspace. In L. Strate, R. Jacobson, and S. J. Gibson (Eds.), *Communication and cyberspace: Social interaction in an electronic environment*. Cresskill, NJ: Hampton Press.

Press, L. (1995). McLuhan meets the net. *Communications of the ACM*. July, 1995.

Rubin, A. (2002). The uses and gratifications perspective of media effects. In J. Bryant and D. Zillman (Eds.), *Media effects: Advances in theory and research*. Mahwah, NJ: Erlbaum.

Schwartz, T. (1973). *The responsive chord*. Garden City, NY: Anchor/Doubleday.

Schwartz, T. (1983). *Media: The Second God*. New York: Anchor Books.

Signorelli, N., and Morgan, M. (1990). *Cultivation analysis: New directions in media research*. Newbury Park, CA: Sage.

Theall, D. (2002). *The Virtual McLuhan*. Toronto: McGill-Queens University Press.

Walters, R. (2007). Effective internet advertising. http://www.catalogs.com/info/gadgets/effective-internet-advertising.html

Warren, K., and Guscott, J. (2000). Wild ideas Lecture Series. *The battle for your mind: Proaganda, PR, and Psyops*. http://www.lkwdpl.org/wildideas/propaganda.html.

Zettl, H. (1996). Back to Plato's cave: Virtual reality. In L. Strate, R. Jacobson, and S. J. Gibson (Eds.), *Communication and cyberspace: Social interaction in an electronic environment*. Cresskill, NJ: Hampton Press.

Chapter 14

Alexander, A., and Hanson, J. (2003). *Taking sides: Clashing views on controversial issues in mass media and society*. Burr Ridge, IL: McGraw-Hill/Dushkin.

Amft, J. (2004). Psychographics: A Primer. www.psychographics.net.

Baker, R. (1997). The squeeze. *Columbia Journalism Review*, Sept.–Oct.

Borchers, T. (2002). *Persuasion in the media age*. Burr Ridge, IL: McGraw-Hill.

Borchers, T. (2005). *Persuasion in the media age*. New York: McGraw-Hill.

Chaffee, J. (1998). How advertising informs to our benefit. *Consumers' Research*, April.

Cuneo, A. (2002). Creative execs stress the importance of the Internet. Accessed Nov. 13, 2002, at www.adage.com using QuickFind Id: AAO20F.

Dollas, C. (1986). Butterball turkeys: An examination of advertising theory and practice. Unpublished starred paper, Department of Journalism, Northern Illinois University, De Kalb.

Espejo, E., and Romano, C. (2005). Children and media policy brief. *Children Now*, Spring, pp. 1–8.

Feig, B. (1997). *Marketing straight to the heart: From product to positioning to advertising—how smart companies use the power of emotion to win loyal customers.* Chicago: American Management Association.

Goodkin, O., and Phillips, M. (1983). The subconscious taken captive. *Southern California Law Review*, 54, 1077–1140.

Hogan, K. (2005). Covert subliminal persuasion: 7 facts that will change the way you influence forever. *The Science of Influence Library*. Eagan, MN: Network 3000 Publishing, Forthcoming.

Honomichl, J. (1984). *Marketing research people: Their behind-the-scenes-stories.* Chicago: Crain Books.

Key, W. B. (1973). *Subliminal seduction: Ad media's manipulation of a not so innocent America.* New York: Signet.

Key, W. B. (1977). *Media sexploitation.* Englewood Cliffs, NJ: Prentice-Hall.

Key, W. B. (1980). *The clam-plate orgy and other subliminals the media use to manipulate your behavior.* New York: Signet.

Lander, A. (1981). In through the out door. *OMNI*, Feb., p. 45.

National Public Radio. (2006). *All things considered.* January 3.

Oates, J. (2006). MSN launches study on changes in advertising. *Brand Republic*, July 5, 2006. p. 1.

O'Guinn, T., Allen, C., and Semenik, R. (2009). *Advertising and integrated brand promotion.* Mason, OH: Thomson-Southwestern.

O'Toole, J. (1985). *The trouble with advertising.* New York: Times Books/Random House.

Parente, M. (2004). *Advertising Campaign Strategy* (4th ed.). Mason, OH: Thomson-Southwestern.

Phillips, M., and Goodkin, O. (1983). The subconscious taken captive: A social, ethical, and legal analysis of subliminal communication technology. *Southern California Law Review*, 54, 1077–1140.

Rank, H. (1991). *The pitch.* Park Forest, IL: Counter Propaganda Press.

Ries, A. (1996). *Focus: The future of your company depends on it.* New York: Harper Collins.

Ries, A., and Trout, J. (1986). *Positioning: The battle for your mind.* New York: McGraw-Hill.

Rothschild, M. (1987). *Advertising: From fundamentals to strategies.* Lexington, MA: Health.

Schudson, M. (1984). *Advertising, the uneasy persuasion: Its dubious impact on American society.* New York: Basic Books.

Schwartz, T. (1973). *The responsive chord.* New York: Anchor Doubleday.

Thompson, S. (2002). Frito-Lay reports Doritos online ad success. Accessed Nov. 18, 2002, at www.adage.com using QuickFind Id: AAO21A.

Trout, J. (1995). *The new positioning: The latest on the world's # 1 business strategy.* New York: McGraw Hill.

Valdivia, A. H. (1997). The secret of my desire: Gender, class, and sexuality in lingerie catalogs. In K. T.Frith (Ed.), *Undressing the ad: Reading culture in advertising.* New York: Peter Lang.

Vestergaard, T., and Schroeder, K. (1985). *The language of advertising.* London: Basil Blackwell.

Wentz, L., and Cuneo, A. (2002). Double-digit Hispanic ad growth continues. Accessed Sept. 16, 2002, at www.adage.com using QuickFind Id: AAN95S.

Winkelman, P. (2004). *Emotion and consciousness.* Eagan, MN: Network 3000 Publishing, Forthcoming.

Wrighter, C. (1972). *I can sell you anything.* New York: Ballantine Books.

Index